KU-482-872

The Russians

HEDRICK SMITH

R.T.C. LIBRARY, LETTERKENNY

947

085

SPHERE BOOKS LIMITED
30/32 Gray's Inn Road, London WC1X 8JL

The author is grateful to the following for permission to quote:

Joseph Brodsky, 'A Halt in the Desert' from *Selected Poems*. Translated by George L. Kline. Penguin Modern European Poets, 1973: Penguin Books Ltd., London; Harper & Row, Publishers, New York. Copyright © 1973 by George L. Kline.

Bulat Okudzhava and Aleksandr Galich, 'Night Patrol'; 'Magnitizat: Uncensored Songs of Dissident.' Translated by Gene Sosin in *Dissent in the U.S.S.R.*, Rudolf L. Tokes, ed. Copyright © by The Johns Hopkins University Press, Baltimore.

Yevgeny Yevtuchenko, excerpts from 'Envoys Are Going to Lenin', and 'The Night of Poetry' in *The Bratsk Station and Other New Poems*. Copyright 1966 by Sun Books Pty. Ltd., South Melbourne, Australia; reprinted by permission of Doubleday & Company, Inc., New York.

First published in Great Britain by Times Books 1976
Copyright © by Hedrick Smith 1976
Published by Sphere Books 1976
Reprinted 1977 (twice)

TRADE
MARK

This book is sold, subject to the condition that
it shall not, by way of trade or otherwise, be lent,
re-sold, hired out or otherwise circulated without
the publisher's prior consent in any form of
binding or cover other than that in which it is
published and without a similar condition
including this condition being imposed on the
subsequent purchaser.

Set in Intertype Baskerville

Printed in Great Britain by
Hunt Barnard Printing Ltd., Aylesbury, Bucks.

To Ann, who shared it all.

CONTENTS

Beneath the flat surface of society in Russia, as presented by *Pravda*, a rich and complex life abounds but it totally lacks any means of communication. We are not a 'one dimensional society' as Westerners believe.

Communist Party official;
quoted by
K. S. Karol, 1971

FOREWORD

Journalists are supposed to focus on what is new and fresh. Typically from Moscow that has meant the big breaking news on the diplomacy of détente, power shifts in the Kremlin, space shots, sudden new purchases of American grain, or the latest arrests of dissidents. But other newsmen, pundits, scholars and Kremlinologists have already provided Western readers with an ample stock of works on these topics so I have touched little on high politics, the anatomy of the Soviet economy, the Communist party structure, or the maneuverings of diplomacy.

What struck me as fresh and new to convey to readers was the human quotient, the texture and fabric of the personal lives of the Russians as people. Experts can study various facets of the Soviet system at their leisure from a distance. What the reporter on the scene can uniquely provide is the tactile sense, the feel of what it is like to sit among Russians in their apartments and watch them raise their children, to go with them to their bathhouses and hear their jokes, to stand in line with them in stores or relax with them in the dacha country of the elite, to share their tales about what really happens inside factories, to listen to them tell how they see the outside world and what Russia means to them.

It was these details of life that others had often passed by that fascinated me – not just *any* details, but those which illuminated the enduring characteristics of the Russians as a people and which defined the society and the times in which they live and move.

No single volume can embrace all that is Russia, especially one based on the personal experience and observation of one correspondent at one period in time. In over three years as *The New York Times* Bureau Chief in Moscow, I ranged as widely as time and the Soviet authorities would permit. What I am now reporting is based on what I saw or learned personally. But I have tried to reach beyond the mere recording of interesting impressions to analyze the meaning of my experiences and of what Russians told me about themselves and their way of life.

As a police state, Russia poses special problems for a journalist, not only while he is reporting but also when he sits down to write. Many of the most important insights I gained came from people I cannot name or portray in detail because they would face reprisals for their candor. Wherever possible, I have identified the people I knew, and wherever a double name appears (first-and-last, or first-and-middle, Russian-style), it is the name of the actual person. But where I felt compelled to camouflage identities, I have either left my informants anonymous or given them only a fictional first name and altered minor details of their lives to protect them. Their comments and quotations are genuine and descriptions of them are accurate in the essentials. I did not use a tape recorder but I kept special, copious notes for this book – in addition to regular reporting notes – during or immediately after score upon score of interesting encounters. I supplemented these with recorded interviews with half a dozen recent Soviet emigrants immediately after my departure from Moscow, but even these people requested not to be named out of fear of official action against relatives still living in Russia.

This book is intended for general readers and I hope that specialists will forgive a few conventions that I have adopted to make it easier for ordinary readers. I have used 'Russia' and 'Soviet Union' almost interchangeably though technically speaking, Russia, or the Russian Republic, is only one of the 15 Republics that make up the Union of Soviet Socialist Republics. But it is the largest and most dominant, and many Russians and other non-Russian Soviet citizens themselves call their country 'Russia'. Usually I have called the people Russians, for they predominated among those I met. But wherever an ethnic group or nationality carried special significance, I have used 'Russian' to denote only ethnic Russians and 'Soviet' to cover all other nationalities unless I had special reason to specify them individually.

For the same reason, I have identified *Izvestia* and *Pravda* (and various journalistic kin of *Pravda* such as *Komsomol-*

skaya Pravda or *Moskovskaya Pravda*) by their Russian names because they are so well known in the West. But otherwise I have translated the names of publications, such as *New World* magazine. Whenever Russian words are well enough known to general readers to use correct Russian endings, such as *apparatchiki,* I have done so. But where I thought the ordinary reader would be confused by grammatical endings, I have made plurals by adding the English 's' – for example, *izbas* (peasant cabins).

I alone bear responsibility for the reporting and judgments in this book but there are a number of people to whom I wish to express my thanks for help in preparing the material. To my researchers Linda Amster and Teresa Redd for their timely, painstaking and resourceful assistance; to my *Times* colleagues in Moscow, Ted Shabad and Christopher Wren for their friendly suggestions and contributions; to several academic and government specialists who generously shared their time and insights – Murray Feshbach of the U.S. Department of Commerce; Wesley Fisher of Columbia University; Henry Morton of Queens College; William Odom of West Point; and Keith Bush and Gene Sosin of Radio Liberty. I am particularly grateful to Steve Cohen of Princeton University for his thoughtful comments on the manuscript. Roger Jellinek, my editor, has been an invaluable and imaginative counselor and friend. And I have a special, priceless debt of gratitude to Ann, my wife, and to those Russians who cannot be named but who made this book possible.

H.S.
Larchmont
September 30, 1975

INTRODUCTION

Not long before leaving for Russia in mid-1971, I ran into Marvin Kalb of C.B.S. whose memory of his first day in Moscow was still fresh. He had gone there in January 1956, the uncertain time after Stalin's death just before Khrushchev had secretly exposed the Stalinist purges. As a junior diplomat, Kalb was given the first morning off to stroll around Moscow to get his bearings. Riding the subway to Red Square, he caught a glimpse of a man nearby eyeing him. The thought flashed through his mind that this might be a tail, but he dismissed it as a foolish fantasy. Still, when he left the subway, the man went with him like a shadow. When he would stop to look in a store window, the shadow would also stop and look. When he crossed the street, his shadow crossed the street. When he walked slowly or speeded up, the shadow kept pace. Finally, though it was a cold winter day, Kalb went up to one of those ice-cream vendors that operate on Red Square oblivious to the seasons. He bought two eskimo sticks and without even turning around, extended an arm backward offering an eskimo. The shadow took it without a word. They continued that way all day, in tandem, never speaking.

His story was like a page from a bad spy novel except that it actually happened. It was the kind of eerie little episode that sticks in your mind if you are headed for Moscow. And it posed an implicit challenge to me as a journalist setting out for Russia with the objective of getting through to the Russians to try to see them as they see themselves.

Very quickly, however, I had an experience which made me think that getting through to the Russians would not be so much of a problem after all. One evening, after a concert by Duke Ellington, courtesy of the Soviet-American cultural exchange, my wife Ann and I were driving home in the office car, a large black Chevrolet Impala that seemed indecently ostentatious next to the spartan little compacts that Russians chugged around in. Although it was only about 11 p.m., downtown Moscow was practically deserted, the sidewalks bathed in the iridescent bluish glare of Soviet street lights. Here and there, people were waving down cabs or hitching rides from passing motorists. To my surprise, one knot of young couples gaily hailed us despite what I had presumed were the risks of unauthorized contact with foreigners. So we picked them up. They had just come from a wedding party in a restaurant and were in no mood to quit partying. As we drove toward their part of town, they impulsively invited us in for a drink.

It was a very Russian encounter. All of them, men and women, were doctors or graduate students in medicine, married and in their mid-twenties. Misha, a slender, pale-faced, thoughtful young man who turned out to be our host, spoke quite passable English. The others said they read it but spoke little and we jabbered in a mixture of tongues. They insisted on sitting all together, and somehow seven of them crammed into our back seat. All were fascinated by the American car, its power, its size, its comfort, its speed, its gadgets, and they were enthusiastic at the chance to talk with Americans. We parked kitty-corner from their apartment building rather than right out front. Misha cautioned us not to speak English as we entered the building and slipped past the *dezhurnaya*, the old woman robed in baggy sweaters, sitting by the elevator, watching the building's comings and goings.

Misha's apartment, the first Russian home we had seen, was small and sparsely furnished but comfortable for two – one bedroom-living room, a tiny kitchen, a hall, a washroom, and a toilet. Nine of us sat in a tight little group on and around the bed, which did double-duty as a couch. The talk, awkward at first, was about the Ellington concert (none of them had gone because tickets were impossible for ordinary Russians to buy), about Western music and fashions, about our family, my job, about life in the West and only a bit about Russia. Misha and his almond-eyed wife, Lena, newly wed, had little to offer except what Russians consider most necessary: a couple of bottles of vodka carried off from the restaurant under someone's coat, two large pickled cucumbers still wet with brine, and a heel of brown bread. A motley assortment of jiggers, juice glasses, and cups materialized for the vodka which, according to Russian custom, we drank neat – tossing back the head to knock down a shotful in one quick gulp.

This was our initiation to this essential ritual of Russian life and the others were amused by our timidity. They quickly gave us a short course on how to endure the lethal punch of the vodka: exhale before you gulp; instantly chase with food. The girls, grimacing terribly after each drink, would hurriedly take a bite out of one of the pickles which passed continuously around the circle. Others gnawed at the bread. Misha explained that during the war, when bread was short, the hardy drinkers passed the crust around the circle and simply took a whiff, not a bite. For them, the whiff was enough to counteract the vodka. He demonstrated, and then handed me the bread and a shot-glass. I downed the vodka, took a sniff of bread, and came up coughing. The room dissolved in laughter. Misha urged me to try again. I shook my head. No, he meant only the bread, and this time insisted I breathe deeply. So I inhaled that moist, rich, sweet-sour earthiness of Russian brown bread. And I nodded to him, without understanding how this whiff, no matter how nourishing to the nostrils, would cool the fire that was still in my throat.

So it went, very innocently, until the vodka ran out – at about three in the morning. Before we parted, we all exchanged phone numbers and heart-warming expressions of friendship. Once again, Misha whispered a warning not to speak English and ferried us past the sleepy-eyed grandmother by the elevator. We bade farewell outside, but not before Misha and Lena urged us to keep in touch. 'We must get together again,' Misha insisted.

Ann and I drove home, amazed at the ease of communication, the friendliness of the young people and their unquenchable curiosity about America. We had learned little about Russia beyond how to drink vodka, but we had passed through that seemingly impassable barrier to human contact. As we pulled away from the curb, I had a moment's pang of uncertainty when headlights flashed in the rearview mirror. They did not follow us, though they may have stopped at Misha's building. Still, we congratulated ourselves for having gotten through to some young Russians so quickly.

The next day, as a gesture of thanks to Misha and Lena, I

18

43087059

wangled two tickets for them to an Ellington concert and telephoned their apartment to let them know. I kept getting no answer or wrong numbers. Other reporters had already warned me about the unreliability of the Moscow phone system, so I doggedly persisted. But after pestering one woman twice in a row, I decided something was amiss besides the circuits. That evening, Ann and I delivered the tickets in person.

The *dezhurnaya* was gone and the elevator was not working. We walked up the eight stories. Lena was at home, surprised but happy to see us again so soon and delighted with the tickets. I mentioned the trouble with the phone and we double-checked the number. It was absolutely correct except for the last digit. Instead of 6, Misha had written 7. It was not a question of illegible handwriting. The figures were neat and clear.

We corrected the number and went off, conveying greetings to Misha and accepting Lena's promise to get together after the concert. Over the next few weeks, I phoned several times. Misha was always out – at work, away on a trip, visiting his parents. But Lena always sounded happy to talk. Once we even discussed where we might meet when Misha was free. One evening when I called, Lena told me I could catch him at his parents' apartment and make the arrangements. She gave me the number. When I called, Misha answered. But when I gave my name, he hung up. I tried again. The phone was busy. I called Lena back and told her that obviously Misha did not want to see us again, and I apologized for bothering them. 'I'm so sorry,' she said. 'You understand?'

I hung up, discouraged but wiser. Although I had not been so blatantly tailed as Marvin Kalb in my first days in Moscow and had made a quick contact, it was now plain that getting to know Russians and making real friends among them was going to be a much more formidable task than it had first seemed. I ran into other Westerners who had also made 'one-time Russian friends' and had been unable to pursue those contacts. Some weeks later, talking with an experienced American diplomat who had served in Moscow in different times – under Stalin, Khrushchev and Brezhnev, I mentioned our experience with Misha and Lena.

'Oh,' he said, 'so you have discovered that the Iron Curtain is not barbed wire on the border of Austria and Czechoslovakia but it is right here in Moscow at the end of your fingertips. You can reach out, you can live right here among them and not really know how they live. The controls are so tight they shut you out. One night, one evening you can talk and drink with them – especially if they can explain it away later as an accidental encounter. But the next morning, they think it over and decide it's too risky to go on.'

Sadly, the diplomat seemed to be right. Yet surely he had caught only part of the truth. For I sensed in Misha's conflicting emotions a hint of a society more complex than I had first assumed and a people with more sharply contradictory drives than I had imagined. Clearly there had been a conflict between Misha and Lena over whether to continue seeing us and later I met other Russians who felt similar ambivalence about friendships with foreigners. In an almost childish way, Misha had exulted in the experience of riding in an American car, admiring its chrome and its horsepower. Yet he was knowing enough to warn me in advance to park kitty-corner from his apartment house and not to talk English as we passed the elevator lady. Even more unsettling to me, his society had so conditioned his political reflexes that even while we were hoisting vodka glasses and toasting our friendship, part of his brain was concentrating on changing that last digit of his telephone number. There was in Misha, then, not one Russia but two – the official Russia, the Russia of police controls and *Pravda* and retreating from unauthorized foreign friendships, and poised against this the other Russia, more human, impulsive, emotional, and unpredictable.

The problem, it seemed to me as I began to pull together the threads of what I was seeing, was that established images of the Russians did not capture this complexity, this ambivalence. The model of the totalitarian state entirely omits the fascinating eccentricities of life beneath the surface, the readiness of people like Lena to disobey the unwritten rules of the system. The opposite, comfortable assumption of most Westerners that Russians are not much different from the rest of us misses the important conditioning that the Soviet system had built into Misha. At almost every turn, the improbability of the down-to-earth realities of Russian life constantly forced me to correct my own preconceptions. The painstaking dissections of Western Kremlinologists, for example, had exposed the fiction of the Communist Monolith but did not quite prepare me to hear a dissident's wife disclose that she was a Party member or to spend an evening listening to a Party *apparatchik* tell me cynical jokes about Lenin and Brezhnev.

The longer I stayed in Moscow, the more I began to wonder whether anomalies weren't the rule. I found that in spite of the climate of aggressive state atheism, there are twice as many church adherents as card-carrying Communists; that in a society that has enshrined state ownership of property, more than half of the living space is privately owned; that in a system of rigorously collectivized agriculture, nearly 30 percent of farm output is grown on private plots and much of it sold through sanctioned free enterprise markets; that six decades after the czars were overthrown, there is a surge of interest in Russia's czarist past and its artifacts; that in spite of the rigid ideological conformity imposed from above, large numbers of people are politically indifferent and privately mock the inflated claims of Communist propaganda; that in the land of the proletariat, people are far more rank-, class- and status-conscious than in the West.

Before going to Russia I had set aside the myth of the classless society but I was still taken aback the first time I heard Russians talking about rich Communists – millionaires, even. Initially, when two writers calmly referred to someone's being 'rich as Mikhalkov', I presumed that Mikhalkov was some merchant prince of old who had built a fortune from furs or salt mines in czarist times. But I was informed that this Mikhalkov – Sergei Vladimirovich – was a Communist, an immensely successful children's writer, a literary watchdog and bigwig in the Writers' Union who later became the first person publicly to call for exiling Aleksandr Solzhenitsyn and who issued other literary pronouncements. The writers told me, and mentally toted up the figures out loud, that along with Mikhail Sholokhov (*And Quiet Flows the Don*) and perhaps another writer or two, Mikhalkov had legally earned a million rubles or close to it, from the multiple editions and collections of his books and from lucrative prizes awarded for loyal service. They said he had two country mansions, a chauffeured car, a fancy in-town apartment, and the life-style as well as the bank account of a capitalist. Moreover, this seemed to run in the family. For he had two sons making their way in the literary world and a son-in-law, Yulian Semenov, who specialized in spy novels and television serials that glorified the KGB (secret police) and earned 100,000 rubles * at a whack.

The Mikhalkovs notwithstanding, I had to learn that money is a poor yardstick in Russia. Earnestly, I asked Intourist guides, queried my Russian office interpreters, went to factories or engaged people in conversation in restaurants, inquiring how much they earned, how much they spent on food or rent, how much it cost to buy a car, trying to compare living standards. I busily went on making computations until Russian friends tipped me off that it was not money that really mattered but access or *blat* (the influence or connections to gain the access you need) – access to cities like Moscow where the stores have food, clothing and consumer goods in quantities and qualities unavailable elsewhere; access to the best schools and to good vacation spots or government cars, or to that most prized of privileges, the opportunity to travel abroad and mingle legally with foreigners; or access to a system of special stores for the elite where a new Soviet-made Fiat-125 Compact costs not the usual 7,500 rubles ($10,000) but only 1,370 rubles ($1,825) and the waiting time for delivery is a couple of days instead of the normal two or three years.

I also had to unlearn the notion that Russia had become a modern industrial state on a par with the advanced West, for that concept obscures as much as it reveals. Behind the mask of modernism, of missiles, jets and industrial technology, is concealed the imprint of centuries of Russian history on the structure of Soviet society and the habits and character of the Russian people. For it remains an intensely Russian land in ways that newcomers, especially Americans with our penchant for instant understanding, our impatience with history, our fixation with Communism, are slow to comprehend. Here and there, the traveler glimpses signs of a very traditional country – women patiently sweeping city streets with long-handled twig brooms, peasants bent over the fields hoeing by hand, store clerks adding up bills, click-clack, on ancient wooden abacuses. But it was months before I began to appreciate the weight of the Russian past on the Soviet present.

* 100,000 rubles is officially about $133,000. I have avoided the tedious computations of the buying power of the ruble (since the black market rate was about 30 cents). I have also ignored fluctuations in official exchange rates from 1970–1974 and used the average figure throughout of one ruble equals $1.33.

Behind the majestic stage-setting of the five-year-plan, I also came to understand, there is an erratic, helter-skelter scramble of production which plays such havoc with quality that Soviet consumers know to check the date of products (much as American housewives check for fresh eggs) to avoid the undependable goods made in the frantic, catch-up final ten days of every month. Instead of one economy, it turned out, Russia has five – defense industry, heavy industry, consumer industry, agriculture, and an illegal counter-economy – each with its own standards. The first and last seemed to give the best performance. The rest were mostly muddling through. The propaganda vision of shockworkers tirelessly building socialism was quickly dispelled for me by the undisguised goldbricking of waitresses, repairmen or builders. 'This is the workers' paradise – the greatest place in the world for workers to goof off,' a young Russian linguist chirped to me. 'They can't fire us.'

It was this latent anarchy in Russian life that surprised me the most – the irrepressive unruliness of human beings in a system of rules. I knew something beforehand about corruption in Soviet society, but I had not grasped how expert Russians were at finagling ways to beat the system and how much it affected the fundamentals of everyday living until I came across Klara, a Moscow State University coed. Klara's family lived in a dingy little provincial town. She was desperate to avoid being sent there or to Siberia on government assignment as a teacher after graduation. She found it impossible to get a job in Moscow because she could not get registered for Moscow housing. (The passport controls are designed to put a ceiling of 8 million on the city's population.) But Klara hit upon the scheme of marrying a Moscow lad to qualify for city housing as his wife. One of her close friends told me that Klara paid 1,500 rubles ($2,000 – a year's pay in her first job) for a bogus marriage to the brother of another friend, never planning to spend a single night with him. In fact, the groom ducked out quickly after the wedding ceremony. All Klara wanted was to use the marriage certification in her passport and six months of 'married life' to obtain her Moscow *propiska*, her resident's permit. A scientist later told me of a couple living in a provincial city who went to even greater lengths for the privilege of living in Moscow. They divorced and each married a Muscovite to obtain a *propiska*. Then they divorced their Moscow spouses and remarried. When I eyed him skeptically, the scientist insisted it had truly happened that way. Other Russians told me that literally thousands of people resorted to 'marriages of convenience', as Russians call them, to live in big cities like Moscow, Leningrad and Kiev and to escape what they regard as exile in the provinces.

It fascinated me that there were such cunning devices for foiling the authorities and that Russians, of all people, supposedly being a nation of sheep, would resort to such expedients. For the notion of the totalitarian state, perhaps useful for political scientists as a bird's eye view of Soviet society, misses the human quotient. It conjures up the picture of robots living a regimented existence. Most of the time, it is true, the vast majority of Russians go through the motions of publicly observing the rules. But privately, they are often exerting enormous efforts and practicing uncommon ingenuity to bend or slip through those rules for their own personal ends. 'Slipping through is our national pastime,' a woman lawyer smilingly commented to me.

Russians, I was also comforted to see, have not lost any of the madcap improbability of Dostoyevsky's characters. I was prepared to hear dissidents curse their KGB interrogators, as many did, but not prepared to hear others say their interrogators were polite or to learn that over the years the chasers and the chased sometimes develop personal ties. It came as a surprise, for example, when Joseph Brodsky, the poet who later emigrated, told me that his KGB interlocutor fancied himself a writer, too, and whenever they met, he would show Brodsky his prose and ask for suggestions and criticism.

Such a relationship is hardly typical since dealings with political police in any country are fundamentally unequal and intimidating. I knew of cases of sadism and vindictive meanness. Yet I also knew Soviets, especially those who had been through labor camps and were not easily intimidated, who jokingly referred to security agents rather possessively as 'my KGB man'. A Jewish family, embittered at having been kept under tight house arrest during President Nixon's visit to Moscow in 1974 to prevent their demonstrating or issuing statements, told me how their police guards had gone to buy groceries for them. And they laughingly remembered how later on they had seen 'our man' in some food store and nodded in recognition across the sacks of sugar.

One reason why Soviet life is so deceptive is that Russians

24

are masters at the art of lying low, of adopting the protective coloration of conformity in order to get by with something or to pursue some special interest that would be crushed if discovered. Important elements of Russian culture and intellectual life have survived this way. During the scientific ban on genetics under Stalin and Khrushchev, for example, some biologists managed to find refuge in institutes of chemistry and physics. They secretly kept their science alive by covering up their real work with phony experiments in other fields or by doing experiments at home in their kitchens, as one scientist told me. Cybernetics had a similar *sub-rosa* existence when it was in the doghouse as a 'bourgeois science'.

Again, while Western rock and jazz were being publicly condemned by the stodgy guardians of Communist morality in the Soviet press, a few Soviet musicians quietly organized rock groups and played 'forbidden music'. Somehow, a futuristic electronic music studio has been operating in the heart of Moscow, developing far-out combinations of the most modern Western rock or cosmic-sounding electronic music accompanied by expressive modern dance, and pulsing to strobe lights and laser-like beams. The whole scene, an offshoot and strange beneficiary of the high priority attached to radio electronics by the Soviets, is far beyond the bounds of official tolerance. Yet, I was told, some authorities know about it and are prepared to pretend that it does not exist so long as it does not attract attention, does not 'raise a scandal', as Russians put it.

The electronics expert and music lover who took me to the studio and arranged a mind-blowing performance of its sight-sound-dance compositions asked me not to write a newspaper story about it at that time because publicity just then might jeopardize the studio's precarious semiofficial sponsorship. Similar precautions were urged upon me when I was taken to a private concert of very hard rock. 'Until this sort of thing gets official acceptance of some kind,' a jazz musician advised me, 'our survival depends on people not knowing about us. That is the way our life is. The most interesting things are going on in private where you can't see them. Not only you as a foreigner but other people, Russians, as well. To you that sounds crazy, I know, but to us it is normal.'

The odds against foreigners finding out about such things are formidable. For Soviet authorities raise many obstacles to normal, easy open contacts between Russians and foreigners. Those who travel to Russia for brief visits are usually escorted about in delegations and tour groups to official meetings or tourist sites and are kept occupied with group activities by guides and interpreters who shepherd them from morning to night. (Although I went to Russia skeptical of such tales, one Intourist guide informed me that guides are required to report to the secret police on those foreigners who stray from the group, speak Russian, or have Russian friends or relatives whom they try to contact. He even showed me the room off the lobby of the Intourist Hotel and described the back room on the top floor of the Metropole where KGB officers received their reports. 'Some guides are conscientious about this, and some don't bother much,' he said, 'but everyone is supposed to do it. If you don't, they call you in after a while to ask why not.')

Those who go to Russia as residents live a cloistered existence. On the final approach of our first flight into Moscow, I remember Ann's fleeting notions of freedom. As she peered out of the window of the Austrian airliner flying low over the Western outskirts of the city, she exclaimed: 'Look, there *are* houses! Maybe we can live in a house out of town instead of a foreigners' apartment.' But the choice was not ours. The houses she saw were the little bungalows, the *izbas*, of the peasants or the country cottages and dachas of the Soviet elite. Like nearly all other diplomats, businessmen, and journalists who work in Moscow, we were simply assigned to an apartment building, one of half a dozen foreign ghettos around the city provided by Soviet authorities for foreign residents. We did not even have the choice of apartment. Living where we wanted – out among the Russians – was completely out of the question.

Around our foreign community was stretched a *cordon sanitaire*. The courtyard of our eight-story apartment building at Sadovo Samotechnaya 12/24 was crudely closed off from the adjacent apartment houses of Russians by a ten-foot-high cement wall constructed so close to our building that it was awkward driving in cars to park. The only way to enter our building was through a single archway past uniformed guards who manned a sentry box 24 hours a day. They wore the uniforms of ordinary policemen but actually worked for the KGB.

26

Soviet authorities tried to maintain the transparent fiction that the guards were there for our protection but it broke down on numerous occasions. Once, a 12-year-old Russian school friend of our daughter Laurie telephoned from her home in fright, saying that the guard had stopped and interrogated her closely as she tried to visit us. He had sent her home and she was afraid to come back unless Laurie came out and got her (and she was unique, for other school friends did not dare to come at all except as a group for birthday parties). When I protested to the guards for interfering with the children, one lamely replied that they were only trying to protect us from 'hooligans'. On another occasion, Aleksandr Gleizer, an art collector, rather foolishly tried to bluff his way past the guards to my office which was in the same building, by speaking a few words of English. They seized him, and for more than an hour held him in the sentry box – I could see his terrified face through the window – while I argued with the guards to let him go. Only after a group of other correspondents gathered and the guards evidently feared a lot of unfavorable publicity over such a minor incident, did they release him. Once again, the excuse was that they were trying to protect me from an impostor, though I knew him well and had told them so.

It would never have dawned on most Russians even to venture near our contaminated zone. There was a group of specially screened translators, maids, chauffeurs, janitors, repairmen, and clerks supplied by UPDK, a Soviet government agency, to foreigners and embassies, whose faces were known to the guards and who could enter unhindered. Official and other prominent Russians could pass the guard-barrier for diplomatic receptions and other special occasions by showing written invitations to the guards. But ordinary Russians were challenged and interrogated. In more than three years in Moscow, I found practically none prepared to risk that ordeal. It was possible for us to go out in the car, pick up Russian friends, and drive them into the compound past the guards, but when we did that on two occasions, the guards ran up close to us either to try to identify our guests or to scare them. Other people, even world famous writers or poets, refused invitations to dinner, mostly without explanation. I remember one writer, with a shiver, saying, 'I can't stand being in that atmosphere.'

In another Russian couple we knew, the wife – who came

from a Communist Party family and who prided herself on her independence – maintained that it was not fear that deterred her but the embarrassment of having to answer the guard's questions about her identity and her foreign friends. Her husband disagreed violently. 'How can you say that? How can you pretend you are not afraid?' he gasped and he turned to me and said in a quiet voice, 'Maybe she is not afraid, but I am afraid.'

Such fears gave a lopsided tilt to our Soviet friendships: we went to their homes, but they never came to ours. Life was hampered by other controls, like tapped telephones, special white-on-black license plates for foreigners to make their cars recognizable to all in an instant (our code was K-04: K for correspondent, 04 for American), and the ban on travel more than 25 miles from the Kremlin without special permission (a cumbersome procedure that took a week at a minimum and frequently ended in failure). Once the tap on our office phone was so clumsily installed that the wires got crossed with police headquarters. I was away but my colleague, Chris Wren, kept getting calls for *pult*, the switchboard. It took several calls before he tumbled to *which* switchboard and to the fact that it was police officers and others calling in complaints. When we reported the problem, we got the swiftest, most solicitous attention on any repair job during my time in Moscow.

Yet, in all honesty, it was not merely controls that inhibited foreign contact with ordinary Russians. Because of the obvious obstacles very few foreigners make a serious and sustained effort to meet and get to know Russians, other than their few designated official contacts. A rather comfortable paternalism envelops the foreign community. The lack of choice in housing may be an affront to a Westerner's sense of freedom but it spares him from house-hunting and simultaneously insulates him from that kind of humdrum encounter with ordinary Russians. The same is true with shopping. Soviet authorities provide special hard currency food shops which, though they periodically run out of ordinary things like tomatoes, tuna fish, orange juice, or strawberry jam, are far better stocked and cheaper than ordinary state stores. The result is that few foreign women even bother to go to Russian stores or experience what shopping is like for Russian women. Similarly, most foreigners travel by car and miss a chance to mingle with Russians who almost all have to ride the bus, tram or subway. The ghetto existence is reinforced by foreign schools – a French school, a German school, an Anglo-American school for the children of foreigners, run by Western embassies. UPDK, the government agency that supplies maids and translators, also provides special ballet classes, language tutoring, exercise groups, and occasional tours to occupy the diplomatic wives.

Each major embassy has its own country house for rural outings, picnics, and parties. About 100 miles northwest of Moscow, at Zavidovo, there are some government lodges on the Volga River which foreigners can rent for a taste of rustic Russia. (A Russian friend who had a boat that he operated on the river said he was sternly warned by guards to stay away from the areas used by foreigners.) West of Moscow, beyond a lovely pine forest, there is a 'diplomatic beach' on the Moscow River. But the foreigner who tries to edge further down the riverbank where Russians swim and fish may be stopped by militia men who jot down license plate numbers and shoo the wayward foreigners back to their own section. Stopping on the road that passes through the dacha-land of the elite is also forbidden.

The consequence of this privileged segregation is that most foreigners – even East Europeans – stick to the beaten path. They pass their Moscow tours entertaining each other and going occasionally to museums and tourist haunts. Except for official functions with Russians, life soon comes to resemble a long cruise on a luxury liner with the same old bridge partners every evening.

Yet surprisingly, all these mechanics of segregated living do not make it impossible for a curious, purposeful Russian-speaking foreigner to meet and get to know Russians. What the restrictions do insure, however, is that by and large those with whom foreigners tend to mix are special people, almost all unusual in some way. And this obviously affects and colors an outsider's view of Russia.

An entire veneer of people, running into the thousands, has been created by the Soviet system for dealing with foreigners. We used to call them 'official Russians' but we did not mean merely government officials. For the veneer extends to high-level journalists specializing in foreign affairs, to Intourist guides, translators, specialists at the Institute of the U.S.A. and Canada or the Institute of World Economy and International Relations, executives in foreign trade organizations, Party scientists and administrators. Practically every Soviet institution from the Red Army to the Writers' Union or the Russian Orthodox Church has its foreign department set up to deal with outsiders. So fixed is the circuit for foreigners that I found on a trip to Lake Baikal and Irkutsk in Siberia, I was taken to the very same specialists whom Ted Shabad, another *Times* reporter, had met ten years before.

These 'official Russians' who have a license, in effect, to deal with foreigners have the task of projecting *Pravda*'s Russia, the Russia of scientific success, socialist workers' democracy, and the modern welfare state. Although I had working relationships with about 30 such people, it was very hard – though not impossible – to find out what they thought about life and to get to know them personally. Mine was far from a unique experience. I knew a Scandinavian Ambassador who had served several years in Moscow and who complained that he had never been invited home by his opposite number in the Soviet Foreign Ministry. Even when the Russian official's mother died, the Ambassador said, he was held at arms' length. He called the Foreign Ministry to obtain the official's home address to send condolences and flowers, but the Ministry refused to give it out. He was instructed to send his flowers to the Ministry. Other foreigners have been treated differently, but the results are often the same. Sargent Shriver, the international lawyer and presidential aspirant, told me that he had not only gotten the official red carpet treatment in Moscow but that he had also been invited home by several foreign trade officials and executives. The hospitality was cordial, he said, but the talk was dry. 'I've had what they call in diplomacy an exchange of views,' Shriver said, 'but I've never had with any Russians what you and I would call a conversation.'

It is hard for someone sitting in the comfort of a Western living room accustomed to the give-and-take of an open society, to grasp what an obstacle this uncommunicative façade poses. I have often been asked by people in the West whether censorship is a problem for reporters in Russia. Not literally. Censorship on outgoing dispatches was ended by Khrushchev in 1961 and most newsmen now send out their stories direct by telex or cable (though photos have to go through censorship). The Russians have other ways of dealing with reporters who poke into things they prefer left uncovered. The most common is constantly to hound, scold, reprimand them for their dispatches, usually in private but sometimes publicly in the press. Occasionally, tires are punctured or reporters are beaten up by police goons to deter them from making unauthorized contacts. Once during my tour, two Western newsmen were interrogated by the KGB in investigations of criminal cases against dissidents, which put a chill on everyone. More frequently, the Soviet Foreign Ministry simply refuses to let reporters travel outside of Moscow or to get official interviews if the Party takes offense at their writing. It happened to me several times. Once, as punishment, I was excluded from a group interview that Brezhnev held with American correspondents on the eve of a summit meeting. And finally, correspondents are expelled or forced to withdraw as were at least four correspondents during my stay in Moscow.

Yet, these harassments in fact represent less of a problem than censorship. Not the censorship which most Westerners immediately call to mind but the self-censorship of most Russians that inhibits them from speaking candidly with outsiders about their society. For most people, this is a habit born of fear and loyalty. But ultimately it springs from a national mania for dressing up reality at all costs and covering up the secret vices or virtues of Russian life or the awkward truths that do not square with Communist propaganda. Nearly everyone is coopted to some degree into not revealing that Soviet life does not measure up to the Party's pretensions – whether the artless fiction that Soviet writers do not have to submit to censorship, the counterfeit claim that more than 100 Soviet nationalities live in happy harmony, or merely the petty pretension that under socialism, waitresses do not need or want tips.

Plenty of Western officials and politicians, of course, squirm mightily to avoid admitting inconvenient facts, but rarely do they resort to the blatant and often baffling extremes of Soviet posturing and prevarication. Soviet officials will blandly deny to an American legal delegation that the Soviet Union imposes the death penalty (though the Soviet press occasionally reports executions); contend to Congressmen that emigration by Jews and others is completely free; insist that the Soviet labor camps have an excellent medical

31

system (after the death of a well-known political prisoner operated on for an ulcer by another prisoner because no professional medical care was available) ; and make other claims that immediately cause a foreigner to raise a skeptical eyebrow.

What makes the Soviet false fronts so much more misleading than those of other countries is the lack of public controversy and independent information to provide a corrective context. The visitor can peer in vain at power stations, truck factories or private cars for an understanding of Soviet Russia. It is not a monolith but it can wear a pretty monolithic façade and the outsider can miss entirely the intangibles and the invisible mechanisms that set it and its people apart from America, the West, and even Eastern Europe.

Another problem is that individual Soviets will sometimes quite consciously shut out the foreigner even when he thinks he is enjoying a moment of personal confidence. I remember a Jewish scientist telling me how, on a trip to America, he had been asked by a Midwestern scholar whether there was academic discrimination against Jews in the Soviet Union. The two were alone and yet this Soviet scholar told me that he lied to the American and told her there was no discrimination even though he had been personally very upset by repeated cases in his own department. He had been afraid, he said, that if he told her the truth, somehow the word would get back to Moscow and he would be denied further trips abroad. He said he was confessing this to me only after having decided to emigrate to Israel and having broken his ties with the Soviet system.

Societies, of course, play down their problems, put their best foot forward and try to make a good impression on visitors, but Soviet society, with the special vanity of its utopian ideology, takes this tendency to extremes. No more dramatic example of staging a show to impress foreigners took place during my stay in Russia than the facelifting given Moscow just before President Nixon's visit in the summer of 1972. Entire blocks of old buildings were burned down and carted away. Hundreds of people were moved out. Streets were widened and repaved, buildings repainted, trees and lawns planted, fringed with fresh flowerbeds put in practically on the eve of his arrival. Even our building, far from the Kremlin, was spruced up a bit on the odd chance that Nixon might show up. Under the czars this was called

'Potemkinizing', after the prince who erected fake villages along the highway used by Catherine the Great to impress her with the wealth of his region. Nowadays, Russians call it *pokazukha*, for show.

Pokazukha can cover anything from the hard currency shops, the fancy imported goods in the windows of G.U.M. department store (goods which usually *cannot* be bought inside) to the model farms and factories where foreigners are taken, down to a little thing like elaborate menus in tourist hotels. Printed on glossy paper, Russian menus can run for pages, spinning out an impressive list of selections in four languages. Only when it comes to ordering does the visitor confront the reality that only about one-third of the plates listed are actually available. So common is this phenomenon that a colleague of Sol Hurok, the impresario, told me that whenever Russian waiters used to present Mr Hurok with a menu and ask what he wanted, he would reply, 'Never mind the menu and the "What do you want, Mr Hurok?" Just tell me what you've got.'

I was myself once accidentally caught up in a *pokazukha*-in-the-making. On one trip to Baku, I was staying in a hotel by the Caspian Sea when word came down that a delegation of foreign ambassadors was about to make an official visit. Like the provincial bureaucrats of Gogol's rich satire *The Inspector General*, the staff scurried about in a frenzy to make the hotel more presentable. The corridor lady collected all the room keys so that workmen could paint new numbers in gold lettering. A cross-eyed electrician began replacing burnt out light bulbs. Maids went to work washing windows and dusting. The front door and the railings on the promenade along the seashore were given a fresh coat of paint. The regular glass ashtrays disappeared from the dining room tables and new, more decorative ashtrays appeared. Large white carnations were placed on each table, along with fancier, shinier, and higher priced menus for the Ambassadors. Not only was this done at the hotel, one Ambassador told me, but at other installations which they visited.

At times pulling the wool over foreigners' eyes approaches a national sport. 'We do it naturally,' a bright young government consultant on foreign policy admitted to me one evening in the privacy of his apartment. 'It is to our advantage. Deceit is a compensation for weakness, for a feeling of inferiority before foreigners. As a nation, we cannot deal with others equally. Either we are more powerful or they are. And if they are, and we feel it, we compensate by deceiving them. It is a very important feature of our national character.' When I observed that his own comments were some disproof of what he was saying, he smilingly responded that he was the exception proving the rule.

Fortunately, he was not unique, for I found a fair number of other exceptions as well. Like Sargent Shriver and many others, I have spent untold hours in uncommunicative dialogues across green felt-topped tables that are a fixture in practically every Soviet institution. But in other settings, out of earshot of others and either to show their own sophistication or because they were tired of the false front, some official Russians opened up. Politics might be taboo (though not always), but like other peoples, Russians like to talk about their personal lives and in the process reveal much about their society. They are usually flattered when foreigners speak their tongue and they are so generously tolerant of the linguistic mistakes of foreigners that I quickly found I greatly enjoyed talking with them in Russian and they, too, felt more relaxed.

On a lengthy car trip through the Caucasus, for example, I had one escort-interpreter (helping me but also keeping me insulated from too much exposure to Soviet life) who slipped into a sad discussion of her problems as a working woman and the hard life of Soviet women generally. At a trade fair, ignored by others and perhaps eager to share a common parental problem, a Communist Party man fell into talking to me about the difficulty of bringing up his sons to be good Communists when all they were interested in was Western rock. In his office, a Soviet intelligence man whose job was to oversee travel and interviews for foreign correspondents, told me of his amazement at the openness of American life and showed off one of the nicely tailored suits and bright wide ties he had brought back from an American trip. There are many other examples I cannot cite for fear of exposing friends to reprisals. The point is that characteristically, taken out of the official setting, Russians begin to reveal something of that other human Russia beneath the official façade. Their instincts, like Misha's, are friendly. Perhaps that is why the controls are tight and official Russians almost always meet foreigners in groups.

There are other types of people who have less sanction

than official Russians to mix with foreigners but often have more personal incentive and show less restraint in doing so – establishment intellectuals, young people, underground artists, dissidents, emigrating Jews. Some establishment intellectuals are interested in little more than maintaining a liberal reputation in the West, wangling an invitation to America, or drinking embassy gin and whisky and keeping a safe distance. Some young people want no more than to buy the jeans off your legs or the latest Western records, the artists to sell their paintings, and the Jews and dissidents to publicize their protests. But in all these groups, I found individuals who were genuinely interesting and revealing, people who were capable of seeing their own society critically though not disloyally, eager for outside contact, and anxious to share ideas and experiences. Some of them became very warm friends.

Being Moscow Bureau Chief for *The New York Times* was an advantage. It gave me more entrée than most other foreign newsmen to senior Soviet journalists at *Pravda, Izvestia,* and elsewhere. Those who had traveled abroad tended to be less obviously dogmatic than government officials who were ill at ease with Western newsmen and generally inaccessible anyway. These newsmen had their professional self-respect to maintain among their Western competitors. Among ordinary Russians being from the *Times* was a help, too, because the Soviet press so frequently quotes the *Times* to try to gain credibility and it is well known to Russians. I made it a practice to inform people who I was. A few were immediately wary. But others, even those who said suspiciously, 'Oh, a journalist,' were intrigued. Some even seemed to make a point of making petty disclosures or complaints, evidently feeling that if they remained anonymous to me, it was safer to tell their thoughts to a foreigner than to another Russian.

At one period, I was pestered by phone by an elderly lady with a quavering voice who insisted on meeting me. Reluctantly, I went. She described how she and her invalid husband and his invalid father were squeezed into a one-room apartment in violation of all housing norms and how officials refused to give them better housing. She was unbelievably plucky for not only had she protested to the Communist Party Central Committee but she thought that if I wrote about her plight, the Soviet authorities would have to solve the problem. (My reaction was the opposite – that a story using her name would get her into serious trouble.) More common was the case of the man who somehow got my home phone and called one night, speaking with a Baltic accent, to tell me how he had been mistreated by the Soviet guards when he approached the American Embassy . . . and the line went dead before he finished.

The most surprising to me, however, were the chance encounters with people all over the country. Ann and I found that the farther we went from Moscow, the less inhibited and less strictly indoctrinated people seemed to be. In minority republics like Georgia, Lithuania, Armenia, Uzbekistan, Estonia, Azerbaijan, Moldavia, even the Ukraine, people were usually more candid than politically sensitive Muscovites, and a fair number of them were critical of the Soviet system because of their outspokenly anti-Russian feelings. The problem always was to find the time and the setting, whether in a restaurant, a theater, on a train, or in an airport, for an opportunity to talk.

Westerners, especially Americans, are always in a hurry when they travel. In Russia, we almost always went by train because we found Russian trains comfortable and because it was a good way to get to know people. I have sat in a dining car with a wiry little state farm director for a couple of hours spooning up borscht and drinking sour, watery beer while he explained how he got one-up on socialism by raising his own private herd of sheep. I have been accosted by a Latvian engineer with thick glasses who read somewhere that the Americans had invented eyeglasses that correct color blindness and would I please help him get a pair, and wound up talking about the foibles of Soviet construction. I have swayed in the aisle of a Baku–Tbilisi overnight local churning through the Caucasus mountains, while a construction worker unfolded to me the mysteries of getting a job abroad, going through a labyrinth of security clearances and indoctrination, and finally enjoying the benefits of overseas pay bonuses. I have played backgammon with two Soviet fighter pilots for several hours while one of them chug-a-lugged vodka and whisky, hugged my wife because her name was the same as his sister's, and kept slapping me on the back and saying, 'So you're a real American,' because the only other Americans he had ever seen were the American pilots of reconnaissance planes against whom he flew wing-tip to wing-tip in a Cold War game of chicken over the White Sea.

In some ways, when we were away from Moscow, life in Russia became a picaresque experience, as we caromed off one individual onto another. Hard as it was to adjust to this fleeting contact, Ann and I came to cherish some of our one-time friends as much as our closer, longer-term Russian friends in Moscow – whether the Armenians who impulsively invited us to attend their church wedding and their long family celebration afterward because they had an uncle in San Francisco, or the nervous Lithuanian artist from whom we bought a couple of modernistic graphic etchings. There was something about the setting, the difficulty of breaking through the barriers of mistrust and fear, and finding the sudden human warmth that made these encounters precious occasions. I remember once in Leningrad an accidental acquaintance that Ann, who is a teacher, struck up with a Russian teacher to whom she turned for help in a store. The woman spoke some English. Before we knew it, we were invited home. Strange as it may sound, we formed a sudden fast friendship with this Russian woman and her husband. For hours on end, they devoured what we had to say about life and culture in the West and we devoured what they told us about their own lives and emotions. We ate plain cheese sandwiches and soup, and lingered long into the night while they showed us slides of their camping trip in the Caucasus Mountains and we told them about our family camping in the Blue Ridge and Smoky Mountains of Virginia and Tennessee. Through other Americans who later met this couple bearing notes from us, we heard that they had been terribly afraid about having made contact with us after my name was mentioned on Voice of America broadcasts. And yet they got over it and sent these same intermediaries back to us with notes and gifts of remembrance.

The tragedy is not that communication is impossible but that so much effort is expended to prevent it, for these are often precisely the unplanned, uncontrolled contacts the Soviet authorities seem determined to obstruct – not the friendship and emotion, but the revelations that go with them. During my time in Moscow, several reporters were beaten up and temporarily detained for contacting dissidents and Jews. Most of us were tailed at times. In Yerevan, the capital of Armenia, I remember looking for an American-born Armenian schoolteacher who had once talked with other American reporters. It was morning and I was trying to find his school. I kept stopping to ask school children the way. I happened to look back and 30 paces behind me, a man in a dark suit would stop and question each school child with whom I talked. I found the teacher at school before classes started and asked him when it would be best for us to meet and, evidently having paid painfully for his last talk with American reporters, he replied, 'It would be best for us not to meet at all.' In Riga with Mike McGuire of the *Chicago Tribune*, the team of surveillance agents that followed us for three days was so obvious that we developed nicknames for them – Chief, Shorty, the Veteran, and so on – and watched them change shifts. In Moscow, I would sometimes spot cars tailing mine, once so openly that Ann and the children watched him follow us from our apartment to the hard currency food store, hanging out the car window to keep an eye on us. I also remember the wan smile of a young Army officer who had been caught talking with us in our train compartment and was hauled off for interrogation by the military police. We had only been sharing impressions of Leningrad with him.

Sometimes foreigners get overly paranoid about being under surveillance or the dangers of sexual provocation by the KGB. Diplomats loved to swap old stories about Soviet *femmes fatales* and this made most men hyper-alert. I recall a dinner in a skimpy little hotel restaurant in Siberia when I had to share the only empty table for a late dinner with three local women just deserted by some Russian boyfriends. All had been drinking and found it a lark to have an American at their table. They were quite forward. As we talked, the flowsy-haired young brunette nearest to me tried holding hands, rubbed my knee and urged me to go with them for some late night fun. I began to wonder whether this was the start of a frame-up. Someone tapped my shoulder. I turned around to find a husky Army officer looming over me. He motioned me to the hallway. *Is this the way it happens?* I wondered. Figuring the safest place to be was right in that restaurant with a crowd watching, I refused to budge. He insisted I come with him. I refused again, but he kept insisting. The girls tried to get rid of him, but he wouldn't leave. I looked closer and sensed that he, too, had been drinking, though not much. And I was anxious to quiet down the fuss being made over me, so I agreed to go out in the hall. When we were alone, he turned and shook my hand, apologized profusely for my misfortune in having fallen in with local whores, and urged me to leave the table. He only wanted to help me. I had to laugh at my own fears for he was the furthest possible person from an agent trying to entrap me. Nor do I believe that the actual tailing of correspondents was continuous and systematic. It did not have to be. The simplest method of keeping track of us was to surround us most of the time with Soviet translators, guides and chauffeurs in Moscow and with escorts from the Foreign Ministry, Intourist or Novosti Press Agency when we traveled elsewhere.

Even then, in my experience, the system of insulating foreigners from Russians was afflicted with the same bureaucratic muddle and inefficiency that plagues other elements of the Soviet system, and we had a lot of time to ourselves. Sometimes, too, the most elaborate precautions of Soviet security officials would backfire.

Michael Parks of the *Baltimore Sun* told me of a trip he took to the provincial city of Ufa, 900 miles east of Moscow, to cover a traveling American exhibition and to see what provincial life was like. He was given only an overnight visa but when he was ready to come back to Moscow on Saturday evening, Aeroflot, the Soviet airline, had no seat for him. This produced great consternation because Aeroflot flights are notoriously overbooked and such an obvious security infraction as allowing him to stay on until the next flight on Monday was impermissible. The solution of the airport security officials was to haul nine Russian passengers off one flight to Moscow to make room for Parks. Why nine? For security reasons. Parks was placed in the middle seat of one row of three seats. Both seats on either side of him were emptied and so were the complete rows in front and behind him. For a few minutes he sat there in splendid isolation while the security men disappeared and a volcanic argument exploded among the unhappy Russians who had been kept off the plane. One of the stewardesses, oblivious to the security problem, appeared and demanded why Parks was sitting all alone. Parks said he didn't know and the stewardess, more concerned with appeasing the roiling mob outside, filled all the seats around him. On one side sat an Army colonel's wife, and on the other the wife of a petroleum engineer. Both talked to him steadily all the way to Moscow, the engineer's wife complaining about how little there was to buy in the shops in Ufa and the colonel's wife telling him how happy she was that her husband was in armor and finally out of paratroops because so many paratroopers were breaking their limbs and having accidents. They had heard about the American exhibition but had been unable to get there and they wanted Parks to tell them all about the American cars and consumer goods.

I had similar experiences – precisely the kind of contacts the KGB wanted to prevent.

PART ONE
The People

I

THE PRIVILEGED CLASS
Dachas and Zils

> . . . every Leninist knows (that is, if he is a real
> Leninist) that equalization in the sphere of require-
> ments and individual life is a piece of reactionary
> petty bourgeois absurdity . . .
>
> Stalin 1934

Pick any weekday afternoon to stroll down Granovsky Street
two blocks from the Kremlin, as I have, and you will find two
lines of polished black Volga sedans, engines idling and
chauffeurs watchfully eyeing their mirrors. They are parked
self-confidently over the curbs, in defiance of No Parking
signs but obviously unworried about the police. Their attention is on the entrance at No. 2 Granovsky, a drab beige
structure, windows painted over and a plaque that says: 'In
this building on April 19, 1919, Vladimir Ilyich Lenin spoke
before the commanders of the Red Army headed for the
[civil war] front.'

A second sign, by the door, identifies the building simply
as 'The Bureau of Passes'. But not just for anyone, I was told.
Only for the Communist Party Central Committee staff and
their families. An outsider, not attuned to the preference of
Party officials for black Volgas and untrained to spot the telltale MOC and MOII license plates of Central Committee
cars, would notice nothing unusual. Now and then, men and

41

women emerge from 'The Bureau of Passes' with bulging bags and packages wrapped discreetly in plain brown paper, and settle comfortably in the rear seats of the waiting Volgas to be chauffeured home. Down the block and out of general view, other chauffeurs are summoned by loudspeaker into an enclosed and guarded courtyard to pick up telephone orders for delivery. A white-haired watchman at the gate shoos away curious pedestrians, as he did me when I paused to admire the ruins of a church at the rear of the courtyard.

For these people are part of the Soviet elite, doing their shopping in a closed store deliberately unmarked to avoid attracting attention, accessible only with a special pass.

An entire network of such stores serves the upper crust of Soviet society – the bosses or what one Soviet journalist irreverently called, 'Our Communist nobility.' These stores insulate the Soviet aristocracy from chronic shortages, endless waiting in line, rude service, and other daily harassments that plague ordinary citizens. Here, the politically anointed can obtain rare Russian delicacies like caviar, smoked salmon, the best canned sturgeon, export brands of vodka or unusual vintages of Georgian and Moldavian wines, choice meat, fresh fruits and vegetables in winter that are rarely available elsewhere. Once, a Russian woman told me an old joke about a little girl asking her mother the difference between rich and poor people in Russia and getting the answer: 'The rich eat tomatoes year-round and we eat them only in summer.'

Certain stores also provide the elite with foreign goods the proletariat never lays eyes on (at cut-rate, duty-free prices): French cognac, Scotch whisky, American cigarettes, imported chocolates, Italian ties, Austrian fur-lined boots, English woolens, French perfumes, German shortwave radios, Japanese tape recorders and stereo sets. In other stores, VIPs are even supplied with hot, ready-cooked meals to take out, prepared by Kremlin chefs. So superior is the quality of this food to the common fare in state stores that one well-connected Muscovite told me that she and her friends patronize a 'diet' food store in the Old Arbat district because it gets leftovers from 'The Bureau of Passes' on Granovsky Street.

The Soviet system of privileges has its protocol: perquisites are parceled out according to rank. At the top, the supreme leaders of the Communist Party Politburo, members of the powerful Party Central Committee, cabinet ministers, and the small executive group that runs the Supreme Soviet, or parliament, get the *kremlevsky payok*, the Kremlin ration – enough food to feed their families luxuriously every month – free.* (By contrast, an ordinary urban family of four might spend 180–200 rubles a month, easily half its income, on food.) The very top leaders get home delivery or supposedly use stores right inside the Kremlin and Central Committee headquarters. Deputy ministers and the Supreme Soviet executive group have their special shop at Government House, a hulking gray apartment building next to the Shockworker Movie Theater on Bersenevsky Embankment Road. Old Bolsheviks who joined the Party before 1930 and are now on pension get their Kremlin ration at a special shop in a three-story building on Komsomol Lane. The value and quality of the rations are arranged in descending order, according to the rank of those receiving them.

Other special cut-rate food stores cater to Soviet marshals and admirals, to top-flight scientists, cosmonauts, economic managers, highly-decorated Heroes of Socialist Labor, to Lenin Prize-winning writers, actors, or ballet stars, to senior editors of *Pravda*, *Izvestia*, or other important publications, to the Moscow city hierarchy. The Central Committee apparatus has three levels of officials and employees, I was told by a man who often visited officials there, and they shop at three different, graded shops and eat in cafeterias at Party headquarters provisioned strictly according to the pecking order. Middle-level functionaries in the Party, major ministries, the armed forces general staff, or the secret police have middle-level stores with fewer luxury items, and they pay more than the big bosses.

In many government agencies the higher-ups are rewarded with what are known as 'special distributions', actually passes granting them access to special stores located on the premises. Each official, one bureaucrat told me, has some specified quota of money that he can spend in the store, marked on an

* A former Central Committee official, writing in the British quarterly *Survey* (Fall, 1974 – A. Pravdin, 'Inside the CPSU Central Committee') reported there were two categories of Kremlin ration for top Party people – one technically worth 32 rubles and the other 16 rubles. But, the defector said, this was misleading because the vouchers are 'paid in their gold equivalents [and] the actual value of the "ration" must be increased 15 to 20 times to reflect their real purchasing power.' That would make the best ones worth 480–600 rubles ($640–800) a month.

identification card, and fixed according to his rank. The amounts are kept secret from subordinates. Tucked away on the third floor of G.U.M., Moscow's main department store emporium, is Section 100 – a specially stocked clothing shop for part of the elite. In the basement of Voyentorg (Army-Navy store) on Kalinin Prospekt, there is a secret shop for military officers. Dotted around Moscow are tailors, hair-dressers, launderers, cleaners, picture framers, and other retail outlets – about 100 in all including the food stores, I was told by one man with access to the network – secretly serving a select clientele. 'I couldn't believe my eyes . . . I wanted to buy everything in the store,' a middle-aged woman journalist confided to me after she had been smuggled into one store by a powerful friend. 'For *them*,' added her husband, 'Communism has arrived.'

For another privileged sliver of Soviet society there are eight hard-currency *Beryozka* shops in Moscow where Russians with 'certificate rubles' can buy imported goods or hard-to-find Soviet items at bargain prices. Certificate rubles are a special currency usually issued to those who have earned money abroad – diplomats, trusted journalists, poets, and the like – which they must change back into Soviet money. But well-connected government officials supposedly get part-pay in these certificates, which trade on the black market at up to 8-to-1 for regular rubles. Almost anyone who deals regularly with foreigners – Intourist guides, interpreters for govern-ment agencies, journalists who escort foreigners, language tutors who teach diplomats – gets some allowance in certifi-cate rubles to spend on an imported scarf, a colorful shirt or tie, a pair of platform shoes to spruce up an otherwise pedestrian Soviet wardrobe. In addition, higher-ups who occasionally entertain foreign dignitaries are supplied with restaurant catering for parties and, I heard, are even loaned furs for their wives for special occasions. One American dip-lomat even noticed the security man who had tailed him shopping in a *Beryozka* store. Many Russians are infuriated at the existence of these stores which are, in effect, a con-sumer goods sector where Soviet currency is not accepted. 'It is so humiliating, so insulting to have stores in our country where our own money is not valid,' fumed a white-collar worker. Not only is the money no good, but people without permission to shop there are turned away by door guards – a sore point with some of my Russian intellectual friends because it so brazenly flouts the proclaimed ideals of socialist equality.

The store on Granovsky Street, which is only the visible tip of the valuable array of perquisites, epitomizes the system of privileges: by and large, these are favors money cannot buy.* They are beyond the reach of ordinary citizens because they are a dividend of political rank or personal achievement in the service of the state. In the West, the plumber or butcher or storekeeper who is willing to blow his cash can buy himself as big a Cadillac, eat as fancy a meal, take a room at as swanky or secluded a hotel, or hire as expert a surgeon as the governor of his state. Not under the Soviet system. It reserves the best exclusively for what Milovan Djilas, the Yugoslav Communist, called 'the New Class . . . those who have special privileges and economic preference because of the administrative monopoly they hold.'

This privileged class is a sizable chunk of Soviet society – well over a million and, counting relatives, probably several million.† Its precise size is one of many elusive things about Soviet society, since the Russians do not admit it exists. Officially there are only two classes, the workers and peasants, and a 'stratum' of employees – white-collar workers and intelligentsia. It is only the upper portion of this intelligentsia which constitutes the real privileged class. Its core is the apex of the Communist Party and the Government, the political bureaucracy that runs the country, joined by the senior economic managers, most influential scientific administrators, and the princes of the Party press and propaganda network.

* Salary levels are a deceptive measure of privilege in the Soviet Union. Brezhnev's official salary, according to what I was told, is 900 rubles a month but his other perquisites make his real income far higher, though incalculable. That is true for many others in the power elite. On the surface, however, Brezhnev looks less well off than a Soviet Marshal (top salary 2,000 rubles monthly), key defense research scientists and administrators (also in the 2,000-ruble range) or a leading writer whose royalties can run to 150,000 rubles for a book that gets picked up by television or the movies. Not only do the power elite get more of the privileges that money cannot buy but Soviet insiders talk of special secret pay-packets for key Party officials, though this is something impossible to calculate with any certainty.

† Western experts have long puzzled unsuccessfully at defining the size of the Soviet elite. T. H. Rigby, *Communist Party Membership in the USSR, 1917–1967* (Princeton, 1968), p. 348, lists 936,000 Party members in the Party, government, and economic bureaucracy. But the privileged class extends as well to the elites of other walks of life – science, culture, and the military, among others.

The nerve center of the system is known in Soviet parlance as the *nomenklatura*, the nomenclature or secret roster of those who hold the most sensitive positions and who are selected by the Party bosses. *Nomenklatura* exists on practically every level of Soviet life from a village to the Kremlin. At the top, the *nomenklatura* of the Politburo – that is, the posts filled by direct appointment of the Soviet rulers themselves – are the Cabinet ministers, the head of the Academy of Sciences, editors of *Pravda* and *Izvestia*, Party bosses in all the republics and provinces, deputy ministers of the most sensitive ministries, the ambassador to the United States and a few other key ambassadors, and the secretariat of the Communist Party Central Committee. This secretariat, a body more powerful than the White House staff, then names more people to thousands of other important jobs – lower, but still very important. And so on down the line to republics, provinces, cities, districts, villages, in a huge patronage system.

It is this patronage system à la Tammany Hall, in this same careful hierarchy, that is being rewarded through the network of special stores and other facilities. The system spreads out across the country, and even in provincial capitals a similar network of closed stores and other privileges exists for the local elite, on a smaller and more modest scale, of course. *Nomenklatura* operates like a self-perpetuating, self-selecting fraternity, a closed corporation. Rank-and-file Party members do not enjoy the dividends of the corporation, only those in positions of Party leadership or in jobs within the Party *apparat* – the *apparatchiki*.

The one other avenue into the Soviet elite, the one other criterion of status and privilege in the Soviet system, is the ability of an individual to contribute to the power and prestige of the Soviet State in some demonstrable way. For outstanding service to the state, a leading scientist, prima ballerina, cosmonaut, Olympic champion, famous violinist, or renowned military commander can earn status in the Soviet elite – status, but not power, and that is the essential difference that marks off the political elite from all others.

As performers in the display of Soviet power and success, cultural and scientific celebrities must demonstrate loyalty to maintain their standing and privileges. The Party holds the monopoly of awarding them lavish financial prizes and bestowing on them the orders and ranks that guarantee a life of ease, or simply deciding who gets profitably published. The

46

Party also punishes. It can withhold official recognition, as it did in the early years in denying Aleksandr Solzhenitsyn the Lenin Prize; or it can withdraw privilege when it is offended, as it did in suspending the right to travel abroad and even to perform at home for Mstislav Rostropovich, the famous cellist who came to Solzhenitsyn's defense. But normally, both as a token of success and as a means of co-opting those who are already successful, the Party bureaucracy grants to the cultural and scientific elite titles of People's Artist or Lenin Laureate, and privileges like comfortable country homes, much as the Russian czars through the centuries granted estates and titles of nobility to the service gentry who performed valiantly for the crown.

After the Revolution, Lenin decreed that talented specialists should be paid more than ordinary workers and that scientists should get special food rations, in spite of Communism's egalitarian goals. John Reed, the American Communist who wrote *Ten Days That Shook the World*, recorded his uneasiness at Soviet leaders' arrogating privileges to themselves. But it was Stalin who really developed the system of privilege and boldly defended it with capitalistic logic – on the grounds that certain people, certain groups, who were especially valuable to the state, merited special pay and rewards. Now, an entire department of the Party Central Committee known by the innocuous title of *Upravleniye Delami* – 'the Administration of Affairs' – and with a secret budget, operates and equips an extensive stable of choice apartment houses, country dachas, government guest houses, special rest homes, fleets of car pools, and squads of security-screened servants for the power elite. A Moscow journalist explained to me that these servants have to sign a statement saying they will not gossip about how the elite conduct their private lives. They are richly rewarded for their discretion, he said, because they have their own special stores and dacha complexes.

The most conspicuous symbols of rank and privilege are the chauffeur-driven limousines of the *nachalstvo* (the bosses), with their gray curtains discreetly shrouding VIPs from curious glances. They race down the centers of streets while policemen frantically motion other traffic to the curb. At the corner of Granovsky Street, along Leonid Brezhnev's route home from the Kremlin, a loud buzzer warns the traffic cop to halt other vehicles when one of the bigshots heads out of the Kremlin toward the green-belt villa settlements of the most mighty. Word gets radioed ahead to other police on the route.

The cream of the elite, about 20 people in all – Politburo members and national secretaries of the Communist Party – get to use black Zil limousines, handtooled and worth about $75,000 apiece. I once peered into a parked leadership Zil until a security man waved me away. It looked like an elongated Lincoln Continental with a posh interior – soft vinyl armchair seats, plus carpeting, air conditioning, radio telephones, and other gadgetry. An engineer, a student of the trappings of power, told me that Stalin was known for using a convoy of six cars – five Zils and one old luxury Packard, using a different car each time so that no one would know precisely where he was. Khrushchev cut it back to four. Ever since a disgruntled lieutenant took a shot at Brezhnev's car at the Kremlin's Borovitsky Gate on January 22, 1969, Brezhnev has usually moved in a four-car motorcade.

For the second echelon who don't quite rate a Zil, the most prestigious car is the Chaika, a bulky, high-bodied limousine that looks like a pregnant Fifties style Packard. So well known are Chaikas for barging down the special center lane of main avenues, the lane reserved for VIP cars, that it has colloquially become known as 'the Chaika Lane'. Cabinet ministers, admirals and marshals, and important visiting foreign dignitaries and delegations rate Chaikas. Some Western embassies and businesses have bought them for 10,000 rubles ($13,300). Ordinary Russians sometimes rent them for wedding parties.

So vast are the fleets of chauffeur-driven state cars (mostly black Volgas) that ordinary Russians take luxury cars for political bigshots for granted. But I have heard people complain that limousine drivers charge through narrow intersections without slowing down, scattering pedestrians like so many chickens on a country road and forcing other motorists to the curbs. An American black woman, attending the Soviet-sponsored World Congress of Peace-Loving Forces in 1973, was so uncomfortable at the lordly way the Chaika driver was racing through the crowds with her official delegation, that she complained that it reminded her of stories about the disdainful way czarist nobility dashed down the centers of roads, splattering mud on the peasants. 'Shhhh,' cautioned the official Soviet guide, 'that's not nice to say.'

As ostentatious tokens of rank and privilege, however, the chauffeur-driven cars are atypical. Generally, the Soviet political elite enjoys its privileged life in privacy and inconspicuous consumption, unseen by its own public. I was a bit surprised myself in 1974 at the glittering reception held in the cool elegance of St George's Hall in the Kremlin in honor of President Nixon. I was only a few feet away from the leaders when they entered the hall and stood in a row for the playing of the national anthems – there was Nixon in his blue serge suit; Party Leader Leonid Brezhnev pursing his lips and sporting a wide, Western-style, wine-red tie; President Nikolai Podgorny with a button nose; and Prime Minister Aleksei Kosygin, looking bored, his eyes wandering like a small boy impatient for the ceremony to end. The banquet tables, that seemed 100 yards long on either side of the room, groaned with delicacies – several kinds of caviar, smoked salmon, roast suckling pig. Waiters in white livery moved under the large crystal chandeliers passing hot snacks while an orchestra in the balcony played songs from *South Pacific* for a guest list of hundreds from the Soviet elite. It was only natural for American reporters to mention the regal hospitality of the Soviet leadership, but the Soviet press kept a discreet silence. And not a single glimpse of this sumptuous ostentation appeared on Soviet television. This is typical of the Kremlin leaders, for their lives are unseen. They dwell in exclusive residential ghettos, spend their leisure hours at their own holiday hideaways or in clubs segregated by rank. When they travel out of Moscow they use a special airport, Vnukovo II. The man in the street may be vaguely aware of their privileged existence, but he is kept well at a distance.

The Kremlin itself is enormously imposing. But Moscow has no official residence to match the White House. Soviet leaders put greater stock in their country dachas than their in-town apartment residences. Brezhnev occupies one floor in the rear wing of a heavy old nine-story apartment building at 26 Kutuzov Prospekt, with Secret Police Chief Yuri Andropov and Internal Security Minister Nikolai Shchelokov on the floors above and below. Kosygin has the most enviable in-town location: a modern apartment building perched on Lenin Hills, overlooking downtown Moscow from across the Moscow River. Podgorny, I was told, lives in a tall, well-groomed, yellow-brick apartment house on Aleksei Tolstoy

Street. There are several other important in-town ghettos for the political elite and Moscow Party apparatus. To the discerning eye, these high-rise apartments have telltale trademarks of power – clean, modern design, yellow-brick construction, unusually big picture windows, recessed balconies, well-kept lawns and landscaping – posh for the Soviet scene.

It is the interiors, however, that dazzle less exalted Russians. An actress with friends in the Moscow hierarchy told me she was astonished to see their kitchens equipped with built-in cabinets, formica-top counters and Kuppersbusch West German stoves and refrigerators, living rooms furnished tastefully in Finnish modern, bought at discounts and imported duty-free. The equipment was so much fancier than anything normally available on the Soviet market, she said, that mechanics had to be specially sent to West Germany to be trained to install and maintain the kitchens of the elite.

Not only the gadgetry but the spacious quarters of higher-ups – the luxury of living one to a bedroom and not having to sleep in the living room – impresses other Russians. A graduate student whom I knew frequently visited the family of General Stefan Mikoyan, a well-established son of long-time Politburo member Anastas Mikoyan, and was awed by their expansive, seven-room apartment (not counting kitchen and baths) at Government House. He made it sound like the best of Park Avenue, private rooms for everyone in the family, a study, living room, and a dining room spacious enough to accommodate a grand piano once played by Van Cliburn, an unthinkably luxurious use of space for 99 percent of the population. Even the ceilings in the flat had struck him as almost indecently high, just as most Soviet apartment ceilings strike Westerners as uncomfortably low. He was unusual in catching a glimpse of how they lived because not many Russians get to see behind the curtain of privacy that the privileged class draws around itself.

'Everything is *maskirovannoye* – masked,' said Pavel, a young government foreign policy specialist, himself the grandson of a Communist who had fallen out of favor. I was walking with him through the Sivtsev Vrazhek district where many elite families live and where he had friends from the exclusive institute which he had attended. 'In these apartment buildings live Central Committee members,' he said, with a wave to one side. 'And look at those shabby buildings across the street. No comparison, is there? Around the corner, over there, is the Central Committee Hotel. No sign. Nothing to tell you what it is. People walk past and barely notice it. That is where they put our friendly, high-level guests – from North Korea, Mongolia, Poland. I had a friend who was assigned to go to Austria. He was dying of curiosity to know what was inside that hotel, to see the furniture and what it looked like inside. So he went in. Before he knew it, a receptionist wanted to know what he was doing there. He got into an argument before he could get back outside. That led to trouble and they canceled his assignment to Austria. It ruined his career, that one mistake. Here, you don't ask questions and poke your nose where you have no business.'

I slowed down to glance at this forbidden building with brass footplates and a long thermometer by the door, curtains blocking any view, and a glassed solarium on the roof. I paused to jot down the address.

'Don't stop here,' Pavel said anxiously. 'Keep walking. Otherwise the *dezhurnaya* [duty-woman] at the entrance of this apartment building will take notice of us.'

We walked on until we were opposite an ungainly, old five-story pseudo-classical building, surrounded by a high fence. It was faced with burnished red granite and had a black-pillared portico. What had once been two stone guardhouses had sunk into the ground and now listed toward each other. The iron gate for what was formerly the main entrance was now permanently chained shut. People were using an entrance to the left. Parked outside were black Volgas with the telltale MOC and MOII license plates. One driver, who wore the flat, short-brimmed fedora and dark blue raincoat of KGB plainclothesmen, was pacing beside his vehicle. Another sat in a car with gaudy red seatcovers minding a little girl in the back seat. Out came a lady in a chic, well-tailored, fur-trimmed coat and imported knee boots. She got in the car with the red seatcovers and was driven off.

'That's the main Kremlin Clinic,' Pavel explained. 'You see the big cupola on top and the heavy columns, the false Greek columns? That's Stalinist style.'

People had spoken of the Kremlin Clinic often but this was my first glimpse. Actually, it is not one clinic but a system of clinics and hospitals loosely known as the Kremlin Clinic. The most conspicuous is across the street from the main entrance of the Lenin Library, around the corner from the Granovsky Street store. It, too, is unmarked except for reliefs of the hammer and sickle by the door. But on occasion, I saw Politburo Zils parked out front, while KGB agents killed time gossiping in sidewalk groups and a chauffeur wiped a rag across a smudged fender. My Russian friends thought it unlikely, however, that Brezhnev or other bigshots actually went there for treatment because, as one journalist said, 'When *they* get sick, the doctors go to *them*.'

The VIPs prefer treatment in secluded places like the hospital at Kuntsevo, in the elite dacha area, where East European leaders like Walter Ulbricht and Erich Honekker, of East Germany, get special medical care. By Soviet standards it is so plush that Aleksandr Tvardovsky, a noted liberal establishment editor once treated there, quipped to friends, 'That's Communism for 80 beds.'

Stalin used an even more exclusive hospital at Fili in the thick pine forest off the main highway to Minsk. Other sanitoria and clinics are dotted along the Baltic Coast, the Black Sea and near health spas, run for the nobility of the *nomenklatura* by what is euphemistically referred to merely as 'The Fourth Administration', meaning the Fourth Administration of the Ministry of Health. Once during an officially arranged interview, a pretty young woman blurted out by mistake that she worked for the Fourth Administration after I asked about her job. You'd have thought she had admitted something awful, like being a spy. Instantly, she dropped her eyes, hoping I would not notice the gaff, and the chief doctor steered the interview away from that conversational shoal.

Other prestigious institutions, like the Academy of Sciences or the Bolshoi Ballet and Opera Company, also have special clinics, hospitals and doctors, far above average. The reputation of their staffs is so far above the average that some of their doctors and dentists do a tidy, illicit private practice on the side. But Moscow Jews told me a little ditty: '*Poly parketnye, vrachi anketnye*,' which challenges the whole notion. Literally translated it comes out something like, 'Floors are parquet, doctors are okay.' What it means is that the facilities may be as fancy as parquet floors but the doctors must be politically okay, which usually rules out Jews and others who may be less reliable politically but much better professionally. Hence, maybe these facilities do not always offer the best doctors. Also, when it comes to medicines, which are very cheap but in such chronic short supply that the Communist press periodically complains about it, the elite get the best.

Pavel, the young foreign policy consultant, used to borrow the I.D. cards of elite friends to sneak into the Kremlin drugstore for new eye-glasses or even to get ordinary items like mustard plaster or folk medicines like the natural tranquillizer, oblepikh bush oil. From others, including a medical scientist, I heard it was very hard to get Valokordin for heart patients, gaminolon for neurological disorders, or synthetic antibiotics like sigmamitsin, as well as Western-made medicines, except in the Kremlin Clinic or other special hospitals.

The greatest perquisites of high status, however, exist outside the city. The leaders and their families have entire communities of hideaway dachas that, individually, may not rival Richard Nixon's luxurious Palm Beach and California retreats but which offer Brezhnev the variety of the mild climate of the Crimea or Pitsunda on the Black Sea, the bracing weather of the Central Russian hunting region around Zavidovo where, like a German baron of old, he enjoys taking foreign guests like Henry Kissinger boar-hunting, the calm of the pine-wood retreat outside of Minsk where he quietly secluded himself with Georges Pompidou of France, or the modern glass-and-teak, Finnish-built state guest houses not far from Leningrad.

Practically any major center in the Soviet Union, and many a minor one, has special state residences for the elite or high-level visitors – located out of sight, down a road, behind a fence, in a stand of pines or birches. Once in the rough West Siberian oil town of Surgut, I was among a group of American reporters quartered in a guest house previously used by Prime Minister Kosygin. The rooms were pine-paneled, rustic, pleasant, a complete escape from the neighboring architectural monotony of prefab dormitories for working-class families. The double rooms were spacious and light, equipped with comfortable beds and rheo-stat lighting, though the plumbing leaked. The private dining hall was well provisioned with fresh fruits and vegetables, unheard of in Siberia in such early spring months.

On another occasion, I accidentally encountered Kosygin's middle-aged daughter, Ludmila Gvishiani, and her family on a train headed to a government vacation spot in Latvia. With Mike McGuire of the *Chicago Tribune*, I fell into conversation with her husband, Dzhermen Gvishiani, a well-known specialist on East–West commerce, whom I had met at a press conference. We chatted about trade and Soviet vacation spots. Gvishiani, a handsome, dapper Georgian given to well-tailored suits and Dior ties, could pass anywhere as a Western executive – and does. He confided that his family preferred the beaches and the cool weather on the Baltic because he found the hot summer weather at Sochi on the Black Sea aggravated his bad back.

Then, in a break with Soviet custom, the family was brought dinner from the restaurant car, six cars away, to their compartment as we were talking. We excused ourselves, only to find that we, too, as presumed acquaintances of the Gvishianis, were offered the privilege of ordering dinner in our compartment, with the gracious explanation that this was a service of the Latvian Railroad line. But when we tried to order dinner in the compartment on the return trip, the startled young woman porter quickly turned us down asserting that, 'This is never done.'

At Riga, too, our path diverged from the Gvishianis. We joined the general jumble waiting for taxis, finally gave it up as hopeless, and walked to our hotel. They were met by five persons, two women carrying bouquets of flowers and three very solemn men in dark suits to handle the luggage and security, which had seemed surprisingly relaxed on the train. The Gvishianis were whisked off in a large Chaika to a Council of Ministers' guest house at a secluded spot 20 miles from the crowded beaches of Riga Bay. So sheltered was that spot, Mrs Gvishiani had told me on the train, that you could 'walk for hundreds and hundreds of yards and commune with nature alone' – an unthinkable luxury for most Russians who cannot escape the teeming throngs at Soviet holiday spots.

At places like the Crimea and the Black Sea Coast, the dachas of some Politburo members, most notably the one built by former Ukrainian Party boss Pyotr Shelest – are so sumptuous that they have raised eyebrows among more puritanical Party officials. With the Crimea as a subdivision of the Ukraine, Shelest could command the use of whatever labor force and materials he wanted. Other Ukrainian leaders built their beach homes, too. But I was told by a scientist who knew the area well, that Shelest like some Southern California movie mogul had Ukrainian workmen erect him a spacious four-story palace on a half a mile of shoreline near the lush Nikita Botanical Gardens at Yalta.

Sand was especially trucked in for his beach, along with all kinds of furnishings for his home. Seawalls were built. Breakwaters tumbled down among the tropical groves across the waterfront into the surf, and security men stopped swimmers or strollers from venturing too close to the premises, according to this scientist who had wandered near the grounds while visiting the Botanical Gardens.

Whatever misgivings other Soviet leaders may have felt about Shelest's opulence, he was not forced to give up his dacha until he was ousted from the Politburo and lost his Ukrainian post. On this, Party protocol is usually merciless: Loss of position means loss of the state dacha, though as a high-ranking deputy premier, Shelest undoubtedly got a more modest dacha even after he was demoted. The system works the opposite way, too. Foreign Minister Andrei Gromyko showed off his new Politburo dacha in the Crimea to Secretary of State Henry Kissinger in June, 1974, while they were cruising off the coast of Oreanda during Brezhnev's talks with Nixon. In 16 years as Foreign Minister, Gromyko had never rated the top-rank dacha until admitted to the Politburo in April, 1973!

The most notable exception to privilege-protocol is Anastas Mikoyan, the grand old Armenian master of Party intrigue who has survived, as Soviets say, 'from Ilyich to Ilyich' – from Vladimir Ilyich Lenin to Leonid Ilyich Brezhnev – outlasting both Stalin and Khrushchev. Although retired in 1965 as a crony of Khrushchev by his successors, Mikoyan has managed to retain not only a handsome villa near Gagra on the Black Sea, which reputedly has two marble-lined swimming pools, one for salt water and one for fresh, but also a huge mansion and princely estate outside Moscow with servants and a waterless moat. Appropriately, in pre-Revolutionary days it was owned by an extremely wealthy Caucasian merchant.

Dacha is one of those magical elastic words in Russian that conceals more than it reveals. Above all, it signals escape from the crowded city into the calm of the Russian countryside. Rather conveniently it blurs social differences; sometimes it sounds far grander than reality; sometimes, more modest. Perhaps that is why Russians are so fond of using the word. Many will talk about 'having a dacha' somewhere with a certain light in their eyes. But neither their twinkle nor their tongue reveals what kind of place it is. For a dacha can mean anything from a little, oversized toolshed or a one-room cabin on a tiny plot of ground, surrounded by a development of identical little cabins with no privacy, to a modest but pleasant four-room country cottage without plumbing in a plain Russian village, to a grand mansion taken over from the old aristocracy or a more up to date, rambling country villa built in the forties by German prisoners-of-war. There is one other essential distinction among dachas: some are state or organizational dachas that come free-of-charge or for a token payment of 200 or 300 rubles ($267–400) a year, and others are privately owned, gifts from the state in the Stalin era for outstanding service to the Soviet Union, or built through some legal cooperative venture, or perhaps bought and sold several times through a bit of skulduggery or flexible interpretation of the rules. One five-room dacha near Vnukovo, southwest of Moscow, had three owners in a decade and shot up from 15,000 to 65,000 rubles ($20,000 to nearly $87,000) in the early Seventies. Usually the high-priced private dachas belong to prize-winning loyal writers, movie directors, composers, and opera stars who can afford them.

The Party leaders themselves have mansions with several acres of land that come cost-free from the state. Their homes are surrounded by high green fences that, as one Muscovite told me, ordinary Russians learn from childhood not to approach too closely. Many lie just off the road to the village of Uspenskoye, where foreign embassies have a communal beach on the Moscow River. The access roads that lead off to clusters of elite dachas tucked away in cul-de-sacs in the pine woods are marked with 'no entry' signs pointing outward to keep away curious intruders. The most exalted personages have uniformed police guards posted at the main road junctions to stop wayward drivers from straying accidentally onto the approach roads, not to mention plain-clothes guards deeper in the woods.

Muscovites find this entire life-style such a mockery of Marxist ideals that they make fun of it with a joke on Brezhnev. While I was in Moscow, his mother was still living, and, according to the anecdote, Brezhnev wanted to impress her with how well he had done. He decided to invite her up from their home in Dneprodzerzhinsk, in the Ukraine and showed her through his ample in-town apartment but she was nonplussed, even a little ill-at-ease. So he called the Kremlin, ordered his Zil, and they sped out to his dacha near Usovo, one used previously by Stalin and Khrushchev. He took her all around, showed her each room, showed her the handsome grounds, but still she said nothing. So he called for his personal helicopter and flew her straight to his hunting lodge at Zavidovo. There, he escorted her to the banquet room, grandly displaying the big fireplace, his guns, the whole bit and, unable to restrain himself any longer, asked her pleadingly, 'Tell me, Mama, what do you think?'

'Well,' she hesitated, 'it's good, Leonid. But what if the Reds come back?'

The gently-rolling hills west and southwest of Moscow contain a number of important dacha communities. Probably the best-known abroad is the writers' colony at Peredelkino, where Boris Pasternak lived and wrote, where Kornei Chukovsky, the much beloved children's writer also lived, where *Pravda* has a network of dachas for its top editors, where Victor Louis, known in the West as a special Soviet intelligence operative, has a large, handsome, two-story home with a huge oak fireplace, sauna, walls covered with religious ikons, and a tennis court that he freezes over in winter for skating; where Andrei Voznesensky and Yevgeny Yevtushenko have rambling frame dachas alloted through the Writers' Union, and where there is a small Orthodox Church as brilliant and wild in its colors and as improbably beautiful as St Basil's Cathedral on Red Square.

In Nikolina Gora, about 25 miles west of the Kremlin in a splendid forest, are the summer homes of academicians, journalists, writers and government officials like Nikolai Baibakov, head of the State Planning Committee. On a high bluff overlooking the diplomatic beach are the dachas of people like Pyotr Kapitsa, a world-famous physicist, and Sergei Mikhalkov, the children's writer. All of these communities are within a few miles of each other, all very close to Zhukovka, which Stalin's daughter, Svetlana Alliluyeva, mentioned as her last home in the Soviet Union.

Zhukovka is a fascinating place, the heart of the dacha country of the high and mighty of Soviet politics, science, culture. It epitomizes the surprising narrowness of Soviet society at the apex. Until friends opened up for me the geography of Zhukovka, it was always puzzling to hear some Muscovites refer to their city as 'just an overgrown village'. That muscular, brawny, sprawling, industrialized metropolis, eight million strong, with races and people as varied as New York a village? I didn't get it for a long time. What they meant, I finally understood, was that if you were inside the network, if you belonged, information and lots of other things passed the same way they do in a small town because people know each other, have the old connections. For a city of its size, for a country of its size, the Moscow network is surprisingly small, because Moscow is the center for everything in the Soviet Union, the way London is in England, or Paris in France.

Americans, thinking of the Soviet Union as a continent more than twice the size of the United States, have difficulty comprehending this. The headquarters of the American auto industry is in Detroit, the movie industry is in Hollywood, the steel industry is around Pittsburgh; atomic energy has Los Alamos and Oak Ridge; the political capital is Washington; the financial, publishing and television capital is New York. But in the Soviet Union, Moscow is the Big Apple in every field. Moreover, if Western societies can be crudely conceived as diamond-shaped in social structure, with a relatively small aristocracy or elite at the top, a great bulging middle class in the center, and a narrowing once again at the bottom, then Soviet society is shaped like a pyramid, very broad at the bottom, narrower in the middle, and finely tapered at the top. Actually, it is not one pyramid, but a series of pyramids, one in each field, all meeting at the top – and with the top all meeting in Zhukovka.

So unimposing is Zhukovka that untutored outsiders ride through in a minute, noticing no more than clusters of typical Russian peasant cabins of rough-hewn logs with outhouses in the vegetable gardens. The only landmark of note is a low, though unusually large cement-block village store complex with an open parking area beside. Foreign diplomats and correspondents who have tried to stop and shop there have been quickly and firmly chased off by uniformed police who materialize from nowhere. Unknowing Russians who have come upon it fairly innocently were surprised to find it very well stocked. 'Frying pans, enamel casseroles, French and Italian suits, all kinds of things that you can't find in Moscow,' one startled middle-aged lady told me. It was built for the elite in their surrounding dachas under Nikita Khrushchev. Officially, Khrushchev is a forgotten, ridiculed and unmentionable non-person in Soviet society but he lives on in subtle and amusing ways: For among the elite of Zhukovka, this store is known even now as 'Khrushchev's store'.

One reason that Zhukovka is so disarmingly bucolic and gives the impression of a struggling collective farm village is that it is in fact not one but three settlements. What the passing motorist or tourist glimpses is known colloquially as Zhukovka village, on the right-hand side of the road coming out from Moscow. Across the road, unseen in the deep forest and situated mostly across the railroad spur that runs to Moscow, are two more villages, antiseptically designated 'Zhukovka-1' and 'Zhukovka-2'. The locals, however, call Zhukovka-1 'Sovmin' for *Soviet Ministrov*, or Council of Ministers. Zhukovka-2 is known as 'Academic Zhukovka'. The Sovmin village, for Cabinet ministers and their top deputies, is surrounded with a brick and iron fence. Entry is only by special pass, and the pecking order is strict. In fact, not surprisingly, Sovmin has grown from the early days and now consists of two settlements – one for lower, though still very important officials, nearer the road, and the other, for the upper crust, on the more secluded side of the railroad tracks.

The dachas are allotted according to rank and protocol. Once, a well-placed scientist told me of a high-ranking scientific administrator whom he knew being promoted to deputy minister and being told he would get a state dacha in Sovmin. The man gracefully tried to decline on grounds that he had purchased a nice dacha of his own in a scientific settlement and did not want either to move or to have to give up his expensive piece of property, despite the honor. He was sternly admonished: 'Are you trying to insult the system of *nomenklatura*? You must sell your private dacha and take the state dacha that goes with your position.' He complied.

Sometimes, exceptions are made to let people of extraordinary rank keep their dachas even after they lose their eligibility. Vyacheslav Molotov, the stern, now frosty-haired Foreign Minister and henchman of Stalin, still has a dacha in Sovmin. So does the dictator's grandson, Yosif, who has become a doctor.

Academic Zhukovka, which is a looser, more informal settlement, got its start in the early postwar years when Stalin rewarded the inventors of the Soviet atomic and hydrogen bombs and the creators of the first cyclotron with two-story country homes near the Sovmin area. In the Khrushchev era, the space age scientists were added, and the community has grown now to about 150 dachas. Here is where top scientists like Andrei Sakharov and Yuli Khariton, who pioneered the hydrogen and atomic bombs, have their summer homes. In recent years, people who have made their mark – and a bundle of money – in the cultural world, have bought summer homes in Academic Zhukovka from the widows of the scientists who originally received them as gifts from the state. That is how composer Dmitri Shostakovich and cellist Mstislav Rostropovich obtained country homes here. Indeed, for a time, Solzhenitsyn lived in the gardener's cottage of Rostropovich's dacha.

In the simple village of Zhukovka itself, new dachas have been sprouting in recent years among the little log huts and the comfortable old unpainted clapboard country homes. Here the KGB general whose division monitors intellectual dissent has an old-fashioned dacha. There, across from him, a KGB general in the border security forces has built himself a modern dacha of imported yellow bricks, amidst the more simple dwellings that villagers rent out in summertime to officials, writers, actors, journalists, artists and other moneyed people.

Academic Zhukovka backs into the huge estate of Anastas Mikoyan and the Central Committee Sanitorium on the Podushkino Highway. A mile or two further in toward Moscow, past Barvikha, lives Mikhail Suslov, the Party's top theoretician and reputedly the kingmaker who put together the coalition that overthrew Khrushchev. In the opposite direction, two hamlets past Zhukovka and opposite the settlement of Usovo, are the most exclusive, most secluded mansions of Brezhnev, Kosygin, Kirill Mazurov, Kosygin's first deputy premier, and Foreign Minister Gromyko, who moved from his ministerial dacha at Vnukovo, out to the 'Brezhnev' enclave when he made it into the Politburo.

Anyone who has spent a summer afternoon in Zhukovka can understand why the high and mighty are drawn to this place. It is softly enchanting, in a very Russian way. The village sits on a bluff overlooking the slow-moving Moscow River and the gently undulating Central Russian plain. In the pine groves, it is sometimes hard to walk because the ground is gouged and uneven where there are remnants of trenches.

'These are the scars of war,' explained Lev Kopelev, a

husky, towering full-bearded Russian writer who was in the camps with Solzhenitsyn and who likes to walk with a heavy stave fashioned from a tree branch. 'The trenches were prepared for the defense of Moscow. But the Germans did not come this way. There were no battles here.'

It is a lovely, tranquil, timeless place, less than 20 miles from the throbbing city of Moscow and yet a world away. At sunset, one can sit high on the river bank, and look for miles and centuries at changeless Russia. The fields and shrubs and undergrowth here are wild and untidy, free of man's intrusion. The sky has a soft tint, not the bright orange or red of Florida or California sunsets, but a light, whitish glow because the region is so far north. The breeze carries the rich smell of pines. Muffled noises reach the ears – a dog's bark, a fish jumping, children far off laughing in the woods. Unpleasantly, a jet soars overhead and Lev softly predicts, 'Someday someone will make a fortune for inventing a silent jet engine.'

Like some patron of the district, though dressed like a lumberjack, he pauses to bid good evening to chance acquaintances out walking and welcomes them to Zhukovka where he and his wife, Rai, have summered for 20 years. 'It is my favorite place in the whole world,' he says, a boyish gleam in his eye.

'Once you could swim here but now it is forbidden,' says Rai. 'It is also forbidden to fish without a special license. This is a protected water zone. It supplies Moscow.'

But down through the trees, we can see fishermen with lines out, visible through the birch saplings and the underbrush. Teen-aged boys are horsing around by the water's edge, skimming stones and climbing over fallen trees. Up on the bluff, a young girl in new imported jean jacket and pants, with an American lapel button – signs of a high-ranking, world-traveling father – sits on a pine stump gazing quietly at the countryside.

'Over there,' says Lev, pointing westward about three or four miles, 'you can see where Brezhnev's dacha is. See the water tower. It is for Brezhnev's dacha, Kosygin's and Mazurov's. You can't see the dachas. But they are right underneath. People call Brezhnev's dacha "Dacha No. 1". When Stalin lived out in that area, it was called the "far dacha". Khrushchev had that big dacha when Nixon came in 1959. You can see the dacha from the river, or you used to be able to see it from the river. We saw it in Khrushchev's time. We were there on the river when Khrushchev took Nixon on that river tour in his launch. It is really a beautiful mansion, beautiful grounds, lovely river banks with marble stairways going down to the river. But now it is forbidden to go on that part of the river, even for us Russians.'

As we walked back toward the village along a path, no wider than a rabbit run, winding among the cottages, Lev began to discuss the geographic intimacy of the Soviet elite.

'You know,' mused Lev, 'if you had stood at the Khrushchev store one morning in the fall of 1972 or the spring of 1973, you could have seen everyone. About nine, Sakharov and his wife would have come by, headed for a dip in the river. Then, Brezhnev, Kosygin and Mazurov would have hurried by in their Zils on the way to the Kremlin because in the good weather, they all live in their dachas. About ten, Solzhenitsyn would have appeared to buy milk for his sons at the store. He was living then in the gardener's house of Rostropovich in Academic Zhukovka. Soon, you might have seen Molotov coming to shop for something, walking from Sovmin. Once Solzhenitsyn crossed Molotov's path and said later that he had wanted to approach the old man and say, "Come Vyacheslav Mikhailovich, let us have a talk together," and then he tried to imagine what Molotov would have said. Solzhenitsyn thought Molotov would have used the same wooden language that he had used all his life. "Because he believed it?" I said. "No, he did not believe it," Solzhenitsyn said. "Simply out of habit." '

From others, I heard that Molotov had been standing in line for tomatoes at the Khrushchev store in the summer of 1972 when a woman complained, 'I don't want to stand in line with an executioner.' Without a word, according to this story, Molotov left the line and walked out of the store.

But Lev was talking about the store as a crossroads. After Solzhenitsyn and Molotov, he suggested, 'would have come Stalin's grandson, Yosif, Svetlana's son. Then, Khariton, the big man of the Soviet A-bomb. Then Rostropovich and Shostakovich from Academic Zhukovka. Rostropovich would always come late. He is an artist. Then from Nikolina Gora, the cars of Pyotr Kapitsa and Sergei Mikhalkov would pass. Perhaps Mikoyan would drive over from his dacha near the Barvikha station. For twenty years, he used to ride his horse around the area. But he doesn't do it any more. So you had the big names of science, culture and politics, all passing this one little country store.'

But the Soviet elite who hobnob together in the hidden dacha settlements around Moscow and in other choice colonies around the country have arrogated to themselves a larger system of privileges than merely being far better clothed, fed, housed and medically cared-for than the rest of the population. Their lives simply take place on a different plane from the rest of society. As the chauffeured cars of the upper crust suggest, they enjoy an ease of living unknown to ordinary people, whether they want to travel at home or abroad, indulge their fancy for Western music or movies, arrange a good education or job for their children, or simply go out to dinner. The system has institutionalized a double standard in life-styles for the elite and for the masses, with some shadings in-between for some of the people part way up. And the elite take these advantages for granted with an arrogant disdain for the common man that often surpasses the haughtiest rich of the West.

'On any railroad train, any Aeroflot flight, in any hotel, at any performance, the managers know that they have to set aside a certain number of places for the *vlasti* [the powers-that-be],' an Intourist guide confided privately. 'It happens everywhere, all over the country, not just in Moscow. In other cities, seats are held for higher officials from Moscow, officials from the provincial Party headquarters, officials from the city Party headquarters, just in case *they* may order them. Rooms are held for *them* in hotels and people turned away just in case *they* may show up. Same thing on airplanes. Then if they are not needed, the tickets are put on sale, say, half an hour before flight-time or before the theater performance. This is the practice everywhere. Space is saved for the *vlasti* just in case.

'Or it can happen the other way around. Some poor guy can have an air ticket and be all set to go somewhere and *they* come along and tell him, "No, you can't go, we need your seat. You wait until the next flight." So he gets bumped by some Party bigshot and maybe he has to wait five or six hours or more at the airport. That's just the way it is. There's nothing he can do about it.' I heard about this insulting treatment from any number of ordinary Russians who chafed but were ultimately resigned to it; and from a couple of moderately important journalists who bragged about being able to pull rank and get hotel accommodations when ordinary Russians were being turned away. They took this as a natural right of rank.

The political and cultural elites also have a host of clubs and special closed restaurants where they can eat comfortably without having to stand outside waiting in line for admission like ordinary Russians or enduring the poor service at the wretchedly overcrowded restaurants of Moscow. The highest officials dine at places like the Party Central Committee and Cabinet hotel-pensions near the Khimki Reservoir. Less powerful but still prominent people eat out in professional clubs like the Writers' Union, Architects' House, the Armed Forces Officers' Club, House of Journalists which offer caviar, steaks, top-grade vodka (normally only for export) and polite, quite prompt service.

When it comes to travel or entertainment, not only Brezhnev, Kosygin and Podgorny are given quick service or the royal box, but the larger political elite, and behind them, the cultural, scientific and economic elites get their pick, too. The Communist Party Central Committee, the Council of Ministers and other important agencies, for example, have special ticket offices where the upper crust can have aides make travel reservations or get them tickets to the top events, which are always in desperately short supply and for which people will commonly spend all night waiting in line. In September 1972, just before the first Soviet-Canadian hockey competition which attracted enormous popular interest, a Canadian diplomat friend of mine was at the main ticket office at Luzhniki Park when a well-heeled young man walked in with an attaché case, set it on the table, and identified himself as the man from the Central Committee 'for the tickets'. The officials there dropped everything else to help this man. The diplomat's eyes bulged as the Central Committee man was given 3,000 tickets per game for each of four games. That was more than one-fourth of all the seats, enough for every other person at the Central Committee headquarters to see every game, while the rest of a city of eight million people had less than one chance in a thousand of getting in.

'No one complained, no one thought it wrong,' the diplomat said. 'This is just the way things are done here. I didn't complain. I just wanted my 200 tickets for the Canadian Embassy.' Top Soviet sports clubs, especially the military ones, and other influential people got their cut. By the time this private split was over, there was nothing left for ordinary hockey fans except perhaps a few dozen tickets as a token box-office sale. This happens again and again, every time some big foreign cultural show is touring Moscow or even when the star Soviet attractions like the Moiseyev dance troupe or the top Bolshoi Ballet performers return from foreign tours. 'For things like that,' said one middle-aged woman, who rarely got to see such shows, 'tickets aren't sold. They are allocated.'

Equally important to some members of the elite is simply the right to enjoy things normally forbidden to others. Ernst Neizvestny, for example, is one of the more iconoclastic Soviet sculptors and painters, denounced and later admired by Khrushchev, wealthy from the gravestones he does for prominent personages but constantly in a struggle with the authorities because the art he really loves to do is too unintelligible, too symbolic and pessimistic for socialist realism. Ordinary Russians never even get a chance to see his art but I was reliably told by a friend that one of Brezhnev's personal aides, Yevgeny Samoteikin, has modernistic Neizvestny graphics in his apartment. An American who had visited the apartments of several high-level foreign trade officials said that he had seen not only unorthodox works by Neizvestny and other modernistic Soviet artists but abstract art objects obviously brought back from trips to the West. More startling, I knew of famous Soviet writers who have the banned works of Solzhenitsyn and other literary contraband quite openly on their bookshelves, a sin for which dissidents have been jailed. But, establishment status provided them protection.

There is hardly any more striking double-standard between the life-styles of the elite and ordinary Russians than the established access of the privileged class to things Western – magazines, books, movies, cars, travel. The privileged, I was told, can catch movies like *Blow-up, Easy Rider, Midnight Cowboy, Bonnie and Clyde, The Conformist,* or *8½* – which are banned by censors for normal Soviet eyes. These forbidden films are shown at closed screenings at Moscow Film Studios, in the professional clubs, or at Dom Kino, a club for the film crowd. Access to such showings becomes a matter of highly prized status for intellectuals. At the very top, the dachas of the power elite are equipped with home movie-projectors where Western films are shown regularly along with Soviet ones. Visiting foreign troupes are sometimes asked to put on their gaudiest and most daring spectaculars for the Soviet art crowd and Ministry of Culture officials in *private* even though the Ministry forbids them from displaying these allegedly corrupt bourgeois art-forms to the general public.

I knew a balletomane who was admitted to what he regarded as a sexy, closed performance by a French dance troupe and he came home eyes rolling, absolutely titillated by the taste of forbidden Western fruit. Others were equally exhilarated by the closed movie-showings. 'You cannot imagine the pleasure, the sense of doing something forbidden and at the same time belonging to a group of special people that you get from going to see a movie like $8\frac{1}{2}$,' an auburn-haired woman editor said to me. Her family was part of the upper intelligentsia but not so high-ranked that she enjoyed the access to things Western as often as she would have liked. 'In Rome or New York you Westerners can go buy a ticket and see any movie you want. But here, it is really something to be able to do that.' With her, as with the balletomane, it was clear that the excitement of sharing something taboo to others was as great as the enjoyment of the movie itself.

In material terms, the most exclusive status symbol that the Soviet elite has borrowed from the West are high-priced Western luxury cars. As détente has proceeded, Brezhnev has made them very fashionable. He is well-known for his stable of Western models (Rolls-Royce Silver Cloud, Citroën-Maserati, Lincoln, Mercedes, and Cadillac), given him by foreign leaders because of his fetish for posh executive cars. Less known, however, is the fact that other Soviet bigwigs go for Western cars too: President Podgorny has driven a Mercedes 600; economic planning czar Nikolai Baibakov has a Chevrolet Impala; Maya Plisetskaya, the prima ballerina of the Bolshoi, has favored a Kharman Ghia 1500 while male dancers like Vladimir Vasilyev and Maris Liepa had a Citroën and a VW bus; Boris Spassky, former world chess champion, owns a British Rover sedan; Victor Louis, the journalist with the KGB connections, has a Porsche, a Land Rover, and a Mercedes 220, the car favored by composer Aram Khachaturian, among others. The list is growing longer each year, for Soviet journalists and diplomats returning from posts abroad as well as highly paid touring cultural figures are smitten with Western cars.

The critical objective for all of them, the *sine qua non*, is getting to the West in the first place so they can indulge their acquisitive instincts. 'Money in the Soviet system is nothing,' complained a highly paid writer who had never been allowed to go West. 'You have to be able to spend it. A Central Committee member does not get much pay but he gets all kinds of things free. He can get his children in the best universities or institutes, or get them abroad.' Then he paused and added sarcastically, '*They* (the leaders) are all sending their children abroad now, exporting them like dissidents.' And like a ten-year-old American boy recalling baseball batting averages, he peevishly rattled off the names indelibly imprinted on his memory because it galled him that they could go and he could not: Brezhnev's son, Yuri, ten years in Sweden as a trade representative, not to mention other trips; Kosygin's daughter, Ludmila, who often accompanied him abroad, and his son-in-law, Dzhermen Gvishiani, the trade expert; Gromyko's son, Anatoly, a high Embassy official in Washington and before that, in London; Igor Andropov, son of the secret police chief Yuri Andropov, a traveler to the West who did research in the United States for a graduate thesis on the American workers' movement; Mikhail Mazurov, son of First Deputy Premier Kirill Mazurov, a zoologist who spent a couple of years in Kenya and traveling abroad; one of the sons of former Ukrainian Party boss Pyotr Shelest, a marine biologist who did research trips to Florida during his father's political heyday.

For many, the system of direct privilege is reinforced by the informal network of connections that enable a general to call a scientist to get his son admitted into an institute, a scientist to wangle a draft-deferment in return, or a movie script-writer who has produced a good Soviet spy film to call the security services to get permission for his wife and daughter to travel West. *Blat*, as the Russians call influence, is a constant, vital and pervasive factor of Russian life. 'We have a caste system,' a senior scientist told me. 'Military families intermarry. So do scientific families, Party families, writers' families, theater families. Sons expect their fathers or fathers-in-law to promote their careers through *blat* and fathers take it equally for granted that they should do this. Others do it. I did it for my son. Why not?'

Certain universities and institutes have become known as the province of the Party, government and military elite for their offspring. At Moscow State University, the faculties of journalism and law, since they are largely 'political' fields, and the Foreign Languages Institute and the Moscow Institute of International Relations (MIMO), because they lead toward foreign travel and foreign careers. These are known as places where some of the highest ranking Party and government people place their sons and daughters or grandsons and granddaughters, quite frequently by using *blat* to get flunking grades on entrance examinations falsely changed to A's.

'You have to have very good Party and Komsomol recommendations to get into MIMO,' one graduate told me, and he mentioned a score of sons and daughters of Party and Government officials who got in through connections. He himself came from a Party family, and said the whole student body had a clubby elitist aura. Few 'ordinary' students make it because, although this is not a secret institution, it is not listed in the normal handbook for Soviet institutions of higher education for prospective applicants. My friend said he knew of an instructor at MIMO, a Party member, who had been fired for refusing to obey orders from the dean to give top grades to children from elite families, derisively known among some Russians as *Sovetskiye detki*, 'the Soviet kids'. In his time, he said, there were any number of students from ranking families who did poor work but were protected from expulsion by family connections. The most illustrious goof-off, he recalled, was Igor Shchelokov, son of the Minister of Internal Affairs, who had a reputation for partying and drinking at his father's dacha, driving in to school in the Mercedes that his father had given him, and making no bones about expecting to be given passing grades regardless of his performance. In English, this young man said, Igor got so many D's that by the normal rules he should have been flunked out, but instead in his fifth year, as a 'practical assignment', he got the unusual privilege of being sent to the Soviet Embassy in Australia temporarily, though his grades should have disqualified him.

Other young friends, as a lark, offered to smuggle me into

MIMO one day for a look around – although it was one of those closed Soviet institutions, with no sign on the door indicating its name or function and with guards posted to keep out the unwanted. A sign at the entrance said plainly, 'Present your passes – in open form', but my friends assured me – and I found they were right – that a firm, knowing nod of the head and a steady stride would be enough to get me past the guards. My escorts showed me the posted academic curriculum and the library with its special 'holdings' of Western newspapers and books. But I found it all disappointingly similar to much more ordinary Soviet institutions and not very exotic, for all its elite status. The bulletin boards had articles about military preparedness with passages underlined in red to show how much Western countries were spending on defense, and the classrooms reminded me of an old school building built in the Twenties with simple wooden desks and tables, scarred and doodled upon. I saw none of the fancy visual-aid equipment that is normal for an American college.

But an American girl who attended a dance there with some East European friends – for the institute was also a haven for the sons and daughters of East European Communist leaders – said that at private parties MIMO had a strictly Western ambience. Her friends pointed out to her the grandchildren of Brezhnev and Kosygin among the dancing couples and Foreign Minister Gromyko's grandson playing the guitar in the student combo. 'He was good,' she said. 'I don't think the group played a single thing all evening that was Russian. It was all Beatles, Rolling Stones, and other Western stuff, sung in English.'

Other organizations, such as the Novosti Press Agency (which puts stress on political reliability and which Western intelligence services regard as an arm of the KGB), or the Institute of the U.S.A. and Canada, have gotten reputations as places where the political elite like to place their children in jobs. Others, through pull, land cushy posts in publishing houses or research institutes dealing with foreign affairs. Russians themselves comment that the upper class feeling today seems increasingly like Russia before the Revolution. An engineer observed to me that what Marx had predicted for capitalist society – increasing concentration of economic power in fewer and fewer hands and a widening gap between the elite and the masses – seemed to be happening in the Soviet Union today. In many ways, the elite show a sense of

69

class, at all age-levels. The wife of a well-heeled writer remarked that her eight-year-old son had been shy about inviting other boys home from school until he came across the son of a well-known Army General 'because he didn't want the others to see how well he lived. But he felt the general's boy was just right.'

The one unwritten rule of the power elite seems to be that they cannot push their offspring into the Communist Party hierarchy, and surprisingly few of the children of the present leaders have shown either the inclination or the ability to follow political careers. Gromyko's son, Anatoly, the No. 3 man in the Soviet Embassy in Washington, is a noteworthy exception. Kosygin's son-in-law, Gvishiani, now deputy chief of the powerful State Committee on Science and Technology, is another.

This limitation on passing political power as well as preventing inheritance of state dachas and other direct perquisites of office, are cited by Soviets, including Marxist-minded dissidents, as evidence that Soviet society has not actually given birth to a new elite class. 'A class has to have permanence and stability,' Zhores Medvedev, the dissident Marxist biologist, contended to me. 'Under the old system, the old nobility could be secure in its status. But that is not true now. Everyone is insecure in his position. If he loses it, he loses everything. He cannot pass on his position and his privileges to his children. These are not immutable birthrights.'

This argument has some validity, especially on the matter of political power or when the analogy is made narrowly to the practice by which the Czarist nobility inherited titles, estates and all the trappings of official status. But by placing their children and grandchildren in the most prestigious institutes and using their influence to get them jobs and careers in select agencies and organizations, the power elite is providing long-term status for the next two generations. Moreover, in other fields, such as science and culture, high-ranking fathers do succeed in passing on private wealth and property, such as dachas, apartments, cars and money, as well as career opportunities and status to their offspring.

Also, rather than instability and insecurity, one of the striking features of the Soviet elite is precisely its stability and longevity in office. This has been one of the more notable trends of the Brezhnev era – the glacial pace of administrative change, which has allowed the state and Party bureaucracy at the top to become more entrenched than ever now that it is free of the threat of Stalin's purges and Khrushchev's unpredictable reforms. In America, Cabinet officials and corporation directors experience a much more rapid turnover than do Soviet ministers and industrial executives, some of whom hold their posts for 10–20 years, consolidating not only their positions but the social status of their families for the future. Indeed, one ranking official in an industrial ministry complained to a friend of mine that one of the problems with the Soviet economy in the Seventies was that 'no one above director of an enterprise ever gets demoted.' He favored more shake-ups for efficiency's sake, but he was not typical of the New Class.

For Milovan Djilas' contention that Communism has created a New Class was focused not on individual office-holders but on the political-economic bureaucracy as a stratum of society with a monopoly of power and privilege to protect, with the individual having a sense of solidarity because his privileges depend on corporate survival. It is undoubtedly true, as Russians and Western scholars assert, that the Soviet *nachalstvo*, the ruling bosses, are not a monolithic group. The elite has its fundamentalists and its modernizers, its hard-line police and security men, its strict ideologists and its efficiency-oriented technocrats in industry and science. The cultural elite has conservatives and liberals. But in the Brezhnev-Kosygin years, whenever frictions have appeared publicly the leadership has repeatedly made conservative compromises to preserve unity and set aside differences. Thus, despite these frictions, the Soviet elite is still bound together by its loyalty to the Party and the system of *nomenklatura* which guarantees both power and privilege.

Some Western sociologists have contended that the gap between the richest elements of the Soviet elite and the poorest Russians is still much less than the gap between the richest and the poorest elements in America. In pure money terms, that is surely true, though the hidden incomes of the Soviet elite in the form of their large discounts at special stores, the use of cost-free state cars, dachas, and other government facilities is hard to feed into a precise equation. In any case, money is an inadequate measure because the benefits enjoyed by the Soviet elite depend on influence, connections, and access that money cannot buy.

71

To me, the life-style of top Soviet government officials, foreign trade executives, fêted writers, and high-ranking journalists with their frequent foreign travel, their ample expense allowances, imported clothes, their environment of creature comforts, or that of the political VIPs with dachas, servants, Kremlin-cooked meals, special stores and free home delivery of choice groceries is as far beyond the ken of a Russian steel worker or a milkmaid on a collective farm as the life-style of the jet-set Americans skiing in Switzerland one week and yachting in the Caribbean the next on money made through clever investments and fast tax write-offs is from the life of a Detroit auto worker or a migrant farm laborer in California.

Unlike America, however, the rarefied life-style and hidden wealth of the Soviet privileged class has virtually no impact as a public issue. A few dissidents like Andrei Sakharov and Roy Medvedev have attacked the system of privilege, but even among dissidents this has been secondary to many other issues. Among ordinary Russians there is general awareness that the power elite and scientific-cultural celebrities have privileged lives, but the extent of the privileges is disguised by the custom of discreet rather than conspicuous consumption and by the total lack of publicity about the private lives of the privileged class. Then, too, for all its advantages, the Soviet New Class is still far from being as cultured, as idle and as jaded as the czarist aristocracy portrayed by Pushkin in *Yevgeny Onegin*. Nor has it yet accumulated such great wealth as some of the merchant princes of pre-revolutionary Russia who lived cheek-by-jowl with abject poverty.

Moreover, this is a risky issue for Russians to discuss openly, and most of those who grumble about it, do it very privately. An elderly lady, passing a dairy known to supply the special stores of the elite, burst out bitterly to Ann, my wife, one night: 'We hate those special privileges. During the war when they were really our leaders, it was all right. But not now.' Svetlana Alliluyeva wrote about fistfights and altercations with a tinge of class antagonisms between the elite youth living in dachas in Zhukovka and the local village farm boys. In Tashkent, I watched a line of tired people grumbling curses at a high-ranking military officer for going to the head of a long taxi line and seizing the first vacant cab for himself, but no one made any vocal protest or physical move to stop him. A mechanic who had helped install air-conditioning and kitchen appliances in apartments of top-ranking military officers later vented his anger to a Russian friend: 'Look at all they have! Why did we fight the Revolution?'

The most striking episode of protest that I came across involved the wife of a very well-known poet whose outburst came at a party given by Dmitri Polyansky, an important Politburo member and Minister of Agriculture. Everyone was fairly high, including the poet's wife who went off to the bathroom. Soon, other guests heard a terrible racket. It was the poet's wife smashing bottles of Mrs Polyansky's French perfumes – Lanvin, Schiaparelli, Worth – and swearing bitterly. 'The hypocrisy of it all,' she fumed, 'this is supposed to be a workers' state, everybody equal, and look at this French perfume!'

But more typical was the impotent frustration which a physicist told me he felt one day after noticing that a precious monkey carved from pure amber and on display for years in the Amber Store in downtown Moscow had disappeared from the window, though everyone had understood the monkey was not for sale. He and some friends went inside to inquire what had happened.

'We sold it,' a sales clerk said uncommunicatively.

'But we thought it wasn't for sale,' objected one of the group.

The woman shrugged helplessly.

'Who bought it?' someone asked.

'Brezhnev's daughter, Galya,' said the woman, anxious to shut off the conversation.

'It's a good thing she didn't go shopping in the Hermitage,' one of the men commented, and they left, crestfallen but resigned.

Resignation is the characteristic Soviet reaction to the privileges of the high and mighty. In Russian history, it has long been that way, Russians say, and this is fatalistically accepted. The thing to do is to find a piece of the action for yourself, as a young American exhibition guide said he had learned from ten months of daily conversations with thousands of Russians. 'People don't want to change that part of the system, they want to beat it,' he said. 'They don't say the system is wrong. They want exceptions made for them personally.'

II

CONSUMERS

The Art of Queuing

> Our goal is to make the life of the Soviet people
> still better, still more beautiful, and still more
> happy.
>
> > Leonid Brezhnev, 1971

> To live a life is not so simple as crossing a field.
>
> > Russian proverb

It was late afternoon when I reached my friend's apartment.
He was out. But his mother, a gaunt and aging lady who had
weathered 18 years in Stalinist camps and exile after an early
romance with Communism, fell to musing about the differences among generations in Russia and the new mood of
materialism.

'The middle-aged people, the people from 30–40 years old
and a bit older, are what I call "the generation of hungry
children",' she intoned quietly, dark brown eyes peering at
me. 'In their childhood and youth they saw enough hardship
for a lifetime. Today, their attitude is, "Give us food, a roof
over our heads, and work, and do whatever you want politically. Give us the material minimum. We won't ask for
more." '

These people, she was saying, were the Soviet counterparts
of the American 'Depression kids'. As she explained the moti-
vations for their nascent materialistic urges, the pale winter
sun slowly expired. But the shadows did not disturb her and
she went on without putting on a light. 'I know a family,' she
said. 'The father was a poor worker, absolutely unskilled and
barely literate. His wife was a simple woman, too. They had
eleven children. He worked in a factory and the family lived
in a dormitory – in a barracks, really. All lived in one big, big

74

room. They had a curtain which they pulled across it, and they put the beds behind the curtain. They used to sleep in shifts. That was during the war. And after the war, too. Those were terribly hard times. The mother died right after the last child was born.

'Now, the children are all grown up and married and have their own children. They are still working-class families, but they live much better than their parents. Each now has his own apartment. Small. One or two rooms. But with conveniences – a stove, maybe a refrigerator. One has a car. Those eleven children have become 40–45 people now, including all the grandchildren. They get their subsidized passes through the trade unions for summer vacations. They work in different factories – one at a food enterprise, one in an electrical power plant, one at Likhachev Automobile Plant, the others in other factories.

'They all know how much better they live now than during the hungry years of the war and after the war. They simply cannot imagine that life could be any better. They think they have everything and that this is the result of their hard work and the system. They don't know anything else. Of course, they are less interested in politics than people were in the first years after the Revolution. Then I remember we were hungry, we were cold, but we were building socialism and so we were willing to endure all that. But then after 15–20 years, we found that socialism was not all that good. And in 1937, things got so awful with the Stalinist terror. But people nowadays do not think so much about that. They think only about how their own life has gotten better.'

After the grim years of Stalin and the war, this lady applauded the new materialism. But other Bolshevik elders deplored and resented the new bourgeois mood. The press, too, sometimes sounded the foreboding note that Spartan socialist idealism was being eroded by acquisitiveness. 'One-sided orientation toward satisfaction of consumer demands, especially when it is not followed by the necessary indoctrination is fraught with the danger of spreading social "ills" such as individualism, egotism, and greed,' bleated *Planned Economy*, the bible of central planners, in early 1975.

But this represented a rear-guard action. For Leonid Brezhnev himself set the tone for the Seventies when, after consumer riots in Poland in December 1970, he pledged a five-year-plan favoring the consumer and 'saturating the market with consumer goods'. No such dramatic inundation occurred while we were in Moscow but living standards did improve in enough ways for long-neglected Soviet consumers to feel they were enjoying their best years since the Bolshevik Revolution.

One of my own earliest impressions in Moscow was that people were better dressed than I had expected. There was nothing especially fancy or stylish that caught my eye. We arrived in Fall and the sartorial colors were somber, almost funereal. But I observed a cloth-coat proletarian respectability on the sidewalks. Even if Muscovites were not sporting the latest mod clothes, they still had a petit bourgeois instinct for keeping up appearances. They shunned the deliberately grubby dress or ripped, faded jeans that many urbanites in the West affected. Women's dresses were plain; men's suits were simple but durable-looking, even if unpressed, and in the parks I noticed coeds in miniskirts and plastic knee-boots, usually in outlandish pink or garish purple. I did not then fully comprehend how much better off Muscovites were than others (the Russians have a saying about this: 'Moscow is downhill from all the Russias', meaning that the best of everything flows down into Moscow). But almost everywhere I traveled later it was apparent that while American bourgeois materialism might be officially censured, the American middle-class way of life embodied the aspirations of a growing number of Russians, especially in the cities. People wanted their own apartments, more stylish clothes, more swinging music, a television set and other appliances, and for those lucky enough, a private car.

We saw life slowly improving during our three years. Self-service stores and prepackaged foods edged into the market. Some people felt affluent enough to afford wigs, pets and even face-lifting. Scientists announced that diets had improved so much since the war years that Russian children were 2–3 inches taller than their parents. At second-hand shops, wives of generals and regime-writers bid against each other for Czarist antiques and pre-Revolutionary nicknacks that were ideologically taboo a decade ago. Some columnists complained about the occasional sale of cut-glass chandeliers for 1,000 rubles ($1,333), women's rings for 2,000, and sable coats for 4,000. Readers debated in letters to *Literary Gazette* the ethics of young girls' admitting that they judged prospective bridegrooms by how much they could earn and provide.

Andrei Voznesensky and Yevgeny Yevtushenko satirized the new materialism in verse, but one columnist boldly declared in a youth newspaper that top workers merited ten times the pay of lazy ones and young people were right to demand more money for good hard work.

Nothing more dramatically captured the onset of bourgeois acquisitiveness during my years than the belated Soviet romance with the private car. To provide an incentive for the elite and the growing middle class of engineers, technocrats, and middle-managers, the Soviet leadership invested about $15 billion to build up its automotive industry from 1965–75 (a large chunk of that went for truck factories and a fair share of the eventual auto output was slated for export at cut-rate prices). Automobiles, once ridiculed by Khrushchev as 'foul-smelling armchairs on wheels', were making it in Soviet society at last.

The West might be struggling to divorce itself from the pollution, congestion and fuel problems born of its early marriage with the internal combustion engine, but in the Russia of the early Seventies there was a giddy, newlywed excitement about cars. A Western ambassador told me that his wife had stopped one day for a red light in their imported Lincoln Continental and a swarthy pedestrian, evidently from Soviet Georgia, motioned her to lower the window and then offered her 30,000 rubles ($40,000) for the car. When I was traveling in Armenia, a factory director proudly gestured to a couple of dozen cars parked in the lot outside his 5,500-worker plant and boasted to me, 'Those are the private cars of our workers.' An engineer whom I knew felt positively liberated by his car (until it had a breakdown) and talked ecstatically about the pleasures of 'traveling wild' (that is, not bound by organized groups, bus routes, or set-package itineraries for vacation). In the warm summer and early fall, the woods and fields around Moscow were sprinkled with the boxy little Zhigulis (Soviet-made Fiats) of people escaping the city.

During my three years in Moscow, the number of private cars in the Soviet Union rose from 1.8 to 3 million (compared to nearly 100 million in America). Still, the private car remained well beyond the means of the average factory worker (who earns $187 a month). For the Soviet auto industry offered four makes and eight models, ranging from the little Zaporozhets-968, a European mini-car that putts along

77

on 13 horsepower and sells for 3,500 rubles ($4,665), to the Volga M-124, a five-seater that looks like a medium-sized Plymouth but costs 9,150 rubles ($12,200). The popular Zhiguli runs about $10,000. And there is no financing to help out; it's cash on the line. Russian friends told me that if the buyer is not fortunate enough to be on one of the special lists for the privileged class, the wait for a car can run from one to five years. I knew a journalist who had waited for six years for a Volga and predicted, 'It will be another five years before I get it.' Actually, through connections, he landed one within the next several months. Those who have to wait normal rotation on the one, citywide public waiting list, get little choice of color or extras when their number comes up. But this seems to bother no one. Russians are delighted with whatever is available.

The Soviet auto age has other idiosyncrasies that confound the foreigner. Traffic rules permit almost no left turns. The Soviet system is to go past the street you want, make a legal U-turn and then come back. But sometimes the legal U-turn areas are few and far between. Gas stations operate on a pump-it-yourself basis and no teenager comes hustling out to check the oil or wipe the windshield. Gas stations on intercity routes have signs, posted in several languages, that act as a deterrent for anyone's demanding service. I was fascinated by one which said (in English): 'front glass wiping – 15 kopecks; side glass wiping – 21 kopecks; back glass, turn indicators and stop signal wiping – 15 kopecks; tire pumping and pressure checking, per each wheel – 15 kopecks'. Another peculiarity is the Russian custom of driving at night using only parking lights, even on inter-city roads (none of which really qualifies as 'a highway' in the Western sense). This makes driving after dark a nerve-wracking experience. I have nearly run into huge poorly lit trucks or peasants walking by the roadside all-but-invisible in their dark padded jackets. Not surprisingly, the Soviet accident rate is very high – much higher than in America. Unofficially but reliably, I was told that roughly 45,000 people were killed in traffic accidents in 1974, almost as many as the American total of 46,200, and roughly ten times as bad a fatality rate in proportion to the total numbers of motor vehicles in both countries.

Ultimately, however, it is service that is the car owner's main headache. Nowhere nearly enough service centers exist for the cars rolling off Soviet assembly lines. When I left, Moscow had 16 repair centers, three really huge ones but the rest pretty modest, for handling a quarter of a million private cars. Ambitious plans were unveiled in 1972 for setting up a nationwide service system for the Zhigulis but in mid-1974, the press reported that fewer than one-third of the 33 planned service centers had opened and the rest were far behind construction schedules. Even where centers are in operation, finding spare parts can be *kashmar*, as the Russians say, a nightmare, because Soviet industry is more interested in producing new cars than spare parts which do not show much impact on the five-year-plan charts. I knew one car owner who mothballed a Volga sedan for several months because he was unable to replace a rear window. Another friend, an engineer, invited to drive us somewhere for a social outing one evening and had to apologize at the last moment because his car had broken down. A couple of months later I asked him about it, and it still had not been put back in service. The spare parts shortage breeds pilfering of parts, even such petty items as side mirrors and windshield wipers, which are in as short supply as many bigger items. As a defense, Russian motorists generally remove their windshield wipers whenever they park or when the weather is good, and store them in their glove compartments.

One of the most comical images I have of Moscow is the spectacle of busy traffic caught in a sudden, heavy rainstorm: Drivers quickly wheel toward the curb, halt their cars, and then like characters in an old Charlie Chaplin movie jump from one side of the car to the other, bending carefully over hoods in their suits or shirtsleeves, wincing at the touch of the raindrops as they fasten on their windshield wipers. Many is the time that I have joined that army of motorists at the curb in this frantic little jig.

So far, only a small slice of Soviet society has entered the auto age but the Soviet economy has laboriously provided other benefits for people less well-off. By early 1974, two-thirds of the nation's families had television sets, nearly 60 percent had sewing and washing machines, and about half had some kind of refrigerator.* Wages had been rising steadily enough for blue-collar workers in 1975 to be averaging 1,728 rubles ($2,244) a year. Savings deposits had ballooned to more than

* V. Perevedentsev, *Literary Gazette*, April 24, 1974.

80 billion rubles ($92 billion), earning two percent interest. Noting the dramatic changes since the early postwar period, one American expert, economist Gertrude Schroeder, reckoned that from 1950–1970, Soviet per capita food consumption doubled, disposable income quadrupled, the work week was shortened, welfare benefits increased, consumption of soft-goods tripled and purchases of hard goods rose twelve-fold.

But if the progress was striking, the shortfall was also staggering, I found. The dilemma for a foreigner in gauging the Soviet standard of living is deciding which yardstick to measure it by. In terms of the Soviet past, it has come a long way; in terms of industrialized Europe and America, it has a long way to go. As Gertrude Schroeder observed: 'Despite the impressive gains, the level of living of the Soviet people in 1970 was merely one-third of that in the United States, about one-half of that in England, France and West Germany, perhaps a little below that even in Italy and Japan, and well below that in the East European Communist countries of East Germany and Czechoslovakia.'* The gap may have narrowed by the mid-Seventies, but only slightly. Not only Westerners who lived among the Russians reacted that way. An East German scientist who had been working in Russia for several years confessed to me that he was 'appalled at how poorly ordinary Russians live'. Other East Europeans reacted similarly.

For in spite of Brezhnev's promise of a consumer-oriented five-year-plan, the nation's top economic planner, Deputy Prime Minister Nikolai Baibakov, admitted before 1974 was out that this promise and the loudly proclaimed consumer targets had 'proven unreachable' in the 1971–74 period and that in 1975, the leadership was quite openly going to give first priority to heavy industry.

I was given a graphic picture of the hard-nosed priorities that had actually been operating all along by Viktor Perstev, the experienced, red-faced construction boss at the high

* These findings by Gertrude Schroeder in 'Soviet Economic Growth and Consumer Welfare: Retrospect and Prospect' (in a Department of Agriculture Bulletin, Prospects for Agricultural Trade with the USSR, April, 1974), were reaffirmed later by a NATO study, 'Economic Aspects of Life in the USSR' (January, 1975), which carried the findings through 1973.

prestige Kama River truck plant. Three of every four rubles of investment, he explained, were going into the plant construction and only one ruble out of four was going into building an entire city for 160,000 people, with all its housing, stores, services, recreation and other facilities that had to be built from scratch. To speed up the construction of the truck plant and to combat absenteeism, Perstev said, they had imposed a ban on vodka, the Russian worker's solace and his employer's sorrow. With 50,000 workers stuck out in the middle of the windswept plains 650 miles east of Moscow, living in overcrowded dormitories and with limited leisure facilities, I asked him whether the town had a brewery. I found it hard to visualize such an army of construction crews without either vodka or beer.

'No. No beer plant,' he declared. 'Come back in five years and we should have a beer plant. It's in the Plan.' Then he chuckled. 'But don't come back looking for a beer plant before that. We have to build the truck factory first.'

That kind of official judgment about Soviet economic priorities has a fundamental impact on the everyday lives of Russians as consumers. What Westerners are quick to ask for are the statistical comparisons of living standards and they are usually impressed at how astonishingly cheap housing is, how much food costs, and clothing, too. I remember a conversation on a flight to Tashkent with a woman who had nine gold teeth and who worked in a textile plant with her husband. Together, she said, they earned 210 rubles ($280). Two-thirds of it went for food to feed three (they had a three-year-old daughter), she said, and only 12 rubles ($16) for their two-room apartment. The rest – 56 rubles ($75) – was split among clothing, transportation, entertainment, cigarettes, nominal taxes.

But the figures do not begin to convey the texture of Soviet consumer life, and the enormous gulf between the daily ordeal of the Russian shopper and the easy life-style of Americans. My Russian friends were amused to hear about American suburban housewives getting into the station wagon and dashing off to the supermarket or shopping center for groceries a couple of times a week. For they usually walked to the stores every day for food, often quite a long way, and had to go to several shops – one for bread, another for milk products, a third for meat, and so on. Some chose to buy their groceries downtown because the few supermarkets there were better stocked, and then had to lug packages home on bus and subway. Others had to shop downtown because many new apartment subdivisions go without basic stores for two or three years after they are first occupied because construction and commerce are so poorly synchronized. I have read any number of complaints in the press from people who said they had to walk a mile to get a pair of shoes repaired or to find some similar trivial but necessary service.

Shopping generally resembles a grand lottery. I had heard about consumer shortages before going to Moscow but at first it seemed to me that the stores were pretty well stocked. Only as we began to shop in earnest as a family did the Russian consumer's predicament really come through to me. First, we needed textbooks for our children (who went to Russian schools) and found that the sixth-grade textbooks had run out. A bit later, we tried to find ballet shoes for our 11-year-old daughter, Laurie, only to discover that in this land of ballerinas, ballet shoes size 8 were unavailable in Moscow. At G.U.M., the celebrated emporium on Red Square with a water fountain and the baroque atmosphere of a rambling, indoor, 1890s bazaar, I tried to find shoes for myself. They were out of anything in my size but sandals or flimsy, light-weight shoes that the clerk, with one look at me, recommended against buying. 'They won't last,' he admitted. Ann went out to buy some enamelware pans (Russians advised against getting the standard zinc-aluminium because it leaves a taste in the food; stainless steel, copperware and Teflon do not exist). She scoured four major Moscow department stores and several smaller shops without any success. In other words, the stocks that had impressed me at first turned out mostly to be the racks of suits and coats that were poorly made or had gone out of style, or the shelves of pots and pans and other unwanted items that Russian housewives refused to buy.

In spite of the various tinkering reforms, the Soviet economy still operates by Plan from above rather than in response to consumer demand from below and this produces a lop-sided assortment of goods. Goods are produced to fill the Plan, not to sell. Sometimes the anomalies are baffling. Leningrad can be overstocked with cross-country skis and yet go several months without soap for washing dishes. In the Armenian capital of Yerevan, I found an ample supply of accordions but local people complained they had gone for

82

weeks without ordinary kitchen spoons or tea samovars. I knew a Moscow family that spent a frantic month hunting for a child's potty while radios were a glut on the market. In Rostov, on a sweltering mid-90s day in June, the ice-cream stands were all closed by 2 p.m. and a tourist guide told me that it was because the whole area had run out of ice cream, a daily occurrence. A visiting American journalist friend hunting flints for his cigarette lighter was advised by Russian smokers to forget it because Moscow had been without flints for a couple of months.

The list of scarce items is practically endless. They are not permanently out of stock, but their appearance is unpredictable – toothpaste, towels, axes, locks, vacuum cleaners, kitchen china, handirons, rugs, spare parts for any gadget from a toaster or a camera to a car, stylish clothes or decent footwear, to mention only a few listed in the Soviet press. Traveling in the provinces I have also noticed the lack of such basic food items as meat. In cities like Nizhnevartovsk and Bratsk during winter, people had become so accustomed to that fact that the meat departments of food stores had simply shut down. I knew one young man whose family lived near Kalinin, a city of about 380,000 located 150 miles northwest of Moscow. He told me he never went to see his parents without taking meat because they were unable to buy anything in Kalinin but bologna and sausages.

Quality is another nightmare for the Russian consumer. The generally tacky quality of Soviet consumer goods is too well known to require rehearsal here. Russians themselves turn up their noses at many goods as *shtampny* – poured from the mold, the epitome of the cheapest output of mass-production industry, or simply, *brak*, junk that doesn't work or comes apart. Above all, goods without color, shape, style or charm. For some reason shoes are a particular headache. The newspaper *Literary Gazette* reported in late 1973 that one out of eight pairs of shoes produced nationwide had been rejected by inspectors and had to be discarded. When it comes to appliances, the American housewife who reads about Soviet goods and mentally pictures her own would be in for a rude shock. Even a Ukrainian researcher commented in 1972 that 85 percent of Soviet washing machines were obsolete (no spin dry, no automatic controls, each operation has to be hand-started, and they take only 3–4 pounds of clothes), and that Soviet refrigerators are far behind foreign ones (about one-third capacity and few with ice-making compartments). The obvious confirmation to me was seeing innumerable Soviet families still hanging their perishables out the window in a net-bag in cold weather to keep them fresh.

But that is an old story. What is new and revolutionary in the Soviet Seventies is that Russian consumers are becoming fussier shoppers. The country folk may still buy practically anything, but urbanites are more discriminating and fashion-conscious. They may have more cash in their pockets than ever before, but they are less willing to part with it. Yet because the supplies of consumer goods are about as unpredictable as the weather (and there is little effective advertising to help shoppers), Russians have developed a series of defense mechanisms to cope with the situation. They know that some Soviet factories, especially those in the Baltic Republics, produce nice items – women's clothing with a bit of style, brighter men's shirts, good sleeping bags, radios, or outboard motors – and that these items sell out in a flash whenever they appear. So they prowl the stores incessantly, hoping to be in the right place at the right time when, as the slang expression has it, *oni vybrasyvayut chto-to khoroshoye*, 'they throw out something good', meaning put choice items on sale. For just that lucky break, women all carry a string bag, an *avoska*, which comes from the Russian word for maybe, perchance. In other words, a string bag for the odd chance that you find something unexpected, because stores do not provide paper bags. Likewise, almost any man carries a briefcase wherever he goes. I remember thinking at first how studious and businesslike all these Russian men looked with their briefcases. Then one day, I was talking with a well-established scientist in a park and suddenly he reached into his briefcase. I thought that he was going to pull out some paper to illustrate a point he was making. But as my gaze followed his hand into the briefcase, I spotted a bloody hunk of meat wrapped loosely in newspaper. The scientist, who lived outside of Moscow, had bought the meat to take home and was just checking to make sure it was not leaking badly. As time went on, I discovered that briefcases were far more likely to be loaded with oranges, hoards of toothpaste or pairs of shoes than with books or papers.

84

Another precaution is to carry plenty of cash at all times, for the Soviet system is devoid of credit cards, charge accounts, checkbooks, or easy loans. Installment credit is available only on items like the less desirable models of radios and television sets which are grossly overstocked and not moving well. So to be ready for the happy chance of finding something rare, one sturdy blonde woman told me, 'you have to carry a lot of cash. Suppose you suddenly discover they are selling good knee-boots for 70 rubles. You have to get in line right away. You don't have time to go back to your apartment and get money. The boots will be gone by the time you get back.'

One of the attractive qualities among Russians that this situation has fostered is an almost frontier readiness to share cash with friends and co-workers to help them make the big purchases. Paradoxically, Russians have less money than most Americans but are more instinctively generous with it to friends. People think nothing of borrowing – or loaning – 25, 50 or 100 rubles until the next pay day, if they can spare it – and sometimes even if they can't. For most people, money is less important than a good opportunity to use it.

Another cardinal rule of Russian consumer life is shopping for others. It is an unforgivable sin, for example, to run across something as rare as pineapples, Polish-made bras, East German wall-lamps or Yugoslav toothpaste, without buying some extras for your best friend at work, your mother, sister, daughter, husband, brother-in-law, or some other kin or neighbor. As a result, I was amazed to discover, people know by heart the shoe, bra, pant and dress sizes, waist and length measurements, color preferences and other vital particulars for a whole stable of their nearest and dearest to be ready for that moment when lightning strikes a store happen to be in. Then they spend until the money runs out.

One middle-aged Moscow woman also told me how office-workers organize shopping pools, the way American housewives operate car-pools, and rotate the daily chore of shopping for food. In their little office 'collectives', she said, someone goes out to buy basic food items for all during the lunch hour to help everyone escape the terrible crush in stores after work. Often the women also take turns sneaking out during regular working hours to scout the main downtown stores for something special and return to sound the alert if reinforcements are needed for bulk-buying. In such cases, a bit of petty profiteering on the resale is perfectly normal. A young man told me how he had seen one woman get on a bus with 20 tubes of popular Yugoslav 'Signal' brand toothpaste in her *avoska*. She was immediately inundated with questions about where she found it and a few whispered offers to buy some at a premium.

Buying imported goods is another line of defense among ordinary consumers, as well as the privileged class. Although few Western goods are available, even goods from Eastern Europe and Third World countries have a certain snob appeal and Russians will readily pay exorbitant premiums for them even when Soviet goods are adequate. 'I would rather pay twice the price for imported shoes than for Soviet-made shoes,' a young tour guide in Vladimir told me. He was wearing Spanish shoes that cost him 35 rubles (nearly $48), or more than one-third of his monthly salary. Sales clerks even push the foreign items over Soviet-made.

I stopped one night in G.U.M. to buy some Soviet toilet goods as an experiment. But when I motioned to a box marked simply 'Shaving Cream' in Russian, the salesgirl steered me to a competing brand.

'Is it Soviet?' I asked.

'No,' she said. 'Made in GDR (East Germany). It's better than ours.'

I then asked her about toothpaste. She recommended 'Merri' from Bulgaria.

'But what about Soviet toothpaste?' I asked. 'Do you have Soviet brands?'

'Yes, of course,' she said, regarding me as a rather odd customer, 'but this Bulgarian one is better.'

I insisted on a Soviet brand – orange-flavored. After one try, I understood why she had recommended the Bulgarian. It was a sour orange flavor that didn't blend with the dentifrice.

'Everyone wants imported things,' a scientist observed. 'I remember an important lady, a friend of my wife who was a high Party official at Moscow film studios. She was director of a department that "edited" movies.' And he glanced over his glasses at me to be sure I caught his meaning. 'I remember – and this was 15 years ago – she used to say, "I don't care if they say the material is bad, I want a dress that is imported." Even such a person! Of course, it had no effect on her beliefs or her loyalty. But she wanted things from abroad because she regarded them as better and as prerequisites of the good life. In those days, people used to call them *importny* goods. Now they like to think they are more sophisticated. So the new term is *firmenny* – from a firm with a trade mark. But actually, it means the same thing. People want something that is not Soviet – anything, a shirt, a tie, a handbag, any little thing at all. It makes them feel better than other people.'

The urge for a touch of class, for something better than others have, has put new pressure on that classic Russian institution – the queue. Customers the world-over wait in lines, but Soviet queues have a dimension all their own, like the Egyptian pyramids. They reveal a lot about the Russian predicament and the Russian psyche. And their operation is far more intricate than first meets the eye. To the passerby they look like nearly motionless files of mortals doomed to some commercial purgatory for their humble purchases. But what the outsider misses is the hidden magnetism of lines for Russians, their inner dynamics, their special etiquette.

The only real taste of stoical shopping vigils in recent American history were the pre-dawn lines at service stations during the gasoline crisis in the winter of 1973–74. That produced a wave of national self-pity in America. But it was temporary and only for one item. Imagine it across the board, all the time, and you realize that Soviet shopping is like a year-round Christmas rush. The accepted norm is that the Soviet woman daily spends two hours in line, seven days a week, daily going through double the gauntlet that the American housewife undergoes at her supermarket once, maybe twice a week. I noted in the Soviet press that Russians spend 30 billion man-hours in line annually just to make purchases. That does not count several billion more man-hours expended waiting in tailor shops, barbershops, post offices, savings banks, dry cleaners and various receiving points for turning in empty bottles and so on. But 30 billion man-hours alone is enough to keep 15 million workers busy year-round on a 40-hour week.

Personally, I have known of people who stood in line 90 minutes to buy four pineapples, three hours for a two-minute roller coaster ride, three and a half hours to buy three large heads of cabbage only to find the cabbages were gone as they approached the front of the line, 18 hours to sign up to purchase a rug at some later date, all through a freezing December night to register on a list for buying a car, and then waiting 18 more months for actual delivery, and terribly lucky at that. Lines can run from a few yards long to half a block to nearly a mile, and usually they move at an excruciating creep. Some friends of ours, living in the south-west part of Moscow, watched and photographed a line that lasted two solid days and nights, four abreast and running all through an apartment development. They guessed there were 10,000–15,000 people, signing up to buy rugs, an opportunity that came only once a year in that entire section of Moscow. Some burned bonfires to keep warm out in the snow and the crackling wood and din of constant conversation kept our friends awake at night.

Yet despite such ordeals the instinctive reaction of a Russian woman when she sees a queue forming is to get in line immediately – even before she knows what is being sold. Queue-psychology has a magnetism of its own. Again and again, I have been told by Russians that anyone's normal assumption on seeing people up front hurrying to get in line is that there must be something up there worth lining up for. Never mind what it is. Get in line first and ask questions later. You'll find out when you get to the front of the line, or perhaps they'll pass back word before then. A lady lawyer told me she once came upon an enormous line stretching all through the Moskva Department Store, and when she asked those at the end of the line what was on sale, 'they said they didn't know or else snarled at me and told me not to interfere. I walked up 20 or 30 yards asking people and no one knew. Finally, I gave up asking.'

Nina Voronel, a translator of children's literature, said she happened to be at an appliance counter one day buying an ordinary hand mixer for 30 rubles ($40), when a clerk carried in a box of East German wall-lamps. 'I told the salesgirl, "I'll take one. Put me down for one and I'll go pay the cashier." And while I went to the cashier, a line of about 50 people formed. How they found out about it, I don't know, word spreads – that is the way we always learn here. Practically everyone in the store was there. It didn't matter whether they needed the lamps or not. People here don't just buy what they need, but whatever they see that is worth having. Some may sell those lamps. Some may give them to

88

friends. But mostly they keep them on the shelf. A lamp is always needed. Good fabrics are always needed, fur coats, fur hats, good winter boots, bright summer dresses, floor rugs, dishes, enamel pots and pans, kettles, good woolen cardigan sweaters, umbrellas, a decent purse, a nice writing table, a typewriter, a good woman's bra – not a floppy, ugly Soviet one with no support and no adjustments, made for big-bosomed country girls. But a Czech bra or a Polish one, white and pretty instead of blue and baggy with rose buds. That is why people are so quick to join a line. It might be any of those things.'

People form lines in a rush like ducks in a pond racing for a piece of bread. In a Kiev department store once, I was not far from the women's gloves counter when a voice nearby pronounced the words 'imported gloves'. I was nearly dashed against the counter in the crush. One particularly aggressive young couple squirmed to the front, examined the gloves over the head of another shopper, pronounced them not to be imported and squeezed their way back out of the crowd. A few others near the front also drifted off. But the tail of the line held firm in its ignorance until a blue-coated store clerk passed down the aisle behind them pushing a cartload of nice looking men's padded windbreakers. Like an ebb tide, the wave of shoppers flowed away from gloves and literally washed this poor clerk into a corner. Clearly, she was un-prepared to sell right there, but she escaped with her cargo into an elevator only when the front ranks had thoroughly quizzed her about prices, sizes and which department would sell the jackets.

Once formed, moreover, Soviet lines are more fluid than they appear. Eddies and undercurrents work within them. In most stores, for example, the shopper's ordeal is prolonged by the requirement to stand in not one, but three lines for any purchase – the first to select her purchase, find out its price and order it; the second to pay a cashier somewhere else in the store and get a receipt; and the third, to go pick up her purchase and turn in her receipt.

But in a dairy store one Saturday morning, I found out that the game is both simpler and more complex than that. I went in to buy some cheese, butter and bologna sausage which were, unfortunately, in three separate departments, each with its own line. *Nine lines!* I groaned inwardly. But rather quickly, I noticed that veteran shoppers were skipping the first stage. They knew what most items cost, so they went directly to the cashier for their receipts. After a bit of studying prices, that was what I did, too. Then, receipts in hand, I went to the cheese line, the longest – probably 20 people – to get the worst over with first. But I was in line less than a minute when the lady in front of me turned around and asked me to hold her place. She darted off to the butter-and-milk line. The cheese line was moving so slowly that she got her butter and milk and returned before we had moved forward three feet. I decided to take the risk, too, and got back with my butter while the cheese line was still inching along. Then it dawned on me that the entire store was churning with people getting into line, holding places, leaving, returning. Everyone was using the cheese line as home base. That was why it was barely moving: it kept expanding in the middle. So once again, I got the elderly gentleman behind me to hold my place and went off to buy my bologna. Once again, it worked. In the end it took me 22 minutes to buy butter, sausage and cheese and instead of being furious, I felt oddly as if I had somehow beaten the system with all those shortcuts.

Line-jumping, I was later advised by more serious shoppers, is accepted for ordinary items but not for scarce ones. 'Things get tense,' several women said. 'People know from experience that things actually run out while they are standing in line,' advised one young blonde. 'So if the line is for something really good and you leave it for very long, people get very upset. They fly off the handle and curse you and try to keep you from getting back in when you return. It's up to the person behind you to defend your place in line. So it's a serious business asking someone to hold your place. They take on a moral obligation not only to let you in front of them later on but to defend you. You have to be stubborn yourself and stand your ground in spite of the insults and the stares. And when you get to the front of the line, if the sales clerks are not limiting the amount, you can hear people, maybe six or eight places back, shouting at you not to take so much, that you are a person with no scruples or that you have no consideration for other people. It can get rather unpleasant.'

This competitive shopping gives a surface tension to Russian life, which as much as anything sets ordinary people off from the elite. An American journalist once compared shopping to going through Army basic training where sergeants deliberately cut new recruits down to size. He had in mind the surly, high-handed attitude of sales clerks who are poorly paid, often overworked, or simply lazy. Stories about waiting an hour in a restaurant for a waitress to take your order and then waiting half an hour more for her to inform you that they are out of what you ordered are legion. In Tashkent, an elderly woman told me she had gotten to the head of a meat line in a food store after a long wait and then had to endure five more minutes while the butcher gabbed about sports with a friend. When she asked for some meat, she said, he wheeled on her grumpily and said, 'Next, I suppose you'll want me to cram it in your mouth for you.' So stereotype are rude sales clerks that Arkady Raikin, the leading Soviet comic, always makes a hit with a sales lady who totally ignores the request of some Soviet Caspar Milquetoast asking for a gift for a middle-aged lady and insists on selling him a toy cannon. The attitude of sales clerks is part and parcel of the entire complex of the Soviet seller's market. 'They think, "I am one and you are many, so why should I hurry? You have to wait for me anyway," ' a government worker explained to me. 'And they're right, of course. Where else can you go if they have what you want?'

In many stores, shoppers cannot help themselves because they are warily kept at arms-length from merchandise stacked behind counters, out of reach until the clerk is ready to serve them. Bread stores are an exception. There, customers are provided with metal forks for testing the freshness of the loaves. But in big department stores, customers are admitted only in small, controlled groups into roped-off sections for women's coats, children's boots, or sports gear. The advent of self-service food stores has begun to alter this chilly aloofness. But the change has been glacial, in part because Russians are so tradition-bound. At the two-story food market on Kalinin Prospekt in downtown Moscow, for example, I noticed that people were used to bagged flour, sugar and dry noodles, but many still preferred waiting in line to watch the sales girl ladle out fresh yogurt into a jar brought from home than picking up a pre-packaged container, even if it was quicker. Others have been deterred by what they regard as insulting spot-inspections of shoppers' handbags in checkout lines, conducted to combat shoplifting.

The Russian shopper's gauntlet is also complicated by the unpredictable interruptions of service and store closings. Far more than in other countries, Soviet stores observe 'cleaning days' and 'inventory days' when business comes to a halt. Or the shopper can unexpectedly come upon a shop door marked *remont*, which means repair but which amounts to a universal cover-up for 'out to lunch indefinitely'. In the provincial cities especially, stores just shut down to suit the staff regardless of posted hours of operation. 'They work like their own bosses,' a dejected country woman said to me in a Caucasian village, as we shared frustrations outside the only food store in the neighborhood. 'If they feel they have something to sell, they're open. If not, not.' Other establishments arrange their own breaks with scant thought for customers, such as the buffet in the lobby of the Ukraine Hotel which is closed from noon to 2 p.m. Or Moscow's Gorky Park, which has the delightful practice in winter of flooding the pathways to permit skating through the woods, but regularly shuts down at prime time – Sunday afternoons from 4 to 6. What is more, as I learned painfully, ticket ladies refuse to sell admission tickets after 3 p.m. 'Not enough time for you to get ready,' barked one woman, and no amount of persuasion could reverse her arbitrary edict.

Russians are surprisingly phlegmatic about it all, but they look upon shopping generally as a form of physical and psychological combat, much as New Yorkers brace themselves for rush-hour in the subways. People barge into stores, bump into each other with faces set in glum, combative expressions, not bothering to thank someone for holding a door or stepping aside. Muscovites, as hardened city-dwellers, have a reputation among other Russians for being particularly brusque. Periodically some columnist will upbraid them for crude manners. Still, Russians, who are marvelously warm-hearted in private, are often surprised to hear that foreigners find them dour and unsmiling in public. 'You have to understand,' said a kind, gray-haired literary critic, 'that for as long as we can remember, shopping was a struggle. Life is a struggle. Where you stand in line is serious business. That goes back to the war years when, if a boy did not get up early enough to get near the front of the line, he came home without bread that day. Of course, things are better now. But people still get that tense feeling when they shop.' And the daily wear and tear – not just from shopping but work, diet, other strains of life – shows on them; they age more rapidly. Among people over 30, I found, Russians tend to think

Americans are 8–10 years younger than they are and Americans think Russians are 8–10 years older than they are.

One positive result of the consumer's eternal gauntlet, however, is that any unusual purchase is a possession to be prized and cherished. Russians are less materialistic than Americans and yet they have a warm sense of extra pleasure and achievement over relatively simple things, much more than do Westerners for whom the buying is easier. 'In America, if your wife has bought a nice new dress and I notice it, I will say, "Oh, yes, that's nice," and that's all,' suggested a woman journalist who had seen America and mixed with Americans. 'But in Moscow, when I get my hands on a pair of shoes that I like, it is an achievement, a feat, an exploit. It means that I have managed to work it out in some complicated way through a friend or perhaps I have found a sales clerk to bribe or I have gone from store to store to store and I have stood in line for hours. Notice how I put it, not simply "bought some shoes" but "got my hands on a pair of shoes". So when I get the shoes I like, I am *very* proud of them. And friends say to me, "Oho, you have new shoes! Tell me, where did you get them?" And it is not just an idle, polite question, it is a real question. Because they are thinking, "Maybe she can help me get a pair. Maybe I can get a pair of nice shoes like that for myself." Americans simply cannot grasp that, can they?' She was right for I have seen that look of triumphant excitement in the eyes of women who have stood in line for an eon and just come away with a nice chignon or a Yugoslav sweater. It is a heartwarming sight.

For most Russians, however, it is other elements of economic life which compensate for the obvious shortcomings of their consumer system and make them prefer their socialism to the freer but less secure life style of Westerners. The economic crises of the West in the Seventies have made some of them more confident about their own system lately, for all its faults. The double-digit inflation, unemployment, high cost of housing, medical care and college education in America, all dismay them. For many, the benefits of low-cost housing, free medical care, subsidized university education and a guaranteed job – above all, that job security – outweigh the disadvantages of the marketplace. I remember one evening during a dinner in the apartment of an environmentalist who was an admirer of O'Henry's short stories and who entertained Ann and me with melancholy songs of the Volga on his guitar before the talk turned to economics. 'We know life here is not as good as it is in America, that your best workers make three and four times as much as ours and your apartments and homes are bigger than ours,' he said. 'But we don't have to save for unemployment here. I bring home my pay, give it to Lyuba and she organizes the household. What do I have to worry about? There is enough money. You make much more than I do. But you have to save. You have to have reserves because any time you can become unemployed and you have to worry about your retirement. Not me. I never have to worry. I have a specialty. I can walk out of my institute and get another job in my specialty and I will make the same money, 220 rubles a month, without any problem. I can count on my 220 rubles. That is the big difference. I don't have to worry about the future, and you do!'

These are comments repeated daily in the press and practically as often when Russians meet Westerners, especially Americans. They have a certain validity, especially the point about unemployment.

Soviet statistics about welfare programs always sound impressive, though the reality behind them often turns out to be a good deal less impressive. Government officials, for example, are fond of proclaiming that roughly 20 billion rubles are paid out annually in pensions. But when you discover that this sum is split up among 41.5 million pensioners, it works out to an average of 40 rubles ($53) a month, which is below the unofficial Soviet poverty line. In practice, many grandmothers and grandfathers have a cushion because they live with their grown children and many also continue to work after legal retirement as low-paid watchmen, cleaning ladies, elevator operators, coat clerks or maids – and the Government encourages them to do so. But, after all, that is not retirement.

Similarly, the Soviet economy has been spared the rampant inflation of Western economies in recent years. But it has not been as inflation-proof as government officials claim. It is true that Russians still enjoy a subsidized subway ride for 5 kopecks (about 6.5 cents) as they did 20 years ago. Rents in state housing are fixed and held very low; 6–8 rubles ($8–11) a month for two rooms, kitchenette and bath. A

94

half-liter of standard grade milk costs 16 kopecks (about 35 cents a quart) now as it did a decade ago. Potatoes in the state store are still fixed at 10 kopecks a kilogram (about 6 cents a pound). The beef price ceiling in state stores is nominally unchanged at 2 rubles a kilo ($1.20 a pound). Travel is cheap. A Russian can ride a train or plane 1,000 miles and spend only 50–60 rubles ($66–80). Hotel rooms, usually shared with strangers, go for a ruble or two a night per bed. Subsidized vacation passes remain a great boon – 120 rubles ($160) for 26 days' room and board in a modest rest house. Children's Pioneer camp costs 9–15 rubles ($12–20) for three and a half weeks. But for things like hotels, trains, vacation passes or camps, the trick is getting space.

Moreover, in my final weeks in Moscow in late 1974, ordinary people were privately scoffing at official claims that the retail price index had actually gone down 0.3 percent since 1970. One middle-aged woman asserted that what had cost five rubles a few years back now cost seven. A linguist estimated that to feed and clothe her family of four, including two growing boys, was now twice as costly as in 1970. A doctor more modestly estimated the increase at 20 percent. Some Western economists have guessed that hidden Soviet inflation is running about five percent a year.*

In a few cases, prices have been openly increased. In 1973 they were doubled overnight on such luxury items as caviar, smoked salmon, furs and jewelry though prices on some television sets and radios came down about 20 percent. But the more frequent technique is to substitute new items at higher prices with little or no change in quality and to withdraw the older, lower-priced items. Another form of inflation takes place because of shortages that force people into the peasant free market in food staples where meat and vegetable prices have risen greatly. In 1970, that universal currency of Russian life, vodka, went through a tricky, hidden price rise. The famous old brands like Stolichnaya selling at 2.87 rubles a half liter simply disappeared from the Russian market (to be exported) and a newer, harsher brand simply named Vodka came out at 3.62. In 1974, the old Zhiguli-1 car (the Soviet version of the Fiat-124) began gradually to be replaced by the Zhiguli-3 (a Fiat 125). The new Zhiguli has a bit more

* Keith Bush in *Economic Aspects of Life in the USSR* (NATO, Brussels, 1975), p. 13.

power, more attractive interior, a warning light to show when the door is open, more chrome and a few other minor modifications. But the price increase was enough to make both Italian and American car-makers envious: the old one cost $7,333 and the newer one $10,000 – a hike of 36 percent in one fell swoop.

More mundane items are hit by such gimmickry, too, from stockings to boys' outdoor jackets or food. One housewife, talking about chickens, told me that 'the cheaper varieties of young friers have disappeared. Now the choice is mostly the better variety at 2.65 rubles a kilo ($1.59 a pound) or imported Hungarian or Danish that cost more or, if you are really desperate, 3.40 a kilo ($2.04 a pound) for cleaned chicken. That is the main means of inflation here. The cheapest varities cannot be found. Medium price items are rare and the most expensive is what is offered. So the cost of living goes up even without changing prices.'

One vital sector that has been essentially inflation-free has been medical care. And freedom from crippling medical bills is one of the prides of the Soviet system, especially in a period of sky-rocketing medical costs in the United States.

My personal exposure to the Soviet medical system was limited to a couple of tours to clinics that were scrubbed spic and span for foreign visitors. Once, our children went for medical examinations to the diplomatic polyclinic, a faded beige building behind heavy iron gates in downtown Moscow, where people brought their 'samples' in *Nescafé* jars, water bottles and other assorted vessels (because no medical containers were provided) to a lab that was open for one hour a day. It took several calls to complete the examination. But the doctors, all middle-aged women, were pleasant and seemed competent, and Ann was very impressed with how thorough the medical examination was.

In travels to Central Asia and elsewhere, I was struck that the general gains in Soviet health care were among the more dramatic achievements of the system in the half-century since Lenin declared, 'either the lice defeat socialism or socialism defeats the lice.' Epidemics have largely been curbed. Infant mortality has come close to the levels of the 15 most advanced countries. Life expectancy is up to 70 years. By 1970, the Soviet Union had the highest ratio of doctors to population in the world – 23.8 doctors for each 10,000 persons (compared to 15.8 in the U.S.) and it had more hospital beds than

America (10.6 vs. 8.2 per thousand, though one reason is that Russian doctors hospitalize some kinds of people treated as outpatients in America, such as chronic alcoholics). By Western estimates, the Kremlin spends about 5–6 percent of its gross national product on health care, compared to 7 percent in America.*

Soviet officials never tire of telling that security from financial disaster because of health problems is one of the most important and popular aspects of the system. Russians whom I knew cited acquaintances of modest means and position who obtained, virtually cost-free, health care that would have been inordinately expensive in the West, including operations or treatment in distant hospitals and institutes.

But privately, many Russians complained to me that their health system, like the rest of the consumer sector, was plagued by overworked doctors, shortages of medicine, poor equipment, and generally low quality service. They mainly blamed the government's low pay to doctors and other medical personnel (financially, doctors, who are mostly women, are near the bottom in pay scales, making about 100–130 rubles a month, $133–173, less than average factory workers). Andrei Sakharov, the dissident physicist, rated the quality of health care as 'very low' and sent his wife abroad for eye treatment. The head of the Soviet Academy of Sciences, Mstislav Keldysh, used an American specialist for heart treatments. Another well-known scientist said cautiously of the Soviet medical care system: 'It's spotty. Some doctors, some hospitals, clinics are good. Others are poor. You can't tell which will be good and which, poor. I'm talking about Moscow, of course. Out in the country, it's worse.'

A medical scientist who emigrated to America in 1974 after working at one of Moscow's leading medical institutes praised Russian doctors as 'more humane' than profit-oriented private physicians in America and endorsed the concept of socialized medicine. 'But you cannot imagine how poor is the general quality of medical service,' he said. 'In Ryazan [a city of 400,000] where I grew up, they have very bad equipment. They lacked very simple things – medicines

* These summary comparisons are based on 'Health As a "Public Utility" or the "Maintenance of Capacity" in Soviet Society', by Mark G. Field in the new book which he has edited, *Social Consequences of Modernization in Communist Societies* (Baltimore, Johns Hopkins, 1976).

for example. The qualification of the doctors is much lower in Moscow. But the worst problem in the system is poor organization and bad nursing service. The nurses do sterilization very badly. After operations, even in our institute which is one of the very top ones, we had a lot of sepsis, festering wounds, infections, and suppuration. The nurses were not clean enough. They made mistakes in operations. Our institute director became very angry because he would do beautiful operations and then there were these infections. So often. You know, the middle-level personnel do not receive good pay and they are not reliable, not competent. Once I was in Kharkov, and I had to be operated on for appendicitis in an ordinary district hospital. It was so dirty that you cannot imagine it. The sheets were gray from such long use. The clothes of the hospital workers were not clean enough. They took special care of me because I was from this important institute in Moscow. Still, I got an infection and so did others. I saw one man die in my presence after an appendicitis operation because of this problem.'

As some Soviet doctors emigrated along with other Jews in the Seventies, both American and Israeli doctors who were trying to help them adjust to foreign medical systems were surprised to find Soviet doctors generally less qualified than they had expected. 'The gap is huge,' I was told by a New Yorker helping to retrain Soviet physicians. Another was surprised to learn that a lady doctor from a leading Leningrad child-care clinic did not know how to use an otoscope, a device for examining ears, and said when he asked her how she told whether the children had infections, she replied, 'We were taught to pull on the ear lobe and if the child cried, it had an infection.'

An East German gynecologist whom I met in the Caucasus and who worked for three years in Leningrad shared this American assessment. 'The Soviets like to make big propaganda about their health system,' he told me, 'but I have worked in their clinics and their ambulances, and the care is not good. They have very little medicine and medical supplies. There is a shortage of necessary equipment. Of course, they have research institutes or special hospitals like the Kremlin Clinic for important people which are probably on the same rank with your American hospitals, with good specialists and supplies. But we in East Germany are, say, 15 years behind you in the general quality of care and the

Russians are way behind us. The government simply does not invest enough in ordinary clinics and hospitals. Ambulances take too long to get to people. In many cases, they are called out to pick up drunks and a patient with a heart attack must wait for two hours. Hospitals are overcrowded. Now they are building them with smaller rooms, say six to a room, but the ones I saw had many beds. Not a very pleasant atmosphere. The food is poor. Most families bring food to their relatives in hospitals and they give money or gifts to the *saniturki*, nurses' aides, so that bed linens will be changed regularly and things will be kept cleaner.'

The overcrowding and delays in getting admitted to hospitals are mentioned by many people. 'For emergencies, it is not a problem to get into a hospital – emergencies are treated at once,' said a Moscow doctor. 'But for "planned operations" [non-emergencies, dealing with chronic conditions and therefore scheduled by plan], it is a problem everywhere.' A Moldavian power engineer told me he had waited several months for an abdominal operation in Kishinev. At Moscow's Institute of Cardio-Vascular Surgery, 'three years, even five years' is not an unusual wait, said one scientist. At less prestigious institutions, the time-lag is shorter but considerable.

The East German doctor dismissed my comments about the diplomatic polyclinic in Moscow. 'You have a special hospital (for foreigners) where the service is much better than in hospitals for Russians,' he said. Even so, I knew Western patients who had been hospitalized there and were unnerved by the unsanitary conditions. Others were surprised to learn that in minor operations, such as abortions and appendectomies, Russian doctors use novocaine rather than general anesthesia, and that almost all dental care, except tooth extractions, is done without any pain-killers.

The cheapness of medicines – often under a dollar for prescriptions – is one of the great pluses of the system, but it is frequently canceled out by shortages. This is one problem that Russians complain about quite openly. Even the press periodically chides the drug industry for shortages of such standard medicines or medical ingredients as glycerine for heart patients, tincture of iodine, ammonium hydroxide, novocaine, even first-aid kits and tourniquets, let alone sophisticated antibiotics. One doctor told me that there were standing instructions for doctors not to prescribe medicines they knew were out of stock. Like many other foreign residents in Moscow, I was frequently approached by Russian friends with urgent pleas for help in obtaining critically needed medicines, unavailable at any price in Moscow. Nonetheless, for most Russians such problems are outweighed by the improvements over the past. They regard the system of free health care as one of the most positive features of Soviet socialism.

Housing, perhaps more than anything else, illustrates the peculiar combination of triumph and tragedy for Soviet consumers. Staggering achievements have been made, yet staggering shortcomings remain. In the 20 years since 1956, roughly 44 million new units of housing have been built by the state, private and cooperative builders, more than in any other country in the world.* In the first half of this decade, 35 billion rubles (nearly $48 billion) were allocated for housing construction and in 1975 alone, the target was to give more than 11 million people better living quarters, more than half of them in new buildings.

The visible impact of the Soviet housing program is striking. Westerners return after a 10-year absence and marvel at the rows of paneled prefab 9-story, 11-story, and 14-story apartment houses that dominate the outskirts of Moscow and other large Soviet cities. The monotony of their architecture and their inhuman size are numbing and their interiors are much humbler than their grand façades. But the scale of effort is impressive. Almost everywhere that I went I encountered scholars, engineers, workmen, teachers boasting about their new apartments. They might be modest by Western standards but they were bright and airy enough to produce a new outlook on life for those who previously had been crammed into communal flats, sharing kitchen, bath and toilet with four to six other families. 'You cannot imagine how important a change that is for people,' a middle-aged teacher asserted.

Yet so massive and aching is the housing shortage that

* Henry W. Morton, 'What Have the Soviet Leaders Done About the Housing Crisis?' in Henry W. Morton and Rudolf L. Tökés, eds., *Soviet Politics and Society in the 1970's* (New York, Free Press, 1974), pp. 163ff. Many of the statistical comparisons in this chapter are drawn from Morton.

Western economists like Gertrude Schroeder still reckon that the Soviet Union is 'the most poorly housed of any major country in Europe – and poorly housed also by comparison with the [Soviet] government's minimum standard for health and decency.' The Russian 'sanitary housing norm' was set back in 1920 at nine square meters of living space – equal to a ten-by-ten-foot room – as the minimum for each person. Yet more than half a century later, Henry Morton, an American expert on Soviet housing, found that 'the great majority of Soviet people in urban areas have not reached the 1920 minimum level.'

More than 25 percent of them still live in communal apartments, Soviet officials concede and Western specialists think the figure may be closer to one-third. In 1972, the national average was 7.6 square meters of living space per person in Soviet urban areas – or about one-third the space of American city-dwellers and one-half the space of people in Western European cities. And within the Soviet Union, Moscow and the Baltic capitals of Riga and Tallinn were far better off than less developed cities like Tashkent, Yerevan, and Dushanbe in Central Asia and the Caucasus.

The problem, however, is more human than statistical. To give me a picture of it, Moscow friends took me one gray November afternoon to an old section near the Rzhevsky bathhouse, just off Peace Avenue. Hundreds of people were milling about for hours, like pickets on strike: Hands thrust into their pockets, scarves wound tightly against the cold, carrying placards or hand-scrawled signs pinned to their leather jackets and sturdy cloth coats. Occasionally, they would pause to converse quietly in twos and threes and then walk on. Despite the resemblance, they were not picketers. They were walking want ads – Muscovites advertising their apartments for exchange, anxious to improve their living quarters.

One modish young couple passed us offering an attractive 'split' – the exchange of a four-room apartment, very large by Soviet standards, for two smaller ones because, as newly-weds, they wanted to move out from living with their in-laws. An elderly woman was trying to coax a man in a dark fedora to take single rooms in two different communal apartments in exchange for his separate one-room flat (kitchenette, bath and toilet are automatically included except in communal flats). Everyone understands that dining rooms are nonexistent and that day-time parlors become bedrooms at night. Four people – a couple, their child, and a *babushka* – living in two rooms is standard, even good, if the rooms are big. Trades were slow that Sunday. It was mostly a day for looking, asking, mumbling, conferring, rejecting and passing on.

At the far end of the lane, however, there was action. There, students and military officers were swarming around a few landlords offering a small apartment, a room or even just a bed for rent. One young woman, surrounded five deep on all sides, had a single room in a downtown location but rejected a well-dressed Army major as a tenant, evidently afraid he would bring his wife and child from out-of-town into the apartment. Her place was too crowded for that, she said. A tall, husky man with wavy silver hair and a thick navy blue jacket caused a stir by offering a two-room flat in an old building with gas heat.

'The water and toilet are in the backyard,' he said. That turned off two young men.

'Who wants that?' said one, as they left in disgust.

But a middle-aged woman, terribly intent, was undeterred. She wanted it for her daughter and a friend, two girls in medical school. 'They are very good girls – straight-A students,' she said.

'I don't care if they get A's or D's,' the landlord replied. 'I don't want students. They'll turn it into a dormitory.'

'You want a family?' asked a brown-haired young woman at the fringe of the circle around him. He nodded, and she shouted over her shoulder, 'Kotik, come here.' Everyone laughed. Kotik means pussy cat, usually a private endearment in Russian. Kotik came over, dark, curly-haired, handsome in a zippered jacket, about 26. Questions about the apartment flew back and forth. Then the landlord cross-examined the prospective tenants.

'What's your profession?' he asked.

'I'm a post-graduate,' Kotik answered.

'You have registration to live in Moscow?' the landlord wanted to know, obviously anxious to avoid what is a long and usually fruitless wrangle with authorities to get such registration.

'Yes, temporary registration,' said Kotik.

'And what about your wife?' he asked, looking at the young woman.

'I'm not his wife,' she said candidly.

'Well, what about *her*?' said the landlord to Kotik, less interested in personal relations than official documents.

'She has Moscow registration,' Kotik assured him. 'How much is the apartment?'

'Fifty rubles a month, paid a year in advance,' the silver-haired landlord declared confidently. The figure was triple the price of a similar apartment in a new building which would offer indoor plumbing and other conveniences that this apartment lacked. But the housing squeeze is so tight that the couple happily took it on the landlord's terms, sight unseen. The three of them walked off to fill out the necessary papers.

The Rzhevsky bathhouse housing exchange is one of 30 in Moscow, one of hundreds across this vast country of 250 million people. Many cities, like Moscow, put out a local apartment exchange bulletin. People become expert at reading between the lines, sorting out less attractive, noisy, five-story 'Khrushchev housing' from better-built, more up-to-date apartments. 'Avoid the top floors, because the roofs usually leak,' one Moscow apartment-hunter advised, 'and the bottom floors because they're noisy and you don't have privacy. A flat that comes with a telephone is a real advantage. Otherwise, it's almost impossible to get one. Check for whether the building has garbage chutes.'

Exchanges often take months to work out because of the intricacies of meeting various space restrictions set by the state. They can involve five, six, seven, even a dozen families in one huge 'musical chairs' arrangement.

A wiry, mop-haired underground artist whom I knew had a two-room apartment but wanted more space after the birth of a second child. He and his wife searched for weeks without luck. They persuaded his well-off parents to throw their four-room apartment into the bargain in hopes of getting two three-room apartments. But that, too, fell through. Finally, they found one three-room apartment, but it was being used as a communal home for two families and a single elderly man. So the artist and his wife set out to help all these people arrange their own intricate little exchanges. When the deal was finally consummated, it involved six apartments and eight families. The elderly man, not entirely happy with his new quarters, had to be paid 500 rubles cash to move. Then the entire arrangement had to be registered with city authorities who scrutinized every detail to insure that no one was violating the Byzantine restrictions of maximum and minimum living space for different categories of people (scholars, certain officials, and war invalids get special allowances, and so on). And the police had to check that everyone was legally registered in Moscow to guard against interlopers from the provinces.

'It took an enormous amount of time and effort but it was worth it in the end,' the artist told friends. 'We got a very nice apartment.'

Sometimes the endings are not so happy. Yuri Trifonov, a well-known fiction writer, published a story called *Exchange* that illustrated the ends to which people can be driven by the housing squeeze. In his story, a son and daughter-in-law connive to move the man's mother, who is dying of cancer, out of her lifelong apartment in order to expand their own living quarters before she dies and her apartment automatically reverts to the state. Other writers and many private individuals blame the housing squeeze for the high divorce rate in the Soviet Union, among the world's highest. A Leningrad playwright, in a moving drama, *Don't Leave Your Beloved*, captured the pathetic agonies of a couple who go through divorce and then are forced to continue living together afterward because they cannot find other housing. Nor is this just fictional fantasy. I was told of specific cases where it happened in real life.

Soviet demographers attribute the small size of Russian urban families, usually one child per family, to tight housing. The press frequently blames high labor turnover in Soviet industry to the failure of enterprises or construction projects to provide adequate housing. Often, housing is more important to workers than pay scales. One engineer-physicist whom I knew quit his regular job for a year and a half to help build a new apartment house outside Moscow in order to get a new apartment, a tactic used by many to improve their housing. This man was living with his family of three in a nine-room apartment with 54 other people. Eventually, they got a two-room apartment of their own but they found the new housing area largely bereft of stores and convenient public transportation. The wife told me it took nearly two hours commuting each way to their old jobs. After a couple of years, they gave up and moved back to their old communal apartment. By then, only 27 people were living there.

One reason why demand for housing remains so strong is

that Soviet rents, heavily subsidized by the government, are so low. But the main reason for the housing shortage, in spite of the construction of the past two decades, is the appalling legacy of the Stalin period when housing was given near rock bottom priority. Add to that the rapid growth of cities and the devastation during the war in European Russia, Byelorussia and the Ukraine, and you have the ingredients of the desperate housing situation after the war. Too, much of the effort in recent years has gone into keeping up with population growth and migration into cities. While 44 million new housing units went up from 1956 to 1975, population also grew by 45 million.

Since 1962, one outlet for more affluent families has been the development of cooperative apartment groups at governmental agencies, enterprises, scientific institutes, or cultural organizations. The normal Soviet practice requires a 40 percent down payment and then 15 years to pay the balance. As demand has risen, so have prices. Friends told me that a comfortable three-room apartment that used to cost 6,000–6,500 rubles ($8,000–8,660) in 1966 would now cost from 8,500–10,000 rubles ($11,450–13,300) in a new cooperative. Although Westerners would regard that as cheap, Soviets on monthly salaries of $400 or so, find it steep. Moreover, cooperatives are available only to affluent Russians, and they account for only about three percent of all urban housing.*

In many ways, the housing situation typifies Soviet consumer life in the mid-Seventies. Their standard of living is improving noticeably, but it is still nowhere near the level of the West, especially America against which Russians are keen to measure themselves. The Kremlin has made concessions to consumers, but Russia is far from being a consumer society. The commitment to consumers, for example, was repeatedly downgraded in the first half of this decade rather than let anything interfere with the Kremlin's tremendous drive to achieve nuclear parity with Washington, to build up the Soviet navy or to continue heavy Soviet economic aid to the Arabs. The average Russian, it seemed to me, is still regarded

* Intriguingly, Henry Morton calculated that the private apartment co-ops combined with the fact that the overwhelming majority of country people live in their own homes, meant that more Soviets today live in private than in State housing.

by his leaders more as a producer than as a consumer, and the concessions made to him are made with that in mind – to provide incentives for greater production.

It is true that expectations of Russian consumers are rising. But what is often surprising to Westerners is that, given half a century of sacrifices, they are not rising more rapidly or more insistently. Despite its worries, for instance, the Kremlin never faced the kind of explosive consumer dissatisfaction that shook the Polish government in 1970, toppled Gomulka and forced concessions to Polish consumers. The Soviet leaders have been more successful than those in any other industrialized economy in persuading their people to defer gratifications, to take less now for promises of a better, though ever-receding future. They are willing to stand in line, literally or figuratively, far longer than most people. In the Caucasus once, I fell to talking about Russian cars with a chauffeur in his fifties who was taking us on a long tourist excursion, a man who was then making 95 rubles a month ($127) after 25 years as a driver. I asked him which car was best in his opinion – Volga, Zhiguli, Zil or Chaika, or some other car, meaning possibly a foreign one. He began his answer with prehistory.

'The Pobeda was good in its time,' he ventured. 'The old model Volga was good in its time. This new model Volga is better. I've never driven a Zhiguli or a Zil or a Chaika. Technology develops. Each one is better than the one before. But each was better in its own time. All were good in their time.'

To me it was a terribly Russian reply. It projected the total unawareness of the ordinary Russian, especially of people past 40, that at each stage there had been better cars produced somewhere else, as well as the uncritical acceptance of each model as it came along. The young and the urban middle-class intellectuals might lust for consumer items from abroad, but more ordinary working folk like this driver took life as it came, with modest improvements. Paradoxically, even some of those who gripe about Soviet goods and shortcomings also comment in their next breath that their lives are better than ever.

'It may be hard for you to understand but you must understand that the majority of people here are satisfied with their lives,' I was told by a scientist who was himself highly critical of the Soviet system. 'Many of them have city apartments.

106

They may seem small to you, two or three rooms, small rooms. But these people remember that their parents lived in the countryside in those *izbas*. You know what they are? Those wooden houses with absolutely no conveniences. Now, here they are with their city apartments. And there have been other improvements. These people don't even stop to think that there have been improvements elsewhere in the world, too. They don't compare themselves with you. They compare their situation with their own past, with their parents and they see that there have been great improvements. So they are satisfied.'

R.T.C. LIBRARY
LETTERKENNY

III

CORRUPTION

Living Na Levo

Thieving as a social phenomenon is one of the
incurable concomitants of capitalism. The entire
development of capitalist society is accompanied by
a tremendous growth in crimes of property.
Great Soviet Encyclopedia, 1951

Very soon after my arrival in Russia, I found myself in
Leningrad, staying at the Yevropeiskaya Hotel, and frantically trying to locate a taxi. Intourist had ordered one by
phone but with no visible results after 20 minutes, I was late
for an appointment. I walked out on the street to look for a
taxi stand, just as a Chaika limousine from the Admiralty
rolled up and disgorged a delegation of high-ranking Soviet
naval officers in blue and braid. They ran through the rain
into the hotel with their briefcases, and their chauffeur
parked nearby. With nothing even remotely resembling a taxi
in sight, I walked over to the Chaika to ask in rather unsteady
Russian where to find taxis in that neighborhood.

'Where do you want to go?' the driver asked.

I explained. It was another hotel and I was mentally preparing to walk, wondering how long it would take.

'Come on,' he said, waving me into the Chaika. I ran to get
my guide and off we rode in the Admiralty's limousine, rather
pleased with the tassled curtains and the old-fashioned
upholstery.

'This is getting it *"na levo"*,' my Russian guide instructed,
meaning that the driver was not just doing me a favor but
was using the Navy's car to make some money for himself.
Literally, *na levo* means 'on the left' but comes across as 'on
the side' or 'under the table'.

'Doesn't he have to worry about those admirals coming back out?' I inquired.

'They're probably having lunch at the hotel,' he said. 'He has time. Maybe they gave him time off for lunch and he's using it to suit himself.'

At our destination the chauffeur asked for a ruble – more than the meter fare but, as I soon learned, the minimum going rate for gypsy cab rides. The driver headed off, away from the hotel, so perhaps he had other business in mind.

Like any traveler who has just bumped into a character on the street offering to sell religious ikons or change currency illegally I presumed I had experienced one of those bits of petty commerce that the natives in many countries practice on tourists. There is plenty of that in Russia – the students trying to buy American records or mod clothes from you on the street, or the headwaiter at a big-name Moscow restaurant who delivers the bill and whispers in your ear, 'It's 72 rubles, but if you want to pay in dollars, cash, it's $50.' The businessman who actually took the risk of that bit of illegal legerdemain saved himself $46 (72 rubles = $96, officially). And the waiter, with dollars fetching 4–1 or better on the black market, made about 130 rubles. But I presumed that this, too, was just the tourist trade.

Nor did I give it much thought when a Moscow woman mentioned that a repairman who had come for what was supposed to be a preliminary inspection of her refrigerator, offered to fix it right away, saving her months of waiting her turn, and then pocketed her 30 rubles for himself. But I began to appreciate the dimensions of the phenomenon when a chemist, whose thick glasses gave him a scholarly look but who distilled vodka at his institute, told me that he had a small car for five years and never once took it to a gas station. The gasoline always came to him. Regularly, Friday afternoons. The drivers of cars for state enterprises and government motor pools would visit areas where private car owners garaged their cars. They would siphon off gas from their tanks – gas bought by their agencies with subsidized government coupons.

It intrigued me that this underground trade was so systematic, but my chemist friend said it was 'nothing special'.

'Everyone is so used to the operation that when the drivers come by, you just hold up two, three or four fingers – for twenty, thirty or forty liters [5, 7.5, or 10 gallons]. The price for 76 octane is usually 40 liters for a ruble [12.5 cents a gallon]. The gas doesn't cost the driver a kopeck so he makes a ruble profit, and it costs me only about one-third the regular price. I know one guy who has had a Moskvich for 11 years and must have bought 10,000 liters [2,500 gallons] of gas but never once had to go to the gas station.'*

Nor was gasoline unique. All the car owners in his part of Moscow had another headache. Their brick garages had been built on naked earth without floors or foundations and that area was very muddy. So they had to install cement floors for themselves, a task which I imagined as well-nigh impossible given the difficulty of obtaining building supplies through normal state outlets. But the chemist said he had managed like the others.

'The easiest way is to go out on the Ring Road – you know, the big circular highway around Moscow – pretend you need a ride, and wait for one of those big cement mixers,' he said. 'There are plenty of them out there all the time. Pretty soon, some driver will pick you up. You ride with him a while and then tell him, "Look, I need some ready-mixed cement. How much is it?" He nods, asks you how much you want and you agree on a price. For me, the driver delivered it right to my garage. In a few minutes, the deal was done. He had ten rubles in his pocket. I had my cement and there was still a lot left for his construction project. Nobody noticed. Nobody cared. The concrete really doesn't belong to anyone anyway.'

On another occasion, Ann and I were having dinner with a young biologist and we marveled at the good, freshly butchered beef that his wife had served. It was far better than the meat I had seen in state stores. But he said he had bought it at an ordinary state store, for 3.20 rubles a kilo ($1.92 a pound), about 60 percent over the fixed price. I asked how he had arranged it.

'Very simple,' he confided. 'I have a butcher friend at the state store near one of those skyscrapers that Stalin built. VIPs live there so they get good supplies. In the afternoon, they usually get about 50 pounds of fresh beef. I go there and check with my friend to see if they have any good cuts left. If

* *Izvestia* disclosed on January 1, 1975, that more than one-third of Soviet private motorists were driving on state-owned gasoline in 1972–1973. From other Soviet statistics, Radio Liberty estimated that this amounted to 150 million gallons of stolen gasoline annually, worth 60 million rubles.

he says they do, I go to the cashier and pick up a receipt for 20 kopecks regardless of how much meat I'm going to get. Then I carefully wrap a *treshka* [a three-ruble note, the Russian equivalent of a five-dollar tip] inside the receipt, so that no one can see it. I get in line and hand in my 20-kopeck receipt with the *treshka* tucked inside and my friend gives me a kilo of top-grade meat. I get the meat, he gets the *treshka*, and the state store gets the 20 kopecks.'

'But where does the butcher get the meat?' I inquired. 'Doesn't he have to account for it to the manager.'

'Supposedly. But they just snip a bit here and a bit there from other customers, give them less than they are supposed to get, and little by little, the butchers scrape together what they sell *na levo*.'

'They?' I queried. 'I thought you said you had one butcher friend.'

'Well, that's how it started, but now they all know me. They're all doing it. I think they have about 50 clients they take care of like me.'

'How did you find out about them, about their being willing?'

'A good friend of mine, a woman, took me and introduced me. She told the butcher, "This is my brother. Take care of him."' And then he laughed at the thought of it. 'So they take care of me like her brother.'

The people who are on the take are not always interested primarily in money and they are not always engaged in illegal operations. They may simply be providing friends and good contacts with hard-to-get items. One night, Ann and I were enjoying a dinner of unusual fish delicacies and other special Russian *zakuski* (the hors d'oeuvres that are the heart of a Russian meal, more important than the entrée), with Andrei Voznesensky and his wife, Zoya, when the phone rang. Andrei has an unusual phone; it twitters like a bird. He answered and chatted tautly at a great clip. Putting his hand over the receiver, he asked me at one point whether I knew how he could get two tickets for the final, decisive game of the World Hockey Championships between Sweden and the Russians for the next night. It so happened that I had two extra tickets and had brought them to Andrei that night as a gift but had not had a chance to tell him. He was delighted, told his friend and hung up all smiles.

I presumed that he himself was going with his friend so I

was disappointed to learn that he intended to give both tickets, very much prized in Moscow at that moment, to the lady on the phone.

'Never mind,' he reassured me. 'It is much more important for me that this lady have the tickets as a gift. Do you know who she is? She is more important to us than the government. She is the director of one of the largest food stores in Moscow. She sells us our best food. She provided this whole meal which we are eating tonight, all these *zakuski* which are impossible to get. You cannot pay her extra money for such things. She is terribly rich because so many people have already given her so much money. She does not need money any more. But she is a fanatic hockey fan. She could only get one ticket to that game herself so she gave it to her husband. But she needs two more because she wants to go with her lover. So it is a great thing if I can give her two hockey tickets. It is better than money. I am grateful to you. It is a great thing.' Andrei, when he speaks English, emphasizes and draws out the word 'great', so that it comes out 'greaaat'; 'I am graaateful'; 'it is a greaaat thing'.

Sometimes, it is not the highest officials but the humblest who are in a position to do the greatest favors. In the depth of winter, when fresh fruit disappears from Moscow tables, Irina, a television journalist, offered me a luscious plate of grapes spilling over a few, slightly bruised apples as we talked in her kitchen. When I raised an eyebrow, she told me that her friendly contact was an odd little fellow, Sasha, the fruit porter, at a nearby fruit and vegetable store. Such jobs are so undesirable, she said, that management will put up with anyone willing to do that kind of menial labor. The technique at that store, Irina said, is that fruit shipments are largely written off by the manager as spoiled or bruised and no good for sale, regardless of their actual condition. Then, Sasha privately peddles them to regular clients in nearby apartment buildings, at the standard price plus a ruble.

'He keeps the ruble and half the price of the grapes for himself,' she said, 'and the manager of the store gets the other half of the price.'

In my early months, I began to glimpse the broader dimensions of illicit trade in the Soviet Union through other encounters. In Baku, I met a young cab driver who told me that in his village it took a 500-ruble ($667) payoff to the local police to get occupancy of a plot of ground and permission to build a private home there, and about 400 rubles ($533) to get a job as a cab driver in Baku. A workman told me he had paid 50 rubles ($66) to the surgeon in a state hospital for operating on his legs after he fell down an elevator shaft, and a chauffeur said he paid 150 rubles to have three of his wife's teeth capped. At a music store in Yerevan, Armenia, the clerk whispered to me that for 50 rubles above the set-price, he could sell an imported accordion better than the one that I was examining in the display case. In Tbilisi I was told it took a 13,000-ruble bribe to get into the medical institute. On a train, the head of a state farm explained to me the ruble-and-kopeck calculations for raising, fattening, slaughtering and selling his private herd of sheep (far above the legal quota).

The personal operation that intrigued me most of all, however, involved an engineer who had swiped enough spare parts at a large automobile plant to construct himself a complete camping trailer, an unheard-of and practically non-existent luxury in Russia. A balding linguist, who knew the engineer personally, told me that this engineer had assembled his trailer, piece by piece, right on the premises of the Zil factory in Moscow which manufactures luxury limousines for the Politburo. Presumably, other workers were either in on the operation or thought the trailer was being constructed for some VIP and discretion required them to keep quiet about it. Somehow it went undiscovered but the engineer was not without his problems.

'Several weeks ago I was talking with him and he was worried that he was not going to be able to get the trailer out of the factory,' the linguist told me. This is because each factory has guards and watchmen checking against larceny of state property from the premises. 'The engineer was worried that he would not be able to find the right guard to bribe to let him get out of the plant with his trailer. But a couple of weeks later I saw him again and he told me that finally he had gotten the trailer to his dacha. He had found the right guy.'

Corruption and illegal private enterprise in Russia, 'creeping capitalism' as some Russians playfully call it, grow out of the very nature of the Soviet economy and its inefficiencies — shortages, poor quality goods, terrible delays in service. They

113

constitute more than a black market, as Westerners are accustomed to thinking of it. For parallel to the official economy, there exists an entire, thriving counter-economy which handles an enormous volume of hidden or semi-hidden trade that is indispensable for institutions as well as individuals. Practically any material or service can be arranged *na levo* – from renting a holiday cottage in the country, buying a raincoat or a pair of good shoes in a state store, getting a smart dress made by a good seamstress, transporting a sofa across town, having the plumbing fixed or sound-proofing installed on your apartment door, being treated by a good dentist, sending your children to a private playschool, arranging home consultation with a top-flight surgeon, to erecting buildings and laying pipe in a collective farm.

This counter-economy has become an integral part of the Soviet system, a built-in, permanent feature of Soviet society. It encompasses everything from petty bribing, black marketing, wholesale thieving from the state, and underground private manufacturing all the way up to a full-fledged *Godfather* operation which was exposed and led to the downfall of a high Communist Party figure, a candidate member of the Politburo. It operates on an almost oriental scale and with a brazen normality that would undoubtedly incense the original Bolshevik revolutionaries. Yet, ordinary people take it for granted as an essential lubricant for the rigidities of the planned economy. What the elite get legally through their special stores and system of privileges, ordinary people are forced to seek illegally in the country's counter-economy. 'It's what helps keep our socialism human,' smiled my chemist friend.

Once I asked Andrei Sakharov, the Nobel Prize-winning dissident physicist, about the size of the counter-economy and he estimated it involved 'certainly ten percent or more' of the gross national product, or, something like 50 billion rubles ($66 billion). I have heard both higher and lower guesses. Professional Soviet economists, even those who acknowledge privately that its scope is tremendous, won't venture a figure. 'It is very big, especially in the (retail) trade sector, but statistics on it cannot be serious – no one can know precisely,' observed a former Moscow State University Professor of Economics, a recent émigré.

No one, however, denies the existence of the counter-economy. The press runs many articles about corruption, thieving and illegal profiteering though, characteristically, it never publishes broad statistics that would portray the over-all dimensions of underground operations. But there are always several publicized each year in which economic criminals against the state are sentenced to death for operations that run into hundreds of thousands of rubles and occasionally top a million. (The death penalty for economic crimes was reinstituted in 1961, obviously because the problem was getting more serious.) In 1966, one press report revealed that one-fourth of all crimes in the country involved misappropriation of state property. In September, 1972, *Pravda* disclosed that there had been more than 200 cases of large-scale theft from the state in the Russian Republic (about half the population) in a recent period, and that more than half of the most serious cases had been long-term operations run by crime syndicates.

So serious is the problem that the Ministry of Internal Security has a special branch, known as the Department for the Struggle Against Plundering of Socialist Property (OBKhSS, in Russian initials), operating nationwide. Not only has this agency failed to lick the problem but Russians I knew talked of unpublicized cases where OBKhSS agents had been bought off like narcotics squad men in the West subverted by dope racketeers. In addition, press accounts indicate that in many cases the elaborate array of supposed checks and controls at warehouses, factories, farms and a slew of other organizations failed because the controllers were part of the conspiracy.

Corruption is not new, of course. Even under strictest Stalinism, Russians told me, it went on (to wit, the death penalty for economic crimes was first imposed in 1932 by Stalin during the forced collectivization and forced industrialization, and lifted only after the war in 1947). But Russians insisted that it had risen sharply as Soviet society became more affluent in the late Sixties and Seventies. One Westerner with old friends in Moscow told me how he had come back in 1972 after a long absence and asked one couple what had been the biggest change in the past decade. With one voice, they exclaimed, 'the corruption'.

'It has grown enormously,' complained the husband.

'You don't know what our corruption has become,' shuddered his smartly tailored wife. 'Before, it was mostly people doing favors for each other – ballet tickets for cigarettes, a

115

bit of caviar for the dressmaker. Now, everything costs money, real money,' and she rubbed her thumb over her fore-fingers in that international gesture for cash.

The Soviet counter-economy has its own lore and lingo, its channels and conventions, understood by all and employed by practically everyone on an almost daily basis. Its mutations and permutations are innumerable. But the most common and innocent variety is what the Russians call *blat* – influence, connections, pulling strings. In an economy of chronic shortages and carefully parceled out privileges, *blat* is an essential lubricant of life. The more rank and power one has, the more *blat* one normally has. But actually almost everyone can bestow the benefits of *blat* on someone else – a doorman, a railroad car porter, a cleaning lady in a food store, a sales clerk, an auto mechanic, or a professor – because each has access to things or services that are hard to get and that other people want or need. *Blat* begins to operate when someone asks someone else a favor with the understanding of eventually doing a favor in return. Technically, *blat* does not involve money. '*Blat* isn't really corruption,' an actress con-tended, 'it's just *ty mne i ya tebe* (you for me and me for you).' In other words, 'I'll scratch your back and you scratch mine.'

Almost any transaction can work *po blatu*, by connections, or through acquaintances, *po znakomstvu*, as the Russians say, from the hockey tickets that Andrei Voznesensky passed on to the food store director as a favor, to a general's getting a professor to give his son a good grade on a university entrance examination and the professor's getting the general to arrange a draft deferment for his son (a real case). The actress mentioned above wanted to get her boy enrolled in a children's swimming club class. Her son was not much of an athlete, and had not passed the test. So she was eager to get her hands on a copy of *Playboy* as *blat* for the coach. In an-other case, a Ukrainian lady landed a job in the Bulgarian Consulate in Kiev through *blat*. The only problem, she told friends, was that some acquaintances started avoiding her because they assumed that any Soviet citizen employed by a foreign embassy or business also worked for the secret police, and this made them wary of her – unjustly, she said.

Olga, a young secretary whom I knew, got a free ride on

Aeroflot to many points in the Soviet Union through *blat*. One of her classmates in school had become an Aeroflot dispatcher in charge of passenger lists on certain domestic flights. When Olga got the itch to travel, she would check with her dispatcher friend about upcoming flights and destinations, and on the appointed day, the dispatcher would put Olga at the head of the line of passengers waiting to board the selected flight. Even without a ticket, Olga would get one of the first seats. If the plane were filled or had an overflow, a regular occurrence, the dispatcher would tell the hapless souls at the end of the line that someone had mistakenly overbooked the flight and they would have to wait for the next one. This happens so often that while it causes aggravation, it doesn't raise a scandal. Olga was never checked for a ticket, thanks to her friend. I never learned what she gave the dispatcher in return, though it must have been something good.

But *blat* is only the tip of the iceberg. Bribery is just as widespread. What the Arabs call *baksheesh*, Mexicans call *mordida*, Americans call 'greasing the palm', Russians call *vzyatka*, literally 'the take'. Its most common form is the ubiquitous price-scalping by lowly paid ($80–120 monthly) sales clerks in Soviet stores and the 'tips' paid to service people. As a computer specialist said to me, 'No one can live on his regular pay. You know, in Odessa, they have a saying that if you get really mad at another person, you put a curse on him – "let him live on his salary". It's a terrible fate. No one can imagine it.'

As I mentioned earlier, one of my first impressions in Moscow was that people were better dressed than I had anticipated. But when I began comparing what they wore with what was actually on sale in stores, the two didn't jibe. Obviously, there was more to shopping than met the eye. It was the under-the-counter bribery of sales clerks for those desirable and perennially scarce items that Russians call *defitsitny*, deficit goods. The custom is simply for the sales clerks to stash away a portion of any shipment of attractive *defitsitny* items and sell them off surreptitiously to steady customers who have either left a bribe in advance or can be counted on to pay a premium on delivery. Ten to fifteen rubles on a 60-ruble raincoat is standard.

So common is this practice that the Soviet press is always flailing away at it vainly. I remember an article in *Leninist Banner*, the provincial newspaper for towns around Moscow,

117

in February 1973, exposing a typical case of price-scalping at the unusually well-provisioned Chaika store in Shchelkovo, a suburb for select space technicians, scientists and defense workers. In one check, the paper said, investigators found illicit scalping in 35 *defitsitny* goods – fur hats, fur collars, 'Alaska' brand women's boots, wet-look shoes and boots, sweaters, Icelandic plaid blankets, handkerchiefs from Orenburg, wool rugs, gloves, tea sets, briefcases, mohair scarves, and so on.

Lampooning this practice, *Krokodil*, the Soviet humor magazine, once did a takeoff on a floorwalker promoting some newly arrived items: 'Dear customers, in the leather goods department of our store, a shipment of 500 imported women's purses has been received. Four hundred and fifty of them have been bought by employees of the store. Forty-nine are under the counter and have been ordered in advance for friends. One purse is in the display window. We invite you to visit the leather department to buy this purse.'

The black market begins where price-scalping leaves off because, as *Krokodil* suggested, clerks themselves buy *defitsitny* items and then illegally retail them on their own time or else customers hoard choice items and then resell them. The press is always thundering at these *spekulyanty*, speculators. So normal is this practice that people take it as routine to have to pay four or five rubles for an ordinary two-ruble theater ticket; and a hot show costs far more. One young man told me he had bought a pair of knee boots for his 'sister' through a *spekulyant* who had paid the state price of 60 rubles (plus a 20-ruble tip for the clerk) and then charged him 140 rubles. Students who get discounts on travel fares profiteer on the resale of their subsidized tickets. But the operations are often more substantial, like the woman who had bought up 200 scarves, 800 handkerchiefs, and a load of sweaters through contacts at state stores and was finally arrested for marketing them from suitcases at the open-air market in Dushanbe, or the ring that was selling rabbit fur hats for 30 rubles (state price, 11 rubles) and blue mink coats at 500 rubles (state price, 260).

The black market has no single locus. Often it is simply the apartment of either the buyer or seller. As a person-to-person operation, it is literally nowhere and everywhere. But segments of it do have established sites. One Moscow woman told me that the most active black market in lipsticks and cosmetics in Moscow was in the women's public toilets down a sidestreet from the Bolshoi Theater. This became a favorite spot for hustlers because male police officers could not intrude. The black market in imported shortwave radios, cassette recorders, and hi-fi equipment, I discovered, centers spasmodically on the Sadovo Ring Road in front of the second-hand commission shop specializing in electronic goods.

In a small Moscow park, near the statue of Ivan Fyodorov, the first printer in Russian history, is the black market in books, both legal and *samizdat*, or self-published underground books. While I was in Moscow, a *samizdat* version of Solzhenitsyn's *Cancer Ward* fetched up to 100 rubles there and a three-volume Western edition of the complete poetry of the late Anna Akhmatova brought 200 rubles. Some books printed in Russia itself command huge markups because they come out in limited editions that do not begin to satisfy demand. I remember the sensation in late 1973 over a one-volume collection of three novels by the late Mikhail Bulgakov, including *Master and Margarita*, his satire of Stalinist Russia. Officially, 30,000 copies were printed but 26,000 were reported to have been sent abroad for sale. ('To impress you Westerners with how liberal we are,' groused one writer.) The 4,000 copies left in Russia were gone overnight. But I was told that the publishing house had actually printed, *sub rosa*, 900 extra copies which insiders sold at a staggering profit. The book's official price was 1.53 rubles but the black market prices ran from 60 to 200 rubles.

In Moscow, however, the two most prolific sources of high quality black market goods are the travelers who go West in sports teams, in ballet troupes, and on official delegations, and come home laden with all kinds of goods from the capitalist West on which they can make a hefty profit; and the network of Beryozka, hard currency stores to which some Russians have access through foreign earnings (diplomats, specialists who go abroad to work, writers who get foreign royalties, people receiving gifts from relatives abroad, etc.) or through the privilege of special pay bonuses in 'certificate rubles'.

The Beryozka stores are an open invitation to black market profiteering because of their cut-rate prices on scarce items. Buying in the Beryozka and selling on the black market has a guaranteed multiplier effect like buying stocks on margin –

but without any risk. A Jewish scientist who received money from abroad told me that in late 1974, for example, brightly colored Japanese umbrellas were a very hot item. They cost four certificate rubles at the Beryozka and sold for 40 rubles on the street. When a shipment of Italian-made 'Super Rifle' jeans came in, he said, they cost 7.50 rubles in the Beryozka and sold for 75 or 80 rubles on the black market. The mark-up is not always so steep but it is enough for top-grade certificate rubles (there are several categories) to be selling at as much as 8–1 against ordinary rubles.

One special wrinkle of the Soviet counter-economy is the gray market that exists in all sorts of goods, especially the gray market in used cars – which sell for more than new cars. Throughout the country, the state has set up *Kommissiony*, commission shops, which market second-hand items in everything from electronic goods or clothing to potted plants. These state-run stores set a price for each item and take a seven percent fee for handling the sale. When it comes to cars, the state prices are so low, given the vast pent-up demand, the long wait for new cars, and the fact that many people are never able to get on lists for new cars anyway and must settle for buying a used one. This has produced the gray market, the double-tiered set of prices at car commission shops – the state-fixed prices, and the price actually agreed upon by the individual buyer and seller.

With a friend I went one overcast October afternoon to the Moscow used car market to see how it worked. It was a shabby, muddy field, littered with cement blocks from a nearby construction site, and swarming with cars of various makes and vintages from a little old Moskvich to brand new Zhiguli sedans, or a black Mercedes Benz and a tired 1968 Ford Fairlane (both bought years before from departing diplomats through a Soviet government agency). Little knots of people gathered around various cars to inspect them or dicker with the owners who sell their own cars.

I watched one transaction unfold. It was a commercial flirtation over a battered old yellow Moskvich (a compact-compact in which the Russians somehow manage to squeeze four people), between a pretty dark-haired woman and a young man with a goatee. In any other country or setting, you would have thought they were bargaining over something else. She, the owner, sat in the car, window rolled down, and answered his quiet questioning and gave him a gentle come-on. Her commercial teasing aroused the interest of a few onlookers. He walked around the car and she got out to preen it, rubbing the windshield clean with a soft rag. Coquettishly, she moved away, wiping a fender and then the headlights while he pursued her, still asking questions, looking at the car, lightly kicking the tires. Finally, they both got in the car, talked a couple of minutes and drove off.

'This is the most important moment,' my Russian friend coached me. 'The excuse for driving away is that the buyer wants to test the car. But they both want to get rid of unwanted attention and negotiate privately on the price.' Officially, price speculation is illegal but it is an open secret that practically no one buys or sells a used car for the price set by state appraisers, even though the Moscow used car market is seeded with police informers posing as prospective buyers. Once the real price is struck during that drive around the block, usually several thousand rubles over the state price, buyer and seller return to the field and go through the motions of getting the state's evaluation and filing official documents, all of which takes three days before the car changes hands.

I have no idea what the dark-haired woman got for her Moskvich, but the asking prices on other cars may give a clue. The Ford Fairlane and the Mercedes Benz were each asking 20,000 rubles ($26,600) despite high mileage. More amazing to me, no one batted an eye when one well-dressed couple appeared with a new white Zhiguli-3 sedan, its interior still swathed in protective plastic sheeting and only 493 kilometers (306 miles) on its speedometer and asked 12,000 rubles (a markup of 4,500 rubles from the new car price). I knew a scholar who had gotten 12,000 rubles for an old Volga sedan which had cost him only 5,500 rubles new and which he had driven nearly 50,000 miles. Two Moslem brothers from Azerbaijan, planning to use it as a profitable gypsy cab, were delighted to get it at any price.

'They practically flew in the windows in excitement,' my friend recalled. 'They never looked under the car or checked anything. In three minutes, they bought an old car for the price of two new Cadillacs, without driving or testing it. They could hardly speak Russian or understand it. After they bought the car, one of them asked me, "please drive us to our hotel. I have a driver's license, but I am afraid to drive the car in Moscow." ' My friend obliged them.

Like the used car market, moonlighting is another sprawling component of the counter-economy which shades from the gray into the black market. Technically, it is legal for Russians to engage in some limited private translating, typing, tutoring or renting an apartment room to vacationers and lodgers, provided income taxes are paid and the prices and scale of operations are modest. But the practice has long since exceeded those bounds and the profits are surprising. An engineer in Moscow told me of a lady across the hall, a language teacher, whose pay at an institute was 110 rubles a month but who could earn 500–600 rubles a month coaching high school students cramming for college entrance examinations. Notices posted on bulletin boards all over Moscow indicate how large is the private sector in tutoring. Word even got around of one ambitious tutor with a flair for self-promotion and a good position in an educational establishment who told a gathering of 500 prospective examination candidates about his services and signed up more than 4,000 rubles' worth of business on the spot. The attraction of such tutors, parents say, is that they are geared toward results and avoid the stiff, uninteresting, repetitious lessons given at Soviet schools. 'We teach them what is not taught at school – to think,' bragged one tutor.

The coming of the private car like the competition for university places among a middle class with some money to spare, has given real impetus to another realm of illicit service operations. Stories of taxi drivers or chauffeurs of state cars swiping gasoline or spare parts to sell at a killing are legion. Anyone with mechanical skill to boot is in constant demand. I was told of an auto mechanic who used to supplement his regular monthly pay of 200 rubles with at least 700–800 rubles a month in private auto repair work. 'He made so much money that he could afford private tutoring for university entrance examinations for both his sons,' an engineer told me. 'One boy had to be tutored in three subjects – math, physics, and English. It is very expensive to pay for private lessons like that, for several months. It cost the mechanic over 1,000 rubles for that one boy. But he was making enough himself *na levo* to afford it.'

The list of services provided by the *shabashniki*, as Russians call moonlighters, is endless. Women eager for the kind of flair or fashion in their clothes that Soviet industry has not learned to provide will get hold of material and go to a private dressmaker or bribe a seamstress in a state-run shop to copy a pattern or a picture from a Western magazine. Some intellectual and elite families send their children to discreetly operated private nurseries (Solzhenitsyn and the literary critic Andrei Sinyavsky used one for their children). I knew of a dentist for a famous international artistic troupe who had a thriving private practice in his apartment which he had furnished with equipment painstakingly removed from his regular clinic and reassembled at home. Unlike dentists in state polytechnics who drill without novocaine and pull teeth at the sight of a serious cavity, this man took gentle care of patients. 'He can really cap a tooth nicely, or make false teeth or a bridge,' I was told by an American woman who went to him on the sly.

Prices in the counter-economy can be fairly steep. Murray Fromson, a C.B.S. correspondent, once hired a free-lance Soviet cameraman to do some work on the side and was stunned at the fee demanded by this private operator – three rubles ($4) for each frame that he shot.

'It's the spirit of free enterprise,' the Soviet photographer said in self-defense.

'Yeah, without the spirit of competition,' Fromson countered. 'In a free market, you'd price yourself right out of business.'

It was amazing to me, however, how many people got into the act, how much money was circulating in the counter-economy, and how many people – desperate for timely service or decent workmanship – would happily turn to *levaki*, the people who operate *na levo*. So shoddy is Soviet housing construction, for example, that repairs are commonly required for brand new apartments. On occasion, I have seen press articles suggesting that workmen deliberately did a poor job hanging doors and installing windows, left leaky plumbing, failed to connect light switches, doorbells and the like, just in order to return and offer their private services at a price. In what was probably a modest estimate, *Literary Gazette*, the Writers' Union weekly, reported that in Moscow alone new apartment owners had paid out at least ten million rubles one year to illicit operators for basic repairs.

That figure only begins to hint at the dimensions of the illegal operations and the extent to which people depend on them. For stories come to light periodically in the press indicating that not only individuals turn to the counter-economy for service but so do collective farms or industrial plants. *Literary Gazette* carried a report in mid-1974 about two collective farm chairmen who had been convicted of buying stolen property from illegal operators, not for their private profit but merely to try to fulfill the economic targets of their farms. One badly needed apple crates and the other was desperate for pipes for a cow-shed, and neither could get what he needed on time from the normal state sector.

Farms and enterprises also turn to private construction gangs to meet deadlines they cannot otherwise fulfill. This practice, I was told, is especially widespread in Siberia and the North where even with hardship pay bonuses companies find it hard to hold regular workers. Although officials are supposed to observe rules for hiring stray workers, press reports and private comments of Russians make it clear that work crews which are, in effect, little 'private companies' often sign contracts with state farms, enterprises or construction agencies to put up certain buildings, lay piping or asphalt roads by a given deadline for a fixed price. These gangs have a reputation for working longer hours and much more rapidly than the regular construction crews which are notorious for slack work, cost-overruns and time-lags.

Usually, it is the small-time operations of the counter-economy that Russians talk about from their own experience, but occasionally the press exposes large-scale Soviet corruption. In 1973, newspapers reported one ring that had mis-appropriated 260,000 rubles' worth of textiles and fabrics in Lithuania, another which had illegally marketed 650,000 rubles' worth of fruit juice in Azerbaijan, and a third which had stolen 700,000 rubles' worth of gems from a Moscow diamond-cutting enterprise. In early 1975, another group went on trial in Moscow and its leader was sentenced to death for a *sub rosa* trade operation that netted about two million rubles. The key figure, Mikhail Laviyev, manager of the Tadzhikistan Shop on Gorky Street, was accused of brib-ing state inspectors to understate the value of silks, wines, and specialty foods from the Tadzhik Republic which his store marketed at steep prices, and he kept the difference.

But the prize example of the black market operations, the one that combines all the ingredients of the counter-economy, from thieving, phony bookkeeping, to manufacturing, sales and distribution, is the complete underground private in-dustry. Here and there, they come to light. In 1972, an entire plant in Bashkiria was uncovered making plastic goods, table-cloths, women's summer shoes, and other items. Two years later, the press wrote up a gang in Odessa operating an illegal fur factory that siphoned off raw furs from the state and produced chic garments sold for very handsome profits.

Nothing in recent years, however, has matched the sensational scandal over underground industry in Soviet Georgia.

Life in Tbilisi, the Georgian capital, has a Latin flavor all its own. In its people, its mood and mores, it is much closer to the Mediterranean world than to Moscow. The streets of Tbilisi are more often named for poets than for commissars. In the soft evenings, dark-eyed Georgians stroll languidly along Rustaveli Avenue, and in the morning heat, workmen water down the dusty central squares. Narrow, hilly, cobble-stone roads wind like dry riverbeds under the iron-grilled balconies of the old quarters, evoking the back streets of Beirut or Algiers. Modish young men motion foreigners into pastry shops or hair-dressing salons to offer 50 rubles for a pair of wingtipped English walking shoes or 30 rubles for a bright shirt. Evening crowds stop to stare at police chasing youths through moving traffic and, unlike Russians, no one makes an effort to cooperate with Authority. One catches the unmistakable scent of Sicilian unruliness.

In 1893, an anonymous French traveler recorded that the city had 126 tailors, 104 bootmakers, 40 barbers, 4 master goldsmiths, 5 clockmakers, 16 painters, and 8 balalaika players, testifying to the Georgian taste for finery and good living. Even in the Soviet era, Tbilisi has flaunted a conspicuous consumption that somehow seemed indecent for this socialist commonwealth. The tailors are still producing expensive clothes and Georgians will consume half a case of wine singing their mountain songs in downtown restaurants. Impulsively, they send gift bottles to strangers who catch their eye. At a hotel buffet, Bob Kaiser of the *Washington Post* and I were once sent brandy at breakfast as a gesture of hospitality.

Among other Soviets, Georgians have a reputation for paying the biggest bribes to storeclerks for *defitsitny* goods, bidding the highest prices for used cars, renting private rooms at the old Sandunovsky baths in Moscow and banquetting

125

like grandees on special succulent lamb shashlik flown in — with servants — on an illicitly chartered plane from Tbilisi. The hook-nosed Georgian farmer, in flat cap and little comb mustache, is a fixture in the farmers' market of Moscow and other northern cities — marketing tropical fruits or jauntily demanding a ruble apiece for flowers flown up to Moscow in midwinter in his suitcases.

The Russians tell the joke about a little Georgian who was on an Aeroflot airliner bound for Moscow when a hijacker broke into the cockpit, brandished a pistol and demanded that the plane go to London. The pilot changed course and soon a second hijacker, with two guns, burst in and ordered the pilot to head for Paris. Another change of course. Finally, the wiry little olive-skinned Georgian entered with a bomb and declared, 'Take this plane to Moscow or I'll blow it up.' The pilot agreed, and changed course a third time. When they landed in Moscow, the first two hijackers were carted off to jail and the little Georgian was congratulated by a high-level delegation.

'Tell us, Comrade,' said one slightly incredulous dignitary, 'why did you divert the plane from Paris back to Moscow?'

'What was I going to do with 5,000 carnations in Paris?' the Georgian replied.

In the two decades since the death of Stalin, who was born in Georgia, the Kremlin tolerated the idiosyncrasies of the quick-tempered, warm-hearted, wine-drinking Georgians. When I first went there in the fall of 1971, having heard rumors of underground millionaires from Soviet friends, these were stoutly denied by Georgian officials. One Soviet journalist told me he had visited a Georgian who lived in a palatial residence with a marble staircase and backyard swimming pool. In Tbilisi, a slender scholar talked of illegal factories producing carpets, textile goods, eye shades, and beachwear. But Mrs Viktoriya Siradze, then an officious, auburn-haired Deputy Premier of the Georgian Republic, dismissed all this as scurrilous innuendo. 'We don't have millionaires,' she insisted firmly to me in an interview. 'It is our collective farmers who are millionaires.'

But on my next visit, ten months later, the mood had changed — and so had the Party line. People were talking about the *chistka*, literally, the cleaning — the purge that was shaking the Georgian way of life to its foundations and was exposing underground wealth and at least one well-known millionaire. (Actually, the investigations had been underway when I had seen Mrs Siradze, led by her closest political patron.) The Kremlin had finally tired of the free-wheeling Georgian style of commerce, evidently because it had actually disrupted the normal fulfillment of Georgian economic goals set by Moscow. As the new Party chief in Georgia, the Politburo picked a former cop (Interior Minister), Eduard Shevardnadze, a man of Cromwellian rectitude.

On my way in from the airport in 1972, a cabbie told me: 'The new boss is tough. He likes order. He won't let the *spekulyanty* get away with so much. He will give everyone a warning and then . . . ' He trailed off with a meaningful shake of the head. Later, I heard that Shevardnadze had begun by summoning all the Cabinet ministers together, asking them to raise their left arms, and then – with their expensive imported gold wristwatches showing, ordered them to toss these symbols of bourgeois living into the center of the table and signal the start of a new era.

But the kingpin, the man who turned out to be the Soviet version of the *Godfather*, was an unlikely former chauffeur and one-time economics student who had not finished university, named Otari Lazishvili. Since the late Sixties, Lazishvili had built up a network of underground private enterprises in cahoots with other businessmen and had amassed a fortune. Several Russians told me he had such high connections with the former Party boss of the Republic, Vasily Mzhavanadze, that he and his business cohorts could arrange hiring and firing of Republican ministers and high Party officials in the city of Tbilisi and even Party Secretaries for the entire republic of Georgia, the highest officials in the region. Although he masked himself modestly as the head of a small experimental synthetics laboratory, the Soviet newspaper *Trud* said, Lazishvili was 'an underground millionaire who laid tables for a thousand rubles at restaurants in Moscow, Kiev and Alma Ata on the occasion of victories of his favorite soccer team', and who had two dachas with swimming pools, one near Tbilisi and another on the Black Sea Coast in Abkhazia.

Trud, the trade union newspaper, disclosed that Lazishvili and his cohorts – 82 of them were indicted in one case – had swindled the state out of 1.7 million rubles' worth of goods. Using the lab as a blind, the ring catered to Soviets willing to pay high prices for scarce consumer items. It produced turtleneck sweaters, scarves, plastic raincoats, beach slippers, and colored nylon net bags that are a 'must' with most Soviet shoppers. 'In reality, it was a private concern called Lazishvili and Company,' said *Trud*. 'At the time of the investigation, police found more than 100,000 rubles' worth of artificial leather jackets, sweaters, knitwear and other goods [on the premises] – none registered in [government] documents.' Later stories revealed that at least three other factories were operating, one in a mountain hideaway, and two others within regular industrial enterprises in Tbilisi.

The basic technique, as the Soviet press explained it, was for the private entrepreneurs to take advantage of slipshod planning to bilk the state out of the raw materials needed for their production. For example, one factory was supposed to be producing nylon bags, each requiring 14 ounces of synthetic material, when in fact only about one ounce was actually needed per bag. The rest went for contraband goods. The established state production norms could be met easily in one shift but the shop worked a second shift secretly. It even acquired five extra machines to increase output.

Lazishvili's undoing was evidently a slowly developing blood feud with Shevardnadze that began years before Shevardnadze became the Party boss in 1972. In the old days, Lazishvili was a frequent guest of Mzhavanadze, the former Party boss installed under Nikita Khrushchev. Mzhavanadze, an alternate member of the Politburo in Moscow, was known as a hard-drinking, high-living, vain, weak-willed leader much influenced by his wife who had a reputation for welcoming expensive furs, jewels, and many other extravagant gifts from businessmen, ministers, and officials. In Moscow I was told by Party members and people with good Party connections, that Mzhavanadze and his wife had become millionaires several times over during his 19-year tenure as Party boss of Georgia.

In his hey-day, Lazishvili allegedly numbered the Party chiefs of the city of Tbilisi as his protégés. At one point he is said to have tried to arrange the removal of his nemesis, Shevardnadze, from a key Party job from which he was beginning to harass Lazishvili's underground industrial empire. Ultimately, however, Shevardnadze, a tall, slender, handsome *apparatchik* with a modest life-style, mousetrapped one of Lazishvili's accomplices with a forged lottery

128

ticket and arrested the man when he went to pick up the prize – a new Volga car. Despite appeals to high patrons in Moscow, Lazishvili was ultimately arrested and convicted – though his sentencing, in February 1973, contained an open hint that he still wielded influence with the Georgian courts. Whereas much smaller fry elsewhere had been sentenced to death for more modest economic manipulations, Lazishvili got only 15 years.

With the *Godfather* out of the way, the purge swept all kinds of Party and government officials out of office and a few middle-level officials into jail. The Soviet press published revised economic statistics revealing how disastrously Georgia had performed in years past and how riddled the economy was by corruption. According to Roy Medvedev, the dissident Marxist historian who has made a career of studying Party affairs, the new Georgian prosecutor wanted to go after Mzhavanadze, the former Party boss dropped from the Politburo in September, 1972. Although Medvedev said there was 'more than enough evidence' to warrant searches of the Mzhavanadze apartment on Tbilisi's Barnov Street and his luxurious country houses at the resorts of Pitsunda, Ikhnete and Likani, the Kremlin leadership blocked the investigation. The case was hushed up. Drawing the obvious contrast with Watergate, Medvedev noted that in the Soviet Union, interference by Party leaders in criminal prosecutions 'is not considered a crime in our country'. Party officials, he said, are investigated only with the approval of their superiors.

This actually happens considerably more than outsiders realize. Investigations and trials of Party officials are held in secret so as not to sully the Party's public image. A Soviet journalist informed me, for example, of a secret trial against four important Party officials in the Voroshilovgrad province on corruption charges in late 1973, leading ultimately to the forced retirement of the Party boss of that province, Vladimir Shevchenko. But in such cases, Soviet insiders say, the principal motive is not usually an urge to wipe out corruption within the Party, but internal political feuding among rival Party factions. In the Voroshilovgrad case, the journalist said, Vladimir Shcherbitsky, the Ukrainian Party chief, had long been looking for a way to remove Shevchenko, an important member of a rival faction, and corruption provided a useful pretext. Many, many other cases of corruption within the Party go unpunished, according to Party members. 'They have become so bold and open about it!' a Party member from a Northern city, a woman engineer, complained to a friend of mine. 'In our city, the Party chiefs just call the fur factory and order fur coats sent over to them for nothing.' Another well-placed Muscovite said that the official in charge of the special stores for the Moscow Party apparatus had 'become a millionaire' through illicit trade.

The most celebrated case during my tour in Moscow involved Yekaterina Furtseva, the Minister of Culture, once a favorite of Khrushchev. During his leaderhsip, she had become the only woman in Soviet history ever to become a member of the Politburo, then known as the Presidium. For years after Khrushchev's removal, reports circulated about efforts to get rid of her because she had been a Khrushchev holdover. But she hung on to her Ministry, energetic, capable, hard-drinking, rough-talking, alternately hard and moderate in cultural affairs. Then in the spring of 1974, word seeped out that she was slipping and would lose her seat in the Supreme Soviet, long an automatic post for her, and possibly her Ministry. The pretext was a scandal over an expensive dacha (costing about 120,000 rubles – $160,000) which she had built in the elite dacha country for her grown daughter, Svetlana. Already, Miss Furtseva and her husband, Deputy Foreign Minister Nikolai Firyubin, had two dachas – one in the Moscow suburbs and another on the Black Sea.

What raised the scandal, first among workmen for the Moscow construction trust that built the new dacha and later in Party circles, was not the fact that this was her third dacha, but that she had paid wholesale cut-rate prices for the construction materials, and that she was building it openly in her daughter's name, passing on the perquisites of power to the next generation too brazenly to suit some Party officials. One version I heard was that the director of the construction trust had gone along with the cut-rate costs because he felt beholden to Miss Furtseva ever since he had won an important state prize while she was chief of the Moscow Party organization in the mid-Fifties. As the gossip spread, the Party leadership reportedly decided that she should pay the full price of the dacha by reimbursing the state about 60,000 rubles (about $80,000), a sum that she managed to produce within a couple of days, itself a startling indication of the substantial wealth accumulated by some high officials.

Despite the reimbursement, private reports persisted that Miss Furtseva would be forced out of her Cabinet post. When news of the scandal hit the foreign press, she was said to have gone twice to Brezhnev to plead for her job, at least until after the formal installation of the new Cabinet in June, 1974. As predicted, Miss Furtseva did lose her seat in the Supreme Soviet. But her appeals to Brezhnev and the implications of the scandalous publicity abroad evidently persuaded the Kremlin to retain her as Minister of Culture rather than openly admit the scandal by dropping her. She died in office on October 25, 1974.

Setting aside such sensational cases of abusing official positions, only a small part of the operations of the Soviet counter-economy would be considered criminal in the West. To be sure, the Soviet Union has embezzlers, car theft rings, prostitutes, narcotics-traffickers, armed bank robbers, and an occasional band of extortionists posing as police units complete with uniforms, handcuffs and documents, shaking down the innocent – offenders who would be criminals anywhere. But much of the private hustling on the black market would not be illegal if Soviet Communist doctrine permitted the kind of small private trade sector that exists legally under Hungarian, Polish or East German brands of Communism. For most operations *na levo*, as one venturesome newspaper commentary in *Komsomolskaya Pravda* in October, 1974, dared to imply, the system is at fault for not meeting the basic needs of consumers.

Occasionally, but only very occasionally, evidence surfaces that someone in the Party hierarchy is toying with legalizing some aspect of the current *na levo* private enterprise. In March, 1971, in his major report to the 24th Party Congress, Brezhnev said it was necessary to consider creating conditions so that certain people 'either at home in an individual capacity or forming themselves into cooperatives could take up some work in the field of service.' Sixteen months later, an article in the *Literary Gazette* suggested that the Russians could learn from East Germany, Hungary, and Poland to permit individuals 'certain freedom of action in the sphere of services'. The author had in mind small shops, cafés, dressmaking emporiums, little restaurants and repair shops. But

nothing came of the idea. That activity remains on the wrong side of the law.

Strangely, for all its protestations about corruption, the regime seems to have ambivalent feelings toward the counter-economy. Any system so intent on centralized control is bound to regard as anathema activities carried on independently of its own planners and regulations. The authorities are genuinely dismayed by the huge losses of state property and the amount of time people obviously take away from their jobs to engage in illegal moonlighting during working hours. The Party worries about the moral decay and cynicism bred by pervasive corruption.

But the regime faces a dilemma. As one Russian, echoed by many others, observed to me, 'Everyone in the Soviet retail trade is a thief and you can't put them all in jail.' The pragmatic policy of the authorities is to catch, expose and punish the biggest illegal operators (so long as they do not embarrass the Party directly), but to do no more than place obstacles in the way of the millions of small-time operators. In a way, one economist suggested, the authorities reluctantly tolerate the personal commerce of 'the little people' as a necessary outlet for their consumer frustrations and a diversion from any more serious challenge to the system. The Party knows, he reasoned, that people who are chasing after illegal goods in the counter-economy, are not worried about reforms. Moreover so long as the public takes the counter-economy as a necessary and desirable fact of life, there is scant hope of collaboration for strict enforcement.

Inevitably, the Russians have a laughter-through-tears joke that conveys their fatalistic attitude toward corruption and makes a virtue out of this vice.

'I think,' says Ivan to Volodya, 'that we have the richest country in the world.'

'Why?' asks Ivan.

'Because for nearly 60 years everyone has been stealing from the state and still there is something left to steal.'

IV

PRIVATE LIFE
Russians as People*

Comrades, we are building not a land of idlers
where rivers flow with milk and honey but the most
organized and most industrious society in human
history. And the people living in that society will be
the most industrious, conscientious, organized and
politically conscious in history.

Leonid Brezhnev, 1972

When the door opened, I thought for a moment that Boris
Pasternak had come back to life. Those same craggy features
were before me. Sensitive, soft, thoughtful eyes looked out
over prominent cheekbones. The gray hair looked windblown. The forehead was a bit higher, the chin a bit longer,
but it was the same strong, lean head and slender, vulnerable
neck. The man at the door was not quite as tall as I had
imagined Boris Pasternak from photographs. But the resemblance was so striking that I stood motionless for an instant
before introducing myself and my wife to the poet's elder son,
Zhenya, who welcomed us with gentle warmth. Over the
months and years we came to know Zhenya and his wife,
Alyonya, their boys, Boris and Petya, and their little
daughter, Lisa, well.

On Pasternak's advice – Zhenya always referred to his
father as 'Pasternak' – Zhenya had forsaken the arts as politically too precarious. An engineer by training, he had become
a specialist in automated control systems but his real vocation
and passion, in the face of the regime's ambivalence toward
Pasternak, was laboring to preserve Pasternak's prestige and

* Wright Miller, an English writer, published an excellent book by the
title *Russians as People* (Dutton, New York, 1960) from which I gained
many an insight.

133

to keep the memory of him fresh by finding letters and other unpublished writings to put into print. Together Zhenya and Alyonya appealed for a museum to Pasternak to be opened at the rambling country dacha in Peredelkino where Pasternak had lived, but the appeals went unheeded and the dacha reverted to the Writers' Union though the family retained a small cabin on the grounds.

Not only was *Doctor Zhivago* still banned 15 years after the furor over Pasternak's winning the Nobel Prize, but the family had never seen the Western film version. Through an embassy friend, we arranged to have it shown one evening to the Pasternak family in the creaky, high-ceilinged living room of their Moscow apartment. Paintings done by Pasternak's father and others came down from the wall to accommodate a makeshift screen. The movie disappointed some family friends, who thought the characterizations shallow and were offended by what seemed a propagandistic ending in which a young couple strolled off beside a huge dam, so like an official Soviet film and so unlike Pasternak. But Zhenya, more tolerant, thought the film had captured Zhivago's free romantic spirit and had been true to Pasternak in the essentials.

What stuck in my mind was the moment when everyone, foreigners and Russians alike, broke out laughing at the movie's portrayal of the meek, milquetoast welcome given by young Zhivago and his step-parents to his step-sister returning to Moscow by train from Paris. It was abrupt and cool, a quick, flat, unemotional Western peck on the cheek and a handshake, obviously directed and acted by people unaware of the effusive, emotional outpouring that occurs when Russians greet or part at a railroad station. They immerse each other in endless hugs, embraces, warm kisses on both cheeks, three times, not just kissing in the air for show, but strong, firm kisses, often on the lips, and not only between men and women, or between women, but man-to-man as well. Westerners used to discount this as an idiosyncrasy of Nikita Khrushchev with his famous bearhugs of Fidel Castro in fatigues and beard. But it is the Russian way. Russians relish the joy of reunion with gusto and they linger over the anguish of parting as if there were no onlookers and it were a private occasion. So tame and out of character was the movie version that night that the Russians were still chortling about it after the movie ended. Indeed, all through the movie, except for Zhivago and Lara, the characters did not sugar their conversation with those affectionate little mutterings and diminutives which families, friends or even close neighbors lavish upon each other unthinkingly. These petty verbal intimacies are one of the pleasant features of close relationships among Russians that foreigners often fail to perceive amidst the general gruffness.

More typical of Russians in public is the totally impassive reaction that I noticed one day at a jazz lecture. The speaker, Leonid Pereverzev, was a real authority on American jazz. He put life and enthusiasm into his talk and used excellent jazz recordings to illustrate it, a rare treat for a Soviet audience which has little chance to hear such classics. And yet not once did a single head bob in rhythm. Not one pair of fingers was snapping or clicking to the music. No feet were tapping. No spontaneous applause broke out. People were studious, immobile, unexpressive. It was an audience of 1,000 young people for whom tickets had been very hard to get. They listened intently to both music and commentary. Yet they betrayed no emotion or rhythm indicating that the music had touched them in any way. Their universal coolness so baffled me that I later asked a young teacher what was wrong, why had the audience not reacted to the music, did they dislike it.

'Oh, no,' she said, 'we feel it inside. But it is just not accepted here to show emotions in public at a lecture or concert like that. We check ourselves.'

This perplexing dichotomy between the warm outpouring at the railroad stations and the self-restraint at the jazz lecture is one of the most puzzling phenomena of Russian life. As a people, the Russians have won a wide reputation for their virtues of endurance, resilience, hardiness, patience and stoicism that enabled them to persevere and eventually to wear down the armies of Napoleon and Hitler in bitter Russian winters. Often this external toughness comes across in public as coarse indifference, passive fatalism, and pushy discourtesy. Western visitors have commented on the glum, shuttered faces of Russian street crowds, and the brusque, negative surliness of service people. In our early months, I remember nodding at Russians, or saying hello if their eyes met mine at close range in public but all I ever got in return was an impassive stare. A Russian told me that Soviet agencies like Intourist, whose employees work with foreigners, get special instructions to smile more than usual because Westerners expect it.

It is true that Russians, especially Muscovites, often come across as gruff, cold, mulish, and impersonal in public. But in private, within a trusted circle, usually the family and close friends but often embracing new acquaintances very quickly if some personal chord of empathy is touched, they are among the warmest, most cheerful, generous, emotional and overwhelmingly hospitable people on earth. I am not talking about the false bonhomie that Soviet officialdom manufactures at the drop of a visiting delegation, usually by forcing more vodka on visitors than they want to drink, but genuine, selfless, heartwarming friendship. 'Russians,' Joseph Brodsky, a freckled, Irish-looking poet told me as we strolled one cold afternoon in Moscow, 'are like the Irish – in their poverty, their spiritual intensity, their strong personal relationships, their sentimentality.'

This dichotomy of coldness and warmth springs in part from some deep duality of the Russian soul and temperament forged by climate and history. It makes the Russians, as a people, both stoics and romantics, both long-suffering martyrs and self-indulgent hedonists, both obedient and unruly, both stuffy and unassuming, publicly pompous and privately unpretentious, both uncaring and kind, cruel and compassionate.

It was Dostoyevsky who had written that Russians were half-saint, half-savage, an Egyptian journalist reminded me. 'Russians can be very sentimental but also cold and cruel,' his plump Russian wife added. 'A Russian can weep at a piece of poetry at one minute and kill an enemy on that same spot a few minutes later.' Wright Miller, an English writer with great insight into Russian character, recalled in 1973 in his book, *Who Are the Russians?*, that Ivan the Terrible murdered his own son in a rage and then knelt in paroxysms of remorse, or plundered monasteries and then gave them funds. I have experienced this quicksilver change in mood and morality on a much more mundane scale. At the Moscow Art Theater one evening, it surprised me to see a Russian audience moved to tears by a shallow, maudlin drama that ended on a predictable note of human kindness. The women around me were wiping their eyes, unable to join the applause, and yet in a minute or two these same women were pushing and knocking each other about during the furious scramble in the cloakroom as if the play's message had left no imprint whatsoever. 'Both the crying and the shoving are gut feelings – they come from the stomach, not the mind,' Andrei Voznesensky remarked to me later. 'And that is very typical of Russians.'

There is, however, another root for the dichotomy in Russian behavior. In their authoritarian environment, from childhood onward Russians acquire an acute sense of place and propriety, of what is accepted and what is not, of what they can get away with and what they had better not attempt. And they conform to their surroundings, playing the roles that are expected of them. With a kind of deliberate schizophrenia, they divide their existence into their public lives and their private lives, and distinguish between 'official' relationships and personal relationships. This happens anywhere to some degree, of course, but Russians make this division more sharply than others because of political pressures for conformity. So they adopt two very different codes of behavior for their two lives – in one, they are taciturn, hypocritical, careful, cagey, passive; in the other, they are voluble, honest, direct, open, passionate. In one, thoughts and feelings are held in check. ('Our public life is a living lie,' caustically commented an experimental physicist.) In the other, emotions flow warmly, without moderation.

Even the scale on which public and private lives are acted out is vastly different. The exterior landscape of Moscow, for example, is one of grandiose façades. Stalin planted seven mock-gothic skyscrapers that tower over the city like ungainly drip-castles of sandstone, their spires crowned with Red stars. The newer subdivisions are a forest of massive prefab apartment blocks, numbing in their monotony (and duplicated in cities all across the country), pockmarked and graying with the instant aging that afflicts all Soviet architecture. They are left naked without grass or shrubbery or shutters or flower boxes, like fleets of dowdy ocean liners gone aground on some barren shore and dwarfing their passengers with their inhuman scale. One of the favorite landmarks of the city fathers is the Hotel Rossiya, a monument to their infatuation with gigantic structures. It is supposedly the largest hotel in Europe with 3,076 rooms, 5,738 beds, nine restaurants, 20 cafeterias, six banquet halls, ten miles of corridors and no air conditioning. The dimensions of streets, too, are Olympian. The main boulevards that cut through the city are ten, twelve, fourteen lanes wide, so immense that New York's Fifth Avenue by comparison, seems like a neighborhood side street.

Another grandiose fixture of public life is the heroic statuary. In Moscow the central shrine is Lenin's tomb. In other cities, the central square is presided over by a powerful statue of Lenin, usually in a wind-furled overcoat, confidently striding toward a brighter future or, hand raised and eyes agleam, exhorting the proletariat to unite. The energetic civic consciousness of this genre is strikingly conveyed in the towering World War II monument in Volgograd, a 160-foot-tall Mother Russia on a hillcrest, sword raised against the foe, her dead prayerfully buried around her feet. The ultimate in statue clichés of socialist realism are the huge, stylized stainless steel Figures of Communist Construction in Moscow—the muscular young worker, one fist clenched around a hammer, and the other brawny arm locked in grip with a stalwart farm maid holding aloft her sickle. Nearby, on the other side of the Exhibition of the Achievements of the People's Economy, a dramatic upswept rocket riding a tail of exhaust that must be 15 stories high, shoots skyward in monumental commemoration of Soviet space exploits.

The scale of these monuments is an important clue to their public appeal and an insight into the Soviet spirit. Russians like awesome structures, impressively broad avenues, sweeping vistas, and images of titanic exploits that convey power. They have a Texan's love for exaggerated bigness that outdoes the American love of bigness, much as the Soviet national economic growth ethic has surpassed the now-shaken American faith in the automatic blessings of economic growth. With the spirit of Paul Bunyan, Russians take pride in the sheer magnitude of the hydroelectric dams they have thrown across the broad rivers of Siberia. They revel in the size of their heavy trucks, their steel plants, and their huge intercontinental rockets. Size is power.

Yet in their private lives, they seek escape from the titanic. They reduce things to a human scale. The interior landscape of Moscow, or any other city, is vastly different from the grandiose exteriors. Passing through the quiet, footworn, unkempt courtyards into the darkened entryways and up the creaky, wooden, old-fashioned, double-doored elevators, I found myself adjusting to a life-style that is less affected, less belittling, more human. The better connected and more affluent families have their sets of lacquered furniture. But many more of the dozens of apartments we visited were furnished by a motley assortment of tables and chairs that looked as if taken from different attics. The rooms lacked brightness or color but that mattered little to the Russians. They took it for granted that beds would serve as couches in daytime. Sometimes a curtain in a large room separated the sleeping quarters of a child from that of the parents, especially in a communal apartment where there were five doorbells on the one outer door, and each large room housed an entire family. Rugs were a sometimes thing. Dining rooms did not exist, but a writing table in the largest bedroom would double for meals. Many apartments seemed to be in a state of permanent but comfortable disorder. Nor were they likely to be hastily and specially neatened up for visitors any more than their occupants were likely to change out of old clothes for new arrivals. That happens on holidays or when Russians are officially prepped to be ready for foreigners. The life-style in Russian homes is natural and unvarnished. I found this one of the most attractive qualities of Russian life, and it is of a piece with the general unpretentiousness of their private lives. Russians are troubled much less than Americans, for example, by compulsive worrying about appearances, keeping up with the Joneses, being brightly scrubbed, having a well-deodorized body, perfumed breath, and a constant fresh look. In Russia, a person can be acned, homely, sweaty and seedy-looking and still be accepted.

We found, too, that visitors who are truly welcome in Russian homes are usually ushered immediately to that most humble and yet most homey of places – the kitchen table, if the kitchen is large enough to accommodate more than a couple of people. The table, whether in kitchen or sitting room, has a central place in the Russian home, a tradition carried on from country life. Unlike Westerners with their cocktail hours and their drawing rooms, Russians go right to the table when friends call. It is usually a small table, overcrowded but in that way more intimate, since Russians, living close to one another all the time, like the physical proximity.

One Sunday lunch at the Pasternaks, we were ten around a table no larger than one in an American breakfast nook, children mixed in with adults and a grandfather in no par-

139

ticular order. Knees bumped unselfconsciously all during the meal as Russians bump each other while shopping or standing pressed together in church. Had we been special guests, a special table might have been laid but we were *en famille*, and the table was set accordingly – dishes of different sizes and from different sets, ordinary restaurant kitchen knives, forks and spoons. The meal was wholesome but simple, the portions adequate but modest – sour cabbage in vinegar and oil, brown bread, a watery broth over vegetables, veal patties, potatoes and peas, and for dessert, a sweetish lemon coolade over cut apples. It was, after all, the midday Sunday meal. Ordinary meals can be very meager – buckwheat porridge, some cheese and a bit of salted or smoked fish, heaps of brown bread, perhaps some sausage, and tea.

The table, however, functions as much more than a place where Russians take their meals. The table is a meeting ground. For hours, Ann and I have sat with Russians around a table drinking strong tea, always a deep, rich, mahogany color – for Russians love their tea piping hot, well-sugared, and very strong (sometimes even 'black') – or else guzzling something stronger yet, nibbling on hard toast or cheese or other simple fare and talking all afternoon, evening and into the night about practically anything. In the Russian home, the table takes the place of the American den, family room and fireplace. It is the center of social life, a bridge between humans, a place for communion.

It is here in their house that Russians find refuge from the sterility and hypocrisy of public life and the aggravating hassle of the marketplace. Among family and friends, they become the wonderful, flowing, emotional people of Tolstoy's novels, sharing humor and sorrows and confidences, entering into a simple but profound intimacy that seems less self-centered and less self-conscious than what one generally finds in the West.

Precisely because their public lives are so supervised and because they cannot afford to be open and candid with most people, Russians invest their friendships with enormous importance. Many of them, in cities at least, are only-children whose closest friends come to take the place of missing brothers and sisters. They will visit with each other almost daily, like members of the family. Their social circles are usually narrower than those of Westerners, especially Americans who put such great stock in popularity, but relations

140

between Russians are usually more intense, more demanding, more enduring and often more rewarding.

I knew of a couple sent off to Cuba for a two-year assignment, and another family put up their teenage son in an already crowded two-room apartment. When Bella Akhmadulina, the poet, married for the third time she and her husband were broke, and their friends bought them an entire apartment full of furniture. Let a dissident intellectual get in trouble and real friends will loyally take the terrible political risk of going to his rescue. Ann and I, too, have felt the warmth and impulsive generosity of Russians. A leading ballerina in Leningrad, hearing of our difficulties in finding ballet shoes for one of our daughters, asked her foot size and instantly got up from the table to fetch one of her own pairs, especially made for one of her roles. A couple in Tashkent, with whom we established a quick and open friendship on first meeting, were so moved they gave us as a memento a rare book of photographs of archaeological finds in Uzbekistan, out of print and personally inscribed to them by the author. In another home, my wife admired a rather expensive set of large teacups which the hostess had just bought and she immediately made them a present to us. In the Caucasus, a dark-haired Alpine guide learned that my mother was ill with cancer and very movingly offered me his entire, pitifully small but precious supply of 'mummy', a medicinal paste made from herb grasses that grow high in the mountains and are gathered with difficulty by climbers. When friends fall sick, Russians will go to enormous trouble to help, regardless of inconvenience.

Friendships are not only compensation for the cold impersonality of public life but a vital source of personal identity. 'Friends are the one thing we have which are all our own,' a mathematician confided. 'They are the one part of our lives where we can make our own choice completely for ourselves. We cannot do that in politics, religion, literature, work. Always, someone above influences our choice. But not with friends. We make that choice for ourselves.'

The choice, among intellectuals at least, is made with special care for one essential ingredient of Russian friendships is the political test of trust. This gives them special depth and commitment. Americans, spared the violence of Soviet political purges, repressions and constant pressures for ideological conformity, do not have to make the vital, acute judgment of sorting out true friend from devious informer. Soviets must make that judgment often, and always unerringly.

'Human relations are a deadly serious business here,' a scientist remarked to me. 'We resent it if a foreigner comes to a party and brings along Russian friends. It ruins the evening for us because it takes us a long time to know someone and come to trust them.' Although the situation has improved since the Stalin era when members of families were turned against each other, this self-protective mistrust of all but a handful of people is one of the most depressing and corrosive effects of political controls which divide people against each other involuntarily. 'You can't trust anyone but your pillow,' one young man cursed bitterly to me after learning that one of his long-time friends had informed on him to the KGB. Among the underground artists who frequently mingled with Western diplomats, more than one quietly confessed concern about which of their group were the *stukachi* (informers) or *seksoty* (KGB secret collaborators) keeping tabs on the rest. It was taken for granted that several people among the artists were informers.

Most people develop an animal sense about each other. 'You never tell the real truth to anyone who is not a real friend,' an auburn-haired editor of children's books explained. 'You know, we have lived next door to another couple all our lives practically. I have known the wife since childhood and yet I have never told her the honest truth. We have always been friendly. We have known them well. They have come to our apartment and we have been to theirs. But they are different people from us. We could sense it.'

'How?' I asked.

'The husband is a nice guy, a scientist,' interjected her stout, curly-haired husband, a science writer. 'You can drink with him, talk with him about pretty girls and that sort of thing. But nothing serious. You know, when you meet with people, you sense whether there is that critical faculty or not. It doesn't matter whether they are peasants, workers or intellectuals. You sense whether they think for themselves. If not, you don't say anything important.'

For safety's sake, Russians hold each other at bay. 'We don't want personal relations with that many other people,' one man said bluntly. They commit themselves to only a few, but cherish those. Within the trusted circle, there is an intensity in Russian relationships that Westerners find both exhilarating and exhausting. When they finally open up, Russians are looking for a soul-brother not a mere conversational partner. They want someone to whom they can pour out their hearts, share their miseries, tell about family problems or difficulties with a lover or mistress, to ease the pain of life or to indulge in endless philosophical windmill tilting. As a journalist I sometimes found it ticklish because Russians want a total commitment from a friend. They do not understand a journalist who regards it his job to maintain open contacts with all and professes ideals of independence and nonpartisanship. Russians are not after decency or fair play; they want allies, partisans. This goes for officials, dissidents and people in between. Their friendship is tribal – inclusive and excluding, and they gauge each other by friends, cliques, groups, reckoning these ties – in high politics as well as in personal relations – as far more meaningful than some abstract loyalty to the system or the Party. They seek, and offer, a personal commitment from friends and cohorts that Westerners rarely accord more than a very few people in their lives.

Normally, Russians keep their emotions under lock and key and take them out to be shown only to relatives and close friends, or on special occasions. But I found that some little twist of fate – a genuine calamity, a joke, a gesture, the presence of a child, a personal liking – can open Russians up and then that sense of intimacy and involvement can envelop one even on first meeting if the Russian feels he has found a soul-brother, and especially if there has been some vodka to tide the flow of friendship. It is this directness in the Russian character, this tendency to startling openness that makes Americans feel Russians are like them in temperament, more so than the complicated French or the restrained British and Germans. Russians call this openness their broad spirit, *shirokaya dusha*, and they pride themselves on talking openly *dusha-dushe*, heart to heart, or literally soul to soul.

There is a public side to this trait – the maudlin sentimentality of Russians. For the great suffering which they have endured not only toughened them into a nation of stoics but also softened them into a nation of incurable romantics. The outside world knows the stoicism, the phlegmatic fatalism of the common man so aptly captured in the national catchword *nichevo*, which literally means 'nothing' but comes across as never mind, don't let it bother you,

143

there's nothing you can do about it, so don't bother me. It conveys uncomplaining endurance, indifference, futility, refusal to accept responsibility. To someone on the wrong side of *nichevo*, it is crippling and rarely is it accompanied by an apology. One American newspaper editor, flying from Moscow to London, rose at 5 a.m. and took the long ride to the airport to his flight only to discover that it did not leave on the date written on his ticket, but the next day. No flight was even scheduled on his day; his ticket had been written incorrectly. No other space was available for 24 hours so that he had to miss some London appointments. *Nichevo*, they said.

But the opposite face of the Russian character is that a genuine calamity will sometimes ease or suspend the rules because it arouses compassion. We learned that in dire and urgent family need the Foreign Ministry and Visa Office would issue exit visas in two days instead of the usual four or five. Such compassion is something ordinary Russians approve of whole-heartedly, for in spite of all the official rhetoric about work discipline and devotion to the Economic Plan, they are moved more by someone's personal warmth than his work performance. 'A man can be a good worker but work is just a *thing*, a balding government economist explained to me. 'What really matters is his spirit, his relationship to others. If he is too scrupulous, too cold, people will dislike him. We have a word, *sukhovaty* – dryish.' His nose wrinkled in disapproval. 'But *sukhoi*, dry, is worse, and finally *sukhar*, which means dry like a bread crust – no human touch at all – is the worst.'

In its public face, this sentimentalism shows itself in the Russian love of the lush melancholy of Tchaikovsky and the fairytale world of romantic ballets like *Swan Lake* and *Sleeping Beauty*. What the ornate productions of the Bolshoi do for the Russian soul is to blend grandeur with make-believe and provide escapism on an exalted scale. Nothing appeals more to the Victorian, 19th-century tastes of Russians than the organdy frill of ballerinas' skirts whirling in endless pirouettes. The modern intellectual compositions of a choreographer like Jerome Robbins leave most Russians unmoved. I saw one man stalk out of the New York City Ballet Company performance of some Robbins numbers one night in Moscow, perplexed by the lack of story line and complaining, 'That is not ballet!' Strange as it may seem for a Communist state, the greater the pageantry of royalty, the more

144

shmaltzy the music, the more extravagant the sets, the fancier the masked balls, the more melodramatic the emotions, the larger the world of make-believe, the greater the pull at the heartstrings, the more the Russians enjoy it.

They fell in love with Van Cliburn as the handsome young American who played their Tchaikovsky with heart. When La Scala Opera and Chorus toured Moscow, the Russians were literally overcome by the power and emotion of their Verdi 'Requiem' and showered the chorus with applause, bravos and flowers. For Russians, flowers are a special sign of admiration and affection. One of their nicest customs is to arrive at someone's apartment for dinner bearing flowers, even if only one wrapped in cellophane. At Novodeviche cemetery, burial ground of the famous, they will buy flowers and stroll among the gravestones, laying a bloom here and there where they feel special respect. In theaters, the management carts out potted plants or bouquets for stars as a ritual, but you can tell when a Russian audience has been powerfully moved. Flowers rise up out of the audience. The response to La Scala was no accident, for Russians are like Italians in their love of strong emotions and undiluted heroics. In spirit, they are the most northern of Latin peoples. 'We have always felt very close to Spain,' a literary critic once mused. 'Not just because of the Spanish Civil War. But we have felt a kinship for the Spanish. They are a noble people. Spain is a country of chivalry and romance. We like Don Quixote very much.' And it is true – Quixote could be a Russian hero.

If sentimentality is the counterpoint to Russian stoicism, then the folksy, traditional, peasant ways of Russians are the anti-thesis to the inflated rhetoric of Marxism-Leninism about the New Soviet Man. Not only are Russians easy-going, indolent, and disorganized rather than scientific, rational and efficient, but they are as simple and homespun in their leisure as their friendship. Martyrs of self-denial they may be in time of crisis, but otherwise they are lusty hedonists, devoted to such sensual pleasures as feasting, drinking and bathing. And in open contradiction to the strictures of scientific socialism, they are a mystical, religious, superstitious people at heart.

My politically orthodox, middle-aged language teacher tried to persuade me that superstitions were *passé*, only for poor, uneducated people or those plagued by illness. People who are healthy and well off, she insisted, have no need of them. An elderly writer agreed, but added that it was the ailments and ordeals of Russian life which made Russians such great believers in omens, signs and portents, such paganistic worriers about the evil eye, such apostles of old wives' tales and folk cures. I recall a poet seriously counseling me once never to go back to my apartment for something I had forgotten because it was bad luck to return and to have to leave a second time. A pretty teacher cautioned that if someone gave a girl an affectionate pat on the rump, he must immediately tug her skirt or else no one would ever make love to her. A well-educated lady instructed our family on having all members of the household sit for a moment of silence before anyone departed on a journey, evidently a holdover from religious practice, for when she rose, she said, 'Go with God.' Others were careful not to mention the precise destination of trips so as not to attract the attention of the evil eye.

Our Russian maid informed Ann that on New Year's eve it is common practice to put three slips of paper under your pillow – labeled 'Good Year', 'Bad Year' and 'Medium Year'. In the morning you reach a hand under the pillow and pull out one slip to find out what kind of new year is in store. The maid said she did not dare try it because she couldn't bear the burden of knowing she was in for a bad year. We knew other Russians who, like Orientals, put their faith in the zodiac names of the years. Still others, including intellectuals, swore that leap year is unlucky, and attributed the disastrous harvest of 1972, among other calamities, to that cause. The coming of anything so precious as a child invokes all manner of precautions. It is bad luck to pick a name in advance, bad luck to buy a present ahead of time, even worse to discuss the likely date. Unwittingly, I once asked a prospective father when the child was due and a family friend cut in to admonish me, 'It's not good to ask.' The father, a technical man, shyly replied, 'I don't know,' and the woman approvingly told him, 'That's the best answer.' Russians also regard it as a bad sign, perhaps more out of conformity than superstition, if a child is left handed. The moment they catch it starting to eat or draw with the left hand, they 'correct' it into right handedness.

So strong are the inhibitions against shaking hands across

the threshold, for fear that it foreshadows a quarrel, that I came home to America hesitating to reach my hand through an open door. Russians do not knock on wood so much as we but they spit figuratively over their left shoulders for the same purpose. Thirteen persons is bad luck at a table though Russian engineers do dare to put 13th floors in their buildings. Friday is a melancholy day, perhaps going back to Good Friday, but what intrigued me was that Monday is so widely regarded as inauspicious for launching a new undertaking. Not until some friendly Soviet journalist put me wise did I understand why trips for foreign correspondents so often began late Sunday rather than Monday morning. Any cat, not just a black cat, is a bad omen crossing one's path. But when you get a new home, Russians said, a cat should be the first creature to enter. If a bird flies in a window, it is a very bad portent of impending tragedy, possibly death or jail. The roots of many of these superstitions seem to lie in the countryside, like the Russian fondness for proverbs or their belief in folk remedies. City people as well as peasants often prefer medicinal herbs and grasses or mustard plaster over modern drugs for simple ailments. An American friend was advised to apply a copper coin to reduce swelling. We saw Russians wearing garlic cloves around their necks to fight off a cold.

Russians have a wholesome, old-fashioned simplicity to their pleasure, too, a way of turning back to nature or improvising simple, inexpensive pursuits. Television, except for sports, is pretty dull and the Soviet Union is a land of far less manufactured entertainment than the West – no drive-in movies, pinball machines, roller-skating rinks, no stock-car speedways and practically no bowling alleys or amusement parks to match Coney Island. Ask Soviet officialdom about leisure activities and they rattle off how many millions are involved, either actually or on paper, in organized sports or taking union-subsidized vacations at sanatoria. These cut-rate vacation passes, *putyovki*, which are sometimes very hard to get, are among the greatest boons the Soviet system provides the common man. For like the Germans, the Russians are strong on health cures, sulphur treatments, and mud baths. Several times on official tours, I saw workers at sanatoria with legs or arms immersed in tubs of warm mud, or women inhaling sulphur fumes, and proclaiming that a 26-day, $200 visit to a sanitorium was an ideal vacation.

But official facilities and official programs take care of only a small fraction of Soviet leisure. Most activities are much more informal and modest. The men, old and young, gather in huddles around park benches to play – chess, I had presumed – but more often it turned out to be dominos, and usually with a good bit of betting. (Russians love lotteries, too.) So much have pets come back into vogue as a hobby that on Sundays a massive business is done at Moscow's 'Bird Market', a sprawling, muddy, open-air flea market where people sell birds, guppies, tropical fish, rabbits, cats, dogs, guinea pigs and other pets that they have raised as well as the homemade paraphernalia to house and feed them. The rage among the young is collecting souvenir lapel pins, a practice that seems to have surpassed stamp and coin collecting as a fad and led to the minting of hundreds of millions of little emblems by every city, club, agency, enterprise and organization in the country. Foreign tourists are often waylaid by small boys offering handfuls of badges, known as *znachki*, in exchange for chewing gum. I remember that Canadian hockey players and fans were absolutely besieged by *znachki* collectors hunting prized Canadian pins. So widespread and sophisticated has this hobby become that professional collectors meet, usually surreptitiously, in an underpass near Gorky Park to swap, compare and sell unusual specimens, mounted on felt boards, carefully covered with transparent plastic and carried in attaché cases. Considerable profiteering has developed. *Pravda* once wagged its disapproving finger not only at adult collectors but at public enterprises for spending huge sums to design and put out *znachki*. What is more, *Pravda* took offense at the Chelyabinsk Dog Club for producing a pin that resembled a prestigious military decoration, and bridled at a plumbers' group in the Azerbaijan Republic for putting out a miniature toilet seat pin with the inscription, 'Best Plumber of the Azerbaijan Sanitary Technical Assembly Enterprise'. When it comes to entertainment, Russians have lost none of their traditional enthusiasm for the classic one-ring circus with dancing bears and unbelievable feats of gymnastics and acrobatics. Even when they go out on the town at a spot like the Sofia Restaurant, with its all-girl band, the frolicking of most people has a wholesome athletic exuberance. Some go just to get drunk. A few young couples are pretty up-to-date with

Western dances. But most people do a bouncy jig that is more sport than dance.

Left to their own devices, however, the majority of Russians turn back to nature for relaxation. They will take an *elektrichka*, an electric commuter train, out into the country and simply wander through the high grass in their floral-print calico dresses or lie by a riverbank guzzling beer. On Friday nights, the railroad stations are crowded with young people carrying crude backpacks and bedrolls, headed for the country to hike and sleep in the open air. In fields and forests, anywhere there is space, I have seen them playing volleyball, even in the snow, and sometimes just popping the ball around a human circle if they have no net.

But the Russian outdoor hobby par excellence – one that always bemuses Westerners – is mushroom-picking. In the fall, it approaches a national craze. Connoisseurs treat the location of their favorite hunting grounds for premier species as top secret. Less dedicated souls creep through any old forest or glen for hours on end, clutching pails, satchels, or kerchiefs and caps converted into makeshift containers and scanning the earth for hidden treasures or pausing to gossip and picnic. At peak season, competition gets so keen that groups organize expeditions, rent buses through their factories on Friday, spend the night in the bus on a country road, catnapping or warming themselves with tea or vodka so that at daybreak they can be the first to get a crack at tender new mushrooms. So numerous are the varieties that it takes a practiced eye to distinguish poisonous from nonpoisonous. To aid rank amateurs, Soviet magazines blossom in the fall with charts that approximate racing forms, giving pointers on the seasons and surroundings in which various specimens perform best. But the charts are so complicated that when we tried it, we spent more time studying our chart than hunting mushrooms.

This is a sport that has more significance than initially meets the eye. Connoisseurs insist that each species of mushroom has its own proper drink. 'The milk mushroom is best with refined brown vodka, known as petrovka,' one old hand told me. 'The little redheads demand clear vodka, crystal clear and very cold so that the vodka does not numb your sense of taste. In fact, some people gather all kinds of mushrooms just to have another excuse for drinking vodka of any kind.'

But the real point of mushroom-hunting for most people is

to escape into the country, to stroll, to get away from it all. Russians have a passion for their countryside. City people, like American urbanites, revel in roughing it at some rented peasant cabin, cooking on a stove tucked out in a shed, using the outhouse in the garden, hooking pots and pans over the weatherbeaten wooden fence palings to dry. The sun playing through a stand of birches or the coolness of the majestic pines casts a spell. But for a long time I found the open countryside a disappointment. Instead of offering dramatic scenery, Russia is a vast flatland, stretching beyond every horizon to fill a continent, like the open, limitless prairie of Kansas. It lacks the breathtaking vistas of Switzerland, the picturesque hills of Bavaria, or the hedgerows and stone walls that give the English countryside its charm. Russia is plainer, more rambling, wilder, undisciplined.

'I love the well-tended English garden,' a Russian walking companion remarked to me as we passed into a private enclosure outside Moscow one day, 'but the Russian garden does something for my soul.'

This puzzled me: Here, behind the green fence was a Russian garden, wild and uncombed. I would not have called it a garden at all; it was just a fenced-in chunk of woodland. Shrubs, trees, grasses grew freely in no pattern, shaped by no hand. And then I realized that this was precisely its appeal to the Russian soul. In its rambling, wild, deliciously undisciplined disarray, it provided release from their over-tended, over-crowded, over-supervised lives. Russians need to break the bonds, burst the limits, spiritually take off their shoes and run barefoot – and they do that in their countryside.

On another occasion, Ann and I went to Dombai, a mountain ski center in the Northern Caucasus, 800 miles south of Moscow. Two rickety chairlifts hiked us up only about 650 feet to an open meadow at the foot of the mountains. Even for the most modest run, we had to hike half a mile and then climb up a hill on our skis. There was no tow. Climbing uphill 400 yards or so for each little run became even more of a chore because the surface snow turned slushy before midday in the warm March sun. But the Russian vacationers did not mind in the least. The setting was truly beautiful, evoking the Alps. They had a chance to commune with nature, never mind the skiing. And with the sun blazing away, these pasty-faced northerners happily peeled off almost all their clothes and sun-bathed in swimsuits or underwear

150

on every available outcropping of rock.

Except for beaches, the only place where I saw more Russian flesh than on that slope was at the *banya*, a venue that is as thoroughly Russian as the gathering around the kitchen table and just as important a meeting ground. The Russian *banya*, or bathhouse, is a cross between the Finnish sauna and the steamy Turkish bath. Its purpose, with a special twist of Russian masochism, is to make you sweat in order to flush out dirt through the pores. 'It can cure most diseases,' one veteran told me. But like mushroom-hunting, it is not merely the act of bathing that counts, but the entire process – the expedition to the baths; the careful ritual of weighing-in, of soaping, steaming, rinsing, weighing and beginning all over again; and the masculine conviviality, the small talk and joking *au naturel* that go with communal bathing. The regulars get to know each other. I could overhear them chatting – 'Haven't seen you in a long time.' 'Yes, been away on assignment.' 'How's the steam today?' 'Fine.' For the *banya* is a complete form of recreation in itself, the closest thing that Russian males have to a men's club (women are segregated), but priced within everyone's reach, which is one reason why, like mushroom-gathering, it is so popular.

For 60 kopecks (80 cents), the customer pays the price of admission, gets a rough sheet which Russian bathers drape around themselves like a Roman toga, and rents a *venik*, a bundle of leafy birch twigs that Russians use to flail themselves in the steam room to help the steam do its cleansing and, at the same time, leave the gentle fragrance of birch in their pores. Although Russian friends told me that the intelligentsia, blue-collar workers and government officials tend to patronize their own favorite bathhouses, the *banya* as an institution struck me as one of the few real levelers of Soviet society. In the change room, where there are no lockers but only clothing hooks on the upright benches and for a tip the attendant watches your wallet, I have seen business suits and military officers' uniforms hanging beside rough work clothes or worn peasant jackets. Most of Moscow's bathhouses predate the Revolution and were favorite haunts of rich merchants who used to feast in private rooms, take dips in marble pools, and generally enjoy a high life. Today, things are more proletarian. The gaudy, ornate Sandunovsky Bath has faded to the point that its tile floors and statuary are chipped and its chandeliers, as one Russian friend quipped, 'are so vulgar

151

that they are almost attractive'. The steam room resembles a boiler room with open piping, but Russians don't mind the seedy surroundings so long as they can savor the folksiness of their communal cleansing.

The *banya* is supposed to produce a sense of well-being but in my experience Russians do not really enjoy that without a preliminary dash of masochism. Like the Finns, they like the steam room kept so hot that the air burns the nostrils when you breathe. They consider the choicest spot to be the hottest balcony, up six or seven stone steps, where the moisture burns the eyes and where the veterans endure their agony and lose their pound of flesh. 'Five to seven minutes is all you should take,' one Russian advised, spotting me as a tenderfoot. Another insisted that if I wanted to stay longer, 'You'd better wear something on your head – an old felt hat or something.' I sat among them, blinking away the sweat, trying to keep still, soothed by the swearing and contented grunts of other bathers thrashing themselves or each other into rosy pinkness with their birch twigs. ('Here, do my back, will you?' or 'More on the legs, *the legs*.') Their low-keyed muttering was periodically punctuated by the inevitable bickering over whether to throw more water on the fire-bricks in the oven. Some veteran, not sweating to his own satisfaction and spotting a newcomer entering the steam room, would command, 'More water!' and the new man was duty-bound by custom to bring in one or two zinc tubfuls of water to dash on the fire-bricks. 'Enough, enough,' came a chorus of gasps from those overcome by the hot, heavy air. Some bathers favored mugfuls of beer or tiny amounts of eucalyptus scent to perfume the steam. But the key was not aroma but striking the delicate moisture balance: Too much water or beer made the heat unbearable but too little robbed the *aficionados* of their necessary quotient of suffering.

Like so much of Russian life, relief comes at the moment of escape from self-torture when bathers flee to the change room outside. There, they lounge around naked or wrapped loosely in their sheets telling jokes, arguing over last night's hockey game against the Canadians or a Spartak-Dynamo soccer game. It is a pleasant place where people eavesdrop freely and butt into conversations, proffering unsought advice on how to handle women, where to find *defitsitny* goods, or how to keep young in old age. I remember one white-haired gent telling me and a friend to take plenty of time with our baths.

'You young people are always rushing about and it does no good,' he admonished. He was 75 but he looked ten years younger and the secret, he asserted, came from a book written by a Bulgarian who told all about baths and explained a technique for massaging the face with a hot wet towel daily. 'Do it like this,' our acquaintance advised, demonstrating how to wipe the towel around the eyes and down the jaw bone, 'and you'll never look old.' Nearby, workmen with tattoos – eagles, women, or *rodina* (Motherland) in inky outlines – wandered around in their black underwear while a couple of other men sat in the corner reading and another group watched a domino game in progress.

Practically everyone sends the *banshchik*, the attendant, out to the hallway for mugs of watery Zhigulovsky brand beer. Plenty of bathers, playing hookey from work, arrive with bread and salami or canned sardines to wash down with their beer. But the favorite delicacy, one for which I can vouch, is *vobla*, a dried, boney, salted fish that you chew and suck on – the Russian answer to pretzels, potato chips and salted peanuts. Some contend that the best time to visit the *banya* is in the morning 'because the steam is drier,' as one veteran explained; many more prefer the evening for socializing. But everyone counts on making it a real outing. 'No one goes for less than two or three hours,' said one government official. 'An hour and a half is too little.' Our office driver, Ivan Gusev, used to take his teenaged son once a week and spend all evening, enjoying the clubby camaraderie, the food, beer, and the sense of sensual contentment that Russians call *lyuks* – luxury.

Russians seek that feeling most in feasting and drinking. They love a party and seize upon any holiday and even the unexpected arrival of a stranger as a pretext. We knew Russians who used the historic change of the calendar and both secular and religious holidays to get in four celebrations at the turn of the year – old and new New Year's and old and new Christmas. Moderation and frugality do not come naturally to Russians; they live for the moment. So when an occasion for partying, and especially drinking, arises, they will throw an entire bonus or a huge chunk of pay – more than they can sensibly afford – into a single evening of mad jollity and emotional Slavic self-indulgence. They may go

153

out on the town with friends to a restaurant with a loud dance band and fling themselves into bouncy fox trots, mazurkas, polkas, and athletic mutations of the twist, monkey or some pseudo-rock numbers, returning to a table well fortified with vodka, cognac or sweet Soviet champagne to keep the party mood afloat. Or, as most prefer, they may kick in 20 or 30 rubles a couple for a grand holiday feast at someone's apartment.

On such occasions, Russians abandon themselves to the orgy of feasting and drinking with a gusto that echoes a memory of hungrier times. In advance, they will prowl the stores and use all their connections to wangle some black and red caviar or smoked salmon, the rare luxuries that give Russians the feeling of high-life merely by their presence on the table. For days, the women work preparing *zakuski*, the hors d'oeuvres that are justifiably the most celebrated part of a Russian meal. When the guests finally sit down, the table fairly groans with food. *Zakuski* are never consumed without a string of good-natured toasts, each punctured by everyone's gulping down a shot-glass of chilled vodka. Russians will consume marinated mushrooms and vodka, salted herring and vodka, smoked salmon and vodka, salami and vodka, caviar on brown bread and vodka, pickled cucumbers and vodka, cold tongue and vodka, red beet salad and vodka, scallions and vodka – anything and everything, and vodka.

'You cannot imagine what a treat a holiday is and how important that feasting is for us,' a middle-aged journalist declared. 'You know that just before the main holidays, the state stores are supplied with good food that is generally not available. Normally, we eat terribly – but we get used to it. People don't care. But on a holiday, then we must eat well. It makes up for all the rest of the time.'

Holidays, however, are more than a time of joyous release. For what begins in good fellowship around the table all too often ends up in gluttonous inebriation, self-indulgent alcoholic escapism from boredom, frustration and the cold. 'Demon vodka', as the Russians have been calling it for centuries, is a national vice, a calamity of the destructive proportions of the drug problem in America and harder to uproot.

The West has nothing equivalent to vodka, the way Russians drink it. Like corruption, vodka is one of the indispensable lubricants and escape mechanisms of Russian life. The mere mention of vodka starts Russians salivating and puts them in a mellow mood. It would take an encyclopedia to explain all the vodka lore from the gentle tap under the throat which signifies drinking to the scores of ditties Russians have invented to convey the message, 'let's go drink'. Vodka eases the tension of life. It helps people to get to know each other, for many a Russian will say that he cannot trust another man until they have drunk seriously together. Vodka-drinking is invested with the symbolism of machismo. Roy Medvedev, the dissident historian, told me that as a young teacher out in the Urals, going around a village to encourage parents to keep their children in school, he was told by three elders in one home that they would not even talk with him unless he downed a tumblerful of vodka. When he performed that feat, they regarded him as a man they could trust. Among working men and peasants, vodka is so popular that the $4.80 half-liter bottle is better than cash as pay for odd jobs.

Those who have not been exposed to Russian drinking do not appreciate how hard Russians drink but travelers to Russia, astonished by it, have remarked about it for centuries. In 1639, Adam Orleans, who represented the Duke of Holstein's court in Moscow, observed that Russians 'are more addicted to drunkenness than any nation in the world'. In 1839, the Marquis de Custine, a French nobleman, picked up the Russian aphorism that 'drinking is the joy of Russia'. It still is, but this does not mean Russians are relaxed social imbibers. They know no moderation. Once the vodka bottle is uncorked, it must be finished. There is no such thing as putting it back on the shelf, a notion that amuses Russians whenever a Westerner mentions the idea. Russians drink, essentially, to obliterate themselves, to blot out the tedium of life, to warm themselves from the chilling winters, and they eagerly embrace the escapism it offers.

In Tashkent, one afternoon, I watched two well-dressed Russians in business suits sit down for a late lunch and order a half-liter of vodka with their meal. The plump one, facing me, was Pickwickian in his round-faced, round-stomached good humor which blossomed when the vodka appeared. The vodka was quickly poured, glasses raised in a brief toast, and clinked. Down went the vodka with a quick jerk of the head, a 'pah' on the exhale as his fork jabbed a bit of herring and stuffed it into his mouth, chased by bread. At quick intervals, the process was repeated. Soon a soft blushing pink flooded the cheeks of the Pickwickian Russian. It was amazing to see how rosy the vodka had made his life. He wore a blissful look. When I paid my check the vodka was gone and a modest decanter of cognac had appeared. The rest of their day was clearly done for. I have witnessed the final scenes elsewhere. If a woman is involved and someone asks her to dance, it can end in an ugly mood. Or, as happened one night at the Berlin restaurant in Moscow, two men went so rapidly through the vodka that by the time dessert came, one glassy-eyed gent bent down to his ice cream dish, preparing to eat it with his mouth, and simply nose-dived into the ice cream. His friend and the waiter had to prop him up and wipe him off, whereupon he proceeded to eat the ice cream with a knife.

Periodically, the press and political leadership inveigh against the national disaster of alcoholism. High officials have disclosed that intoxication is the major factor in the majority of all crimes (90 percent of murders), accounts for more than half of all traffic accidents, is a major cause in 40 percent of all divorce cases, figures in 63 percent of all accidental drownings, one-third of all ambulance calls in Moscow. It is the prime cause of the absenteeism that plays havoc with the Soviet economy. Still, I found it difficult not to be skeptical of the state campaigns supposedly intended to curb drinking when alcohol production by the state liquor monopoly rises annually, when the rate of consumption is five times what it was in 1940, and when the pathetic little country stores always seem to have vodka even when they are out of less volcanic wares. Drunks, stiff as boards, or crumpled into heaps, litter the city sidewalks at holiday times, not just in skid row areas, but almost anywhere. Heavy Sunday daytime drinking is just as common as a Friday or Saturday night binge. Women drink less than men but more heavily than in the West. I have seen 14-year-olds drink vodka neat.

Nor can foreigners spend much time in Russia without having their livers threatened by vodka. For centuries, Russians have been flooding Westerners with vodka as a form of hospitality which conveniently numbs the travelers' critical faculties. Baron Sigismund zu Herberstein, Ambassador of the Hapsburg Emperor to the Court of Ivan the Great observed in 1526 that 'The Russians make every effort to get their guests drunk' concocting toasts and pretexts for drinking when no good reason exists. The guest who hesitates or sips instead of joining in the Russian 'bottoms up', is sternly told that he is insulting the host, for Russians take no little pride in drinking foreigners, especially Americans, under the table. In my three years in Russia, I am sure that I consumed more alcohol than in all the rest of my life.

Only once did it get out of hand, but it taught me something essential about Soviet life. In Bukhara, Ann and I met two scholars, an Armenian and an Uzbek, when our taxi broke down and they generously offered us a ride back into town. From that came an invitation to dinner to sample Uzbek rice pilaff. But when we arrived for dinner, it was clear that the purpose of the evening was to drink with an American. Half a dozen men had been assembled, all teachers at the local pedagogical institute. They had left their wives at home so that Ann was the only female. When we sat down, there were six or eight bottles of liquor on the table. One man bowed out of drinking as the driver of the car, as did Ann. Three other men, the elder trio, preferred cognac. A quick calculation showed that there were four bottles of vodka (equal to two quarts of scotch) for just three of us – for me, the little Armenian and a handsome muscular young Uzbek who had spent all day in the fields harvesting cotton (the institute where all these men taught was shut down for six weeks so that students and faculty could help pick cotton). Food normally provides some protection and an excuse to slow the drinking, but this table was discouragingly barren except for a few chocolates, some marinated tomatoes, and a plate of green onions.

The Armenian was impatient and did not want to waste time waiting for the meal. I tried to stall by talking to another man about his children, but there was no denying the iron imperative of the occasion. We drank to our meeting, to Soviet-American friendship, to peace, to détente, to our women, to a record cotton harvest – at which point the muscular young Uzbek gave me blessed relief by rising to recite selections from Omar Khayyam from memory, while I prayed for food. I did not like the tomatoes; but nothing else appeared. The cognac drinkers were nipping lightly but my two vodka partners insisted that our rounds be 'bottoms up' to prove our friendship. I still felt all right as we toasted to our children, to all children of the world, to the wish that our children would never make war against each other, to the cousins of the Armenian whom he thought were in San Francisco, to Armenia, to Nixon, to Brezhnev, to the host's home-made wine – a sickly sweet potion that mixed badly with vodka, to so many other things that I cannot recall them. By then, the conversation had all the clarity of the mad, disjointed drinking bouts of Dostoyevsky's novels but, like a true vodka drinker, I was insisting to my wife that everything was still under control. My two drinking companions were now talking with me heart-to-heart, *dusha-dushe*. By the time our plump Uzbek hostess finally appeared with the celebrated pilaff about three hours later, all the vodka on the table was gone and we were all so numb that no one but Ann could eat.

Vodka, as any Russian will tell you, has a delayed punch that strikes at the base of the neck with guillotine suddenness severing brain from body. The blow hit me as we went out to try to find a cab home, for the nondrinking driver had disappeared with his car. In true Russian fashion, my two drinking partners, convinced they had found in me a soul-brother, insisted on riding home with us. They waited outside the hotel for an hour or so while I tried to sober up by walking around the town parks until two police officers steered Ann and me back toward the hotel which, by then, was shut for the night. With some difficulty, we got someone to open up whereupon both my drunken compatriots and the police all lurched behind us up to our hotel room where a great commotion ensued. Ultimately, the police led off our two unfortunate friends.

What is indelibly etched in my mind is the next day. One blessing of vodka is that it does not leave the headache or nausea of other liquors, but it totally demobilizes its victims. When I arose and applied the standard wake-up treatment of dashing cold water on my face, I felt nothing. My face was still numb. Somehow, we managed that morning to fly to Samarkand, but I spent the day in bed, not sick but totally useless, unable to function. It was this crippling devastation of the vodka bout which so impressed me. I have never experienced that before or since. On that occasion, I had wound up in that helpless state somewhat accidentally. But the little Armenian and the handsome young Uzbek – and the millions upon millions of Russians who drink that way – had set out deliberately to destroy me and themselves from the very beginning.

V

WOMEN

Liberated but Not Emancipated

> To effect [woman's] complete emancipation and
> make her the equal of man, it is necessary to be
> socialized and for women to participate in common
> productive labor. Then women will occupy the
> same position as men.
>
> Lenin, 1919

Mariya Fyodorovna Maksheyeva is an imposing woman in
her late forties with the looks and tall stature of a Russian
Ethel Merman and a fondness for singing sad romances
about her youth. She has a firm jaw, a strong handshake, a
wide smile, and a self-confident gregarious manner that I
found as commanding as it was comradely. I was introduced
to her in Murmansk – the Arctic port made famous by Allied
war convoys during World War II – by Nikolai Belyayev,
editor of *Polar Truth*, the local Communist Party newspaper.
Clearly he was in awe of her.

Like any foreigner who has traveled much in the Soviet
Union, I met a number of 'representational women' in posts
of public prominence – a Deputy Premier in Georgia, a President of the Yakut Republic of Siberia, a Peace Committee
leader in Moscow, a senior trade union official in Latvia.
Most were really examples of Soviet tokenism, women who
held figurehead positions rather than exercising real authority. But Mariya Fyodorovna was the most memorable
career woman I encountered in Russia because she had
achieved genuine responsibility and power.

Not only had she single handedly reared two sons to join
the Murmansk fishing fleets but she had bulldozed her way
into the top strata of the Murmansk power hierarchy to
become boss of the Rybkombinat, the fish processing plant

159

with 4,500 workers under her command. She had earned a seat on *Gorkom*, the Communist Party Committee that runs the city. With her black hair tied back in a bun, simple gold earrings, and wearing a plain sea green dress, she cut quite a different figure from glamorous American feminists like Gloria Steinem – but she was a kindred spirit. In America, she would have been called a rugged individualist with all the assertive personal characteristics which that implies. Sturdy of build, energetic, efficient, intelligent, strong-willed, she epitomized the Russian women who boldly stepped into industry in the postwar years when Russia was most grievously deprived of her men and – very unusual even for that era – she had made her way in the man's world of management. I was struck that she was more poised than many Soviet men I met for, unlike most officials who gather a phalanx of aides as reinforcements for any meeting with foreigners, she met me alone.

When I asked how she had fared in the masculine domain of management, she replied with a wide smile that exposed two perfect rows of teeth. She had supervised men, she said simply, and it had been no problem. With amusement, she recalled occasions when at banquets, as the only woman among male executives and important officials, she would hear some man give a toast to the women whom they had left at home. Puckishly, she would rise to offer a rebuttal toast to the men, reminding them that not all the women were at home.

To Mariya Fyodorovna, it was only natural that a woman should hold her $800-a-month job as director of the fish processing plant. 'Eighty-five percent of our workers in this plant are women,' she asserted. 'How could they have such a plant without a woman in charge?' Her predecessor had also been a woman, but before that the plant had been run by men. She twitted me and Belyayev good naturedly about how hard we would have to work in her plant because of the high standards she maintained. With a docile nod, Belyayev agreed she was a no-nonsense boss.

There were snow flurries in the air when we toured the nine rambling factories, warehouses, refrigeration lockers and docks that she was in charge of. I saw only three men on the job. But women were everywhere. Outside, burly women in padded blue cotton jackets, orange safety shirts and layers of thick woolen stockings chopped ice, shoveled snow or worked

160

in the holds of fishing trawlers. Inside, young women – girls they seemed to me with their slender, sallow faces – slithered around a water soaked floor in rubber boots and aprons, lugging ponderous frozen slabs of fish and hoisting them with difficulty into bins. Elsewhere, teams of older women, hair tied back in kerchiefs, cut off the heads and tails of herring, cod or sea perch, and, with incredible speed and dexterity, trussed them up in little slings to be hung on racks for smoking. Thanks to an automatic 50 percent pay bonus for working in the Arctic region, the women in Mariya Fyodorovna's factory made anywhere from $150 to $400 a month, and clearly they worked hard for it. Many of them were the wives of the fishermen who brought in the catch.

Mariya Fyodorovna, who had spent 20 years in the plant, knew most of the workers personally and joked with them in her hearty patronizing way, all the while explaining to me the processes of smoking, curing, treating the catch, canning it, and describing where the $190-million output of her plant would be marketed. 'People want less salt on their fish nowadays than before,' she said, 'so we have to make it tastier.' As we walked along, she remembered coming to Murmansk 25 years before from Shatura, a town near Moscow, after graduating from a fishery institute. She had known a rough life in this cold northern outpost. Her marriage had ended unhappily, but she had never been tempted to go back to the milder climates of Central Russia. She had become so accustomed to the severe Arctic weather that doctors had advised her against vacationing in the far south because it would be bad for her heart. 'I can't stand too much heat,' she confessed, tucking a loose hair back in her bun.

Mariya Fyodorovna is the kind of woman that Soviet officials like to have foreigners meet because she substantiates their claim that Soviet women are the most equal in the world. Long ago the Stalinist constitution of 1936 declared their 'equal rights with men in all spheres of economic, state, cultural, public and political life' which American women's libbers were still battling to get added to the American Constitution in the mid-Seventies. On paper, Soviet women already have it made. They are officially liberated. Abortions are legal. Four-month paid maternity leaves are written into law, and jobs must be kept for new mothers for a year. A network of state-subsidized day-care centers has been set up nationwide and cares for ten million preschoolers. Equal pay for equal work is established as a principle. A higher proportion of Soviet women work than in any other industrialized country and a modest number have achieved career successes. Vast numbers have completed higher education and work beside men in science, industry and government.

Yet despite these achievements and the enormous propaganda hoop-la about women in the Soviet media, Soviet women remain a distinctly second sex. If any large segment of the population has been exploited by the system, it is women. Even three decades after World War II, when educated urban women are watching their figures, chasing Western fashions and worrying more about their femininity than Russian women ever found time to do in the past, women still do the bulk of the low-paying, backbreaking, dirty manual labor. They shoulder a wearisome double burden of work plus what Lenin termed 'domestic slavery'. Justifiably, they complain of inadequate relief from the competing tensions of career and family.

From afar or on hurried visits to the Soviet Union where they have met occasional feminine successes like Mariya Fyodorovna, some American women speak enviously of their Soviet counterparts. But life looks different up close. No American woman I encountered who had lived among Russians long enough to have a genuine feel for what their lives entail, would think of swapping places. The main reason, as Russian women themselves say, is that contrary to Lenin's dictum, mass access to the job market has not proven the panacea that either Lenin or some Western feminists presumed. In many ways, it has made life more trying. Some Russian women even feel so disadvantaged that one confided candidly to an American woman I knew: 'I hope my child is a boy, not a girl. As a boy, his life would be so much easier.'

In spite of the declared Marxist-Leninist commitment to feminine equality, the strong tradition of male chauvinism in Russian life has been only mildly moderated by the Soviets. The enduring assumptions of male superiority and feminine subservience come through in Russian humor, so often revealing of deep-set attitudes. I remember a popular stage skit put on by a Leningrad satirical troupe in which four husky women sit at home, playing cards, getting roaring drunk, singing raucous songs and telling old war stories while a hen-pecked husband caters to their whims. As the women grow more boisterous and uncontrolled, the timid man, wearing a ridiculous little apron, bounces obediently from one thankless chore to another. He tries vainly to end the drinking bout by substituting tea and sandwiches for the vodka bottle but the four women snap at him about the food, bitch about the dirty table and clutch at the vodka. When they finally break up for the night, they reel around the stage in helpless inebriation while the woebegone husband strives to jam them into their coats and ferry them out the door. With the others gone, he begins helping his own wife to bed by pulling off her shoes, but she pinches him on the butt. 'Don't touch me!' he squeaks, and they launch into a spat over whose paycheck was frittered away on the vodka. Russian audiences find it all deliciously funny. They love slapstick. And they immediately understand the parody as a complete reversal of typical roles in Russian households where the wife does the chores while the husband lounges about reading the paper, watching television or getting drunk with friends.

Not long before I left for Moscow, an American woman of Russian descent gave me a couple of booklets on Russian proverbs. I was surprised at the blatant male chauvinism in a number of them: 'A wife isn't a jug – she won't crack if you hit her a few'; 'When you take an eel by its tail or a woman by her word, there's precious little stays in your hands'; or, 'A dog is wiser than a woman – he won't bark at his master'. Working-class women nowadays still take rough drinking and rough handling from their menfolk very much for granted. A Western diplomat's wife told me how her Russian maid had questioned her about her husband and after discovering that he did not periodically get drunk and beat up his wife, pronounced her very Russian verdict: 'He must not be much of a man.'

These are inbred attitudes drawn basically from peasant life, as was the most embarrassingly candid joke about male superiority that I heard in Russia. Intriguingly, it was told by a young man, well-educated, married, and an urbanite. According to him, it is an apt caricature of male Russian attitudes. It is one of those jokes about testing the national character of Spaniards, Frenchmen, Englishmen and Russians by putting two men and a woman from each nationality on a series of desert islands. The scientist left them for several months and when he returned to the island where he had deposited the Spanish trio, he found the woman alone and asked about the men. 'Oh, they have shot each other dueling over me,' she said in disgust. At the English island, the three people were standing in the same separate corners where they had been left. When the scientist asked why, one of the men replied, 'You forgot to introduce us properly.' At the French island, things were in perfect order and one man was tending a well-manicured garden. How had it been so well organized and where was the other couple, the scientist inquired. 'Simple,' explained the gardening Frenchman. 'For three months, he was her lover. For three months, I was. Now it is his turn again and they are off somewhere while I do the gardening.'

Finally, at the Russian island, the scientist came upon the two men holding a meeting, seated at a green felt-topped table, drinking bottled *narzan*, soda water, and making boring speeches to each other.

'Where is the woman?' the scientist asked.

'The masses,' declared one man with masculine condescension, 'are in the fields working.'

Among educated people, such attitudes are more muted. In some families we knew, the wife was more assertive than the husband and, as my experience with Mariya Fyodorovna showed, career women are occasionally more outspoken and self-confident than men. But in my experience, these were not the typical cases. In Russia as in the West, women generally defer to men, wait on them, play a more retiring role, and complain that male officialdom treats women less seriously than men. On occasion, I have seen educated men treat serious matters as 'not for the wives', much as stuffy European diplomats cling to their segregated, after-dinner cigars. Once I asked a dissident who was campaigning for human rights why more women did not sign dissident statements. 'If women signed those statements, people would laugh at it,' he said. 'You don't understand that we still live in the Middle Ages.' Another time, I was talking with two young establishment husbands about Solzhenitsyn's *Gulag Archipelago* which they had surreptitiously read and found impressive and devastating. Yet when I asked one of their wives her opinion, she shrugged helplessly. 'Oh, we don't give those books to our wives – we just read them ourselves,' her hus-

164

band hastily explained, oblivious to the slur on her intellect. In fairness, he represented only part of the story for we knew other couples where husband and wife shared their intellectual life fully and equally.

Moreover, in most Russian families, the women take such complete responsibility for managing the household that husbands simply turn over their paychecks to their wives as a matter of course and leave the rest to them. In Estonia, a Russian bank cashier told me she was having trouble with her Estonian husband because, in typical Estonian tradition, he wanted to control the family budget whereas she wanted to follow the Russian custom of the woman managing the finances. This young lady mentioned several other mixed Estonian-Russian couples with similar problems. In some cases, she said, the ethnic frictions ended in divorce. Ordinary Russian women take it for granted that they are the binding force in the family and sometimes laugh at the helplessness of their husbands. 'My husband can go out and buy the bread or milk, simple things like that,' a waitress in an airport restaurant told me with a twinkle. 'But I can't trust him with anything bigger. If we wanted to buy something really big, like furniture, we'd save money and decide on it together. Otherwise, I buy everything – even his clothes. I always go with him. If I didn't, he'd come home with terrible junk.'

Her assumption of responsibility is shared by most Russian wives though in practice it is limited to the chore of keeping the household afloat and functioning and minding the children. The man is the real head of the household. I recall one leading Russian journalist, back in Moscow after a visit to the United States, unhappily contending that 'American men are under the thumbs of their wives'. When I asked him why he felt this way, he told me about an evening he had spent at the home of a well-known Washington journalist. 'He was busy all the time fixing drinks, cooking steaks, and I fell under the power of his wife,' the Russian complained. 'The whole evening I had to listen to his wife talk – about clothes, children, prices, shopping, women's talk. It was awful. I hardly had a word with the poor man. If that is your women's liberation, I hope we don't get it here.' What appalled him was not only that this American woman was boring but that her husband had accepted such a subservient role.

* * *

As Mariya Fyodorovna's experience suggests, the male vacuum of the immediate postwar period drew millions of women into the economy and was the springboard toward success for some of today's middle-aged women. Women now account for nearly one-fourth of the Soviet equivalent of Ph.Ds, close to one-third of the ordinary judges, nearly one-third of the 1,517 members of the Supreme Soviet (parliament), about 70 percent of the doctors, and about 15,000 members of the professional unions of journalists, writers, artists, architects, composers and film workers. More than five million women have had some higher education, not too much of a lag behind the men. In part, this is a result of the lopsided feminine majority in the population after the war. Yet even as peacetime birth rates have begun to even out the Soviet population and build up the male share, the government has kept up intensive recruiting to draw every possible woman out of the household into the labor force. Women are actually a larger proportion of the work force today than in 1950. During the 1960s, more than 16 million additional women were put in jobs – a staggering figure. Even though the rate of growth slowed in the Seventies as the reservoir of unemployed women was depleted, roughly 60 million women were at work in 1974, close to 85 percent of all working-age women – the highest percentage in the industrialized world* (in America the figure was just about 50 percent).

Most Soviet women by now take a job as part of the natural order of things and find it hard to imagine not working. So strongly ingrained in them is the work-ethic that there is a stigma to being simply a housewife. The weight of propaganda steadily emphasizes the *duty* to work. One movie, *Let's Live 'Til Monday,* for example, showed a teacher publicly criticizing a tenth-grade girl for answering a free essay question, 'What do you want to be?' by saying her dream was to become a mother with many children. The teacher castigated this as a shameful response. For many Soviet women, the traditional American woman's role of homemaker, mother, raiser of children does not seem adequate; they feel unfulfilled without a job. Even some whom I heard complain

* For help with these and other statistical computations on working women in the Soviet Union, I am indebted to Murray Feshbach, a specialist on Soviet labor resources and manpower problems for the U.S. Department of Commerce.

bitterly about having too much to do, said in the next breath that they reluctantly preferred the exhaustion of too many burdens to the 'spiritual death', as one young teacher put it, of being unemployed, bored and idle at home.

But this is more than the urge to work. It is a matter of total life-style. For not only is Soviet society geared to get women into jobs but home life, especially in the cities, has much less to offer than in the West. Apartments are small and confining. Few urban couples have more than one child. Most sports and other leisure hobbies are a luxury. Russian women have no parallel for the range of volunteer and community activities or adult education enjoyed for their own sake which absorb so much of the time and energy of non-working American wives. Only at work can most women have a life of their own.

'Don't American women want to get out of the house?' Zoya, a 30-year-old Intourist guide, asked incredulously when Ann mentioned that she had given up her teaching job to become a mother full-time. Zoya may have been a bit unusual for she admitted that she had no taste for childrearing (most Russian women dote on children). She had turned over her own baby at three months to her mother-in-law, a classic *babushka* (grandmother), who lived with the family. So Zoya was unsatisfied by Ann's explanation that raising four children as we moved from one foreign assignment to another kept her busy. 'Don't you want to work?' she demanded. 'Don't you want to earn money and get some independence?'

That feeling of financial independence is an asset prized by younger educated women especially. An attractive chestnut-haired divorcee with a nine-year-old son told me that having a career had been essential to her even daring to seek divorce. Without a separate income, she said, she would not have been able to raise her son on alimony (which, for one child, is usually one-fourth of the husband's salary). 'You don't have to listen to some man talk to you *that way* if you have your own job,' she asserted. Others simply enjoy the social life provided by working companions. Many an institute, factory or enterprise will organize group excursions, theater trips, nature outings and picnics – not just once-a-year holiday parties like those in American offices, but more frequent occasions, where the working woman can enjoy her time off apart from her family if she chooses.

Yet for all this, it is basically the economic imperatives –

167

both for the government and the individual – which really leave Soviet women no alternative but to work. Most of the day-care centers and other supporting institutions which Soviet propagandists so constantly ascribe to the state's benign solicitude for feminine liberation are actually indispensable requirements for keeping as many women as possible on the job. Several Russian women commented rather bitterly that the network of state nurseries, kindergartens and children's summer camps were less to aid their self-fulfillment than the fulfillment of production norms at the factory. Indeed, Western economists have noted that a fair share of the Soviet economic growth over the past 15 years has come through increasing the size of the labor force, especially by getting more women – and pensioners – to work.

On a personal level, few Soviet families could enjoy the luxury of having only one parent at work. Most fathers earn too little (average factory workers' pay in 1974 was $187 monthly) to support a family of three, let alone four or more. One of the most persistent reactions to American life that I encountered among Russians was their surprise that large numbers of American families could be supported by the father alone. Even middle-class Russians, who were my counterparts in Soviet society, were incredulous that in a family of six, my wife did not have to work to contribute to the family budget. Finances in Russian families with children are often so touch-and-go even with both parents working that some women do not even use all the unpaid maternity leave to which they are legally entitled because their families cannot afford to live on the husband's salary alone. I knew one couple where the husband, a government worker, made a good salary of about $350 a month, yet his wife went back to work after only nine months' maternity leave because they felt a financial squeeze. For the overwhelming majority of urban women, the practical choice of not working simply does not exist.

One irony is that these financial imperatives have created a strong undertow of what might be called a counter-lib feeling among some educated Soviet women – in my experience, the same, well-educated, rather well-heeled segment of society which in America has furnished some of the most vigorous and active women's libbers, for whom a career is the panacea. Where the Americans are rebelling outwardly against having to be housewives, the Russians are rebelling

168

inwardly against having to be breadwinners, a necessity that can transform work from a means to self-fulfillment and independence into drudgery.

I have heard quite a few educated Russian women voice resentment at having to work. A literary critic in her sixties said that three of her four grown daughters, all with higher education, would much prefer not to work. A mother of three, related to a famous poet and financially well enough off not to have to work, mentioned the envy of her friends at her freedom from work. Others said privately that they would prefer part-time jobs, if the Soviet system were flexible enough to allow that, and occasionally the idea surfaces briefly in the press, but it never gets seriously developed because it obviously goes counter to what the authorities want. I remember the wry reaction of one veteran woman editor, whose years in publishing houses and on newspapers had left her with perennially weary eyes, when I asked her reaction to American style women's lib. 'Away with your emancipation!' she retorted. 'After the Revolution when they emancipated women, it meant that women could do the same heavy work as men. But many women prefer not to work but to stay at home and raise their children. I have one child but I wanted more. But who can afford more children? Unfortunately, we cannot *not work* because the pay our husbands earn is not enough to live on. So we have to go every day and make money.'

In their careers, many Soviet women complain of discrimination just as vehemently as Western women. Superficially, this may seem surprising because women are so visible in Soviet public life. For Soviet politicians are just as sensitive to a show of 'ticket-balancing' as American politicians are and usually arrange to have women's representatives or women's delegates prominently placed at any public occasion. Propagandists never tire of boasting about Soviet women in figurehead positions, disregarding the reality that men really run things. The press, for example, brags frequently that more women sit in the Supreme Soviet 'than in all the parliaments of the capitalist states combined.' But this is a spurious comparison. The Supreme Soviet is for show, a sweetener for women (or minority nationalities) that often misleads foreigners. It is a rubber-stamp body that has unanimously approved every single measure put to it.

Within the Communist Party, the real apparatus of power, Soviet women have fared no better and probably not as well as American women in the political life of their country. Not one of the 15 members of the ruling Politburo, which makes all the key decisions, is a woman. Nor is there any woman among the nine national secretaries in the Party Secretariat, which runs the day-to-day operations of the Party. Half a dozen women are members of the powerful 241-member Party Central Committee, a proportion slightly smaller than the number of women in Congress (though a couple of these women were token representatives of labor rather than people of real power, as most Central Committee members are). Like America, the Soviet Union has notably lagged behind countries such as India, Israel, Ceylon or Great Britain which have put women at the head of their governments or a major political party. In roughly six decades of Soviet power, the one woman who made it into the Politburo was Yekaterina Furtseva, a favorite of Khrushchev who was soon demoted but served from 1960 until she died in 1974 as the only woman in the Soviet Cabinet. Even at Republic and provincial levels, almost no women have risen to positions of command. America may have had only four women governors, but no women have had comparable posts of power as Party bosses of a Republic or a major province. Occasionally in Russia, as in the West, the inbred unselfconscious male chauvinism comes out in embarrassing ways, but none during my tour topped the official announcement of the Soviet Commission for International Women's Year in 1975 – headed by a man.

In the economy, the picture for women is better but not a great deal. Khrushchev, in a candid observation to a large meeting of agricultural supervisors, is supposed to have surveyed the scene and remarked disapprovingly that 'it turns out that it is the men who do the administering and the women who do the work'. Women do comprise roughly half the work force in industry, yet nine out of ten plant managers are men. Women represent nearly half of those engaged in scientific work but only ten percent of the senior professors or members of the Academy of Sciences. Close to three-fourths of Soviet schoolteachers are women but three-fourths of the principals in the basic eight- and ten-grade schools are men. About 70 percent of the doctors are women but men get

170

the lion's share of the prestigious jobs as top surgeons, department supervisors or hospital directors. Those figures may not compare too unfavorably with the West, but given the numbers of women in the Russian work force, they do undercut the contention that Moscow is far ahead in granting women equality.

In Russia, equal pay for equal work is an accepted principle, but getting the equal work is the problem. Millions of women are shunted into the lower-paying, less prestigious fields. Teaching and medicine are prime examples. These are practically at the bottom of the pay and status scales and these are the professions in which women are most heavily represented. In industry, women work mostly in the light, consumer sector where, according to Soviet studies, pay and all other benefits are well below those in heavy industry (where men predominate). In farming, women provide the core of the low-paid, unskilled field hands while men operate the machinery and get better pay. Perhaps most indicative of the situation nationwide, one major Soviet economic study drafting a working-class family budget assumed that the husband would earn 50 percent more than the wife.*

When women do break into more desirable careers, they often complain of a double standard. 'I used to work in a design bureau with about 10 architects, all women, but the chief of our section was a man,' an articulate lady architect in her mid-thirties told me. 'He was a very mediocre architect and everyone knew it, except him. Some of the women were mediocre, too, but some were quite talented. One of the talented ones should have been the section chief on the basis of merit alone. There was a lot of resentment against this man who was conservative, not very bright, and who would reject projects with unusual ideas. It was impossible to argue with him. He would say, "Oh, you are just a bunch of women with silly ideas." And if you argued that sex had nothing to do with designs, he would say that he had to clear the drafts with his superiors and they were all men. So he would insist that we do it over again. It was frustrating.'

'Women don't like that sort of thing,' chimed in a slender blonde artist who had been listening, 'but we have to accept

* Cited by Mervyn Matthews, *Class and Society in Soviet Russia* (Walker & Co., New York, 1972) p. 82. The comparison between light and heavy industry appeared in a series of articles in *Literary Gazette*, November, 1972 through January, 1973.

it. What can we do about it? It is always said that men can take a more serious attitude toward their jobs than women because they do not have the distractions of children and housework, and no interruptions for childbirth. Men are simply regarded as superior.' What bothered her equally was that the double standards applied to private life as well. 'A man can fool around with other women, drink, even be lackadaisical toward his job and this is generally forgiven. But if a woman does the same things, she is criticized for taking a light-hearted attitude toward her marriage and her work.'

To American feminists, this comment may sound like a frustrating replay of their own problems. Yet there are some crucial differences between the predicament of Russian women and American women. For example, Soviet women already comprise so much larger a proportion of the work force than elsewhere that the most talented ones feel that women have earned a larger share of supervisory jobs. Nonetheless Soviet women lack a real public outlet to campaign for better treatment. While their problems do constitute one of the few areas discussed with some candor in the Soviet press, the censors obviously consider blunt charges of sex discrimination on the job taboo. Only veiled hints or occasional mention of outlandish cases get through so that improvements depend largely on masculine goodwill rather than the vigorous public pressures, political action or court cases that Western women can use as leverage.

Moreover, as a school teacher commented to me bitterly, 'In Russia, women do the dog's work' – the grubby, low-paying work that in America is consigned to blacks and wet-backs. Indeed, most Western tourists arriving in Russia for the first time are forcibly struck by Russian women cracking asphalt on the highways and hefting shovelfuls into trucks (while the male truckdriver watches), using crowbars to pry loose old railroad ties, sweeping streets or shoveling snow and cracking ice in winter, carrying hods, hoeing potato fields, slapping paint on buildings in the coldest weather, or heaving coal onto trains along the Trans-Siberian Railroad. 'How can one fail to feel shame and compassion at the sight of our women carrying heavy barrows of stones for paving the street?' Aleksandr Solzhenitsyn asked in his open letter to the leadership before he was exiled. Some Soviet officials privately share the embarrassment of having women work like beasts of burden, but many Russians are not shocked by it because it has been so long part of their scene.

Finally, the financial imperative to work and the chaotic inefficiency of consumer life puts the working Russian woman in a crucible that very few American women experience and that Soviet welfare programs only partially relieve. Soviet women find themselves inescapably mortgaged to two worlds: work and family. Unable to succeed in either they are left to race, as one Soviet writer put it, like 'squirrels in a cage'. This predicament is not unknown in the West, of course, but in Russia, it is the norm. In the words of one joke that a Moscow friend told to me: 'Under capitalism, women are not liberated because they have no opportunity to work. They have to stay at home, go shopping, do the cooking, keep house and take care of the children. But under socialism, women are liberated. They have the opportunity to work all day, and then go home, do the shopping, do the cooking, keep house and take care of the children.'

Several times when I asked Soviet friends about their lives as 'liberated' professional women, they recommended that I read a story called *One Week Like Any Other*, by Natalya Baranskaya and published by the magazine *New World* in 1969, under the liberal editorship of Aleksandr Tvardovský. Written in the matter-of-fact prose of a weekly diary, it immediately touched off controversy because it so directly challenged the official slogan-image of the New Soviet Woman proudly and happily serving as 'a good mother and a good production worker'. It is now out of print but was more daring than what was permissible in the early Seventies.

Olga, the heroine, is caught in the dilemma of trying to hold a full-time job in a scientific institute, keeping up with new developments in her field, and trying to raise two small children without help from a live-in grandmother and precious little assistance from her husband, who is also a scientist. She is always late, always racing to catch-up, always tired and uncombed, almost never able to find a moment to herself, and afraid of losing her job. It is, as she says, a life of 'eternal haste, permanent anxiety, fear.' As her work week begins Monday morning, she and her women co-workers find a questionnaire asking how they allot their time. Among the headings is leisure.

'Akh, leisure, leisure – it's a rather awkward word,' she muses to herself. And then, satirizing official slogans, she thinks on, '*Women. Struggle for Cultural Leisure!* It is something alien – leisure. Personally, I am attracted to sports – to running. I run here. I run there. With bundles in each arm. I run up. I run down. Into the tram, into the bus, into the subway and out. We don't have any stores in our district. We have been living there more than a year, but still they are not built.' So Olga shops downtown and lugs home her groceries daily, fighting with the bus and subway crowds. At the office, someone turns up with two spare theater tickets but she must turn them down because there is no one to care for the children. Except for grandmothers and grandfathers, Soviet society does not have evening baby-sitters – Russian mores don't permit children to work for money.

American women with small children would recognize Olga's recitation of the ratrace of cooking, mending, tending, changing, washing, scrubbing, soaping, sweeping, vacuuming and falling into bed at midnight exhausted, only to wake in the wee hours to comfort a sick child and then drag herself, weary, from bed in the morning. But some things Soviet readers take for granted Americans would overlook: Diapers, as one Russian mother advised me; there are no diaper services, no buyable, disposable diapers, no rubber panties, so that each diaper must be immediately changed, washed, rinsed and hung up to dry on the radiator or a makeshift line in the bathroom. Soviet industry has not yet produced a clothes dryer. Washing itself is a nightmare. I knew one woman who, like many others, still did it by hand in old zinc tubs, sometimes in cold water, in an old building that had no running hot water. But most women in big cities now have small Soviet washers. They are called semiautomatic, but they take constant attention and manual operation – put in the clothes, turn on the tap to run in water, turn off the tap, push prewash button, come back in a few minutes, turn off the machine, set the switch to drain, wait while it does a feeble spin-dry, pour in fresh water, and so on. On some models, rinsing requires lifting out the clothes and doing the rinse by hand in the sink. Soviet models do three-to-four pounds per wash compared to 14 or 15 for American models so that a small laundry can take all morning. Dishwashers are unknown. Refrigerators either come without freezer sections or they are so small that frozen TV dinners are out. They do

174

not exist, anyway. Precooked or ready-to-cook meals are almost nonexistent, though some restaurants have carry-out service. Mostly, women cook meals from scratch. That makes for a plain diet. Olga, for example, serves eggs, cheese, sausage, potatoes or buckwheat porridge at night.

In the middle of her week, over sandwiches at the office, she and her co-workers fall to discussing another point on the questionnaire: why don't Russian women have more children? And do women have children for personal reasons or in the public interest? (A question that reflects the official drive to promote larger families, especially among ethnic Russians, because the leadership is worried about Russians being outnumbered by more prolific ethnic minority groups.)

Olga raises her hand to speak and, sarcastically mocking the stilted rhetoric of Soviet propaganda campaigns to stimulate 'socialist competition', she declaims:

'Comrades! Permit a multichilded mother to have a word! I assure you that I gave birth to two children exclusively for state considerations. I challenge you to a competition and I hope that you defeat me both in quantity and quality of products.'

An empty argument boils on in that same sterile language while Olga privately recalls how she dreaded her second child. Kotik, her son, was only 18 months old when she discovered she was pregnant again. 'I felt horrid; I wept. I signed up for an abortion,' she remembers, 'but I didn't feel entirely in favor of it.' A sympathetic doctor coaxed her out of abortion by encouraging her to hope for a daughter. Her husband, Dima, wanted the abortion, but he relented and took a second job when she quit work to give birth and nurse the baby.

One of the more unusual passages is the open criticism by both husband and wife of the much-vaunted Soviet nurseries for one-to-three-year-olds. They complain that 28 children in one group is too many for one 'upbringer' to handle. They are disturbed that their little daughter misses Olga so much that she clings desperately to her at night and resists going to the nursery in the morning. And they are upset that their children so frequently get sick from other youngsters. In all, Olga has missed 76 days (nearly one-third of her working time) in the past year for children's sick leave. But fearing the consequences of missing yet another day, she takes her daughter to the nursery one morning despite a night of vomiting.

Yet so essential is a job to Olga's self-esteem that she reacts in fury at Dima's suggestion that she quit work for a few years to concentrate on raising the children. 'Do you want to destroy me?' she shrieks in tears.

Olga's work week is not entirely without bright moments – a brief period in the library reading international scientific journals and leafing through other foreign magazines; a small triumph when an under-the-table tip gets her a cute haircut after the regular hairdresser carelessly leaves her face looking like 'an equilateral triangle'; an impulsive walk part way home to enjoy nature; sledding with the children and her husband between chores on Sunday. But the marital frictions are unrelenting, though Olga describes Dima as a good husband compared to others. He helps with the dishes, does some shopping, watches the children part-time on the weekend, and occasionally helps dress them. But Olga resents every moment he sits sipping tea and reading professional journals in the evening while she does housework. On Sunday night, after failing all week to find time to sew one button back onto her dress, she explodes when Dima asks her to iron his pants. Sunday night, she falls into bed overcome by life: 'I'm really lost – lost in a blind alley of chores and cares.'

To an outsider, the portrait may seem overdrawn. But several women told me they were 'real-life' Olgas, and I am confident that the Olgas far outnumber the success stories like Mariya Fyodorovna. The frequently published complaints of Soviet mothers about their household burdens and the rasping replies of husbands who refused to be goaded into doing more household chores were further confirmation that Olga's story reflected central tensions in many Russian families. The high divorce rate (about 28 percent in 1974 compared to 43 percent in America, though in Moscow it was said to be about 50 percent) is further evidence of the strains of modern urban life, intensified by pressures on working women and the housing squeeze which allows individuals little privacy.

Nonetheless, Olga's story was untypical in three respects: unlike most Russian urban women, she had a second child; she was lucky to get places for both children in day-care centers, something only about one-half of urban families can do because there are not enough places for all (in rural areas, only about one-fourth of the children can be handled), but she had no *babushka*, or grandmother, living in to care for the children when she was unhappy with the day-care centers.

Although life-styles are changing under the pressures of urbanization, the tradition of the extended family, where three generations from infants to *babushkas* or *dedushkas* (grandfathers) live all together, is still a strong Russian institution. Baby-sitters are built in. To me, one of the most attractive features of Russian life is the strength of family feelings and the deeply felt sense of responsibility from generation to generation. Indeed, so well known are the strong family ties that I was surprised to learn about the high divorce rate and the widespread practice of taking separate vacations – children off to a Pioneer camp and husband and wife going their separate ways at separate times. (Partly, this is because husbands and wives find it impossible to arrange simultaneous vacations, though a number of Russian men told me they preferred it that way. As one Soviet diplomat smilingly explained, it was not a vacation if his wife went along.) But in normal day-to-day living the family is of necessity very close. A *babushka* may add to the crowding and squabbling in the family apartment, but she is an indispensable aide to the working mother and very few families willingly get along without her. The recompense to the elderly is that in a society which has the reputation for cradle-to-the-grave welfare but which, from what I heard, has only a limited and not very attractive institutional system for caring for the aged, families care for their own elderly at home. Thus paradoxically at both ends of life – in childhood and old age – the system's deficiencies are strengthening the importance of the family.

The greatest tragedy for most urban Russian women, to hear them tell it, is that they feel forced by circumstances to forego the pleasures of having more than one child. 'Children are the greatest riches in the world and we have been deprived of them because people cannot afford them,' sadly mused a grandmother whose one grown son was an outstanding computer specialist. A dark-eyed woman, a writer, offered the bigger epigram that, 'Soviet women have been put into production and taken out of reproduction.' Literally dozens of other women, upon discovering that we had four children, would blossom with smiles and exclaim, 'You are rich people!' – meaning not wealthy but blessed. 'Very many women would dream of having two or three children, not just one,' a woman journalist commented. 'But that happens mainly in the countryside or in Central Asia. There isn't enough money, enough space, the right conditions for most people to have more than one child if they live in the city. We had one and that was all I could manage, and if you hear of someone with two children, it is some kind of heroism.' This sense of deprivation comes out not only in random conversations. *Literary Gazette* in July 1973 published a survey of 33,000 women which concluded that the vast majority of women want two or three times as many children as they actually have. Another survey reported that only three percent of the women thought one child was the ideal, yet 64 percent had only one child and 17 percent had none.

The state has tried to encourage larger families with all kinds of propaganda, including publicity about Mother-Heroines with ten children. Small taxes are imposed on bachelors and childless couples, and allowances of a few rubles monthly are paid to women with three or more children. In November 1974, the government instituted a new child-support allowance of $15 monthly to families where monthly income fell below $67 per person to help large families, but this seems too modest a measure in itself to stimulate bigger families and stem the steady decline of the Soviet birthrate. The natural population growth is now one of the world's lowest, less than one percent annually – a worrisome fact to a political leadership that regards large population as one element of national power.

For all their emotional attachment to children, many Russian women dread childbirth, from what some told Ann and me. This is partly because little pain-killing anesthesia is used, but probably more fundamentally because of the archaic Soviet attitudes toward sex education and general preparation for birth.

Western preoccupation with sex and sexual problems is matched by almost total silence in Russia. The one so-called sex manual that appeared during my time in Moscow turned out to be mainly a discussion of abnormal cases and of little use to ordinary people. Privately, Russians have a lively, earthy approach to sex-in-the-flesh whether on university campuses, in writers' homes or in any other mixed group setting that lends itself to promiscuity. Privately they relish dirty jokes and gossip about other people's infidelities. But in public, they have a Victorian squeamishness about candid discussion of the biology of sex, and 'in public' can mean just two people. Not only did I hear Western students express astonishment at the prudery and biological naiveté of young Russians, but periodically the Soviet press ran some pathetic lament from a pregnant teenage girl pleading for frank advice because her mother literally dropped her knitting when she mentioned the subject of sex. Still, the advice is not forthcoming except in the form of wary warnings that men are wicked, vulgar language is naughty, and chastity should not be surrendered lightly. So total is the sexual puritanism of Soviet public life, so much at odds with the free-love 'sex-is-a-drink-of-water' avant-gardism of the early Bolshevik years that, sitting in Moscow, I could hardly help but be amused by alarms in America that sex education in American schools was a Communist plot.

One practical impact of Soviet puritanism is that birth control winds up being more a matter of reacting after pregnancy than of planned prevention. To begin with, the arsenal of birth control methods and information about them is limited. Dr Yuri Bloshansky, the silver-haired chief gynecologist of Moscow, told me that five sizes of diaphragms are available to women but my Russian women friends said they could find only two and that, without jelly or cream, these were pretty useless. The supply of birth control pills, mainly a Hungarian variety known as Infekundin, was so limited and erratic that many young women dared not start for fear of running out at the wrong time. Those who had tried Soviet varieties complained of bad side effects – liver and blood problems – and doctors at one maternity home which I visited confirmed this as a serious problem. Soviet condoms are so thick and clumsy that they destroy all sexual pleasure and men told me they refused to use them. The loop, late in catching on, is coming into wider use. I was told most couples use rhythm or practice withdrawal. Not too surprisingly, then, when one American woman asked relatives in Russia what gift they would most appreciate, they said contraceptives.

For the main method of birth control is abortion, re-legalized in 1955 after Stalin had it outlawed in the Thirties.

Officially, an abortion costs nothing for a working woman and only five rubles ($6.67) for a woman who does not work, though several people told me that women, or girls, pay 30–40 rubles ($40–50) or more to get a private abortion if they want it hushed up or want to get into a good clinic and have nice treatment. Nominally, the Soviet medical establishment frowns on abortions. 'We do not consider abortion a good method of birth control,' Dr Bloshansky said. 'We prefer other methods – the pill, the loop, diaphragms, condoms, rhythm. But if a woman wants an abortion during her first three months of pregnancy, that is her choice. After that she can have an abortion only for medical reasons.' As with so many other fields, the Soviets do not publish abortion statistics – and have not done so for years. 'For each birth, we figure two abortions,' Dr Bloshansky said. 'In Moscow we have almost the same statistics as New York – about 200,000 abortions [in 1973]. That includes both abortions and miscarriages. Abortions are about 85 percent [or 170,000].' If that were typical nationwide, it would mean roughly five million abortions annually – a staggering figure but one that cannot be confirmed.

What was clear to me, however, was that many women have repeated abortions. Having two or three is common. Nurses in Moscow and provincial hospitals spoke of women having four, five, six, and I heard higher figures, too. Soviet doctors, though they try to discourage abortions, say that medically there is no limit to the number that one woman can endure so long as she is in good health and there is at least a six-month interval between abortions. The official explanation from officials like Dr Bloshansky is that all are done with light anesthesia and by the modern vacuum suction method, as may be the case in the best hospitals. But women who have been through more ordinary gynecological hospitals complain of unsanitary, overcrowded and unpleasant conditions and say the old scraping method is used. 'It's like an assembly line, very crowded and you hear the others being sick and nurses shouting at them,' one pretty young married woman recalled. 'The atmosphere is traumatic. Any kind of gynecological care is so unpleasant, even at a gynecologist's office, that any woman puts off going as long as possible. I found having an abortion a very unpleasant experience.' Nor were her feelings unique.

More than one Moscow husband joked that the primary

methods of birth control were the housing shortage, the total lack of double beds in the Soviet Union, and the exhaustion of their working wives. 'The married Russian woman who already has a child has no time for sex,' groused one frustrated middle-aged husband. 'By the time she's finished doing everything else, she's too tired for sex,' his wife agreed. And that is obviously a common feeling for I remember an audience at the Moscow Art Theater getting a great kick from a line in Chekhov's *Sea Gull* when Masha, an unhappy young woman, leeringly comments, 'When I marry, there will be no time left for love.' And with the way she said 'love', the audience took it physically.

Some women privately retort to the complaints of their husbands that the way Russian men make love, the women do not get much sexual satisfaction anyway. 'There is no question of being satisfied sexually,' said one woman, an unusually candid Jewish writer. 'That is why it is not discussed. It is considered shameful to discuss. It's no problem for *them*, but for us? . . . ' She said a doctor had told her of women who were afraid to reach climax because they feared it might increase chances of becoming pregnant. The writer's husband, a scientist, tacitly agreed with her assessment of the love-making of Russian men for he told me that on travels to the Caucasus, he had heard the dark-haired, dark-eyed Georgians, known as a race of Romeos, boasting that Russian women liked to sleep with them because they paid more attention to the pleasures of foreplay than Russian men who have a reputation for a slam-bam-thank-you-mam approach to sex. Nonetheless, Soviet demographers report that extramarital and premarital sex is on the rise in many age groups, so much so that one study published in *Our Contemporary* magazine in June 1975, disclosed that one out of ten children is illegitimate, or about 400,000 every year.

Childbirth in Russia is very different from in America. Some women, but not a lot, take natural childbirth courses. (They are told to breathe deeply because oxygen helps relieve pain, and except for novocaine, anesthesia is not often used.) In theory, women go to their local district maternity home, but in big cities many prospective parents shop around to find the maternity hospitals with the best reputations. One couple in Leningrad told me they blamed poor medical practices for the loss of a first child, a breech birth, and they carefully researched several others before picking the best maternity hospital in the city for the second birth.

There, as elsewhere, the wife was kept for more than a week. Soviet doctors, who hold new mothers for 8–10 days, are shocked that American women are allowed to leave the maternity hospital in 3–4 days. Another Soviet practice is to keep husbands and other relatives segregated from mothers and new babies. They are not allowed to enter the hospital except to bring needed items from home, and nurses are strict about what is allowed.

'Haircurlers are absolutely forbidden – I don't know why,' Viktor Grebenshchikov, one of our office translators, told me just after the birth of his daughter, 'and the nurses seem to have an uncanny way of spotting haircurlers no matter how they are hidden in packages. Only new books are accepted. Old books are rejected – perhaps it is dust. The hospital food is pretty dull, so the women all want food – cookies or chocolates, cheese and sausage – but the nurses have a list of what is permitted and what is not. It doesn't matter because we have a system for getting around all these restrictions. The relatives all gather outside the windows of the maternity wards and the women lower down strings. We tie things onto the strings to be hoisted up. It is a marvelous scene: Fathers and brothers and grandfathers, all happy and delighted, passing up little bundles on the strings. Unfortunately, my wife is in a room on the third floor directly over the nurses' room. Before we can tie on any packages, our group of fathers has to make sure that the nurses are not there. So we have some volunteer go to the message room [for official transfer of messages to mothers] to make sure the nurses are busy down the corridor. Then hurriedly, everyone ties the packages on the strings and the mothers are shouting down at us from the third floor and relatives shouting up answers. Everyone is in a good mood. The strings are left behind by each group of mothers as they leave – for the next group.'

It is a quintessential Russian scene: an unnecessarily complex set of rules laid down by hospital authorities, ordinary Russians engineering ways to beat the system, and the nurses probably fully aware of what was going on, simply blinking at the practice. To the foreigner, it is touching, amusing but a bit bizarre that people have to go to so much trouble. To Russians, it is perfectly natural – that is the way so much of life operates. And they take special delight in their small private victories.

The rules carry over into the early days and weeks of parenthood. In maternity hospitals, mothers have to wait 24 hours to see their babies who are very tightly swaddled – legs, bodies, and arms, in the traditional Russian *kosinka* – a mummy-like wrapping. The freedom of movement given American babies is not permitted. If hands are left free, a Russian nurse told me, babies will scratch their eyes and cheeks. Legs must be held out straight. Only the little round head peeps out from the *kosinka*. Russian babies are always laid out on their backs. Viktor, our translator, voiced the Russian belief that babies laid on their stomachs would suffocate, and was skeptical when we mentioned that millions of Americans had begun life on their stomachs. Most Russian babies are nursed, often up to a year. Doctors and mothers believe in the natural way. Besides, practically no ingredients for bottle formulas are sold. Many urban Russian parents regard the instructions of the local nurse or pediatrician as law. The Soviet market cries out for books like those by Spock or Gesell. Soviet counterparts are too stuffy and formalistic to be of much practical use, a young Russian mother told me. Spock was her favorite, and evidently for many others because the translation sold out long ago.

Despite the impression in the West that Soviet children are almost automatically turned over to well-subsidized state nurseries right from the cradle, it came as a discovery to me that most preschool children are actually raised at home. The main reason is that although subsidies put the cost of day-care centers as low as $14 a month to the parents, the state had enough spaces in 1974 for only about one-third of the 30 million preschool children from ages one to six. The older three-to-six group is better covered than the one-to-three group. Cities are about twice as well served as rural areas, though city women frequently have to hunt for spaces and occasionally protest to the press about long crosstown bus rides to distant and inconvenient nurseries.

At Kindergarten-Nursery No. 104 in Southwest Moscow, Zoya Lissner, a cheerful blonde mother and Communist Party member, told me how she had reluctantly surrendered a good $265-a-month job at Likhachev Automobile Plant, one of the high prestige plants of the country, when her son was born. She could not put up with the crosstown work and nursery runs and decided to raise her son at home for the first three years. Eventually, she was able to place him in the local kindergarten by taking a $100-a-month job there herself as a nanny.

I found her case significant because it reflected not only on the shortage of space in nurseries but also on the preference of a fair number of women – and the better educated, the higher the proportion – for bringing up children at home rather than turning them over to nurseries. Most Soviet mothers are enthusiastic about kindergarten playschools for three-to-six-year-olds. Blue-collar mothers often have no choice but to use the one-to-three-year-old nurseries to protect their factory jobs. But apparently a growing number of urban women, especially professional women who can sometimes arrange part-time work, dislike using nurseries and make great efforts to avoid them. 'The children can learn from grandmother and they are better off with her,' said a lady lawyer.

Nor is this merely the reaction of mothers. From time to time, respected Soviet scholars voice misgivings about group upbringing during the first three years. In September 1974, the noted demographer, Viktor Perevedentsev, wrote in the monthly *Journalist* that 'negative aspects' of nurseries 'are becoming more clear: a lag in education compared with "family raised" children [and] a greater rate of sickness.' He recommended cutting back on nurseries and using part of the funds saved for expanding kindergartens rapidly for the older group as well as 'paying mothers an allowance to enable them to raise children of nursery school age by themselves'.

This would involve a major break with the state's policy on working mothers and a significant revamping of the day-care-center system. Hence, the surprise in some quarters that Perevedentsev's critique appeared, though it was only a few sentences buried at the end of a long article extolling the Soviet social welfare system. But Perevedentsev said other demographers shared his views, and the fact that his article appeared in the organ of the journalists' union suggested backing from some fairly powerful people in the press and perhaps in the Government or Party. These proposals – to let mothers raise their own children in the early years and to give them some financial allowance for doing so – are privately welcomed by many professional women.

Probably the most moving appeal for turning child-rearing back to mothers has come from Arkady Raikin, the stage comic, who often ends his programs with a touching monologue on motherhood. It is about Slavik, a small boy, whose grandmother has died and whose mother has more than she can handle with her job, her shopping, her son and her housework. Because she cannot always be handy when the boy needs her, she asks neighbors to help. On the way to work, she calls on a pensioner in a nearby apartment to see that the boy gets up in time for school. She asks a nurse to feel his forehead on the way home from school, to make sure he is well. She asks the neighborhood cop to keep him out of fights. Then gently, Raikin concludes: 'I think that none of the people can replace a mother who sings lullabies, who can answer any question, and who feeds and comforts her child. Mothers should probably work less and pay more attention to their children. Everyone would benefit – children, parents, and the State.'

VI

CHILDREN
Between Parent and Teacher

> The school apart from life, apart from politics, is a
> lie and a hypocrisy.
>
> Lenin, 1920

Discipline, it turns out, is a problem in Soviet schools, too.
That is not the way it seems when foreign visitors enter a
classroom and girls in their black dress-and-apron uniforms
inherited from czarist times and well-scrubbed boys in bus
driver gray suits rise in unison and greet guests with a
chorused 'Good morning.' Nor is it what you would think
watching Soviet children leaving school in the afternoon
neat, mannerly and subdued, compared with the hectic,
kinetic spill-out of kids from an American suburban school
singing, shouting, teasing each other or racing in all directions with shirttails flying. But it is what Ann and I discovered when we went to our first parent-teachers' meeting
at Work-Polytechnical Middle School No. 30 of the Sverdlov
Borough, Moscow, attended by two of our children, Laurie,
11, and Jenny, 8.

With about 30 other parents, we crouched in the little
green wooden desks (attached in pairs as in an old country
schoolhouse) in Jenny's second grade while the teacher, Irina
Georgiyevna, a small brown wren of a woman, explained
lessons in grammar and short division and then read the riot
act to the adults for the behavior of their children. Like all
teachers, she was known by her first name and patronymic
and addressed students by their last names.

'Ivanov, A.,' she called out. Parental heads swung around
and scanned the room until a large man in the back, looking
uncomfortably out of place in his business suit squeezed into a

small green desk, raised his hand. Irina Georgiyevna lit into him.

'Your Sasha is regularly late to school,' she admonished sternly, while the other parents either stared at the father or self-consciously looked away. 'He comes in the middle of morning exercises. We begin at 8.15 and he arrives at 8.30. You cannot be late for your work like that. If you are, you are setting your boy a bad example. We cannot have one boy disrupting our class routine like that. I have spoken to him about it. But you know, it isn't the boy who is guilty. It is the parents. It is your responsibility as a father to see he is on time. Please look after it.'

The sharpness of her tone surprised me. Irina Georgiyevna was a short woman with wispy brown hair and a kind of uncertain look. She wore a large wool scarf over her shoulders, like a shawl. She had taught for many years. A couple of days before school opened, when we had gone over to meet the teachers and see the classrooms, she had been friendly and comforting to Jenny who was overwhelmed at going to a strange school in a strange language. But in the classroom, Irina Georgiyevna was anything but meek and mild. She was a firm disciplinarian, whether dealing with her 30–40 students or with their parents, whom she addressed in the same authoritarian manner as her second-graders.

'Semyonova, N.,' was her next target. More shyly this time, a mother's hand went up – it was mostly mothers who were there; only a couple of fathers. Irina Georgiyevna held up a notebook and turned the pages slowly for all to see. 'Look at this,' she said. Here and there I could see an empty page, a scrawl, an ink blot; one page ripped out and pasted in again. 'This is very bad work,' Irina Georgiyevna scolded. 'And this is typical of yourNadya. She is messy. Do you allow her to leave messes at home? Can she just throw her clothes anywhere? Here, you see,' and she pointed out what she regarded as an offensive page, 'she writes wherever she pleases on the page.' That particular page did not look so bad to me. But looking more closely, I could see that the child's letters were not all evenly placed on the lines, though the work was legible and otherwise reasonably neat for an eight-year-old.

'My God,' I winced inwardly, 'what is she going to say about poor Jenny who can barely read and write Russian.' Irina Georgiyevna spared us a personal critique, but she did not spare the Russian parents. One after another, she found

187

fault with their children at school or in their home upbringing. 'Kiryukhin,' she called out. 'He talks constantly in class.
He is always bothering the others. He can't stop talking.'
Then she mentioned another girl by name. 'Oh, she's a bright
girl but she cannot sit still, cannot sit straight. She wiggles all
the time.' Another boy was not only behaving badly in class,
she said, but he was arriving home at 3 or 3.30 in the afternoon, a couple of hours after second grade was out. This
meant, she declared disapprovingly, that the parents did not
know what he was doing, did not follow his behavior. She
went through a list of a dozen more children and concluded
by saying, 'I have a request for the parents of these children
– please put them in order.' Finally, Irina Georgiyevna went
to her desk and came back toward the cowed group of
parents with a miscellaneous collection of small balls, strings,
parts of plastic airplanes and tanks, and one open knife with
a hefty four-inch blade, like a fish knife. 'These things were
confiscated in class from your children,' she remonstrated.
Then she held up the knife for all to see. 'What is a second-
grade boy doing with such a knife? In school? Playing with
it in class?' she demanded. Silence. The parents accepted her
bawling out without complaint, protest or explanation,
acknowledging guilt by acquiescence and not challenging her
authority. From Russian friends we heard that such criticism
sessions were a regular ritual, dreaded and yet paradoxically
looked forward to by both parents and children, as a source
of considerable gossip afterward as both parents and children swapped stories from family to family about what the
homeroom teacher said about everyone.

Upstairs, in the sixth grade, the atmosphere was less tense.
By the time we arrived, Natalya Ivanovna, a pleasant, oval-
faced blonde, had finished her child-by-child critique and
was explaining the new geometry and algebra to parents,
some of whom were evidently out of their depth trying to
understand their children's homework. Firmly she cautioned
parents against doing the actual work for their children and
urged them only to check it over afterward. But her manner
was that of a friendly counselor, not a martinet. Once we had
sat down among the others, she reminded them there was an
American girl in the class and gave a public critique of
Laurie's academic work. It was even-handed, a balance between a frank assessment of Laurie's early shyness and a
modest compliment on her more recent recitation of

algebraic definitions. Laurie's grades were posted publicly on a bulletin board, along with everyone else's, according to the customary Soviet practice. In this class, the main bone of contention was that the art teacher had given out a lot of 2s (flunking Ds; 5 is the highest grade in Soviet schools) for what she considered sloppy work. One father complained that the teacher was being too strict in marking children down for not using a certain kind of graph paper that was then unavailable in stores. Natalya Ivanovna sympathized but no marks were changed.

In the larger, schoolwide parents' assembly, a visiting lecturer from a teachers' college told parents they should pay more attention to their children's television viewing habits. It sounded like something out of Scarsdale: a bad idea to ban television entirely but equally bad to be totally permissive. He recommended not only imposing time limits but also watching some programs with children and discussing them afterward to make television an educational, family activity. When he finished, one father rose to complain that there were very few programs for children under 14 and those few that did exist were shown too early for working parents to follow his advice. Other parental heads nodded. And after some discussion, the principal, Mikhail Petrovich Martynov, steered the meeting back to the school's real concerns: kids not doing homework, discipline problems, the need for parental cooperation. He did not go into details but Laurie and Jenny told us that spitballs and shooting paper airplanes behind the teacher's back is as normal for Russian boys as Americans. Girls got their long hair dunked in ink wells and fought back by jabbing the boys with sewing needles. Smoking was strictly forbidden but the boys' toilet during recess, Laurie said, was known for its mushroom cloud of smoke.

The principal, a balding grandfatherly man with steel-rimmed spectacles and a pleasant smile, was not so stern as the second-grade teacher had been. But I could hardly help reflecting on how different were the entire set of relationships from an American PTA meeting where parents go proudly to see their children's work posted on bulletin boards and to hear heart-warming praise of their progeny from homeroom teachers, and where if anyone raises public complaints, it is usually parents upset with the principal. I later learned that some Russian parents, like Americans, do work in class committees with teachers on discipline problems or such projects as helping poorer children get textbooks. Moreover, as the brief dialogue about television illustrated, better educated Soviet parents are less intimidated than earlier generations by educational experts or school officials and occasionally speak up at parents' meetings. At one Moscow school, a Russian friend recalled a mother who had the nerve to ask why the principal, also a history teacher, had been instructing history classes that Christ was one of the gods of Greek mythology. 'What are you attacking him for?' defensively muttered a *babushka* nearby. 'There are different theories.'

Overall, however, that first parents' meeting introduced us to several essentials of Soviet educational philosophy. The technique of public shaming for misbehavior or poor performance, brutal as it seemed to us, is central to the Soviet system, whether in bringing up children or making adults toe the line in any walk of life. From an early age, all learn the futility of arguing back with authority, of disputing public criticism, as the passivity of the parents indicated. What is more, everyone seemed to accept the idea that school is supposed to know best about bringing up children and that teachers should coach families and set standards for them, not vice versa.

A sharp dichotomy exists, nonetheless, between the supervised, rule-ridden lives of children in school, and the lax atmosphere at home where children are pampered, spoiled and protected. At heart, Russians are soft on children. The common rationale, which I have heard from officials again and again, is that children must be given privileged treatment 'because they are our future'. The real reason, I suspect, is more emotional. Russians are moved by sentimentality to dote on children: They envy and fancy the innocence of childhood.

At the farmers' market, the collective farm women loved to give free flowers and other little gifts to Lesley, our three-year-old, while they chucked her under the chin and muttered endearments to her. Stern customs inspectors would mellow at the sight of our children and let us pass sometimes without a check. Waitresses in restaurants, ignoring other customers, would stop and make a fuss over children. Once we arrived in Leningrad by car from Helsinki and the hotel administrator could not find a record of our room reservation. Although it was well past dinnertime and we were hungry, she told us to wait while she handled a group of 70 students who had arrived after us. But when I plopped Lesley on the counter, another room-clerk immediately took pity on us. 'Olga,' she gushed, 'they have a little one.' Rooms were hurriedly found.

This tendency has an official side, too. At collective farms I visited, the nursery was often the brightest and certainly the cleanest spot on the premises, an obligatory stop on the official tour of the farm because the powers-that-be were so proud of it. In the oil town of Almetyevsk, I was taken with a delegation of foreign newsmen to the Pioneer Camp of the local oil trust, also one of its proudest installations, and justifiably, for it was a pleasant, secluded, well-kept hideaway in the woods. In Murmansk, where for two months the sun does not rise during the long, arctic winter night, I was told that children were given top priority for fresh food, vitamins, and sunlamp treatments. At Nursery-Kindergarten No. 101, Ann and I watched one group of toddlers strip down to undershorts, don goggles and then, like players in a children's game, line their toes on a chalked circle.

'All right, children,' clucked Dr Tamara Ponomarova. 'Hands over your heads.' And fifteen pairs of hands wriggled in the air while bare tummies were bathed in the eerie iridescence from the ultraviolet sunlamp in the center of the circle.

'It's dark in here,' objected one tot with a hairbow, tugging at her sunglasses.

'Masha,' cautioned a white-gowned matron, 'don't take off your glasses.'

In a jiffy, they were turned around to be toasted lightly on the back side. The treatments, I was told, ran up to six or eight minutes a day at depth of winter. And in the dining room, the cooks showed us the little shredded-carrot salads and the slice of fresh lemon (for tea) given to the children. 'We save the best for the children,' Dr Ponomarova advised me. 'They are our future.'

At home, family life practically revolves around children, especially when they are small. So many urban families have only one child that all the possessive physical affection and intrusive fussing of Russian parents is focused on the one little creature. 'They treat us like dolls rather than people,' whined one unusually independent 14-year-old. This boy wanted to be more adult but most children bask in the spoiling given them. We had a language teacher who adored to dress up her little two-year-old Lisa in pleated skirts and to put white organdy bows in her hair. The father indulged Lisa with an extravagant array of stuffed animals and dolls, many of them imported; the kind of luxury he much more sparingly allowed himself and his wife.

A Russian art historian, with one daughter, tried to distinguish between Russian spoiling and American spoiling of children. 'You let your children *do* as they please and we *give* them what they please,' this woman said, 'and our children grow up selfish. Many times it is because the parents have had a hard life and they want their children to live better. But the children come to expect it and they do not appreciate it. I know a woman who works in three different places so she can have the money to buy her daughter the best clothes. The mother herself dresses very plainly. She takes nothing for herself. But the daughter thinks she must have the latest of everything, and she is not even grateful. In other families, children get the choicest portion of good food. If there is any extra on the table, it is always put aside for them.' Indeed, one family we knew, very well off because of the father's high position in a ministry, allotted black caviar to the six-year-old boy almost daily. Typically for a small boy he balked at the taste, while adults in the household salivated enviously. But all accepted the tradition of giving the best to the youngest.

Along with this spoiling goes lavish parental overprotectiveness. Its most obvious manifestation is the fetish for overdressing children to go outdoors. They are transformed into walking cabbages, stuffed with layer upon layer of oversized sweaters under a surrounding leaf of fur coat two sizes too large, and around it all, a scarf tied like a ribbon at the midriff. I never quite understood how these ambulatory balls of humanity got much exercise but the parental sense of protection was satisfied. And in the parks, I have seen many a *babushka* poised on a bench ready to jerk a small body to its feet if its wayward rump should accidentally settle into the sand of a sandbox. All Russian toddlers have to master the art of squatting to avoid the cold touch of Mother Earth that so worries their elders. When small fry play in the snow, parents hover over them protectively. When seven-, eight-, or nine-year-olds walk to school, along goes the *babushka* who usually lingers to take off their outer garments at school. It was striking to me how rarely we saw children under ten or eleven in public without some adult. And Russian parents were surprised that we allowed Jenny at 8 or 9 to ride the bus alone or with Scott, who was 5 or 6, even if only for a few stops to the American Embassy.

But let a child somehow get lost and Russians take communal responsibility for it. Friendly, protective hands materialize in a moment. Once in Gorky Park, when we were ice-skating on a small rink, a Russian mother rushed from a bench to gather up little Lesley who had been left to play in the snow at rinkside – though still where we could easily watch her. As Ann skated back, the Russian woman waved her away and volunteered herself as a baby-sitter for half an hour, seating Lesley on her lap and amusing Lesley with her own children, so that Ann could enjoy skating.

At home, parental protectiveness usually spares children from household chores. An auburn-haired journalist I knew was chagrined by the paradox. At school, she said, her 16-year-old daughter took care of her clothes, carried her tray in the cafeteria, took turns with other children dusting, washing windows, and cleaning up classrooms or the playground. 'But at home, Masha doesn't do anything,' this mother told me. 'She comes home, sits at the table and expects to be waited on. I told my mother to let her wash her own dishes. But mother made up some excuse: "Masha does such a terrible job – it's easier for me to do it myself." It's the *babushkas* who spoil them the most.' A Russian engineer, a father of three, called it 'a kind of Jewish spoiling – we fear for our chlidren, that they won't be healthy, they'll go off to the Army, that some misfortune will befall them – because we have seen so many hardships ourselves.' Let some family encourage self-reliance by arranging for a teenager to get a paying job and the community disapproves. A scientist told me about a doctor's family where the parents got their daughter a summer job as a clerk in a telegraph office. The girl was pleased, but when word got around to family friends, they considered it so shameful of the parents to make a youngster work that they hounded the parents until the girl quit the job.

The envelope of family protectiveness also makes Russian school children more dependent on their families than American children and less obsessed with the cult of their peers, though it is changing. School-age children have fewer games and diversions outside the home than in the West and are often thrown back on their families for entertainment. It is true that in summer, millions go off to Pioneer Camps, which vary in quality as greatly as adult institutions. The best camps, like stores for privileged adults, are very impressive (and hard to get into). More ordinary camps, I was told by a couple of boys, are pretty boring and rule-ridden. My auburn-haired journalist friend, explaining why her daughter didn't go, said that 'in summer children want relief from the discipline and at those camps, they have to "live by the bell" with exercises and activities all on schedule.' In the long fall and winter months, entertainment can be more of a problem. The circus, puppet theater and children's theaters are very popular as is ice-skating in the parks. Another big hit is the movie and television cartoon series *Nu Pogodi!* (Hey, Wait a Minute!) in which an evil wolf chases a lovable rabbit through all kinds of ridiculous escapades. Our children liked it as much as the *Roadrunner* cartoons in America. But pickings are slim compared to the West, and public facilities are far too few to handle more than a fraction of the demand. A Soviet diplomat just back from Washington, whom I encountered accidentally one day out picnicking with his family in the woods, volunteered to me how bored his children were with Soviet television and how meager the park and playground equipment seemed to them in Moscow (which has the best the Soviet Union has to offer). Perhaps less well-traveled children did not notice so much. The smaller ones play in courtyards outside, but older ones have a hard time finding the independence that youngsters seek around 12 or 13. The weather forces them indoors and they automatically become an appendage of the adult circle. No matter what age they are, children are usually taken along as a matter of course when their parents go out to call so that their own social lives are mainly as part of the family group, listening to adults.

Sometimes the close living in Soviet apartments makes for emotional and explosive disciplining, I was told, but the Russian families we knew were quite permissive. Several times I saw children act fresh, come and go haphazardly from the table, ignore repeated parental requests to eat, to be quiet, to sit still, and the parents let it go. I remember one seven-year-old child who spent an hour jumping on and off a chair and a bed only a few feet from the dinner table where we were eating and her family thought nothing of it. Nor is this just laxity in a few random families. A Moscow kindergarten director asserted to me that one major justification for Soviet kindergartens was to socialize 'only' children spoiled at home. A grade school teacher in Latvia told me that the conflict between family permissiveness and strict school discipline often causes tensions among children who miss kindergarten. This young woman was as critical of the rigidity in schools as of the laxity in homes. 'If the horse has been galloping fast and free,' she said, 'you can't stop him all of a sudden.'

Letting go of their children is something Russians find hard. The first day of school outside the red brick School No. 30 where our children went was a scene of such excitement and emotions that it reminded me of Americans sending children off to camp for their first prolonged absence rather than the mere surrender of youngsters for a few hours. Fathers climbed on windowsills and stood on their tiptoes to get snapshots of the children all lined up outside in the courtyard, class by class, in front of their teachers. Mothers shouted advice. Finally, the principal made a speech and the children marched into school. Not a few mothers were crying and I even came across an Army captain around the corner of the building wiping away tears. The Russian parents simply could not tear themselves from the school and began peering in windows. 'Please, parents of first-year students, don't put more pressure on your children,' the principal pleaded over a bullhorn. 'They are already excited. Please go home. Don't stay near the windows. Let them start the first lessons in a quiet atmosphere.'

People in the Soviet Union today still have the idealistic reverence for education that Americans had before the urban school crisis of the Sixties spawned disillusionment. Along with Communist Party membership, education is one of the two main avenues for moving up in Soviet society. It is still popularly regarded as a great social leveler though, as in America, reality is far from that ideal. But the first six decades have produced impressive educational achievements in mass terms. From an illiteracy rate of about 75 percent and a school enrollment of 10 million before the Revolution, the Soviet Union has moved close to full literacy and roughly 50 million children in its schools. Nor are these merely abstract statistics. I remember a toothy little Tadzhik peasant named Sultan Mirkhalov on a state farm outside Dushanbe whose family embodied the educational transformation that had taken place in three generations. John Shaw of *Time* magazine and I were taken to his home during an official tour and given a feast of lamb pilaff and local wines, served on the traditional raised outdoor dinner table typical of Central Asian homes. We were sitting as cross-legged as our poor unaccustomed Western legs would permit while Mirkhalov told us about his father who had been a poverty stricken, illiterate share-cropper before the Revolution. But now, he said, seven of his eight children had received high school or college education and the eighth, who was 11, would do so, too. Then, with great pride, he announced that at 54, he himself had been inspired by his children's example to 'go back to school'. He was taking a correspondence course in viniculture and other subjects and, he said with a chuckle, 'my children help me with my homework.'

Yet in spite of such achievements, stark inequities remain. The 1970 census showed that more than half of all Soviet adults had gone no further than seventh grade and only 5.5 percent had any education beyond high school. Also, in spite of a nationally standardized core curriculum set in Moscow, variations in the quality of Soviet education are so great that both Soviet and Western scholars now suspect that the educational system is rigidifying and reinforcing the class structure of Soviet society.

The very top schools are half a dozen specialized *phys-mat* (physics-mathematics) schools, patterned after the Bronx High School of Science in New York and reflecting the high prestige of science in the Soviet system. At one such school in Novosibirsk, I was told, 300 whiz-kids from all over Siberia are admitted annually out of a million who begin an academic Olympiad that selects the most promising talent. Like similarly competitive science schools in Moscow, Leningrad and Kiev, this one tapped university professors as teachers and experimented with methods far more flexible and stimulating than in ordinary schools. As a special question in one quiz, the rector told me, a teacher had asked students to propose substitutes for the internal combustion engine. In five minutes, one 14-year-old had come up with three ideas, two so practical that adult Soviet scientists were already exploring them. At the affiliated Club of Young Technicians, adults were pushing the far-out imagination of these bright youngsters to inventions. One lad had produced his own small laser machine. Another had devised an elaborate hydraulic push-me-pull-you machine for skimming across Siberian swamplands without getting stuck. Elsewhere, a few teachers' colleges run selective experimental classes where marking is done away with. We knew a family who were delighted to have their daughter in an experimental school where children were allowed to argue with each other in class and occasionally allowed to lead the class in place of the teacher – something unheard of in normal schools.

At the other extreme are poorly staffed and equipped rural schools, provincial schools which sometimes run on two and three shifts because of overcrowding, or the roughest schools in worker districts, some of which were described to me by Russian teachers as 'Soviet blackboard jungles'. Vasily, a dedicated young math teacher in a Moscow workers' district school, told me that 15 of his 80 eighth-graders had medical slips classifying them as mentally retarded or having a mental debility that excused them from exams or, in some cases, attending school at all. 'Dead souls,' he called them sadly. Along with a portion of able students, Vasily said he had many others who could not keep up with homework partly because of broken families or alcoholism at home. Still, he faced severe pressure from the school administration to pass all but one or two because of the official drive to claim that all children were getting secondary education, even if in name only. (Completion of eighth grade became the compulsory level nationwide in 1973.) So bad is the atmosphere in some blue-collar schools, I was told, that teachers will endure an inconvenient, time-consuming commute in order to keep jobs in the older, better schools in central Moscow rather than accept transfers to working-class schools closer to their homes.

'Practically all of my students are "illiterate" but I closed my eyes to that,' I was told by Nedya, a middle-aged woman who taught literature to eighth- and ninth-grade classes in Moscow blue-collar schools for years. 'Out of 40 students, I always have five or six boys who fight all the time, smoke and drink. They are real hooligans. They get into gang robberies

197

and some of the girls get pregnant. I had one 15-year-old girl last year who was in school for only half a year and was convicted of prostitution. But you can't give flunking grades because the principal wants to fill the quota for passing students. It has to get 98–99 percent. If the principals don't fill that norm, they get reprimanded. One teacher was fired a year ago for giving too many failing grades. The students know that. They will tell you right out, "You cannot fail me." Once I gave a C to one pretty good student and he was upset. "Why do you give me a C when you give a C to that other guy who knows absolutely nothing?" he asked me. I told him, "I want to pass that other boy out of eighth grade, so he can leave school altogether. Then next year I can teach you and the others who really want to learn!" '

What she meant was that after eighth grade, poorer students drop out completely or are shunted off to vocational schools. This has become a touchy issue. Periodically, the press runs unhappy letters from parents complaining that there are not enough places in ninth and tenth grades – college preparatory levels – for the eighth-graders. In our own neighborhood, children took a week of exams in eighth grade to be classified for specialties, and weaker ones were diverted into vocational schools, including one around the corner that trained garment workers. The problem has become increasingly acute because Soviet authorities have made a great push over the past decade to increase enrollment in high schools (ninth and tenth grade) without expanding higher educational institutions to match. Now, the state and many parents are in conflict – the state needing more well-qualified blue-collar workers and the parents intent on getting their children higher education and the more prestigious jobs that go with it.

What has apparently happened is that the Soviet intelligentsia has now become large enough to replenish itself, a change from the long period when revolution, civil war, purges and world war wiped out so many people that the state always needed fresh blood from below. Now, well-heeled parents who have their eye on the Soviet equivalent of the Ivy League – Moscow State University, Leningrad State University or a few other prestigious universities or institutes – make great efforts to place their children in 'special schools'. These, like the one our children attended, offer special courses in English, German, French, Spanish,

198

the sciences, or music (starting as early as second grade) plus a better caliber of general education. Since big-city Soviet schools run straight through from grade one to grade ten in one building, entrance is essential from the start. Technically, special schools serve geographical districts like others, but they do not accept all comers. Quietly, they weed out slow learners by giving unofficial entrance tests. Some neighbors told us that at our School No. 30, prospective first-graders were asked to read from a book (though normally preschool reading instruction is not given in kindergarten), to recite nursery rhymes, tell some fables, and to describe the different seasons. To grease the skids, many parents use influence and 'gifts' to school principals to get their children enrolled in these schools, if they live outside the neighborhood.

The class consciousness of parents, and sometimes the antagonisms between blue-collar workers and the intelligentsia, passes by osmosis to children. We knew a family who lived in a cooperative apartment building occupied by what Soviets call the intelligentsia (Americans would call it the middle class – engineers, scientists, army officers, educated people). Around them were all blue-collar workers' apartment buildings. The life-styles in the two groups, our friends said, were quite different. The talk among workers was about sports; the children were pointed toward sports clubs; and lights went out at 10.30. In the cooperative, people took greater interest in culture, gave their children music lessons and lights burned until midnight. Socially the two groups mixed little. Nor did our friends or other Russians know of more than a few isolated marriages across class lines.

Children from the two sets of families went to the same neighborhood school, but from an early age they had different aspirations. Workers' children expected to finish high school and become taxi drivers, policemen or factory workers and intellectuals' children expected to go to college. 'There are exceptions of course,' said our friend, a systems analyst, 'but basically, there are two groups and everyone knows to which he belongs. The children almost never invite home children from the other group. They sense the social difference. When they play together, they are enemies.' Then he paused, considering that too strong a word. 'Rivals?' I suggested. 'No, rivals is not strong enough,' he countered. 'Something between enemies and rivals. In any case, the children in the other buildings think of the children in our building as coming from the intelligentsia. They assume they are richer and they look up to them.'

Whatever the differences, one common denominator is the collectivist, political indoctrination to which all children are exposed in nursery, kindergarten or school. Academic instruction may vary but not social character training. 'The objective of educational work in socialist society is the formation of a convinced collectivist, a person who does not think of himself outside society,' a leading pedagogical manual asserted in 1974. 'The formation of Communist, all-people morals . . . is the unifying foundation of the requirements for teaching children.'* In other words, the main precept of Soviet child psychology is that by creating the proper group atmosphere, the school insures that children will grow up properly. Leonid Vladimirov, a former Soviet journalist who defected, explained that children at the tender age of three or four develop political antennae from the 'upbringers' in their nurseries. 'The young boy or girl gradually acquires what is an extremely important faculty in Soviet society. He develops an understanding of which questions one can ask or discuss and which ones must be avoided,' Vladimirov wrote. Beyond that, youngsters are instilled with a conformist, collectivist zeal. 'The greatest offense a child can commit in kindergarten is to be different,' observed Vladimirov. 'Few nations make it easy for the individual who wants to swim against the current of prevailing mores, but the Soviet Union makes it almost impossible.'†

The kindergartens that I visited, which Russian friends said were way above average, were usually bright, pleasant places, well-stocked with toys, plants growing in some corner and a smiling, benevolent portrait of 'Uncle Lenin' in almost every room. There, the children learned to play and work together, even to look after disciplining each other, under the warm but firm maternalism of the 'upbringers'. In Murmansk, at Kindergarten-Nursery No. 101, I saw one group of toddlers where the tea tables were perfectly set up for all the dolls. When the children started to play, large women in

* V. M. Korotov, *Razvitiye Vospitatelnyx Funktsy Kollektiva* (*Development of the Educational Function of the Collective*, Moscow, 1974), pp. 3 and 28.
† Leonid Vladimirov, *The Russians* (Praeger, New York, 1968), pp. 34–35.

white gowns enveloped one child after another and guided them, in warm tones, where to sit, how to sit, how to handle the dolls, how to play in general. Although this instructing, countermanding and supervising was done with obvious affection, it seemed bound to smother initiative and spontaneity. The children could hardly move without some instruction. Jean Ipsa, a young American child psychologist who was doing research at Moscow nurseries, was also struck by this 'very warm but intrusive' guidance. 'Psychologically, it makes the kids very dependent because they don't want to lose the warmth by doing something wrong,' she said. At Moscow Kindergarten-Nursery No. 104, the director, Lidiya Aleksandra Agareva, described to me how older children play scenario games where the teacher manages them from start to finish, arranging the games to teach the ethic of collective cooperation. And if a child was selfish or misbehaved badly? I asked. The punishment, she said, is usually exclusion from the game and ostracism from the group.

Although our five-year-old son Scott spent only about three months in Soviet kindergarten, we had an opportunity to notice the friendly but enforced conformism there. On one occasion, the children were being disciplined collectively for a good hour by having to sit still in their chairs. On another occasion, Ann came home talking about both the neatness and the uniformity of the art work. 'Twenty little children made clay rabbits and every one of them is the same size, the same shape, the same position. You couldn't tell Scott's from Masha's or Misha's!' she exclaimed in disbelief. Later, it was daisies – every picture showing the flower in the same position, with the same number of petals, in the same colors with the same three leaves on the stem. In Georgia, we saw an art exhibit by ten-year-olds – decorative, colorful, well drawn and the space well used, but there, too, no trace of individuality or spontaneity, in concept or technique. In vain, we looked for those artistic fantasies that most children love. This was socialist realism in miniature. The children were obviously imitating a teacher's model or each other.

One subject which little Soviet children are forbidden to draw, a former nursery teacher told me, is Lenin. He is too sacred, she said, 'and they draw too badly'. The political content of nursery, kindergarten and school propaganda, especially based on Lenin, staggers most Westerners. Russians say it is less oppressive and crude than under Stalin when children used to be instructed to scratch out the eyes or blacken the textbook portraits of high officials as they fell victim to Stalin's purges, used to sing worshipful hymns to the dictator, or, at the peak of the Cold War, learned slogan ditties against the West ('Stalin is candy, Roosevelt is yuk, Churchill is crap' – the words rhyme in Russian).

Now the emphasis is on patriotism and Lenin-worship. One Soviet reader begins not with Dick-and-Jane prose, but the assertion: 'The first country of socialism in the world became the first country of children's happiness in the world.' From two or three upward, children are immersed in songs, games and little holiday performances filled with red flags, scarlet banners, red stars, and paeans to the October Revolution and the Motherland – 'Best in the World'. One young Muscovite I knew recalled a kindergarten song in his childhood about a child who finds a button, gives it to a border guard, and that helps catch a foreign spy – with the obvious moral about avoiding foreigners. That song was missing from one current children's song book given to me but among patriotic songs, there was a heroic little tune about the border guard always on duty, eyeing ravines where an enemy might be lurking, ready to repel the foe.

Unlike the Stalinist era, no living leader is idolized; all affection is focused on Lenin. Two- and three-year-olds, teachers are told in their manuals, should be taught to recognize, love and respect Lenin's portrait; four- and five-year-olds, to decorate paintings of Lenin with ribbons and flowers on holidays; and six-year-olds, to lay flowers at his statue in their hometown. The innumerable songs about Lenin give him the aura of a combined George Washington, Santa Claus and Christ figure, the most perfect human who ever lived and, in the words of one tune, 'always the best friend of children'. Some songs imagine him coming back to life, playing hide-and-seek, picking strawberries, bouncing children on his knee, and the children loving him better than their own grandfathers, telling him, 'We want to be like you in every way.'

Not surprisingly, this political conditioning is heady stuff. I have listened to eager young children in an Armenian village, Baku, Moscow, or Murmansk, enthusiastically singing about Lenin. Our own Scott came home one day to announce that 'the czar was like the English king but Lenin's team was stronger and Lenin won!' When I mentioned this to a Soviet diplomat, he smilingly replied, 'Give us time. We'll make a Bolshevik of him.' A four-year-old nephew of some Russian friends, very excited one evening by holiday fireworks, asked his mother if he could shout. She agreed and this tot piped out with, 'Glory to the Communist Party of the Soviet Union' – a kindergarten outlet for holiday excitement. A writer told me he was mildly amused one day when his three-year-old daughter admonished him: 'Uncle Lenin says to brush your teeth every day, not the way you do.' But when he tried to use Lenin to reinforce family discipline, it backfired. He warned his daughter to behave 'or Uncle Lenin will eat you up.' Evidently the daughter carried word back to the teacher for she contacted the mother and humorlessly remonstrated that this was no way to talk about Lenin to children. But the biggest jolt came to a Swedish couple who had sent their six-year-old son to Soviet kindergarten. Trying to assert paternal authority over him one day, they asked him what grown-ups he respected. Instead of naming mother or father first, he said, 'Lenin.' Well after that, who? And the boy went right down the line through the Soviet political hierarchy from Brezhnev to the District Communist Party Secretary without mentioning his parents.

The sense of collective responsibility, disciplining, and group activities begun in kindergarten is carried forward through the school years in the classroom and in a succession of children's organizations – the Octobrists, Young Pioneers, and Komsomol. The Pioneers (9–14) have a Boy Scout-Girl Scout ethic of doing good deeds for the school and community, except that their indoctrination and activities usually have an ample political quotient, reaching a crescendo around Communist holidays. A scientist in his mid-twenties recalled his passion as an 11-year-old Pioneer for the romantic revolutionism of books about a youth named Timur and his gang that somehow mingled a feeling of links with the Red Army and its fight against Fascism during World War II to the gang's secret good deeds, recovering stray goats, helping foil bad boys who stole apples, and watching over the homes of women whose men had gone off to war. Now, Timur gangs have been institutionalized, to promote self-sacrificing, patriotic, collective exploits among youth. 'I remember how horrified I was,' the scientist went on, 'when I learned that capitalists encouraged their children

203

to make money by doing little odd jobs. I still find that un-attractive. Once I was in downtown Moscow when some Americans asked me for directions. From school, I under-stood a little English and I led them to the building where they were going. I was very offended when they offered me a tip.'

The classic Pioneer hero and martyr is Pavel Morozov, a 14-year-old who, in 1932, reported on his own father for hiding grain from the state during the harsh period of farm collectivization. The boy was murdered by private farmers who opposed collectivization. He was later immortalized by the Party. Pavel Morozov is less vigorously celebrated now than under Stalin, but the code of Young Pioneers still promotes not only civic duty but political consciousness among youth: 'A Pioneer is loyal to his Motherland, the Party, Communism. . . . A Pioneer has the heroes of the struggle and work as his models. A Pioneer keeps the memory of the fallen fighters and prepares to become a defender of the Motherland. . . .'

Many Soviet classrooms have a so-called system of self-discipline which amounts in practice to institutionalized tattling, in which one child, known as the *zvenovoi*, or leader of a link, reports to the teacher on the conduct of children in his row. Laurie and Jenny said this was not done in their classes, but it did go on in other schools. One Russian mother described the system to me this way: 'Each morning, the teacher asks for a report and first one *zvenovoi* gets up and says, "Sasha came to school late today," and the second reports, "Nadya did not finish her homework," and the third, "Petya was fighting with Marina and has a dirty shirt."'

Under another scheme, known as *sheftsvo*, the best students are designated by the teacher to help weaker ones with classroom work or homework. (Laurie used to help Russian children with their English lessons and vice-versa, though they did this out of friendship rather than because of en-couragement by the teacher, so far as she knew.) The *sheftsvo* and *zvenovoi* systems have greatly impressed some American educators – most notably Urie Bronfenbrenner, whose book, *Two Worlds of Childhood, U.S. and U.S.S.R.*, makes much of the collective responsibility Soviet children take for each other. Bronfenbrenner also favorably cited the practice of older children in Komsomol students councils summoning errant youngsters, such as a group of boys who went swimming one evening without supervision, and punishing them.

In real life, these systems work less ideally than in the model situations which Bronfenbrenner was shown. According to Soviet parents and children, most youngsters – especially those over 10 – roundly dislike the *zvenovois* and sometimes beat them up at recess for tattling. Others regard the behavior of model students, who get an ego-kick out of helping teachers or weaker students, as very much like teachers' pets anywhere in the world, girls being more zealous about it than boys. The unique Soviet element is that many teachers encourage children to report on each other's conduct and try to institutionalize the practice. 'They are training little informers,' said one mother bitterly. In lower grades it works; but by the time children are 11 or 12, our friends said, most children refuse to cooperate.

My own impression, moreover, is that Bronfenbrenner's prime examples – including the Komsomol student council – were really disciplinary techniques manipulated by adult authorities, coaching and using children as proxies, rather than student democracy and self-initiated responsibility at work. 'Children don't initiate organized punishment of each other,' one mother said, in answer to my questions. 'They go to those Komsomol council meetings the way adults go to their meetings. They can't not go. So they go and take their cue from the leader. They sense what is expected of them, and they do it.' Generally, Soviet youngsters are more 'law-abiding' than American children, but in my view this is primarily because they have been taught from nursery upward to submit to authority.

The obvious discipline problems that crop up by the time Soviet children reach 12 or 13 suggests that values of self-discipline have not been internalized in the absence of authority or strong group pressures to keep them in line. The corruption and furtive rule-breaking in adult society would tend to confirm this. At School No. 30, not only did our children notice classroom misbehavior behind teachers' backs and smoking in the toilets, but rather brazen cheating in class and the practice of teachers locking classrooms during recess to keep better control of children. Russian parents told us of similar precautions at their schools and teachers complained privately about discipline problems. They complained of difficulties with hookey, occasional vandalism,

205

drinking and what the Soviets loosely term 'hooliganism'. From time to time, the press carried articles that hard drinking as well as smoking begins around 14, that illegal 'radio hooligans' – young ham operators – interfere with government channels, and that juvenile crime is a problem. There are never broad enough statistics printed to allow comparison with other countries. I would guess that juvenile problems are growing but are not yet as severe as in America. During a candid morning with Aleksandr Semeyusov, deputy mayor of the Siberian city of Bratsk, I learned that among his city's major headaches were car thefts, radio hooliganism and delinquency among 14–16-year-olds. He told me the police force was being expanded with university graduates to try to cope with the most troublesome youngsters in a more sophisticated way. 'The problem of bringing up the young is everywhere,' he confessed with rare candor for a Soviet official. 'You have it – and we do, too.'

Academically, Soviet schools start late but move fast, much faster than early grades in American public schools. Children do not enter school until age seven and at kindergarten they normally get little or no instruction in the three R's. The first years quickly make up for that. A Soviet school reform in 1970 compressed work formerly done in four years into three. By the end of second grade, our Jenny had been exposed to the lower multiplication tables, some short division, number sets, algebraic concepts and other elements of the new math. Russian parents we knew were groaning at their inability to understand their children's homework, let alone help with it. We found the reading, grammar and penmanship impressive. So rapidly do Russian children move along that most American children transferring into the Russian system nomally go back a grade, and this puts them in with their normal age group.

One reason for the rapid progress, we discovered, is the workload. School runs six days a week and from September 1 to May 30 with very short holiday periods. Laurie and Jenny found the homework load heavy, and not just because they were foreigners. Russian children work hard too. 'I take about four hours a night and this is normal for good students,' a bright and conscientious 16-year-old told me. 'The poorer students have to work longer, I guess.' (Frankly,

I guess not, from what Vasily, the teacher in the blue-collar schools said.) Laurie put in a good four hours including language tutoring and homework sessions with one friend, Marina, without whose help she would hardly have survived in the early months. Russian parents have complained about the overload and even some Soviet pedagogues have wondered aloud in public whether the accelerated pace was causing tensions, illness and possibly impairing eyesight, but most students cope somehow.

The classroom atmosphere seems deliberately to over-compensate for the sentimental indulgence of Russian families in home life. Our girls were immediately told they could wear no rings, jewelry or cosmetics and were advised to cut their hair or keep it well combed back. Russian boys said that some instructors objected to Western haircuts and fashions. The uniforms lent the flavor of what I would imagine in an Imperial German *gymnasium* – which was where Stalin supposedly obtained the heart of the Soviet curriculum – or a strict American parochial or military school. Nothing could be further from the individual-oriented trends of American education in recent years. In general schools, electives are out of the question. Laurie's sixth grade had a dozen set subjects: math, physics, biology, Russian literature, Russian grammar, Russian Medieval history, geography, English, drawing, singing, physical culture, and work (sewing for girls, shop for boys).

The emphasis was on drill, drill, drill and straight memory work, often unchanged for generations. In literature, for example, Laurie struggled to memorize a passage from Gogol that her 26-year-old language tutor and our 55-year-old office translator had both memorized in their day ('What a wonder is the Dnieper River in tranquil weather when, smoothly and freely, it speeds its generous waters through forests, hills and dales. . . . '). Not only did algebra require memorizing rules, definitions and theorems to be regurgitated letter-perfect in class but singing required memorizing verses of Pushkin.

Written work was monitored with the finicky strictness of a French lycée. The younger children worked not with pencils and erasers or even ballpoint pens but with fountain pens. And as Irina Georgiyevna demonstrated in her lecture to parents, one blot in the copy book was as heinous a sin as in David Copperfield's day. Laurie submitted a drawing once for art that had taken her an hour and a half and the teacher rejected it because the pen line was too thick. It had to be done over. Blackboard notes recopied in student notebooks must reflect exactly the capitals, indentations, underlining and double underlining of the teacher's original or students are marked down. 'You have to line up your books and notebooks at the upper right hand corner of your desk, the edges in line with the front and side of your desk,' said Jenny. Laurie told us that Russian teachers did not like children going to the bathroom during class but permitted it only during recess. 'And you can't just get up and go to the pencil sharpener or get a drink of water if you're thirsty the way we could in Washington' [where she last went to school], she said. 'You are supposed to do that during the class breaks.'

American parents who worry that American schools are too achievement-oriented would boggle at the success ethic and failure phobia of the Soviet system. Performance is gauged almost daily in every subject when children are called on to recite their homework. (Other children often whisper helping words and phrases and some teachers wink at the practice.) And the daily grade goes in the book. Our children were amused that this mark-mania extended even to Physical Culture where Jenny said her second grade class was graded on somersaults and tumbling.

For the most part, little is done in Soviet schools to liven up classes. In the schools we visited, Ann (who is a former teacher) and I looked in vain for book corners or science tables and projects where students could work or dabble at their own pace. In Murmansk and Baku, I saw high school science classes which consisted of rote recitation, lecturing by the teacher or by his doing an experiment in front of the class. Although there was a separate science 'study room', I did not see enough lab equipment for the pupils to learn by doing. Their role was passive. Vasily, the young math teacher in the blue-collar schools, said dialogues in his classes were rare. 'Students almost never ask questions,' he said. Russian parents confirmed that their children's classes were teacher-dominated. 'In an American school sometimes you wander off the subject and get into a discussion that is interesting,' Laurie commented after her year was over, 'but it seemed as though that never happened in Russian school. You know how you can have some games, like spelling bees or mathematical puzzles or games? Well, they don't do that.'

I don't want to leave the impression that the institutional life of Russian children is entirely bleak and cheerless. In big cities like Moscow, Leningrad or Novisibirsk, I saw impressively equipped Pioneer Palaces or Clubs of Young Technicians where the most fortunate and energetic youngsters could join radio groups, make up their own inventions, film movies, go through mock training and exercises for cosmonauts, study animals or stuff birds. The big trade union federation, the Army, the police and other organizations sponsor sports clubs for youngsters. One uniquely Soviet institution is the sports school where potential athletes are selected at an early age and given daily training for sports careers. In the Central Asian city of Frunze, I visited a swimming school for 700 children where the coaches applied sink-or-swim tests to first graders and took only those who kept afloat and looked well-coordinated. 'As a rule swimming champions are 14 or 15 years old, so we pay attention to developing sports among children,' I was told by Aleksandr Kumysh, the director of the Frunze Agricultural Machinery Plant which sponsored the school. A coach explained that out of 1,500 children who try out annually for the school, less than one in ten is admitted. Then they swim an hour or more daily all through school and more during vacations. The same thing is done for soccer, track and field, for hockey players and other athletes. The difficulty for most children is that such schools and the programs of the big sports clubs handle only a privileged minority. For the rest, the diversions from academic life are more limited.

The positive side of the no-nonsense Soviet approach to classroom education is that great gobs of materials are committed to memory and children are drilled to mastery of fundamentals. In subjects like math and the natural sciences which lend themselves to that method in the early years, results are impressive. Laurie learned so much in a year of Russian school (where she half-skipped a grade) that she coasted for the next full year in mathematics in the Anglo-American Embassy School in Moscow. Another correspondent's son, Steven Shabad, who attended the same School No. 30 for four years in the Sixties, found himself excellently prepared in math and sciences when he entered Columbia University but way behind in essay writing and the humanities.

209

For the cost of the stifling conservatism of the Soviet method is in the lost spontaneity of students and in the Soviet system's failure to teach them to think creatively for themselves or to ask imaginative, probing questions. In sixth-grade math, Laurie's homework included a heavy dose of complex, intricate exercises that tested her ability in all the mechanical tasks she was supposed to master, but word problems were almost unknown. In class discussions, even at higher grades, precious little time or effort, if any, was devoted to Socratic dialogue. Nadya, the literature teacher, remarked that many Soviet teachers thought they were helping pupils 'to think independently and creatively – but in fact, they did the opposite.' Both she and others told us that the emphasis was on giving 'right answers'. This can be a problem anywhere, but it seems far more acute in Soviet schools because their authoritarian approach is aimed, as one teachers' manual put it, at correcting 'unfounded ideas, debunking incorrect, mistaken conceptions'. The humanities, especially history which treats the past and particularly the Russian past as one long ineluctable prelude to the glorious era of Soviet rule, are taught with simplistic ideological rigidity. 'The course of history at the secondary school must bring home to pupils that the downfall of capitalism and the victory of communism are inevitable, and disclose consistently the role of the popular masses as the true makers of history,' one Soviet syllabus asserted.* Steven Shabad told me that in his days in Sovet high school, 'We had one teacher in history who used to say, "Don't look in the book – think, think, think!" But she didn't mean, "Think for yourself." She meant, "Think: Remember what you have been taught." '

The problem of rote-learning has bothered not only a few maverick teachers and iconoclastic parents whom I happened to meet, but prominent Soviet educators as well. Periodically the press – especially the Writers' Union weekly, *Literary Gazette* – has carried fairly tart critiques of Soviet scholars for the mechanical stuffing of students with facts and figures that leaves them ill-prepared for university or modern application of their knowledge. Mikhail Prokofiev, the Soviet Minister of Education, scorned Soviet high schools in the late Sixties for drenching students with memory work and leaving

* Fred M. Hechinger, 'Education: Triumphs and Doubts'. In Harrison Salisbury, ed., *The Soviet Union: The Fifty Years* (New York, 1968) quotes this syllabus on p. 147.

'no scope for reasonable initiative'.

One of the primary impulses of the 1970 educational reform – undertaken, ironically, as an answer to the American reforms that followed the American panic after Sputnik in 1957 – was the desire to break out of the mechanical teaching methods. One of its chief prophets, Leonid Zankov, a senior member of the Soviet Academy of Sciences, wrote a book called *Conversations with Teachers* designed to show that children were far more ready for inventive, analytical, inductive teaching than most teachers thought.* His more flexible approach was adopted in some schools but the unrelieved complaints of parents and a few outspoken educators in the mid-Seventies indicated that the reforms had not really made much of a dent. Indeed, just before I left Moscow at the end of 1974, the assistant dean of Moscow State University's Philology Faculty lamented in the press that literature candidates were unhappily subjecting the classics of Chekhov and Pushkin to the schematized stereotypes of the class struggle because of the way literature was taught in Soviet schools.

Probably the sharpest blow to the spirit of educational reform and experimentation in recent years was the emasculation of Phys-Mat School No. 2 in Moscow in 1971–1972. As one of the half dozen elite schools for young scientific geniuses, it had flourished for several years, not only feeding top students into the best universities but regularly placing winners in nationwide student olympiads. Prominent scientists and other scholars had worked without pay in many cases to develop an experimental curriculum. To a Westerner the curriculum would not seem especially innovative, but to the Soviets it was a daring departure. University professors taught classes. I was told by former students and their parents that the school developed genuine intellectual ferment unique in Soviet secondary schools. One teenager said he had even discussed Solzhenitsyn's works with other students and informally with one unusually liberal and daring teacher. According to the *Chronicle of Current Events*, an unofficial human rights publication put out by dissident scientists and intellectuals until its suppression in 1973, students excelled 'in establishments of higher education, not

* Susan Jacoby, *Inside Soviet Schools* (New York, 1974) presents an excellent insight into the reforms and cites the positive application of Zankov's principles at Moscow School No. 607.

211

only by virtue of their high-level grounding in physics and mathematics but also because of their love of literature, their keen interest in social problems, the nature of the questions they asked lecturers in ideological disciplines, and their habit of not taking on trust anything that had not been proven.' Applications to the school soared to three or four times the number of places available.

As the logical extension of some of the educational reform theories, the intellectual climate at the school obviously troubled Communist Party conservatives. The percentage of Jewish students was very high and so was the proportion of Jewish scholars on the faculty, according to my Moscow friends. When in early 1971, one of the teachers, I. Kh. Sivashinsky, applied to emigrate to Israel, the authorities moved in on the school and began administrative harassments. According to Igor, a tall, lanky recent graduate, the pretext for administrative inspections was that New Year's Eve 1971 had been celebrated with a roulette game. Another pretext, he said, was that a group of students had visited the Jewish synagogue in Moscow and would have gotten away without trouble for the school except that one boy wrote the school's initials on a fence near the synagogue. Purges of the faculty and student body were carried out in spring 1971, and again a year later. In one action the director and three assistants were fired; later, teachers of history and literature were forced out, an indication that the real reasons for the purge were ideological. Several other teachers, I was told, resigned in protest at these firings. Marxist-Leninist indoctrination courses were stiffened and students who did poorly in those fields, no matter how talented in science, were called on the carpet, and outside lectures by university professors dwindled to nothing.* By fall, 1972, the previous flood of applicants had fallen off and in Igor's words, this once elite school had become 'a spiritless, gray, sorry spectacle'.

One of the unique qualities of this school, I was told by several people, young and old, was that in its prime it had been not only a place of academic experimentation and excellence but of unusual candor and confidence between students and teachers. More typically, several intellectual families privately told us, children learn quite early in life about the schizophrenic split between talking freely at home but care-

* Much of this account comes from issue No. 27 of the *Chronicle of Current Events*, October 25, 1973.

fully conforming and concealing their views in public. 'Any family whose level of education is high enough to have many books at home, talks differently at home than beyond the walls of its home and the children can feel it,' said Vasily, the young math teacher. 'Maybe no one tells children specifically not to speak out, but they are canny and they learn the cynicism from their parents.' Nadya, the literature teacher, acknowledged it, too. 'We are part of official life,' she said. 'Once children pass beyond the innocence of those first years when they will do anything a teacher says, they watch what they say in front of their teachers.'

In rare cases where children, in innocent naiveté, buck the political values of the system, it has a way of backfiring. I knew a 16-year-old boy, a quiet, artistic, independent lad, who told some school friends that he did not plan to join the Komsomol (Young Communist League) though it is virtually obligatory for all. His father was a Communist Party member, though passive and unenthusiastic. He knew nothing of the incident until being summoned to school the next day by the homeroom teacher, whom the family regarded as a flexible and sympathetic lady. She told the father what had been reported to her by another student. 'I would rather not know this,' she said, itself an unusually liberal remark for a Soviet teacher who is supposed to take seriously the Party's exhortations to monitor the moral upbringing of her students. 'But you know this can be a serious matter. You are an intelligent and sophisticated father. Tell the boy that he can think what he wants but he cannot say what he wants.' So the boy joined the Komsomol.

Poignant as that was, I was even more touched by an incident that affected another family in which the father was an establishment figure of some rank with a good official job. Somehow he and his wife had obtained a copy of Solzhenitsyn's *August, 1914*, and their teenage son found it at home. It was a time when the book was under sharp attack in the Soviet press. At school, the boy's literature teacher had denounced Solzhenitsyn and that book specifically. 'The teacher said it is very bad, it is anti-Soviet and the West picks up everything that is anti-Soviet,' the boy said to his father, shrewdly adding, 'Don't we pick up everything that is anti-Western?' The son wanted to read the book at home but the parents forbade it. The father told me he had sternly warned his son not to let anyone know that his parents had the book or that they had discussed it. 'I have to choose between lying to my son about what we read and what we think or teaching him to lie,' said this man, in a moment of searing honesty. 'I prefer to be honest with our son. I love him. He will never be happy because he will understand too much. But at least he will not grow up like a stupid ass.'

VII

YOUTH
Rock Without Roll

> Just because we dig Jimi Hendrix doesn't mean we
> are any less ready to fight for our country.
> > Young Russian rock fan, 1974

Rock. Hard rock. Live. That unmistakable driving, pulsating
rock beat. Amplifiers way up. A kid in a leather jacket works
the dials and periodically dashes half way up the aisle to
check the decibels. Tall, lanky Valery Vernigor belts out
Evil Woman and *Spinning Wheel*, hits made famous by the
American group Blood, Sweat and Tears. He sings with feeling. In English. It could be the original except for sharp
brassy riffs from trumpets and trombones. At the electronic
organ, throbbing with rhythm, is a goateed dandy in a
flaming red shirt. The drummer, lean and intense, is developing a handlebar mustache. A bank of electric guitarmen in
neck-length hair give out with the vacant-eyed look and
rolling body motion that go with rock. At center stage Lyosha
Kozlov, with stringy beatnik hair and a full Solzhenitsyn
beard, works over a wild, rippling alto sax. The room swims
in sound. Then, sharp enthusiastic applause all around me.
And Makhurdad Badi, a Moscow-born Persian lad with a
high wavering tenor and kinky hair falling to his shoulders,
joins in a medley from *Jesus Christ, Superstar*.

Almost anywhere else in the world, this scene may be
standard. But this was Moscow, March 1974. Not the underworld exactly but a libertine delight savored surreptitiously.
A crowd, 400-strong, mostly young, on a Thursday afternoon,
packed into a nondescript meeting hall lost somewhere in the
sprawling and pretentious exhibition grounds built by Stalin
to advertise 'The Achievements of the National Economy'.

215

Not only was the setting improbable for live rock, so is Aleksei Kozlov, the combo's leader. Lyosha, to his friends, is one of those intriguing Russians who live double lives because their real passions are taboo, or borderline: Abstract artists who design theater sets or do graphic illustrations for a living; sculptors with a bent for religious figurines or pornographic metal sculpture who earn handsome commissions doing tombstones for the high and mighty; satirists who live off writing children's fairy tales; a jazz piano teacher whose regular job is assistant professor of automation and telemechanics at the Moscow Physical-Engineering Institute, which founded and still sponsors the Moscow Jazz School – evidently because more appropriate institutions were not prepared to embrace jazz.

Kozlov himself is an architect by training. Since 1962 his official employment has been as specialist in industrial design at the All-Union Research Institute for Technical Aesthetics. He is also Moscow's top free-lance jazz-rock musician, a man now in his early forties who began listening to Western radio broadcasts of jazz in the early Fifties and has experimented with Dixieland, swing, hot jazz, be-bop, cool jazz, rock and is now developing his own style. For years, he had to practice in places where people, including his parents, did not go for the Western sound. So he sewed himself a heavy velvet bag with three holes in it – one for the mouthpiece and one for each hand. He stuck his saxophone inside the bag and then, like a bagpipe player, tooted away at muffled sax with less bother to the neighbors.

On stage, he is alive with music, directing his own arrangements and compositions when he is not playing that slithery saxophone. Off stage, he is so relaxed, he looks as if he had no bones. 'I economise all my energy to put it into playing,' is his explanation. Modest of build and manner, Lyosha doesn't drink much and doesn't smoke but plays cards seriously, the way he plays music. In the Sixties, he played saxophone in several Soviet stage bands which are still doing Fifties-style dance music, and was sent by the Young Communist League to the Warsaw Jazz Jamboree in November 1962, as a Soviet representative. But gradually, Lyosha Kozlov has drifted away from official music. Once, in the mid-Sixties Leonid Pereverzev, a sonic engineer whose love and encyclopedic knowledge of jazz has made him a leading commentator, gave a jazz lecture on Moscow television, illustrated with

216

pretaped numbers by an earlier, milder Kozlov combo. But 'the editors', as one musician put it delicately, snipped out one number, because the swaying, rhythmic gyrations of Kozlov and his musicians were deemed too unorthodox and suggestive.

Kozlov drifted further away from officially approved pop music and is now guru to young musicians, some of them classical music students at Moscow Conservatory, who want to master rock. Actually, what Kozlov creates is a hybrid of jazz and rock, a combination of the heavy rhythmic drive and loud electronic acoustics of rock with jazz improvisation and brass techniques from the big band era. Russian youth obviously dig what he does but he must tread carefully. During my years in Moscow, his music was not banned but it was officially regarded as shady.

So sought-after is the Kozlov group by youth-in-the-know that even though it is strictly unofficial, essentially nonprofit and totally unadvertised, it plays fifteen to twenty concerts a year, each one privately organized and carefully arranged for a closed audience, like the concert I saw at the fairgrounds. Invitations come from young auto workers, mining engineers, technical designers, oil institute students, and groups in cities like Donetsk, Dnepropetrovsk, and Kuibyshev where sometimes the unknowing authorities are less politically stingy about music than Moscow bosses. But Kozlov is careful not to let things get out of hand and spoil the music. Once, in late 1974, an enthusiastic audience at the Moscow House of Scientists began cheering and shouting in the tradition of rock audiences the world over but well in excess of Soviet norms. Kozlov politely asked them to go easy. 'I consider rock a branch of contemporary academic music,' he cautioned. 'We are trying to treat it that way, so we ask you to react to it in the same spirit.' The audience got his message.

Moreover, the lid is on for the general public. Outside the *aficionados*, the Russian public is unaware of Kozlov's existence. Catching one of his concerts, like getting in on almost any of the more interesting subterranean happenings in Russia, is like spotting a shooting star. It flashes across the heavens briefly. If you happen to be outside on the right night at the right time and looking in the right direction, you see it. But otherwise, at all other moments, the sky looks normal and you'd swear there were no shooting stars. With

Kozlov's music, you need a tip in advance, and also the connections to wangle your way in. What is striking to me, however, is that the Soviet youth scene today is studded with would-be Kozlovs in little combos all over the country, because pop culture has seeped right through the ideological walls that conservative elders have tried to erect.

Generalizing about Soviet youth is as impossible as generalizing about American youth. In sophistication and life-style, a university student from a prominent, foreign-traveling Moscow family is a world apart from a young factory worker in Ryazan, only about 100 miles down the road but still provincial and isolated; let alone the rough youth in the Far North or a Siberian village. The one language that comes closest to speaking to all of them is pop music. Back in 1971, the newspaper *Soviet Culture* carried a letter from a girl in Kuibyshev saying 'the Beatles are understood by and are close to millions of my contemporaries'. Three young men from Gorky indicated how badly they ached for a change of pace from the diet of patriotic music, Red Army marches and semioperatic ballads fed them on Soviet radio and television. 'We young people need recreation, and light recreation at that,' they wrote. 'There is scientific and technological progress. One has to keep in step with everything. How can you suggest our singing ballads and listening to marches after a difficult, strenuous day?'

Traveling across the Soviet Union, I have run into 'pop groups' or 'beat groups' ('rock' remains too explosive a word for official Soviets) not only in cities like Moscow, Leningrad, Riga, or Tallinn but in the once Islamic city of Bukhara in Central Asia or in Siberia, 10,000 miles from New York. In Bratsk, one group that I met had put together a large library of tapings from Voice of America (this was while V.O.A. was still being jammed) of The Beatles, Rolling Stones, Jefferson Airplane, Engelbert Humperdinck, and other Western stars. None of them really understood English, but they happily and skillfully mimicked the English lyrics and disc jockeys. So 'up' were they on Western rock idols that they peppered me with questions about the private lives of stars I had never heard of, and then excitedly got me to help them transcribe the words to a recording of Mahalia Jackson's 'He's Got the Whole World in His Hands'. I don't think they had the vaguest idea it was a jazzed-up rendition of a spiritual. What interested them was not the message, but the

218

music. And what they played privately for their own enjoyment was far different from what they were allowed to play in public.

For after discovering that stonewall resistance to Western pop culture simply would not work, Soviet authorities have compromised on more sophisticated methods for siphoning off the down-beat urges of their young. In the Sixties pop groups began sprouting under official sponsorship – at factories, institutes, universities, and local Palaces of Culture, as Russians pompously call their community centers. But pop groups, like dachas, run the gamut. They range from the bland, loyal and uninteresting majority to the far-out, authentic rock of the Kozlov combo. The tamer variety are encouraged to take part in nationwide talent-hunts with local and regional competitions building up to the nationally televised play-off. But their repertoire and lyrics, even their dress, movements and their politics, I was told by several young musicians, are monitored, vetted and purged of anything that is morally, sexually or politically suggestive. Often innocent tunes whose only flaw is their Western parentage are dropped. When some provincial groups audition for television, a hip young guitarist said, they are told 'they have to do the *agitprop* songs – you know, about economic achievements and space heroes', adapted to the modern idiom. Since they need official affiliation to get a place to rehearse or the right to perform, and sometimes even to obtain certain instruments, they bow to controls.

The irony is that the more proficient and professional pop groups become, the more they are controlled and co-opted, the guitarist said. For that reason, he had no intention of turning pro, though he was talented enough to make it in the West. From others I heard that the best groups are in academic institutes – unknown amateurs with flamboyant names like The Time Machine, The Violent Catastrophe, The Ruby Attack – rather than the professional groups with tepid names and official repertoires like The Singing Guitars, The Jolly Guys, or The Troubadours. These professionals are recorded but far less well-known and less followed than the imported Western rock sounds. The reason, according to the guitarist, is that professional Soviet combos cannot show their stuff. On television, he said, they are forbidden to use their loudest, best amplifying equipment to keep their music from being too wild. In concerts, they are given a quota on how

219

much Western music they can play (typically, 15 percent because they have to play 65 percent Soviet compositions and 20 percent East European). Equally crippling is the refusal of music-monitors of the Komsomol and Ministry of Culture to permit groups to play their own compositions on grounds that these tunes were not written by official, regime-approved composers.

Nor has détente helped things much. In Tallinn, the most 'open' of Soviet cities, a restaurant-band pianist told me that officials were becoming increasingly touchy about having Western tunes performed publicly, as détente proceeded. Restaurant bands and sometimes even those playing for fairly private occasions have to watch their step, I was told, because the authorities seed the clientele with informers to double-check the band's performance against its approved repertoire. Once at the Berlin restaurant in Moscow, some friends of ours recognized the band playing the Lara theme from *Doctor Zhivago*, strictly *verboten*. After a few minutes, one of them asked the band to play it again.

'We didn't play that song,' said the combo's leader.

'Oh, yes,' my friend insisted. 'I heard it myself and so did my friends. We recognized it.'

'No, you must have been mistaken. We didn't play it and so you didn't hear it!' The reply was spoken in that frozen Soviet voice that is less a denial of the actual truth than a rejection of an inconvenient one.

Occasionally, groups try to defy the authorities or put one over on them, but it rarely works. The Pesnary, a Byelorussian group, tried to insist back in 1970 on their own program for a television appearance, and the argument reportedly got so heated that they were not only blocked from that appearance, but a lot of other performances were canceled until they were ready to submit again. The Kvasary from Bukhara gave Soviet-style protest titles to Beatle songs in the belief, as one musician said, that 'nobody pays attention' to the lyrics. But they got caught, had to trim their hair, were banned from playing at weddings where they had made side-money, and faced review of their repertoire. Some music enthusiasts feel restrictions have tightened since the Sixties. One avid rock fan told me of wild nights at the Evening Restaurant on Kropotkin Square in downtown Moscow in the early Sixties when Beatle music first took Soviet youth by storm. 'The Komsomol sponsored jam sessions and the kids went wild,' said this tubby 30-year-old. 'They would scream as if someone were being killed. It was a terrible racket. Furniture got bashed in and windows smashed. So that ended that. Then they used to have the Blue Bird Cafe, with guards at the door and admission only by special Komsomol tickets, but that has stopped, too.' In January 1974, the Komsomol in Moscow made plans to open a new jazz cafe, with live music, at the Glass Restaurant in Gorky Park. A writer got us tickets for opening night, but it was called off at the last minute because higher-ups did not approve. The jazz cafe never opened, leaving Moscow without any public place regularly offering live jazz or rock, though several cafes play recordings of Western stars like Aretha Franklin and Otis Redding slipped in among Soviet selections.

The conclusion seems inescapable that authorities are less afraid of Western records circulating *sub rosa* than of genuinely popular homegrown Soviet rock groups. If homegrown groups were allowed real freedom and developed mass followings, they could become even more difficult to control than some big-name writers, athletes, or scientists. Willy-nilly, as an alternative, the authorities have turned a blind eye to the greater leakage of Western rock records sent or smuggled into the country in recent years.

So large is the black market traffic in records and other paraphernalia of Western rock culture that one American coed studying at Leningrad University compared it to the way pot and drugs circulate on American campuses. The *fartsovshchiki*, blackmarketeers, are the Soviet counterparts to the drug pushers, the pros, the money men. Some use student sub-agents whose payoff comes in cheap jeans or rare records; and sometimes the police use student informers to trap professional operators. Once, with a Russian friend, this girl was walking in downtown Leningrad: 'There they are!' popped the Russian, pointing to a knot of dark-coated men with briefcases on a street corner, circling each other like dogs, sniffing and checking until sufficient trust was established for actual bargaining to begin. No records were exposed until the title and price had been set. Then a couple of men would ease down the street far enough to feel safe exchanging disc for money. In their time, LPs of *Hair* and *Jesus Christ, Superstar* could command 100 rubles ($133) or more, usually earned back amply on retapings at ten rubles a throw. Typically, the contraband entered the country with tourists or returning Soviet travelers. Sometimes records slipped past customs agents or mail censors because someone had thoughtfully tucked them in record jackets for Strauss waltzes or Bach Cantatas.

But never have live Western groups been allowed into the country. As part of the Soviet-American cultural exchange in early 1972, the American Embassy proposed The Fifth Dimension, not one of the wildest American rock groups but sufficiently gutsy to have had a sensationally successful run through Rumania, Hungary, Poland and Czechoslovakia. Moscow rejected the proposal flatly and asked for something else. Not long afterward at a diplomatic luncheon, I was sitting next to Vladimir Golovin, then deputy chief of Goskontsert, the Soviet State agency which handles all bookings. When I asked him why The Fifth Dimension had been rejected, Golovin tried to put me off by saying he did not think they were very popular – 'at least not popular enough to fill concert halls' for a six-week tour of the Soviet Union.

'Hard to understand,' I countered, given the enthusiasm of a young audience I had recently seen in Moldavia for a pop group from the Mari Autonomous Region. The entire hall, 1,000 seats, was sold out for one of the milder, relatively unknown professional Soviet pop groups. One cleaned-up Beatles song, *Back in the Old U.S.S.R.*, I said, had been enough to bring down the house.

'The Fifth Dimension are not The Beatles,' Golovin sniffed.

'Well, how do you think The Beatles would go over with Soviet audiences?' I tested.

'The Beatles are already old fashioned,' he parried.

'They are classics, you mean?'

'No, not classics. I didn't say that. Old fashioned,' he insisted primly. So much for The Beatles, too.

The next day I happened to have an unusual chance to talk with a successful, orthodox pop song composer who said she made a whopping 25,000 rubles ($33,333) a year doing pop-style patriotic tunes for Soviet youth. When I told her the Americans had proposed sending The Fifth Dimension, she and her colleagues were wide-eyed. Would the group have any trouble filling the halls? I asked. Silly question, they replied. Why not have them? I pursued. 'Ask Goskontsert,' said the pop song composer. When I said I had talked to Golovin, they were eager to know his response. When they heard it, they winced at his transparent evasions.

Soviet authorities have dared to invite Polish, Bulgarian and Hungarian combos and the crowd-crush has been immense. East European musicians, one Polish performer confided, regard these as 'duty trips' to Russia to balance off more desirable trips to the West, so that Moscow will not scold the East Europeans about their allegiance. But what is a chore for them is sheer heaven for Russian youth, the closest thing to a glimpse of the West, indirectly reflected through East European styles and costumes bolder and gaudier than Soviet homegrown. The authorities, however, remain wary of admitting the genuine article, a big-name Western rock group, for fear of an uncontrollable reaction.

The hunger for Western music and the paraphernalia of the pop culture is evidence enough of a generation gap in Russia, a generation gap in reverse, at least among the middle-class and the establishment youth. Whereas the American youth rebelliously turned to jeans, copping out, and the folk-rock ambience in defiant rejection of parental affluence, precisely what Soviet youth want is affluence and the good life. They are in the vanguard of the new materialism. Young men will take summer construction jobs in Siberia if they can get 1,000 rubles in hard cash and secretaries will scrimp on food to save money and blow almost an entire month's pay for such Western symbols of easy living as flared slacks, wigs, knee-boots, or platform shoes.

This trend goes for young marrieds as well as teenagers. Vadim, a young engineer, and Svetlana, a teacher, are typical though better heeled than most. The hall of their apartment is decorated with bright cut-outs from slick Western fashion magazines showing models in leopard skin bikinis and huge, moon-shaped sunglasses, jet-set squires in mod sport clothes, or swanky modern home interiors. Their own two-bedroom apartment is cozily furnished by Soviet standards, but much more modest. Vadim's pride is a five-band Grundig shortwave transistor radio for which he shelled out 400 rubles (two months' pay), and the wide ties Svetlana made for him from imported material. He will happily stand in line two hours for a good Polish jazz record. An original Paul Desmond LP transports him with delight. Svetlana favors bright Japanese scarves and hip-tight slacks which she makes herself. Anything to break away from the Spartan styles of the prewar and wartime generations and the general stodginess of their own postwar parents.

So far, the trend toward modish dress has been mild compared with the peacock revolution in the West. The notion that clothes express the individual personality has not taken root. Russian youths do not sport psychedelic get-ups or deliberately create the freaky look. Moscow has its small tribe of hippies, but most young people know that slovenly dress is an invitation to trouble with the authorities and dare not risk it. The Soviet mod trend consists mainly of catching up with more established Western fashions. But this fashion-consciousness grew visibly during our three years in Moscow. When we arrived in 1971, university students complained they had to shave their neck-length hair when they went to collect their university stipends or they would be turned down. When we left, there was still some resistance but much less, and neck-length hair even occasionally showed up on television, the most conservative of Soviet media.

The drug scene, too, made an appearance. Not on anything like the American scale, but enough to prompt worried Soviet authorities to tighten up antinarcotics laws several times, imposing stiff penalties on narcotics rings and repeaters. One set of decrees, issued in May 1974, indicated that a major source of illicit drugs was theft from health clinics of medicinal narcotics, and the use of bogus or outdated prescriptions. Privately, a young doctor from Odessa confirmed this. Several times he had been offered hefty bribes for a volume delivery. 'You could get a new car for it,' he said. Although he had not gone along, this doctor said such traffic 'is everywhere' in a port like Odessa which had a reputation long before the Revolution as a bad city. According to him, the traffic fed largely off laboratory technicians who manufactured drugs in government institutes and from other state employees who were swiping hard drugs from clinics. Morphine, he said, sometimes came from war veterans who had become addicted during World War II, while being treated for wounds. Under the Soviet health system, they are given booklets entitling them to regular dosages from the State and either the booklets or the morphine, the doctor said, reached the underworld.

In 1972, a biologist told me about a scandal at Moscow's Institute for Natural Compounds after authorities uncovered some LSD made by researchers there. Not a word appeared in the press, but tough instructions went out to other biology and chemistry institutes to tighten controls against such activities. But this did not halt the trade because a year later an acquaintance of mine attended a party at Moscow University where LSD was in use. More common, however, is hashish from the mountainous regions of Soviet Central Asia or the Caucasus. A young man offered me some – showed it to me – in Tbilisi, the capital of Georgia. Several people in Moscow mentioned its use. And a veteran Soviet journalist pointed out the high-columned Motherland Movie Theater, not far from Izmailovo Park in Moscow as a known trading point. There, he said, a small, half-thimble-sized ball of black hashish, enough for one reefer, went for five rubles ($6.67). Yet despite these and other vague tales of narcotics traffic, the overwhelming impression of Soviet students and foreign exchange students who lived among them was that the drug action on Soviet campuses did not begin to compare with the West. Far more of a problem is alcohol – the vodka which Soviet students, like their elders, drink with the same self-obliterating intensity of Western drug addicts who seek oblivion on a high.

When it comes to sex, Russia is certainly no land of strolling lovers. Few and far between are the necking or petting couples in parks and other public places. That kind of public display of affection is frowned upon. Candid discussion of sex in public, or even in private, is virtually taboo. The Western cult of the body simply does not exist. Nor, for all practical purposes, does nudity on stage or screen. One Russian friend jokingly remarked that the biggest public kicks Russians get are sexy *pas de deux* at the ballet. A man in his forties re-called his personal shock in 1952 when for the first time he saw a modern oil painting of a nude on exhibition – a plump, healthy Russian country maid emerging from the village bathhouse in the altogether while snowflakes danced around her pink flesh. 'For our socialist realism,' he smirked, amused at the memory, 'so daring!'

In one recent and rather candid play about young lovers, *Valentin and Valentina*, the Moscow Art Theater tried a fleeting nude tableau after the couple had spent their first night together in someone else's apartment. At the premiere, in 1971, Prime Minister Aleksei Kosygin allegedly felt so offended that he let his views be known, and the lovers were covered up. Other companies performed that play but no one ventured a nude moment. In another youth drama in Leningrad, *The Przhevalsky Horse*, a pair of young lovers at a Komsomol construction site got no further than sunning themselves in their underwear on boards six feet apart, reaching out to touch hands, and then a fast blackout. One striking exception to this artistic prudery was the scene of mass pagan nudity in Andrei Tarkovsky's masterful film about the Russian ikon painter, *Andrei Rublev*, which was delayed by censors four years and released only after it had won international recognition.

For all the talk of free-love in the Revolutionary period, what carried the day and still sets the public tone were Lenin's views which sound like those of a Victorian British boarding school headmaster. Deploring what he called 'excessive interest' in 'the sex question', he wrote:

> Young people particularly need the joy and force of life. Healthy sport, swimming, racing, walking, bodily exercises of every kind and many-sided intellectual interests . . . that will give young people more than eternal theories about sexual problems . . . The Revolution demands concentration, increase of forces . . . It cannot tolerate orgiastic conditions. Dissoluteness in sexual life is bourgeois . . . Self-control, self-discipline is not slavery, not even in love.*

Stalin carried forward this Victorian puritanism, but the public reticence toward sex in Russian life predates the Revolution. Tolstoy treated sex gently as did even so stormy and emotional a writer as Dostoyevsky. Pushkin was the most ribald of classic Russian writers, a real-life Don Juan who supposedly kept a detailed list of his own 103 love affairs, but almost nothing of his erotic poetry is printed today.

From all evidence, there is at least as much Pushkin as Lenin in the modern generation. A Leningrad professor may warn that 'premarital sex can be a source of severe psychic disturbances and can lead to social impoverishment of the personality', but a sociological survey of university students at Leningrad University in 1969 turned up the results that 85 percent of the men and 70 percent of the women had had premarital sex before age 21. And though Leningrad, as a cosmopolitan city, may be abnormally liberal, one social

* 'The Emancipation of Women' from the Collected Works of V. I. Lenin (New York, 1966).

scientist commented that 'nevertheless, the figures are very indicative'. Given the shortage of men after World War II, Russian women have gained a reputation for being forward. Tales of village youths being chased by girls and having several affairs at once crop up occasionally in Soviet fiction, and evidently more often in real life. One graduate student in Moscow told me that Russian girls sometimes go to the Caucasus for affairs with dark-haired Georgians the way some British girls are said to go to Spain. But sleeping together in university dorms is easy enough.

For reasons of economy, Soviet universities turned to coed dorms long before American universities did. Moscow University among others has strict rules against men being in girls' rooms after hours and conducts periodic corridor searches as a deterrent. But students told me that Soviet student Romeos hide by slipping outside on the window ledges of the 26-story building. Russian roommates are also more tolerant than Americans might be, having grown up in more crowded living conditions. They are housed three, four, or five to a large room but, as one girl said, coeds simply turn their backs if a guy spends the night with one of their room-mates. 'People get away with that a lot,' she said, 'so long as the roommates don't complain about its being a nuisance.' In some classes, an American exchange scholar told me, the authorities try public shaming to deter sexual affairs by reading out the names of girls caught after 11 p.m. with boys in their rooms. 'Funny,' he added, in a very American comment, 'that would never work in the States. The guys would all laugh and take down the names of the girls.' Affairs in working-class dormitory buildings, Writers' Union hideaways, and hostels are reportedly so common, that Russians joke, 'We don't need prostitution, we have hostels.'

This laxity reaches down into teenage. A sociologist in Odessa reported in 1973 that in a study of 14- to 17-year-old high school students, 25 percent admitted having had intercourse. The boys had developed what he called an 'industrial psychology' toward sex which 'regards love as a physical necessity'. A young doctor in Moscow added that with health campaigns having reduced the dangers of venereal disease, with young people living at a faster tempo and with religion no longer providing moral guidance, promiscuity was naturally on the rise. 'People have neither faith nor fear,' he shrugged.

The major problem of the young is finding privacy. Unlike Americans, Soviet youth cannot just check into some hotel or motel. That requires a passport inspection and embarrassing questions about why someone needs a room in his hometown. Floor ladies also keep an eye on unregistered roommates. Most young people live at home with parents, cheek by jowl. Their quandary was aptly conveyed in that play, *Valentin and Valentina*, which had the two lovers meeting in libraries and subway stations or smooching in elevators. Their one big night came when Valentin got the apartment key of a single friend who had gone out of town. Such frustrations often prompt Russian young people to marry early, in an effort to find privacy and independence.

By Western standards, the typical Soviet wedding ceremony is pretty plain. Constant demands are made to infuse marriage with more meaning by adding to the wedding ritual, but it still comes across as a tinsely, assembly-line affair. An American preacher considers himself overworked if he does three or four weddings on a June day, but 30 or 40 is not uncommon on a Saturday at a Soviet Wedding Palace.

Vadim and Svetlana, the couple mentioned before, come from well-off educated families who spent a small fortune on their wedding celebration, even though the parents did not attend the ceremony. Like many Russian girls, Svetlana wanted a full length white lacey wedding dress, with sleeves to the elbows. Being well-to-do, she had another dress, short, stylish and wine-red, for the party afterward. Together, they cost nearly 200 rubles at the dressmakers, and white shoes cost another 30 rubles. For more ordinary families, special wedding shops offer much less expensive and not very well made wedding outfits. Vadim was also unusually elegant in a black suit, white four-in-hand tie, and winged collar shirt, all of which cost a pretty penny. But he, too, was unusual; most young men come in in an everyday suit – a new one, if they can afford it, and their regular suit, if not.

One month before they planned to wed, Vadim and Svetlana went to declare their intentions to the civil authorities and paid 1.50 rubles to register for a date. They wanted a Friday or Saturday wedding, the most popular because of the following days off, and had to wait three months for a place in line. On their wedding morning, they went off with their two best friends, a girl witness for Svetlana and a young man for Vadim. Sometimes parents also go to the ceremony but just as often, not. There is no tradition of 'giving the bride away'. In Svetlana's case, the young foursome went off alone in a rented taxi decorated with streamers and balloons, but no 'just married' on it. Tied to the front grill was a doll (some couples prefer a toy bear) to symbolize their wish for children.

Wedding Palaces are usually crowded with waiting people – nervous couples doing last minute primping in an ante-room, and fathers anxiously looking at their watches or complaining to the staff that the rented taxi will leave unless the ceremony gets under way soon. The ceremony lasts only six or seven minutes but with the mass production line, it inevitably seems to run late. I did not see Vadim and Svetlana's wedding ceremony, but they said it was very much like the ones I saw conducted by Mrs Aleksandra Suvorova, the director of the Wedding Palace at 33A Leningrad Prospekt in Moscow.

Mrs Suvrova, a handsome, friendly, gray-haired lady who is a deputy in the Moscow City Council and an academic specialist on marriage, wore a full-length purple gown for the occasion. Draped across her bosom was a red sash bearing the emblem of the Russian Republic and the legend, 'Proletarians of the World Unite'. The large, high-ceilinged wedding room was stark and empty except for Mrs Suvrova's desk at one end and behind her, a faded mosaic of the Soviet Hammer and Sickle. A glass vase with red carnations stood on the desk. As the doors at the far end of the room opened to admit the wedding party, loudspeakers played a well-worn recording of Tchaikovsky's First Piano Concerto. Ten feet from the desk, at a signal from a lady in a plain gray suit, the wedding party and the music stopped abruptly. Everyone stood for what was less a wedding ceremony than an official registration of the act of marriage.

'The Executive Committee of the Soviet of Working People's Deputies of the City of Moscow has empowered me to register the marriage of . . . ' Mrs Suvorova began in an official, impersonal voice. The young couples before her – bride and bridesmaid with long-stemmed flowers wrapped in cellophane and groom and best man with hands at their sides – looked as nervous and uneasy as young couples all over the world, until the lady in gray called forward the bride and then the groom to sign the marriage papers. Mrs Suvorova picked up two plain gold wedding bands from a container on the desk, walked out to the young couple and had them exchange rings – without vows. Then, warmly and much more personally, she spoke to them briefly about the obligations of marriage, and the need for mutual love and respect. 'Do everything together,' she told one couple, 'in happiness and in grief, in hope and in doubt, in defeat and in victory, in all family affairs.' Then she pronounced them married and the lady in gray prompted: 'The young newly-weds congratulate each other.'

As they kissed gently, the gray lady switched on the recording again, this time a Strauss waltz for gaiety, though more than once she had missed the proper stopping point for the entry march, and the second playing began with a snipped-off snatch of Tchaikovsky, a scratchy pause, and then the Strauss. Mrs Suvorova shook hands with the couple, gave them their passports, in which the marriage was already registered, and ushered them out. Champagne and sweets were optional down the hall for a fee, but most couples preferred going off to their own wedding parties. Often I saw young couples on ritual stops at the eternal flame for the Unknown Soldier, where the brides laid their flowers, or riding up to Lenin Hills for a view of the city and photographs. Vadim and Svetlana skipped those rituals. 'I did not want that,' said Svetlana firmly. 'If you go to Lenin Hills on a Saturday afternoon, you see ten brides in their white dresses every hour. They look so embarrassed. What do you need that for?'

Either way, the highlight of the day, the time of personal enjoyment and family warmth, is the wedding party afterward. Like many couples, Svetlana and Vadim had their banquet in a private room at a public restaurant, the Crystal Cafe. For hours, more than 70 guests feasted on food and champagne, vodka and cognac, dancing to the music of some of Vadim's university friends who had an informal pop combo, and singing Russian songs. The poor newlyweds were constantly badgered by cries of 'gorko, gorko' (bitter, bitter) meaning 'life is bitter, give us something sweet'. This is a call for the young couple to rise and kiss to lusty cheers from their friends.

For many, this great feasting proves a catastrophic expense. One thousand rubles is a figure that occurs often enough for the press to run periodic laments of young couples who have gone into terrible debt to finance the partying. Some complain of gate-crashers at restaurants like the Crystal, which run several wedding parties at once. Poorer families economize by partying at home and preparing their own meals for smaller gatherings. The Western tradition of the honeymoon, however, is not so elaborate among Russians. Some couples manage to arrange special travel passes for a couple of weeks. Others take a weekend trip somewhere. But it is equally common, as in Vadim and Svetlana's case, for parents to move out of the family apartment for a few days to let the newlyweds have a home to themselves before all begin to live together.

The generations may live together for awhile but this does not bridge the generation gap or ease what Russians have called the problem of 'Fathers and Sons' ever since Turgenev wrote a novel of that name. The intriguing thing to me about the Soviet Seventies was that it was the parents who were worried by the materialistic self-indulgence of their children and who, as members of the establishment, were upset by the political apathy of the rising generation, rather than vice versa, as in the West. In their day, middle-aged Russians lived a hard life but they were philosophically committed. Now, they see their young growing up spoiled and uncommitted.

'Our children want everything right away!' a buxom matron with an unblemished Party record complained to an American friend. Her moral indignation reminded me of the Calvinist code of old-fashioned, self-made American entrepreneurs who came up the hard way and were convinced it had been good for the soul. 'The young get married these days and they want to have their own apartments and polished furniture,' she said. 'It took us years to get our own apartment. Why should they be in such a hurry? People should wait for these things and then they would appreciate them more.' Mrs Suvorova at the wedding palace told me, with a worried look, that half the couples she was marrying were under 20 and were unprepared to have a family. She considered it one of her main functions to talk many of them out of marrying so young. Another woman, an ambitious, energetic, self-willed writer, born into an old Party family though not a Party member herself, felt the younger generation had simply gone soft. 'I am disappointed in my children,' she fretted to me. 'They are weak-willed, lazy, not self-disciplined. Our son is extraordinarily bright and able academically. But this is not backed by an ability to work or to make a schedule for himself or to sort out what should be done first. I know you Americans regard this as normal for students and teenagers, but at 15, I was already working at a factory, earning my own bread.'

The response of the young is that Russians have been waiting long enough to enjoy life and there is no reason why they should have to repeat the hardships of their parents. 'Young people want to have, have, have,' an openly cynical young government interpreter told me in a Moscow cafe. 'They don't have time to think, to ask questions. We are at the point, I guess, where you Americans were in the Fifties. Young people want to be better dressed, get a car, enjoy the high-life.'

Some parents feel that the materialistic self-indulgence of the younger generation has fostered a disturbing political indifference. 'I left school after the ninth grade to join the Army,' recalled a Foreign Trade official, a Party man who often travels to the West and has two sons studying at the prestigious Institute for International Relations. 'I was big and powerful in those years. You know, the young boy who thinks he is already the man. My mother was against my joining the Army. But my father was an Army officer and all I wanted to do was go off and fight Germans. My boys don't understand me. When the war movies come on television, my wife and I like to watch. We remember what we lived through. But the boys are uninterested. They say, "Oh, again, it's about all this shooting and bombing. Why do you like to watch that?" For me, it's interesting. But they prefer to go dancing somewhere. All they care about is that modern pop music which I dislike. They know all the stars. Not just The Beatles. That's nothing. I mean the latest stars. Once, they met an Englishman and asked him all kinds of questions about stars he never heard of. And they were very disappointed when he couldn't answer them. It seems to me they're crazy over that stuff. I don't understand them.'

Not only individual parents but Party ideologists worry about ideological backsliding among the younger generation – what *Pravda* decries as 'parasitism', 'nationalist tendencies', 'inadequate attention to atheistic indoctrination among youth', or just plain 'indifference to ideological issues'. One sign of the insecurity of the powers-that-be is the exaggerated play the press gives to statistics that half a million young people under 30 have been 'elected to organs of state power' or more than 20 million have joined the Komsomol. I did encounter university students like the dark-haired Komsomol activist who kept Lenin's collected works in her room for bedside reading and watched when Russians mixed with foreign students in order to step in before fraternization became too easy. Moreover, American youth come away from joint sessions with Komsomol delegations astounded by the dogmatic rigidity of the younger activists, those around 20. 'The younger ones are really frightening,' remarked a dazed, disbelieving American graduate student after a week's seminar. 'The older ones, nearer 30, know something about Stalin and are a bit more flexible about politics. At least a bit. But the younger ones were absolutely rigid.' They may have been putting up a good front for when *Pravda* trumpets, as it did in mid-1974, that 20,000 young people were enthusiastically trooping off to build the Baikal-Amur Mainline Railroad in the Far East or to help reclaim Central Russian farmlands during the summer, it quickly adds that ideological work among youth must be stepped up. (And privately, a Komsomol leader told me later that only a few hundred of the 3,000 Moscow Komsomol members pressured into signing up for the railroad project actually went.)

Middle-aged people who are not even ardent Party supporters note the loss of idealism among the young. A journalist turning fifty, a huge man with wavy hair, an ample belly and glasses that slid down his nose, recalled his own enthusiasm a generation ago. 'I joined the Komsomol during the war,' he wheezed. 'We were all excited then. It was a big event in our lives to join the Komsomol. But not my son. It meant nothing to him. When he was nearly finishing high school, I asked him if he were going to apply to the Komsomol. But he said, "No, if I try this year, I have to ask them. And next year, they will ask me. Better to wait."

'It was only in his last year at school when someone told him it would help him get into university to be in the Komsomol that he got around to it. He simply went to the office, signed up and they gave him a Komsomol card. There was a little ceremony. But it meant nothing to him. He was happy if it would help him get into the university. And at the Komsomol office, they were happy to get another member for their quota. But in fact, neither he nor they cared. My son was so uninterested that he even stopped paying his dues – something like 20 kopecks a month. My mother-in-law, being from the older generation, didn't think this was right. So each month, she would take the bus and go and pay for him. When he got into the university, they told him he would have to do a "social assignment" in order to get his stipend. So, he said, "They made me chairman of the group for training internationalists." Him! When I asked him what does that mean? he said, "Oh, Papa, who needs to understand?" '

That may be an extreme case but a number of unpublished sociological studies, seen by Western scholars, indicate that as youth rates itself, ideological conviction is very low. 'I don't know anyone who joins the Komsomol out of ideological enthusiasm,' said a very pretty young blonde who had been a Komsomol leader in a provincial factory town a few years ago. 'I was an idealist in school, but I changed. Some of the most unpleasant days of my life are associated with Komsomol.' And she rattled off for me the obligatory Komsomol assignments and *subbotniki,* 'voluntary' working Saturdays, she had had to put in, checking on other factory workers. 'The only Komsomol jobs people liked were the construction brigades because the boys could earn big money, and the agitbrigades because we made up songs and went off to sing them in distant parts of the country. That way we got free trips all over the country.' Others said they regarded the Komsomol as the best, and often the only, ticket for the young to get trips abroad, to Poland or East Germany, and on rare occasions even to the West. A few spoke of harvest brigade work as times of youthful camaraderie but it was clear that their generally apathetic mood was a far cry from earlier years when 'building socialism' was a rallying cry for Soviet youth.

Cynicism, there is. But rebellion, no. By world standards, Soviet youth is abnormally quiescent. The assumption of many a Westerner that political ferment and a dissenting counter-culture necessarily ride the coattails of rock music, jeans, long hair and beards, runs aground in Russia. For some youth, especially out in the conservative-minded provinces, neck-length hair is indeed a mild symbol of personal protest. For the children of the elite, Western borrowings sometimes connote rejection of life-long parental preoccupation with career-building and political power. But in the big cities, especially among the educated upper-middle class, pop culture imports from the West have become so common and so tolerated by the establishment that they have lost political thrust and content.

'Jeans in the West are a symbol of protest,' observed Alex Goldfarb, a thoughtful young Jewish scientist from a good family, 'but here they are a symbol of the good life. If you are looking for some kind of counter-culture against parents or against the authorities and you think jeans are part of this, it is absolutely wrong. For you [Americans], this all developed organically. Jeans became popular in the West among young people opposed to the war in Vietnam, to the life-style of their parents. They are a symbol of poverty, deliberate poverty, because American young people considered it fashionable to look poor. But here, the evolution was entirely different. Jeans and the pop culture came from outside. With us, jeans are a symbol not of poverty but of the good life, of wealth. That is why they are the most inflated item on the black market. Perhaps they cost ten rubles new in America and good woolen slacks cost 25 rubles. But here you find people will pay 75 or 80 rubles ($100–106) for a pair of jeans, 200 rubles ($267) for a jeans suit, and maybe only 15–20 rubles ($20–26) for slacks made of much better material. Jeans have snob value.'

Alex paused to let me absorb this idea. We were sitting in his kitchen sipping very hot, strong Russian tea and eating chunks of hard cheese. He sipped a bit and then told me of a fascinating confrontation that illustrated how little political significance the absorption of Western pop culture had had. Alex is a sleepy-eyed young man with a bushy black beard given to wearing a rumpled, slept-in jeans outfit that made him look more like a fugitive from the Berkeley campus than a former research scholar at one of the most prestigious Soviet scientific institutes. He was an active dissident, a Jew in his late twenties who was actively campaigning to emigrate to Israel and confronting official resistance. (He was eventually allowed to leave in 1975, after I had departed Moscow.)

But Alex came from a prominent scientific family and his social connections reflected this solid establishment background.

Not too many months before, Alex said, he had been at a party where he met the son of Vladimir Semichastny, former chief of the KGB, a very high-ranking Party official with a reputation as a strict hard-liner. 'I was in my jeans and he (Semichastny's son) was in his jeans,' Alex recalled. As they talked casually, the two young men discovered that both possessed records of *Jesus Christ, Superstar*, then the hottest item on the pop black market. The Semichastny lad was wearing his Komsomol pin in his lapel, and when the two talked politics, they clashed.

'As long as we talked about pop culture, we talked the same language,' Alex told me. 'But when we talked politics, we were completely different. He got so mad at me when I criticized Soviet aid to the Arabs and defended Israel, that he told me that if he were in the Middle East and I were there, too, he would not hesitate a moment to shoot me. And I told him that I would shoot him, too. So there you are. We both had our jeans and our *Superstar* records and it didn't mean a thing except that both of us were from elite families – he, from the political elite, and I, from the scientific elite. He got his jeans through his father's position and I got mine because my father could travel abroad and get them in the West. But the jeans themselves had no political meaning.'

It was an observation echoed by other young people, talking not only about jeans and rock music, but about acquaintances listening to Western news broadcasts or surreptitiously reading the banned novels of Aleksandr Solzhenitsyn and other underground literature and yet pursuing conservative, compliant, conformist public lives. 'They go to work dressed properly, acting properly and talking properly,' as one miscast young editor for a right-wing Moscow magazine put it. Another young man, a Komsomol leader at an academic institute but a political liberal and a fanatic fan of Western rock music, affirmed his basic loyalty to the established order. When an American friend remarked to him that he sensed no stirrings among Soviet youth against the universal draft, no campus ferment for a greater voice in university affairs, no tendency to debunk their country the way American youth does, this young Russian said bluntly: 'Just because we

236

dig Jimi Hendrix [the American rock singer] doesn't mean we are any less ready to fight for our country.'

The political conformism of Soviet youth is not so surprising given the institutional environment in which they live for when the stakes are high, as they are at Soviet universities where only a small minority is admitted to begin building their careers, the system does not tolerate the kind of iconoclasm that the West has come to take for granted on its campuses. Once, I asked a British exchange student his dominant impressions of Soviet students at Moscow State University (MGU) and without hesitation he replied: 'Sat upon!'

'What do you mean?'

'I mean they lack life and spontaneity. Not just politically. At MGU, there is much less just plain tomfoolery than you would find at any university in the West.'

The basic reason obviously lies in the general political climate of the country in recent years and in the controls. But the controls are so different, so much more basic, complex and effective than most Westerners imagine, that it is worth describing the institutional grid in which Soviet youth live and mature. These are not the controls of the KGB against dissenters. That type of control touches an infinitesimal portion of the young. A far simpler, more innocent, and yet more powerful web of checks and controls is built into the Soviet system of higher education and career-building. They are a function of the unified, state-controlled system of education.

The system provides college youth not only with tuition-free education and modest stipends for living, but also with very structured lives. In rough outline, they go to an engineering school, an agricultural institute, a graphic arts college, a literary institute, and graduate as certified engineers, agronomists, graphic artists or writers. The economic planners each year put in a quota for each category and once the students have completed their courses, they are guaranteed a job in their own field – not only guaranteed that job but assigned to it.

'We produce engineers and agronomists like we produce cotton,' Gulan Aliyev, the white-haired rector of the Tadzhik Agricultural Institute told a group of visiting American correspondents in May 1974. 'We have a plan for producing the numbers of specialists, which are needed, and we distribute them according to the "orders" (requests) we get.' In other words, he explained, the state and collective farms in the republic put in requests for the trained specialists they need and these go up through the planning commission in each republic, perhaps all the way to Moscow, and come back down to various institutes in the form of quotas for agronomists or water engineers who are parceled out after graduation. It works that way in other fields. When I was in Irkutsk, the rector of the university there told me that the most rapidly growing faculty was the law faculty because so many Siberian cities were requesting lawyers. One reason was, it turned out, that police forces wanted law-trained university graduates to help cope with juvenile delinquency.

Actually, the quota system sounds more inhuman than it is. The individual has flexibility in choosing which field he or she wants to compete for and which institution he wants to try out for. Unlike the American college board system which allows multiple applications, the Soviet system requires most candidates to pick one VUZ (higher educational institution) and one faculty in that VUZ for which to take exams. The student puts all of his eggs in one basket.

Success means a virtual guarantee all the way into the job market, because so few students flunk out of universities and institutes once admitted. But, as a University Rector in Georgia acknowledged, it is almost impossible to change fields once you enter a faculty. You go straight through in a field you picked before you entered. The curriculum is standard, often centrally determined in Moscow. Electives are few. It is a system geared toward inculcating technical skills rather than being concerned with such liberal arts intangibles as learning to think or personal growth and self-expression. It is difficult to imagine a more direct contrast with permissive, experimental, individual-oriented trends in American education than the uniform, strict, conservative Soviet system which is focused so heavily on performance and mastering a fixed body of material.

Failure at the university examinations is a personal watershed. Usually, it means waiting a year before trying the examinations again. Roughly seven million students finish secondary school each year and only about one million get into university-level courses, nearly half of them in night school or correspondence courses. Transferring into regular universities from such programs is extremely difficult. Many young men who fail exams are drafted into the Army, rather than getting the relatively cushy reserve officer training and commission of university students. A lot wind up in manual jobs, though some go to college after the Army. But failure to get in is a blow, for despite all the propaganda about the workers' state, Soviet sociological polls among high school students have regularly shown the strong preference for 'intellectual careers' and the low prestige of manual labor. And the experiences of families we knew personally was ample evidence of the intense disappointment of failure since, in many cases, it has an almost guillotine finality.

The result is terribly intense competition, cramming and tutoring for university examinations, enormous tensions for high school seniors and their families, a fair amount of string-pulling with admission boards and other educators, and academic scandals about bribery of examining officials, usually in outlying areas so as not to embarrass important people in Moscow. Theoretically, no one is supposed to be able to approach the Rector of Moscow State University, the Minister of Higher Education or other top officials to influence the admissions process. 'But,' said one pushy career woman who went through an extensive and eventually successful lobbying campaign for her own son, 'if you could see the reception room of the Minister of Higher Education and his deputy at this time, you would not believe it – cosmonauts, actresses, journalists, officials. Everyone wanting to make appeals. If you try to get into the Minister's office, the secretaries – those ladies who sit outside his door saying, "No," to everyone without even checking what they have to say – will tell you, "it's no use, there is already a crowd in there." '

A taxi driver complained at what he felt was the unfairness of the system. 'My kid can't get into university but the children of the general can,' he griped. 'A general's son gets a five (A) on the exam, but a worker's son gets a three (C).' The implication that grades are all stacked may be unfair, for the government makes periodic efforts to give workers' and farmers' children a better chance. In 1973, the philological faculty at Moscow State University was ordered to take in 70 percent of their freshmen from the workers' night schools, a teacher told me. According to this account, they managed to find only 40 percent who could qualify. But the resulting class was so weak, that in 1974, they disregarded the social background requirement entirely and went by grades alone. And the workers' family contingent fell way off. Soviet sociological studies through the Sixties, showed that the children of the intelligentsia had two to eight times as good a chance of making it into universities and institutes as workers' or farmers' children. At the high prestige institutions, the bias is even more lopsided. Richard Dobson, a Harvard sociologist, told me he had read an unpublished Soviet dissertation that showed the trend in favor of the intelligentsia was increasing at Moscow State University. In 1960, it showed that 70 percent of the students came from educated families and by 1970, that was up to 80 percent. Moreover many students who come from factories or state farms, with the financial and political sponsorship of those institutions, are sent to technical institutes under the control of industrial ministries and are committed to returning to their factories or farms after graduation.

This moment of assignment after graduation, known as *napravleniye*, is another critical juncture for Soviet youth. It is a time when educational performance, political record, and family connections all come into play, because most young people are terribly anxious to stay in the big cities, where life is more interesting, rather than getting sent out to the provinces. The initial obligatory assignment may only be for two or three years, theoretically to pay back the state for one's education, but the force of inertia is compelling. The vast majority of people whom I met in the north, in Siberia or other far off jobs said that they had initially come on *napravleniye* and decided to stay. Once in the provinces they found it very hard to get back to the cities. This process, like the admissions process, puts a premium on a clean political as well as academic record.

Throughout their university careers, Soviet university students are given compulsory political education – five full-year courses in the History of the Communist Party of the Soviet Union, Dialectical Materialism, Historical Materialism, the Stages of Capitalism and Socialism, and the Basis of Scientific Communism. Privately, they gripe constantly about these courses and crack cynical jokes. But the political atmosphere makes active alienation and protest unthinkable for almost everyone. I remember one tall, lanky, rather shy teenager who wears horn-rimmed glasses and comes from a prominent dissident family describing a student meeting at the university which he attended: The military instructor for the class presented a resolution to the class on its 'socialist obligations' – supposedly volunteer duties. After it was read aloud, this young man had raised his hand to object that the resolution said it was 'approved unanimously'. This was impossible to say in advance, he contended, since it had not even been discussed yet. Silence. The others stared at him in disbelief. The military officer denounced him.

'How can you talk that way?' the officer demanded. 'Are you a Komsomol member?'

'No,' answered the lad. 'I'm not in Komsomol.'

'Then you are a Trotskyite!' the officer insisted. That was enough to assure unanimous passage without discussion.

'Our university students are not radical or progressive – they belong to the silent majority,' commented a middle-aged mother. 'They have to be loyal, obedient people or they would not be where they are, especially at such places as MGU (Moscow University). 'There are so many ways of putting pressure on them – their stipends, their dormitory rooms and most important their places in university. If you realize that only a minority of young people can get places in universities, and even fewer get into the really good ones, you understand how much students want to protect their places and not get thrown out. It means protecting a career. Black marks get written down and follow you the rest of your life. Get thrown out of one university and you cannot get into any other. So the students want terribly to stay in. Not necessarily for monetary reasons but out of interest in their field. If someone loves biology or physics or history, he cannot take the risk of being thrown out of a university for any reason, because that means he is throwing away a lifetime. No wonder our students are conformists.'

Another very important difference from Western youth which tends to reinforce the political orthodoxy of Soviet young people is their dependence on their parents and their close sense of family. Before, during and often well after their college years, many have to live at home because of the housing shortage. Some chafe at this. Others regard it as normal. But all know they can do almost nothing about it. The well-traveled wife of one high-ranking Foreign Ministry official recalled having told her university-age son,

241

much like a Western parent, 'It's time for you to go find some work and earn some money and make yourself more independent.' But the boy was unmoved: 'Okay, Mama, you find me an apartment, and I will do it.'

'Of course, it's impossible to find an apartment easily,' she went on, 'so he still lives with us in our three-room apartment. He goes to the university and he is away from home a lot. For two months, he quit university and disappeared somewhere. I don't know where. But he came back and returned to the university and, of course, he lives with us again.'

Living at home is crucial. It may create frictions because it makes it harder for the young to find the privacy they want. But it also maintains family ties longer. It means that parents remain involved in ways that American young people would probably regard as an infringement of their independence. For example, a chemistry student told me he saw nothing unusual in taking his university stipend, paying his Komsomol dues, and turning over all the rest to his mother for the family budget, rather than keeping the cash for himself. Others, who live on campus, say that their stipends of 40 rubles monthly are not enough to cover room and board, let alone other personal expenses which several rather well-off young people reckoned at 120–150 rubles a month (probably considerably less in the provinces). For the balance, they said, they depended on their parents. Another link to the older generation.

Moreover, the cultural differences with the West are significant. The youth cult of America has no counterpart here, and the authority of parents remains relatively strong. Soviet students do not knock their parents as much as Americans do. Many young people defer to their parents, consult them about courses, trips, jobs, marriage, and some will fly home to a parental birthday or celebration more readily than would Western students. The importance of family connections, especially in better-heeled families, also reinforces parental authority, especially when young people follow their parents' careers, as so often happens in the Soviet Union.

For all this, today's youth generation is more cut-off from its own past than any other in Soviet history. It is difficult for

Westerners, especially Americans who have passed through their moral anguish over civil rights, the Vietnam war, and the Watergate scandal, to appreciate what it means to grow up in an historically deaf-mute environment. For the greatest moral issue in Soviet history, Stalinism, has been suppressed and, from all outward signs, the youth generation of the Seventies is growing up with a severely stunted historical memory of that time. The Party elders have decreed that the Stalinist repressions are a closed book, already dealt with and buried with the Party, not to be publicly exhumed.

Privately, of course, families talk about the issue, but sometimes the generations wind up on different sides than I would have expected. I remember a tall young Russian, so fanatic a rock fan that he took the incredible risk of sneaking past the armed Soviet guards into the American Embassy one night to see a movie of The Beatles' famous *Concert for Bangladesh* and got away with it. He argued with his father, a Party man, about Stalin. Like so many kitchen conversations, theirs rambled but at one point the dialogue got quite sharp. The son spoke in defense of Stalin's violent imposition of collectivization and the harshness with which he forced industrialization on the country in the Thirties, to the chagrin of his father, who was older but more liberal despite his age or perhaps precisely because he had been closer to the terrible events they were debating and thus knew them at firsthand. It was a stunning reversal of the usual roles that Westerners assume are played by the father and son in Russia when Stalin is discussed:

'I think the country needed a Stalin at that time,' the young man, a Komsomol activist, declared.

'What?' challenged the father. 'At the cost of 20 million lives?'

The son backed off a bit, but held to his basic argument. 'Well, obviously the terror was excessive and unfortunate. But maybe Stalin had to use such force to pull the country together and hold it together. It was necessary for that time.'

This case was far from unique. Yevgeny Yevtushenko, now in middle age, told me how he had felt compelled to describe the dimensions of Stalin's terror to a group of young people in Siberia after one of them rather naively proposed a toast to Stalin around their campfire, knowing virtually nothing about the purges. A senior Soviet diplomat privately told another American reporter, an old friend, that he was astonished at his own teenage son's favorable opinion of Stalin and tried to argue him out of it. What made it remarkable was that the son had been exposed to the West by living there, and had been greatly taken with American television, pop culture and entertainment generally.

Other young people are candidly disturbed by how little they know about much of Soviet history, the artistic and intellectual ferment of the Twenties as well as the Stalinist repressions. One young man protested vigorously to the father of a university coed he was dating: 'We don't know our own past, our political history, our literary history. We have the 20th Party Congress [at which Khrushchev exposed Stalin secretly in 1956], but we have never seen the documents so that we cannot make up our own minds about the past.' Some young people, like those around the Siberian campfire with Yevtushenko, are unaware even of the extent of their own ignorance of the past, cut off as they are by censorship from those parts of Soviet history which do not fit the Party line at present. I knew one irreverent young man who kept posted on his wall an old picture of Brezhnev and Chinese Premier Chou En-lai hoisting their hands aloft in a gesture of solidarity. He said his friends were so historically illiterate that many refused to believe it was a genuine picture and suspected him of fabricating a montage.

Westerners forget that far from the scene, they sometimes know more about some Soviet historical events than young Russians themselves. Rarely was this brought home to me more starkly than in hearing about an incident involving Arkady Raikin, the famous Soviet stage comic. He had been hospitalized one winter by a heart attack and was being visited by his 18-year-old grandson, according to a family friend. Suddenly, Raikin bolted upright in bed, startled at the sight of Stalin's closest living deputy, Former Prime Minister and Foreign Minister Vyacheslav Molotov, passing the door of his hospital room.

'There he goes!' gulped Raikin to his grandson.

'Who?' asked the lad, not recognizing the figure, banished from the pages of the Soviet press almost throughout the boy's lifetime.

'Molotov,' mumbled Raikin.

'Who is Molotov?' asked the boy in stunning ignorance.

This historical deafness, one middle-aged scientist remarked, has made this a generation of youth without villains or heroes, except possibly the Western rock stars. It is, he suggested, a eunuch generation not exposed to moral judgments and moral choices.

In that, the generation of the late Sixties and early Seventies is different from any previous Soviet generation. The Revolution and Civil War period left a distinct ideological brand. The generation of the Spanish Civil War, now in its sixties, experienced antifascist fervor and the intimidation of Stalinist repressions, emerging either with a mentality forged by Stalin or an outspoken bitterness against him. The World War II generation, now in its fifties, again felt the clearcut call of antifascism and national patriotism. The generation of the Khrushchev thaw and de-Stalinization, now in their forties, is now cowed but ideologically unconvinced, and privately prepared to render judgments against both Stalin and Khrushchev. It is difficult to get a sense of the Brezhnev generation, the youth generation of Czechoslovakia and détente.

'Our youth is alienated,' remarked a Party journalist with two grown children. 'They want to think over their problems without consulting us. They are introverts compared to us. We were extroverts. We started with the Spanish Civil War and we had the war against Hitler. We knew which side we were on. This generation acts as if ideology were irrelevant. A lot of them think it is irrelevant to them. They have not had any cataclysms. They are not engaged. They are not committed.'

PART TWO
The System

VIII

RURAL LIFE
Why They Won't Stay
Down on the Farm

> Villages, villages, villages with graveyards,
> As if all Russia converged on them. . . .
> You must know after all that the Motherland
> Is not the city where I lived festively,
> But these hamlets in which our grandfathers strolled
> With simple crosses on their Russian graves.
>   Konstantin Simonov

Vasily Pochinkov is a rare man for the Soviet system. His job is to promote private enterprise.

As I entered his second-story office in a building almost as large as Madison Square Garden, he rose from his desk, stout and prim, wearing a white smock over his suit like a druggist. For a long hour we talked about budgets and profits, ten-ton trucks for rent, warehouse space and laboratory inspections; about procedures for renting space and uniforms, setting prices and providing rooms in his dormitory hostel for people who come from Moldavia, Central Asia, Azerbaijan, Georgia, Byelorussia and sometimes Lithuania and Latvia to do business in Moscow. Then we toured the premises.

Pochinkov is manager of Cheremushki Farmers' Market, one of 30 in Moscow, one of 8,000 in the Soviet Union where peasants can legally bring billions of rubles' worth of produce from their modest private vegetable gardens or slaughter their calves, chickens and rabbits and sell these wares on the free market with a style of come-hither commerce unlike the rest of the Soviet economy.

We found the farmers' markets a godsend and so did many Russian families. Sometimes housewives balked at prices that came close to rivaling room service at the Waldorf – lettuce jumping from 30 cents a pound in summer to $1.50 in November before disappearing altogether; cauliflower at $2.50 a head in winter; sweet pears from the southern Ukraine at nearly 50 cents apiece; and roses from Georgia at $1.35 a stem in January. But the quality is better, the selection far wider than in state stores. And the Russian housewife succumbs to the flattery of coaxing and catcalls, to aromas of ripening produce laid out for her to inspect, and to competition for her favor and her purse.

'Come over here, *dochka* (little daughter),' a white-haired grandmother clucked at Ann one afternoon, using one of those folksy Russian endearments to entice her to sample jugs of thick, tawny honey. 'Taste and see how good and sweet it is, little mother,' she coaxed. 'Let the little one have some.' And the peasant *babushka* offered a lick of honey on a wooden popsicle stick to Ann and Lesley, our three-year-old, as she bragged about the freshness of dripping honeycombs just taken from the hive.

Let the browsing shopper hesitate by one vendor and the competing chorus begins. Here, an unshaven peasant missing some front teeth offers skinned rabbit. There, a rolypoly Russian shows off farm-fresh eggs in earthy hands. An old woman, head wound in scarves like a mummy, offers a hunk of *tvorog* (sweetened homemade cottage cheese) on waxed paper, or a sample of *smetana* (sour cream) from a white enamel bucket. A swarthy, flat-capped Georgian will carve the skin off a pear, eyeing the shopper craftily, and then extend a succulent sliver on his knife. In the far corner, women in rough country clothes beckon you toward dried mushrooms dangling on strings like necklaces of corks. The peasant women water down their wares constantly so that the long stone counters are lined with glistening mounds of cucumbers, red beets and radishes, or piles of fat, stubby carrots that resemble the peasant fingers that tend them, but surprisingly sweet. The pungent tang of dill quickens the nostrils.

A hungry shopper can tide herself over to the next meal, meandering among the stalls at the Central Market or the one at Cheremushki, sampling not only honey and cream cheese, but little spoonfuls of vinegary sour-cabbage, bites of dill pickle still dripping with brine from the barrel, a nibble of pomegranate or little handfuls of pistachios and small purple grapes from Samarkand. But the country folk are wary of Muscovites trying to make too much of a good thing. 'All right now,' a canny vendor will caution. 'How about a kilo? Are you buying today or not?'

The private plots that produce these goods are small and mostly farmed part-time but the volume of their output is so enormous and essential to the Soviet economy that the nation's 250 million people could not be fed without it. Since that is an ideological sore point, the regime is loath to publicize the performance of this private sector, preferring instead to trumpet 'the heroic achievements of socialized agriculture'. But one unusual article in March 1975, revealed that 27 percent of the total value of Soviet farm output – about $32.5 billion worth a year – comes from private plots that occupy less than one percent of the nation's agricultural lands (about 20 million acres).* At that rate, private plots are roughly 40 times as efficient as land worked collectively. In hard, crop-by-crop terms the 1973 Soviet economic yearbook showed that in terms of value, 62 percent of the nation's potatoes, 32 percent of other fruits and vegetables, more than 47 percent of the eggs, and 34 percent of the meat and milk in the homeland of Communism came from the private entrepreneurs of the countryside who number about 25 million strong. One explanation is that the big crops are the ones farmed collectively – mainly, grain and cotton. Another is that farmers get better prices for produce marketed privately than through the State. A third reason for these staggering statistics is that roughly half of what farmers produce on their private plots goes to feed themselves and neighbors, without reaching the marketplace. But it is also clear that

* A. Yemelyanov, 'The Agrarian Policy of the Party and Structural Advances in Agriculture', *Problems of Economics*, March 1975, pp. 22–34. The crop figures are computed from those in *The Economy of the U.S.S.R. in 1973* (Moscow, 1974), p. 353.

peasants farm their own plots much more intensively than they do collective land.

Ultimately, the Communist ideal is to have this last embarrassing – but necessary – vestige of private enterprise wither away as industrialized state farming grows in scale and output. Nikita Khrushchev, in spite of rural roots, pursued that end vigorously and earned the enmity of the peasantry. He cut the size of private plots to a maximum of half an acre and made life difficult for the farm market trade. I was told by Russian friends that Ukrainian peasants became so irate that they stopped selling eggs as food and made paint out of them. 'Egg whites make very durable paint,' a Moscow painter commented to me.

Under Brezhnev things have improved. The maximum plot went back up to an acre and measures were taken to improve farm market operations. Soviet figures show that private farm output grew nearly 15 percent from 1966–73. Although the state sector grew even faster, it is obvious that the centuries-old habit of personal farming will die hard among Russian peasantry. Even under serfdom, serfs had their own plots to work when the lord's needs were met. With his permission, they could trade their surplus in the town markets. Under Communism, this system was perpetuated after Stalin's brutal collectivization as a means of stemming migration from farm to city. Now, whenever rumors circulate, as they did in 1974, that some agricultural reorganization will wipe out the plots, high officials quickly issue denials, evidently fearful that abrupt change would engender serious peasant resistance.

In the Soviet era, private plots have provided a vital margin against poverty. Not enough in themselves to bridge the large gap in living standards between city and countryside, they have meant the difference for many families between bare subsistence and something better. For if you follow the farm folk after they sell their produce, they head for Moscow shops to buy what is unobtainable in their grim little country stores. The fortunate Georgians, Uzbeks, or Azerbaijanis from the South who grow high-priced tropical fruits and flowers or winter vegetables go off to bribe salesgirls for *defitsitny* goods, buy toys and trinkets for children, splurge at restaurants, or occasionally pick up secondhand cars. But those from the stingy soils of Central Russia, whose harvest is cheap potatoes, carrots or beets, head for state stores to stock up on great long sausages and coldcuts or to purchase thick winter stockings, heavy cloth overcoats or aluminium pots and pans.

Follow the country folk toward home at night, in the railroad stations, and you see what Russians call the *narod*, the masses, of whom officialdom and intellectuals privately speak with condescension or contempt. They are coarse, raw, simple people, weatherbeaten as the log cabins in which they live, hardy and enduring as Maine fishermen, toughened by a lifetime of battling the elements. I remember one evening walking through Kazan station, one of nine stations that funnel more than a million travelers through Moscow daily. At 11 p.m. the waiting room was overflowing with a couple of thousand people. Every available seat was taken. Men lay on tables and floors trying to sleep. The whole sea of humanity reflected a niggardly, strenuous existence – the cheerless expressions, the rough apparel, the meager belongings, the subdued demeanor, the long wait. Russians often brag about how much they read. But I saw only half a dozen people glancing at newspapers. The peasant women with broad, flat faces and cheeks worn smooth as the wood of a well-used washboard, were sturdy as workhorses. They sat on benches like men, legs spread, hands clasped around their bellies, not a trace of femininity about them. The contours of their bodies were lost under layers of faded, shapeless clothing. I studied one old crone. Under her frayed, black velvet vest-jacket was a gray wool sweater; under that, an ankle-length housecoat in a flowered print; under that, another sweater, a calico dress and so on. All had long since lost their color, for each garment had obviously been made to survive from harvest to harvest, like its wearer. The young, teenage girls in bright jackets and plastic boots or even soldiers in khaki, seemed colorful by comparison. The peasant men were silhouettes of darkness – dark, rumpled, tieless jackets and pants; thick, dark, scratchy wool overcoats; dark workmen's caps or fur hats; black rubber boots or black shoes unshined for generations. Everywhere was improvised luggage – cheap cardboard suitcases, string bags stretched to accommodate impossible parcels, scavenged pieces of burlap or newspaper thrown around new belongings. As trains were called, people lumbered off with their awkward bundles.

Follow the *narod* into the countryside and the modern world peels away with astonishing suddenness. Not only the

250

peasantry but the countryside presses in close around Moscow. It surprised me to see that just ten miles from the Kremlin, near the village of Little Mytishchi, city life and its modern conveniences simply come to an end. New apartment buildings give way to *izbas*, squat, low peasant log cabins. Side roads are suddenly no longer paved but turn to dirt, often no more than two ruts or footpaths dribbling off among garden fences. Thanks to Lenin's belief in electricity, most peasant homes have lights – and television. But plumbing remains a luxury for the future. Each vegetable garden has its outhouse in the corner. Along the roadside every few hundred yards there is a hand pump and a well. In the soft warmth of summer, or in the bitter cold of winter, I have watched country people crank up pails of water and then labor homeward with two buckets balanced carefully on a wooden shoulder-yoke. Off the main highways, I have seen peasant women doing their wash by hand in the fresh cold waters of country streams, with the onion domes of a church visible over the trees.

In some villages outside Moscow, especially along the tourist route to the famous monastery of Zagorsk, about 60 miles to the north, peasant cabins have storybook decorations of carved, aqua-colored window frames. Their fences are neat and sturdy and their villages have a fairly prosperous look. But much of Russian village life is shabby, drab, untidy and, above all, muddy – with a mud that immobilizes life and movement. In the 'nonblack earth zone' of north Central Russia, a region roughly as far north as Hudson Bay and with an inhospitable climate to match, the writer Boris Mozhayev lamented not long ago that village life is 'decaying, slowly disintegrating'. He described what I myself have seen on drives north of Moscow: peasant cabins listing from neglect, and the unkempt pastureland slowly giving way to the returning underbrush. It is as if modern civilization radiated outward from the cities in concentric circles and the further out, the fewer amenities, the harder the life.

This is what I was told by Gennadi, a chubby, fast talking accountant who was born and educated in Leningrad but worked at three different state farms, outside the city. In the pecking order of Soviet socialism, state farms are considered a higher order than collective farms, which are theoretically voluntary associations (though withdrawal from them is exceedingly difficult). Both types can be very large, incorporating thousands of acres and several villages. State farms pay their workers a regular wage, whereas collective farmers get a share of the communal harvest, in cash and kind. The salaries of state farm workers are higher and they get other social benefits, such as state housing, but they have much smaller private plots and for that reason sometimes actually make less money than collective farmers, though they are cushioned against bad harvests by their fixed salaries.

'On the stronger, larger state farms not far from Moscow or Leningrad, or those built for show,' Gennadi told me, 'conditions are better in every way – stone buildings, separate apartments for each working family, a sewage system, running water. This was the way it was on the first two state farms where I worked. They were each about an hour from Leningrad. But the third state farm was further out – about two hours. It was a weak farm. Wooden buildings. It lacked all conveniences. No central heating system. No sewage system. No running water. The greatest problem on all three was the lack of meat. There was almost none. As far as other food goes, the closer to Leningrad, the more the stores were selling. The further from Leningrad, the less they were selling. That was the rule. Apples you could get. But oranges, tangerines – only in Leningrad.' His comments were confirmed by the few stops I made in country stores around Moscow, which offered only a scant selection of basic goods like brown bread, a couple of kinds of cheese, lard, canned fish, pears, a few dried staples and, very rarely, bologna. Some also carried a few housewares and a skimpy selection of clothing. They were dreary shops with neither the bulging shelves nor the cracker-barrel warmth of the traditional American country store.

Yet even this glimpse of rural life in Central Russia left me unprepared for what I heard from Galina Ragozina, the petite, blonde Kirov ballerina who married and later emigrated with Valery Panov. 'I saw chickens to eat for the first time two years ago when I came to Leningrad (1970),' Galina said. She had grown up in the Ural Mountains, about 800 miles east of Moscow, an industrial region off limits to foreigners. Galina thought the travel ban might have been imposed because the authorities did not want Westerners to see how poorly people lived in the Urals, though my presumption was that it was because of the defense installations and possibly because of nuclear accidents of the Sixties, which some of my friends talked about.

'We never ate chicken,' Galina recalled. When I expressed astonishment, she shoved a saucer with two little tangerines at me. 'This is only the third time in my life I have eaten these.' Meat used to be available about once a month in her Urals childhood. Even attending the excellent ballet school in Perm, she found things little better. 'Most of the year, there was nothing fresh to eat – absolutely nothing in winter and a few fresh vegetables in summer,' she said. 'I remember that at 13 (in 1963), every other girl in my class at ballet school had liver trouble. They would all get yellow. The water was terrible for drinking. From all the industry there. My hair used to fall out. I think it was because of the water, because it has stopped now. Leningrad has good water. We could get milk, of course, but only in the mornings. If I came to the store after noon, they were out.'

This is a side of Russia that foreigners rarely see. I remember a Russian woman, who married an American, telling me that her greatest surprise in coming to America was to see how narrow was the gap in living standards between city and country, compared to that same gap in Russia. Roughly 100 million people live in the Soviet countryside. It is as impossible to generalize about them as about Soviet youth. For the farmers from the Southern Ukraine, the Caucasus and Central Asia with year-round growing seasons and lucrative cash crops, are much better off than the peasants of Central Russia. Everywhere, too, rural life has its hierarchy – the farm directors, chief agronomists, better paid tractor and combine drivers, accountants, and engineers who stand well above the milkmaids, cowherders, and ordinary unskilled field hands. It is these last, the least skilled, who constitute the opposite end of the social spectrum from the privileged class of Party and government bosses with their special stores and chauffeured cars. And the actual state of their lives is just about as hard for the outsider to learn about as is the privileged life of the elite.

Soviet authorities are extremely sensitive about the countryside and the impression it makes on Westerners. Even in cities, when I would notice the old log cabin homes, which have a certain rustic warmth next to the tasteless stamped-from-the-mold prefab buildings, officials would quickly describe plans to demolish the old *izbas*. Stone, it seemed, was a symbol of modern construction whereas wooden dwellings were deemed a shameful sign of underdevelopment. The *izbas* did not fit the self-image of the nation that proclaimed itself the vanguard of socialism. In the countryside, too, peasants would emerge to protest against our taking pictures or jot down our license plate if we stopped by the roadside. The Foreign Ministry balked and stalled at requests to spend any length of time in the countryside. For three years, I sought permission to go live on a state or collective farm for several days to gather a well-rounded impression of rural living. I proposed harvest time because I presumed that it would be a high point of activity and therefore the most flattering time, though I was willing to accept any season and any farm they chose. When the Virgin Lands Region was having a record grain harvest, I asked to go there, but a Foreign Ministry official told me that people there were too busy and besides, he said, 'The people there did not like what you wrote about Armenia.' (Among several articles on Armenia, I had done one about Armenian nationalist feelings that had irked authorities in Moscow.) I said that I was surprised to hear that *The New York Times* had readers in the Virgin Lands, but this quip did not budge him.

Like other foreigners, I was occasionally taken on brief chaperoned tours to model farms, usually in southern places like Moldavia or Uzbekistan where climate and soil not only made farming more productive than in Central Russia but made ordinary living easier. In the Hungry Steppe in Central Asia, I was impressed by dramatic land reclamation projects which had recovered tens of thousands of acres of land from semiarid desert and now provided record crops of cotton. An engineer described how they had built 70-yard-wide irrigation canals, a real feat of engineering, slashing through the dusty, dry earth, giving life to man and plant. Farm chairmen rattled off imposing statistics that incredibly made peasants sound richer than high-level government bureaucrats or senior scientists. With other reporters, I was taken to freshly whitewashed homesteads where the master of the house was a Hero of Socialist Labor, or some equally atypical specialist who gave away the game by warmly recalling previous visits by foreign delegations to his immaculate home – a museum piece with its lace curtains, overstuffed furniture and large television set on the corner table. Occasionally I would meet some ordinary soul but in the company of so many official onlookers and kibitzers that realistic conversation about everyday life was impossible. It was always: 'Life is good. We have everything.'

Once, in Armenia, a collective farm chairman was telling Bob Kaiser of the *Washington Post* and me that ordinary field hands averaged 350–450 rubles a month year-round and was offering other figures so out of line with published Soviet statistics that we simply stopped taking notes. But he droned on. As we walked to his house, some matter detained him and I used the occasion to slip off independently to have a word with a farmhand who told me he made 150 rubles a month at harvest time and less out of season, and that without his private plot he could not make ends meet. But before we got into particulars, the Chairman came rushing after me, broke off the conversation, shepherded me into his house where he fed us a huge meal well-laced with his strong homemade 'grape vodka' and toasts to Soviet-American relations. We never did get to tour the farm, see people at work and talk to them. It was a pattern repeated often – the interrupted conversations, the enforced drinking, the close chaperoning, the lack of time to mix freely.

Under Brezhnev, much has been done to raise rural living standards by raising government procurement prices for crops, reducing compulsory delivery quotas to the state, and increasing basic wages of collective farmers, though they still lag behind the national factory workers' average of $187 a month. As an antipoverty measure to aid the poorest families, the government introduced a program in November 1974, to pay child support allowances of $15 monthly to families in which annual income fell below $800 per capita. Press articles indicated that most of the 12.5 million recipients would be from large rural families.

Inflation of food prices in the farmers' markets in recent years has also benefited collective farmers, especially those with the most lucrative cash crops. Indeed, their forays into Moscow to sell produce and then raid the stores to hoard up on meat, sausages and clothing has produced jealousy among city dwellers. I heard urbanites complaining that their country cousins were better off because, even on lower pay, money went further in the countryside and they could raise their own food. A chemist told me of his surprise when he picked up a hitchhiking peasant in his car one day and discovered that the man had 3,000 rubles in the savings bank (but no car). There is some evidence that average savings in rural areas may actually be higher than in cities. This reflects how little there is to buy in the countryside.

For in spite of recent improvements, rural Russians remain second class citizens. The most obvious indicator that they themselves feel this way is the great exodus from the land into the cities (21 million people from 1959–70). Occasionally such respected scholars as Viktor Perevedentsev, the demographer, candidly acknowledge 'the extreme backwardness of everyday life in the countryside'. The most humiliating stigma for decades has been the government's refusal to issue collective farmers the domestic passports possessed by other citizens. Technically, without them, the peasantry is almost as tied to the land as serfs used to be. Many are embittered by that. Yet so many found ways to get around the problem, especially by sending their children somewhere else to register for their first passports at age 16, that the government finally promised in 1975 to issue passports to peasants. But it is in no rush. The process will take until the end of 1981.

By any measure of living standards – income, schools, social life, welfare, health care, consumer goods, leisure outlets, transportation – rural people are worse off than city residents. Millions live at or below what would be the poverty level in any other industrialized nation, as the government tacitly acknowledged with the new child support program. From bits and pieces in the Soviet press, I sensed in rural Russia that same demoralizing, self-reinforcing combination of conditions found in American pockets of rural poverty – social stigma, poor schools, physical isolation, bad working conditions, low wages, poor morale, limited leisure, and chronic alcoholism. These are conditions that make rural poverty in Russia such a hard-core problem, passed from generation to generation, because the most able and energetic young people depart for the cities, leaving the less able and the elderly to man the farms.

The rural syndrome sets in early and ends late in life. Rural pensions average 20 rubles a month ($26.67), half the national average. Rural children have about half as much chance of getting into day nurseries or kindergartens as urban workers' children. They have less protection against child labor. And their schools are notably inferior, as the press repeatedly points out, mainly because educated city people wriggle out of assignments as country teachers.

'Children from country schools are not stupid,' Nadya, an experienced Moscow high school literature teacher, told me. 'But there is no comparison between the education they get and what we give our children. They aren't taught anything. One of their tenth graders would go into our seventh grade. Often they don't even read books themselves in the literature course. They just listen to the teachers read them and do textbook exercises.' And, though she did not say, sociological studies show they have far less chance of getting into university than urban children.

When it comes to farm mechanization, Soviet movies and television newsreels always seem to show spanking new tractors or combine harvesters moving in perfect echelons through sunny, windblown fields of wheat or geometrically ordered rows of cotton. From the cab of a tractor, the typical feature film hero, with a careful smudge on one cheekbone, often a woman with a bandana round her hair, a firm set to her jaw and her eye on an impossible quota, declares, 'What the Party wants is impossible, Vasya, after this bad weather, but we have taken our socialist obligations and we will fulfill them for the Motherland. Don't worry, we'll do it somehow.'

But as I drove at random through the countryside, I was usually struck by how much back-breaking farm labor is still done by hand. It is true that mechanization, irrigation, and industial farming techniques are expanding. Nonetheless, my mind's eye has an indelible image, from repeated occasions, of a drab brown field worked by women in heavy padded cotton jackets and boots, bent double over the earth, digging potatoes or heaving heads of cabbage onto a flatbed trailer. In that scene, the only mechanization is the tractor hooked up to the flatbed truck for hauling the produce away. Or in Central Asia, I remember seeing children, 12 or younger, dragging canvas bags through rows of cotton, hand-picking the bolls that combines had missed – roughly one-third of the crop.

These visual impressions were confirmed not only by the loudly trumpeted fall campaigns for city folk to go into the countryside to help harvest potatoes and other crops, but also by periodic complaints in the press. One sticks in my mind. In 1975, several mothers in Turkmenia complained to

Pravda that schools had shut down for three months so children could help gather cotton. The mothers wanted to know why this took so long. *Pravda*, obviously anxious to bawl out the farm equipment administration – a traditional *bête noire* of Soviet agriculture, answered candidly that this was because one-fifth of Turkmenia's farm machinery was down for repairs. Even more striking to me was the acknowledgment in print by V. Kirichenko, an economist, that in 1970, more than 80 percent of work in the socialized farm sector was still done by hand* – obviously a big reason why Russia still has four or five times as many people in farming as America.

One major obstacle to mechanization is the fact that the most modern mechanically oriented people, the young, are leaving the countryside. To try to stem this human hemorrhaging, farm managers save the best mechanical jobs for the young men and give them good pay. Some young men do remain, for in those fields where women were digging potatoes, I noticed that the lone tractor driver was always a man, and usually a young one. 'A tractor driver, from April through October – the busy season,' Gennadi, the state farm accountant, told me, 'could earn as much as 250 rubles a month, working every day, 14–15 hours, with no days off. In other months, 80–100 rubles.'

For the young, however, pay is not the prime cause for drift into the cities. It is the ennui, the Tobacco Road emptiness of village life where entertainment is sometimes no more than sitting on a bench outside the green fence that shuts in the vegetable plot and keeps out the rest of the world, and watching an occasional truck or car pass by. It is difficult for Americans with more than 100 million private cars, many of them pickup trucks or jalopies of farm families, to appreciate the sense of isolation in Russian villages. For sheer voice contact with the outside world, a state farm of 3,000–4,000 people, Gennadi said, may have only a half-dozen telephones – in the main offices or in the homes of the top officials. A roadside hamlet may have none. (In 1970, the Soviet Union had 11 million phones compared to 120 million in America.) An emergency at night, Gennadi said, requires tracking down some farm official to get him to open up the offices to call an

* Cited by Murray Feshbach and Stephen Rapawy, 'Labor Constraints in the Five-Year Plan', *Soviet Economic Prospects for the Seventies* (Joint Economic Committee of Congress, Washington, 1973), p. 489.

258

ambulance, and then the phone network is not always reliable and ambulances take hours in coming.

Travel can be a worse headache. In winter, people get closed in by snow. In spring, the coffee-colored mud gets deep enough to sink a big truck to its axles and human movement comes to a halt except on a few main roads. Out-of-the-way villages become isolated for weeks. Children cannot get to rural district schools. Even in good weather, travel is a burden. Driving through the countryside, I have been struck by the numbers of people gathered to wait at bus shelters or walking alone in the open country, anxiously flagging us down for a ride. When we picked them up, they spoke of an interminable wait and the irregularity of bus service. Aleksandr Ginzburg, a dissident banished to Tarussa, about 90 miles from Moscow, told me that only about half the scheduled buses from there actually ran and if he hit it perfectly, it took a minimum of three hours to bring his child to Moscow to see a doctor because the one pediatrician in his region was away. Another family, living in Moscow, said they would get up at dawn to go visit rural friends 150 miles away and felt pleased to get there by dinner, traveling by bus all day.

It is this cut off, provincial feeling more than anything else that seems to drive out the young. I remember one fall Sunday afternoon in the small town of Pasanauri in Soviet Georgia, about 60 miles from Tbilisi. Time hung over that hill town in the Caucasus with a dead weight, as it does in American Appalachia. The village elders had gathered for a funeral and talked idly in knots along the main street. A boy scampered past several houses showing neighbors the fox he had trapped. At the Intourist guest house, serving tourist traffic to the mountains, a cow clambered up the front steps and a waiter had to chase her away three times. In the next block, women in dark shawls poked at a few linens on a sidewalk stall while others inspected a new shipment of dented aluminium pots in the general store.

Beside a stone house, I fell into conversation with a square-jawed young Georgian worker who had quit the town and gone to Tbilisi even though he lost money doing so. True, he said, he made only $135 a month as a factory worker and his father made twice that much doing carpentry and odd jobs in Pasanauri, some official and some *na levo*. True, too, he said, the sturdy stone homes of Pasanauri villages were more

259

spacious than state apartments in Tbilisi, though they lacked plumbing. Also true, this being sunny Georgia, that when the orchards and vineyards yielded plenty of fruit and grapes for Georgian wine and cognac, some farmers could earn enough to buy a car. But in the factory, he said, brightening, you worked with machinery; but here, with your hands. Tbilisi had restaurants and girls and things to do. It was modern.

'There's nothing to do here, no way to amuse yourself,' he said glumly. Then gazing up at the leafless trees and long lines of burnished hills on either side of the valley, he added: 'There's no movie theater. Nothing. Nothing to do but hunt and drink.'

It was a tale I heard elsewhere. Gennadi, an educated man in his early thirties, felt stir crazy in the state farm villages around Leningrad. 'On a state farm you have mud and impassable roads and you walk around all the time in boots,' he groaned. 'It's boring. Such terrible boredom! And this is at a farm only a couple of hours from Leningrad. There is a club, an old wooden building, damp, cold, and besides they show old films you've seen twice or four times. Everyone is, as they said, *pod etim delom* – drunk. Young people want to go to the movies in Leningrad. To go around the city *not in boots*, but in shoes! Just to feel yourself not an animal, but a human being. If you're in the city, you're a human being.'

Given such sentiments, it is remarkable that the exodus from the countryside has not been greater. This says something not only about administrative restrictions but also about the conservatism of the Russian peasantry and their roots in the countryside. Yet leading writers of the current 'village school', like Fyodor Abramov and Boris Mozhayev, who exalt the long-suffering moral character and evoke the hardships of the peasantry, write that many feel alienated from the land and that the earth has become orphaned. What they seem to mean is that the peasantry no longer feel attachment to communal fields. In less literary terms, Party officials squawk that field hands work poorly on collective land and sneak off as much as a third of the time to work on their private plots.

The Party's response to this and other chronic problems of Soviet agriculture has been to pour immense investments into farming (roughly $150 billion in 1971–75), especially into grand schemes that will promote large-scale industrial farming. In some ways the increasing use of chemical fertilizers and modern irrigation techniques is paying off. Cotton output has reached record highs, and even in bad years when Moscow has to shop for grain in America, the grain harvests are 10–15 million tons larger than they were under Khrushchev. Brezhnev's new departure in the mid-Seventies has been to promote formation of collective farm conglomerates that would put construction, animal husbandry, and various other tasks on a joint, industrial basis. Brezhnev's second plan, similar to Khrushchev's Virgin Land Scheme, was to announce a 35 billion ruble (nearly $48 billion) program to revitalize the long-neglected farmlands of Central Russia, the non-black earth region. I was told by a journalist that this had been pushed by Russophiles, the pro-Russian ethnic faction, among the Politburo, including Mikhail Solomentsev, premier of the Russian Republic, and Agriculture Minister Dmitri Polyansky. In the long run, both programs seem intended not only to industrialize farming but to reduce the role of private plots.

Largely unnoticed abroad, a small band of liberals and economic rationalists, working on the basis of industrial reforms of the mid-Sixties, have tried the opposite tack. They have sought to decentralize agriculture and to revive the peasantry's attachment to the land by trying to use the principle of private plot incentives on collective farmland. 'Capitalism in socialist clothing' was how one reformer privately described it to me.

The idea was to turn over sizeable tracts of state or collective land to farm 'links' – small working units of 6–12 qualified specialists whose pay depended solely on harvest from their tract. According to this concept, which surfaced in the early Sixties, the link would have machinery as well as land at its disposal and thus have responsibility not only for land cultivation but also for machine maintenance – a perennial headache in the Soviet farm system and always a serious factor in bad harvest years. In effect, each link was a small cooperative enterprise in itself. The theory was simple: If pay depended on results and the work force was organized in small enough units, each individual could see the benefit of producing well, just as on a private plot.

The main difference from the existing system was that,

normally, collective farmhands move all over huge areas, working one field and one task one day, another field the next, having no sense of responsibility and no direct dependence on the results of their labor. A tractor driver, I was told, is paid by the size of the area he plows so that it behooves him to plow rapidly and in shallow furrows in order to cover more territory even though the best crop yields require plowing more slowly, more carefully and deeper into the soil. The same with weeding and other tasks. The link was supposed to combat this quota-filling mentality.

One celebrated exemplar of this system was Vladimir Pervitsky, a Hero of Socialist Labor from the Krasnodar Region, who showed in one experiment that his 10-man link could triple the yield of a tract normally worked at various times by 80 people. His link plowed, planted, weeded, reaped and protected their land better than normal workers. They came to feel it was 'their land', I was told by Aleksandr Yanov, a former Soviet journalist who was forced to emigrate by the secret police because the reformism of his press articles had gone too far. I met Yanov in New York City in December 1974, two days after he left Moscow. The link idea was supported well enough during the mid-Sixties to gain token acceptance on many farms – with one or two small links on each very large farm – though it encountered opposition from both farm administrators and ordinary workers who, according to Yanov, saw themselves becoming superfluous if the smaller links proved too efficient. It would expose the gross over-staffing of most state and collective farms. Gradually, the Politburo sponsor of the links scheme, Gennadi Voronov, lost power, and conservatives neutralized the link experiment.

Nonetheless, Yanov told me of another reformer of unusual energy and daring who made a fresh attempt in the early Seventies to put the link system with its built-in profit motive on an even larger scale. He was Ivan Khudenko, a burly, red-faced, outspoken, veteran Communist who resigned as a Senior Agricultural Official of the Kazakh Republic in the 1960s in order to pursue his radical experiments. According to Yanov, Nikita Khrushchev was toying with using some of Khudenko's ideas to reform Soviet agriculture when he was overthrown in October 1964. Yet Khudenko's efforts were so little known publicly that they were news to me when Yanov mentioned them in New York.

Khudenko was Yanov's idol, a model for Soviet reform. 'We thought the link system, especially Khudenko's approach to it, would be the salvation of Russian agriculture,' enthused Yanov, who wrote many articles on farming and other economic topics for Soviet newspapers and journals. 'We thought it would change the face of Russia completely.'

After one abortive experiment on a collective farm, Khudenko persuaded a state farm director to let him use a large tract of marginal, unused farmland in the steppe around Akshi, in Kazakhstan. He wanted to test whether a limited group of farm specialists would show greater productivity than normal state farm workers, if they operated on the link principle. With tractors and materials for building their own homes, borrowed from the parent state farm, Khudenko and his 60 picked specialists conducted their experiment in 1972 – a disastrous farm year for the Russians.

'Khudenko's idea was that with the link system on this larger scale, he could compete with the best farm enterprises in America and Western Europe. He not only said it, but he proved it,' Yanov told me. 'Unfortunately, the experiment lasted for only one harvest and then it became clear that if Khudenko was right, the entire agricultural leadership was wrong. The experiment was a success. They demonstrated that labor productivity on this farm was 20 times higher than on neighboring farms. The Kazakhs were so pleased that a local journalist wrote a play about Khudenko. It had its final "inspection preview" for a select audience on January 7, 1973.' The preview was attended not only by censors but a number of reform-minded journalists and economists.

'The next day, Khudenko was arrested and charged with trying to steal 1,000 rubles from the state,' Yanov bitterly recalled. 'It was a trumped-up charge. The agricultural powers in Moscow were against the experiment.'

It appeared that Khudenko had been framed in a bureaucratic maneuver. The decree closing down his experimental farm at Akshi was signed by the Minister of Agriculture in Alma Ata but Khudenko claimed that this was an incorrect procedure because such action required a decision by the entire Council of Ministers, and he went to court to sue for 11 months' back pay for himself and his 60 men. A local court in Kazakhstan upheld his suit, actually exceeding its authority, though Khudenko did not know that. For when he took the court order to a bank to collect the funds, Yanov said, he was arrested on charges of trying to obtain state funds under false pretences.

According to Yanov, there was high-level, behind-the-scenes intervention at Khudenko's trial and the judge, thought to be leaning toward Khudenko until the last moment, handed down a verdict against him and two of his closest aides. Khudenko was sentenced to six years in jail. Although economists and scholars in important institutes in Moscow sympathized with Khudenko's efforts and friends like Yanov tried to rally support for him, very little was done to defend him. The leadership had rejected his approach which would have put Soviet farming on a more flexible pragmatic basis, and had decided to push ahead with a more centralized, industrialized program for upgrading Soviet agriculture. Khudenko died in prison in 1974 at the age of 62.

IX

INDUSTRIAL LIFE
Skoro Budet—It'll Be Here Soon

As long as the bosses pretend they are paying us a
decent wage, we will pretend that we are working.
Soviet workers' saying, 1970s

'The tempo of work is different for each ten-day period of
the month,' said Rashid, a stocky, honey-colored factory foreman from Uzbekistan, who was explaining what work was
like at the Tashkent Tractor Parts Factory. 'Do you know
the words – *spyachka, goryachka* and *likhoradka?*'

Literally, I knew they meant something like hibernation,
hot time and feverish frenzy, but I did not immediately
associate them with his factory, so I shook my head. Rashid
smiled at my innocence and rubbed a calloused hand across
his cheek.

'Those are the nicknames we give the "decades", the ten-
day periods into which each month is divided,' he said. 'The
first decade is the sleeper time, the second decade is for hot
work, and the third decade is like fever.' He paused to let me
absorb that and went on. 'The tempo of work also depends
on pay day. Normally, we have two pay days a month: one
between the 15th and 20th and the other in the first days of
the next month. Two or three days before pay day, there is a
preholiday feeling and no one is in the mood for working.
And two or three days afterward, people are practically sick
from drinking and they have to drink off their hangovers.'

With variations and embellishments, it was a story repeated by others including Yosif, a tall, slender, middle-aged
engineer from a big city in southern Russia who chain-
smoked as he talked about the plants where he had worked.
To hear his description of Soviet factories that made air-

265

conditioning and refrigeration units was to pass through a Soviet looking glass and to discover a world inside Soviet industry that seemed almost a travesty of the Command Economy imagined in the West to be functioning with monopolistic harmony and monolithic discipline.

'Storming' is what Rashid and Yosif were describing. It is a practice so endemic and essential to the Soviet system that Russians have coined the fancy word *shturmovshchina* to denote the entire national phenomenon of crash programs and the wildly erratic work-rhythm of Soviet factories, large and small, civilian and military. Storming to fulfill the monthly, quarterly or annual Plan turns every month into a sort of crazy industrial pregnancy, sluggish in gestation and frenzied at the finish.

'Usually, at the start of the month an enterprise is virtually paralyzed after the storming in the final days of the preceding month,' Yosif explained. By his account, the work force was in a state of exhaustion not only because of drinking but because so many skilled workers had been pressed into long overtime shifts during the storming campaign. 'A lot have to put in two shifts a day during storming,' he said. 'They work all day both Saturdays and Sundays, their normal days off. Management doesn't have the right [to pay them for overtime] because it has a ceiling on its payroll and financial inspection organs check on that. Sometimes if a worker is badly needed, he can get time-and-a-half or double time off to compensate for his overtime. But whether or not they get time off, workers have to put in those extra days [Black Saturdays, they are universally called] without extra pay. So usually there are a lot of workers off at the start of the month and the enterprise is in a state of paralysis.'

'Plants couldn't operate at normal capacity anyway because they do not have a lot of the materials and components needed for operation,' Yosif went on. 'In spite of the Plan and seemingly definite delivery deadlines, suppliers don't fulfill the Plan or meet delivery schedules. So manufacturing plants cannot work rhythmically. Normally, not enough parts and components are available until about the 10th or 12th of the month. Some items can be assembled almost completely, but they lack certain parts. A large number of items cannot be shipped out and accumulate in store rooms. They are held as late as the 20th of the month because parts aren't ready or certain components are missing. Finally

266

comes the third decade (20th to 30th). It's a good month if absolutely everything required is actually on hand by the 20th. When everything has finally been received, the storming of the Plan can begin. Immediately work starts in many sections simultaneously.'

Yosif spoke about it matter-of-factly, making clear this was a normal state of affairs for Soviet industry, not some aberration peculiar to factories where he worked or to particular seasons of the year, though December, being the end of the year, is worse than other months.

'In other countries, production normally goes on throughout the month,' Yosif observed, 'but here, it can only begin on the 15th or 20th when all materials have been received. So factories must fulfill about 80 percent of the Plan [quotas] in the last 10–15 days. No one cares any longer about quality. Volume is the main thing. Some workers are sent to finish the items that were partly assembled and kept in storerooms. Some of the production is no longer finished in factory conditions but often in the open air. Water, dirt, and dust can fall in the equipment which, of course, lowers its quality and cuts down its life span.

'The whole population knows all about this because everyone works,' Yosif commented. 'So normally, when someone buys a household appliance, he tries to buy one with a certificate saying that it was produced before the 15th of the month and not after the 15th. [Soviet goods carry tags with production dates.] If the item was made before the 15th, obviously it was not made in a rush and the customer thinks, "maybe it will work". If it was made after the 15th, there's a good chance it will stop working pretty quickly.'

Other Russians with whom I talked were more flexible than Yosif who, as a technical man, may have had higher standards than most. They reckoned it was not too great a risk to buy something made as late as the 20th. But no matter what the object, the candid advice of one middle-aged Moscow woman, echoed by others was: 'Don't buy if it was made after the 20th.'

Her husband nodded in agreement and with a typical Russian laughter-through-tears sense of humor launched into his favorite joke about storming. It concerned a hapless Soviet worker who died and found himself in purgatory confronted by an official who addressed him in the stilted, condescending rhetoric of Soviet bureaucrats: 'According to your moral qualities, you will not be permitted to enter heaven. Your papers are not in good enough order to be accepted. You may only enter hell. My duty is to warn you that there are two sections of hell – capitalist hell and socialist hell. You have a choice.'

The worker inquired about the difference.

'In the capitalist hell, they will drive a nail into your butt every day all month long,' the official said curtly.

'And does the same thing go on in the socialist hell, too?'

'The socialist hell is different, comrade,' the functionary advised. 'There, the Devil gets drunk a lot and there is a chronic shortage of nails.'

'Well, in that case,' said the newcomer, brightening, 'I'll take the socialist hell.'

'All right, that is your choice,' the official acknowledged, 'but it is my duty to warn you that all the same they'll drive those 30 nails into your butt in the last five days of the month.'

That irreverent view of the workings of the Soviet economy has the kind of insight into Russian reality that prompted Dostoyevsky to describe his native land as a sublime, universal, ordered chaos. It is a far cry, however, from the picture that Western visitors derive from officially guided tours through spruced-up Soviet industrial installations, from the image of technological prowess given by live television coverage of the Soviet Soyuz spacecraft docking with an American Apollo, or from the impression projected to the world-at-large by the Kremlin's perennial boasting about overfulfilling its Five-Year-Plans.

The plan is proffered by Soviet Marxists as the key to scientific management of manpower and resources, the unerring lever for achieving maximum growth and rising productivity, the Utopian device for assuring the coordinated functioning of the world's second mightiest economy. The Plan comes close to being the fundamental law of the land. 'Fulfill the Plan' is one of the most incessant incantations of Soviet life. Publicly, the Plan is treated with almost mystical veneration, as if endowed with some superhuman faculty for raising mortal endeavor to a higher plane, freed of human foibles.

It is the Five-Year-Plans, launched in 1928 by Stalin to

force the pace of industrialization, that are officially credited with multiplying Soviet output 50-fold from 1913–1973 and building the backbone of the Soviet economy. Indeed in six decades, Moscow has transformed a backward though emerging continent into an industrialized state. It has developed the world's largest network of hydroelectric power stations, opened up the incalculable mineral riches of Siberia, produced atomic ice breakers, space platforms and mechanized moon explorers, and surpassed America in such basic measurements of industrial muscle as output of steel, cement and oil.

But the Plan, as some internal critics have noted in their Aesopian language, has hardly assured the clockwork functioning of the economy. Along with dramatic growth, it has spawned rigidity, waste, and lopsided development. In some ways, the Soviet system has seemed less a planned economy than a system for concentrating on principal targets so that the Kremlin could set priorities and mobilize mass effort behind them. (Like most other Westerners, I had been unaware, for example, that the Soviet leadership had been so successful in putting its population to work that in 1970 the Soviet work-force numbered 122 million – compared to only 85 million in America, including the unemployed.) Through the mechanism of the Plan, Soviet leaders have made enormous investments in heavy industry, military production and science and, especially during the sharp growth of the Stalin era, financed this mainly by exacting heavy sacrifices from Soviet consumers.

As one Western expert commented, Stalin 'bequeathed to his heirs both a great industrial power and an inefficient economy.'* His enshrinement of the centralized Plan was probably more suited to the rapid, muscular build-up of the economy than to the present period when the Soviet economy faces more sophisticated problems of modernization. Soviet growth rates have slowed in the Seventies, though Western specialists still reckon that on the average the Soviet economy was growing twice as fast as the American economy from 1968–1974.† With economic controls and centralized

*Moshe Lewin, *Political Undercurrents in Soviet Economic Debates* (Princeton, 1974), p. 119.

†In July 1975, C.I.A. economists calculated that from 1968–1974, the Soviet Gross National Product rose from $555 to $722 billion while American GNP rose from $1,090 to $1,266 billion, giving the

pricing, Russians have cushioned themselves from the gyrations of boom-and-bust and double-digit inflation that have rocked Western economies. Largely unperturbed by serious debates about environment or the wisdom of maximum economic growth that now perplex Western leaders, Soviet officials from Brezhnev to the lowest village Party secretary rattle off production statistics and Plan quotas with a kind of undiminished 19th-century infatuation with the sheer magic of output enthusiastically expressed by Marx. They point with pride to massive industrial conglomerates made possible, they feel, only by the Plan's awesome ability to focus vast resources on projects of top national priority.

The Kama River Truck Plant is the Soviet crash project par excellence, the showpiece of the 1971–1975 Five-Year-Plan. I've seen other Soviet installations, like Bratsk High Dam, that rival Western facilities for modern technology. I have met Western businessmen who waxed eloquent about electronics plants at Riga and Leningrad or encountered American aircraft specialists raving about what Soviet engineers were doing with modern metals like titanium at the Voronezh Aircraft Plant which makes the TU-144 supersonic transport. But none of these matches the Kama River Truck Plant as an archetype of the gigantomania of Soviet planners, as a symbol of the Soviet faith that bigger means better and the Soviet determination to have the biggest at any cost.

Kama is the kind of massive crash project that appeals to Russians. It embodies industrial might created from a vacuum and materialized in a furious five-year flurry of storming. It emanates brute strength. In 1971, Soviet construction brigades started from scratch to build the world's largest truck plant in the open, rolling, wind swept plains about 600 miles east of Moscow. By the time I got there in mid-1973, what had been empty rye fields near a sleepy rural community of weather-beaten peasant cabins had been transformed into a throbbing, rapidly growing city of 90,000. High-rise apartments for construction workers stood wall-to-wall across the horizon. Close to $700 million worth of the

Soviet economy an annual growth rate close to 4.7 percent compared to about 2.4 percent for the American economy. In 1968, the Soviet GNP was almost exactly half of American GNP. In 1974, with the American economy in recession and GNP falling, the Soviets were up to 56 percent of American GNP. All figures were calculated in 1973 dollars.

most modern industrial machinery from the United States, West Germany, Japan, France and elsewhere was on order and construction crews were being exhorted to enclose the frames of factory buildings before winter so that equipment could be installed.

For hours our group of correspondents were driven by bus, slithering through ankle-deep mud (in July!) past mile upon mile of pipelines, covered conveyor belts, giant factory skeletons. The sheer magnitude of the project was staggering. Soviet engineers informed us that Kama was not just one factory but six, all huge: a foundry, a forging plant, a body plant, an engine plant, an instrument-and-repair plant, and an assembly plant, to be linked by 175 miles of computer-run conveyor belts and assembly lines. The production complex, costing in the billions, occupies 23 square miles, an area larger than the entire island of Manhattan. At full capacity, Kama is slated to produce 150,000 heavy trucks and 250,000 diesel engines a year, dwarfing anything in Detroit or the German Ruhr.

As the premier project of the national Five-Year-Plan, Kama has enjoyed vast advantages over run-of-the-mill Soviet industries. Yet for all its exalted priority, it has been plagued by chronic problems that bedevil the Soviet economy in spite of planning. In 1969, the cost of Kama and its satellite city was reckoned at about $2.2 billion; by 1975, the figure had ballooned to $5 billion, a sign not only of higher prices for Western machinery but industrial inflation at home as well. For all the Plan deadlines and Kremlin attention, the construction schedule has slipped badly. When I was at Kama, huge banners urged: 'Let's give [the Motherland] the first Kama truck in 1974.' Yet by fall, 1975, it had yet to appear.

In any case, I found it hard to understand why the rush, except as a way of whipping up national fervor and projecting Soviet prestige. The explanation of Soviet planners was that Kama trucks were needed to break the national transportation bottleneck. But the Soviet highway network, let alone the auto service network, is hardly in shape to handle an enormous new fleet of heavy trucks. It is only about one-fourth as large as the American highway system and 60 percent of it is dirt or gravel roads, impassable to heavy trucks. Moreover, I couldn't help wondering whether there would be enough Soviet customers ready to put the Kama trucks

271

to efficient use. For one of the most baffling aspects of traffic around Moscow was the hordes of trucks, barging through traffic, belching black fumes, but empty. Russians and foreigners alike used to chuckle at all the empty trucks. This numbing waste of truck capacity made the ambitious production targets for Kama reminiscent of the breakneck race to put Bratsk High Dam in operation by 1961 even though the Bratsk aluminium plant, its main customer, was not completed for another decade. Bratsk was a planning goof that even some Soviet economists had criticized.

Nonetheless, at Kama, Plan targets had an iron logic of their own. Despite delays, Russians claimed – and Western industrialists conceded – that they were building this vast facility more rapidly than would be done elsewhere. Yet the enormous haste imposed by arbitrary Plan deadlines made waste. Theoretically to save time, the Russians plunged headlong into constructing factory buildings before technical plans had been drafted, before Soviet foreign trade firms had contracted for the equipment to be installed in the plants, or before designs for Kama trucks had been produced. One result was that some buildings later had to be altered to accommodate the equipment and some expensive Western machinery, waiting to be installed, was stuck in makeshift warehouses or left outside to rust.

In 1973, Soviet bosses at Kama complained to American newsmen that Swindell-Dressler, the American firm hired to design the metal foundry, was falling behind schedule and upsetting the whole timetable. Months later, I was privately told by Swindell-Dressler executives that the holdup was because Soviet engineers, born and bred in a system of secrecy, would not give Americans the specifications for Soviet equipment to which American machinery was to be connected. Without specifications, it was impossible to draft engineering designs. Another obstacle, they said, was the terrible delay caused by protracted Soviet dickering over prices with Western equipment suppliers. Technical plans had to wait until Soviet buyers made up their minds.

Even where work went swiftly, the Soviets paid a price in quality. Engineers like Viktor Perstev, the red-faced veteran construction boss at Kama, were fond of bragging that Soviet construction brigades could throw up a 14-story apartment building (300 units) in a month. From a distance, the apartments looked good enough. But up close, they were falling apart soon after occupancy, victims of the instant aging that afflicts almost all Soviet construction. Floors were uneven; windows and walls cracked; kitchen and bathroom plumbing fixtures were crude and badly joined. Generally, the workmanship was shoddy, as it is almost everywhere. When an American correspondent asked a Russian why it was all so poorly done, the Russian shrugged: 'It belongs to no one so no one cares about it.'

In short, the mechanistic Soviet Economic Plan seems to cut against the grain of Russian nature. In the world at large, Russians have a reputation for discipline because of their seemingly docile obedience to authority. But this is a discipline imposed from outside. Left to their own devices, Russians are generally an easy-going, disorderly, pleasantly disorganized, and not very efficient people. (Significantly, the Russian language had no word for efficiency and had to borrow one from English.) The typical Soviet office, often unseen by foreign visitors, is a supercrowded, disorderly muddle with a little propaganda corner and not enough desks to go around for everyone, I was told by Moscow friends. Factories through which I was taken were usually neat, though I was struck by the terrible din of machinery and by how few industrial safety signs there were. But Soviet friends insisted these were *pokazukha* factories, spruced up for show, and that the run-of-the-mill Soviet factory was 'a bordello', as more than one put it.

Moreover, the foreigner can tour plenty of installations and stare at machinery without learning about 'storming' or understanding that the Russian sense of time is at once enchantingly and frustratingly loose or nonexistent. It bears little relation to time in a commercial society. Most tourists learn to their consternation that just ordering dinner in a restaurant can require an hour or more. A one-hour press conference begins nearly an hour late and runs for two more; a short answer can take 45 minutes; a 10-minute drop-in with friends invariably stretches to three or four hours; staying late, until 2 or 3 a.m., is one of the more attractive Russian vices; a week's job takes three weeks; elevators break down and stay out of order for a fortnight or more; other repair work consumes unpredictable gobs of time; construction timetables nationwide run years behind. Russians are genuinely put off by the impatience of Westerners, especially Americans, who go up the wall with frustration at the dawdling uncertainties of Russian life. The innocent Western visitor, assuming that the Soviet Union is an advanced society, is often bruised when he first bumps against the essentially underdeveloped tempo of most Soviet commerce. It takes a while to learn that *skoro budet*, literally, 'It'll be here soon,' is really *mañana* stretched to eternity. For procrastination is built into the Russian temperament. Perhaps that's the main reason for constant propaganda hounding Russians to finish the Plan on time.

Although Russians are capable of great exertion if pressed to produce, sustained hard work is not a national characteristic. They do not have the work ethic of Americans, Germans, or Japanese. 'Americans work hard, put in long hours, get ahead and also get ulcers,' was the comment of a Soviet editor who admitted that he rarely strained on his job. 'Russians don't work very hard or try very hard. And we live more relaxed lives.' A schoolteacher told Ann, that she considered her job the best part of her life 'because no one pushes me there'. Martic Martentz, an Armenian-American Communist who voluntarily returned from New York to try living in the Soviet Union, told me he was astonished at the Soviet image of Americans. 'They think everyone [in America] is rich,' he gasped. 'They don't realize how hard people have to work in America.'

A movie script writer suggested that one reason many Russians don't work harder is that generally it doesn't pay enough. If one doctor in a polyclinic gets a reputation for good, conscientious work, she winds up with extra patients and a lot of overtime work but she cannot be paid for overtime, the writer said, whereas those who get ahead are usually doctors who speak up in Party meetings and curry favor with Party officials. Another reason, Russian friends reminded me, is that the Soviet Union is still not as money-oriented as Western societies. 'Money alone is not enough, you have to have something to spend it on,' remarked a young scientist. 'Connections matter more than money. With connections you can find the deficit goods and spend the money. Without them, it's not worth the effort.'

Playing hookey from work is a national pastime so common that Arkady Raikin, the comedian, has gotten censors to approve several skits on that theme. In one, he plays an engineer who lolls all day on a bed the size of a putting green and rationalizes skipping work by recalling how little he does on the job. 'I'm doing them a favor by staying away,' he quips. In another, three men sneak out during working hours to the barber shop but get lousy service because the barbers themselves are trying to sneak away. One barber wants to buy oranges, another, to get some gadget repaired, and the third, to visit the dentist. The barbers return defeated, only to discover that the grocer, repairman and dentist are the three customers sitting in their chairs. 'That's just what happens,' a Russian confessed to me during intermission. 'My wife goes out shopping during working hours. It's the only way, because after work the crowds in the stores and the lines are simply terrible. Everybody does it.' A linguist told me her friends would duck out of work just to pay social calls or see a movie.

If part-time hookey is a pervasive problem among white-collar workers, full-scale absenteeism among blue-collar workers reaches such disaster proportions, especially around pay days, that the Kremlin leadership and Soviet press periodically inveigh against 'slackers' and 'bad labor discipline'. The Moscow manager for a Western airline told me his Soviet ground crews were so unreliable that his Western technical chief had to check personally that fuel was available, ground service ready, and de-icing and other equipment prepared for their incoming flights. On the days that their planes came in, the technical chief would pick up his Soviet mechanics and workmen at home to insure they would be on the job.

Soviet managers have a great deal of trouble disciplining factory workers not only because it is almost impossible to fire them but also because labor is generally short and a disgruntled worker knows he can quit and find another job easily. Theoretically, Soviet Marxism holds that workers are not alienated under socialism because they enjoy the full fruits of their labor, and Soviet propagandists seek to maintain this fiction. But occasional sociological studies and press items revealing that 2.8 million workers changed jobs in the Russian Republic alone in 1973 undercut that contention. Poor working conditions and lack of side benefits, such as housing, rather than pay are cited by workers as reasons for dissatisfaction.

From a few limited contacts with blue-collar workers I

gathered that there are more labor-management frictions over pay and work norms than I had imagined. One man, who later became an engineer, said that when he was 17, being taught by an older worker how to operate a lathe, he had asked whether it could not be operated faster. 'Yes, but shut up,' the older man said. 'Next month they are revising the norms, so we slowed it down on purpose.'

Soviet industry is run on the old, 19th-century company town basis and Soviet unions, as company unions, are more interested in doling out vacation passes and welfare benefits or helping to keep workers in line than in battling with management over bread-and-butter issues. In fact, very few cases of group job actions in Soviet industry ever come to light. The press suppresses that news and if word reaches Westerners, it is often months or years later.

Nonetheless, through Moscow friends I met several factory workers who told me that slowdown protests occasionally do take place on assembly lines. Yuri, a burly young metalworker, mentioned two instances in his metal-pouring plant near Moscow but did not want to discuss them for fear the news might be traced back to him. He did, however, describe to me how three brigades in a neighboring textile plant had shut down their assembly lines for several hours to protest introduction of automatic knitting machines with higher work norms, resulting in lower pay.

The technique of Soviet management in such cases, Yuri said, was artificially to select one brigade as *peredoviki*, model workers, and to grant them large pay bonuses and other privileges based on phony output figures on the new machinery. Their results then became the pretext for raising norms of the three other brigades. The ordinary brigades found out they were being finagled; hence the protest. Although the shutdown lasted only three hours, it was serious enough for the plant's security section to investigate, Yuri said, because it involved three different lines. 'If it had been just two, they figure that it's nothing unusual because two brigades could get into an argument,' he explained. 'But three lines is an emergency. It means someone organized it. That's very serious. I don't know what happened to the organizers but I heard that the bosses had to back down and lower the norms.'

In an effort to increase output the Communist Party resorts to various moral inducements, from special awards to

276

model workers, to 'socialist competition' between work brigades or factories, to the perennial technique of 'socialist obligations'. Before every great holiday, work collectives across the country take upon themselves obligations to exceed their work norms. They solemnly pledge to implement Party decisions, to 'increase their ideological level', and to raise their output. Steel mills promise to roll out 110 percent of their quota of steel, candy factories vow to produce a year's output of sweets in just eleven months, and libraries take an oath to insure that an unprecedented number of books by or about Lenin will be read in the next three months.

Another favorite gimmick of Soviet propagandists is the *vstrechny plan*, literally, the Counter Plan, or the Plan the workers themselves put forward to meet, match, and exceed the official Plan fixed for them. Theoretically, it is spontaneously offered. But the entire ritual is widely viewed as such cynical humbug that factory workers have contrived their own raunchy put-down of the *vstrechny plan*. According to this joke, a factory worker arrives home late one evening and to protect himself from his wife's scolding, he explains that he was delayed by a long factory meeting on the *vstrechny plan*.

'What is this *vstrechny plan*?' asks his skeptical spouse.

'Well,' he says, 'it's as if I proposed that we screw twice tonight and you come back and propose we screw three times when both of us know damned well we couldn't do it more than once.'

The two young Russians who told me this joke as we walked along a Moscow boulevard broke into loud guffaws and were disappointed that I was not similarly moved by their earthy humor. 'At least you get the idea about the *vstrechny plan*?' one asked. I nodded.

Despite the Party's attachment to such gimmickry, industrial managers seem to rely on more pay as the best incentive. High priority projects, especially those in hardship conditions such as the Siberian oil fields or gold mines, often pay triple or quadruple the average Soviet blue-collar wage of $187 monthly. The Soviet economy is laced with a bewildering maze of bonuses and premiums for fulfilling Plan quotas but workmen like Yuri said that basic premiums are quickly taken for granted as a fixed part of workers' pay and thus lose leverage.

Yuri's picture of political and social attitudes among his

fellow-workers corresponded surprisingly to American blue-collar ethnic conservatives attracted by Alabama's Gov. George Wallace. On the job, he said, they have a certain camaraderie. The men cover for each other within the work brigade if one is sick or has a big event like a wedding or a birthday to celebrate. But they dislike habitual drunkards and model workers – drunkards because they impose extra burdens on others, and model workers, Yuri said, because they are usually picked by the Party 'for political reasons or by management to raise the norms'. Class feelings are strong. Like the Wallace constituency with its sniping at 'pointy-heads' and intellectuals, Soviet laborers, according to Yuri, talk contemptuously of intellectuals as *nakhlebniki*, parasites living off the bread of others. (He quoted a workers' proverb deriding the intelligentsia: 'A fish begins rotting from the head.') The workers were loyal to the Soviet system and the Party, Yuri affirmed, but they bore no love for the big factory bosses riding around in chauffeured black Volga sedans. 'If there were ever a second Revolution, it would be first against the bosses in the black Volgas,' he said. But he hastened to add, 'Of course, there won't be any second Revolution.'

President Nikolai Podgorny once grandly called the Soviet factory director a 'plenipotentiary representative of the socialist state and Communist Party' and a Soviet woman whom I met said her husband, who had run a 12,000-man factory in Central Russia, was like 'a prince' within his domain. Although nominally his salary was 450 rubles a month ($600), he actually earned twice that much through a series of regular bonuses. Moreover, he could command free services from the factory and received special monthly food cartons – free – from elite stores in Moscow. His family was assigned choice, cheap, comfortable housing, and they could buy meat, eggs, and produce from neighboring state farms for a song. They vacationed for practically nothing at Council of Ministers' guest houses and enjoyed such other privileges as a direct telephone line to the Kremlin. 'All the people in the village would say, when I would go by, "There goes the wife of the big boss," and they would hypocritically be nice to me, flatter me and so on,' she said. Compared to others, her family lived like nobility.

Nonetheless, this woman regarded her husband's job as a nightmare, and steered her sons away from such career ambitions. As she told it, July was 'the hottest month' because her husband spent all his time 'beating down the Plan', wrangling with his ministry to lower targets for his plant in the coming year. It was vital, she explained, for the factory director not to disclose his plant's real capacity and never to exceed his current Plan targets by more than one or two percent because otherwise his quotas would be raised too steeply next year. One constant worry was that the chief engineer, traditionally regarded in Soviet factories as 'the Ministry's man' appointed by higher-ups independently of the director, might undercut him.

Like other factory directors, she said, her husband always kept plenty of extra workmen on his payroll so that he had enough hands to successfully storm the Plan. Then, too, he could loan workers to other factories in return for equipment or favors that he wanted because, as she put it, 'There isn't a single successful factory director who operates by the book – you can't do it.' Nor was the Plan his only big worry. He had to keep on the good side of local Party bigwigs and that meant supplying them with workers for the harvest, for road construction and other pet projects. Never mind how padded payrolls undermined efficiency. A factory director knew, she said, that if he got into trouble, it was more likely to be because he failed to keep the Party hierarchy happy than because his efficiency was slipping. Ultimately, she disclosed, it was politics, not economics, that cost her husband his job in the early Seventies.

The most constant headache, as she saw it, was the unending struggle with supplies. Thefts were a serious nuisance. Whole rail carloads of raw materials or parts would disappear or simply never show up. But more often, it was simply the delays. 'At home, the phone would ring all night,' she said. 'People telling my husband, "The metal hasn't come yet from Siberia or the parts aren't here from Odessa." All the time. Sometimes for a factory director it's helpful when raw material is late in delivery because he can use that as an alibi for getting his Plan lowered. But not all raw materials are top priority and can be used as an alibi. Those which are lower priority, he must "beat out" of the system himself.'

That aspect of her story was corroborated by a Soviet journalist who landed by chance in a Leningrad factory director's office when one of his shop superintendents informed him the factory was out of metallic lacquer and would have to shut down temporarily.

'The director got on the phone and called the Party Committee of the Province, the industrial department,' the journalist told me. 'Why them? Because toward the end of the month, a general redistribution of shortage materials takes place. There is a hierarchy of enterprises: in the first rank, military factories; in the second, heavy industry; and in the third rank, light [consumer] industry. All the reserve materials that have been accumulated by light industry are withdrawn, confiscated for the sake of heavy industry. The director called them to take the metallic lacquer from some light industry factory. But he was too late. They told him, "It's not possible to do anything for you. Someone else has already stolen it." That's exactly what they said – stolen. "You've got to steal some lacquer for our factory or we won't fulfill the Pan," the director told them. And they said, "We would have stolen something for you with pleasure but a more important factory has already had time to steal it. You were late. You should have called us two days ago." '

According to my journalist friend, the factory director was in such a jam that he called the Party boss for the Province, hoping that through personal influence he could obtain lacquer from a Party boss in a neighboring province. 'The Party bosses have permanent connections with each other,' the journalist said. 'Today, one helps the other. Tomorrow, it is the other way around. His Party boss agreed to get the material – but only the day after tomorrow. That meant today and tomorrow the workers would have nothing to do and still there would be hardly time enough to fulfill the monthly Plan. So the director decided to let the workers have a day off but make them work a Black Saturday.'

The chronic shortages of supplies, which the Plan does not take into account, force industrial managers to cut corners and adopt shady practices that, technically speaking, the system frowns on but simply has to tolerate. *Izvestia*, the government newspaper, once held up a factory director as a bad example for hoarding huge stocks of metal to cushion himself against shortages. But he had a ready reply: 'You know the saying, "If you want a two-hump camel, you must order a three-hump camel. The system will shave off the extra hump." ' Theoretically companies can sue each other for late delivery of supplies but it is such a cumbersome procedure and yields such unsatisfactory results that most factories use *Tolkachi*, or pushers – legendary, semi-illegal Soviet middlemen, to bludgeon or bribe their suppliers into sending materials on time or to finagle complicated swaps with other plants, outside the Plan. The fundamental problem is that since everybody's output is someone else's input, shortages at one stage of production have a domino effect. Caught in a squeeze, many factories simply shortchange customers by cutting down ingredients to stretch out their supplies.

A canning engineer admitted to a Soviet friend of mine that such hanky-panky was standard practice in his industry. 'If we add less sugar to jam than the jam needs or disregard quality standards for the fruit, we can produce more canned goods and meet the Plan,' he said. This had once caused him embarrassment during an international canning conference. 'We were tasting Bulgarian canned goods and we were almost thrilled with the high quality and good taste,' he recalled. 'We asked the representative of the Bulgarian firm how they managed such high quality. He looked at us in surprise: "Why – we always follow your Soviet recipes and technology without change." His reply put us in an awkward position because we could never afford to follow our own recipes.'

Sometimes the deception practiced is more blatant. A poultry breeder from Central Asia explained that his state farm, one of the nation's largest, regularly fudged its figures to show it had met the Plan. The daily target was 100,000 eggs, he said, and the farm consistently ran about 30,000 short. The breeder said he would report the accurate daily total to the director who gave a false report to regional superiors. 'The director reported that the day's Plan had been fulfilled,' the breeder said, 'and the next morning he would order me to write off 30,000 to 40,000 eggs as if they had been broken and fed to the chickens, even though those eggs never existed.' Similarly, he said, feed shipments would regularly arrive at the farm with 1.5–2 tons out of 30 tons missing, indicating that someone else was meeting his Plan by short-weighting.

It is a tale told in one form or another by people from all walks of Soviet life. Cooking the books and double-counting, occasionally exposed in the official press, are so widely practiced that many Soviets simply disbelieve official claims about Plan fulfillment. Not many months after my arrival in Moscow, a chemical engineer told me that the central government made innumerable adjustments lowering various Plan targets during the year so that, technically speaking, at year's end the overall Plan was 'fulfilled'. Public confirmation came later, during a purge in Soviet Georgia, where the Plan had regularly been reported as fulfilled. The new Party boss made a series of speeches, chastising Georgian industry and agriculture for poor performance and revealing how disastrously, in fact, the Georgian economy had fallen short of original targets. Something similar happened later in Armenia.

By the time I had left Moscow, I had no reason to doubt that jimmying the Plan went on everywhere. Indeed, one dissident economist, writing under a pseudonym and buried somewhere in the state administration, circulated an underground document showing how in category after category the economy had fallen short of the 1966–1970 Five-Year-Plan targets even though overall growth of national income had met planned objectives.* Hidden inflation covered up most of the shortfall.

Month-in and month-out, the pressure of the Plan has undoubtedly forced Russian workers to disgorge a greater volume of output than would have emerged without Plan deadlines. But the Plan mentality has also spawned a chaos all its own. Because the Plan, and ultimately that means the Kremlin leadership operating through Gosplan, the state planning agency, has demanded more than can be reasonably delivered by an economy of chronic shortages, the Plan has engendered storming, featherbedding in factory work forces, the end-of-the-month hassle over raw materials, the short-changing, phony figures, and systematic deception at all levels. Sometimes, it is self-defeating in ironic little ways. A

* In a pamphlet called 'Free Thought' circulating in December 1971, an economist, using the satirical pseudonym, A. Babushkin, made a comparison of openly published Soviet statistics showing that from 1966–1970 only 26 percent of the planned number of cars, 40 percent of tractors, 50 percent of paper and cheese, 58 percent of canned goods, 65 percent of textiles, 70 percent of electric power, 71 percent of steel, etc., had actually been produced, in spite of Party claims in 1971 that all major indices of the Plan had been fulfilled, with ruble figures on national income theoretically supporting that claim. Babushkin also recorded a few items actually over-fulfilling the Plan but far from enough to fulfill the Plan in absolute terms as the Party claimed.

scientist related to me how his institute, shocked to discover near the end of one year that it had not exhausted its fund allotment for new equipment, quickly bought an expensive, very fancy but totally unnecessary piece of gadgetry rather than risk having next year's allocations cut back because this year's were not used up. At a more humble level, a school-teacher confessed her panic when she had found 800 unspent rubles in a school fund. 'I went out and bought 800 rubles' worth of cactus plants for the school,' she said.

An American military attaché in Moscow irreverently compared the Soviet economic system to the U.S. Army. 'It's a bureaucracy,' he said, 'where the rules are: "Don't buck the system", "Don't make any waves", "Don't go looking for extra work", "Don't push for reforms because that means changing the way of doing things", just "Cover your ass".'

Nowhere, it seems, is the cover-your-ass philosophy more assiduously applied than in the construction industry where projects are solemnly proclaimed complete for the sake of holding a ceremonial opening on schedule even though projects are not ready for operation. The classic case was reported by my colleague, Ted Shabad, who found an article in *Trud*, the trade union newspaper, on June 14, 1973, admitting that an elaborate ceremony marking the start-up of a new Siberian power generator at Nazarovo in December, 1968, had been phony and that nearly five years later the generator was still not in operation. At the time of the supposed commissioning, the Soviet press carried inflated front-page articles hailing the start-up at Nazarovo as 'the beginning of a technological revolution.' But *Trud* disclosed that actually, the 500,000 kilowatt steam-turbine generator had burned out on the factory floor during testing and was not even at the power plant for commissioning. Contrary to earlier Soviet press accounts reporting on how new power from Nazarovo surged into the Siberian power grid, *Trud* admitted that 'the needles of the instruments indicating power output did not move. There was no current and how could there be any since the manufacturer had not even supplied the generator. The inauguration ceremony together with band music and speech-making was therefore purely symbolic.'

For the controlled Soviet press and the hypersensitive Soviet leadership such an open admission is unprecedented. But Soviet friends told me that the Nazarovo incident was far from unique. Avgust, a balding Jewish construction engineer from Latvia with an impish smile, spent an hour or two one afternoon rattling off construction cover-ups from his own experience. Once, he said, not until the banquet celebrating commissioning of a factory was it discovered that the interior piping had not been hooked up with the outside sewer lines. 'We knew it would take a lot of time and effort to fix this,' Avgust said, 'but the "act of commissioning" had already been signed and nobody wanted to take responsibility for so shameful a mistake.' So it was agreed that the building would officially be considered complete – and, in effect, ready to operate – but the plumbing disaster would be listed in the small print among certain 'imperfections'. On another occasion, he said, an iron rolling mill was all complete except for delivery of some key machinery. His construction organization was eager to write off the factory as finished in order to qualify for its end-of-the-project bonuses. The client enterprise finally agreed to accept the factory as in a state of 'starting operations for adjustment'. That suited both sides, Avgust said, because in that condition the factory had no Plan targets but received state funds to test and adjust its machinery. 'It went on that way for two years before the machinery came,' Avgust said.

More typical, according to Avgust, was the situation at a textile plant. Because the machinery was not delivered until the last minute, construction crews left 20-by-20-foot holes in the outer factory walls for inserting it. Literally on the eve of commissioning, Avgust said, the last equipment arrived, was put in place, and construction crews quickly closed up the holes. 'We put in bricks, plaster and painted all at once,' he said. 'Each of these operations takes time and requires waiting before the next. Brick-laying requires time for shrinkage. Plaster should dry before painting, and so on. But we had no time for waiting and did everything contrary to the rules: while bricklayers were doing the brickwork, plasterers started plastering from the bottom up, and painters started painting the wet walls. Everyone knew that within two or three months, paint would peel, plaster would flake off, and brickwork would crack. But it didn't matter. Our only worry was to finish on time.'

When I heard that, my thoughts flashed back to the shoddy construction in the apartments at the Kama River Truck Plant and in so many other buildings I had seen in city after city. The sad letters-to-the-editors in Soviet newspapers from new apartment-dwellers were ample testimony that this is a standard technique used by construction organizations bent on claiming completion of so many square meters of floor space by the deadline in order to qualify for Plan-fulfilling bonuses. Government officials knowingly connive with them out of eagerness to proclaim how many new apartments they were providing.

In its oafish way, the Soviet economy muddles through in spite of such chicanery. As the Kama River Truck Plant project suggests, Soviet planners count on industrial brawn to compensate for lack of finesse.

The real drag on the Soviet economy – and one that has worried the Brezhnev-Kosygin leadership even though it does not show up in statistics on economic growth or Plan fulfillment – is the inability of Soviet socialism to generate enough good modern technology and to convert it into production fast enough. Over the decades Moscow may have produced impressive growth rates, though the pace is now slowing, but the dynamism of innovation has been missing. The planned Soviet economy lacks the driving force of competition that stimulates technological development in the West, and Communist planners and theorists have yet to devise an adequate substitute.

Practically the entire system, top to bottom, resists new inventions, new products, new ideas. Deterrents are woven into the very fabric of the Soviet economy. Generally, innovations seem to emanate from decrees issued on high with little input from ultimate consumers. They are developed in huge research institutes which operate independently from industrial enterprises and which take more pride in having some special, one-of-a-kind, hand-tooled sample gadget for show (*pokazukha*) in a Soviet industrial exhibit than in getting it into production. Even pushed by some agency, a new proposal must thread its way through a labyrinthine process of approvals from the central bureaucracy, immobilized by a maze of technical regulations.

One Soviet executive was quoted in the press as complaining that in order to produce a simple aluminium cup, he needed 'consent from 18 organizations – not only in Moscow but in other cities.' Vladimir Dudintsev's famous novel, *Not by Bread Alone*, was the tale of an inventor's unbelievable struggle against the bureaucracy to see his breakthrough metallurgical invention accepted. The newspaper *Kom-*

somolskaya Pravda, has run periodic articles exposing active suppression by the bureaucracy of new ideas, from efficient shoe-making machinery to new orthopedic treatments. The very institutes assigned to develop new techniques, it reported, often take the lead in squelching ideas from outsiders. In October 1972, *Pravda* recounted the ordeal of a factory in Omsk which had done market research and come up with a proposal for making clothes trees (Soviet apartments have no closets and most people dislike naked hooks on the wall). It had to ask Moscow for a high-level decision on the price. No word for three months. Then came a request from the All-Union Institute of Furniture Design and Technology, asking for an entirely new application, in triplicate, with pictures. More waiting. The factory sent an executive to Moscow and discovered its file had been lost. When *Pravda* printed its story, the factory had been waiting ten months and faced a damage claim filed by a trade organization that had ordered 2,000 clothes trees and was tired of waiting for them. Still no answer.

The canning engineer who had been embarrassed by the good Bulgarian jam related a case of stupefying resistance to change. Normally his cannery in Mordovia pickled green tomatoes but when some shipments, delayed in transit, began arriving with ripened red tomatoes, he quickly adapted and began pickling red tomatoes. 'They weren't standard but they were really good and they saved the state thousands of rubles,' he said. 'But I was not rewarded and praised for it – just the opposite. A special commission arrived to inspect my work. They didn't want to believe that I had intended to save those red tomatoes for the state and not for myself. They suspected me of stealing and although they had no evidence against me, this incident caused me endless troubles. There was a chain of Party meetings and I was almost expelled from the Party. Just in time I remembered an old wartime instruction about using all kinds of raw materials, whether standard or not, and it saved me.'

Russians tell innumerable stories of such inbred, bureaucratic, nitpicking opposition to innovation in their society. This occurs in other societies as well. But what was particularly Russian about the canning engineer's experience was the deep suspicion, the overreaction and the narrow escape from drastic retribution over something so trivial. Quite properly Western economies, especially the United

States, are chastised by critics for squandering natural resources, energy, the environment, and being prodigally wasteful of things like cars, appliances, and gadgetry produced with built-in obsolescence. But the West is far less wasteful of people and ideas than Soviet society which stifles not only dissenters but able engineers, researchers, and people with an urge to improve their system, whose ideas are regularly aborted or stillborn because the system so sternly resists originality.

The structure run from the top-down is essentially to blame, but not all bottlenecks are in the central bureaucracy. Brezhnev once supposedly remarked that Soviet factory managers avoid innovations 'the way the devil shies away from incense'. He did not add that inflexible Plan requirements are the main reason for this attitude, but an experienced Soviet newsman laid it out for me this way:

'In a planned economy, a man with a new and more efficient machine is dangerous to everyone. I'll tell you why. The Plan demands 100 percent production, 12 months a year, 24 – maybe 30 – days a month. Everything is all calculated out: productivity of machines in the factory, size of the work force, amount of steel and other materials needed. Planners know just about what can be produced. If you introduce new machinery, you have to shut down the plant, or part of it. That means that the Plan will not be fulfilled. That is bad for the factory director and the workers. They will not get the bonuses that sometimes comprise 20–30 percent of their pay. It is bad, too, for the ministry in charge of that factory, because it will not fulfill its Plan. And if you stop the plant to install new machinery and that takes several months, you have to stop delivery of steel and other output from that plant which goes to other plants. And they will have trouble fulfilling their Plans. That is the problem with the planned economy. The Plan is a brake on its own growth, on improving the efficiency of the economy.'

During my years in Moscow, the Soviet leadership was obviously concerned about this. One indication was the decision to make labor productivity, the Soviet code word for efficiency, a principal indicator for successful Plan fulfillment.Yet despite constant reports of success, the efficiency gap between East and West did not noticeably narrow. The Soviet economy may rank second to the American in terms of total output, but even by Soviet statistics its output per capita in 1973 ranked 15th, and by American calculations, it ranked 25th – behind the United States, Canada, West Germany, France, Britain, all of northern and central Europe, Japan, Australia, New Zealand, several oil-producing Arab states, East Germany and Czechoslovakia. What I noticed traveling through Russia – that factories, stores, farms, restaurants, or barbershops always seemed to have an inordinate number of spare people on the job – is borne out by statistics. The 1973 Soviet economic yearbook rated Soviet industry as just about half as efficient as American, construction industry about two-thirds as efficient, and agriculture about one-fourth. Occasional articles by some efficiency-minded Soviet economists have pointed out that when Russia has bought plants from the West, it has sometimes employed up to eight times as many laborers, neutralizing the efficiency of Western technology.

All of this seems hard to square with Soviet cosmonauts in orbit with Americans or with dire warnings from generals and admirals of the West threatened by new generations of multiheaded Soviet missiles or nuclear submarines. How can the Soviets look so good if reality is so bad? The answer to this paradox is twofold.

One element of the answer lies in the Russian psyche, the Soviet obsession with overcoming historic Russian backwardness in relation to the West. This is not just a matter of power but of national self-respect. Like the czars before them, Soviet leaders are driven by a burning sense of inferiority and a determination to overcome Russia's historic backwardness. No less a figure than Stalin gave voice to this compulsion in 1934 when he declared:

> To slacken the tempo would mean falling behind. And those who fall behind get beaten. But we do not want to be beaten. No, we refuse to be beaten! One feature of the history of old Russia was the continual beatings she suffered because of her backwardness. She was beaten by the Mongol khans. She was beaten by the Turkish beys. She was beaten by the Swedish feudal lords. She was beaten by the Polish and Lithuanian gentry. She was beaten by the British and French capitalists. She was beaten by the Japanese barons. All beat her because of her back-

wardness, military backwardness, cultural backwardness, political backwardness, industrial backwardness, agricultural backwardness. They beat her because to do so was profitable and could be done with impunity.

It is almost impossible to exaggerate the importance of this gnawing inferiority complex as a clue to Soviet motivation in relations with the West today. The Russians are determined not to be backward, not to be second best, but to be *seen* as the *equals* of their chief rival in the world arena today – the Americans. By today's standards the greatness of a state is measured by its might as a nuclear power and its prowess in space. Hence, the Russians will make the sacrifices necessary to attain equality with America, or at least to project the image of equality, especially in those fields. By Western estimates, for example, Russia spent $45 billion on manned space flight from 1958–1973 compared to $25 billion spent by America. After the Americans landed on the moon, it was crucial to the Russians to have the Apollo-Soyuz flight to link up with the Americans in space, in order to erase the image of being behind and to project the picture of parity.

The second element of the answer lies in the split-level nature of Soviet society. In the West, military technology is closely related to the general level of technology in the entire economy. Not so in Russia. If something matters vitally to the state, it is specially done and the chances are that it will be done quite well. If it is for the leadership or for premier scientists, ballet troupes, writers, athletes, people important to the state and its image in the West, no effort or luxury will be spared, though ordinary Russians have to tighten their belts to pay for it. An American doctor, noting this split quality in Soviet society, remarked to me, 'The Russians can put a man in space but they can't keep elevators operating. They can do the most sophisticated viral research, but they cannot treat common sicknesses very well.' To me, it is not only a question of capability but of choice. Shoddy consumer goods for the hoi polloi should not be taken as a gauge of the caliber of what is provided to the elite or to the Defense Ministry.

Not only do defense and space efforts get top national priority and funding, but also they operate on a different system from the rest of the economy. Samuel Pisar, an American lawyer, writer, and consultant on East-West trade, made the shrewd observation to me that the military sector is 'the only sector of the Soviet economy which operates like a market economy, in the sense that the customers pull out of the economic mechanism the kinds of weaponry that they want. Generally speaking, the Soviets have a push economy – products are pushed out to consumers on orders from above, essentially repeating past production, without tapping the inventions and new technology of Soviet scientists in laboratories and institutes. But the military, like customers in the West, has a pull effect. It can say, "No, no, no, that isn't what we want." Also, it can try out its tanks or its Sam-6 or Sam-7 missiles by selling them to the Arabs for a good profit and testing them in the field, and then come back with a "market reaction" for Soviet producers.'

Moreover, the Defense Ministry not only has its own system of 'closed' factories engaged in military production but throughout Soviet industry, the military operates on different standards than the normal civilian economy. Yuri, the metalworker, told me that his plant had three separate categories of products, with different assembly lines and different work brigades, earning different levels of pay even though they were making the same items. One was for the armed forces; the second, for export; and the third, for 'common' domestic use. 'For a nail, a tack, a teapot; for metal, uniforms, blankets, mittens; or for some apparatus, this is the way it is done with everything,' he said. Yosif, the refrigeration engineer from southern Russia, reported the same. 'Common production pays less,' he said. 'Export and military production pay better, but requirements are higher. More time is spent on the work and quality specifications are higher. Such work is usually given to highly qualified workers.'

Rashid, the Tashkent Tractor Parts Factory foreman, said that whenever military orders came to his factory for 'switches or lights or something like that, say, for rockets, the Armed Forces sent detailed instructions for checking the quality of parts. I myself signed papers saying that our production did not meet military specifications and then we sold the same things to collective and state farms – various instruments, tools, wrenches, screwdrivers, spare parts, and so on.'

Another friend, a systems analyst who had worked on automated control systems in many factories, some of them 'closed' defense plants as well as mixed civilian-military plants, said there was no comparison in the quality control, even on ordinary items. 'The efficiency of the military and space programs rests in procurement checks,' he advised. 'Military officers sit in each factory – in the big factories, these are generals – and they operate with strict military discipline. They are empowered to reject *brak* [junk, substandard items] and they reject great quantities of *brak*, often at great expense. But the budget is padded to allow for that. Workers in the very same factories produce good refrigerators for the military and refrigerators that are largely junk for the civilian market, but nobody cares because there is no real quality control. I have seen how they made transistors. They would make 100 and the military representative would select only one or two. Some would be thrown out as defective and the rest would go to the [civilian] market.'

Even so, in the high priority items of crucial importance to the state, in its military and space programs and in key civilian projects as well, Soviet standards do not match those in the West. The Russians are reckoned to be up to 10 years behind America in the computer field. In early 1975, a Soviet Academy of Sciences bulletin reported that the Soviet Union had only about one-tenth as many computers as America, most of them the slower, second-generation, transistorized computers rather than the faster, third-generation, micro-circuit computers in wide use in the United States. Nor is the difference merely one of outdated hardware. More than one Soviet computer expert privately told me that Soviet programming is far behind Western programming. An electronics engineer with years of experience in defense factories complained that unreliability of computers and other electronic gear was an even bigger headache. 'Our computers break down all the time,' he said. 'There is no comparison in the down-time [time when computers are not operating] of our computers to yours. Yours are much more efficient.'

Nor have the special quality standards for Soviet export goods raised the caliber of Soviet technology enough to make it attractive to the West. Perhaps the easiest yardstick for gauging the relative difference of economies East and West is the lopsided flow of technology between them. According to the Soviet monthly, *Foreign Trade*, the advanced West in 1974 bought only 170 million rubles' ($220 million) worth of Soviet machinery and equipment – in other words, technology – whereas the Soviet Union bought two billion rubles' worth ($2.67 billion) from the West. A ratio of nearly 12–1 against Moscow. Were it not for oil, natural gas, gold, chromium and rare metals – the exports essentially of an underdeveloped economy – Moscow could not afford trade with the developed West. Precision mechanics, precision technology, precision biochemistry are fields that Soviet scientists acknowledge that their system is weak on. 'It is easier to produce an atomic bomb or isotopes than to produce transistors or biochemical medicines,' said a physicist. 'We have never had that kind of capability for precise technology. We are years behind.'

By concentration of effort and resources, the Russians have made important gains in the space and military fields, forging ahead of all countries but America, in part because no others make the effort. But the best Western estimates still reckon that in development of sophisticated missilery and in manned space flight, the United States has a lead of several years, though the Russians pursue doggedly. The Apollo-Soyuz rendezvous mission in July 1975 was an indicator of the American advantage. In the period leading up to the joint flight, one Soviet manned space mission was aborted at launch and others failed in docking. During the joint flight itself, Russian cosmonauts had considerably more trouble docking with the American Apollo than vice versa. In fact, the mission plan deliberately assigned the more active role to the American spacecraft.

As I watched it on television, I was reminded of a comment made to me by Vance Brand, one of the American crewmembers, at a July 4th reception at the American Embassy in Moscow in 1974, a year before the flight. Brand and the other American astronauts had come to the Soviet Union to get acquainted with the Russian cosmonauts and their spaceship. When I asked Brand his general impressions, he sipped a glass of juice and tried to duck my question. Finally, he said, 'Well, after seeing the Soyuz up close, my admiration for the Russian cosmonauts has increased tremendously.' Another American space official, interpreting this, said the American astronauts had been astonished at how primitive the Soviet Soyuz seemed in comparison with the American Apollo that had gone to the moon and back. 'The cosmonauts just go along for the ride,' the American said. 'They are just passengers. They have nowhere near the control, the chance to change the mission in flight, that our astronauts do.' The Americans, who deliberately avoided making public comparisons embarrassing to Moscow, were also surprised at how limited the life-support and safety features of the Soviet spacecraft had been originally, and also at how the Russians went about fixing some malfunction. The Russians simply patched up the particular problem, the American official said, whereas American technicians, using a systems approach, usually asked what other parts might be causing trouble, checked the whole system, and tried to do preventive maintenance. It was a measure not only of a gap in technical thinking but also of a difference in their whole management outlook.

Management, ultimately, has been the *bête noire* of the Soviet economy. Half a century ago, Lenin told his Bolshevik comrades to study American management techniques. Now Prime Minister Aleksei Kosygin's son-in-law, Dzhermen Gvishiani, among others, is preaching a similar message. Curiously enough, influential elements within the Soviet military establishment are also, behind-the-scenes, among the more vigorous advocates of managerial reform in the Soviet system. Occasionally, a journal like *Communist of the Armed Forces* discreetly criticizes the rigidity of Soviet planning and urges more flexibility. Privately, too, I heard a very trustworthy report relayed in late 1973 through a ranking West European Communist leader with high-level contacts in Moscow, that there was great uneasiness among the military high command as well as top industrial technocrats over deficiencies in Soviet economic management. By this account, these men wanted drastically to reduce interference by the Communist Party Central Committee apparatus in the operation of the economy.

That, of course, had been one of the major objectives of the economic reform pushed in 1965 by Prime Minister Kosygin. The theory then was that the Soviet economy could break out of technological stagnation and be revitalized by giving the heads of industrial enterprises much greater control over their own operations. The approach was to deemphasize gross output as the chief indicator of economic success and to emphasize profitability instead, to promote efficiency, as advocated by some economic reformers practically since Stalin's death in 1953. But by the late Sixties, the

Kosygin reform had been sabotaged both by the Party hierarchy and central ministries jealous of their power and reluctant to relinquish any authority to industrial enterprises. Soviet friends contended, too, that Moscow's scare over political by-products of the liberal economic drive in Czechoslovakia in 1968 also helped kill economic decentralization in the Soviet Union.

In April 1973, another approach was pushed, this time by Brezhnev: formation of large industrial conglomerates, called production associations, which were to be given broad new powers, including some greater authority for direct dealings in foreign trade. In support of this approach, *Pravda* ran an astonishingly forthright article by a leading liberal establishment economist, Abel Agenbegyan. He reported that in a poll of more than 1,000 industrial managers, 90 percent said they needed more flexibility in decision making and 80 percent blamed their problems on interference in normal operations by higher authorities.

The most candid shot of all in this apparent campaign was a blisteringly honest critique (by Soviet standards) of Soviet industry's inability to compete in the world market, written by Nikolai Smelyakov, a Deputy Minister of Foreign Trade who had once headed Amtorg, the Soviet trading company in America, and had traveled widely in the West. Smelyakov, writing in the December 1973 issue of *New World* magazine, implicitly challenged some of the canons of Soviet economics – quotas, indices of Plan fulfillment, marks of quality, and output norms – by emphasizing that in the tough arena of international trade, competitiveness was the only yardstick. Facing up to that, he declared, would be 'good medicine' for Soviet industry. His critique made it plain he felt the hidebound Soviet bureaucracy was too rigid, constipated, and unimaginative, and that Soviet industry was too weak in promoting its products, adapting to the needs of the customer, and in follow-through with service and spare parts.

'While our planning and distribution organs wrote treatises on how many and what machines could be allocated for export and whether it was possible to provide less and earn much more – without providing the necessary spare parts,' Smelyakov wrote, 'while they argued about whether it would not humiliate our dignity to make goods better for export than for domestic consumption, or was it not possible to sell abroad machines unsaleable inside the country or was it not possible to refrain from exporting machinery in great demand domestically, the highly developed capitalist countries already occupied the markets, straddled them, dug in, took commercial root, and developed exports of machinery and equipment on a colossal scale and monopolized whole branches of industry tc work on exports.'

With that kind of blunt critique, presumably backed by someone on high like Brezhnev, it looked as though winds of change were blowing for the Soviet economy. Word leaked that in November, 1973, Brezhnev was pushing for some shake-up in planning and management during the secret session of the Communist Party Central Committee, for the sake of more efficiency. About the same time, some modern-minded mathematical economists were advocating relaxation of the ironclad input-output form of central planning set up by Stalin and still in effect, by which Moscow sought to decide on every last economic detail, generally for five years at a time. They wanted to substitute more flexible planning. They favored setting only general development targets and options, loosening controls, and openly revising the general Plan every year.

Within months, however, the conservative bureaucracy was beating back this idea and President Nikolai Podgorny was telling the Soviet hierarchy not to worry about radical changes in the system. By early 1975, it was clear that Brezhnev's program of production associations was being emasculated even while it was technically being put into effect. A few big industrialists openly complained in the Soviet press that the ministries and the state planning council which report to Prime Minister Kosygin, had multiplied the amount of interference and had increased from five to 80 the Plan indicators that industrial managers had to worry about. In short, decentralization was being blocked again – by rivalries within the Politburo leadership and by the conservative opposition of the top Party and state bureaucracies.

'It's a stalemate,' a high-level Party journalist told me not long before I left Moscow. 'Our economy needs reform, but nothing will be reformed so long as Brezhnev, Podgorny and Kosygin are still around. They can't agree on what to do. And none of them, even Brezhnev, is powerful enough to push through any big change against the will of the other two.'

X

LEADERS AND LED
Nostalgia for a Strong Boss

> Russians [have] gloried in the very thing foreigners
> criticized them for – blind and boundless devotion
> to the will of the monarch, even when in his most
> insane flights he trampled underfoot all the laws of
> justice and humanity.
>
> Nikolai Karamzin, 19th-century Russian historian

'What difference does it make to you that America has a new
President?' an inquisitive Intourist guide in Kiev asked me
after Richard Nixon had been forced out of the White House
by the Watergate scandal.

'Before, we had a dishonest President and now we have an
honest one,' I replied. 'That makes a big difference.'

'No, I mean to you personally, as a journalist,' she persisted. 'Now that there is a new President are you being called
back to America?'

At first, I did not get the connection. But as we talked it
slowly came through to me. This well-educated, English-
speaking young woman was reasoning from Soviet experience. She knew that the senior correspondent in Washington
for *Pravda* would be a Party man trusted and picked by the
Party hierarchy. So she assumed the Moscow bureau chief
for *The New York Times*, which many Soviets take as a
direct counterpart of *Pravda*, must have connections to the
Nixon White House. And since the Nixon faction had just
lost out, presumably I was in political hot water, too.

'No,' I said, as we strolled past the Mariinsky Palace where
Nixon had stayed in Kiev in 1972. 'We have no relationship
to the Government, no connection at all.'

'But who pays your way when you travel in the Soviet
Union?' she wanted to know.

'*The New York Times,* my newspaper, pays my expenses,' I replied.

'Not the government?'

'No,' I said, '*The New York Times* is not a government newspaper. In fact, the *Times* disagreed with Nixon on Watergate. We called for his resignation. We are an independent newspaper. We do not have government or party newspapers in America the way that *Pravda* is *the* authoritative paper for the Communist Party leadership here.'

Even though this discussion took place after the climax of Watergate, a topic on which this young lady had posed to know something, she eyed me with disbelief. She started to challenge my comments about the American press, stopped in midsentence, shook her head and then dropped the subject, evidently regarding it as hopeless.

Watergate was something the Russians could never fathom. Not the break-in, the eavesdropping and the cover-ups. That part they understood well enough from a history of bloody intrigues and cabals under both czars and communists. No, the baffling element was the scandal that followed. It took place in a political dimension beyond their ken, and their reactions revealed much about their own political mentality.

The notion of the purposeful division of political power and of the ruler's being subject to restraints of law was something that met skepticism from even the most sophisticated Soviet analysts of American affairs for many months. Having seen Presidents Johnson and Nixon pursue the Vietnam war despite intense opposition in Congress, they found it hard to credit Congress with real power. For a long time, these Russian specialists on America were inclined to dismiss the furor over Watergate as some charade of democracy that would fade away. In mid-1973, nearly a year after Watergate had been percolating in the American press, an important, well-traveled editor of *Pravda*, whose responsibility was to watch Western politics, remarked that he always skipped over the Watergate news to save time. 'There is too much to read and that is a minor matter,' was his judgment.

Later, the Deputy Prosecutor General, Mikhail P. Malyarov, voiced what seemed a common view of high-level officials. Disdainfully, he brushed aside the contention of dissident physicist Andrei Sakharov that Watergate was proof that American democracy worked. 'It is calculated just for show,' Malyarov shot back. 'All Nixon has to do is show a little firmness, and the whole thing will come to nothing.'

I do think that was not merely a cynical put-down of American politics because some dissidents, too, spoke in that vein. Aleksandr Solzhenitsyn treated Watergate as a petty partisan tempest in a teapot. I was told, moreover, by an American scholar that one top Kremlin Americanologist admitted privately during the winter of 1973–1974 that it was impossible to explain Watergate to the supreme leadership because the Kremlin would not take it seriously. The Malyarov answer had caught the characteristic Russian attitude – a show of toughness from the top and the whole affair would melt away. Nixon was just toying with his critics.

Nor did this seem to be just a miscalculation of the political odds for or against Nixon. (Some Americans, after all, misjudged them too.) The problem for the Russians was much deeper: They simply could not grasp the fact that many Americans regarded the Watergate break-in and cover-up as an intolerable transgression against the essence of democracy. They could not fathom why the affair had engendered such strong public reactions. They found it incredible that Nixon's hand-picked 'Politburo' – for that is how some Russians I knew referred to Haldeman, Ehrlichman, Mitchell & Co. – would have to endure the indignity of standing trial like common citizens and that Vice-President Agnew and President Nixon would be forced from office.

Not only were they incredulous but deep down they questioned the wisdom of it all. A few free-thinkers privately applauded the American political system. But other Russians, even intellectuals wary of their own press and regular listeners to foreign radio stations, were mystified – even horrified – that the American Congress, judiciary, and press could – and deliberately would – shake the foundations of American leadership. It went against the grain of their own political habits. Their history had given them no way of comprehending the legal, moral and constitutional issues about the limits of Presidential power or the President's responsibility before the law in our system. And so, within the framework of Marxist-Leninist clichés and their own political experience, they tended to regard the Watergate affair as a factional plot within what the Soviet press calls 'American ruling circles' or as some power play by the Democratic opposition.

'When will Senator Jackson become President?' a fairly well-informed Moscow lawyer wanted to know after Nixon quit.

Again, from the Soviet standpoint, it was a natural enough question. The Soviet press had given Watergate only scant coverage right up until the end. Some of my Russian friends suspected this was not only to protect the image of Richard Nixon, Brezhnev's personal partner in détente, but to avoid giving the Soviet public dangerous ideas about challenging established authority. Between the lines, however, the Moscow media conveyed the implication that Watergate was a maneuver against détente. 'I would like to emphasize that the impulse of the affair came after the Democratic Party suffered defeat [in 1972],' said Leonid Zamyatin, Director-General of Tass and Kremlin spokesman, in the only televised postmortem of Nixon's resignation. 'It [Watergate] was, in fact, used as the chief weapon in the interparty struggle and was given the coloration of a conflict between the Executive, in the person of the President, and the legislative power, represented by Congress.' As with other Soviet coverage, he never mentioned the break-in at Democratic Party headquarters or Nixon's income tax difficulties but complained that 'a very definite brainwashing of public opinion has been taking place both on radio and television' against Nixon, clearly labeled as the Soviet friend in détente.

The Soviet lawyer who asked about Senator Henry Jackson of Washington taking over the White House had drawn the logical conclusion from this kind of commentary. From Voice of America and even the Soviet press, he knew Jackson was the most powerful Democratic critic of détente in Congress. He took it as a foregone conclusion that Jackson would become President. Ford he regarded as an unknown interim figure. The Soviet mind, thinking back to Stalin's death in 1953 or Khrushchev's sudden ouster in 1964, expected a new strong man to emerge. American talk about legal procedures sounded like window dressing. In April 1974, four months before Nixon's resignation, when Senator Edward Kennedy came to Moscow and solemnly declared that American political institutions would be stronger once Watergate had run its course, I remember Russians taking this as under-

299

standable Democratic Party blarney. Kennedy and the Democrats would gain perhaps. But the idea that a political system as a whole could profit from a frontal assault on its own leader was so foreign to the Russian concept of national power and authority that it had no credibility.

'What are you people doing to your President?' the translator for another correspondent asked me late in the Watergate affair. This was a Russian sympathetic to America and it exasperated him to see America in such turmoil. 'What are you people doing to your country?' he burst out at me.

'The question ought to be, "What is Nixon doing to our country?"' I demurred.

'Oh, well,' he responded, 'but that sort of thing happens everywhere. Don't you think we have it here, too?' and he quickly cupped his hand to his ear to signal the bugging. 'Of course, everywhere. If something like that happens here, it is just hushed down and no one finds out about it, or if an official is really caught doing something bad, then he is just transferred to some other job – on the same level. The big bosses, of course, don't have to worry. There is no need to ruin your country for something like Nixon did.'

He, and many like him, felt no different after Watergate had run its full course and Gerald Ford had made his journey to Vladivostok to reaffirm détente. The traumas of democracy made no sense to them.

If Watergate puzzled Russians, then the nostalgia for Stalin among ordinary Soviets surprised me – and they are warp and woof of the same political fabric. I went to Russia thinking of Stalin not only as the wartime commander and stern tyrant whose harsh programs of forced industrialization and collectivization had built up Soviet power, but also as the dictator whose bloody purges ranked with Hitler's persecution of the Jews as the gravest mass inhumanities of the 20th century. To me as to other Westerners, Khrushchev for all his flamboyant unpredictability, his blustering over Berlin and his missile gamble in Cuba, was something of a hero for having dared to debunk Stalin, expose his terror and rehabilitate some of his victims. I knew, of course, that the Brezhnev coalition had reversed Khrushchev's line on Stalin. It had gradually rehabilitated him, erecting a statue over Stalin's grave, allowing flattering literary and cinematic portraits of him, and sweeping the purges out of sight with the semantic whitewash of the term 'personality cult', which made it sound as if Stalin's only sin had been his vanity and not his murder of millions. But it came to me as a discovery that Stalin had great latent prestige among ordinary people and that Khrushchev was widely regarded as a boor and bungler practically without redeeming attributes, except among the liberal intelligentsia and the rehabilitated victims of the purges who had been direct beneficiaries of his policies.

Stalin's favorite wine was Kinzmarauli, a hearty red from his native Georgia, hard to obtain now even as it was during his lifetime. Its mere appearance on the table is sometimes enough nowadays to set off rounds of toasts to Stalin at private parties. A Swiss diplomat related to me his astonishment one evening at hearing Stalin warmly toasted several times over glasses of Kinzmarauli by a group of middle-level Foreign Ministry officials, a gathering at which he chanced to be the only foreigner. Some other friends, Russian intellectuals for whom Stalin was anathema, were equally shocked on a visit to working-class relatives for a big holiday feast to find the crowd singing old war songs, including one with the refrain: 'Let's drink to the Motherland. Let's drink to Stalin.' And up went the vodka glasses for the dead dictator.

Soviet Georgians are accepted as a maverick people, fiercely nationalistic, and so their devotion to their native son, Yosif Dzhugashvili, who rose from a cobbler's son to rule the Kremlin, was taken as one of their idiosyncrasies, a way of lording it over Russians. Not only did Georgians drink to Stalin and face down Russian critics of his rule, but I was shown photos of state holiday celebrations in which Georgian officials were carrying Stalin's portrait down the main streets beside Lenin, Marx and Engels, a public act of reverence forbidden elsewhere. But in other parts of the country there were many people who were perhaps more discreet but still felt nostalgia for Stalin.

An Azerbaijani taxi driver in Baku, asked about the photographs of Stalin pasted on his windshield, asserted: 'We love Stalin here. He was a strong boss. With Stalin, people knew where they stood.'

A factory director in his fifties on the train from Odessa to Moscow, after complaining about the long hair and untidy look of Soviet youth and the unruliness and unreliability of workers in his plant, said: 'They are all slackers. We have no discipline now. We need a strong leader. Under Stalin, we had real discipline. If someone came five minutes late to work . . . ' And he slit his throat with a finger. That was a time he longed for.

A 30-year-old Russian librarian in Tashkent: 'Stalin carried the entire, gigantic war effort on his shoulders. He built the power of this country. Of course, mistakes were made in his name. By other people. He should not have trusted them so, especially Beria. But look what Stalin achieved. They never should have removed his body from the mausoleum [in 1961]. The ordinary people did not like that. It was Khrushchev's idea. He was crude and stupid. He wasted money on his crazy schemes, like trying to grow corn in Kazakhstan. And he made a fool of himself, and of our country.'

Gennadi, the state farm accountant: 'The intelligentsia may dream of democracy but the huge mass of people dream of Stalin – his strong power. They are not reactionary but they are being mistreated by their petty bosses, who cheat and exploit them, suppress them. They want a strong boss to "put shoes on" the petty bosses. They know that under Stalin [economic] conditions were not as good, but the state farm directors and other officials were not robbing them under Stalin, were not mocking them. There was a check on local authorities.'

Yuri, the young metallurgical worker in his twenties: 'You want to know what the workers think? Do you know the saying, "The Russians need a broad back"? It means that Russians need a leader who is strong, to stand behind his broad back. That saying was more important under Stalin than now. But it is still important. That is how the workers feel. They want a strong leader, like Stalin, and they don't think Brezhnev is that type.'

A linguist in her fifties: 'The present leadership has no sense of decorum. Stalin knew how to impress people. When he was alive, other countries respected and feared us more.'

A writer in his sixties, who spent eight years in Stalinist labor camps, trying to explain the latent sympathy for Stalin among workers and peasants: 'Out there, Stalin has a real hold on the *narod*, the masses. They feel that he built the country and he won the war. Now they see disorganization in agriculture, disorganization in industry, disorganization everywhere in the economy and they see no end to it. They are bothered by rising prices. They think that when there was a tough ruler, like Stalin, we did not have such troubles. People forget that things were bad then, too, and they forget the terrible price that we paid.'

The forgetfulness is hard for Westerners to appreciate because for them Stalin's name is inextricably linked with the mass purges, a memory refreshed by biographies of Stalin and by Solzhenitsyn's *Gulag Archipelago*. But Russians suffer from historical amnesia, produced by the Soviet rewritings of history. That sounds a bit fantastic, I know, but it came home to me in that story of Yevgeny Yevtushenko.

He was very agitated when we rendezvoused one snowy Sunday afternoon near the beautiful old church in the writers' village of Peredelkino. Solzhenitsyn had been arrested only a few days before and Yevtushenko had gotten in hot water for sending Brezhnev a telegram of mild protest. He greeted me in a blue warm-up suit but he looked far too solemn for a man really out for a jog. Perhaps it was his 'cover' for meeting me at the church. In that tense raw voice of his, he talked at breakneck speed about reading *Gulag* furtively and in a rush because only a handful of contraband copies were then circulating in Moscow. One had only 24 hours to devour the book whole. People spent all night reading and passed it to others. Yevtushenko was agitated because a scheduled reading of his poetry had been canceled and he had circulated a document explaining his position.

What struck me most was not his ambivalent defense of Solzhenitsyn but his unqualified anguish over the frightening ignorance of the younger generation about Stalin. The summer before, around a campfire in Siberia, he wrote, a young coed had shaken him by proposing a toast to Stalin. He asked her why Stalin:

'Because then, all the people believed in Stalin and with this belief, they were victorious,' she answered.

'And do you know how many people were arrested during the years of Stalin's rule?' I asked.

'Well, say, 20 or 30 people,' she answered.

Other students sat around the fire, and they were about her age. I started asking them the same questions, too.

'About 200,' said one lad.

'Maybe 2,000,' said another girl.

Only one student out of 15 or 20 said, 'It seems to me about 10,000.'

When I told them that the figure is reckoned not in thousands but in millions, they did not believe me.

'Did you read my poem, *The Heirs of Stalin?*' I asked.

'And did you really have such a poem?' asked the first girl. 'Where was it published?'

'In *Pravda*, in 1963,' I answered.

'But then, I was only eight years old,' she answered, somewhat at a loss.

And then I suddenly understood as never before that the younger generation really does not have any sources nowadays for learning the tragic truth about that time because they cannot read about it in books or in textbooks. Even when articles are published in newspapers about heroes of our Revolution who died in the time of the Stalinist repressions, then the papers fall silent about the cause of their deaths. In a volume of [Osip] Mandelshtam, which has been published just now, there is not a single mention of how he died – from tortures in a camp. The truth is replaced by silence, and silence actually is a lie.

It would be wrong to leave the impression that Stalin's terror is universally forgotten or that he is universally admired. Not only the Yevtushenkos and the victims of the purges and their families – and there are many thousands of them – refuse to toast Stalin. Others, too. A journalist told me of liberal friends in the Communist Party hierarchy who secretly fear and oppose neo-Stalinists because they do not think they would survive another era of purges. I heard, too, of people like the Army officers who privately condemned Stalin's decimation of the top command in the purges, or the factory director who cursed Stalin's failure to anticipate Hitler's attack in 1941 and his refusal to accept Marshall Plan aid from America after the war. Yet beside the constant derision of Khrushchev, these criticisms of Stalin seemed minor. To a taxi driver, Khrushchev was the erratic bumbler. The press regularly slights him by emphasizing how the Party put policy right after Khrushchev fell, or by its awkward silence at his death. Khrushchev was being abused in part because his successors found him a handy scapegoat, a butt for popular discontent, but it seemed to me that more fundamentally the present leaders wanted to cut him down because his exposure of Stalin had called into question the infallibility of the Party. He had cast doubt on the deeds and personal sacrifices that millions had made in Stalin's cause with Stalin's name on their lips. He had made so many look so foolish or so guilty for their silent adulation of Stalin.

Today, setting the purges aside – and that is what most Russians want to do, set them aside – those who are nostalgic about the good old days under Stalin yearn most of all for his style of leadership. Time has dulled the memory of his awful malevolence, his paranoid suspiciousness, his capricious tyranny. As the leader who forged a modern state, who steeled a nation in wartime to emerge victorious, and then made the rest of the world tremble at Soviet might, Stalin embodies power. Significantly, when Soviet officials or tour-guides talk of the watershed between Czarism and Communism, they do not talk about the Soviet constitution as Americans would or about the coming of the Fourth or Fifth Republic as Frenchmen would. They refer to the 'establishment of Soviet power'. Nor is this a matter of mere semantics or loose translation. It is a vital clue to the Russian political mentality. For them, the point is that one form of power replaced another. In that essential equation of Russian history, constitutions and republics do not figure.

This language of power is the language many Russians use when they recall Stalin, for they like a powerful leader. In their most admiring moments, Russians praise Stalin as the *krepki khozyain*, the strong master. He held society together in his grip and they liked that feeling. So essential was Stalin to the concept of how Russia should be ruled for many middle-aged and elderly people that they now recall their panic at the time of his death. As one intellectual recalled to me, 'We literally did not know what would happen to the country, how we would survive without Stalin.'

Nor is this an attitude restricted to the ruler at the very pinnacle of the state apparatus. At factories, farms or power projects, I have heard workmen or farmers or construction engineers speak proudly of their own chief as 'a strong boss', making a hard fist and pumping their right arm to illustrate his muscle. They like the feeling that someone above them is firmly in charge.

I recall a technical specialist lamenting what he regarded as the inevitable decline of the Soviet space program after the death of its leader, Sergei Korolev in 1966. 'After that,' he said, 'we could not compete with you Americans. There was confusion, disorganization. Too many "chiefs" and not one boss. You can't get anywhere without a big man in charge.' After the Soviet Tu-144 supersonic transport crashed at the Paris Air Show in 1973, an engineer had similar misgivings. 'If there had been a good strong man in charge, he would have run things properly and prevented such mistakes,' he said. I found it especially striking to hear such reliance on a strong leader from a young, technically trained intellectual whose education should have given him an appreciation for the teamwork, management and intricate dovetailing of complex technology to make such a project successful. But scientists, too, told me that institutes, or entire fields of research, suffered for lack of a single commanding leader. A sports fan offered the strong-man diagnosis when the Soviet national hockey team lost to Czechoslovakia 7–2, during the world hockey championships in April 1974. He blamed it on a soft coach. 'Tarasov was a dictator,' he said, recalling the former coach. 'He was crude, but he made the team train and train and train. Under him, they played better. With Russians you have to be firm, very firm.'

The brilliant 19th-century writer, Mikhail Saltykov-Shchedrin, satirized this Russian worship of strong rulers in his story, *The Tale of One City.* A Russian friend recalled for me the moment when Russian characters, having suffered at the hands of enemies, cry out: 'Even if they put us in a heap and set fire to us from four sides . . . we can endure because we know that we have our bosses.'

This underscores a fundamental difference between Russians and Americans, who are often moved to seek similarities in their national characters. They may share an openness of spirit but Russians and Americans differ sharply in their attitudes toward power and authority – and not just because of Soviet Communism. Inbred mistrust of authority is an American tradition. We are wary as a people of bigness when it is accompanied by unchecked power – Big Government, Big Business, Big Labor, big anything. Part of us welcomes strong leadership but we also want laws written to curb monopolies and political power hemmed in with restrictions, subdivided institutionally. We want Watergate Presidents removed for overreaching their power.

Not so the Russians. Bigness and power are admired almost

without qualification. Size inspires awe – huge Kremlins, cannons, churchbells under the czars; huge dams, missiles, atom smashers under the Communists. Marxism-Leninism has provided a rationale for large-scale production and concentrated power in the hands of Party leaders and central planners. But six centuries of authoritarian rule from Ivan the Great and Ivan the Terrible forward had made Russians monarchists in their bones long before Lenin and Stalin came along. They have no heritage of common law with its *habeas corpus*, no long, well-established historical traditions of public political debate, no panoply of institutions designed to disperse power and buttress the individual against the state.

'Under the czars we had an authoritarian state and now we have a totalitarian state but it still comes from the roots of the Russian past,' I was told by Pavel Litvinov, the dissident grandson of Maxim Litvinov, Stalin's foreign minister. 'You should understand that the leaders and the ordinary people have the same authoritarian frame of mind. Brezhnev and the simple person both think that might is right. That's all. It's not a question of ideology. It's simply power. Solzhenitsyn acts as if he thinks this has all come down from the sky because of Communism. But he is not so different himself. He does not want democracy. He wants to go from the totalitarian state back to an authoritarian one.'

So much has been inherited from the past, that a Russian takes for granted elements of political despotism that are instantly an affront to a Westerner. History has conditioned Russians differently. The cruel tyranny of Stalin was prefigured by the bloody reign of Ivan the Terrible in the 16th century and the iron rule of Nicholas I in the 19th century. Peter the Great, celebrated for opening Russia to the West and introducing a more modern Army and state administration, is less well known abroad for having also improved the efficiency of authoritarian controls, some of which survive today. It was Peter who set up the first political police administration and who officially instituted censorship and the practice of issuing internal passports to keep Russians from traveling away from their permanent homes without special permission.

Nor were the czars all that different in their treatment of dissenters than Soviet leaders today. Peter had his own son, Alexis, tried and sentenced to death for passive opposition to his reforms. By some accounts, he killed Alexis with his own hands. In a preview of Soviet ambivalence toward détente, Catherine the Great first opened and then shut the door to Western ideas. Like Soviet leaders, czars cast themselves as censors for the most troublesome writers. Nicholas I was the personal censor for Pushkin. Count Leo Tolstoy, like dissident writers today, smuggled some of his controversial works to the West for publication, and Dostoyevsky was banished to Siberia. The Soviet practice of putting dissidents in mental hospitals had its precedent in the famous case of Pyotr Chaadayev, an eminent early 19th-century scientist and thinker who was officially branded insane for an essay that condemned Russia as backward and advocated Westernization and Catholicism as a panacea. It would be naive to contend that nothing was altered by the Revolution. But the historical parallels are powerful.

Whether under the czars or commissars, Russians have traditionally had a deeply ingrained fear of anarchy and the centrifugal forces that tug at the unity and stability of their vast state. Montesquieu wrote that absolutism is inevitable in a country so huge and backward as Russia. Inevitable or not, centralized despotism with the czar or Party Leader projected as the personification of the state has been Russia's historic answer to the chaos which it feared.

A history of invasions from the Mongols and Napoleon through Hitler, of peasant revolts and civil wars, of czars and boyars mounting secret cabals or royal father out to kill royal son just as Stalin intrigued against and liquidated his fellow revolutionaries has made Russians prize order and security as much as Americans prize freedom. Most Russians, it seemed to me, are so genuinely dismayed at the unemployment, crime, political assassinations, drugs, and labor strife in American life that they prefer instead the disadvantages of censorship, police controls, arbitrary arrests, labor camps and enforced intellectual conformity. As I listened to older Russians describe their terrible ordeals, it gave me some appreciation why they recoil from any threat of instability. Some have lived near the edge of the apocalypse most of their lives.

'Think of it,' said Lev Kopelev, the dissident writer, bright eyes dancing above his white beard, 'I know people who have lived through the Revolution, the Civil War, the time of Stalin – industrialization, collectivization, and the Terror – and then the war. They have lived through hunger such as you have never known. They have endured this cold. Think

308

of it, in one lifetime, to have lost a father under Stalin, then a brother in the war, not ever to have seen your grandparents alive, and to have had to struggle to hold on to life itself.'

He paused, as if picturing it to himself, and then abruptly asked me, 'Have you ever eaten a "cutlet" made of potato peels?'

Then smiling at the black humor of it (he called it 'cemetery humor'), Lev said, 'Think how much more experienced we are than you.'

It is not only the chaos around them but the anarchy within themselves that Russians seem to fear. Their outer conformism and self-restraint and their obedience to Authority have given them a reputation as a disciplined people that to me seems exaggerated. Russians are not Germans. Theirs is an imposed discipline, not an ethnic instinct for regimentation. 'The Russian is lawless in his soul,' a woman playwright remarked to me. 'In Russia, the law means nothing. The only thing that matters is custom.' I would amend that: what matters most is power. The Russian obeys power, not the law. And if Power is looking the other way, or simply does not notice him, the Russian does what he thinks he can get away with.

This undercurrent of lawlessness and unruliness in the Russian temperament comes out in the many odd bits of life that authorities cannot control. The pervasive corruption is one sign of it. Another is the blatant jaywalking and erratic driving habits of ordinary Russians. So impulsive and undisciplined are Soviet motorists that one Russian, exposed to New York traffic, commented to me in amazement: 'Americans drive real neat!' But it is pedestrians in Moscow, the unvarnished country Russians, if you will, who pose the greatest hazard. Still uncertain about the rules or, more likely, oblivious to them, Soviet pedestrians will suddenly freeze in midcrossing at the sight of an oncoming car, even while within their rights walking across a zebra-striped safety zone. Or else without warning and against all common sense, they will lurch abruptly from the curb into the street against the traffic light and try to pick their way across a busy ten-lane boulevard through moving traffic, lane by lane, like some hiker crossing a rapids leaping precariously from stone to stone.

In private, or otherwise freed of the grip of Party control, Russians are apt to throw themselves into wild, disjointed,

309

free-for-all gabfests like characters from Dostoyevsky. Some Western writers have attributed this headstrong intellectual anarchy to the visionary quality of Russian intellectuals inspired by the broad open spaces of the great Russian interior. But Lev Kopelev suggested to me that it was a hangover from the 19th century when Russian intellectuals indulged in endless political and philosophical vaporings without having to be practical or to compromise for the sake of action because they knew they would never have the opportunity and responsibility for exercising power. This lack of responsibility fed the innate anarchy within.

'If we come together now to try to decide what to do for some political objective,' Lev said of modern Soviet dissidents, 'I will say, "Let us have a statement", the next one will say, "Let us have a demonstration", the third will say, "Let us wait", and the fourth will have another idea. That is normal anywhere, I suppose. But we Russians will disagree and stay disagreeing. After two or three days, we will become rivals. That is how we are different from you. Russians need an ideology and unity from above – democratic centralism – or we disintegrate. We are not practical people like you Americans.'

On another occasion, Bob Kaiser of the *Washington Post* and I were talking with a Russian scientist about the rigidity of Soviet controls. We asked why the authorities resorted to such overkill in dealing with a few dissidents, with errant poets or with seven protestors on Red Square. His answer was to draw a diagram illustrating the insecurity Russians and their leaders feel about their own system.

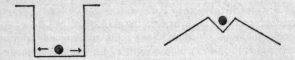

On the left, American society with the established stability of its political system represented by the high walls of the container. This meant, the scientist said, that the ball of human action could move quite freely from side to side and the latitude for human freedom could be very great. In Russia, he said, both the leaders and the led felt a dangerous and inherent instability – illustrated by the shallow pocket for the ball of human action in the diagram on the right. People had to be controlled tightly because the walls of stability were so low and society so vulnerable to violent and dramatic change. To me, the Soviet system always seemed far more stable than that and the Party and police in very solid command. But my opinion was irrelevant. The authorities almost always act as insecure as the scientist said they were.

My own first exposure to the system's obsession with control of the masses was unforgettable. It came after an international soccer match with the Irish team. The Soviet crowd, by international standards, had been pretty subdued. It was a crowd of catcalls or booing. The only genuine emotion that came out was the periodic derisive whistling of impatience at the poor play and dull style of the Soviet team. (Soviet sports teams play almost mechanistically perfect position-soccer or hockey, always showing a picture-book form but no razzle-dazzle.) It never would have occurred to me that this calm Russian crowd would explode into some Latin tantrum after the game. But Soviet authorities were taking no chances. Coming out of the stadium with 100,000 other fans, I saw the streets lined with armed soldiers standing shoulder to shoulder in a wall of khaki. They formed a channel through which the crowd had to flow toward the subways and bus lines. Along another street, the foot soldiers were reinforced by mounted cavalry, also lined up side-by-side. The array of power was numbing.

On that day I avoided the subway crush, but on another occasion I saw what happened when the iron corridors of soldiers stopped short of the platform. Freed of control, the orderly line of Russians suddenly dissolved in chaos as the train appeared. There was a mad scramble to get aboard like a last second, do-or-die touchdown-plunge in a pro football game. When I remarked about it to Russian friends, they laughed and talked about losing shoes or having buttons pop off their coats at such moments. I escaped without property damage and no more than an instant of panic that the moving torrent which picked me up bodily might drop me between platform and train. And I gained a greater appreciation of why the authorities had imposed such strict order on the streets above.

For Russians, the very word for order, *poryadok*, has a special mystique. Language dictionaries render it as proper order, procedure, sequence. To Westerners, putting things in order, tidiness, neatness, organization is an understandable rendering. To Russians it can simply mean that things are okay, hunky-dory. But just as often *poryadok* carries the firm undertone of law and order: things going the way the authorities, the bosses, prescribe – usually the political bosses, but just as easily the factory director, shop foreman, school teacher, even the parents. The echelons above. It is not a frightening word, but a strict one. It conveys a sense of someone standing over you or somewhere unseen but nonetheless keeping an eye on you to make sure things go as they should. In its public life, Soviet society is strong on *poryadok*.

The well-swept streets of Moscow and the city's immaculate subway system are examples of *poryadok* that would make any American mayor envious. The subways, handsome structures decorated with classical busts and mosaics, are free of the trash, vandalism, and self-indulgent *graffiti* that deface the subways in New York City. 'Man, the discipline!' whistled Russell Davis, an awed young American black from the Harlem Street Academy on a visit to Moscow. 'The streets are clean. People get in early. They have a whole lot of respect for the police. You find a whole lot of discipline.'

You also find an unbridgable chasm between the leaders and the led; between 'Them' at the top and 'us' at the bottom. My Russian friends commonly referred to the leaders impersonally as 'Them' or the *vlasti*, the authorities, or more literally, the men of power. Ordinary Russians not only shy away from pronouncing aloud the initials of the secret police (or walking on the same side of the street as its headquarters) but often they avoid mentioning Brezhnev by name by quickly wiping a finger across an eyebrow, an allusion to his heavy eyebrows. It is a gesture that recalls that richly Russian line in *Fiddler on the Roof* when the rabbi is asked whether he has a blessing for the Czar and replies: 'Yes, may God bless you and keep the Czar away from us.' The instinct of the little man is to keep his distance from those on top.

It is not a great problem, for the leaders do not seek exposure politicking among the people. Almost nothing is disclosed about their private lives or families. For the ordinary citizenry, the Kremlin leaders appear only periodically as faces on television at ritualistic state occasions and then disappear from view. The leadership live hidden lives. They seem to prize anonymity as an essential ingredient of mysterious and unchallengeable authority, as if some Russian Machiavelli had long ago counseled that leaders whose personal lives become too much of an open book are no longer so awesome but become human and vulnerable. In Pushkin's *Boris Godunov*, for example, the Czar advises his son that if he wants to hold power and rule effectively, he should not expose himself too much to popular view but retain the aura of aloofness.

For the common man, politics and the power of the leaders are like the natural elements. No ordinary mortal – worker, peasant, intellectual, Party member – dreams of doing anything about them. They are simply a given, a fact, irresistible and immutable. State policy is like the weather. It descends from on high and the ordinary Russian trims his sails with stoic fatalism. He makes the best of whatever comes along, enjoying calm political seasons and trying to find shelter in rough ones. Not too surprisingly, most Russians are apolitical.

'Here, there is simply no identification of the individual with the rulers, with the government,' a linguist from a prominent family, a brilliant but embittered woman, told me over tea and cold toast. 'The individual citizen does not identify with his government here, the way you do in America, in the sense that you feel it is somehow responsible to you. With us, it is there, like the wind, like a wall, like the sky. It is something permanent, unchangeable. So the individual acquiesces, does not dream of changing it – except a few, few people. In America, people feel ashamed about their government, for example, being in the Vietnam war. But here people do not feel shame. I don't feel shame about what my government does in Czechoslovakia or somewhere else. I am sorry for our society and for others. But I don't feel shame about the government's actions because it is totally separate from me. I feel not connected with it.'

The political self-confidence and self-assertion that are essential to democracy are not part of the Russian make-up except for those who wield power or for a tiny handful of dissidents. One of them, Andrei Amalrik, a young historian, put his finger on the crucial difference between authoritarian and democratic mentalities in his book, *Will the Soviet Union Survive Until 1984?*, published in the West – an act for which Amalrik was sentenced to three years in Siberia.

'Whether because of historical traditions or for some other

313

reason, the idea of self-government, of equality before the law and of personal freedom – and the responsibility that goes with these – are almost completely incomprehensible to the Russian people,' he wrote. 'Even in the idea of pragmatic freedom, a Russian tends to see not so much the possibility of securing a good life for himself as the danger that some clever fellow will make good at his expense. To the majority of people the very word "freedom" is synonymous with "disorder" or the opportunity to indulge with impunity in some kind of antisocial or dangerous activity. As for respecting the rights of an individual as such, the idea simply arouses bewilderment. One can respect strength, authority, even intellect or education, but it is preposterous to the popular mind that the human personality should represent any kind of value.'

Russians comment that people nowadays are less submissive to authority than in Stalin's time. I am sure it is true. Yet for Americans who have lived through a generation of demonstrations, war protests, establishment-knocking and the removal of a President, Russian public submissiveness is still remarkable to see. I remember American tourists bridling at dictatorial Soviet militiamen blowing whistles at pedestrians on Red Square, insisting they follow cross-hatched lanes even in areas were no traffic comes and where no visible reason exists for following a prescribed path. But Russians simply obeyed. At a provincial cathedral one Easter, I watched many young people, powerfully tempted to enter to see the beautiful religious ceremony, but deterred even from trying – with some few exceptions – by the presence of a policeman at the door.

On an Aeroflot flight landing in Tashkent one spring, an almond-eyed Uzbek air hostess announced, 'All right, you can get off.' People rose and began gathering belongings but the stewardess objected. 'No, sit down comrades,' she coldly commanded the Soviet passengers. 'I was addressing our guests' – meaning half a dozen foreign correspondents and our Soviet escorts. The Russians all submitted to this slap in the face silently, sat down and began craning their necks to watch us disembark first. It was a scene I saw repeated in many settings.

I was struck that no one refused to comply with such

orders. I did, however, witness one case of vigorous protest against bureaucratic injustice by a group of younger people, typically less intimidated than their elders, and obviously from well-educated and probably well-connected families accustomed to better treatment.

Like us, they had come from one of a handful of modest Soviet ski resorts in the Caucasus and were flying back from Mineralnye Vody to Moscow. Late in the afternoon we all boarded the scheduled plane but because of an insoluble breakdown, we had to get off and spend 17 hours through the night in the airport waiting for a substitute plane to be flown in. Unfortunately, it had fewer seats. After boarding, these young skiers suddenly realized that one of their group was being held off the plane on the ramp. A handsome, curly-haired blond man in a blue windbreaker, about 30 years old, and a well-dressed brunette came to the hostess to try to get their friend on the flight.

'Comrades, there are no seats,' a chubby Aeroflot hostess told them. 'He is not registered on the manifest for the flight.' Another hostess claimed that the man had no valid ticket – hardly likely since he had been aboard the original flight.

'That's your fault, not his,' complained the man in the windbreaker. 'If his ticket is not valid, then neither is mine. We all came together. We are seven in a group. We all did the same thing.'

'There's nothing the air crew can do about it,' the hostess said. 'Go sit down, so we can take off.'

The protest had been very mild and reasonable but the mere challenge to authority upset several middle-aged women sitting near us. Rather than blame Aeroflot, they blamed the young people for protesting. 'Careless young people, irresponsible!' grumbled a woman in a blue mohair hat. 'They'll talk two or three hours and nothing will come of it.'

'Why are they making trouble for nothing?' agreed a rough country woman, joining what was a conflict of generations and social classes as well as between customer and bureaucrat. 'They are holding up all of us.'

By then, the younger couple, joined by four friends, were asking to see the aircraft commander.

'The commander can do nothing about it,' insisted the

315

hostess. 'Go sit!' she ordered, in the deliberately insulting language that Russians use with their dogs.

'Are you children?' complained a male passenger's voice. 'You're making a useless fuss.'

'Our friend's luggage is on the plane with ours,' pleaded one young man. 'He hasn't enough money to buy another ticket if you say that one is invalid. And when will the next plane be available?'

The Aeroflot hostesses did not bother replying. One elderly passenger suggested, 'They should get the police.'

Sure enough, the police were coming across the tarmac, two gray-uniformed officers in a little motorized cart. Up the ramp they came preparing to remove the hapless skier bodily. At the sight of the uniforms, the young skiers on the plane began to disperse to their seats. The middle-aged women scolded them as they passed down the aisle. Everyone backed down but the tall blond in the windbreaker who insisted, 'Well, at least let me get off the plane a moment and give my friend some money.' That was permitted. But there was no telling when his friend would get to Moscow. We had inquired during the night and Aeroflot had said all flights were booked solid to Moscow for the next five days.

Soviet intellectuals can tell stories into the night about the passive obedience of their countrymen. A cybernetics specialist recalled that in 1953, with Stalin fatally ill, the publication *Clinical Medicine* came out with a major editorial, 'Murder in a White Gown', about the so-called 'doctor's plot' against Stalin, prelude to a new purge. But the dictator died, the situation changed, the doctors were cleared, and a second edition was hurriedly issued with a substitute editorial. Subscribers were asked to return the first version, which no longer fit the Party line, and many people did so, obeying instructions rather than taking the risk of being caught with the wrong version at home.

Similarly, the third edition of the Great Soviet Encyclopedia appeared with a long article about Lavrenti Beria, Stalin's secret police chief, who was subsequently executed in a power struggle with Khrushchev and others. The Encyclopedia editors, desperate to blot out the memory of Beria, produced a special article on the Bering Strait. This was mailed to Encyclopedia owners with instructions to paste it directly on top of the Beria article. Again, my friend said, he knew many who complied.

316

The atmosphere today is far less oppressive than under Stalin. In private, among trusted friends, Russians will turn their wit and their curses against their leaders, but I have seen many close the kitchen door and pull the blind before doing so, out of habit if not out of actual fear. They know, moreover, that publicly knocking any political figure is risky – and 'publicly' can mean not in a public place, but simply in front of the wrong people. So inbred is that caution that a middle-aged Moscow woman refused to believe an American correspondent who told her that Americans could publicly criticize their President. (This was early in Watergate.) Sophisticated younger people, making fun of such attitudes liked the joke about the American tourist who boasted to a Russian, 'We have freedom of speech. I can go out on the street and criticize Nixon all I want.' Whereupon the Russian replied, 'We also have freedom of speech. I can go out on the street and criticize Nixon all I want, too.'

Which is not strictly accurate, as a British exchange student attending the provincial university in Rostov-on-Don learned in 1972. He and four friends, arguing with Soviet students about democracy and dictatorship, alluded to the ubiquitous Soviet pictures of Lenin. One Russian shot back that this was no different from the British hanging up pictures of the Queen. To demonstrate the difference dramatically, one Briton pulled down the Queen's picture in his bedroom and tore it up in front of the Russians. Word of this act of political irreverence got to university authorities who were dismayed. They summoned the Britishers and warned that if anything further happened, all five would be expelled.

I don't want to leave the impression that Russians are totally docile. I saw motorists arguing – though not terribly vehemently – with traffic cops; overheard people cursing store clerks or petty bureaucrats; and was told of workers talking back to superiors. Some people send in complaining letters-to-the-editor of Soviet newspapers and carry petty grievances to local Communist Party officials. But most people shy away from confrontations with authority. 'If a person bumps into someone or has an accident, he is ready to stand up for himself,' a young professional woman told me. 'But if he finds out the other one is some official, say, from the District Party Committee, the next moment he is bowing and fawning and trying to avoid trouble. I myself do not make

317

complaints. If you talk too much, they can shut off your path and make things hard in many ways. It's a mistake to irritate officials.' This deeply ingrained sense of impotence, because of the official power of retaliation, and the assertive intrusion of officialdom with personal lives, is something alien almost totally to middle-class Americans and perhaps understood only by blacks and poor people in America. Yet it affects almost all Soviets. I remember the instinctive fear of officials of a prestigious Jewish scientist who had applied to emigrate to Israel and had thus broken with the Soviet system. He had written a very mild open letter to the then Secretary of State William Rogers criticizing the American policy of quiet diplomacy on emigration. He asked me about the wisdom of publishing the letter.

'Do you think it is a mistake?' he wanted to know.

'You have to decide on the risks for yourself,' I replied, 'but what worries you about it?' His answer was deeply Russian.

'I understand things are done differently in your country from ours,' the scientist explained. 'I think quiet diplomacy is wrong and I want to say so. But will it be safe for me if I publish an open letter criticizing Secretary Rogers? Or will he retaliate and take action against me and my family?'

The power of officialdom also leaves most Russians feeling guilty before authority. Several told me that practically everyone assumes the accused must be guilty if the authorities charge them with misdeed, even if only in the press or at a public meeting. Similarly, if accused themselves, I have heard Russians say, their first reaction is to begin offering explanations, excuses, or disclaiming responsibility rather than objecting to unjustified harassment or insisting on legal procedures. One Russian woman, a hardy dissident not easily intimidated, nonetheless described her own surprise at what she regarded as the unusual audacity of an African student friend who got into a scrape with authorities at Moscow's Lumumba University. He had defied their wishes by stopping in Paris en route between Africa and Moscow during his vacation. When he returned, the Dean called him in to ask what he had done in Paris. The African replied that was his affair and perhaps that of the French, but not of the Russians. 'No Russian would have answered that way,' this woman asserted. 'A Russian would have said, "Oh, you know, I have a friend in Paris, and he invited me," or some-

318

thing like that, to try to explain it away. The first reaction of a Russian is to correct his mistake. From childhood we learn to feel guilty before superiors and we try to explain ourselves. Only later, our second reaction is to ask ourselves, "Why do they need to know?" '

The fact that power and authority derive from above not below, has made Soviet society far more rank-and-hierarchy conscious than Western societies – strange as that may seem for a state that preens itself as the protagonist of the proletariat. Power determines rank from top to bottom in Soviet society. The crucial test, in Lenin's blunt formula, is *Kto-Kogo?*, literally, 'Who-Whom?' but more meaningfully 'Who can do what to whom?' It is an unspoken question Russians have in mind constantly as they deal with each other. Hence the enormous attention paid to the pecking order at all levels of Soviet society. It is the inordinate care that the Soviet leadership itself devotes to deciding who stands where in official photographs or on top of the Lenin Mausoleum which gave birth to the Western art of Kremlinology. It was the same under the czars. Centuries ago Western envoys to the Kremlin learned to study certain ikons to discern the importance of various court personalities because their position in processions was often shown not according to real life or the laws of perspective, but according to their rank and importance.

Today, the West has learned some of the symbols of hierarchy in the Soviet system but few people appreciate how religiously they are followed. In the 1974 elections to the Supreme Soviet, for example, despite the fact that it was a politically empty ritual as an election, the Party leadership carefully stage-managed the procedures so that *Pravda* reported Brezhnev receiving nominations as a candidate from 54 electoral districts. Podgorny and Kosygin, next in rank, were nominated by 22 districts each; Suslov and Kirilenko, next in line, 10 each and so on, neatly delineating the ranking of Politburo members by the numbers of nominations. Each man ran, of course, from only one district unopposed and each gave only one 'campaign speech'. Once again, the order of speaking and the importance of the city or region where he spoke was in almost precise ascending hierarchy so that the most junior Politburo members spoke first, in far-off provincial cities, and Brezhnev spoke last, from the Kremlin, on national television.

This devotion to the pecking order permeates all levels, all walks of Soviet life, a contemporary echo of the elaborate system of 14 ranks that Peter the Great established for the government services. Not only political figures but scholars are carefully stratified, from top down, as Academicians, Corresponding Members of the Academy, Institute Directors, full Professors, Department heads, Laboratory Chiefs, holders of the Doctorate Degree, senior researchers, etc. Each rank carries not only its salary scale but special housing allotments and, at the higher ranks, the right legally to hold second jobs and lucrative consultantships. Individual sportsmen, too, are ranked formally by class: Honored Master of Sport, Master of Sport–International Class, Master of Sport Class A, Class B, and so on. At theaters or musical concerts, programs are printed or numbers are introduced with each leading artist, soloist, conductor identified as 'Honored Artist of the Russian Republic', 'Honored Artist of the Soviet Union' (quite a bit higher), 'People's Artist of the Soviet Union' (the highest), and laureate of the Lenin Prize or some international concourse. I have attended televised concerts where the introduction ritual is repeated for each number – even for the very same persons. And if composers are present, their ranks and laurels are also cited.

As a people, Russians love ceremony and relish these pompous titles and symbols of rank and accomplishment, the way small American boys love Cub Scout merit badges. They are greatly offended if their title or honors are accidentally omitted. I remember a Soviet-American news conference on trade at which Donald Kendall of Pepsico introduced Vladimir Alkhimov, Deputy Soviet Foreign Trade Minister, giving his position, a detailed biography and a more elaborate introduction than he would have given any American. But when Alkhimov rose, his first comment was to observe that Kendall 'forgot to mention that I am a Hero of the Soviet Union' – the equivalent of an American Congressional Medal of Honor winner. On the sidewalks I often saw war veterans wearing their decorations on their civilian suits just as Brezhnev sports his Lenin Peace Prize Medal and his honors as Hero of the Soviet Union (military) and Hero of Socialist Labor (civilian) on his breast for speeches and important functions. To an American, this comes across as strangely akin to the British with their system of peerages, knighthoods and orders.

Nor is it all done merely for show or psychic one-upmanship. These decorations, honors and ranks have practical impact. Life runs more smoothly for their holders – who probably run into the hundreds of thousands. At railroad stations, signs at civilian ticket windows state that Deputies in the Supreme Soviet (which automatically includes the most important Party and Government officials), war invalids, Heroes of Socialist Labor, and others honored by 'socialist orders of the third degree or higher' can buy tickets ahead of the line. At military ticket windows, Heroes of the Soviet Union, generals, admirals, colonels and majors, are accorded this privilege. This works at airports, theaters, hotels and untold other public institutions. Each of the 15 individual republics has its own hierarchy of VIPs granted such privileges within its territory.

Similarly, Soviet citizens have little work passes that come in various gradations of size and color. Like the gambling chips at Monte Carlo, they increase in size and change color according to their worth. These little hardbacked pass booklets, a bit smaller than a cassette, are normally blue. But booklets of Communist Party officials at all levels and of staff members at important government institutions are red. The Bolshoi Ballet-Opera Troupe, as a flagship of state, is granted red, and when the Kirov Ballet in Leningrad was accorded this honor in 1972, some Kirov dancers told me, this added to their ease of living. Most booklets are embossed with the name of the institution where the individual works and that, too, gives an instant clue to power and status. Those of the security agencies carry the seal of the Soviet Union. The mere flashing of a red booklet, especially bearing the state seal or the name of an important Party or Government agency, is enough to help many people gain instant admission at a housing office, theater, restaurant or through a police barrier while others stand in those aching lines. Often, I have watched such line-crashing with indignation, yet Russians did not protest. They took it as a given of life. 'You learn not to complain no matter what you feel inside,' said one young woman helplessly.

The most honored and exalted personages have special pass booklets that are vest-pocket size. Valery Panov, the ballet dancer, showed me his, awarded for a high State prize that he had won. It looked like a small diploma, neatly inscribed by some 'court' calligrapher. An ordinary bureaucrat confronted with such a document immediately recognizes rank, and practically genuflects in his effort to please.

No modern Soviet writer has outdone Chekhov in capturing the twofaced fawning servility of Russian bureaucrats to their superiors and their arrogant disdain toward the masses. Two decades before the Revolution, Chekhov did a series of vignettes that are as contemporary as if they had been written yesterday. In *Fat and Thin*, two former schoolmates meet accidentally years later and enjoy the encounter until the thin one discovers that the fat one has risen a bit higher on the scale of ranks than he. Suddenly normal personal relations become impossible. The thin man becomes so obsequious, so awed by his fat old friend's importance, that he is reduced to nervous giggles. Nowadays, Russians told me, it is more often the other way around – the senior person acting so condescendingly that relations with old friends are corroded. Either way, this feeling of subordination or superiority seems almost inescapable in public life. Where Americans take each other's measure in terms of money, Russians do it by rank. And they treat each other accordingly.

Once again, it is Chekhov who sketched that trait so graphically in *Chameleon*, the story of a town bailiff who alternates between menacing self-importance and timid acquiescence in his handling of a stray dog – depending on what onlookers have to say about the identity and rank of the owner. The bailiff is ready to prosecute so long as it appears the owner is a nobody; he wants to drop the case when he hears the owner is a general. As the conflicting versions alternate, he changes like a chameleon. In Soviet life, this is an everyday occurrence. Any foreigner who has lived in Russia has experienced the *volte-face* from cranky arrogance to Uriah Heep helpfulness the minute it appears that people of some importance are involved. Foreigners have more status than most Russians and enjoy certain benefits. A Soviet journalist told me that Russians must sign a slip promising to get out of an Intourist Hotel room at any time of day or night if it is needed for a foreigner. Traveling by train from Murmansk to Moscow, Ann and I were rudely told by a scruffy waiter one evening that we could not get dinner because the dining car was closed. He had taken us for Russians. We knew it was an hour before closing time and we sat down anyway, hoping someone else might help us. The waiter ignored us. So did a fat waitress with a Brunhilda hairdo tinted a glossy auburn, a shade favored by working-class women. But when other diners heard us speaking English and alerted the Brunhilda that we were foreigners, the attitude changed abruptly. We got dinner. On another occasion, *Times'* Foreign Editor Jim Greenfield wanted to visit Moscow but for days Intourist insisted there was not a single free hotel room in Moscow on his dates. Yet once I had engineered intervention from the Foreign Ministry not only was a room discovered but Greenfield and his wife were given the spacious, marbeled VIP suite at the National Hotel.

This sort of thing can happen in other countries, too. Americans, like others, have their own sense of who stands where on the totem pole and of apple-polishing. But it is rarely manifested so baldly as in the rank-consciousness of Soviet life. 'We have a court society and so people behave like courtiers,' a Soviet magazine editor confessed to me. Among common people who work side-by-side in factories or in the fields, I sensed a rough feeling of equality. During World War II, I was told, the national sense of solidarity diminished the normal sense of rank. But Russian life today is marked by status feelings – that some are above and others below, that some prevail and others submit.

Some experienced Western diplomats as well as Russians whom I knew argued convincingly that this kind of attitude colored and complicated Soviet negotiations with the West, commercial as well as political. Compromise, they reasoned, is an Anglo-Saxon concept that assumes a rough equality. It does not arise instinctively in the soul of Russian official-dom. For the Russians the instinctive question is: who is the stronger and who is the weaker (something which makes détente extremely tricky). Inherently, any relation becomes a test of strength. I was surprised at a luncheon one day to hear a Swedish diplomat, talking about this Russian charac-ter trait, vent his bitter frustration at the short shrift given Sweden and small nations by Moscow. 'The Russians respect power,' this vexed young Scandinavian rasped.

'They deal with you Americans with respect because you have power, because there is *something* behind your words. But they don't deal with us that way. We're not powerful. We're a "little" country.'

The 'little man' in Russian society, *malenky chelovek* as Gogol called him, has the same sense of impotence before the apparatus of the Soviet state, except that he has long since steeled himself not to notice too much.

From the flow of dramatic literature about purges, labor camps, and the secret police, Westerners have an exaggerated notion of the extent to which the KGB intrudes in the daily lives of ordinary Russians. It is true that though the terror has eased since Stalin, the secret police still persecute the most daring souls. Their mere presence is enough to keep the vast majority in check. Every Soviet institution has its 'first department', its security section which keeps a steady watch on political reliability and conscientiousness as well as a full, lifetime dossier on everyone. Each time an individual changes jobs, gets a promotion, wants to travel abroad, or does anything unusual, he has to obtain a *kharakteristika*, a character reference that includes not only job performance and recommendations of superiors but a 'social comment', or security evaluation, by the Party and KGB. Mail censorship, telephone bugging, controls on typewriters, copying machines and the like have been too often reported to need cataloguing here once more. These controls form the general environment of Soviet citizenry but they are not the little man's greatest burden. For the quiet erosion of the spirit that takes place daily is caused more by the petty tyrants of Soviet life – the rigid little bureaucrats and the self-appointed busybodies who use infinite regulations and documents to harass, humble and hound the man in the street.

I would have thought that with all the nuisances burdening ordinary Russians they would instinctively have banded together to ease the strain of life. Within their own narrow circles they do. Yet Soviet society in general is peopled by mini-dictators inflicting inconvenience and misery on the rest of their fellow citizens, often it seems, as a way of getting back at the system for the hardship and frustration they themselves have suffered. 'The peasant learns to suffer and therefore to sympathize with suffering,' wrote

Maurice Baring, a British commentator, not long before the Revolution. 'He learns to bear suffering with stoicism, and therefore to inflict it with insensitivity when the occasion arises.' I have heard Russians in more recent years describe this phenomenon as a mass settling of scores on a personal level.

'Put a Russian in charge of a little plot of ground or a doorway somewhere,' a bespectacled scientist ruminated sadly to me, 'and he will use his meager authority over that spot to make life hard on others.' In one way or another, practically everyone works for the state and, on the job at least, adopts the psychology of government functionaries, which typically means a narrow and finicky adherence to the technicalities and a bull-headed stubbornness not to venture an inch beyond the rules for fear that any initiative will later be chastized.

The result is that divisions of grizzled pensioners guard the doors at restaurants, brigades of imperious matrons in mohair hats stand watch as duty officers on the floors of every hotel in the country, and regiments of younger women safeguard gates at airports, stations, or department stores with the mentality of goalkeepers, the tenacity of terriers, the gruffness of bulldogs and the devotion of the French troops at Verdun who vowed: 'They shall not pass.' *Izvestia*, the government newspaper, once pointed out the absurd lengths to which this blind devotion to the rules can be carried. It reported that one poor man leaving an office Friday afternoon, noticed at the door that he had left behind his briefcase but was refused permission by the doorman to re-enter because he was only working there on temporary assignment. The weekend period had begun and temporary employees were not allowed in on weekends. The office worker pleaded desperately that all his belongings were in the briefcase, including his hotel key, and he could not even remember his room number. The doorman was unmoved. Ultimately, someone with normal access appeared and was sent after the briefcase.

One of my more puzzling encounters with this rigidity occurred on the day of a new Soviet-American environmental research agreement. With Murray Fromson of C.B.S. and Murray Seeger of the *Los Angeles Times*, I went to the House of Unions for the press conference. The building, near the Bolshoi Theater, is a large, handsome, columned, pre-

325

Revolutionary edifice used for important occasions. It was a windy, late September day and all three of us were glad to get inside as we entered. The inevitable matron in an inevitable blue uniform asked, as is customary, for our documents before admitting us. We produced Soviet press cards and she was about to let us pass to the cloakroom when she stopped Fromson, who was carrying a cassette recorder. 'You cannot take the recorder through this entrance,' the lady in blue instructed Fromson. 'You must go around the corner to another entrance.' She pointed for him to go back out the door.

At the next entrance, there were two more blue-uniformed ladies whom I half expected to confiscate the recorder. But when we entered they were not only uninterested in this treacherous device but did not even bother to ask to see our press cards. Evidently, they were expecting Americans and were relaxing customary vigilance for this occasion of Soviet-American cooperation. Ten steps beyond this second doorway, we found ourselves on a landing overlooking the foyer of the first entrance and the same cloakroom where we had just been. We descended a few steps to check our coats and nodded at the lady who had refused to let Fromson and his recorder pass. She looked sternly at us but said nothing.

'Now explain to me why the recorder can come through one entrance and not another,' Fromson griped between his teeth.

'I don't know, Murray,' I replied. 'When we understand that, we'll understand the entire country and it will be time to go home.'

After the press conference, we descended to the lobby and picked up our coats. We were heading out the first entrance, which was closer, when the blue-uniformed door-guardian reappeared and halted Fromson once again. 'Excuse me,' she insisted, signalling him to stop, 'but recorders are not allowed through this entrance.' We broke out laughing and all went out anyway.

What goes for door-ladies, goes as well for hotel administrators, housing clerks, police officers, and their bureaucratic cousins in every institution – all reinforced by the Soviet passion for documents. Russians are forever being asked to produce their identity or work documents or a *spravka*, a permit, to prove that whatever they are doing is authorized – be it staying in a hotel, getting medical treatment, selling goods in a farmers' market, taking a vacation, going on a business assignment, buying gasoline with government coupons, entering a library. The Russians have a ditty that runs, 'Without a document, you're an insect; but with a document, you're a human being.' The assortment of required documents is too formidable to recite in full. The most important, however, are the domestic passport, the work book, the institutional work pass (red or blue booklet), the *kharakteristika* (mentioned before) and the special purpose *spravka*. The work book is a lifetime employment record with job description, salary level, disciplinary measures and reason for leaving listed for every position held throughout a person's career. The employee turns it in to his employer to keep until he quits or is fired and must get it back to seek a new job, a certain deterrent to floating and random job hunting, but not always effective. The passport is the key item because it contains not only vital information about birth, parentage, national ethnic groups (very important among Soviets), marriage and divorce data, but, most important, the residential registration with the local police. This is the basic element of control – the residential permit in the passport, known as the *propiska*.

In probably two dozen closed cities – Moscow, Leningrad, Kiev, Tbilisi, Vladivostok, and other principal cities or defense areas – it is extremely difficult for newcomers to get *propiskas* because the authorities are striving to hold down population, overcrowding, housing shortages and general congestion. Any move from one residence to another must be registered and approved by the police. Any visit to another city lasting more than three days must be registered, too. But plenty of people find ways to beat the system for a little while. 'Every rule has its antirule,' the poet Joseph Brodsky smilingly told me one afternoon on a park bench. It was easy to beat the three-day rule, he said, merely by staying with friends or by renting a private room rather than staying at a hotel where clerks automatically registered you with the police. So many people are traveling and so many are renting rooms, legally or illegally, that the police cannot keep up with all those who avoid public accommodations. It is harder to beat the system for a longer period, though in Siberia where the labor shortage is often acute and authorities wink at the rules, groups of workers float from one construction site to another grabbing highly paid work and moving on. Local Party officials tolerate this because they, like the construction bosses, have an interest in getting their work projects finished as quickly as possible, and are glad to get extra workers.

Most of the time, however, Russians are hounded by the need to get some document stamped or inspected as proof that they carried out an assignment, got a permission, reached a destination. In my mind's eye, an almost permanent attachment to many a Russian's hand is a crumpled, well-thumbed piece of graying paper, a *spravka*, held out to be inspected. Once, on a nightmare trip to Siberia, a group of Western correspondents landed after midnight in the airport of the provincial city of Tyumen where, because of lack of accommodations, we had to sleep for several hours on the floor of the VIP lounge. We moaned and groaned until one correspondent discovered that our two Soviet escorts, responsible officials of the influential Novosti Press Agency, could not even sleep. They had to trot around the airport in the wee hours in search of the duty militia officer. They needed him to stamp and sign their travel papers to certify that they had actually stopped in Tyumen as scheduled.

Documents take on special importance for the innumerable closed institutions, events and performances of Soviet life. The most surprising of these to me were the parades on Red Square on November 7 and May Day. I thought they were for the masses. But unlike the Thanksgiving Day parade in New York or the French Bastille Day march down the Champs Elysees, these Communist celebrations were not open to the ordinary public. Only the elite, armed with special invitations, could attend – plus selected foreigners. So tight was the security that I counted passing through nine different checkpoints to get to Red Square. Except for marchers, who were thoroughly monitored and grouped, the streets were clear of ordinary people.

At each of the nine security lines there was a little ritual. A police officer would block my path, demand my press card and my invitation, compare the two, scrutinize my face to be sure it matched the picture, and then grandly usher me through with a *pozhaluista*, 'if you please'.

Russians sometimes laugh at the document mania in their country but they are genuinely baffled that Western societies can operate without a similar array of documents. 'I think one of the better books we have published about England was done by a *Pravda* correspondent named Osipov,' a tall, striking Russian woman told me as we were walking in the woods one afternoon. 'Because I have been to England myself, some of my friends asked me about that book. The chapter that caused the most interest, and the most astonishment, was the one where he described how he put his child in an English school. He simply went to the school one day and said, "Here is my child. I would like to enter him in school" and that was it. For our people, that's astonishing. My doctor asked me, "Lara, is it really like that? How can they do it without any documents? They have no proof that the child lives in the district. They have no proof of the child's age. Just the parent's word. How can they do it?" '

I laughed and then she laughed and we talked a bit about how Russians were constantly having to prove their identity, not for financial reasons like Americans or other Westerners with their charge cards and checkbooks and driving licenses but simply in order to go somewhere or get into some place. 'People are not trusted here,' my walking companion said. 'Why Petrov should want to pretend he is Pavlov, I don't know. If you want a job, you have to take your diploma or otherwise how would they know you had graduated from school or college.'

It offended her, this all-pervasive mistrust. But then she confessed her amazement at American laxity. 'The first question my friends ask, and I wonder about it, too, is "How can they [Americans] find people if they need to? How can they catch criminals?" It is really a problem for us to imagine how society works without having people registered where they live or having to give a passport to hotels when you check in.'

In much the same way, the ordinary Russian takes for granted the latticework of rules and regulations that frames his existence. He chafes sometimes, but they seem as natural as the sun and moon. To an American, Soviet life often resembles living full time in the Army, not only at work but even on vacation.

Outside the Latvian capital of Riga one sunny June morning, the chief doctor at Jaunkemeri Sanatorium explained the regime for a 24-day holiday and treatment period. The entire schedule and the diet were worked out, he said, by a scientific institute in Moscow and were followed nationwide – a staggering thought to me. One guest, Ivan Safronov, a husky, ruddy-faced war veteran with a cushy job on the

People's Control Commission in Tashkent, testified like a schoolboy that he could not go sun himself on the beach without a *spravka* from the nurse which he had to show the beach attendant. Badly as he wanted to swim in the cool Baltic Sea, he vowed that he had not been in the salt water since his hot sulphur and mud bath treatments had begun. His holiday, though it was incredibly cheap ($64 for 24 days) thanks to heavy union subsidies, could hardly be called a fling – up at 7.30, group morning exercises, breakfast, medical treatment, a prescribed walk on the beach (all by the clock); lunch, a free hour, then a mandatory quiet hour in his room; afternoon tea, collective cultural activities or excursions, supper, a prescribed evening walk, a collective show or concert, yogurt at 10 p.m. ('We give it to everyone – we consider it like medicine,' the chief doctor advised). And lights out at 11. The doors were locked pronto at 11 p.m.

'What if someone gets back late, after 11?' I asked.

Safronov, the chief doctor, and my official Latvian escort all shook their heads. The doctor said that no one came back late, implying everyone knew the consequences. The Latvian official removed any doubt. 'I knew of a case of a man who came back late and got in trouble,' he said. 'He was sent home. A report went to his factory. And he could not qualify after that for a *putevka* [a subsidized vacation pass].' I believed his story but, knowing Russians, I am sure that there must be a fair number who found a way to get around the curfews.

At summer camps for Young Pioneers, the daily schedules are just as detailed, from reveille to retreat with not much time for just plain fooling around. At a ski base in Dombai, in the Caucasus mountains, I noticed that beginners were given a fully planned two-week routine worked out so that they spent their first two days far from the slopes – just receiving equipment, learning its designations, studying how to put it on, and listening to lectures on the theory of skiing. Practice came later. (Courses of all kinds are strong on the obligatory combination of theory-and-practice.) Advertisements on city bulletin boards beckon young people to take a four-month course to become a bread store clerk or five months to learn to be a check-out girl, or eight months to become a driver. The course time is divided between theoretical instructions and on-the-job practice. I never could figure out why it took so long. Friends explained that the theory part was boring, senseless and often included lectures on Marxism-Leninism and Party history.

Russians endure this kind of regulated living much better than Americans, Britons, Frenchmen or Italians would. Just as they are more tolerant of the intrusions of self-appointed busybodies who monitor community conduct and proffer unsought advice. These self-commissioned corporals of society, as Chekhov named a pre-Revolutionary forerunner of the contemporary breed, are one reason why the streets and subways are kept so clean. Many people, mostly middle-aged and older, are quick to intervene against 'antisocial behavior'. At an organ concert in a Latvian cathedral, I remember officially appointed monitors shushing people so noisily and unpleasantly that they were more of a nuisance than odd whispers in the audience. On another occasion, Russian friends of mine were setting off to dinner. The wife, in a plaid maxi skirt and her long hair flowing, pleaded with her husband to take a taxi. 'I can't stand those people on buses,' she said.

'Why would they care?' I asked. 'You look lovely.'

'You don't understand,' she said with irritation. 'They don't approve of these fashions and they heckle you the whole trip.'

This busybody trait can have an attractive, friendly, my-brother's-keeper side, too. Strange women have come up and advised us on numerous occasions to bundle up our children better against the cold. Elderly men and once even a policeman kindly advised me to put on a hat. Others solemnly warned that sitting on stone was certain to cause colds or pneumonia and we had better get up from sitting on cement steps. One American friend had her hand knocked away from her jaw by a Russian woman who sternly admonished that this was a sure way to get pimples. Less pleasantly, *babushkas* have remonstrated that our children were disorderly because they were running on park paths (where else?) or that other American children we knew were not neatly enough dressed to be out in public.

One Saturday morning, out walking our dog on a leash near the Ministry of Justice of the Russian Republic, I was sternly accosted by a plain woman in a mud-brown overcoat headed for home with her groceries.

'It's forbidden to let your dog run on that yard,' she announced. Actually, the dog was not running on the yard,

331

only in the bushes along the edge of it, so I paid no heed. 'It's forbidden,' she insisted. 'Take your dog out of there.'

'How do you know it's forbidden?' I asked. 'There's no sign.' Indeed, that was remarkable because the landscape of Soviet cities is peopled with 'forbidden' signs telling human beings where they cannot enter, cannot smoke, cannot eat, cannot be.

'It's forbidden,' she persisted. 'That is a State institution.'

'Do you work there?' I challenged. She shook her head.

'Take your dog over there,' she commanded, pointing at a tawdry little unattached plot of ground 50 yards away.

'The dog likes it here and we will only be a minute anyway,' I stalled, hoping she would go away.

'That lawn is for people,' the woman objected.

'But it is Saturday morning and no one is working there today,' I demurred, unable to imagine people being authorized on the lawn if dogs were not. 'The dog isn't bothering anyone.'

'We are beautifying Moscow for people, not for dogs,' she proclaimed. 'The lawn is for people. Your dog can have a place in that little yard.' And she eyed me steadily until I had tugged Amy, our little black mongrel, out of the bushes and led her away. I confess that one reason for my own stubbornness was resentment at the constant badgering, ordering about, being told that things are 'forbidden' in Russia.

But Russians themselves generally do not take it that way. During a stopover in the Leningrad station one wintry midnight, I watched two female railroad car porters scold and pester a Navy Commander, a man in his fifties, for starting to venture out into the cold night without an overcoat. He just wanted a quick breath of air and he was wearing a thick blue warm-up suit, a costume favored by Russians of both sexes for train travel because it serves as both day outfit and pajamas. But these women hectored him mercilessly.

'You'll catch cold, comrade,' counseled the first.

'It's forbidden without a coat,' commanded the second.

The poor, henpecked man hovered like an uncertain five-year-old in the door of the train, aching to step outside and walk around with the other people on the platform. Yet he accepted this well-meant pestering from two very ordinary women with good humor though many a Westerner would probably have brushed it aside and felt compelled to prove his independence by stepping off the train.

That is not characteristic of the Russian. His way is usually to submit to the busybody just as he submits to the power of the authorities, to the system of ranks and privileges, to the rules and regulations, to the documents, to the myriad controls of his life. I remember an iconoclastic writer telling me that he had learned from the Army: 'Never disobey. Always say, "Yes, sir," and let *them* worry about whether you carry out the orders.'

This caught it exactly. The Russian tactic is not to confront Authority, not to seek reform of the system, but to step back, endure, and look for a loophole or pray that someone else's inefficiency will somehow help you get by. As one Russian proverb has it, 'The wise man does not climb the mountain, but goes around it.' In this trait, today's New Soviet Man is no different from his forebears under the czars. Ivan Novikov, an 18th-century Russian writer, was quoted to me as having observed that 'The good fortune of Russia is in the bad execution of bad laws.' In the same way, Russians today find some comfort in the thought that an easygoing inefficiency in their lives – the opposite of German Teutonic discipline – will temper the harshness of the system.

'Thank God we are not Germans,' gushed Lev Kopelev, the bearded Russian writer. 'If we were, it would be unbearable.'

The proliferation of rules does make for the proliferation of loopholes. For adding to the authority of the bureaucrat with documents and regulations also adds to his powers of discretion. Depending on his whim, mood, personality and connections with whomever stands before him, he can just as well finagle and fix things as forbid them. 'The law,' as Russians say, 'is like the yoke of a cart – it goes where you turn it.' Most of public life is immutable, unalterable. But wherever possible and certainly within their own orbit of relatives, friends, acquaintances and associates, Russians are quietly engaged in coaxing, cajoling, compromising, corrupting and colluding with each other to achieve some modest relaxation of the stern order of public life. And when all else fails, they find refuge in their private lives which they carefully maintain as a separate world.

XI

THE PARTY

*Communist Rituals and
Communist Jokes*

> The Party is the Mind, Honor and Conscience of
> our epoch.
>
> > Lenin

My first, strongest, most enduring image of Soviet Communism was the long line in Red Square; the people waiting for hours for a glimpse of their entombed saint, Vladimir Ilyich Lenin. Newspaper pictures have made that orderly queue of Russians, their passive peasant faces reflecting a patience bred of centuries and their voices hushed by the vast expanse, seem familiar even to those who have never been to Moscow. But the pictures do not begin to capture the mood or meaning of that pilgrimage to Lenin – the central ceremonial obligation of Soviet political life.

One gray November morning, I joined the pilgrims. The line already led across Red Square, ran down a gentle slope beside the Historical Museum, turned a corner through iron gates, passed the eternal flame for the Unknown Soldier, and rambled on for nearly a hundred yards before it dribbled away somewhere in the gardens beneath the towering fortress walls of the Kremlin. It was a cold day. Everyone was in overcoats, hands in the pockets, arms hugging the sides. When our part of the line reached the well-guarded police barrier at the foot of the hill, with the Mausoleum still out of view, police and plainclothesmen straightened out the column and paired us off in twos. After we passed through the barrier, guides began collecting women's handbags, to be returned later. Except for this one long human column, Red Square was swept clear of humanity, like a great coliseum before the spectacle begins. Its emptiness heightened the air of expectancy, imposed a sense of order and discipline.

I was among a group of East German tourists though my march-partner was a tall blonde Russian woman. We talked in respectfully quiet voices as we walked. The column marched us across the cobblestones straight toward St Basil's Cathedral and then, abruptly, in the middle of the square, made a sharp, 90-degree pivot toward the Lenin Mausoleum. At the pivot the visual contrast between those two Russian shrines was startling – first, the chaotic beauty of St Basil's with a kaleidoscope of colors exploding on its onion-, pineapple- and cone-shaped domes, and then the low, sober, unembellished, rectangular, red-granite dignity of the Mausoleum. Here were two sides of the Russian spirit – the exotic and the austere. And Stalin had nearly eliminated one when he threatened to raze St Basil's.

Along our path we had passed several policemen but as we approached the pivot, I caught sight of the blue shoulder boards and collar tabs of uniformed KGB troops posted every few feet. Instinctively, my Russian companion and I stopped talking. Others in the line grew still. Wordlessly, one guard in a military greatcoat reached into the line and physically reversed a couple, to put the man on the right and the woman on the left. Most other pairs were already that way. He wanted perfect uniformity. A few steps further, another guard vigorously motioned me to take my hands out of my pockets.

We made the pivot. Suddenly, the man in front of me, a dark-haired Russian, was jerked out of line by an officer.

'What's that?' the officer demanded, gesturing to a bulge under the man's overcoat.

'Nothing,' answered the Russian. 'Just a package.'

'It's forbidden,' the officer commanded. 'You must leave.' And he pointed across the Square to the exit where we had come in, like a master expelling a stray dog from the yard.

The Russian's friends, the woman beside him and the woman next to me, looked crestfallen. But no one protested. (I don't know whether they knew, for the news had been hushed up, that a bombing had taken place at the Mausoleum some months before, killing at least three people.) A plainclothesman came over and made the Russian, already a step or two out of line, take out the worrisome package. The line began bunching up to the consternation of both guards and tourists. The plainclothesman felt the package, a long slender object wrapped in shop paper. 'What is it?' he inquired.

'A child's toy,' said the Russian sheepishly. 'I just bought it.'

'Okay, let him go,' the plainclothesman told the uniformed soldiers. Then to the Russian, he said: 'Carry it openly in your left hand, down, like this,' and he handed back the package.

The Russian had to run to catch up with his friends who had shuffled along. 'No running,' ordered another guard. Behind me, I could hear a plump lady from Leipzig whispering sarcastically to her companion, 'Tsk-tsk, the discipline.' By then we were approaching the Mausoleum steps. Guards were instructing men to remove their hats and making more checks. Another soldier found a bump in an East German's coat. The line hesitated. It turned out to be only a pair of gloves and the line moved on. We passed between the two immobile, honor-guard sentinels, gleaming bayoneted rifles held in rigid salute, and entered the Mausoleum.

Immediately ahead, a KGB officer directed the column to the left. We were moving quite rapidly now, or so it felt in the cool, black marble interior. Left, then right, down two flights of stairs, and right into the main crypt room. At every turn was an armed, uniformed guard. All kept the column of visitors under close surveillance. The nearer we got to Lenin, the more intense the scrutiny became. In the crypt room itself, I counted at least 13 armed guards, four with fixed bayonets at the corners of the brightly lit glass coffin in which Lenin lies; others at strategic points.

The column made a swift circuit around the coffin. The crypt room is constructed so that visitors enter, immediately turn right and walk up half a flight of steps along the wall, turn left and walk along another wall on a balcony overlooking the glass tomb of Lenin, turn left again and descend another half a flight of stairs, and exit the room. This semicircular route permits a view of Lenin from both sides and from the feet, but never at closer than ten to twelve feet and never with an instant to pause and simply look. While we made our circuit, one guard reached out and pulled a woman firmly by the arm, evidently because she had strayed minutely from the prescribed path. Like the others, I was so busy climbing and descending the stairs, watching out not to bump into the sentries or other tourists that I had little chance to study the figure, to decide for myself whether the body was really the well-preserved remains of Lenin himself or, as Russians privately suggest, the work of some expert waxworks. For all the immense impact Lenin has had on the course of history, he looks remarkably small, lying there in a black suit with a black and red tie. His face and hands, the only visible parts, do look waxy. They show a yellowing and a slight darkening, but otherwise reflect none of the vicissitudes of the half century since his death, including the transportation of the mummy to Kuibyshev during World War II when Nazi forces threatened Moscow, and what are said to be annual rejuvenations by skilled Soviet undertakers.

Even after we had gotten our fleeting glimpse of Lenin, the vigilance did not relax. Mutely, we mounted two more flights of stairs. The line was unbelievably quiet yet still I heard a KGB guard insistently shush people behind me. Not until we got outside and men began putting their hats back on, did I feel as though I could breathe normally again. The Germans were muttering in surprise about the rigid discipline. My Russian companion wanted to know my impression. I told her that I had never seen such a strict regime, such intense scrutiny, at any other memorial. American memorials are usually open, I said, and in Paris at Napoleon's tomb, I had noticed that visitors were let in by groups and were respectfully silent, but without such vigilant security.

'Well, you see,' she replied, 'that is how we guard our *vozhd* [supreme leader].' She was not defensive as Russians usually are at such comparisons and I thought I detected a trace of irony in her tone. But she did not smile obviously or give any further clue that she, too, regarded it all as vastly overdone until we were passing the graves of civil war heroes and former leaders like Stalin, where the security was much less forbidding. Then, with a little nudge and a twinkle in her eye, she quietly observed, 'So, you see, it is more relaxed now.'

It is a commonplace to describe Soviet Communism as a secular religion. But to me that insight had the power of renewed discovery when I first came face-to-face with the full force of the Soviet cult of Lenin. Kremlin leaders resort to a constant, almost mystical incantation of Lenin's name as the source of legitimacy for whatever policies they pursue. Lenin was the founder of the state, the maker of the Revolution, the shaper of history and we follow his course. Lenin was a colossal genius, a fountainhead of wisdom who foresaw how socialism would develop in our country and extend into other parts of the world, and we carry forward his struggle. Lenin was a humane, kind, considerate uncle, with a captivating smile, a warm laugh, a simple modest style of life, the father of a humane society that we make better each passing day.

Whether it is trade with the West, warnings about ideological penetration, construction of electric power stations, slogans about the importance of the press or movies, or observations on nuclear war (which Lenin did not foresee though quotations from Lenin are stretched to claim that he did), Lenin is cited as scripture for today's actions. In a political system which denies the existence of Khrushchev and sidesteps the importance of Stalin, legitimacy is derived from one man – Lenin. It is the Leninist creed on which rests the infallibility of the Communist Party and its leaders.

In terms of public symbolism, Marx is strictly secondary. Just how secondary I was reminded one night when an American diplomat organized a scavenger hunt which required a couple of dozen participants to find a small bust of Marx, among other things. Little busts of Lenin are on sale all over Moscow, even statuettes of Turgenev or Tolstoy. But none of us could find a bust of Marx on sale. One Marx replica was unearthed – a plaque of Lenin, Marx and Engels together, borrowed from a foreign Ambassador. But Moscow store clerks were puzzled by anyone wanting a bust or figurine of Marx. 'We never have them,' one surprised clerk told me. 'No one asks for them.'

By contrast, Lenin is a ubiquitous ikon. The veneration of his bodily remains is reminiscent of the worship of the relics of saints in Christendom and Islam. The effort to perpetuate the illusion of immortality by preserving his remains in the Mausoleum is another obvious parallel with religion. Secular shrines to Lenin, modest or gigantic, are omnipresent in Soviet life, sown like seeds from on high across the full length and breadth of this enormous country. The main square of every city is dominated by a statue of Lenin leading, exhorting, declaiming, gesticulating, or striding boldly into the bright future. No government office is complete without a portrait of Lenin writing, studying, thinking, and above all, guiding.

A gold-painted Lenin figure greeted the children every morning in the hallway of our neighborhood school. Factories, institutes, apartment buildings all have their 'red corners', often dreary little rooms with slogans and charts and photos grouped around Lenin. They draw upon the old Russian tradition of placing ikons of Christ, the Virgin, and church saints in the corners to pray to – either because the Party understood that Russians are by nature a deeply religious people and decided to turn that trait to the Party's purposes, or simply because Russians instinctively put their new saint in the corner when they converted from one religion to another.

At the Lenin Museum in Moscow, just off Red Square, Party researchers and propagandists have assembled more than 10,000 pieces of Lenin memorabilia in 34 huge exhibition halls, filling a grand, old high-ceilinged three-story building. I have seen school and university students taken there in groups, not so much for excursions as for indoctrination sessions. The museum has a number of intriguing exhibits – the first printing press of *Iskra* (*Spark*), Lenin's underground revolutionary newspaper; the false-bottomed suitcases, hollow children's blocks, and inner seams of dresses in which *Iskra* was smuggled into czarist Russia; Lenin's black Rolls-Royce roadster; his red wig and other parts of his disguises; his silver-handled cane. But these are not the exhibits to which the lecture-guides direct attention. They concentrate on reading underlined selections of Lenin's writings, his letters, his newspapers, his instructions to subordinates, his calls to action. Clichés of revolution abound – 'class struggle', 'vanguard of the working class', 'party of a new type', 'the Bolsheviks win'. I watched several groups of bleary-eyed youngsters go through two hours of this nonstop lecturing and then, numbed into silence, disappear in an instant when the guide cut short the tour after only 17 rooms and dismissed them.

Practically every town has some facsimile of the Lenin Museum. Once in far-off Siberia, among the Yakuts, a people who resemble eskimos, I visited a village school where a teacher proudly took me to the Lenin room. Her favorite display was a crêche of the hut where Lenin had supposedly

339

been born, made by some children. In Tadzhikistan, the builders of the giant Nurek Dam used their first spark of electricity to light a mountaintop sign: 'Lenin is with Us'. Banners in Leningrad proclaim: 'Lenin Lived. Lenin Lives. Lenin Will Live.' – a ubiquitous slogan, hung from rooftops or painted on signs along the roads, like 'Jesus Saves' billboards in the American South.

The Lenin cult reaches a climax on November 6, the eve of the anniversary parade celebrating the Bolshevik seizure of power. On that evening 6,000 members of the Soviet elite gather in the Kremlin Hall of Congresses for a ritual celebration: a televised speech from one of the Politburo leaders and an all-star variety show with fragments from the Bolshoi ballet, operatic solos, baritones singing patriotic anthems, and lively folk dances in national costumes. But after the speech and before the entertainment, there is a re-enactment of the sacred Revolution done à la Eisenstein: Shots of Lenin flash on a huge movie screen along with scenes of the assault on the Winter Palace of the Romanov Czars. Lenin leaps about like a figure in a speeded-up silent film, ceaselessly commanding the masses, fanning their fervor, lighting the very fire of Revolution. The battleship *Potemkin* fires its salvos. Red troops rush the palace. The Bolsheviks win.

The year 1917 gives way to 1930 on the screen. A chorus in work clothes chants revolutionary songs of labor while films of construction teams, welders, armies of cranes, trucks, dam-builders, re-enact the feverish industrialization period. Next: 1941. Photos of World War II. Stacks of Molotov cocktails. Rifles are passed out to recruits. Troops and tanks parade in the snow through Red Square and race from the parade directly to the front to stem the Nazi tide menacing Moscow. Children dig Moscow defenses. Winter troops clad in white scramble into battle. By now another chorus, all in helmets, chants Red Army songs. Flares burst in the sky. The Victory Parade.

As the climactic moment approaches, a barrel-chested bass backed by a large choir roars out in song, 'Forward, Communists!' Solo and then echo by the chorus, a dozen times, 'Forward, Communists!' As the lights go on, the huge stage is filled with probably 2,000 singers – men in black suits, strong, full-throated, and bursting with power; the women, in pleated, full-length white gowns like a forest of Corinthian columns; and children in the white shirts and red scarves of

340

Young Pioneers. It is a truly massive chorus. Beside it, the Mormon Tabernacle Choir pales like an octet. And with this vocal phalanx in full voice, the spotlights throw great shafts of light on a magnificent white statue of Lenin which has glided to center stage. The chorus roars like the seas of eternity, Lenin gleams, one hand in his pocket, an open book resting on his other arm – human, reincarnate. The whole purity of the statue projects the resurrection. It is truly a religious moment, intended to awe and inspire, to revive faith among those grown hard, cynical or forgetful. It is a Communist sacrament, of course, but it suits the Russian character, for Russians love grandiose theatrics. The stagecraft is very effective.

Not only Westerners but Russians themselves see this as a religious observance. In private, I have heard them joke about 'Vladimir the Second', comparing Vladimir Ilyich Lenin to Prince Vladimir the Great of Kiev who, in 988, introduced Orthodox Christianity to Russia from Byzantium. Well, too, I remember a dispatch carried by Tass in Novembe 1974 (when the Lenin Mausoleum reopened after a six-month shutdown for repairs) which sought to project a religious aura about Lenin:

> From early dawn an endless line of people formed up across Red Square from the granite sepulchre held sacred by the working people throughout the world. Over the half-century, 77 million people [have] passed in a mournful and stern march by the sarcophagus where the genius of humanity lies in state. From this day onwards new thousands and millions of people will be bringing worship to Lenin from all over the world.

The propaganda overkill surrounding Lenin is the regime's compensation for the waning of ideological fervor. For behind the façade of Communist conformity are puzzling contradictions and a dry rot of disbelief. Zealots exist, of course, but just as surely, friends told me they knew officials in the Communist Party Central Committee apparatus – at the very heart of it all – who privately mock their big bosses and are cynical about the system. Personally, I came to know Communist Party members who were close friends of dissidents like Aleksandr Solzhenitsyn and Andrei Sakharov. I met others who had discreetly had children baptized, held religious weddings and funerals in their families, or who publicly proclaimed their loyalty and privately swapped jokes at the Party's expense. After all, Stalin's own daughter, Svetlana Alliluyeva, was a Communist who underwent religious conversion and made friends with dissident writers. One reason that her defection came as such a jolt to the West was that the cardboard image of the typical Communist true believer left no room for skeptics, cynics, or out-and-out nonbelievers within the Party.

Our own political environment is not a good teacher: In the open political arenas of the West, those who join the Party do so out of conviction. But in Moscow, a cleancut young man will candidly say he wants to join 'to get ahead' or 'to travel abroad, and without a Party card I don't stand a chance'. Others explain Party membership as a matter of family tradition and connections. Middle-aged people recall their patriotic fervor when they joined during the war. Still others, under some Party recruiting quota in an Army unit, factory or institute, were extended a bid, in effect, to join the club. 'People join nowadays almost without a reason,' one middle-aged Party man said, 'the way people in the West go to church – out of habit, not out of belief.' For the ambitious, the Party is the path to power, position and privilege. Creed is secondary.

It is not easy, however, for a foreigner to penetrate the political veneer of Party members, or any Soviet officials for that matter, to discover who are the real believers and who are not – 'radish Communists' (red on the outside, white on the inside), as one Russian called them. Most Communists greet foreigners with such a dogmatic version of the Party line that normal dialogue is impossible. Perhaps that is the point of the exercise, since real conversation in the presence of interpreters, guides or other officials, is too risky for them. I remember my own impatience with one man who repeatedly sounded a particularly hard line at a conference that I covered and my great surprise at learning later that this man had privately approached another American and tried to defect. His shrill politics had been a cover. Muscovites have a joke about the barrier foreigners face when they try to learn what Russians really think. According to the joke, an American scientist visiting Moscow asks a Russian colleague his views about Vietnam. The Russian replies with a verbatim quote from *Pravda*. The American inquires about the Middle East, and the Russian echoes a commentary from *Izvestia*. On other topics the American meets the same results. Finally, he declares in exasperation: 'I know about *Pravda* and *Izvestia* and all those other papers. But what do you think yourself?'

'I don't know,' the Russian replies helplessly. 'I find I disagree with myself.'

But some Russians I came to know well told me how they and others made their bow to the Lenin cult and then found ways to turn it to their personal advantage. One linguist who had been abroad cited to me the excursions 'On the Leninist Path' (a favorite Party slogan) organized by the State tourist monopolies, to take Soviets to places where Lenin lived or had been active. In spite of the heavy doses of propaganda, he said, these tours are very popular because people leap at the chance to travel to Germany, Poland, Czechoslovakia, Finland, and more rarely, Sweden, Switzerland, France, Britain or Belgium – countries visited by Lenin but generally off limits for most ordinary Soviets. An amiable young factory worker from a provincial city outside Moscow told me of cases where factory groups or other organizations from outlying cities would charter buses to make a visit to Moscow's Lenin Museum and then, upon arrival, tell their political guide they had no interest in the Museum but wanted to shop. Usually, he said, they agree to meet late in the afternoon for a brief token visit to the Museum to satisfy the formalities but some groups don't go at all. 'That sort of thing satisfies everyone,' my young acquaintance said. 'The guide gets paid for doing almost no work, the people get to shop in Moscow, which is very important, and the Party people at the Museum and the factory get to write down that workers are studying Lenin.'

Making a bow to Lenin is a favorite technique of some liberal intellectuals who want to stretch the limits of the permissible in art or literature. Artists sometimes use Lenin as a subject to gain approval for experiments in modernistic techniques. One evening Mstislav Rostropovich, the cellist who had been kept from performing solo concerts for months after his defense of Aleksandr Solzhenitsyn, appeared at the Moscow Conservatory playing a Hungarian suite by Aram Khatchaturian. The program opened with an orchestral ode to Lenin, paving the way for the Rostropovich appearance.

'Something for the Party and something for us,' commented one music lover.

For years, journalists, scholars and writers have found that by citing Lenin prominently in their articles, especially at the beginning and end, they can sometimes get otherwise questionable material past censors. A Western scholar, for example, spoke of seeing a book on Africa by a Soviet foreign affairs specialist which he considered well done except for periodic *non sequitur* quotes from Lenin. When my friend talked with the author about it, the Russian candidly said: 'Well, I have an editor and he inserts those passages.' A highly successful free-lance journalist told me that he himself spent hours mastering Lenin's works to bracket ticklish essays to make them more palatable.

In their formal education, Soviet students cannot escape a solid dose of Party history, dogma and Leniniana. But very few develop any passion for mastering fundamentals of doctrine. Some intellectuals even consider it risky to know the talmudic formulations of Lenin too well. I heard a scientist counseling his university-age son one night not to be too precise in reciting Lenin quotations or this would lead to trouble with Party officials who know Lenin's works far less well and would be uneasy that a young intellectual might start quoting Lenin against them. 'You can know Lenin too well for your own good,' the father cautioned. But this was an aberration. Most students groan about the boredom of Party political courses and practically boast about how quickly after their exams they forget the Leninist catechisms.

Their massive indifference, however, is almost never translated into public protest or even lighthearted pranks. With all the millions of Lenin images around the country, I have never seen or heard of one defaced or pockmarked with irreverent graffiti, or even decorated with an extra mustache. In that sense, Lenin is untouchable. Only once did I see an act of public sarcasm directed at the Lenin cult. And by that time, I myself had become so conditioned by the Soviet political environment that I was immediately fearful for those involved.

They were three young couples who had joined a crowd of foreign tourists and other Soviets at midnight one May evening gathered to watch the changing of the guard at Lenin's tomb. The young Soviet KGB guardsmen went through their precise routine: A slow goose-stepping march from the Kremlin out to Red Square, with free arms swinging in wide rhythmic arcs and their bayonetted rifles balanced upright in the butts of their extended palms, and then, at the Mausoleum, a series of sharp, quickly executed turns that smoothly replaced the two old sentinels with new ones. As the old guards were marching away in that same, slow goose-step, the three young couples began sarcastically chanting, *'Molodtsi! Molodtsi!'* At a sports event, this comes across as 'Well done, boys.' But in this case, with their giggling and obvious sarcasm, which I was close enough to catch, it came out more like, 'Well, bully for you!' a sacrilege at the holy of holies. I expected them to be marched off by some police officer, but evidently their shouts were lost in the general scuffle of the crowd as it broke up and they melted away.

For many people, the antidote to the Lenin cult is humor, shared with trusted friends and often, as I noticed, told after someone has cautiously shut the kitchen door or closed the blinds. For foreigners, the problem is that Lenin humor translates badly because so much of it consists of in-jokes that require close knowledge of Soviet history, personalities and the stilted idiosyncrasies of propaganda.

One frequent target is the official practice of attributing all good things to Lenin, as in the little ditty which runs, 'Winter came and went, then came summer. Thank you Lenin for all that.' Another quickie spoofs the sloganeering about Lenin as the constant companion of the good Communist. A mock advertisement promotes a triple bed for the happy Communist couple because 'Lenin is always with us'. A third, satirizing the repetitiveness of revolutionary rhetoric, urges a special gift clock which, in place of the normal cuckoo bird popping out every hour, has an armored railroad car, like the one that carried Lenin across Germany into Russia, with a little figure that pops its head out a window and says, 'cuckoo'. Other jokes, often very raunchy, satirize Lenin's supposed gentleness with allusions to his orders that people be shot, or poke fun at an invented love triangle between Lenin, Nadezhda Krupskaya, his wife, and 'Iron Felix' Dzerzhinsky, the Polish revolutionary who ran *Cheka*, as the secret police were then known. Still others make fun of the constant publicity about memoirs or recollections of people who claimed to have seen Lenin in his lifetime and thereby to reflect his greatness indirectly. In one joke, a husband comes home to find his wife in bed with another man. The husband is outraged, not because his wife is having an affair, but because the other man is a bearded ancient. 'How can you have such an old man for a lover?' bleats the husband. 'But he saw Lenin,' says the wife in self-defense.

Western readers rarely get a glimpse of Lenin humor because Soviet authorities are so intensely sensitive to anything written about Lenin in the foreign press that Western newsmen generally regard the subject as taboo. An Italian journalist, Guiseppe Josca of *Corriere della Sera*, took a chance in early 1972 and paid for it dearly. In an article on the Lenin cult he wrote that the most common statue of Lenin, with his hand raised during a speech, gives the impression of someone waving for a taxi because taxis are so hard to get in Moscow; and he compared the cult of Lenin to the cult of Mussolini in Italy. That article triggered a sharp attack on Josca in the Soviet press, scores of threatening, insulting and intimidating phone calls. The Foreign Ministry charged that Josca had made a sexual play for his government-provided, KGB-cleared Russian secretary, which he vigorously denied and then fired the young woman for concocting the accusation to help the secret police frame him. The KGB frequently followed him and his wife and daughter closely and photographed them up close as a form of harassment. The Foreign Ministry pressured Italian Ambassador Federico Sensi to get *Corriere della Sera* to withdraw Josca. For months both he and the paper withstood the pressures. Finally in 1973, Josca departed Moscow. According to other Italian correspondents, his newspaper agreed to replace him with a politically less active correspondent.

By and large, Russians are a nonpolitical people. Indifference is their main defense to the unrelenting Party propaganda about Lenin and the 'unparalleled achievements of socialism'. For all but a tiny fraction, state politics is too far beyond and above them to care about. Over lunch, ordinary people gossip about work, how to wangle a good travel assignment, who gets the best bonus, or the petty jealousies and illicit affairs of the office. Around the dinner table they will argue about sports or the best site for picking mushrooms, talk about the family, grouse about higher prices or shortages, calculate the black market rate for certificate rubles, debate

346

the best places to go fishing and with enough vodka or in the right company plunge into philosophizing about the tribulations of the soul or start quoting Pushkin or Lermontov. But except for the Jewish emigration question which was a constant buzz during my tour in Moscow, ordinary Russians said they did not usually talk much politics at home. The overdose of propaganda has turned them off.

I knew an historian who was visiting the resort town of Kislovodsk on June 14, 1974, when Brezhnev delivered the main, climactic address of the Soviet election campaign from the Kremlin. 'Tens of thousands of people were there, out walking in the park,' this man recalled. 'The weather was beautiful. Warm and pleasant. All over the park, loudspeakers were broadcasting Brezhnev's speech. I watched the people and for a couple of hours, not a single person stopped to listen to Brezhnev's speech. Under Stalin, everyone would have been listening. They would have been afraid not to. Under Khrushchev, people would have listened from time to time because sometimes he would say something interesting. But now, under Brezhnev, it's just indifference, massive indifference.'

This shows up in other ways, too. Bookstores all have well-stocked propaganda sections selling the Communist classics – works of Lenin, collected speeches of Brezhnev, Prime Minister Kosygin, or Chief Party ideologist Mikhail Suslov. But that is not where the customers are. I would notice them clustering at the other end poring over technical books, literature or photo albums of old Russian churches. In mid-1974 the big Melodiya record store in downtown Moscow was offering a special album of two LPs of a Brezhnev speech on youth for the bargain price of 50 kopecks (67 cents). But when I was there, it was totally ignored by the young who were scrambling over singles of some Hungarian group doing 'Cecilia' and 'Mrs Robinson'.

The indifference is not directed so much at Brezhnev personally as the entire system of propaganda. People tune it out. Like many foreigners I was immediately struck by the huge political slogans hung from the rooftops, draped from bridges and hotel balconies or fixed in a firmament of lights in downtown squares: 'Lenin is Our Banner', 'The Party and the People are United', 'Communism Will Win', 'Lift High the Banner of Proletarian Internationalism', 'Glory to the Soviet People, Builders of Communism', or simply, 'Glory to

347

Work!' It is overwhelming to the newcomer but Russians tune it out. Once during a trip arranged by the Soviet Foreign Ministry, several of us Western newsmen were grimacing at the array of slogans in the city we were visiting. Later a Russian translator for another correspondent approached me discreetly and advised in a low voice: 'I heard you talking about those slogans. But you must know that we Russians simply do not see them. They are like the trees. They are part of the scenery. We don't pay any attention to them.'

There is little the system can do about such passive resistance. What it does require from everyone, however, is participation in the political rites and rituals of Communist society, much as the Russian Orthodox Church used to require proper observance of its rules. For if the church traditionally placed more emphasis on ceremony than theology, the Communist Party today places more stress on ritual than belief. 'Ideology can play one role or the other – either symbol or theory,' a bespectacled Moscow scientist observed. 'It cannot be both. Our leaders use it as a symbol, as a way to affirm the loyalty of others. But it is not a theory they act upon. It is not live.'

On November 7 and May Day, the Party turns Red Square into an enormous outdoor television studio for the march-past of rockets and tanks, of thousands upon thousands of gaily clad gymnasts who execute their figures and pause before the assembled Party Leadership on top of the Lenin Mausoleum to shout, 'Glory to the Communist Party of the Soviet Union! Glory! Glory! Glory!' (One man told me that it took daring merely not to shout as loudly as the parade organizers required.) The portraits of Lenin and the living leaders, all looking 10 to 15 years younger than in real life, are carried aloft through the Square, much as the ikons of saints were borne aloft in religious processions through Red Square in centuries past. The parades are conducted with such Cromwellian seriousness and pomposity that Russians admit to being bored by it all. I knew people who had to be dragooned by Party or trade union activists at their factories or apartment houses to participate. Some connived to get medical slips excusing them. 'My mother said it used to be an honor to march in the Red Square parade before and during the war,' a mustached young government worker remarked. 'But now it is just a duty they impose on people.'

The parades are but one element in the machinery of mass participation organized by the Party to mobilize people – *in spite of* their indifference and their private joking about Communism. And it works. Every fall, students, office and factory workers are trucked off by the tens of thousands to help the farmers bring in the harvest, usually with modest pay. In spring, people 'donate' an unpaid Saturday (a *subbotnik*) to what is theoretically a voluntary mass spring cleanup. In fact, as one Russian friend remarked, most factories, stores and other agencies simply get a day's unpaid work out of their labor force. Indeed, I noticed that in May 1974, *Pravda* happily reported that 138 million people produced nearly 900 million rubles' ($1.2 billion) worth of goods and services on the spring *subbotniks*, confirming that cost-free output was the prime interest in preserving this ritual begun by Lenin. People are constantly being drawn into all kinds of obligatory 'social work' – making speeches to colleagues at work, 'volunteering' for duty with the *druzhinniki* or auxiliary police-vigilantes, serving as *dezhurny* or duty persons in some unpaid political function, made to sell subscriptions of Party newspapers and magazines to fellow workers (many of whom are simply ordered by superiors to subscribe and others of whom have to buy *Pravda* and the heavier, undesired Party propaganda journals in order to get the humor, health, or popular science magazines they actually want). Occasionally, people told me, there is a payoff for the most ardent 'volunteers': tickets to some show or *putevka*, vouchers to some vacation spot that are normally hard to get. The Party needs countless 'volunteers' because it operates so many mass political activities that in Moscow alone, one local paper reported, it has 100,000 professional propagandists giving lectures.

A short, dark-haired Armenian teacher told me how she dreaded it when the Party organizer at her institute informed her she would have to join the normal rotation and give a lecture on Lenin. 'I can't do it,' she said in panic beforehand. But months later, when I saw her again, she was taking her turn routinely, no longer worried about being knowledgeable or interesting but, 'like the others', she said, parroting what was expected, no matter how dull and repetitious. At institutional celebrations like the 200th anniversary of the Bolshoi Ballet School, a former ballerina told me, speeches praising the Party's wise patronage of Russian ballet are obligatory. In factories, workers, too, have 15-minute political sessions in the morning or during lunch breaks twice a week, where the men take turns lecturing each other. I heard from one machine-tool operator that at his plant, workers often did no more than read propaganda articles right out of the press. A former defense plant foreman described to me how he literally had to 'drag workers by their coat collars' into monthly union meetings, heavy with political rhetoric. 'No one wants to go and hear those speeches,' he said. 'If they did not hold those meetings during working hours, no one would show up. In our plant, we could keep the workers in the factory because they needed timesheets to show the gate guards to get out. When there was a meeting scheduled, we would just withhold the timesheets. So they were forced to come to the meetings. I know a construction site where they hold the meetings on payday. Everybody comes to the meeting because they don't pay the workers until the end of the meeting.'

No ritual is more important to preserving the fiction of democracy and the illusion of political participation than the Supreme Soviet elections every four years. Like many Westerners, I had mentally written off these elections as empty rituals (a single slate, 99 percent of the vote, etc.) without ever imagining the personal effort and ordeal of Soviet precinct workers until Vitaly, an intense young graduate student, told me his experience. He sounded strangely like a precinct worker in New York. He was personally charged with getting out the vote – literally 100 percent of the vote, like some production target – and from that requirement, he said, came the phony figures.

Vitaly had not volunteered but was tapped for election work by the Party bureau in his institute to take charge of 150 voters in a downtown Moscow district, mostly pensioners and intellectuals. He had to go see them several times. First, he went around door-to-door to tell them the date and location of the balloting and inform them of pre-election activities at their neighborhood Red Corner. This aroused little interest, he said, so he made a second tour to give them each a little pep talk. Finally, a week before the election, he went out to register them. One job was to provide people who were going to be out of town with absentee ballots enabling them to vote anywhere in the country on election day. Individual districts and candidates are of such little importance to voters that, for example, a Party official like Georgi Arbatov, head of Moscow's Institute of U.S.A. and Canada, could run from a rural hill district near Baku, 1,500 miles away where he was so unknown that local officials were unable to tell touring Western correspondents whether Arbatov had ever visited their district. But if the voters were going to be in Moscow, Vitaly said he would hound them steadily until the election.

'How?' I asked. 'Call them on the phone?'

'Oh, no,' he replied, 'the phone is unreliable. No. I would go around and see them. And it was not a question by then of ideological appeals. Maybe they would tell me that they would vote only if the District Party Committee would help them get a new apartment for which they had been waiting for years. Or maybe they would complain that we had gotten poor entertainment at the Red Corner [the local Party propaganda room]. One complaint or another. And I would plead, "Please come. Just for me personally so I can be free because I have to wait for you to vote." As poll-watchers, we were not allowed to go until every one of our people came to vote or until midnight of voting day. So, of course, you want your people to show up early. Still, some people would not come and you would have to make up an excuse for them. Usually, it was "unexpectedly called away on business". Out of 100 people, you would get maybe five or ten who did not show up. It depended on the district. But it was impossible to get 100 percent. After all, some people fall sick or go away, and some even die. I know sometimes election workers vote people who are dead. And this is in Moscow, the ideological center of the country where the ideological work is the strongest and where people are accessible. So in the countryside, it must be much worse. But no one reports it that way. And I have seen it happen that if a person picks up his ballot [with only one approved candidate] and then does not drop it in the ballot box [which is out where everyone can see], they would stop him and ask him to talk to the voting supervisor. They would ask him to explain why he is not voting. So practically no one challenges the system that openly. If they are really so indifferent, they just stay away.'

The intellectuals we knew said, with few exceptions, that they went through the motions of participating in elections and other political activities despite their private disbelief or reservations. 'You have to go to those political meetings but nobody listens,' said a plump Leningrad schoolteacher in her late thirties. 'It's the same old stuff we had to study in university. Sometimes there is a foreign affairs lecture – on China, Vietnam. Some people knit. I read or grade papers. When the director of our school gives the lecture, he tries to make it interesting. He's a nice man – a Party member but a nice man. But everyone is bored and nobody believes it.'

'What about the person giving the lecture?' Ann asked her.

'Even he doesn't believe what he's saying. The older generation really believed in Lenin and they felt this was the way to build a new society. But my generation doesn't believe it at all. We know it's false. We have no religion, so we have to have Lenin. We can't change the system. We have to just go on living. I have my family and my children. . . . ' And she shrugged helplessly, indicating that economically she could not afford the risk of open protest.

George Orwell so powerfully inserted double-think into our political lexicon and it has subsequently been so overused that by now it has become a cliché drained of human content and meaning. If you had asked me as I headed for Moscow, I would undoubtedly have said that Orwellian double-think was as much fictional exaggeration as reality, or at worst one of the aberrations of the terrible period of high Stalinism when people would say anything to save their own necks. In more modern, less brutal times, I imagined that it was probably a bit passé. So I was hit doubly hard by the number of intellectuals who privately agonized over how routinely they practiced double-think and how pervasive was the practice. A curly-haired architect in his thirties who by his own account had been a model true believer in the enthusiasm of youth and only later became disillusioned by what he considered the cynicism of Party officials, told me of his unease at the facility with which he himself switched from private honesty to public hypocrisy.

'Someone will be talking before a group and telling the same old nonsense and you will be thinking to yourself, "Why does he talk that way, the fool? He knows better." But when they call on you at one of those meetings to get up and speak, you find yourself saying the same things, talking the way our newspapers sound. We have been taught long ago that this is the way one speaks in a meeting so that is how we speak to each other when we open our mouths in public.'

Nor can one easily duck out of political meetings no matter how much one chafes at the enforced participation. A lady mathematician told me that to skip the weekly Wednesday afternoon *politgramota* (political literacy) session at her institute was to invite an official reprimand, which is a serious matter. 'Sometimes we have outside lecturers and sometimes our own people have to give talks,' she told me. 'I have to give a report, for example, about computers and the solution of problems. Thank God it is not a political subject. But, of course, I will have to talk about computers in socialist society. In our institute, the computers work very badly. I will have to lie about that. But what can I do?'

I was surprised, too, that some well-connected establishment writers, journalists, or scientists, not only resented having to take part in the show of ideological conformity, but were willing to reveal their bitterness to a Western correspondent. I recall one senior editor explaining to me, 'It's very hard to describe a Party meeting to someone who has never been to one. Five minutes before it begins, people will be out in the hall, joking with each other, making critical remarks, talking about how poorly the Arabs fight and waste all our military aid. Then comes the meeting. Out go their cigarettes. And these very same people raise their hands and get up and denounce Israel and proclaim the victory of the Arabs. Or someone talks about the "Third Decisive Year of the Five-Year-Plan" and the others will listen solemnly or repeat the same slogans, knowing it's meaningless. It's a game, of course, but you must play it.'

I knew urban intellectuals who worked off their frustrations at this enforced conformity by staging private parodies of political meetings or did take-offs of the extravagant propaganda celebrations held in the Kremlin on big holidays. Still others, so disbelieving of all propaganda, were incredulous at the naiveté of Americans. I remember listening to a Russian who had worked with the Soviet delegation at the Congress of World Peace-Loving Forces in Moscow in December 1973, and who told me of his astonishment at the earnest idealism of American delegates.

'They take it so seriously,' he said. 'They really believe that they can do something about bringing peace and influencing political leaders. And we are so cynical – nothing will happen, nothing will change. I don't mean that the Americans.

liked all the speeches because they did criticize the propaganda. They wanted something more practical. But what I mean is that they think they can actually affect politics. Are all Americans like that?'

Hearing such a frank admission of disillusionment from a member of the Soviet establishment brought up in a Party family sharpened my curiosity about what Soviets actually believe in. Were their antiregime jokes evidence of passive ideological defection or merely a harmless way of letting off steam? Were the private cynicisms a sign of fundamental disbelief or a more limited expression of frustration at the cant and pretense of Soviet public life without signifying some corrosion of rock-bottom faith in the system? Were establishment intellectuals a breed apart, so completely different, say, from Party members that their skepticism reflected the views of a narrow circle rather than a wider mood? Or did the amalgam of ideology and loyalty include belief and disbelief side by side?

After all, the Russian translator who had told me that the Russians paid no attention to the stilted Party slogans posted on buildings had also told me quite firmly, 'Our ideal, the ideal of socialism, of people working for the common good, is much better than your profit motive even if we can see that it is not being lived up to now.' The historian who had recalled the total indifference to Brezhnev's speech among vacationers in Kislovodsk park had cautioned me: 'Don't mistake this as a sign of great dissatisfaction with Brezhnev, either. There is no great grumbling about him.' The factory foreman who had recalled having to drag workers into the political indoctrination sessions by the scruff of the neck and had retold some of the anti-Party jokes that circulate in factories, also said: 'Workers may sound off, criticize – but they only sound off against individuals. I never once heard anyone say that the Party or the system is to blame.'

'They may tell jokes about Khrushchev or Brezhnev,' he went on, fixing his glasses and brushing a muscular hand back through his hair. 'They may draw caricatures of a man with a big belly and big eyebrows [Brezhnev] on the wall newspapers, or they may joke about the way Brezhnev speaks as if he had porridge in his mouth. Workers feel they can be more outspoken than intellectuals about these things – because they have less to fear. They know they are needed in the economy. They see problems around them but they blame their factory director or other officials, not the Party. The system is not to blame. And Lenin, despite the jokes, is really above criticism. What he said, goes.'

No stereotype, of course, would stand for 14 million Communist Party members. It is impossible to compare the attitudes of a life-long Party man in his sixties, who grew up under Stalin, experiencing the romantic Communist fervor of the early years and struggling to survive under the terror of the Thirties, with those of a young Party member in his late twenties who never knew Stalinism firsthand and was born into an established system. Middle-aged Communists who came of age when Khrushchev was debunking Stalin have a special outlook, more disillusioned and dissatisfied than either the older or younger generations. It also seemed to me that the farther one travels from big, politicized cities like Moscow and Leningrad out into the provinces, the more chance there was of encountering simpler people with less ideological pretension but perhaps more genuine ideals. The Party *apparatchiki* with their special privileges and the political pragmatism of organization men, are very different from rank-and-file workers and peasants who are selected for Party membership.

I remember an afternoon drinking beer on a train with a sunburned construction worker, a Party man from the Ukraine. For him the Party had been a ticket to a job on the Aswan Dam in Egypt where in three years he had piled up huge savings in certificate rubles and the right to spend them in special stores. When he got back home, he bought himself all kinds of luxuries including a black Volga sedan like the bosses use. So Party membership had paid off in material terms. On another occasion, I visited the home of a tractor driver in Uzbekistan, a highly honored Hero of Socialist Labor. He, too, was a Party man. But more than that, he came across as a strong, direct, uncomplicated man of the fields who believed in what he and others around him had accomplished, in what he had seen happen with his own eyes – cotton fields created out of the semidesert region known as the Hungry Steppe. Socialism had honored him for his work and provided him and his family with a modest, comfortable home. He now lived better than he had ever dreamed when he first arrived in that God-forsaken region of Central Asia.

His faith was in results rather than slogans, and he seemed uninterested in comparisons with the outside world.

'The great mass of people, whether Party members or not, do not think about ideology, they simply accept things as they are,' a Moscow lawyer observed. It was an opinion echoed many times, among others by Gennadi, the state farm accountant. He had himself become disillusioned but he said he was atypical because he was an intellectual. Ordinary rural people, by his experience, were savvy enough to discount exaggerated propaganda claims about Soviet achievements in the press. 'But they still believe in the system,' he said. 'They know nothing else, and they accept it.'

Motives and attitudes are far more complex, and skepticism more widespread among the intellectuals, bureaucrats, educators, scientists, economic managers and party *apparatchiki* who now comprise the largest component of the Soviet Communist Party, in spite of all the propaganda about its being the party of the working class.* Beneath the surface of Party unity, Stalinist-minded dogmatists try to nudge the system one way while pragmatic-minded reformers seek to whittle down the impact of ideology and modernize the Soviet system with more rational methods of planning, management, farming and sometimes even adopting more flexible cultural and political controls. But the weight of inertia and the Party's jealous hoarding of its powers works against the reformers.

It is impossible for an outsider to gauge and generalize about the ideological zeal and fidelity of people at the heart of the Soviet system. But in private, Soviets themselves, whether Party members or not, privately talk of a loss of fervor, a rise of materialism and opportunism, a growth of corruption and moral decay.

'When you heard Khrushchev declare, "We are moving forward to the victory of communism," you might not agree with him but at least you felt he believed it,' commented an important editor. 'Think of it, here was a man who had been

* The biweekly *Party Life* reported on July 13, 1973, that the 14.8 million Party members consisted of 14.7 percent collective farmers, 40.7 percent workers, and 44.6 percent 'employees' (white collar and up). Even these figures, I was told privately by Party officials, overstate the worker component because a Party member is listed as a 'worker' throughout his Party career if that was his status when he joined. Hence Brezhnev and many other Party officials are carried on the Party books as workers though they have long since left working-class jobs.

356

at the bottom of society. He had made his choice and joined the Revolution when it was not clear who would win. He took the risk. You felt he believed. Even a man like Suslov [the ideological chief of the Party, now in his seventies], probably believes. But these new ones in the Politburo – Polyansky, Mazurov, Shelepin, Grishin – you feel they are just cynical. What they want is power, pure power.'

'How can you sense it?' I asked.

'It is something you can feel. You hear what they say in their speeches, watch their mannerisms, listen to their voices. It is all done smoothly, from habit, but with no feeling, no conviction.'

Russians often scoff at Westerners' attempts to divide Party figures into liberals and conservatives. They insist that power cliques, career ties, relations by marriage, and old established political loyalties or rivalries are more important for divining the flow of Party politics than alleged ideological shadings. They make the Party sound like Tammany Hall. 'It is more important to know if someone was with Brezhnev in Dnepropetrovsk or the Virgin Lands in the old days than whether he is supposed to be a conservative or moderate,' said a systems analyst who enjoyed dissecting state politics. 'Whose man is he? Brezhnev's? Kosygin's? Kirilenko's? Suslov's? That's what counts.'

As for ideology or propaganda, several Moscow intellectuals with friends working in the Party's Central Committee headquarters, the guts of the Soviet power apparatus, have told me incidents that illustrate the ideological dry rot among even such career Communists. A scientist recalled that the director of his institute, one of the most important in Moscow, went to appeal for more funds from the Science Department of the Central Committee. He painted a bleak picture for Soviet science in his field and concluded by saying, 'It is not so good with us,' meaning at the institute. The director was taken aback, he told colleagues later, when the high-ranking Central Committee official, in an unblinking contradiction to the glowing boasts of official propaganda, replied: 'And just where is it good with us?' implying the country generally. After a tough, nuts-and-bolts discussion, the institute director came away amazed at the private realism of the Central Committee officials: 'They're no fools. They understand everything.'

A social scientist told me about friends in another Central

Committee Department who made fun of the political rigidity of Politburo members, among themselves in their offices. A well-placed Soviet journalist described to me a walk in the woods he had taken with a senior official in the Central Committee's Cultural Department who began talking in despair about high-level corruption in the Party. 'Is it possible that the Pope and the cardinals of the church are venal philistines and the church itself can endure?' this official asked aloud. In other cases, the maneuverings of supposedly moderate, realistic Party bureaucrats sound strangely like some American officials during the Vietnam war compromising and submerging their private views in hopes of moderating policy. Except that in Moscow, there is no Congress, no press to leak to, no public opinion, less chance to affect thinking on top.

Politically well-connected Muscovites spoke of an invisible but discernible split within the Central Committee structure: On one level, the leaders who hold the key positions of power; on another, the lifelong *apparatchiki* who serve as aides to men of power but who gain a reputation for being too sophisticated, too educated and worldly to be fully trusted with top jobs. Three different men who closely follow inside political maneuvering pointed out to me, for example, that when the Politburo leaders have a top-level vacancy to fill, they generally reach out to the provinces for candidates rather than promoting Moscow-based careerists who carry the taint of urban sophistication. In the Brezhnev period, Dinmukhamed Kunayev, the Party boss in Kazakhstan (a Brezhnev crony), joined the Politburo; Konstantin Katushev, Party boss in Gorky, was tapped to become national Party Secretary for relations with ruling foreign Communist parties; Vladimir Dolgikh was brought in from Krasnoyarsk to become National Secretary for heavy industry; Mikhail Solomentsev was recruited from Rostov to become Premier of the Russian Republic.

Almost class-like jealousies develop, I was told, between Party technocrats with their *kandidaty* (Ph.Ds) and the heads of Central Committee departments who have climbed through the Party hierarchy as loyal organization men – protégés of some powerful Party patron. One writer told me of several Central Committee friends who made fun of their Department Chief as a political neanderthal and redneck from the provinces, mocked his proletarian habit of wearing a jersey or sweater under his suit rather than white shirt and tie, and yet literally popped to attention when he entered their offices. 'They had to show him respect,' the writer said. 'This man had the power to decide what assignments they would get, whether they could take a trip to the West, when they would get a bigger apartment.' Far more than the Watergate White House of Richard Nixon, the Party inculcates this instinctive ethic of loyalty to superiors. As one scientist explained to me on the basis of his contacts with Party circles, 'A man with his own ideas is in difficulty because the essence of the game is to understand the desires of superiors, or better yet, to anticipate their desires. It is bad to get the reputation of being difficult to work with or being too knowledgeable.'

But loyalty is rewarded, I was assured by a rising and ambitious Party journalist I met in Murmansk. His personal gripe was that bureaucrats who become local bosses through Party connections are so often inept. 'They are plumbers at heart,' he whined. 'But unless they make a scandal by having an affair with the Party Secretary's daughter, they never get demoted. Things may go downhill in their little factory or their theater, but the "plumber" simply gets transferred to another job, running a symphony orchestra or a farmers' market. Being a Party man, he is never demoted from the level of director. That's the way our system works.'

Yet within minutes, this same handsome, well-dressed young man with a taste for flashy ties and pretty girls was talking of his own promotion, a nice post for a man of 30, and was appreciatively reflecting that 'the Party controls everything' and how he, too, had 'good friends'. The Tammany Hall element attracted him, too. And it is this down-to-earth quotient of post-office politics that is so often lacking in abstract notions of the typical Soviet Communist.

Once, during the final Nixon-Brezhnev summit in Yalta, I fell to talking with a high-ranking Party journalist who had seen enough of the West and had mingled enough with Westerners in his career to occasionally take the risk of candor. He was talking about the war, and recalling how he had joined the Party then when patriotic feelings were running high, and I asked him why people joined the Party nowadays.

'They join the ideology,' he answered coyly. I gave him a skeptical look, disappointed at such a cliché response from him.

'What does the ideology mean to you?'

'To me? It means our promise of a future paradise,' he added with a grin, deliberately deflating his previous answer. 'It means a just society of equals with equal opportunity for all people. It means a minimum of work with a lot of time for each person to do what he likes.' He paused, eyed me, took out a cigarette and then decided to go on talking before he lit it. 'Certainly, that sounds idealistic compared with the politics we see every day. Our people see all kinds of mistakes and shortcomings and squabbling going on around them. But they think, "Okay, after a decade or two, the real line of the Party will triumph." '

Someone came along and interrupted the conversation. But when the intrusion ended, I returned to his theme of idealism, sensing from something he had said earlier about American youth and the Vietnam war that he regarded young Americans as more idealistic than the generation of his own grown children.

'There are idealistic people who are trying to build a better society in this country,' I said. 'But my experience is that the real idealists are far from Moscow. I have bumped into them in places like Siberia and Murmansk. But in Moscow, I find more cynics, more opportunists, more people out for themselves.'

'You are absolutely right,' he said a bit gruffly. 'It is more cynical in Moscow. People are more materialistic. You remind me of a French girl who told me once, "We hate you Czechs and you Russians because you want the very materialism which we reject." It's true. Our people are materialistic now. But you must understand why. It has been 56–57 years since the Revolution. People know that half a century has passed, and now they are saying, "We understand about the Revolution and the Civil War and the War with the Nazis and collectivization and the first five-year-plans and the sacrifices that were required. We understand all that, but what about your promises? I have only one life to live and it is short. So give me something for myself. Not always for the future!" So the Revolutionary fervor is declining. It is only natural after so much time.'

And when he turned the talk to Watergate, then approaching its climax, I said that it was painful for Americans, 'but I think it is a good sign not only of troubles in America but of a very genuine political idealism that still works. In fact, I have

360

been surprised in coming here to find that this is a cynical society, by and large, and that by comparison America is not such a cynical society after all, but an idealistic one.'

He looked at me, nodding thoughtfully in agreement but said nothing for a moment. Then all at once he surprised me by saying, 'I love America for its idealism,' and quickly changed the subject.

It would be wrong to leave the impression that this reflects a typical attitude among important Party journalists. I don't know what is typical. I do know this was a genuine expression of feeling in private by one quite liberal newsman at a moment of Soviet-American cooperation. At the other extreme, and far better known, is the image projected by Yuri Zhukov, the graying, pudgy-faced, tweedy propaganda cold warrior of *Pravda* who comes closer to playing the role of true believer than any other prominent Soviet propagandist. He is Moscow's counterpart to Joe Alsop, whom he sometimes quoted in outrage as proof of the dangerous influence of 'American right-wing circles'. On periodic television broadcasts from his book-lined office, Zhukov, a man in his mid-sixties, with two comfortable dachas, a large in-town apartment and chauffeured car, often comes across as the voice of the hardhat Soviet conservatives.

Just before Moscow stopped jamming the Voice of America, he delivered a warning to television audiences against listening to foreign broadcasts which were ideological intruders using the Russian mother tongue to spread falsehoods. In fairness, at a time when Soviet-American trade relations appeared to be blossoming, Zhukov once sought to correct a widespread Soviet impression that American lend-lease in World War II consisted only of canned Spam, by listing tanks, trucks, jeeps, and other equipment sent by the Americans. But his more familiar position has been point-man in the propaganda jousting with the West. After the invasion of Czechoslovakia in 1968, Zhukov was a leading voice crying out about the dangers of 'Czechoslovak counter-revolutions' and making insidious comments about Tito of Yugoslavia. During the long preliminary maneuvering of the European Security Conference, Zhukov accused the West of trying to blackmail Moscow and its allies into opening their borders to 'imperialist' subversion as the price for a big East-West conference that Moscow wanted. In one startling blast, he accused most of the leading papers of the West – *The New*

York Times, Washington Post, Los Angeles Times, London
Times and *Daily Telegraph, Le Monde* and *Figaro* in France
and *Die Welt* in West Germany, of conducting a 'violent
campaign' against a détente. Some of his colleagues at
Pravda told me they were embarrassed by that one.

With the appearance of Aleksandr Solzhenitsyn's *Gulag
Archipelago,* Zhukov made himself the spokesman of the
Soviet silent majority, reading outraged letters from readers
who responded to the book with the kind of gut patriotism
and virulent anger that some Americans felt toward the
peace movement during the Vietnam War. In person, he
comes across much as he does in print. After the *Gulag*
attack, he invited Western correspondents to come in and
share his mail. One afternoon he read us anti-Solzhenitsyn
letters aloud, alternating between Russian and accented,
hoarse but quite adequate English. He sidestepped the issue of
whether he himself had seen *Gulag* but he was stridently
opposed to Solzhenitsyn's effort to revive the issue of Stalinism. Zhukov told us he was not reading the most vitriolic
reader letters on TV because he did not want to be accused
of persecuting Solzhenitsyn and Andrei Sakharov, the
physicist. Had he gotten any letters supporting the two men,
someone asked. 'Unfortunately, not,' he quipped in Russian.
'They were probably sent to *The New York Times.*' Before
we left, he posed for a group picture. A couple of days later,
Zhukov called John Shaw of *Time* magazine to ask if John
had received *Gulag* because he wanted to borrow the book
for a few days. Shaw supplied it to him.

By far my most revealing encounter with a Soviet Communist, however, was an accidental late night get-together
with a young *apparatchik* who reminded me at first of some
budding young American political aide brimming with his
own ideas and self-assurance, but whose conflicting attitudes
eventually pulled together for me many elements of the
puzzle about what makes the professional Communist tick.
Volodya was a man of the new generation, a tall, good-
looking blond with shoulders to match his classic slavic
features, and the kind of winning gregarious charm that
would have made him a successful life insurance salesman or
politician in America. We met at a party after most of the
people had left. It had been an evening of drinking and tell-

ing jokes. Volodya had come late and avoided the limelight but with only a few people left, someone coaxed him to tell some anecdotes. He was known as a raconteur as well as an effective Party speaker. And within minutes, he had lived up to that reputation.

One theme of the jokes that night was Party corruption. Volodya's first one concerned two Party secretaries who had just collected dues from Party members and were walking toward Party headquarters with the money when one suggested they drop into a restaurant for a quick shot of vodka. One vodka led to another, then to *zakuski* (hors d'oeuvres), more drinks, a meal, wine, a second bottle, cognac. By the time they finished, they had racked up such a bill that they had to use the Party dues as well as their own money to pay the bill. As they left, one Party man remarked, 'You know, I don't understand how other people can afford all this eating and drinking without being Communists.'

Everyone enjoyed the joke, especially since a Party man, in fact, the only Party man present, had told it. Everyone but Volodya's wife who was nervous about his telling anti-Party jokes, especially with a foreign reporter in the crowd. But Volodya was a proud man, determined to show he was unafraid – though he did ask someone to get a radio and to turn up the volume before he went on with his stories. We all had another round of vodka, and he began the story about corruption in Soviet Georgia, where a real purge had been underway for two years. Everyone knew about government and Party officials with illegal mansions, mistresses, extra cars, and illicit businesses. Volodya set the scene beautifully, with the Party leadership gathered for a private banquet, the table laden with the most elegant and expensive dishes, several varieties of vodka, and Georgian cognac. The toastmaster asked for permission to speak so that all could drink to the health of the Party boss.

'I want to raise a toast to Aftandil Buavadze,' intoned Volodya, with a suggestive leer, 'not because he has four dachas – because, thank God, none of us has to sleep without a roof over our heads. I want to drink a toast to Aftandil Buavadze, not because he has five Volgas – because, thank God, it is fortunate that none of us has to walk the street. I want to drink a toast to Aftandil Buavadze, not because he has a wife and three mistresses – because, thank God, none of us is a bachelor. I want to drink a toast to Aftandil

Buavadze, not because he has 10,000 rubles stashed away in the bank – because, thank God, none of us has to get along just on our salaries. I want to drink a toast to Aftandil Buavadze, because he is a *real Communist*.'

Volodya told it well, pausing to milk each of the punch lines, and it delighted everyone. Then, somehow, Volodya gradually slipped out of the role of joke telling. A bit later, I had a chance to ask him why he had joined the Party after finishing a good technical education. Now, in his late twenties, he was already in a responsible Party organizer's post.

'Let's say I have a friend,' he replied by way of explanation. 'He and I graduated from the same institute together. We both have the same kind of grades and get similar jobs. I am in the Party and he is not. Along comes a promotion. Now which one of us do you think is going to get it?' He waited for me to nod at him and said, 'That's why I joined the Party.'

'What about ideology?' I asked. By now the radio was playing louder and other people were talking.

'No one believes in the ideology any more,' he said. 'No one needs it.' Then feeling he had overstepped himself, he pulled back. 'Well, maybe some believe. But not many.'

'And why does the Party want you if you have such an outlook?'

'Because they know they've got you when you join. If you are not a Party member, you can sometimes refuse to do what they want. You don't have to take assignments you don't like. But if you join, then you have to do what they say. Discipline, you know.'

'But what about your feelings about the ideology?'

'I have a reputation for understanding Marxism-Leninism very well,' he smiled. 'I learned it well at the Institute. I knew it perfectly when they examined me for joining the Party. When I make a speech, it sounds just right. But what I say and what I am thinking when I am saying it are two different things.'

We got off onto the twists and turns of the Party line and, sounding like some Western political analysts, he noted how many times the Party line had changed but it was always called 'The Leninist Course'.

'In Lenin's time, the Party believed what Lenin sent down. In Stalin's time, the Party believed what Stalin sent down. In Khrushchev's time, the Party believed what Khrushchev sent down. In Brezhnev's time, the Party believes what Brezhnev sends down. It is all "the Leninist Course" even though Khrushchev changed it 90 degrees from what Stalin said, and so on. The only thing you can say about the Leninist course is that it goes around in circles.'

It was an in-joke within the Party. Volodya's wife was getting uneasy again and came over to urge him to go home. But Volodya was showing off and wanted to talk. He enjoyed being the oracle of the Party in this group. Moreover, he wanted to prove his own personal independence of thought. 'I think therefore I am,' he said to me at one point. He was upset that Party instructions were calling for induction of more workers and fewer intellectuals because he thought more intellectuals might make the Party more liberal. He said he had read *Gulag Archipelago* and believed what Solzhenitsyn had written about the Stalinist camps. He was worried that the Soviet Union was now returning to a political mood similar to 1931 when Stalin was carrying out collectivization and people had to conform. His prescription was flexibility to modernize the system. Almost imperceptibly, however, his tone was changing. For all his earlier cynicism and joking, it was slowly becoming apparent that he was a believer in his own peculiar way.

'If I had my chance, I would change things 45 percent, that is, nearly by half,' he said, self-confidently. 'Things started to go wrong in 1920....'

'1918,' objected a Russian friend who had been listening silently until that moment.

'No, 1920,' Volodya insisted. 'When Lenin began to lose a bit of control. Until then, it was right! The Revolution, the Civil War. But after that, it went wrong. If I had been there, I would have agreed that after the Revolution what we needed was one great collective,' and he made a fist, 'to keep the country strong. Otherwise, we wouldn't have made it. But that is not our situation today. We have to develop differently, give people more of a chance.'

In his light and jocular way, he was proclaiming a kind of loyalty and began to talk about 'what I will do when I get a post in the Politburo'.

His friend, Sasha, considerably more liberal, more apolitical, and much less ambitious than he, was horrified and reproved him for aspirations to power that would corrupt him. 'Volodya, that's a terrible thing to hear you say that you want to be in the Politburo some day. If you get there, I'll shoot you.' It sounded like student talk, but both men were nearly 30 and quite serious.

'No,' replied Volodya coldly. 'I won't let it happen. I will remember your words, and I'll make sure that you won't be in a position to find me.'

It was a chilling instant, this sudden mercurial switch from joking and philosophizing to threatening a friend. It passed, but Volodya's mood had changed. He began talking about what he knew of the actual story of the Party's secret investigation of corruption in Georgia, secret as well as public trials of key figures. When I questioned the accuracy of a point or two, he disdainfully called me down, turning to his friend, 'Sasha, you know the sources.' I presumed he meant inside Party information, which Sasha confirmed with a nod, but Volodya decided to drop the subject. We got into détente and trade relations in Europe. Imperceptibly, his pride in Soviet power surfaced.

'The Germans,' he said. 'Not your Germans but our Germans, tried to threaten us once over natural gas.'

'Which gas, when?' I asked.

'Oh, you don't know about the gas?' he queried, exuding pride in his superior knowledge. His wife was worrying again, but he quieted her with 'they don't know about these things'. Then he snuffed out a cigarette and carried on.

'You know, we supply the GDR [East Germans] with gas for their industry. We supply it to them for, say, 43 kopecks, and then buy back other goods from them for a ruble. Economically, we lose. But this is not economics. It is pure politics. We hold onto them with the gas. They told us, "For the development of our industry, we need you to double the amount of gas deliveries each year." And we told them, "We can increase the deliveries a bit, but not as much as you want." And they told us they would get gas from your Germans, even though your Germans were already getting gas from us. In other words, our Germans threatened us with your Germans, but they could not threaten us because *we* have' -- and here he began to turn his hand on an imaginary pipeline valve -- 'we have the taps in our hands. That is very useful to have the taps in your own hands. We have the taps now for both Germanies in our hands. The more they take, the more we have in our hands. So they threaten us, the Germans, and to us such a threat was just a trifle. We stopped deliveries for awhile and they understood what it meant.'

This was evidently the version propagated at internal Party meetings. Volodya moved on to how the Soviet Union had handled difficulties with Hungary, Poland, and Czechoslovakia, too. 'Only three times have the East Europeans challenged us, threatened us,' he said. 'Once in Poland and then Gomulka came in. Once with the Germans, what I just told you. And once in Czechoslovakia – and we all know how that ended.'

'What about Hungary in 1956?' I asked.

'That was not the same kind of threat,' he replied without explanation.

I did not see his logic but I saw that here, side-by-side with his cynicism and his joking about corruption and his seemingly genuine desire for internal reform, was a young man who prided himself in his *realpolitik*, who was driven by personal ambition for a career of power and influence, and who was flattered by the sense of superiority and inside knowledge that being a Party organizer and careerist gave him. He believed in the roots and goals of revolution and though he thought the Party had gone off track under Stalin, he was immensely proud of the powerful nation that Stalin had built and the empire that Stalin had gathered under the shield of Muscovy. He was prepared to do the Party's bidding as he rose up the ladder, unless he could use his Party connections to wriggle out of some unattractive assignment. And he was prepared to pay constant lip-service to the ideology in which he professed not to believe – indeed, he was rather proud at his skill in masking his private views and his reputation as an able Party speaker. In essence, he was an ideal organization man. He kept his cynicism and liberalism to himself and his close friends. I could imagine his maturing over the years as a Party man: his disbelief subordinated to his ambition, his nationalistic pride in Soviet power growing along with his ego kicks at being a privileged insider, and somewhere his threat to remember the conscience-stricken words of the friend who found his ambition too frightening.

For Volodya as well as for some of the Soviet intellectuals I had met, the quintessential Soviet gesture is what the Russians call the *fig v karmane*, the sign of the fig – the thumb thrust irreverently between the second and third fingers in a clenched fist, meaning roughly, 'nuts to you' or 'screw you' or stronger, depending on the force of the gesture and the circumstances. But *v karmane* means in the pocket of one's pants. In other words, making this defiant little gesture secretly, privately, out of sight. The urge to defiance is thus overcome by fear and by the pressure to conform, and so the protest is hidden in the pocket, figuratively speaking.

So, belief or nonbelief in ideology is not the vital issue, so long as the individual submits and does not challenge ideology openly. The system prevails, and along with it the ideological rituals which affirm and legitimize and perpetuate it.

XII

PATRIOTISM
World War II Was Only Yesterday

> Russia's past was wonderful, her present magnificent, and as to her future – it is beyond the grasp of the most daring imagination. This is the point of view from which Russian history must be written.
> Count Aleksandr Benkendorff,
> Secret Police Chief, the 1830s

Eight of us were gathered around Ben Levich's dinner table all talking at once. So many complaints were being raised by Ben's relatives about the vexations of life in Moscow today that I deliberately changed the subject by asking them what had been the best period in Russian history. Conversation came to a halt. Ben, whose round, pink face always had a look of boyish, pop-eyed wonder despite his sixty-odd years, seemed to fumble for thought. As a ranking scientist, he had prospered under the system until applying in 1972 to emigrate to Israel, and he still had the Establishment feelings of a Jew who has long been well-assimilated and comfortable.

'How do you mean – best?' Ben stalled, eyes popping. 'Materially? Morally?'

'That's up to you,' I shrugged. It was a minute or two before he replied.

'The best time of our lives,' he said finally, 'was the War.'

His answer surprised me, and evidently the others as well. Ben grinned shyly, obviously pleased to have caught us off guard. Given the enormous devastation and suffering that all Soviet people associate with World War II, the immediate astonishment was understandable. Moreover, this was a company of skeptics, reluctant to echo or endorse any

cliché of Soviet propaganda. especially one so constantly invoked as the Soviet victory in World War II.

'The War,' Ben repeated quietly. 'Because at that time
we all felt closer to our government than at any other time
in our lives. It was not *their* country then, but *our* country.
It was not *they* who wanted this or that to be done, but *we*
who wanted to do it. It was not *their* war, but *our* war. It
was *our* country we were defending, *our* war effort.'

'I remember I was in Kazan in my room sleeping,' Ben
went on, his choppy Russian speech accented here and there
with a word in English, 'and in the middle of the night,
someone from the *cheka* [secret police] came and woke me
up, and I was not afraid. Think of it! He knocked on my
door in the middle of the night and woke me up and I was
not afraid. If some *chekist* had done that in the Thirties, I
would have been terrified. If it had happened after the war,
just before Stalin died, it would have been just as frightening. [That, too, was a time of blood purges, especially for
Jews.] If someone did that now, I would be very worried,
even though the situation has changed. But then, during
the war, I was absolutely unafraid. It was a unique time in
our history. They wanted me to take part in some very important meeting. They were afraid chemical warfare was
beginning. I was a specialist in chemistry and they wanted
my opinion.'

By the time Ben had finished, the others around the table
were in agreement. In spite of their disdain for Soviet propaganda, these were patriotic emotions they understood. Those
who were old enough to remember, shared the memories.
Elsewhere, too, I learned that these were not merely the
sentiments of an isolated fortunate Jewish scientist in his
sixties, but of people from all walks of life. 'The war was the
one time when poets were writing poetry sincerely,' commented an alienated linguist in her fifties. Other people
often spoke of the war not only as a time of suffering and
sacrifice, but also a time of belonging and solidarity. The
war had meant death and destruction but it had also demonstrated indestructible unity and invincible power. And the
memory of the shared ordeal and triumph in what the Soviet
people call The Great Patriotic War is a primary source of
the unblushing patriotism they feel today.

* * *

In an age grown skeptical of undiluted patriotism, Russians are perhaps the world's most passionate patriots. Without question, a deep and tenacious love of country is the most powerful unifying force in the Soviet Union, the most vital element in the amalgam of loyalties that cements Soviet society. That may sound commonplace for other countries which have no proclaimed political ideology. Indeed, before the Revolution, ardent national patriotism was a hallmark of Russia. The paradox today lies in the fact that Lenin and other Revolutionary leaders – only a minority of whom were ethnic Russians – set out to break that tradition. 'We are anti-patriots,' Lenin declared in 1915. The Bolshevik creed of world revolution and proletarian solidarity condemned narrow national loyalties as heresy. It was Stalin, seeking to rally the people against the invading Nazi armies, who deliberately built up Russian nationalist fervor. In 1928, with the First Five-Year-Plan and again, bit by bit in the 1930s, he had invoked the inspiration of czarist heroes. But by the war he was so intent on promoting patriotic zeal that he even resuscitated the persecuted Orthodox Church. He and the Orthodox Patriarch would make joint radio appeals to the nation. And in the years since the war, the hold of patriotism has grown as Communist fervor has waned, so that today nationalism has more magnetism and meaning for the overwhelming majority of Soviet people than does Marxist-Leninist ideology.

'Nationalism, the worship of the Motherland, has become a substitute for all other forms of belief,' one of my younger scientist friends commented. It may have been an exaggeration, but not much of one. 'Take away national patriotism and what do our people have?' he continued. 'Before the Revolution Russians believed in three things – in God, the Czar, and third, only third, the homeland. After the Revolution, especially in the Twenties but also in the Thirties, people believed in socialist proletarian internationalism. It was wrong to assert Russian nationalism, We against Them. You could get in trouble for that. But with the war, Stalin emphasized nationalism. Since then, it has been growing. Now, people do not have God or the Czar or socialist internationalism. They have Russia, *rodina*, the Motherland, and the Party makes great use of this.'

Others, too, remarked to me on how shrewdly and frequently the Soviet leadership plays upon emotions of national loyalty. It is an appeal that must be managed with great delicacy because of the historic frictions between ethnic Russians and other nationalities, like Georgians, Armenians, Lithuanians, or Uzbeks, who now comprise a majority of the Soviet population and who often privately resent the Russification of their minority republics. What makes World War II so valuable as a propaganda device is that it lends itself to blurring the distinction between the devotion of ethnic Russians to Mother Russia and the attachment of minority nationalities to their own regions. It allows propagandists to meld these peoples together in common loyalty to the broader entity of the Soviet Union. It also enables them to fuzz the line between patriotic pride in the national military victory over the Nazis and political commitment to the Soviet system. In the propaganda of The Great Patriotic War, patriotism and politics are thus fused.

With that same purpose, the Soviet press today heralds Soviet space exploits and international sports victories. Big-time sports in the Soviet system are not entertainment, as in the West, but politics, which is one reason why Soviet sports are so thoroughly subsidized and why top performers are secretly provided extra perquisites and handsome cash bonuses, especially for gold medal showings abroad. Sports champions, so goes the Party line, prove the superiority of Soviet socialism. It is no accident that the Soviets are often the ones who seize every opportunity at the Olympic Games or other international competitions to insist on playing national anthems, displaying national flags, or performing march-pasts and other rituals that cater to national feelings and keep aflame the Soviet sense of patriotism and national pride. Sports, like World War II, are a perfect vehicle for this type of propaganda.

Ethnic Russians, passionate patriots by nature and tradition, readily warm to nationalistic appeals. In almost any situation, they can take their patriotism straight and thrive on it. Where else would long distance trains depart with loudspeakers playing anthems? Where else would an audience sit through a full evening of hymns and paeans to the homeland without feeling it maudlin? I remember one concert hall of Russians moved to tears and emotional applause by a misty-eyed baritone fervently singing patriotic refrains by Yevtushenko against the stirring rumble of timpanies and the sweep of violins:

Motherland of Pushkin,
Motherland of Lenin,
Motherland of our children.
Long live, long reign
The Great Sovereign People.

On another evening, a stout journalist and his wife happily recited to me in their kitchen the lyrics of one of the currently best-selling pop tunes: 'Where does our Motherland begin? With the picture in your little primer? With good and true comrades who live in the home next door? Or maybe it begins with the song that mother sang?' Sensing my uneasiness at such saccharine sentimentality, the husband quickly reassured me: 'It's a very good song. Our teen-age daughter likes it, and so do all of her friends.'

Russians of all ages are as sentimental about Mother Russia as about their own families. My middle-aged language teacher broke into tears one morning as she recalled how she had crossed the border into Russia on a train a few years ago after living abroad on a diplomatic assignment. 'Just hearing the word *rodina* makes me tremble,' confessed a young woman biologist who had known a grim childhood in a rough industrial town and was now generally critical of things Soviet. The emotional force of that word *rodina* for her and other Russians is untranslatable. By the dictionary, it means native land, mother country, homeland, land of one's birth. Yet all these fall short of the evocative power of the word in Russian. *Rodina* to Russians has the ring of 'My Country Tis of Thee' – that singing devotion to country, unreasoning, unquestioning, unstinting, the way a mother loves her smallest child and the child blindly returns that love, a constancy and homage that makes the individual forget all the petty nuisances, harassments, inefficiencies, and entanglements of daily life, and proclaim his loyalty, take pride in it, merge himself somehow with the nation and find there comfort, confidence and a sense of community that nowadays eludes Americans and many other Westerners. For Russians, *rodina* stirs the gut patriotism that freedom and democracy used to do for Americans. It is an umbilical word that expresses much more of what holds the country and people together than a multitude of diagrams about the structure of the Communist Party, for it evokes the blood attachment of Russians to their native soil and to each other. It captures the profound spiritual meaning that the nation has for the Russian psyche.

Even emigrés who have turned their backs on the Soviet Union politically find they are no more immune from the pull of Russia than from the pull of gravity. Cut off from her, many feel a void. David Bonavia, a British correspondent, wrote wisely about the paradoxical loyalty of dissident intellectuals: 'They are like the man who beats his wife, swears at her vilely by day and then crawls into bed to make love to her at night. They love Russia, even those who divorce and leave.' A Moscow friend told me of a Russian woman who had lived 40 years in Paris and who after her first chance to visit Russia, flew back to Paris with the one gift that all of her emigré friends had prayed for – a suitcase full of Russian earth. I have met Jews in the West who fought bitterly for the right to emigrate and then suddenly felt themselves cruelly uprooted and desperately homesick once they were abroad. 'Spiritually, culturally, I am Russian,' one such man protested to me vehemently in New York. In the same vein, the poet Joseph Brodsky, after arriving in the West to live, wrote Brezhnev yearning to be preserved as a part of Russian literature.

The return of Marc Chagall in 1973 after half a century in exile was an emotional homecoming that evinced all the passionate attachments of Slavic peoples to their native soil. When Henry Kamm, a *New York Times* colleague in Paris saw Chagall after his visit, he found the Ukrainian-born Jewish painter positively radiant and rejuvenated. It seemed like the return of the prodigal. Before, Chagall had been read out of the family, ignored, not exhibited, even scorned as an antagonist of socialist realism. None of that had mattered now. Chagall was immensely flattered that the Soviets would want him, would show a few of his works that had been locked up in the vaults for decades, would ask him to sign the murals he had done for the old Jewish State Theater. Back in Paris, buoyant and refreshed, he thrust a vase containing two dried bouquets of Russian flowers under Kamm's nose and commanded: 'Smell! Smell! No other flowers have that smell. I have not known it in 50 years.'

The passionate patriotism of the Russians contains not only this deep and unwavering love of the homeland which

Chagall, even as a Jew, shared, but also a kind of primeval sense of community, a clannish defensiveness toward outsiders and intolerance toward renegades from within, of Victorian pride in national power and empire, of blinding ethnocentrism, and of conviction of moral superiority that echoes America's earlier age of innocence.

Now, as in centuries past, Russians have a love of country that overlooks all blemishes. John Steinbeck, writing of such a love, once said about New York: 'It is an ugly city, a dirty city. Its climate is a scandal. Its politics are used to frighten children. Its traffic is madness. Its competition is murderous. But there is one thing about it – once you have lived in New York, and it has become your home, no other place is good enough.' Russians may not be as brash, cocky or candid, but their loyalty to country is just as dogged and forgiving. As if in response to Steinbeck, Russians today will quote a famous line from Pushkin: 'Even the smoke of our Motherland is sweet and pleasant to us.'

If emigration were suddenly totally free, I am confident that very few Russians, as distinct from Jews and some other minorities, would leave their country permanently. In part this is a measure of their parochial isolation. They are not accustomed to coming and going. For 95 percent of the citizenry or more, the gate to the outside world is never opened or, once opened, it clangs shut forever afterward and painful nostalgia sets in at once. Were the gate left permanently ajar, inertia and fear of the unknown life abroad would be powerful deterrents to many Russians. But most of all, they would be held back by the pull of the homeland and their own folk. For they have an almost peasant, tied-to-the-land-and-clan mentality that is difficult for people from the mobile, commercial civilizations of America and Western Europe to comprehend.

Historically, Russians have been a people of great social cohesion. They are comfortable attached to the group, uneasy cut off from it. Today, as a sacred entity in Soviet mythology, the *kollektiv* ranks second only to the Communist Party itself. The work collective at farm or factory is supposed to do much more than unite a brigade of workers on the job. The farm or factory paternalistically provides housing, schooling and other services, organizes leisure activities and sometimes even monitors private life as well. Workers get a great kick in going off fishing together on a company-provided bus. So much is the collective spirit pushed, that I found people talking about it unselfconsciously all the time. Even in our small office, we and our Russian employees constantly joked about 'The New York Times *kollektiv.*' But the roots of communalism in Russia run much deeper than contemporary Party propaganda. The hardy conquest of wild forest lands by peasants a millennium ago was a group endeavor. Under the later czars, planting and harvesting were organized by the village *mir* or assembly on a communal basis. In the Orthodox Church, confession was a public ritual symbolizing the sinner's return to the community of worshippers, and the individual learned to subordinate and merge himself into the common fold.

The contrast with Western historical evolution is dramatic. From the Reformation forward, Western life has emphasized the separateness of the individual in church and commerce and has proclaimed his freedom to be different. Even the celebrated American penchant for joining civic clubs and other groups provides much looser and more superficial ties than those of the Russian to his *kollektiv* and to his nation. On a personal level, the Russian merges with those around him less self-consciously than the Anglo-Saxon. I was struck by how they bump into each other, touch each other, lean against each other in public quite naturally and without concern. In communal worker apartments or student dormitories, Russians live in closeness that many Westerners would find claustrophobic. They take for granted sharing hotel rooms or six-bed railway compartments with utter strangers. The Russian language does not have a word for privacy. In the natural order of things, the individual simply takes second place to the *kollektiv*. To me, the Russian sense of sacrifice for the group and the nation was an attractive quality. But I was put off by the code of group conformism that tried to get the individual to conceive of himself primarily as a cog in a group machine, making excommunication from the group the most severe social penalty, whether merely the banishment of an unruly child from a kindergarten play group or the forcible deportation of Aleksandr Solzhenitsyn for his dissident writings.

'We learned from our history that to survive, we must band together as Russians,' Anatoly, a 30-year-old government economist, told me. 'The Tatars came and conquered us when we were living in separate princedoms, each one practically with its own borders. We were many more people, we Russians, and the Tatars were few, and still they punched through us like a strong fist. And so we have learned we must band together – rather like the Jews, though that sounds funny. The Jews have banded together and now their nationalism calls them to gather in their new homeland. But our homeland calls on us to stay here, so we stay. It sounds like the opposite thing, but it is really the same feeling. We have many sayings about our sense of loyalty. Maybe you have heard of (Marshal) Suvorov, the great army commander who defeated the troops of Frederick the Great and later Napoleon. He used to say, *"pust khuzhe, da nashe"* (Let it be worse, but let it be ours).'

When I suggested that in English, which he knew, this came across as 'my country, right or wrong', something which we called blind patriotism, he readily agreed. 'We call it *kvasnoi patriotizm* – kvas patriotism,' he said. Like so many essentials of Russian life, the phrase does not readily lend itself to translation, for one has to know that kvas is a fermented peasant drink made from water dripped through burnt bread. Kvas has a malty flavor, and cheap kvas can be like old coffee – bitter, the color of muddy water, with grounds at the bottom. In cities all over Russia, white-coated women serve up glass mugs of kvas from large, saffron-colored, mobile metal kegs in the summertime. Foreigners usually pass up a second mug, but Russians swear by it, and peasants produce their own home brew of kvas. So kvas patriotism represents the earthy, peasanty, intensely Russian brand of patriotism.

'Chauvinism?' I asked.

'Yes, chauvinism and something even stronger,' Anatoly affirmed. It is a patriotism that breeds and believes in legends like those of our own John Paul Jones and Davy Crockett. Such tales tumble from Russian lips readily. Anatoly remembered the brave exploits of the border troops who opposed the Nazis; and the Russian defenders at Brest, fighting valiantly though outnumbered and forced to surrender. This positive heroic devotion to country, however, has its negative McCarthyite side in rigid intolerance and persecution of mavericks and dissenters whom the clan regards as unpardonable renegades.

'People will do almost anything when they believe the motherland is in danger,' Anatoly said. 'This applies not

377

only to a military danger, but to an ideological danger, because the country is being invaded by alien ideas. You see, it is quite natural for people to consider men like Sakharov and Solzhenitsyn as traitors. It is very simple: Sakharov and Solzhenitsyn are turning to foreigners for help [our conversation took place in 1973 after a virulent press campaign against these two leading dissidents]. The imperialists are using these two, and you have to understand that no matter what else is said, imperialism is still our main enemy. So if our enemy is using these people, then naturally it must mean that they are traitors. Sakharov called for the West to punish our country, to keep us from getting most-favored-nation tariffs from the United States. So, of course, he is considered a traitor and it is a normal duty for people to join a campaign to denounce him.' He paused for a minute before expressing disappointment, but not the kind I had expected. 'National feelings are weakening among some of the intelligentsia nowadays,' he said. 'Some people hesitate to join the campaign against Sakharov and Solzhenitsyn. It is not as automatic as it should be.'

Any foreigner who has ever questioned or challenged the Soviet way of life or its government, even mildly, has inevitably encountered this same clannish loyalty. Whatever their private thoughts, Russians close ranks and rise to the defense of their nation against the outsider. Nor is this merely parroting of official propaganda, for I have heard dissidents suddenly switch positions when a foreigner offers the same criticism of their country that they themselves have expressed. National pride before foreigners is an immensely powerful emotion. A magazine editor told me that I was mistaken if I thought Russians had to be coached by officials on what to tell foreigners. Even without prompting, he said, common people exaggerate their standard of living to Westerners visiting their homes and factories. 'It is natural,' he said. 'People feel, "We're Russians. We must appear well before foreigners. We must show them, Americans especially, that we live well." '

What is at work here is an instinctive, tribal-like, loyalty reflex. For just as Russians in their personal relations draw sharp distinction between the inner ring of trusted friends and all outsiders, so in their national feelings, they distinguish sharply between their clan, their nation, and all others. Words like *nash* (our) and *chuzhoi* (other, foreign, alien)

378

crop up constantly in both propaganda and conversation. They have immense force in delineating friend and foe and in fixing attitudes, for Russians think in terms of only two sides – for and against. They have an ingrained skepticism toward neutrality. 'He is *nash* (our) man' – or just the opposite 'he is *chuzhoi* (on the other side)' – is enough to settle an issue.

That same young woman who trembled at the very sound of the word *rodina* remembered her rage as a teen-ager whenever Western radio broadcasts transmitted unpleasant news about Russia. 'When I heard Voice of America, I knew that what they said about Russia was true, absolutely true, but it still made me mad,' she said. 'There was something insulting about hearing it from outsiders. It was as if the foreigners were laughing at us. It did not make me angry so much at our system as at Voice of America.' These same feelings of resentment against the outsider are deftly activated today by the most experienced Soviet propagandists. Yuri Zhukov, the *Pravda* columnist and television commentator, warned Soviet listeners in late 1974 to beware of the sly tactics of Russian language radio broadcasts by foreign stations in terms precisely calculated to raise the hackles of the Soviet patriot: 'In our (*nash*) bright, clean Soviet home steals a stranger (*chuzhoi*) and speaking our (*nash*) language disseminates lies and slander.'

The immensity of Russia and its continental isolation through long periods of history have left many Russians today with a strong streak of moral chauvinism. In part this is sheer ethnocentrism. Like other large nations (China, America), Russia sees the world revolving around it and gauges all others by its own standards. Russians have a traditional saying that all nations see the world from their own belltowers and the Russian tower is the tallest. This sense of moral superiority took root after the Russian embrace of Orthodox Christianity from Byzantium. Under the czars, Russians came to regard Moscow as the Third Rome, the protector of the one true Christian faith after Byzantium fell. This historic ethnocentrism and sense of mission were perpetuated and reinforced by the Bolshevik Revolution, seen by Russians as the major event of the 20th century. The messianic ideology of Marxism-Leninism has not only claimed Moscow as the New Jerusalem but as the only legitimate interpreter of Communism, to which revolutionaries from all over the world must pay court and allegiance.

So far, Soviet Russia has escaped the kind of cultural pessimism that has afflicted the West. With less reason than in a number of other countries, Russians retain a basic unquestioning confidence in their way of life. They gripe about shortages, prices or corruption, or privately dream of some tinkering reforms, but they do not engage in the agonies of self-doubt, the vehement denigration of their own country, or the fits of despair that have tortured Americans or other Westerners in recent years. Indeed, I remember one elderly Russian telling me that Soviet war veterans, no matter how antagonistic toward the American intervention in Vietnam, simply could not conceive of how young American veterans could have brought themselves to throw back their war decorations at Congress in protest over the Vietnam War. It was an insult, not just to the government but to the nation, that Russians with their vibrant patriotism simply could not countenance, he said. Very few Russians, for that matter, ever wonder whether some other way is better or whether their system should be fundamentally changed any more than one wonders about whether to change one's parents. They are confident of Mother Russia as rock and refuge. It rarely seems to dawn on Russians, except for dissidents, that their land may be unvirtuous or guilty of moral transgressions. Their sense of moral innocence is as unshaken today as was that of Americans before the awful agony of Vietnam introduced to some a sense of national guilt and capacity for evil.

Protecting Russians from that sense, I suspect, is one reason why the Soviet leadership has felt it so terribly important to suppress not just the truth about the Stalinist purges, but also the recognition that millions participated in those bloody repressions. For the Red Terror may have been ordered by one man, like Hitler's persecution of the Jews, but it was carried out by thousands upon thousands of people, visiting hell upon their comrades as well as their competitors. This national guilt is what made Khrushchev's exposure of the Stalinist purges not only an extraordinary disclosure but an extraordinary political act, fraught with dangerously unsettling emotions for all people, and undoubtedly for him as well, even though he found it a tactically useful maneuver. This is also what makes Solzhenitsyn such an explosively dangerous author for Russians, especially in his *Gulag Archipelago*. That book and his first works about the camps force Russian readers to face up to the evil that they, or their parents, or their countrymen committed. Instinctively, the regime understands that this awareness must be suppressed not only because it challenges the Communist Party to admit responsibility and risk diminution of power but also because it forces all people to face up to the national capacity for sin, an act that could dilute the national patriotism that is such an essential part of the regime's legitimacy today.

Paradoxically, despite the Russian sense of national moral superiority, much of the gusty boastfulness in the Soviet press about the Soviet Union being first, largest and best in every conceivable field seems a compensation for a deep-set national sense of inferiority toward the West in fields of science, technology and commerce, and in the pragmatic achievements of the modern age. It was Stalin who promoted the Soviet fetish for claiming exaggerated preeminence for Russian achievements, even though he also spoke candidly about Russian backwardness and the compulsion to overcome it. Under his rule the practice of chauvinistic exaggeration of Russian achievements reached ridiculous proportions: encyclopedias were claiming that Aleksandr Popov – not Marconi – was the inventor of the radio; that Aleksandr Lodygin, not Thomas Edison, invented the electric light bulb; that Ivan Polzunov beat James Watt by 21 years to the steam engine; and Aleksandr Mozhaisky was way ahead of the Wright brothers in putting the first airplane into the sky. After Stalin, the official policy of promoting such Russia-first claims was toned down. But the practice still goes on in many publications today. Urban intellectuals with their snobbish preference for things Western, often mock this egregious chauvinism with the sarcastic put-down, 'Russia – home of the elephant.'

But at all levels of Soviet society there exists a very strong, conservative Russian conviction that 'ours is best' (*nasha luchshe*). It is a phrase that pops into conversation frequently, and often without special reason. Riding an elevator in the Intourist Hotel before a large international reception one evening, I overheard two middle-aged Russian women admiring the cocktail dresses of several young Soviet women who were going to the reception. Although they were not as fashionably dressed as some of the foreign guests in the elevator, these two biddies were brimming with pride. 'Aren't our girls attractive?' chirped one. 'Yes, ours are the best,' came the cliché response from the other.

So automatically is this thought expressed by conservative-minded officialdom and by common people whether talking about girls, dams, space exploits, tractors or hockey teams, that more cosmopolitan young people relish the joke about the Communist Party official whose wife has just discovered that her husband has a ballerina for a mistress. She insists on going to the Bolshoi to see her rival. They are just settled in the box with other higher-ups when the curtain rises on a slender fluttering swan. The wife nudges her husband and asks, 'Is that the one?' 'No,' he replies, 'that's Petrov's.' 'I'm glad,' said the wife. 'Her legs are too thin.' A bit later the wife points to another feathery ballerina with a questioning eye. 'No,' says the husband, 'that's Ivanov's.' 'Good,' says the wife. 'Her face is not pretty.' Finally, the husband gestures to a ballerina in the back of the stage. The wife checks the young dancer, settles back in her seat with a smug smile, and clucks, *Nasha luchshe*' (ours is the best).

This national self-esteem regardless of circumstances is reinforced by a Victorian pride in the power and accomplishments of the Soviet Union. Volodya, the young Communist Party careerist, expressed it in his chauvinistic lordliness toward the Germans and other nations dependent on Soviet gas and oil. A British diplomatic friend, who had often visited East Germany and occasionally talked with Russian soldiers, found them envious of the German standard of living but still feeling superior toward Germans, as if their affiliation with the muscle of Moscow compensated for all else. Only a minuscule handful of dissenters protested in Red Square against the Soviet-led invasion of Czechoslovakia. They were arrested even before they could unfurl their banners. Hints of disapproval among some Establishment intellectuals came out in Natalya Baranskaya's story about the professional woman's week, 'One Week Like Any Other', when the wife suggested to the husband that they should discuss serious issues like 'Vietnam and Czechoslovakia'. Keen-eyed Soviet intellectuals spotted that as a deftly dissident equation of Soviet intervention in Czechoslovakia with American intervention in Vietnam.

But beyond the substantial indifference to the invasion on

the part of the masses, many people evidently took pride in the exercise of Soviet power in the same way that 19th-century Englishmen took pride in maintaining their imperial domain. It was one of the attributes of being a super power. A Russian writer I know was vacationing at Sochi in August 1968, when Soviets began to get wind of the invasion from Western radio broadcasts. 'The people down there were really very happy with what happened,' he recalled. ' "Finally," they said, "our troops have gone into Czechoslovakia. We should have done that a long time ago. Now we must go on and do the same in Rumania." These people were glad to see that Russia had used its force. They respect that force very much. They like to see Russian power exercised.' Gennadi, the state farm accountant, said this was true among the farm officials and farm workers whom he knew, as well. 'They believed in the huge wild lie that the Soviet Union had to invade Czechoslovakia to help the people there,' he said. '(The intervention) was a matter of pride in their own nation.' Another friend, the young scientist who had philosophized about nationalist fervor, found himself sharing a hospital ward with a civilian chauffeur who had been a tank driver in Prague during the invasion. The driver, by his account, was a thoroughly likable Russian but as blind and brutal a patriot as American soldiers in Mylai. He told the scientist how he and his comrades had obliterated Czechoslovaks at the mere appearance of what they suspected as opposition. Let a local appear on a rooftop and if he seemed menacing to the tank crew in any way, the driver said, 'We would aim our big gun at the building and blow off the top of it.' The scientist, privately opposed to the intervention, evinced some misgivings about unnecessary killing. But the driver brushed it aside with his *kvas patriotism*. He had no qualms, he said, 'because they were all Fascists.'

As a people, Russians are just as emotionally devoted to peace as Americans. But the official propaganda treatment of war, harping on themes of vigilance and preparedness, is vastly greater than in the West. Because of Vietnam, war is an extremely divisive issue in America, but in the Soviet Union, it is an unchallenged unifying element that serves to justify many of today's policies.

Even in an era of détente, and as an antidote to it, the Soviet leadership has quite deliberately tapped the wellspring of World War II to keep Soviet feelings of patriotism live and vibrant. Not surprisingly, for example, many of the letter writers who were quickest to denounce dissidents like Sakharov and Solzhenitsyn or to warn of the dangers of Western ideological penetration identified themselves as war veterans. Spy movies and war memoirs not infrequently state or imply that the West, even during the wartime alliance, could not be trusted. The constant wartime picture of Russia besieged is an implicit justification for the continuation of the draft, for high school military training, for heavy military expenditures and for the sacrifices that Soviet consumers must make because America, Germany and other capitalist economies of the West are allegedly driven by munitions industries that will never let defense expenditures turn downward.

For most Americans, World War II is now a distant and insignificant abstraction, a chapter of near-ancient history, a drama played on another stage. As a nation, we do not feel in our bone and muscle the wrenching, wounding memories of Europeans. We cannot appreciate how strongly the French, the Poles or the Russians feel in their blood toward the Germans nor can we grasp the emotional impact of old war stories on their present mood. Our relations with Germany have been defined by a new era, a new commerce, a new diplomacy. In America scrapbooks and war medals may be taken out on a rainy afternoon. Occasionally a new book on Potsdam or a film on the Normandy invasion appears. But the palpable feel of the war is gone. Korea and Vietnam have blurred the memory and diminished the importance of World War II as a national experience and as a factor in contemporary politics.

The contrast with the Russians could not be more vivid or more revealing. The war for them has a mystique. In restaurants or hotels or on trains and airplanes, utter strangers will suddenly be swapping war stories after discovering that they had been sergeants or nurses, colonels or correspondents on the same front or passed through the same cities or rail junctions during the same campaigns. Those who had been only children recall with grim satisfaction their having survived years of living on meager bread rations as refugees in Tashkent, Kuibyshev, the Urals or some other far-off point separated from parents while Hitler's armies encircled Leningrad or menaced Moscow. The annual reunions of old war units are occasions that Russians love to attend because, unlike political meetings, they touch authentic emotions. The very words 'at the front' still have an almost religious ring in Soviet life three decades after the war and veterans wear their decorations proudly in public on many occasions. The Soviets seem to take literally the motto, 'Nothing and no one shall be forgotten.' No Westerner visiting the Soviet Union can fail to be struck by the constant harping on the war, the ever-present theme of that holocaust, the war as an explanation for the Soviet economic lag behind the West, and the feeling that for Soviet people the war ended only yesterday.

Entering Moscow by the airport road, the traveler passes a monument of huge, stark tank traps, like three huge jacks, symbolic of how close the Nazi advance came to the capital and where the Russians turned it back. In Odessa, tourists are taken through the grottos where partisans hid out during the occupation by German and Rumanian troops (the Rumanians, now Communist, are conveniently forgotten as former enemies by contemporary tour guides). In Lithuania, a gaunt mother statue epitomizes the sorrow of a little nation caught in the terrible cross fire of two massive armies.

Let President Nixon pay two visits to the Soviet Union and he is taken, on the first, to the Piskarevka Cemetery in Leningrad – acres of graves of the war dead, an awful reminder of the terrible human cost of the 900-day siege of that city; and then, two years later, to Khatyn in Byelorussia where a memorial and a bronze statue of a man, tenderly holding his dying son, commemorates the razing of a village and the burning alive of 149 villagers by Nazi troops who suspected them of aiding guerillas operating behind Nazi lines.

So it is everywhere. Practically no city or village in European Russia, Byelorussia, the Ukraine or the Baltic states is without its war memorial, its grave markers, its eternal flame to the war dead. In a place like the Northern Caucasus, where Nazi forces captured the peak of Elbrus and pushed toward the oil city of Baku, war memorials play up the theme of the multinational defense of the region – the solidarity of Russians, Ukrainians, Armenians, Georgians, the Karachai and Cherkess nationalities. Even a ski resort hotel has its war memorial room.

All too well, I recall another such display in the ancient city of Pskov. In the history museum Ann and I suddenly passed from collections of ikons, silver chalices and drinking cups from czarist times into a room devoted to a panorama of the battle of Pskov in 1944, displays of captured German weapons, pictures of local heroes and their decorations and grisly photographs of five partisans hanged by German soldiers. Two men dangled from the gallows while three others were being led up to them. In another grotesque scene, ten men in simple peasant garb were being shot in the town square in front of women and children who had been assembled to witness the execution. The effort to keep the wound of war from healing seemed masochistic.

Nor is there any sign that the practice is diminishing, for emphasis on wartime memories not only reinforces patriotic feelings but points up the need for vigilance and readiness today. It was striking that in 1975, the 30th anniversary of the Allied victory over Germany brought such an outpouring of war propaganda in the press that some Western experts tabulated the flow as heavier than in 1965 or 1970, on the 20th and 25th anniversaries of victory in Europe. Sometimes, the connection between war propaganda and current issues is quite explicit. A group of American university students, camping through the Soviet Union in 1972 after the first Nixon-Brezhnev summit, came across a program at an outdoor movie theater in a campground near Orel, in central Russia. A belligerent one-hour documentary spliced film clips of North Vietnam being bombed by American jets, Israeli air attacks on the Arabs, and the Nazi attack on the Soviet Union in World War II as well as some wartime tank battles. 'It was all as if the war had ended only yesterday,' one American shuddered later on. 'Why can't they leave it alone?'

Soviet cultural life is saturated with the war theme but almost always painted in heroic rather than gory colors. 'They don't want to raise a nation of pacifists,' a Russian student commented to me. Not only have a slew of such military terms as 'mobilizing the reserves' and working a 'good watch' at the factory become standard vocabulary for the economy, but the war theme is far and away the most popular subject for books and movies. Some are crudely chauvinistic; others are more subtle and interesting because Soviet authors have found that they can capitalize on the political sanctity of the war to attempt experimentation.

A Byelorussian writer named Vasil Bykov has gained a following for his psychological novellas about partisans, playing on which people break down and collaborate with the enemy and which go nobly to their deaths. Konstantin Simonov, a former war correspondent for *Red Star*, the Armed Forces newspaper, has become virtually the nation's most famous author with his diaries and his novels flashing from battle scenes and strategic landscapes to semi-documentary views of wartime leaders. The avant-garde Taganka Theater put on 'The Dawns Here Are Quiet', a very moving and effectively staged drama about some Russian women killed by Nazi forces near the Soviet-Finnish border. Other works chronicle reunions of veterans, the problems of women on the home front, the guilt of a young woman who has been unfaithful to her husband who dies at the front.

War, a pulp novel by Ivan Stadnyuk, stirs a jingoist mood and provides the most adoring portrait of Stalin in recent years. *Hot Snow* by Yuri Bondarev recalls the heroic defense of Stalingrad and inserts another flattering portrait of Stalin, remembered by one character as 'the man whose countenance had imprinted itself onto his mind more firmly, more indelibly than the faces of his dead father and mother.' The granddaddy of the war movies in my years was *Liberation*, a five-part series beside which *Gone with the Wind* pales as a short. It completely bypasses the early war years, when Stalin panicked and the Russian forces were reeling in retreat, and tells the story of the turning of the tide up to the capture of the Reichstag in Berlin. Far too many other war stories and movies come out every year to name even the leading ones. Suffice it to say that in any season war books are always among the best sellers and that for the Soviet screen, the war theme is more important than Westerns are to Hollywood.

Spy movies and spy novels are another addiction of Russians, for in a time of knocking intelligence agencies elsewhere the Soviet spy remains a national hero. Nor are they tongue-in-cheek stories à la James Bond. In late 1974, while the American press was raking the Central Intelligence Agency over the coals for its role in Chile, the Soviet press paid its perennial tribute to the Soviet superspy, Richard Sorge, who, posing as a Nazi correspondent in Tokyo, had

387

informed the Kremlin in advance of the date of the Nazi invasion of Poland and Hitler's plans to attack the Soviet Union. The fact that Stalin ignored Sorge's warnings, however, is always omitted. By the time the C.I.A. was being roasted for domestic intelligence snooping, *New World*, the most liberal of Soviet monthly magazines, was running an heroic novel about the campaign by Smersh, the death-to-spies counterintelligence agency, to wipe out nationalist, non-Communist Polish partisans fighting the Nazis in 1944. The magazine dedicated the novel: 'To the few to whom very many are indebted.' For something comparable in America, the *New Yorker* would have to run a serial romanticizing Allen Dulles and Richard Helms. The two most popular Soviet television serials of recent years were 'Seventeen Instants in Spring' and 'Shield and Sword', tales of Soviet master spies who infiltrated the Nazi hierarchy, run with little concern about the effect on détente. Yet in 1974, when Finnish television screened *Silk Stockings*, a 1957 American slapstick musical about Soviet agents in Paris, the Soviet Embassy protested vigorously.

The Russians have patriotic morality plays for every medium. One of the most striking numbers put on by the Moiseyev Dance Troupe is a brilliantly dramatic dance called 'Partisans' done by dancers in great winged, black cossack-coats that make each partisan dancer a forbidding hawk or raven. First one partisan horseman appears, then another, then a stream of them gliding along smoothly, feet hidden beneath their cloaks and moving at great speed as if riding on a dark night. Suddenly, the dancers unfurl their ravencapes and reveal all the various nationalities and walks of life – young men, partisan girls, sturdy Slavs, Germanic-looking Baltic peoples, Eskimo-like Yakuts, Central Asians, railroad workers, soldiers, parachutists, sailors. The dance becomes a very effective display of the heroic unity and solidarity of all Soviet peoples, splendidly performed. In short, a stirring propaganda reminder of the exploits of war as well as an artistic hit. Soviet audiences love it, and it travels well all over the world.

Few Russians over 35 need much prompting to recall the war. I heard many sad stories of personal ordeals, but a slender, spunky artist once entertained a roomful of people with humorous recollections of his war years as an aviation mechanic. Everyone was frantic, he said, to get his hands on any kind of alcohol to numb the pain, the cold, the fear. One of the favorite gimmicks was to drain the landing gear boxes of fluid and to filter the mixture of oils and spirits through gasmasks. It was a slow, laborious process, but it made a bearable drink. 'Of course,' he said, 'it left the planes tilting to one side after the fluid was removed.'

Another man, a tour guide in the Caucasus, had a more tolerant view of the Germans than most because some German soldiers saved him from execution. As a young teenager in an occupied zone, he was dragooned for a work crew and angered a German sergeant by letting a telephone pole fall against his shoulder. The infuriated sergeant motioned him to walk toward some nearby bushes and unsnapped his pistol holster. Other German soldiers, sensing what was about to happen, shouted at the sergeant. 'Willi, we know you are mad, but don't do such a terrible thing.' Twice, the sergeant started to pull out the gun and the others stopped him. Finally, the Russian said, 'the sergeant cuffed me such a terrible blow that I flew 15 feet. But nothing more. So I can say there are human beings among the Germans. They saved my life.' His views are more charitable than most.

In Murmansk, a marine biologist who had lost a father, an uncle and seven other relatives in the war, could hardly abide the policy of détente with West Germany. 'I know the world needs peace,' he said tautly, 'but I hate the Germans.' Privately, I have heard other Russians voice the fear that Brezhnev was going too far trusting Willi Brandt and the Germans. In Samarkand, I felt the sting of hostility some people still harbor toward Germans. A storekeeper took me for a German when I asked the price of some Uzbek hats he was selling and refused to answer. When I asked again, he snapped at me: 'We don't serve Germans here.' In Moscow, a young German technician who was working and training at a factory about 150 miles from Moscow, toward Leningrad, told me he had been shocked by the antagonism of provincial Russians. 'They don't know in their hearts that the war is over,' he said. 'All they think is, "the Germans want to kill us and we want to kill the Germans." And I told them, "But here I am. I'm a German, and I don't want to kill you. The war is over. We are building socialism in our part of Germany." ' So afraid was this young man of Russian passion that he dared not go drinking with his fellow workers even though he was on an officially sponsored work-study program. He was greatly distressed that these factory workers made no distinction between East and West Germany. 'I spent a whole day arguing with them and telling them that our part of Germany was friends with them and that we were building socialism,' he said. 'But it didn't seem to matter. For them, Germans were Germans and they hated us all.'

The powers-that-be, nonetheless, worry greatly that the patriotic dedication felt by those who lived through the war is not being forcefully enough transmitted to the young. Decrees are issued, movies critiqued, and writers' conferences held to promote that end. From an early age the young get indoctrination in paying proper tribute to the sacrifices made during wartime. One scene indelibly imprinted in my memory is that of young children, boys and girls of 11 and 12, standing as honor guards at war memorials. I recall a windy fall afternoon in Odessa, where one memorial overlooked the sea. The sky was overcast and the wind whipped up whitecaps. Four children in the red scarves, white shirts, blue pants and skirts of the Young Pioneers stood vigil, rigid as soldiers, posted at the four corners of the memorial. I happened to arrive with a tour guide just as the guard was being changed. We stopped to watch. Down a long pathway marched a new contingent, arms swinging widely, their slow pace reminiscent of the measured gait of the KGB guards at Lenin's tomb in Moscow. The crunch of gravel stones underfoot marked the cadence of their steps as they went through the ceremony – silent, disciplined, intensely devoted to the sacred duty of standing guard for the Motherland.

This is of a piece with the actual military training carried out nation-wide in Soviet high schools, the universal draft for 18-year-olds, and the serious way in which Soviet university students are put through compulsory reserve officer programs. Our first exposure to this network of paramilitary activities in civilian life came when our 11-year-old daughter, Laurie, went off to play *zarnitsa* (lightning), a war game, on Lenin Hills, organized for the sixth and seventh grades by a military instructor at her Russian school. It would all have seemed very much like a summer camp game of capture the flag except for the deadly earnestness with which it was done. Laurie came home and told us that the two grades, children from 11 to 13, had first been drilled by a uniformed army instructor in formation marching and making right faces and left faces. In our living room she demonstrated marching and faces. They were divided into two teams, one assigned blue patches to sew on their sleeves, and the other assigned green patches. The blues were given a head start to go scatter in the hills, like partisans, and the greens were to hunt them down, rip off their badges and bring them back as prisoners. 'We couldn't play too long because it was very cold,' Laurie said. 'There was snow on the ground. I got cold because they left me guarding prisoners.' Still, with the drilling and all, the expedition ran about four hours after school. It was a practice carried out in all schools. In the older grades the complexity of the game increased as the instructors introduced primitive field tactics. Playing tennis not far from Lenin Hills, I would occasionally see teams of children darting through the woods playing *zarnitsa*. An American university student whom I knew was amazed one day to have spotted one group of students, dressed in dark navy uniforms, not only capture their rivals but go through the ceremony of lining the captured partisans up against a wall and pretending to shoot them. The victims fell and died very realistically.

That was but one of a number of activities suggesting to me that the line separating civilian and military life, so pronounced in the West, was far less important in Soviet society. The national physical fitness program has the theme, 'Ready for Labour and Defense' (*Gotov K Trudu i Oborone*). The television program 'Come on, Guys' is intended to popularize various military skills among the youth by running regional and national competitions in marksmanship, the art of self-defense, and aspects of Soviet law affecting military service. At 14, youngsters can join the Voluntary Committee for Assistance to the Armed Forces, a gung-ho organization with the stated objective of training civilians 'in the spirit of constant readiness for defense of the interests of the Socialist Motherland.' D.O.S.A.A.F., as it is known by its Russian initials, has no real counterpart in America. It combines the functions of 4-H Clubs, Boy Scouts, the YMCA, Civil Defense, the American Legion and National Guard, with branches at farms, factories, institutes and in city neighborhoods all over the Soviet Union. It is a vast apparatus. I was astonished to hear that a Soviet officer disclosed at a public lecture that the D.O.S.A.A.F. membership was 65 million. The organization gives courses in military history and tactics, develops civil defense facilities, teaches youngsters to drive and maintain all kinds of vehicles, to operate and maintain radios and electrical equipment, to make and design aircraft models, to make parachute jumps, to shoot and to learn professions 'which have military importance', as one Soviet blurb put it. It runs driving clubs and schools. For dog lovers it has a program supplying breeds suitable for military purposes. Those who accept such dogs and enroll them in training programs qualify for extra housing space.

For men really serious about military careers, the Soviet Union has at least 135 military schools and colleges graduating commissioned officers, compared to ten such schools in the United States. The real introduction to military life for the youth of the entire nation comes in ninth and tenth grades, the last two years of ordinary Soviet high school, where boys and girls take an obligatory, twice-a-week classroom course in military training and civil defense. The textbook, which a Russian friend gave me, opens with the black-and-white rhetoric of the Cold War: 'The U.S.S.R. is a peace-loving state. . . . There is no crime which imperialists have not committed.' The 1973 edition had four lines on Soviet-American détente squeezed between warnings that 'the U.S. has not turned away from its aggressive course' and 'the requirements of military readiness have grown in recent years as imperialist circles, first of all the U.S.A., heat up the international situation without any lessening of the dangers of a new world war.' This is for all high school students across the country.

The textbook then moves quickly into a description of the Soviet armed forces, instructions on dismantling weapons, throwing grenades from trenches, firing weapons prone, making tank traps and undertaking field maneuvers. Each summer, the high school boys go off to army camp, from five days to a month. They conduct long marches with a pack, take tactical field training, dig civil defense shelters, and fire weapons like the world-renowned Kaleshnikov submachine guns used by guerillas worldwide. 'The Soviet equivalent of the American basic training camps like Fort Dix and Fort Jackson are in the Soviet high schools,' an American military attaché remarked to me. 'They are paid for, not by the Ministry of Defense, but the Ministry of Education.'

392

In the late Sixties, one Russian lad told me, the enemy in field maneuvers and classroom lectures at summer camps used to be explicitly identified as Americans. But with the coming of détente in the 1970s, some camps fuzzed the identification, though youngsters still understood who was meant. The silhouettes at target ranges, this lad said, all wear wide-brimmed headgear – 'a symbol of the bourgeoisie so that we are "properly instructed in the [Marxist] class approach".' Another lanky teen-ager confided to me that he had found the routine all too realistic, beginning with the first day head-to-toe search to make sure no one had smuggled alcohol or some other contraband into camp. 'The food was so terrible I could hardly eat – I was hungry the whole time,' he moaned. His father, a pacifist, was pleased when his son returned shed of romantic ideas about the Army. 'I didn't like the idea at first,' the father confessed. 'But it has its benefits. Now these boys have a realistic picture of the Army.'

One result is that many young people strive desperately to get into some higher educational institution, any institution, to obtain a reserve commission and to avoid the compulsory two-year draft. But in universities, too, the courses are more serious than American ROTC programs. In addition to the standard drill about ranks, formations and military regulations and a two-month encampment before the senior year, the Soviet Army develops military applications for each student's academic specialty. Language students, one bearded young linguist told me, are prepared to become military translators. 'We learn all the terminology and nomenclature of American weapons in our courses – to be ready for mobilization,' he said. Biology students take courses in health measures in case of nuclear attack and study military parasitology and military microbiology, a girl biologist said. The girls at Moscow State University, and elsewhere, join the boys at the shooting range. 'I lay down next to the colonel who was our instructor and he showed me how to hold the Kaleshnikov,' smiled the biologist, a striking blonde with classic Slavic features made even more striking by her narrow Tatar eyes. 'I shot three times. I couldn't even hit the wall. They couldn't find my bullets. But the colonel liked me. He gave me a C.'

*　　*　　*

Periodically, the intense Soviet propaganda about World War II is used to bolster the policy of détente, especially as a prelude to the visit of some major Western leader. Just before President Nixon's arrival in 1972, Yevgeny Yevtushenko set the tone with an emotional poem about the meeting of American and Soviet troops at the Elbe River that evoked happy memories of the wartime alliance and joint victory over Nazism. I ran into a fair number of middle-aged men with warm personal recollections of collaboration with Westerners – men who served at airdromes where American planes landed or who worked at Murmansk where the huge flow of Western lend-lease reached the Soviet Union. But far more frequently, Soviet propaganda passes over in silence the concrete acts of cooperation and raises points of mistrust and conflict.

In Murmansk, for example, city officials paid lip service to wartime cooperation but in the local museum, many rooms of which were devoted to displays about the war, there was not a single chance for Russian visitors to learn about Allied lend-lease. Amidst panoramic, wall-to-wall photographs of the havoc wreaked on Murmansk by Nazi firebombing, I found an edition of *Harper's* magazine opened to an article by Dave Marlowe, an American journalist who had reached Murmansk on an Allied convoy. He described the convoy under pursuit by German submarines and planes and the relief of the crews at reaching their destination. Then he portrayed the depressing devastation of Murmansk. But the only part translated into Russian was the description of his impressions of Murmansk, without any reference to the gauntlet run by the convoys, the Allied aid, or why an American might be in Murmansk.

Out of curiosity, I asked Yelena Pavlova, the enthusiastic museum director, if she had information on the number of Allied convoys or amount of Allied aid that passed through Murmansk. 'I never bumped into any such figures in all my years here,' she said. She advised trying the city's handsome new technical library. There the director, Vera Popova, a busty, imposing administratrix, proudly showed us around the bright, modern building for a couple of hours. After the tour, I inquired about the convoys. Researchers were confidently dispatched. After an hour or so, they returned with one thin volume reporting that in 1942, 93 Soviet ships were engaged in importing goods for the war effort, but nothing about British or American aid. More searching turned up nothing else, to the embarrassment of my official host Nikolai Belyayev, the editor of 'Polar Truth', the local Communist Party newspaper. The next day, however, he showed up triumphantly with a book that had one passage referring to 'foreign seamen [who] guided their ships here in the days of the war'. But the point of the passage had nothing to do with aid, which was unmentioned. Rather it cited the praise of the foreigners 'for the exploits of Soviet frontier guards' who helped douse fires on their vessels. A couple of ships were mentioned by name, but no nationality or reason for their being in Murmansk was given. Such awkward exclusions could only have been by design, meaning that censors had banned mentioning $15 billion in American and British aid for the Soviet war effort.

Indeed, a Soviet journalist and a movie director later confirmed that to me. As a result, they said, most Russians thought of American wartime aid as no more than *tushenka* (canned Spam) which they belittled. The movie director considered it practically a revolutionary development that in 1973 Yuri Zhukov, the *Pravda* commentator, had mentioned on TV that American aid had actually included planes, trucks, jeeps, spare parts, and other vital equipment. 'That is the first time in many years that our people have heard such things about your lend-lease,' he said. I never heard the program repeated.

For the Kremlin, a full and candid picture of the Western contribution to the Soviet war effort would not have accorded with the ethnocentric Soviet view of the war, a view that usually ignores its global aspect and sees Russia as the center and all else as a secondary sideshow. This is a fault of all nations, of course, but it is carried to an extreme by the Russians through censorship. It would have been a painful blow to national pride to admit that in time of need, Moscow had had to lean on the West for help. Out of some deep-seated inferiority complex, this kind of information has always been suppressed, whether wartime aid, the famine relief in the early twenties from Herbert Hoover's American Relief Administration (treated in the Great Soviet Encyclopedia mainly as a cover for subversion and espionage), or the huge Russian grain purchase from America in 1972.

Nor is the war automatically a symbol of Allied collaboration to Russians. Even today they bear grudges against the West over the conduct of the war. For reasons of ideological solidarity, their celebrations often play on the modest wartime actions of Poles, Rumanians, and Hungarians against the Nazis, and seldom make much of what the British, French or Americans did. But beyond this official line of Communist solidarity, I found myself besieged with the argument that the West had deliberately delayed the Normandy invasion to allow the Nazis to concentrate their force against the Russians. This is widely regarded by Russians as a purposeful act of betrayal. Many quote Stalin on this point though they steadfastly ignore that Stalin's own pact with Hitler from 1939–1941 allowed the Germans to concentrate all their force against the British in the early war years without the distraction of a second front in the East. Most Americans do not think of this when challenged about Normandy. My own response was that we hardly wanted to bleed Russia since we were pumping in billions of dollars of lend-lease through Murmansk, and the Russian retort commonly was that American aid was niggardly – *tushenka*. This response came from a Foreign Ministry official and a well-established journalist, who had reason to know better, as well as from ordinary people who may genuinely have been ignorant. Among those who knew and were prepared to admit that Western wartime aid had been more extensive, the response was usually, 'but aid is only dollars and we paid in blood.'

Another burning wartime grievance which affects the East-West climate today is the widespread belief that in the final months of war the Allies secretly sought to make a peace deal with the Germans through Allen Dulles in Switzerland, behind Moscow's back. That is the main theme of the popular television spy serial, 'Seventeen Instants in Spring', a story which falsifies history to project the picture of double-dealing Americans. The Soviet spy, a handsome emigré named Sterlitz, has wormed his way high into the ranks of the Gestapo and uncovered a plot by Heinrich Himmler, head of the SS, to negotiate a separate peace with the West through Field Marshal Albert Kesselring, the SS commander in Italy. This plot is allegedly blocked only by the brilliance of Sterlitz and the cunning mistrustfulness of Stalin who senses 'Allied trickery'. Although the television film and the story on which it was based were presented to the Soviet public as entirely 'based on facts', Moscow had no known superspy within the high reaches of the SS. Moreover, the author, Yulian Semenov, telescoped the actual time span of events to make the alleged Western betrayal appear more shameful, presenting a version of history contradicted by published diplomatic documents. According to State Department records of Soviet and American wartime communications released for publication in 1968, the talks were initiated by an aide of Kesselring and involved potential surrender of Nazi forces in Italy and only in Italy. The Soviet Government was immediately informed by Ambassador Averell Harriman and was invited to participate in them. Nothing in the documents suggests Himmler's involvement or any broad political peace settlement with any Germans. But they do portray Stalin's near paranoiac refusal to accept the good faith of American invitations for the Russians to take part in the talks, ultimately provoking President Roosevelt to protest in astonishment at Stalin's accusations.

The television series was sufficiently touchy for Soviet authorities to have delayed its first screening until after Brezhnev had completed his visit to America in the summer of 1973. But the caliber of the production – technically and dramatically it was far and away the best television series which I saw in the Soviet Union – made it an instant hit. So popular was it that it was given a rerun that fall and its political message had extra impact with a huge national audience. Not long after the series had run the second time, I discussed the show with an opera singer and an Army captain who were sharing a train compartment with me from Leningrad to Moscow. Both were firmly convinced that there had been an American betrayal near the end of the war and my allusions to the documentary record did not interest them.

'It's a good thing that Stalin found out about it or it would have made trouble for us,' the opera singer declared.

'It's not pretty but that's the way it was,' the captain insisted just as adamantly. 'We have documentary proof of that. Of course, the movie was fictionalized, but we know what was done behind our backs.'

XIII

SIBERIA

High Rises on the Permafrost

> I am not for the sweetly timid daydreamers,
> Childish in their complacency.
> I am
>   for those who are willing to fight
>   not for those who resort to prayer,
> For idealists of action!
> For those
>   who have undertaken to change the world. . . .
>   Yevtushenko, *Envoys Are Going to Lenin*

Russians are connoisseurs of the cold. They relish the onset of winter when snow magically transforms the drab,
gray visage of a city like Moscow into a lighter, more pleasant
countenance by dusting the roof-tops and window ledges
with a fresh coat of white trim, badly needed in any season.
After the rainy, funereal pall of autumn, I myself came to
welcome the liberation of winter with its brief but brilliant
sunshine, its stunning azure skies, and its clear, invigorating
coldness.

I had to be cautioned, however, lest I be misled by its
false beginnings. In my amazement at the heavy, nine-inch
snowfall in mid-October during my first year in Moscow, I
wrote a story about the early arrival of winter. But Ivan
Gusev, our office driver, quoted the peasant lore that winter
comes only after the third snowfall and I should not be
fooled by its first feint. Sure enough, those nine inches turned
to ugly slush and disappeared. So did the second snowfall.
When the third came, it piled up and packed down, and the
Russians exulted in the squealing of the hardpack under
their heels and the frost crystals that webbed their window

panes, firmly taped shut for the hibernation from early November to late April.

In our courtyard the drivers, fidgeting over balky engines and laughingly pouring precious vodka into the radiator of one machine which had somehow escaped more modern prophylactics, would gather in council to consider and savor the first hard frost. '*Skolko gradusov?*' – 'How many degrees?' one would ask. When winter truly arrives, Russians never ask what the temperature is. Only: How many degrees? Degrees below freezing is taken for granted. The other drivers would sniff the air with animal satisfaction, as if that first hard frost had a fragrance akin to the first bloom of spring, then pronounce their verdicts and compare them with the morning weather reports.

As our first Moscow winter began, I was surprised to see that rather than retreating indoors, Russians would emerge and flood the buses or suburban commuter trains with cross-country skis slung over their shoulders and journey into the nearby countryside where they darted off among the sun-dappled birches. The hardier menfolk would hike out on the frozen rivers, laboriously bore holes through the ice, and squat all day watching their lines. That was one of Ivan's favorite sports. Whenever I would kid him about coming home with a pitiful catch of no more than a cupful of minnows, he would grin and reply that he went not so much for the fish but to get out in the country during winter. Always, too, Russians had a tale of a place farther north or farther inland where the frost was harder, the freeze stronger, the air drier, the people tougher. If ever, as a foreign neophyte, I were to comment on the chilliness of the morning to the drivers in the courtyard, one of them was sure to humorously advise that in Siberia spit froze before it hit the ground or that a Siberian toilet consisted of just one implement. 'What?' I would innocently ask. 'A stick to beat off the wolves,' would come the reply amidst a chorus of laughter.

Braving the cold, like downing vodka, is part of the machismo ritual for Russians, women as well as men. One morning in February, when winter grudgingly relaxed its grip temporarily, sixty 'walruses', as Russians call their winter swimmers, took advantage of the 'balmy' 30-degree weather for a bracing dip among the ice floes in the Moscow River. At Gorky Park, I was among hundreds of ice skaters who paused to watch the middle-aged and white-haired bathers come out of the change house in swimming caps and skimpy trunks. It made me shiver to see them march, nearly naked, across the ice and snow to the river bank and then plunge one by one into the murky brown water. A few gamely performed the crawl but most kept their heads above water and dog-paddled or breaststroked as long as they could stand it. A sailor in uniform drew cheers when he jumped in, fully clothed. Several middle-aged women paddled slowly beside a rowboat for photographers.

'See how strong and healthy our walruses are!' gushed an enthusiastic announcer to the fur-capped throngs on the river bank.

'They must be out of their minds,' a warmly dressed militia captain mumbled.

It all seemed like child's play, however, when I flew to Yakutsk in Eastern Siberia, a city as far north as Anchorage, Alaska, yet colder because it is locked in the continental fastness without the moderating influence of a nearby ocean. Yakutsk is the capital of the Soviet Klondike, hard by the Arctic Circle. Fittingly, Erik de Mauny, a British correspondent, once called it 'the end of the line except that there is no line to be the end of' – the nearest trunk railroad is 1,200 miles to the south. Yet here, too, the *siberyaki*, as devoted Siberians call themselves, take a certain masochistic pride in the rigors of winter and their ability to endure.

I remember a brisk wintry walk through Yakutsk one day with two Soviet acquaintances. From the brooding emptiness of the North Siberian Plain came a piercing wind that burned the cheeks and froze the nostrils. Not a howling blast, but silent and sharp as a knife. Tears welled up in the eyes and gloved fingers flexed instinctively. It was mid-March but even a bright sun could not lift the temperature higher than 13 below zero.

It was a greedy, confident Siberian wintriness, devouring the hardy folk who labored along the sidewalks and chasing indoors those whose energies it had already eaten away. The day before, in one cafe, I had seen people banging through the door steadily, taking refuge over piping hot tea and lingering as long as possible in the stale communal warmth. I watched one worker chug-a-lug a half-tumbler of brandy like a dose of antifreeze before having another go at the elements. Outside, people had surrendered any semblance of fashion to the all-consuming struggle to keep warm. They hobbled along in clumsy, black-felt *valenki* boots or animal skins, legs wrapped in woolen leggings, heads buried in fur. Coat collars were raised to hide every last inch of flesh from the merciless wind.

'Stings, doesn't it?' muttered one of my companions, a Ukrainian newcomer to Yakutsk.

'This is nothing,' scoffed Yuri Semyonov, a native Siberian whose grandfather was banished by the czars to Yakutsk when it was no more than a dumpy little village for political exiles, fur traders and native Yakuts tending reindeer herds. 'Our coldest day this winter was minus 72 [Fahrenheit],' he said. 'In Moscow, people don't send their children to school on days like today. But our kids go – down to minus 58.'

'You think of our climate as oy-oy-oy,' smiled Mrs Aleksandra Ovchinnikova, rolling her dark brown Eskimo eyes as I gratefully thawed a few minutes later in her office. Since 1963 she had held the largely honorary title of President of the Yakut Autonomous Soviet Socialist Republic, a region almost as large as all of Western Europe and now exploited by the Soviet state for its incalculable riches of diamonds, gold, natural gas, oil and untold other minerals. 'But it is a very dry climate – good for the health,' she insisted. 'You notice that our people don't get fat. And they live long lives. You have to dress warmly. The women wear woolen tights, one on top of the other – at least three layers, maybe six.'

In Yakutia, wearing layers is a life-style. Even houses and cars do it, as we discovered driving among the straggling settlements of log cabin huts with icicles hanging from the eaves to the ground. In Moscow, Ann and I had become accustomed to double windows but in Yakutia storm windows are triple thick. Each layer has its little *fortochka*, or miniwindow, in the upper right-hand corner to control the airflow. In the Hotel Lena, the scruffy hostelry where we were quartered with an overflow crowd of workmen sleeping in the hallways, the *fortochkas* had thoughtfully been sealed to prevent drafts. In our room, the only link to the outdoors was a stove pipe, thrust through all the window layers. But someone had stuffed it full of old rags. Buses and cars, too, came equipped with double windshields to keep them from glazing over. Vehicles which could not be garaged overnight were simply left running around the clock. 'If they st-stop,' advised our stuttering taxi driver, 'you have to wa-warm them up with special heating devices and it takes three or four hours to st-start them again. It's easier and cheaper just to l-leave them running.' Man, it turns out, is more durable than machines. In December and January, when work at diamond mines or on construction sites slows to a crawl, workmen can take no more than half an hour outside without heading for the warm-up shed. But they have to give up entirely at 58 below because machinery breaks down and steel rods snap like twigs in the extreme cold.

What staggered me was that in spite of these conditions, Yakutsk had grown to nearly 120,000 people and included a university, several scientific institutions, a television relay station, a full-scale port on the Lena River, its lifeline to the south, and several dozen small industrial enterprises. Indoor plumbing, however, was a rare luxury. Even in the most bitter weather, just as the joke about the Siberian toilet implied, people used outhouses. In a workers' neighborhood one evening, I peered into a couple of outhouses and catching sight of frozen piles of excrement, knee-high, I shivered at the thought of the cold midnight dash. 'It's worst for women,' one worker conceded.

Ordinary house water poses a problem, too. Here and there on street corners were electrically heated spigots serving a section of homes. But two-thirds of the city's population lived in sections without such conveniences. Their water came in the form of huge chunks of ice, sawed mechanically from the frozen surface of the Lena River, and delivered by truck or horse-drawn sled to be stored outside or in the 'basement' – a hollowed cave in the permafrost beneath the houses. River ice cost fifty kopecks (67 cents) a square meter and one lady vouched for it as 'the best quality water there is – especially good for the stomach.'

As if remoteness and the rigors of climate were not enough to contend with, permafrost multiplies the difficulties and costs of any human endeavor. Yakutsk lies near the heart of the permafrost zone which covers nearly half of Soviet territory, mainly in Siberia. As the name implies, permafrost is earth that remains frozen year-round to depths of 1,000 feet or more. Unless its iron hardness can be softened, at least temporarily, I was told, man cannot sow his crops, sink mineshafts to tap the mineral wealth underground, or even construct sizable modern buildings.

This last point puzzled me for it seemed that permanently frozen earth would provide the most stable possible foundation for buildings. The problem, according to Rostislav Kamensky, a bearded young scientist at Yakutsk's Permafrost Institute, is that the top five or six feet of permafrost thaw and turn into marshy swamp in summertime. Fine for farmers who manage to grow wheat, oats, cabbage and even hothouse tomatoes in forest clearings, but it plays havoc with builders. I had already noticed homes tilted at rakish angles or ridiculously buried up to their window sills. Any normal building set flush to the ground, Kamensky explained, generates enough heat to thaw the permafrost under it and then sags into its own quagmire. The quirks of permafrost make roads heave and railroad tracks buckle like miniature roller coasters.

The Yakuts have long accepted topsy-turvy cottages as an unavoidable inconvenience. But when modern Soviet engineers want to raise structures more than two stories high, there are obvious perils. The solution they have devised is to set buildings on concrete stilts to allow the icy Siberian winds to circulate under buildings and keep the permafrost frozen. But this means penetrating the permafrost long enough to sink pilings firmly into the obstinate earth. One method is to bore holes. But the most common, if more cumbersome, expedient is to funnel steam at high pressure into the permafrost from a long firehose contraption, thawing the earth temporarily. Then, with an ungodly clanking and heaving, a huge crane rams a 30-foot piling into the steam-softened pit by dropping it over and over and over until the sheer weight of the piling drives a hole to the desired depth. There, the permafrost seals its icy vice around the piling. This technique has caused construction costs to skyrocket but, Kamensky said, it enabled the Russians to build a new seven-story hotel in Yakutsk and a nine-story office building in the diamond town of Mirny (though I never did quite understand why such tall structures were needed anyway).

It had been my dream to visit the diamond mines at Mirny or the gold fields in Aldan, but the authorities refused permission. As a consolation Yuri Semyonov, the slender newsman whose grandfather had come as an exile to Yakutsk and who was my local host, took Ann and me on a fishing expedition that exposed us to other facets of Siberian life.

In a sturdy old Volga taxi we headed for the Lena River, which in summer months is the transportation artery that brings Yakutsk almost all its year-round supplies. As we approached the river bank and were preparing to cross, I suddenly realized; no bridge. But the driver plunged onward and soon we were bounding along on the river in an icy, rutted but well-prepared track. 'It's safe,' Yuri reassured us. 'The ice is plenty thick – about eight feet. Strong enough for trucks.' We were traveling on a regular winter high-way, used from December until late April, linking Yakutsk with settlements to the north and east. For nearly 15 miles we bounced along, passing an occasional truck, car and even one motorcyclist. The curbs, so to speak, were marked not only by drifts but with regular little pine trees to prevent snowblind drivers from mistakenly plowing off into deep snow somewhere in no-man's-land.

We turned off the ice highway and clawed our way deep into the countryside, nearly slithering to a perilous halt in axle-deep snow several times before we came upon 15 Yakuts in a large clearing that turned out to be a snow-covered lake. The Yakuts are an ingenious race of trappers, fishermen, and reindeer herders with as great a mastery over the north as American Eskimos to whom some Soviet anthropologists believe they are ethnically related. Since early morning this team of men had constructed an elaborate fishtrap. Through the ice they had bored about 20 bushel-basket-sized holes, setting them out in a huge oval nearly the size of a football field. Masterfully, they had stuffed large nets under the ice, threading them from one hole to the next. Then they knocked on the ice to drive fish into their nets.

By the time we arrived, they were pulling in their third catch and had about 500 pounds of fish. They teased us into helping them pull in nets and use great skewers to hoist flapping fish out of the freezing water. Within minutes a couple of fires were crackling near a cove of pines and the aroma of fresh fish soup seasoned with salt, green onions and herbs quickened our appetites. The inevitable ration of vodka was produced but before anyone could raise a glass to his lips, a smiling Yakut carpenter with the thoroughly Russianized name of Vasily Androsov, solemnly dashed a portion of vodka on the fire, which flared brilliantly for an instant. It was a throwback to the ancient pagan worship of sun and fire among the Yakuts.

'The custom among our people,' Androsov confided, 'is to pour the first drink on the fire for Bayonai, the god of hunters and fishermen – a god of merriment like your Dionysus. It is for good luck.'

Siberia.

Maxim Gorky once called it 'a land of death and chains'. The great 18th-century scientist Mikhail Lomonosov glowingly predicted that its natural riches would eventually become the source of Russian might and power. Today, the reality lies somewhere in-between – neither so terrifying as the boundless prison without bars used by the czarist, Stalinist and Brezhnev regimes for convicts and dissidents, nor so romantically bountiful as Lomonosov dreamed. Yet both prison and promise remain.

Even now university students in Moscow and Lenigrad shudder at the thought of being dispatched on two or three years of compulsory state assignments at some project in the remote, desolate territory which stretches 3,400 miles from the Ural mountains to the Pacific, officially divided into West Siberia, East Siberia, and the Soviet Far East. But as we discovered, many Siberians firmly proclaim their devotion to the beckoning solitude of the *Taiga* pine forest and vow they would never trade their stern existence or the free outdoor life of Siberia for the overcivilized, overcrowded, overbureaucratized life of European Russia.

'I don't like the West,' a young professional woman in Irkutsk remarked, not meaning London, Paris or New York – but Moscow. 'I have a lot of friends there, but I don't like it. People are rude. They are in too much of a hurry. They are too tense. Out here people are more friendly. They have that broad Siberian spirit.' Again and again, I heard that sentiment. 'Back there, they are bureaucrats,' a bluntspoken Bratsk engineer commented disdainfully. 'Out here, we are democrats, working together.'

For the loyal *Sibiryak*, his is the land of manifest destiny, filling up with strong young people throwing hydroelectric dams across titanic rivers, planting mighty construction projects in the rich but untapped wilderness, building a new civilization, marking out the blueprint for the future. An unquestioning faith in economic growth comes gushing forth in a stream of superlatives about Siberia. 'This is all virgin territory,' boasted our friend Yuri Semyonov, with the kind of pioneer spirit that would have warmed the heart of Horace Greeley. 'People here have much more opportunity than they do back in the West.'

With grit and willpower, the settlers have achieved some striking results over the past quarter century. Hydroelectric dams at Bratsk and Krasnoyarsk, already world famous, are being joined by massive new power projects at Sayan and Ust-Ilimsk. At Norilsk in the far north, a mining industrial complex refines copper, nickel and platinum. Aluminum is being produced at Bratsk, Krasnoyarsk and near Irkutsk. Power lines and pipelines criss-cross the frozen wilderness, pumping natural gas and oil from West Siberia not only to European Russia and Eastern Europe but to Western Europe as well.

Industrial development, growing slightly faster in Siberia than in the rest of the nation, is pushed hardest where it is easiest – in or near established cities on the Trans-Siberian Railroad or in southern regions where the climate is less fierce than in Yakutia. When new towns sprout in the Siberian north, it is to tap vital mineral resources and they are staggering indeed.

The natural gas fields in West Siberia are claimed by the Russians as the world's largest, with bigger reserves than in the entire United States. The oil fields of West Siberia's Tyumen region shot in one decade from dormancy to become the Soviet Union's most productive area, outstripping even Moscow's ambitious plans. Siberia holds 60 percent of the timber of the Soviet Union, 60 percent of its coal, and 80 percent of its water power on giant rivers that, if linked, could circle the globe 25 times. Not only are there lucrative deposits of gold and diamonds in Yakutia, but elsewhere are rare metals like platinum, molybdenum, and wolfram – in fact, practically every element in the periodic table of Mendeleyev. So vast are the reserves that Soviet economists and engineers wave away Cassandra-like warnings of Western scholars that mankind is recklessly depleting the world's natural wealth. Siberia, they believe, can be worked for a millennium.

The messianic enthusiasm of Siberia's boosters, however, ignores very real obstacles, especially the fact that living conditions are so severe that in the Sixties nearly a million more people moved out of Siberia than moved in, despite graduated pay bonuses designed to hold people there. (Each hardship region has a basic coefficient. In Yakutsk, pay is 50 percent over standard wage levels in what Siberians call 'mainland' Russia. For each year in Siberia, the worker gets another 10 percent on top of that, up to five years. In some regions of the far north, bonuses run up to 200 percent.) Only a few years back some Siberian enthusiasts were predicting that its dazzling prospects would lure a population of 60 to 100 million by the year 2000. Yet by the early Seventies, it had reached only 26 million with little likelihood of hitting 35 million by the end of the century. Not only have acute labor shortages slowed construction and put a crimp on overall Siberian economic growth, but ruble-conscious planners in Moscow have discovered that while Siberian mineral resources are plentiful, the cost of developing them and providing necessary facilities to attract workers are double or triple the costs of developing more accessible, if less dramatic, resources elsewhere.

Nonetheless, for a nation that has lost its revolutionary élan without shedding its revolutionary pretensions, Siberia is vitally important as a political symbol of the new frontier. As each big showcase project draws toward completion, a new one is inaugurated. When I left Moscow at the end of 1974, the propaganda buildup was underway for BAM – the Baikal-Amur Mainline – a railway to be carved through 2,000 miles of wilderness from Lake Baikal, the scimitar-shaped natural wonder of East Siberia, to the Amur River near the Pacific coast. The stated objective is to open up a remote mineral-rich zone of the Soviet Far East. Significantly, BAM will also provide a strategic rail route well north of the Trans-Siberian Railroad and hence less vulnerable to any land attack from China, perhaps the real reason for its construction. Poets and pop groups as well as propagandists have been enlisted to churn up a gung-ho spirit for BAM which Moscow claims will be the feat of a generation, if not the century.

'If Siberia did not exist for those projects, the Party would have to invent it,' commented a young Moscow economist. 'Every generation has its big Siberian project. There was the Bratsk generation. Now the BAM generation. I have been on one of those projects and the conditions were miserable. The mosquitoes nearly ate us alive. They got into our hair, our tents, our food, everywhere. We Komsomols worked like slaves, from early morning to late evening. I made nearly 500 rubles that summer. At first it seemed like a lot but I spent quite a bit getting there and living there. It didn't seem like so much money when I got home. But it's a way of getting the country mobilized.'

'People know that the real dirty work is done by convict labor,' added a Leningrader whom I knew. 'They know that most of the young Komsomol brigades are pressured into going out there and that older workers go for the 'long ruble' [the high pay bonuses]. Still, it stirs national pride when people read: "We are building a new railroad across Siberia," or "We have built the world's largest dam." Notice the way these big projects are described. Not so much for their precise economic benefits but for transformation of the country-side. Their importance is more ideological than economic. Without that sort of thing, there would be no idealism left. Without those projects, how else would we know we were "building Communism"?'

The Westerner who has not ventured across Siberia by rail has difficulty grasping the immensity of the Soviet Union. The brain is ill-equipped to comprehend the geographic meaning of a nation that encompasses eleven time zones. It is not ready to absorb the fact that Leningrad is much closer to New York than to Vladivostok. Americans are accustomed to conceiving their own country as continental in dimensions but it shrinks next to the vastness of the Soviet interior. The United States plus half of Canada would fit into Siberia alone. The 3,200-mile trip from Moscow to Irkutsk is like a flight from New York to Los Angeles, and yet that is only half the journey across the Soviet Union.

The omens of a formidable passage appears even before one boards a Trans-Siberian train. Russians, who have a way of taking possession of a train as if it were a motorized wagon caravan, arrive at the station burdened with cheap, battered suitcases, boxes desparately strung together, gifts, toys, lumpy bundles and unraveling packages. Before departure, they provision themselves with whole loaves of brown bread, hunks of cheese, rations of cold, cooked fish or meat patties, and string bags bursting with sticky sweet Russian soda pop or watery beer. Once on board, they flood the interior and transform it into a mobile tenement, changing immediately into blue warm-up pajama outfits, gathering whole clans in their four- and six-bed compartments, the women peeling cucumbers or fondling children while the men, scratching and yawning in their undershirts, play chess or squint at newspapers.

In a world where the passenger train has all but passed away, the railroad still has magnificent mystique in Russia. The old first-class wagons, with their faded wine-colored curtains, quaint lamps and doilies on the writing tables, and curved brass handles on the doors have a turn-of-the-century romanticism that always made my wife feel like Anna Karenina. The borscht or solyanka soup in the dining car may be served in institutional metal bowls, but in each car a samovar chugs and puffs constantly, its fire stoked by a plump and talkative attendant, ready to supply tea and sweet biscuits at any hour. The old Russian cars, built for the widest gauge track in the world, contained a special luxury for me – the longest bunks in my experience of train riding. On trains, too, Russians had the time and the nerve to gossip with strangers, and we talked with them at great length on trains. Our one concern, as we headed for Siberia, was that the train might be cold. It was a needless worry: like all Russian interiors in winter, the train was so over-heated that we burst out for fresh air at every available stop.

The snail's pace at which we crawled was a great instructor in distances. Like some creaking merchant vessel patiently plying a vast inland sea, our train crept across the continental expanse. The Moscow-Peking Express, it was called (5,630 miles in 175 hours, according to a notice on our car). We went only half way, to Irkutsk, but for four long days we stared out the windows at the changeless scene of gently undulating snowfields giving way to forests of birch and larch, giving way again to snowfields. We felt like passengers on an ocean voyage gazing out at the rolling waves. The snowbound hamlets with their weatherbeaten, smoking peasant *izbas*, floated past like unconnected islands, seemingly uninhabited in the sea of snow.

I had imagined Siberia as having been filled up by waves of settlers, much as the American West. But what impressed me most on that train trip was the sparseness of humanity and the enormous emptiness of the land. Cities would suddenly loom up without the warning of suburbs and then, after we stopped briefly, would vanish just as suddenly. The petty barter from ship-to-shore marked the progress of our voyage across the continent. The dining car left Moscow well stocked with fresh apples, oranges, cucumbers, chocolate candy and other little delicacies. At the early stops, town-folk would rush to purchase these goodies from the dining car staff leaning out doors and windows. But later, as supplies ran low and the menu became more restricted, the trade shifted the other way. Although there was only meager fare 'on shore' at Zima Junction, we joined the rush of other passengers to the station kiosks for sweet buns, beer and fresh newspapers. A few old crones, wrapped in black coats and woolen scarves, were hawking homemade pickles and steaming boiled potatoes at 25 kopecks a pound, while other women shoveled coal onto the train or chipped off icicles that had gathered beneath drains or had frozen up the couplings. Once I saw a woman batter off a chunk of metal along with the ice, look at it, and walk away with a shrug.

So modest and disappointing were the Ural Mountains that we crossed them almost without noticing the striped post that marks the continental divide between Europe and Asia, the official beginning of Siberia. But after two more days of travel we were aware of passing into another hemisphere when we reached Irkutsk. Droves of young Soviet soldiers, back on a quick leave from Mongolia or posts along the Sino-Soviet frontier and chasing local girls, reminded us that China was near.

On the train I had heard Russian passengers quizzing the car attendants about life in Peking. Other travelers who had covered the Far Eastern leg of the Trans-Siberian route talked of seeing Russian helicopter pads and troop installations from the passing train, units of the massive garrison of 40 divisions and a million troops that Russia keeps along its disputed frontier with China. Later, I would hear of sealed zinc coffins coming back through Irkutsk in April, 1974, which residents presumed were from some undisclosed border clash. But then, in 1972, after Nixon had been to Peking but before he had paid his first visit to Moscow, Russians nervously pressed me to explain why America was siding with China against Russia. So keenly do Russians feel their rivalry with the Chinese that I was repeatedly asked about our diplomacy with China, especially when I visited regions close to the frontier with China.

On no other issue did private opinion seem to coincide more closely with the official line than in the deep-seated Russian fear and mistrust of the Chinese. Intellectuals talked of the Chinese as the new barbarians: peasants brainwashed in the fields with loudspeakers, life entirely militarized, people mindless with Maoism. That is the way press articles and television shows depicted China. It struck me as ironic that these Russian intellectuals had the same image of China that the West had had of Russia under Stalin at the peak of the Cold War. Indeed, they talked of the Chinese as the new Stalinists. The 'Chinese military threat' was another bugaboo. A Russian journalist back in Moscow from Byelorussia, a continent away from China, told me that people in Minsk were worried about war with Peking. In Moscow, mothers would talk about not wanting their sons to serve draft tours along the Sino-Soviet frontier the way American mothers did not want their boys in Vietnam. In border zones or cities near the frontier, like Irkutsk, the hatred and suspicion of the Chinese seemed especially strong. At times, people spoke bitterly about the bloodshed with the Chinese over Damansky Island in 1969.

Over lunch one day in an Irkutsk restaurant, where we shared a table with a young computer programmer, we got a dose of local anti-Chinese resentment – fanned, we were told by others, in closed political lectures. From the far side of Lake Baikal, less than 50 miles to the east, the computer man said, you could see Mongolia and China. (It seemed too far away to me, but he insisted.) In a candid, imperialistic affront to the nominal independence of Mongolia, he talked genially of that country as 'our 16th Republic' – an insult tantamount to calling Mexico the 51st state. Mongolians he liked, but not the Chinese.

'We used to have many of them here in Irkutsk, in our institutes and in our factories,' he said. 'We taught them everything. Now they are gone and look how they treat us.' He was embittered by the Chinese polemics in the press and on Peking radio.

'Don't any Chinese come here at all anymore?' I asked, meaning civilians or diplomats, but he took it militarily, and bristled with chauvinism.

'No, no, no,' he declared. 'We have enough troops along the frontier to handle them. Here. Everywhere. They can't come into Russia. My brother was at Damansky. We showed them there. And if they try something new, we will show them again.' With that, he made a strong, clenched fist, a characteristic Russian gesture of power.

For Siberians, dams symbolize Russian might, just as do troops and rockets. They embody man's conquest over nature and they are an article of the Communist faith. In his drive to modernize Russia, Lenin preached: 'Communism is Soviet power plus electrification of the entire country,' and his apostles took him so literally that they have zealously been erecting what the poet Yevgeny Yevtushenko called 'temples of kilowatts'. The particular temple that inspired Yevtushenko was Bratsk High Dam, which he immortalized in an epic poem: *The Night of Poetry*.

> In the Bratsk station, Russia, your motherly image
> Shimmeringly unfolded itself to me.

Bratsk epitomizes the New Jerusalem, the Soviet blueprint for Siberia – a huge hydroelectric project feeding a cluster of new industries, a new city hacked out of pine forest beside a gorge on the rushing Angara River at an isolated spot 750 miles further north than Montreal. It was there I met Aleksandr Borisovich Gurevich, a Ukrainian Jew who typified the priesthood of Siberian true believers.

Broad-shouldered, square-jawed, and irrepressibly ebullient, Sasha Gurevich had responded in his youth to the Communist Party's call for eager Komsomols to come build the world's mightiest dam and to hell with the hardships. He was an incurable romantic whose utopian faith in the wonders of industrialization was blended with undimmed 18th-century idealism about the perfectability of man. Perhaps it was only a pose, but true to his intellectual environment, he seemed oblivious to the disquieting insights of Freud or the implications of Stalinist terror as he spouted catechisms of optimism from every culture. At breakfast, for he spent practically every waking moment with Ann and me during our two days in Bratsk, Sasha proclaimed his admiration for Jack London's *Call of The Wild* and for Walt Whitman because of 'Whitman's love of humanity.' At dinner, he entertained and exhausted us with poetic recitations including a flawless rendition, in English and in

412

Russian, of Rudyard Kipling's 'If you can keep your head when all about you are losing theirs and blaming it on you . . . ' Films like *Andrei Rublev*, which portrayed the time of the Mongol conquest, among other things, disturbed him because they showed the suffering of Russia and the dark side of its history. His two all-time favorites were Eisenstein's *Battleship Potemkin* and *Chapayev*, heroic epics of the 1905 Revolution and of the legendary Red Army civil war commander, Vasily Chapayev.

He was annoyed with the life-style of Russian youth with their hunger for Western rock music, their hankering for modern fashions, their political indifference, their lackadaisical attitude toward work. 'What have they ever done that really counts?' he demanded. In his own youth he had been educated as a journalist but had volunteered to come to Bratsk as a rockdriller, he said, because he could not resist enlisting in the army of 54,000 construction workers building the nation's most vital project. 'When the Party says, "You must," the Komsomols answer, "We will," ' Sasha declared with extravagant enthusiasm. (When I repeated that old Komsomol slogan to people back in Moscow, many winced at the cliché loyalty.) But Sasha was a Party man, a lecturer in Marxism-Leninism at the local pedagogical institute, a propagandist who tried to tell me that we were all part of the international proletariat and that I should throw off the mental chains that made me think of myself as a middle-class American.

Sasha claimed to have no regrets about having followed his spirit of patriotism and adventurism to Bratsk. Building that dam had been his finest hour. 'It was our October!' Sasha enthused, comparing the 13-year struggle (from 1954 to 1967) to erect Bratsk High Dam to the October Revolution in 1917.

Like Jay Gatsby watching reruns of old college football games and imagining the roar of the crowds, Sasha took us to a movie on the construction of the Bratsk High Dam at a club where the director, one of his contemporaries now in paunchy middle age, fondly remembered the dam as 'a monument to our youth'. Nostalgically, Sasha relived every agonizing moment of the tedious transport of equipment up the frozen Angara in the depth of winter, the dynamiting of the gorge, the installation of the first stage coffer dams. He relished every miserable cold night without electricity in the early years. 'That's why we had such a high birthrate – no electricity and nothing else to do,' he laughed. He remembered every mosquito bite. 'The mosquitoes attacked us worst in June, just like Hitler's armies, so we called them Fascists,' he grinned.

By any standard Bratsk High Dam is an impressive achievement. As we had flown northward from Irkutsk to Bratsk, we had caught glimpses of the dam from the air – a narrow line holding back a sprawling lake, locally known as 'the Bratsk Sea'. Up close, the dam was mesmerizing as water gracefully tumbled through its spillways and power lines hummed and rasped over our heads. Serenely, it rose a sheer 400 feet blocking the rocky Padun Gorge with a half-mile-wide wall of concrete. A spur of the Trans-Siberian Railroad was superimposed on top. Not only was it gigantic, but it was the brightest, most modern, cleanest, best-maintained Soviet industrial installation that I visited.

Merely seeing it, Sasha was a geyser of more superlatives than the engineers who built and ran it. 'Biggest in the world,' he gushed. 'Well, not quite any more,' cautioned Lev Ablogin, the short, stout, red-faced deputy directory of the dam. It had been the biggest when it was finished in 1967 but its 4.1 million kilowatt capacity had been overtaken by a newer Soviet dam at Krasnoyarsk with 6 million.

'But its output is the biggest in the world,' Sasha insisted knowingly, and Ablogin proudly agreed that as of 1972, no other dam had produced so much energy in one year as Bratsk.

Ablogin kindly took us through the dam and showed us diagrams and a map of the entire complex. Again, Sasha could not contain himself. Bratsk Sea was 'the biggest man-made lake in the world', he asserted. 'Well, almost,' Ablogin responded. The Kariba Dam on the Zambezi River in Africa had backed up a larger lake, but he thought Bratsk Sea was second. Then, as Ablogin was explaining the 'pioneer frontal method' of dam construction, Sasha quickly interjected that Bratsk High Dam was 'the highest in the world' built that way. Again, Ablogin had to qualify by observing that Canada was building a slightly higher dam by the same method at Churchill Falls in Labrador.

Each answer pained Ablogin and pained Sasha even more because like so many Siberians – and like Russians generally – they exulted in those words, 'biggest in the world', with a national pride in bigness that seemed to compensate for the burning humiliation that many Russians feel at being industrially second best to the West. As if suffering from an acute national Avis complex, they grasp for any chance to compensate, which is one reason that so many officials meeting Westerners exaggerate Soviet accomplishments. Ablogin was unusual in his professional accuracy. Sasha was more typical. For most Russians, biggest means best. The dream of building the biggest was what had inspired Sasha and his generation, and Sasha could not bear to have that dream tarnished. His caustic disparagement of the younger generation was a reflection of his anger that they no longer cared about building a Utopia, about being biggest and first.

It was not from Sasha that we heard, for example, that close to half of the original 54,000 construction workers at Bratsk had left for other projects or had gone back to European Russia because they could not stomach life in Siberia. Nor was he the one who mentioned that Soviet economists like Abel Agenbegyan, Director of the Institute of Economics at Novosibirsk, had singled out Bratsk as a prime example of helter-skelter 'unbalanced' development because the builders had rushed ahead too enthusiastically with the dam, producing power by 1961 whereas its main intended customer, Bratsk aluminum plant, began production only in 1966 and was not completely built for several more years.

Piecemeal, the drab realities of everyday life in Bratsk came through to us. In its heyday, as the nation's top priority project, Bratsk had commanded special supplies of food and other consumer goods. But now those priorities had passed further north to Ust-Ilimsk and other new projects. In March, we found the shelves of Bratsk food shops pretty barren. One housewife complained that fresh fruits and vegetables disappeared for the five worst winter months. We saw only a few scraps of meat and people said it was seldom available. In a children's store, I happened upon a furious fight among mothers over an unexpected shipment of girl's underpants. A professional woman complained that cultural life was absolutely dead. 'I could not bear to live here if it were not for my long trip home (to European Russia) every summer,' she groused.

To me what was most depressing was the naked, Orwellian monotony of row upon row of identical gray prefab apartment blocks in the eight settlements of Bratsk, officially designated Bratsk-1, Bratsk-2, Bratsk-3 and so on. The one pleasantly rustic community was the old Padun township where the early construction workers had been housed in wooden buildings, now repainted. The other settlements had been bulldozed out of the pine forest. Hardly any pines were left standing. I was told that Prime Minister Kosygin had chastized city officials for the numbing sterility of the architecture and for stripping the city naked of greenery.

Elsewhere as well I ran into evidence of this dark side of Siberian development yet I marveled at the Russian determination to keep throwing up large new communities (Bratsk had 160,000 people) in the inhospitable regions of the far north in defiance of the elements, both natural and human. By 'dark side' I do not mean the estimated one or two million inmates of Soviet labor camps legally condemned to work in Siberia, but the travails of ordinary people who pay a punishing price for the way the Soviet system has mounted its assault on Siberia. A few Soviet specialists have suggested putting only small settlements in the icy north to work the natural resources, reinforced in summer by labor and construction crews from larger, permanent settlements in more tolerable climates to the south. But so far, that is not the vision of Soviet planners.

The development of towns like Nizhnevartovsk and Surgut in the West Siberian oil country is typical. In the mid-Sixties, both were sleepy villages of a few thousand souls. The oil boom transformed them. Now, at a latitude equivalent to that of Anchorage, Alaska (pop.: 48,000), each has shot up to 50,000 people and Soviet blueprints call for growth to 150,000. They are to become hubs for development of oil and natural gas fields even further north. These two island settlements are set in frozen marshlands that turn into impassable swamps in spring and summer. Roads cost about $2 million a mile to build. The Ob River, the main supply line for all construction materials, is frozen from September to May. The payoff for the state is the 60 million tons (about 420 million barrels) of oil produced by the phenomenal Samotlor field in 1974.

To show us that there was a payoff for individuals as well, local officials produced for a group of visiting Western journalists the chief of a champion oil drilling rig at Samotlor who said he earned, with all pay bonuses and hardship differentials, about $1,500 a month, an astronomical figure compared with the average industrial wage of $187. His pay was exceptional, but other men made $500–600 a month and oil trust officials insisted they had no trouble recruiting workers. Nizhnevartovsk was a classic Soviet company town where the local oil trust not only hired workers for all trades, operated the river port and imported all goods and supplies, but arranged vacation trips, built and ran the bus system, the clinics, kindergartens, schools, and stores, and provided housing. Officials confidently told us that housing and community services were in excellent shape, though whenever we asked for a quick look, we were told our schedule did not allow time for it.

The official version did not square with reports in the Soviet press or a few accidental encounters with local people, which made it immediately apparent that production came first and the workers were treated as pawns. No sooner had we returned to Moscow than *Pravda* ran a sharp critique of the very cities we had visited, chiding local officials for inadequate housing and services, charging that apartment buildings were being occupied without heating, water or sewerage and with inadequate insulation. Other publications later reported that housing construction in the entire West Siberian oil region was only about 40 percent of what had been planned. An engineer from Nizhnevartovsk complained in a letter to the editor in early 1975 that the city had not a single movie house and workers felt lucky if they landed tickets to see old movies at the oil workers' club. Another workman from Surgut wrote that the oil workers' club there had been under construction for seven years and was still not completed, an indication of the low priority of desperately needed leisure facilities. Soviet academic publications estimated that the cost of living in Siberia was 40 to 80 percent higher than elsewhere, eating up much of the pay bonuses. The Writers' Union weekly, *Literary Gazette*, deplored the 'suitcase mood' of the vast majority of workers who were going into Siberia on assignment for a short while, making big pay and clearing out. One article, in August 1973, added the 'unexpected discovery' that 'the most unstable group is the workers with the highest average pay'.

A graphic illustration of the hardships had actually greeted us when we landed in Surgut in a developing snowstorm. The airport was jammed with probably 200 people sleeping on luggage, sprawled on window ledges and enveloped by an air of stale weariness that spoke of an interminable wait. Our two Soviet chaperones from the Novosti Press Agency quickly shepherded us to a VIP lounge segregated from the Russians. But, lingering by a newspaper kiosk, I was accosted by an angry woman with exhausted eyes. Obviously taking me for a Russian in my fur hat and sheepskin coat, she burst out with the proposal that we go together to the district Communist Party Committee to complain. She said her family – and later, I discovered, many of the other people as well – had been stuck in that airport building, with no indoor plumbing, no sleeping quarters and only a pitiful little sandwich buffet, for six days.

'Six days?' I asked incredulously.

'We have been in the airport six days waiting for a flight to Khanty-Mansisk (about 250 miles away),' she repeated. 'We have been living here, washing ourselves in the snow outside. The luggage room is too small to take our suitcases, so we sit on them. My two children should be in school. I have to take care of my family. We've been complaining but nothing happens. Let's go to the Raikon [Party Committee] together and maybe they can do something.'

It was not that there had been no flights, I learned, but that available planes were used for official business or for the main runs, not for local runs like the one she and others wanted. Another woman seated nearby, realizing I was a stranger, tried to stop the woman from talking to me. 'Do you know to whom you're talking?' she admonished.

But the first woman was so desperate she would not desist. 'What does that mean, "to whom I am talking"? You don't need to butt in.' But by then, one of my official Soviet guides reappeared and insisted that I join the group in the VIP lounge. Within a couple of hours, when the weather cleared, we left on another flight, but the crowd in the airport remained.

The common explanation by Soviet officialdom is that the raw new Siberian towns, as rough as Dodge City in its early days, are for the young who can take the bumps. Come summertime, loyal *Siberyaki* insist, the enchantment and freedom of hunting and fishing in the open Siberian country and the arrival of supplies by riverboat compensate for the rigors of winter. To a certain extent, that is true. 'The big cities are too crowded,' a 23-year-old factory worker told me in Bratsk. 'People there are always pushing and shoving. Here it's peaceful and quiet. In summer, I like to go hunting and boating in my outboard on the Bratsk Sea.'

Yet it was in Bratsk that Deputy Mayor Aleksandr Semeyusov rather candidly conceded to me that juvenile delinquency, car theft, and radio hooliganism were a problem among a restless young generation that lacked a strong sense of purpose. That was symptomatic of broader problems. The early idealism had faded, Semeyusov said, and many young people found the new reality bleak and humdrum. It was hard to motivate them. 'It does not sound so romantic to talk about running a timber factory and an aluminum plant as when we were building the dam and a new city,' he acknowledged. In other words, the New Jerusalem of Bratsk had been more successful as a community during the raw muscular enthusiasm of its construction era than as a utopian blueprint for permanent communities of the future.

XIV

INFORMATION
White Tass and Letters to the Editor

> A censored press only serves to demoralize. That
> greatest of vices, hypocrisy, is inseparable from it.
> . . . The government hears only its own voice while
> all the time deceiving itself, affecting to hear the
> voice of the people while demanding that they also
> support the pretense. And on their side, the people
> either partly succumb to political skepticism or
> completely turn away from public life and become
> a crowd of individuals, each living only his own
> private existence.
>
> Karl Marx, 1842

In early August 1972, Moscow was enveloped for days in a
mysterious blue haze. It hung motionless over the city. The
big domestic airport at Domodyedovo, south of Moscow,
had to divert flights because of poor visibility. From our
eighth-floor apartment some mornings, we could see no more
than 300 yards. Muscovites were coughing terribly, wiping
tears from their eyes. Streetcars and automobiles were forced
to use headlights. People were alarmed by rumors that fires
in the fields around Moscow were menacing populated
areas. Yet for nearly a week, the press said nothing. Finally,
one skimpy back-page article mentioned a peat-bog fire near
Shatura, about 60 miles east of Moscow. Two days later
another newspaper added the obvious fact that 'smoke had
reached Moscow' but did not say whether the city was in
danger. The smoke seemed too dense and stable to have
been blown 60 miles.

I knew a middle-aged scientist, anxious to learn more,
who tried to bluff some information out of the Central Moscow Fire Station. Posing as the doctor for the prestigious

Writers' Union, he telephoned the fire station claiming that he had patients sick with pneumonia and in danger from inhaling the smoke. He demanded to know whether they should be evacuated from the city.

'The chief is out at the fire,' the dispatcher told him.

'Then give me the deputy,' the scientist said.

'He's out at the fire, too.'

'Then, let me talk to someone in charge.'

'They're all out at the fire,' the dispatcher insisted. 'I'm the only one left.'

'Then you tell me how serious it is and how long you think it will last,' the scientist said. 'I need to know if it's under control.'

'I don't know,' the dispatcher said. 'They're all out at the fire and they still can't do anything about it.'

My friend hung up feeling more uneasy than when he began. In a few days, however, the smoke abated. Another article appeared, blaming the bad summer drought for fires in the peat-bogs but also announcing regulations against camping, picnicking, and lighting fires in a large, tinder-dry region around Moscow. Obviously a lot was being left unsaid. Much later, some officials were cited for heroism and an obituary of one youth was printed, discreetly placed on the inside pages. Ultimately, in bits and pieces, it came out that fires had broken out in early July, fully a month before the press mentioned them, and had raged over thousands of acres. More than 1,000 firefighters including planes, para-troopers and entire military units had joined the battle. It turned out that some fires were extinguished no more than 15–20 miles from the Kremlin, very close to populated suburbs of Moscow. Yet most of the press printed practically nothing and *Pravda*, the Party's flagship newspaper, ran not a word.

The absence of such routine and obviously necessary information is typical. Russians take it as a fact of life that much of the information they need to know just to get along day by day does not appear in their press. I was talking one evening about this problem with the scientist who had called the fire station. We had gone out for a walk. 'Going for a walk' has a special meaning for Russians because it is the standard precaution for talking frankly about some sensitive aspect of Soviet life safely out of earshot of telephone taps or room-bugs. We were taking our walk not far from the

Foreign Ministry in the Old Arbat, a warren of peeling 18th- and 19th-century homes with fussy stucco moldings and faded Victorian façades, the former homes of nobility or intellectuals like Gogol, Herzen and Scriabin, now museums or communal apartments with laundry hung incongruously behind lace curtains. That evening a mid-October rain had left a penetrating London dampness and deserted streets. I asked my scientist friend what impact the restrictions on information had on people's personal lives.

He told the tragic story of a young woman from Central Asia who had flown the year before from Karaganda to Moscow to take entrance examinations for Moscow State University. She was scheduled to spend a week in Moscow. Her parents waited ten days and became concerned at hearing nothing from her or from friends in Moscow. After two weeks, the father himself flew to Moscow to try to find her. When he got to the University, he was told that his daughter had never appeared for the exams and people knew nothing about her. He called on family friends with whom she had thought of staying but they had not seen her. He went to the police. At one precinct station, an officer suggested trying the airport police detachment. There, as everywhere, he appealed for help in locating his daughter. Only then was he informed confidentially – and instructed to keep the information confidential – that her plane from Karaganda to Moscow had crashed and she had been killed with other passengers. He was stunned: it was the first he or his friends had heard of the plane crash.

The Soviet press does not report such catastrophes except in the rare cases where foreigners or Soviet VIPs are involved, and then only briefly and cryptically. This means that ordinary people are not alerted by the press to the possibility that someone dear to them may have died in an airplane crash. What is more, my scientist friend explained, Aeroflot often does not take down the addresses of passengers or their next of kin. So when a plane goes down, Aeroflot does not know whom to notify. That is why this poor man had to go hunt for his missing daughter and dig out the sad news for himself.

This technique of silence of the Soviet press undermines its credibility. In October 1974, a Jack-the-Ripper murderer was stalking Moscow's streets. Enough women were killed on the sidewalks for Muscovites to suffer a bad case of nerves over street crime and to worry that things had gotten 'as bad as New York', as one plump matron said to me. During that period, I heard more real personal stories from Russians about robbings, burglaries, purse-snatching, and car thefts than I had ever imagined took place. When our office called the Moscow police about the reported murderer, we got the brush-off. But Soviet women told me they were being officially warned at work not to go out at night, and were being cautioned by apartment watchmen not to open their doors to strangers. 'My husband is more gallant than he has been in years,' one gray-haired Russian lady told me, half-jokingly. 'He's never worried about me before. But now he insists on meeting me at the bus stop and walking me home after dark.' Auxiliary police, called in to expand the man-hunt, were given a portrait of a handsome, friendly, muscular young blond with a weakness for women who wore red.

The press printed nothing, though I learned that at one newspaper office the staff was told that seven women had been stabbed to death by a psychopath. From that and other similar briefings, rumors spread. There were said to be not one killer but two, then a gang. For days we heard that a train transferring a large load of young psychopaths from one prison to another had derailed and 200 convicts had escaped and were loose in Moscow. Later the figure rose to 500. Ultimately, on October 28, police officials who had previously shied away from admitting a problem to the Western press, privately told Reuters, the British news agency, that they had arrested a young man believed responsible for 11 women's deaths – three in the previous 24 hours – and had him put under psychiatric observation. This report was confirmed elsewhere. Yet that same day, in an apparent attempt to reassure Moscow's jittery populace, the newspaper *Evening Moscow* quoted Viktor Pashkovsky, deputy chief of the Moscow police, as saying, 'No dangerous crimes have been committed in the city in the last ten days.'

My Russian friends reacted with total skepticism, so great had the credibility gap become. They scoffed at Pashkovsky's ludicrous denial that there had been any killings. They knew better than that from what they had been told privately at work and from comments of individual police officers. But they felt so deceived that they also disbelieved the Western press version that the killer had now been caught and the danger was really over.

'They may have caught one,' said one middle-aged mother whose response was fairly typical, 'but there is a second killer. They still have not caught the main one.'

It takes a great leap of imagination for Westerners, especially Americans who are literally blitzed by information, to picture the poverty of information in Russia. In the past decade Americans have been inundated by news cascading over them simultaneously with events – by the Vietnam war exploding on television screens or a Watergate Presidency crumbling before their eyes. They are submerged by a Niagara of information that Russians are routinely denied – not only inside information like the Pentagon Papers or background information leaked by a Henry Kissinger, but economic information on the latest wiggle of the consumer price index or the unemployment rate, sociological information on crime, smoking or sex habits, opinion polls on politicians or race relations, census information about divorce rates, migration, education, or unsolicited advertising information on fads and bargains.

Russia by comparison is an information vacuum. Strictly speaking, of course, it is not a perfect vacuum because the world of science has its own body of information and because the Soviet press and libraries teem with cheerful official statistics that limn what one Soviet pamphlet immodestly termed 'the story of the unprecedented growth and all-round development' of the socialist homeland and trace 'a path unparalleled in history'. But hard, down-to-earth useful information is rationed out in dribs and drabs. It is restricted, as the Marquis de Custine, a French nobleman, observed on a trip to czarist Russia, by the legendary Russian obsession with secrecy. ('In Russia secrecy presides over everything: secrecy – administrative, political, social,' Custine wrote in 1839, and it still holds.) Like their czarist predecessors, Soviet officials find it distasteful to admit anything has gone wrong or has gotten out of hand, as with airplane crashes or the summer fires around Moscow. They are obsessively insecure about admitting failure. Perhaps they restricted information about the Jack-the-Ripper murderer in order not to panic people or to deny criminals dramatic publicity that would encourage more crime. But I suspect that this, too, is more of the same – covering up awkward facts that suggest something is amiss and reveal that the weeds of crime have somehow grown in the healthy garden of Soviet socialism. Sometimes, too, information is bottled up through sheer bureaucratic clumsiness. More often it is withheld because the powers-that-be (and this can be mere petty bureaucrats) reckon that the ordinary man or woman simply has no real need-to-know.

The first visit to Moscow of President Nixon in May 1972 stands out in my mind as an example of keeping the public unnecessarily in the dark, not just about the high politics but the simple mechanics of the occasion. In advance, the Western press was full of stories about the trip whereas the Soviet press carried only a single advance story (though Muscovites were amply forewarned by the thorough face-lifting given their city and were joking about 'the big *kniksen*', a play on the Russian word for curtsy). On the day Nixon was due to arrive, *The New York Times* ran a map of his motorcade route from the VIP airport at Vnukovo to the Kremlin. But no route was shown in Soviet newspapers. Even the timing of his arrival was undisclosed except to those discerning enough to decipher the real meaning of an item innocuously labeled '4 p.m. – International Program' in the daily television diary.

Thousands profited from that little tip and played hookey from work to try to see the first American President ever to visit their capital. But many of them miscalculated because their information was insufficient. I came across one crowd of about 2,000 still standing eight rows deep at Manezh Square, not far from the Kremlin, fully half an hour after Nixon had been deposited inside the fortress by a motorcade that had used another entrance, blocks away and out of sight.

'Why are you waiting?' I asked several people.

'To see,' replied a shirt-sleeved student with a briefcase.

'Why didn't you wait at the other end of the Kremlin where he was supposed to go?' I inquired.

'Because this is better – a better view,' he asserted in ignorance.

'But Nixon has already gone into the Kremlin – at the other end,' I said. 'I saw him go in. It's all over.'

'Oh,' said the young man, frozen to his spot. I walked away, but the crowd remained, patient, hopeful, and unknowing.

That first Nixon visit to Moscow was a striking illustration of how effectively the Soviet leadership can insulate its own public from political reality. The entire event took place in a different dimension for Russians than for the Western public. Ordinary Russians were too ill-informed to fathom either the trial or the triumph of that summit.

No Soviet citizen outside a narrow slice of the political elite had been given any reason to expect important accords to be signed on limiting the strategic arms race. The acronymic stepchildren of the nuclear balance of terror – SALT, ICBM, MIRV, ABM – never had a chance to become household words because they had rarely been mentioned to the Soviet public. Soviet news coverage of arms negotiations over the previous two and a half years had been limited to the bland, unrevealing arrival-and-departure statements of chief negotiators. So much in the dark was everyone but those at the pinnacle of power that one thoroughly trusted and experienced Soviet journalist foolishly bet me a bottle of cognac that there would be – and could be – no major arms agreement until the Vietnam war was settled. And the bet was made before the crisis over Nixon's mining of Haiphong harbor. The journalist simply knew nothing about the progress already made in the arms talks, which had been quite evident in the Western press.

On Haiphong, too, the Soviet public was spared the agony of being informed. In Washington, the sense of confrontation over the mining of Haiphong harbor was palpable. The world press blossomed with comparisons to the Cuban missile crisis of 1962 and speculation about Soviet minesweepers trying to break the mine blockade. Nixon was accused by Democrats of risky brinksmanship and the White House seemed to encourage the interpretation that it wanted to force a showdown with Moscow.

Given that picture, intelligent Soviets would undoubtedly have found it hard to understand how the Kremlin could stomach such humiliation and go through with the Nixon visit at the price of disagreement with allies in Hanoi who were burning mad over the mining. Pyotr Shelest, the Ukrainian Communist Party boss, reportedly lost his job for urging the Politburo to call off the visit. But because the Brezhnev-led majority chose to slide around Nixon's challenge rather than meet it head-on, the Soviet press kept its citizenry in the dark. For 20 days before, during, and after the summit, the controlled press did not mention the mining except for one brief aside buried in one news item. Moreover, it ignored the return to Moscow during the summit talks of a plane carrying two dead and 20 wounded Soviet seamen back from North Vietnam, casualties of American air raids against port areas. Normally an item for blistering attacks on America, this news was inconvenient to the Kremlin. So it was suppressed.

The result, not surprisingly, was that ordinary Russians took Soviet press denunciations of American air raids against North Vietnam as routine. They knew too little of the dangerous situation to share the real frustration of the Soviet elite – just as after the summit, the Soviet public understood too little to share the leadership's sense of triumph at the agreements reached. For months afterwards, I was asked privately to explain the accords to Soviet scientists, writers, and other intellectuals. No one had bothered to read the texts of the agreements which were printed by the press verbatim without the explanation necessary to make them intelligible. Moreover, the most important document – the protocol that specified the precise number of land missiles and missile submarines for each side – was never printed by Soviet newspapers. To have revealed to ordinary Russians that the two sides had agreed on such a precise calibration of their forces, one scientist told me, would have undermined the Party's campaign to maintain Cold War vigilance among the population and would have made it very difficult to continue to insist that Soviet scientists swear, as they must, that in publishing any innocent, totally nondefense-related academic paper, they are not disclosing anything secret. In other words, the rationale for an entire system of secrecy would unravel if the extent of the arms agreements was really understood by the Soviet intelligentsia.

The Nixon visit ended pretty much as it had begun. At the Kremlin, the day before Nixon's departure, an American reporter traveling with the President noticed a Russian couple approach the plainclothes security man at the Borovitsky Gate to ask when the Kremlin would be open again to the general public.

'I don't know,' the security man said curtly.

'We've come from Leningrad,' the Russians explained. 'We want to rearrange our plans in Moscow to be sure we have time later to see the Kremlin. Can you say when the

American delegation is leaving.'

An impassive, unyielding 'No' was all they got.

At this point the American reporter who had been standing nearby, went up to the Russian couple and explained what was general knowledge to readers of the Western press – that the Nixon party was leaving the next day. 'Perhaps the Kremlin will open after that,' he said.

It was a typical, revealing little episode. For often when Soviet officialdom restricts information available to ordinary Russians – whether street maps, telephone books, advertisements, when the Kremlin will reopen, or other seeming trivia of daily life that Westerners take for granted – it has no deep political motivation. Officials act out of sheer bloody-mindedness or an ingrained, habitual, arrogant Soviet disdain for 'the little man'.

Intourist, for example, would give out train and aircraft schedules by phone but steadfastly refused to disclose whether there were any seats available. Only in person could that be learned (*after* a hassle about travel permissions). Russians told me that if this frustrated us, they suffered much ruder treatment at railroad stations, ticket offices and stores. 'I never bother to phone a store to ask what they have,' one housewife advised. 'It's hopeless.' The only recourse is to go stand in line. Aeroflot seemed to have an unwritten commandment, or perhaps it was actually in writing somewhere, not to reveal whether its planes were departing or arriving late, a matter of some consequence since its service was so erratic that the chances of delay seemed better than 50–50. Yet its divisions of blue-uniformed ground clerks, whether bossy middle-aged matrons or busty young blondes, refused to give anything other than scheduled departure time. The nationwide loss of time over this policy of noncommunication must have been monumental. I personally spent many hours, up to 17 hours at one clip, and I knew other people who spent as many as 24 or 36 hours pinned to the air terminal waiting for planes. Practically everywhere I traveled, Soviet airports were littered with people, draped like wilted flowers over all available furniture, unable to stray from their tedious vigils because Aeroflot refused to inform them of a likely departure time.

428

With good reason, Americans groan about the continual bombardment of their senses by ads and commercials on television and in their press. But they might half reconsider if exposed for awhile to the consumer blackout in Russia. Lack of the most basic consumer information is one of the most enervating and crippling facets of Russian life. It is the main reason why Russian sidewalks are so constantly populated by shoppers earnestly plodding from store to store with their string bags and briefcases engaged in an unending hit-or-miss lottery, hoping to stumble onto a find or to bump into some strange woman on the street and ask her where she got those good-looking oranges.

Soviet advertising is no help to them because it is still so primitive. With the exception of housing exchanges where good detailed information is available, the Soviet consumer depends on expending shoe leather or on the informal grapevine. Soviet advertisements are typically institutional in style. ('Watches make the best presents' or 'If you want to live to ripe old age and be beautiful, modest, thorough and truthful, drink tea.') Most newspapers publish without ads though more popular ones like *Evening Moscow* run weekly ad supplements that are mostly personals and a few vaguely worded store ads. Television commercials, bunched together for short bursts on secondary channels at random hours, are amateurish and almost universally ignored. Rarely, if ever, do they tell listeners where to buy the products advertised, a basic flaw with much Soviet advertising.

The shopper looking for choice meat or a stylish dress has no handy yellow pages to let her 'fingers do the walking' nor the kind of specific daily newspaper supermarket or department store ads that in the West would tip her off where to shop. The closest approach is a 15-minute blurb of commercials on Moscow Radio at 1.45 p.m. (which many of my Soviet friends did not even know existed), where Ready-Made Clothing Store No 142 offers 'a large selection of men's suits, Soviet-made, all wool, half-wool with synthetics, or pure synthetic, from 70 to 150 rubles [$95–200],' or where Electrical Goods Store No 7 offers a 12-ruble [$16] trade-in for used washing machines on new ones. When I asked a mother of two about these ads, she brushed them aside with a disgusted grunt.

'Listen,' she said, 'there are basically two kinds of products: those which no one really wants and which sometimes get advertised, and the good items which are in short supply and which stores don't need to advertise.' This terse judgment was echoed by others.

In other words, Russians either get inside tips from well-placed friends or else do without. One tall, slender linguist with a face like Andy Gump, chortled smugly as he recalled a life-saving telephone call from a friend in December 1971. The friend had a tip that the next day Moscow's only new car outlet would let people sign up for the first 25,000 Zhiguli cars – the city's entire quota for two years. 'The guy told me he could hold me a place in line during the night – in spite of the cold they were already lining up out there to spend the night,' said the linguist. 'But I had to be there by dawn. My friend said it would be a mob scene the next day and he was right. After that, there were no more sign-ups. I had to wait about a year for my car, but I got it. Without that call, I would have been out of luck.' No one bothered to advertise that crucial event. Finding out was a matter of luck or the right connections.

Something as ordinary as a map is also a problem, though perhaps for more sinister reasons. Russians don't seem to miss street maps. Not having cars, they just ask each other general directions and take the bus or subway. But Ann and I liked maps for walking tours. In Moscow, some city newsstands sometimes carried subway and street maps. But almost everywhere else we traveled, it was impossible to get a street map, no matter how crude. When we would ask for them, Intourist guides would flood us with folders enticing us to travel to Yalta or some other distant point, or with brochures showing the local fountains, the university, and the main statue of Lenin. But maps were not part of the kit. We scoured bookstores. No maps. Clerks looked at us as if it were a stupid question. 'Military secret,' said a Soviet journalist opaquely. Another friend, laughing sympathetically at our map frustrations, confided that on the few available Moscow maps, the angles of the streets were purposely just a bit askew to foil Western intelligence. I couldn't tell by looking at them, but he said he wasn't joking.

Another common reference tool that Westerners take absolutely for granted – the telephone book – is an item of almost priceless rarity. One of the momentous events during our three years in Moscow was the publication of a new phone book. Until that moment – and even afterward –

Moscow must have ranked as the largest metropolis in the world without a readily available phone directory. Unlike Western telephone companies, the Soviet Ministry of Communications does not automatically provide phone books to subscribers. Nor are they available at pay phones or in other public places. But then, except for calling friends, Russians seem to use the phone a lot less than Westerners do.

The phone book that went on sale in 1973 was the first directory of personal telephone listings to be published in Moscow in 15 years (though a separate book on offices, stores, hospitals, and other public institutions is printed at somewhat more frequent intervals). The problem with this phone book, as with so many desirable items in the Soviet Union, is that supply made not even the barest pretense of satisfying demand. For a city of eight million people, the printers published 50,000 phone books. They sold out within a few days at city newsstands even though the full four-volume set cost a hefty 12 rubles ($16).

Those lucky enough to have a full set of office and personal directories noticed some oddities. The Moscow Province and City Administration occupied 32 pages of the office directory but the Communist Party Central Committee, the nation's most powerful and important body constituting a complete shadow government that matches the entire structure of government ministries, modestly gave only one number (206–25–11). Most ministries provided 15 or more numbers but the Defense Ministry listed only two. The Soviet space program went completely unlisted. The KGB, or secret police, listed a 24-hour inquiry office (221–07–62). But thousands of foreign diplomats, businessmen and newsmen living in the Soviet Union were entirely omitted, presumably in keeping with the official Soviet effort to isolate foreign residents from ordinary Soviet citizens as much as possible.

Those not fortunate enough to land one of the precious phone books could dial information (09) or go to one of the many little octagonal information kiosks dotted around Moscow. But that is not always so simple as it sounds. I learned that to get a number from the information operator, you needed the full name (first, last, and middle), and an extremely precise address. Once I was asked the year of birth of the person I was trying to reach and was so startled by the question that I apologized and hung up in confusion. I did not want to get the people in trouble and I was fearful that she might be checking extra closely because I spoke Russian with an accent. But Soviet friends later explained that these were routine questions from operators. Because people live in such massive apartment blocks (often several with the same street number but different building numbers) and because so many Russians have similar names and because there are so many communal telephones, the operators need very specific data to sort out one Ivan Ivanovich Ivanov from another.

Getting someone's address can be equally, if not more, trying as I noticed one day passing Moscow Information Service Booth #57 at Petrovka Street and the Boulevard Ring Road. Over the window on the booth was a sign that read: 'For obtaining information about the address of a Moscow resident, it is necessary to know: first, middle and last name; age; place of birth (city, province, district or village).' I could hardly believe my eyes. 'If I were looking for my mother,' wisecracked a young Moscow friend, 'I could do it. But not for anyone else.' Muscovites, he said, did not use the booths much; they were mostly for out-of-towners. And indeed near Red Square they line up for hours at the information kiosk, fresh off the train or plane from the hinterlands.

Knowing the various shortcuts in Soviet life, I was curious to see whether the system at Booth #57 actually operated according to the stated rules, so I hung around studying the schedule of charges while the gray-haired lady inside handled a customer. A man in a flat cap and brown padded coat approached. He fished out some change, pushed a coin through the window, and asked for the address of some friend who had moved. I could actually hear him rattling off full name, age, and birthplace of the other man. A pause. Then the lady slipped him a scrap of paper through the window. He pocketed the information which had cost him five kopecks – as much as a subway ride – and strode off. The schedule of prices showed what other information the lady had: suburban train information (2 kopecks), long distance train or plane information (5 kopecks), information on out-of-town rest homes and sanatoria (8 kopecks), travel information for trips on mixed means of transport – a combination of train, ship or riverboat – (10 kopecks), unspecified information of a legal character (5 kopecks), information on lost documents (10 kopecks), inquiries requiring a long time to fulfill (30 kopecks).

Like the rest of Soviet life, information is not a matter of money, but connections. The better his connections, the better informed a Soviet can be because information, like consumer goods, is rationed out according to rank. Party and government bigwigs, important ministry officials and propagandists for the main central newspapers, for example, receive both special briefings and a special daily news report from Tass. The ordinary service published for everyone and known as blue or green Tass, is the sanitized and censored version of reports from around the country and abroad, that has been tailored to fit the Party line and pruned of objectionable disclosures about the Soviet Union itself. Tass headquarters on Moscow's Boulevard Ring Road also acts as a filtering point for newspapers and magazines from all over the world. A Tass man once disclosed to me that 12 editors worked in the American section of Tass in Moscow in addition to the full complement of reporters in Washington and New York.

'What in the world do they all do?' I asked, 'There aren't but a few hundred words of Tass reports on America in the Soviet press every day. One man could handle that.'

Most of them, he confessed, work on 'service Tass' – meaning the special, secret Tass reports running one hundred pages or more daily, which circulate to government ministries, Party headquarters, and key newspaper offices. Often when I visited senior commentators for *Pravda* or *Izvestia,* I would see stacks of this special 'White Tass' service on their desks. It is a far richer and more detailed selection of foreign news and comment (including digests of dispatches sent out from Moscow by Western correspondents) than ordinary Tass. I was also told that White Tass includes accurate and revealing information on Soviet domestic affairs, such as reports of air and train accidents, statistics on crime, word of health epidemics, serious production deficiencies, crop reports and similar material that the regime would find embarrassing to print openly. Finally, I learned there is an even more rarefied edition of Tass, called 'Red Tass' because its covering summary is – or was – printed on red paper. It supposedly goes only to chief editors, the highest government officials and Communist Party bigshots. Despite this restricted handling, Soviet newsmen told me that the contents were not based on spy reports or special intelligence. Most of it would be ordinary news to a Western newspaper.

The gradations of Tass are but a part of an entire hierarchy of special publications for Soviet insiders with various degrees of trust and responsibility. For its mass propagandists, the Party puts out a weekly, *Atlas*, which contains a bit more detail on current events than most Soviet newspapers. Other organizations do the same but they are very skittish about acknowledging the existence of such special publications. John Shaw of *Time* magazine told me that just before Nixon's visit to Moscow in June 1974, he was at a public lecture in Moscow and noticed the young woman next to him, evidently a trade union activist, reading an article entitled 'What Is Impeachment?' This surprised him because up to then the Soviet press had not carried anything so explicit. He asked her for a look at the magazine. It turned out to be a translation of an East German article, simply explaining the mechanics of impeachment. But it went further than any normal Soviet publication in implying the weakness of Nixon's position. Shaw jotted down the title and phone number of the publication, an internal trade union organ, and noticed that it had a small circulation of about 2,000 – obviously intended for the central leadership and activists. The next day, he had his translator call to ask for a copy of the publication. But the editors insisted that not only were copies unavailable, but that no such publication existed, even though Shaw said he had read it himself.

A parallel phenomenon, vital to the functioning of the Soviet system, is the hierarchy of closed lectures. They are held for Party groups, officials in government ministries, newspaper staffs, scientific institutes, and for all kinds of specialized groups. One former Party lecturer, an intense young man who had become disillusioned by the privileges and cynicism of Party higher-ups, told me the lectures were used to provide more than usually candid explanations of Party policy, to start whisper campaigns against dissidents like Solzhenitsyn and Sakharov if the regime did not want to arouse the West by attacking them publicly, to discuss or explain away awkward developments like bad harvests, industrial accidents, or personnel shifts within the Party or

Government, or even to warn people about problems such as the Jack-the-Ripper murderer in Moscow in late 1974. The candor and the amount of information disclosed, this man said, is strictly geared to the importance and political reliability of the audience. At closed Party meetings, he said, 'if they asked the right questions, we were obliged to answer them. The kinds of information that we could give out, for instance, were what kind of harvest we had, how many tons of grain we bought abroad, and how much gold we paid for it, or things like how much our aid to Vietnam cost – it was costing us two million rubles [$2.67 million] a day. But there were some questions we never answered no matter who asked them. If someone asked what happened to that man who shot at Brezhnev, we did not answer such a question. Or if people asked when would the government lift the temporary price increases introduced under Khrushchev in 1962, we did not answer that question.' Before he left on lecture tours, he said, he was given instructions on what he could reveal to different categories of people – the most to top Party provincial and district officials; the least, to ordinary office workers. But he noticed one general effect at all levels: closed lectures made everyone feel like an insider, trusted and therefore committed.

Beyond these closed lectures, the *Znaniye*, or Knowledge Society runs innumerable public lectures, much blander than the closed ones but still more revealing than the Soviet press because they allow for question-and-answer periods. At these, I heard Russians asking about grain purchases from America, the treatment of Sakharov, the expulsion of Soviet military advisors from Egypt, or elements of the confrontation with America over trade and Jewish emigration. After the end of Soviet jamming of Voice of America and some other Western stations in September 1973, the questions seemed generally sharper than before, reflecting the fact that in big cities like Moscow and Leningrad, some people not only listened to Western radios but tried to use Western information in an attempt to pry more out of their own authorities. This practice, however, ebbed and flowed with news developments that interested Russians. As Western radio stations became more concerned with Western economic problems, the trend eased.

One idiosyncrasy of the Soviet system, aimed at keeping higher circles well informed without contaminating the minds of ordinary citizens, is the production of 'special editions' of significant and politically sensitive foreign books. Plenty of selected Western fiction, from Hemingway, Dreiser, and Galsworthy to Arthur Haley and Kurt Vonnegut, is translated into Russian and sold commercially, especially if it gives an unflattering image of Western life or morals. But important nonfiction of interest to the political elite and deemed too provocative for the Soviet public is translated and published in very limited special editions. Mikhail Agursky, a specialist in automated control systems and a dissident Jew who eventually emigrated, told me that during his establishment years he had seen special editions of books like John Kenneth Galbraith's *Modern Industrial State* or Bertrand Russell's *History of Western Philosophy*. From others, I learned of German linguists who had translated Hitler's *Mein Kampf* for Stalin's edification or William L. Shirer's *The Third Reich* for the contemporary leadership, not to mention English language experts who had translated all kinds of books on American strategic thinking.

These special editions, Agursky said, are marked 'only for service libraries' meaning that only high-level Party officials or Party researchers have access to them. They are easily distinguished from normal Soviet books because they do not carry a fixed price impressed right into their back cover as normal books do. Moreover, Agursky said, they are numbered individually, like highly classified documents in the West, so that no one can get away with a copy without a record of where it is and who is responsible for it.

Not only books but foreign periodicals are also distributed by rank in the Soviet system. Top-level editors, administrators, scientists and other VIPs are sometimes allowed the special privilege of receiving personal subscriptions to Western publications (including the U.S.I.A. propaganda magazine, *Amerika*). One scientist told me that Pyotr Kapitsa, head of the Institute of Physical Problems in Moscow, received his own copies of specialized publications in his field as well as *Science, Scientific American* or a general magazine like *Newsweek*, though at politically sensitive times Kapitsa's subscriptions were cut off. All such publications must, of course, be vetted by international mail censors or a central clearing house for foreign scientific publications. In Soviet technical libraries I have seen Western magazines that have been through this vetting process. The copies of *Scientific American* that I saw in one Moscow institute had odd white spaces in its table of contents and gaps elsewhere for articles that had been removed, evidently because they dealt with touchy issues like arms technology or made critical evaluations of Soviet science or policy. A science writer I knew told me of the awkward efforts of Soviet officials to cover up their excisions of embarrassing political articles in foreign publications. On a visit to the scientific institute in Moscow which receives incoming Western publications and photo-reproduces them, he had seen the originals and the sanitized Soviet reproductions side by side. 'In one magazine,' he recalled, they ran the same advertisement for five pages in a row to try to fill up the space where they cut out an article they didn't like.'

With wry amusement, Zhores Medvedev, the dissident biologist, described the operation of this mail censorship apparatus in his book, *The Medvedev Papers*. Painstakingly, he documented that Soviet censors had become so inefficient that it now took twice as long for a letter to reach him from Western Europe as it used to take Lenin's mail from Western Europe to reach his family in Siberia under czarist censorship. He also told me that in 1972 Solzhenitsyn had sent two letters, one to Karl Gierow of the Swedish Academy in Stockholm and one to his lawyer, Fritz Heeb in Zurich, with a note enclosed to the Soviet mail censors: 'You may read this letter, photocopy it, subject it to chemical analysis. But it is your duty to deliver it. If you do not, I will publish a protest against you and it will not bring honor to the postal service.' Both letters arrived at their destination – minus the slips.

What interested Medvedev more was the system for processing his own academic mail and scientific publications from the West. He carefully noted the various markings that censors put on the material sent in from abroad. After reading his book, I kept an eye out for those markings and before long had noticed a copy of the *International Herald Tribune* in an office at *Pravda* bearing the censor's mark ⟨ 185 ⟩ which Medvedev said meant very restricted distribution. (Theoretically, the *Tribune* is on sale in the Soviet Union. But in practice, I found it was only occasionally available at hotels for foreign tourists, usually kept under the counter and produced only for foreigners, and almost always out of date if not out of stock). Later, in Novosibirsk at the Academic

City's technical library, the director proudly displayed to me file copies of *The New York Times*. These, too, bore the same telltale restrictive marks of the censor which meant that only someone with special permission could read them, though the library director tried to pass the *Times* off as a publication in general use. The copies he showed me looked untouched.

Perhaps no institution more than the Lenin Library, the Soviet equivalent of the Library of Congress, embodies the carefully stratified Soviet hierarchy of information. Outwardly, it has the imposing, columned façade of august public buildings around the world. Inside, it functions by a web of rules out of Kafka. At the *Leninka*, as it is affectionately known among Muscovites, it is clear that the Soviet state regards knowledge as power and controls it accordingly. To begin with, it is almost impossible for an ordinary citizen without higher education to get a library card, mostly because of the crush of people. Those with cards gain access to general reading rooms, but specialists with advanced degrees (Soviet Ph.Ds) get into special reading rooms stocked with more material, especially scientific and technical publications, and occasionally new fiction from the West.

Finally, there are the *spetskhrany*, literally the special holdings, or more accurately, the secret stacks. 'The general alphabetical index is secret,' said Mikhail Agursky, tugging on his magnificent, ginger-colored side-whiskers as we toured the library one afternoon. What he meant was that the *Leninka* is probably the only great library in the world with two entire sets of catalogues, each occupying huge rooms: one of them a limited censored catalogue open to general readers, and the other, the full catalogue of the library's holdings, including the secret stacks, open only to the security-cleared staff.

'It's a problem, for example, to get religious or philosophical literature,' Agursky intoned softly, not to be overheard. 'It's not forbidden. But you can't find it in the catalogue so you can order it [from the special holdings] through a librarian. And even if I happen to have the catalogue number, the librarian will ask me why I need such a book. It happened to me several years ago. I was trying to obtain some old religious books and the librarian asked me, "Why do you need this book? You are a technical specialist. You have very strange interests."

438

'And it was not said with a sense of humor,' Agursky said, eyeing me sternly. 'She refused to get it.'

This kind of problem drives foreign scholars wild. An Indian historian fumed to me over lunch one day, explaining his frustration at having to deal totally through some intermediary who checked the secret catalogue and then the secret stacks. 'I am completely at the mercy of this young woman who may be competent or no good at all,' he said. A British scholar took some small comfort that foreigners were usually allowed to read more things than most Russians until he angrily remembered that he could not get certain historical materials 'until some Russian researcher has gone through to check them first.' An American professor was exasperated by the Lenin Library's refusal to xerox some articles by Freud from the closed stacks. 'We are forbidden to recopy Freud,' the librarian told her. 'He has those sexual theories.'

Far more than Freud or theological literature is consigned to the secret stacks, to be produced only for those with special permission. By the account of Agursky and others, the secret stacks include any foreign literature and periodicals which take issue with the current Communist Party line (in other words, most of it); non-Communist newspapers and magazines and even some Communist ones (during the invasion of Czechoslovakia, I was told, all the foreign Communist press which is normally in open stacks disappeared into the *spetskhrany*); Maoist writings; Communist classics written by proscribed authors like Trotsky and Bukharin as well as lesser-known Soviet works published in earlier periods when the Party line differed from today's (for example, works by Stalin or praising him too slavishly or, on the other hand, works from the Khrushchev era that are now considered too disparaging of Stalin); and Russian literature generally, either pre- or post-Revolutionary if it is unfavorable to the Communist cause or the current Kremlin rulers – unless it is so illustrious (Dostoyevsky or Tolstoy) that the Soviets would be embarrassed before world opinion to conceal it.

Like any system of censorship, this one has its imperfections, its slip-ups, and amusing little inconsistencies. For example, books by or about Trotsky are banned, but it is possible to read Communist newspapers of the Twenties quoting Trotsky's speeches. But generally, the library controls work effectively enough to frustrate any Soviet who is

439

intellectually curious and lacks the rank to command the access he wants.

Indeed, the degree of compartmentalization of information in the Soviet Union is hard for Westerners to fathom. American arms negotiators were stunned, for example, to discover in the strategic arms talks that Vladimir Semenov, the Deputy Foreign Minister who nominally headed the Soviet delegation, and his civilian aides knew practically nothing about the Soviet strategic arsenal. In other words, they were in no real position to negotiate since the Soviet Defense Ministry had not made them privy even to the most basic information on Soviet weaponry. American officials admitted later that they had had to spend the first months educating the Soviet civilians on the nuclear facts of life before the talks could move ahead.

On a much less exalted level, I met a young Soviet researcher who had been given special access to *The New York Times* as part of a research project to which he was assigned at his institute. It was his first exposure to a big Western newspaper and he was amazed at the volume of information which piqued his curiosity for more. One day, killing time near the librarian who handed out foreign publications from the restricted stacks at the institute, this young man found himself absentmindedly pawing through a copy of *Life* magazine that had been left sitting on the counter. He was talking with the librarian as he glanced at *Life* and suddenly realized that she had become quite nervous and was looking at him disapprovingly.

'What's wrong?' he asked. 'Did I say something wrong?'

'No,' she said. 'It's just that with you, *The New York Times* is permitted, but not *Life* magazine.'

Before going to Moscow, I had assumed that Soviet science, because of its prestige and importance to the state, might be spared such problems over information. But later I met Soviet scientists who maintained they had trouble keeping abreast of developments abroad and an even worse time keeping up with new work among their Soviet colleagues because of restrictions on the flow of information or because of the way the Party controls channels of scientific contact with the West. Zhores Medvedev, who specialized in problems of aging, told me while he was still in Russia he found it impossible to obtain full Soviet mortality statistics with a breakdown on the causes of death, even though such data was essential to his work. 'Mortality statistics are treated like state secrets,' he protested. A bio-medical engineer at Moscow's top surgical institute said doctors there could not obtain cumulative figures on patients who died or otherwise suffered from complications after surgery. A French doctor related to me the tragic case of a West German diplomat who had died of spinal meningitis in Moscow because his illness was not quickly enough diagnosed, largely because Soviet health authorities had suppressed information about other recent cases of spinal meningitis in Moscow. More broadly, outspoken nonconformist intellectuals like Andrei Sakharov, the physicist, and Roy Medvedev, the Marxist historian, have charged that Soviet science suffers from what Medvedev called 'the authoritarian atmosphere and lack of intellectual freedom, the dominating role of the censor'.*

As an objective branch of knowledge beyond ideology and as a field which enjoys enormous prestige, science has long posed a problem for the Communist Party. The Academy of Sciences, established in 1726, has been almost unique as an institution that has preserved a modicum of independence from Party overseers. It has repeatedly rebuffed efforts to push ranking Party officials like Sergei Trapeznikov, the head of the Central Committee's Science Department, into its membership and it has balked at expelling such iconoclasts as Sakharov and Ben Levich, the electro-chemist who applied to emigrate to Israel. Lenin himself is supposed to have proposed an amendment to the Academy's statutes exempting all of its publications from censorship, though this has been systematically disregarded.

In years past, Soviet science has paid a heavy price for political interference. The most infamous example was the quarter of a century during which genetics was suppressed while Trofim Lysenko reigned over biology. It was his theory, sold to Stalin and Khrushchev, that characteristics acquired from the environment could be transmitted in

---

* In his book, *On Socialist Democracy* (Knopf, New York, 1975), Medvedev has an excellent chapter on how the entire censorship mentality has constricted Soviet intellectual activity in literature, the arts and science. His brother, Zhores Medvedev, in *The Medvedev Papers* (MacMillan, London, 1971) has a long section on problems of Soviet scientists.

the evolutionary process. Mendelian genetics became anathema; its advocates were dismissed and persecuted, and their leader, the brilliant biologist, Nikolai Vavilov, died in a Stalinist camp in 1942. At other times, dogmatic Marxists opposed the theory of relativity, obstructing Soviet advances in nuclear physics, and fought against the science of cybernetics.

One ranking Soviet scientist told me he felt that it was only as the Kremlin came to see military applications for various fields of modern science that these fields flourished. 'Before the war, science was some kind of plaything for intellectuals,' he said, 'but then Stalin understood the importance of atomic weapons and this gave a great boost to physics' – nuclear physics, particle physics, accelerators, atom-smashers, and the whole paraphernalia for which the Russians are now internationally well known. In 1950, he added, cybernetics was so mistrusted that a leading Stalinist theoretician, Boris Agapov, attacked it in an article, 'Cybernetics: A Bourgeois Pseudo-Science.' But it was kept alive within the military establishment and under Khrushchev, in about 1956, the scientist said, cybernetics was recognized by the Kremlin for its importance in developing computers and ultimately missiles with their complex guidance systems. The official line did a 180-degree turn and the same Boris Agapov wrote a new article, 'Cybernetics: The New Science'. The next beneficiary, he said, was theoretical mathematics which got a lift from missile research as did chemistry, especially the chemistry of polymers, vital for heat-resistant nose cones in rockets. Biology got a push from the post-Khrushchev leaders, the scientist said, because of applications in both agriculture and biological warfare. 'Where the state sees a military benefit,' this man asserted to me, 'scientists have won considerable freedom in their work.'

Internationally, Soviet science has a reputation for some of the world's most brilliant theoreticians in physics and mathematics, but only spotty strengths elsewhere, and general weakness in experimental work. Privately, top scientists blame this on bad management, rigid bureaucracy, political interference and second-rate equipment. These problems hamper experimenters more than theorists. 'We can read about experiments in American scientific journals that we cannot even repeat because we do not have the equipment, the computers,' a dejected Soviet physicist told an American friend of mine. Others say Soviet science inevitably lags behind America in spite of talented individual scientists because information on new developments in world science or Soviet science circulates so slowly.

I have heard several scientists assert that the West overestimates Soviet science. Andrei Sakharov, who gained distinction as a theoretical physicist who helped create the Soviet H-bomb, was once asked by Murray Seeger of the *Los Angeles Times* how Soviet scientists had been able to make breakthroughs in spite of political controls, and he shot back: 'What breakthroughs? Since the Second World War there have been no significant breakthroughs in Soviet science. For every important scientific paper published by a Soviet, there are 30 published in America.' He blamed the stifling intellectual and political climate. Later, in his essay, *My Country and the World*, Sakharov said the diversion of resources to the military and the elite had held back Soviet science and asserted that early Soviet space age achievements 'and certain successes in military technology are the result of a monstrous concentration of resources in that sphere'.* I knew other scientists, while less categorically self-critical than Sakharov, who privately shared his complaint that the general climate of controls – though eased from Stalin's time – still inhibit science, especially in the fastest developing fields.

Soviet science is hurt, they said, by poor communications among Soviet scientists who are terribly compartmentalized. Normally it takes a year or two for new findings to get into scholarly journals, a process that in the West can be cut to weeks or days for important breakthroughs and thus speed scientific progress. The ferment and fast moving exchange of ideas prevalent in Western science, I was told, is largely absent in Soviet science. A rising young physicist complained that even at Novosibirsk's *Akademgorodok* (Academic City), set up in the early Sixties to promote cross-fertilization of ideas among scientists in different fields, this did not go on any more. Nor do Soviet researchers share ideas informally by phone the way Westerners do. 'No one talks about technical matters on the phone,' a Moscow science writer told me. 'People have the habit of not talking about anything that relates to secrecy.' And Russians treat most science as falling in that category, for scientific papers require a

* Andrei Sakharov, *My Country and the World* (Knopf, New York, 1975).

443

special security clearance (known as the *akt ekspertisa*) to be published.

The Russians make a tremendous effort to cull all Western scientific publications for every scrap of useful information through the All-Union Institute for Scientific and Technical Information. While this represents a much more systematic effort to tap Western science than the West makes to monitor what the Soviets are doing, the centralized approach is often slow and cumbersome.

Soviet scientists pointed out to me that at times of experimental discoveries, modern science can move with great speed. Theorists compete to explain any new phenomenon. In this race, Soviet specialists complained that they are at a competitive disadvantage because of the information-lag, among other things. An able mathematician-physicist cited to me the discovery in mid-November 1974, by American scientists at the Stanford Linear Accelerator and Brookhaven National Laboratories, of the new psi-meson particle as an illustration of the shortcomings of Soviet science. The Americans, this Russian said, had done better experimental work to achieve the breakthrough. With the fast flow of scientific information in the West, the discovery was confirmed by West German and Italian scientists within a couple of days. Although the Americans had also informed Soviet experimental nuclear centers at Dubna, Novosibirsk and Serpukhov of their discovery, it was nearly six months before the Russian confirmation came through. My Russian scientist friend attributed this delay largely to Soviet equipment that was less precise than American or other Western equipment – atomic particle accelerators at Dubna and Novosibirsk, for example, that could not achieve the same particle-beam intensity as American accelerators because of lower-grade electronic and magnetic technology. And because of restrictions on the flow of information and the compartmentalization of Soviet science, he said, Soviet theoretical physicists were left in the dark and could not compete with Western rivals in explaining the new phenomenon.

Pravda had run four paragraphs on the American discovery initially but only by chance, he said, did theoretical physicists at Moscow's prestigious Lebedev Institute learn the technical details they needed. A young Soviet physicist happened to be on academic exchange in Switzerland and sent a report by mail to his mentor, the theoretical physicist

Lev Okun at the Lebedev Institute. Otherwise, my friend said, it would have been months before the technical report came into print and filtered through the Soviet bureaucracy to scientists who needed it. So frustrated was Professor Okun that when he briefed a closed meeting of important scientists in Moscow on the American discovery, my friend said, he pleaded for reforms 'to speed up the exchange of information with the West and to solve the difficulties with experimental equipment or otherwise we will simply lag behind completely'.

If science as an objective field of knowledge has to bend to political realities, then politics is presented to the Soviet public in cut-and-dried fashion to make it seem immutable and scientific. The front pages of the big dailies are so similar that they look as if they were laid out by one Managing Editor. (Indeed, I was told that Tass does circulate instructions on how to play stories.) And to the Western eye, the formula that he uses seems fated to kill readership – no scoops, no crime or sensations, no inside dope stories or background leaks, no social gossip columns on beautiful people, no bad news, stock market finals, comics or race results. As one government worker remarked to me, 'Reading our press is like eating dry noodles – no flavor.' The staple of a paper like *Pravda* is an ample serving of what Lenin called 'production propaganda' framed by smiling workers with blowtorches; windy, turgid, repetitious editorials; and political commentaries that cast the world in terms of irreconcilable class conflicts and malignant conspiracies against the Communist cause or the Soviet homeland. It represents advocacy journalism carried to the extreme, with little pretense at objectivity.

But *Pravda* claims the largest circulation in the world for any daily paper – more than ten million – and gives every evidence of prospering even though it runs no ads and only charges three kopecks for a six-page paper. And for all the grumbling that I heard from intellectuals (some of whom made a point of boasting that they never read the Soviet press), it struck me that *Pravda* and other Soviet papers were serving their system rather effectively by their own lights for they left no room for nagging doubts among their readers about the legitimacy of the system.

445

They do, however, make astonishing reading. Soviet history is treated as an unimpeded and uplifting march toward a more plentiful and joyous collective existence. Clichés reach a crescendo at Revolutionary holidays when commentaries embroider the Party's rousing slogans: 'Working people of the Soviet Union! Struggle for a Communist attitude toward labor. Hold public property sacred and multiply it. Strive for savings of raw materials, fuel, electric power, metals, and other materials. Workers in the national economy! Persistently master economic knowledge and up-to-date methods of economic management and administration. More widely introduce in production the scientific organization of labor, advance experience and the latest achievements of science and technology.'

The average 30-minute nightly television newscast consists of a long feature on grain harvesting by 'our outstanding collective farmers' at the Dawn of Communism Collective Farm in the Ukraine, a report that shockworkers at the Magnitogorsk Metallurgical Combine have pledged to fulfill this year's economic plan three weeks ahead of time, and an interview with a Lebanese Communist who manages to answer one question with a nonstop, five-minute recitation that varies only minutely from the latest *Pravda* commentary on the Middle East. These anchor items lead into riot pictures from Ireland, demonstrators outside the American Embassy in Greece, miscellaneous Soviet sports news, and weather reports. Accompaniment for the main items consists of stock newsreel shots of grain pouring into railroad cars, harvest combines in carefully staggered phalanxes rolling across fields, and steelworkers pouring molten steel into troughs or white-hot ingots sliding toward the camera. The themes and pictures are unvaried day in and day out and seem to have very little connection to the date on which they are shown.

Dull as it strikes the Westerner, this kind of propaganda has a long-term subliminal effect on Russians. It plays to the deep-seated Russian instinct of national pride and collective identification with 'our' national achievements. Individuals may privately scoff, but cumulatively this type of 'news coverage' compensates for the obvious shortcomings that people see in their own lives.

Another objective, clearly, is to avoid any sense of excitement. The bigger the news, the smaller the story. When a

Soviet airliner crashed in Moscow in October 1972, killing 176 persons (at that date, the largest civil aviation single-plane crash in history), it merited only two paragraphs from Tass. When the Soviet TU-144 supersonic transport split up in midair at the Paris Air Show on June 3, 1973, *Pravda* tucked 40 words away on the back page. But the epitome of Soviet news management during my tour came when Khrushchev died on September 11, 1971. The next morning, *The New York Times* ran a 10,000 word obituary and a roundup of Communist press reaction from around the world – excluding Moscow. The night he died, I went out on the streets to gather comment from ordinary Russians but people were incredulous about the news and suspicious of me.

'Too bad, he was a sick old man,' said a woman at a sidewalk vegetable stand, anxious to get rid of me.

'How do you know that?' skeptically inquired a movie cashier.

'I haven't seen anything in the press,' parried an elderly man sliding away from me into a phone booth.

It was true. When the man who had ruled Russia for most of a decade died, the Soviet press was struck dumb. For 36 hours we waited for a word about Khrushchev. Finally, there appeared a tiny item at the very bottom right-hand corner of the front page of *Pravda* and *Izvestia* (no other papers ran it) – one solitary sentence announcing the death of 'pensioner Nikita Sergeyevich Khrushchev', squashed beneath a fat harvest report and a profile of the visiting King of Afghanistan.

The main reason for the delay, of course, was that the Kremlin leaders needed time to figure out how to handle Khrushchev, and seven years after his ouster they found him still too hot to handle. But the delay was also typical of the unhurried pace of Soviet journalism. Whenever I visited *Pravda* or *Izvestia*, there was none of the deadline frenzy of the Western press, the rush to beat competition into print. Senior journalists worked in roomy offices rather like American boardrooms done in Spartan furnishings and decorated with inspiring portraits of Lenin; and their pace was leisurely. The reason was obvious: news in our sense was not their primary business. At *Pravda*, editors told me that less than 20 percent of their paper was devoted to breaking news – unless Brezhnev or some other leader delivered a major speech, in which case it was simply printed verbatim. Visiting *Pravda* in late morning, I have frequently seen the next day's paper all ready except for a few blank holes. The page proofs were laid out, meaning that the stories had been put into type two or three days before and gone over with a fine tooth comb. *Pravda*'s 17-member editorial board meets at 11 a.m. to approve tomorrow's paper and put together the days after's. Such advance work enables *Pravda* and other Soviet papers to achieve a typographical perfection that would be the envy of any Western editor or reader. But even if a slip-up does occur, there would be no printed correction because *Pravda* does not admit mistakes (though occasionally, other papers do).

The idiosyncrasies of the Soviet press produce special habits among Soviet readers. They usually pass up blockbuster commentaries and look for the little items with the real news – the 40 words on the TU-144 crash in Paris or the one-sentence obit on Khrushchev. Most announcements of big foreign trips by Brezhnev or Kosygin break the same way: in two-line items at the bottom of massive columns of type on the front page. This leads, of course, to reading from the bottom up.

People also told me they prefer to read *Pravda* from back to front, and the few newspaper polls about which I heard confirm that this generally reflects reader tastes (high on human interest, sports, and articles dealing with social mores, and low on ideology). People know, for example, that in 1957 word of Marshal Georgi Zhukov's ouster as Defense Minister ran in a back-page item labeled 'Chronicle' and that the tip-off for Nixon's arrival time in 1972 was buried in *Pravda*'s back-page television diary. The expulsion of Aleksandr Solzhenitsyn in February 1974 was also a back-page short. But *Pravda*'s back page has other attractions – sports, chess and cultural news, occasional human interest features or satirical exposés. Page five is the newsiest of all in the Western sense because it runs breaking foreign news. Farther forward the going gets heavier.

Soviet readers become expert, too, at culling the kernel of news from the chaff of propaganda. Some intellectuals I knew got the message in 1973 that Egyptian President Anwar Sadat had expelled Soviet military advisers when the Soviet press ran a little item from Cairo saying that the Egyptians had thanked the Soviet advisers for completing their mission (though many other readers missed the point). Others divined the bad harvests of 1972 and 1974 by the failure of the press to run its usual glowing crop reports. One couple I knew figured out there had been a big airplane crash (near Sochi) after noticing five unusual husband and wife obituaries regretting their 'untimely deaths' – a circumlocution often used for accidental deaths. Yet another technique is to work backward from the penchant of Soviet propagandists to project Soviet problems onto other countries.

'If you read in our press about a big airplane crash in America, it means there's been a crash in the Soviet Union,' said a woman from a children's publishing house.

'That's not quite true,' her husband, a journalist, corrected her. 'What happens is this: if in Russia there was an airplane crash, then for the next month, the Soviet press will run stories about airplane crashes in America, West Germany, Formosa – anywhere. That's how you can tell we had one.' The same logic applies, he said, to health epidemics, price increases, crime waves, harvest setbacks, water shortages, jailing of political prisoners, and so on. Western problems are reported as object lessons in the miseries of life under capitalism and to distract people from similar difficulties at home. 'It's very effective propaganda: "Life is bad under capitalism; it was terrible under the czars," ' a young scientist remarked. 'People may not yet be convinced that life here is as perfect as the press pretends. But the masses do believe that it is worse elsewhere.'

In spite of the similarity of Soviet front pages, the Western image of absolute uniformity throughout the Soviet press is inaccurate. The spectrum may be narrow but there are some variations – from the conservative Cold-War right of *Red Star*; the Armed Forces newspaper; stodgy *October* magazine; and the neo-Stalinist *Young Guard* monthly to the more modern-minded youth newspaper *Komsomolskaya Pravda*; and the mildly liberal *New World* magazine. By far the most interesting newspaper in recent years, however, has been *Literary Gazette*, the Writers' Union weekly which has been an important outlet for the tenuous budding of sociology in the Soviet Union. No other newspaper has gone as far in trying to deal realistically with some contemporary

449

Soviet social problems, within the limits prescribed by censors. On occasion *Literaturka*, as it is known among devotees, nibbles at the fringes of policy. It took a lead in the battle against industrial pollution of Lake Baikal in Siberia and has delved into the issues of traffic congestion, pollution, urban transportation, inadequate service and supply of spare parts raised by the belated and uncoordinated Soviet plunge into the auto age. One series, quite impressive to me, documented the sharp disadvantages in pay, housing, and other benefits to workers in consumer industries compared to those in heavy industry. The implication, though nothing was directly stated, was that the Kremlin was not living up to its pledge to give consumers a better deal. *Literaturka* has also run articles probing the causes for the high Soviet divorce rate, decrying the pressures of the university entrance examination system, humorously mocking the disastrous inadequacies of consumer services and once – albeit gingerly and with a protective citation from a Brezhnev speech – even suggesting that the Soviet Union experiment with privately run cooperative service shops to improve the situation.

Nor is *Literaturka* unique in pointing up problems in Soviet life. Criticism of shortcomings is obligatory for the Soviet press. Soviet editors I knew used to brag that they were 'watchdogs for the people' and 'we have our investigative reporters like you'. The analogy is beguiling but misleading.

The Soviet press does have a watchdog role and Soviet officialdom does genuinely fear exposés in its own press. 'Journalists are very dangerous people,' a Soviet sports official once remarked to me. 'You talk to them. They write something down. And if it comes out in ways that other people do not like, you have to answer for it.' He made clear he meant not only foreign journalists but Soviet ones as well. Later, a Moscow journalist showed me a case of choice *Gorilka*, Ukrainian pepper vodka, that he had brought home from Kiev, 'a gift' from Ukrainian officials to persuade him to cover up some malfeasance he had found.

Pravda does its own special kind of muckraking week in and week out. In one month, I noticed for example, that it scolded brewery, tannery, and automotive enterprises in the Siberian city of Chita for building factories without providing housing for their workers; it castigated Yuri Shikhaliyev, head of the Karadag Carbon Black Plant in Baku, for the soot and pollution which his plant was spewing out over the city; it chastised A. Pokrovskaya, forewoman at the Novograd-Volynsky Meat Combine for letting her workers steal hoards of huge salami sausages from work; it upbraided the Ministry of the Paper Industry for failing to provide enough paper for books and magazines; and it ran a revealing report that 'Many [Soviet] villages are still without water, gas, and the entire array of consumer services.'

These 'self-criticisms', as they are known in Soviet parlance, have two common elements. First of all, with the exception of the rural article, they are focused on individual plants, directors, foremen, or ministries. They fit the motto quoted to me by one Soviet journalist: 'Criticize But Don't Generalize'. In other words, it's all right to find fault in a particular situation but don't write general conclusions because that is politically dangerous. This is precisely the point of Soviet 'muckraking' – find flaws to touch up the overall masterpiece. Nonetheless there is an inherent paradox in major criticisms that appear in papers like *Pravda*. Each case of corruption or mismanagement in some distant city or province is treated in print as an isolated shortcoming, and yet by giving it prominence in the national press, the Party bosses are signaling their nationwide apparatus that this is a general problem to be dealt with forthwith.

The second common element is that the criticisms which I cited – and the bulk of those that appear in the press – are made from top downward, on behalf of the leadership, pointing out errors of execution by middle-level management or petty bureaucrats. The infallible wisdom of the Party – of Brezhnev, the Politburo, the Party Central Committee, the Party as a corporate body, and Party policy – is always protected. The very vocabulary of Soviet 'self-criticism' is designed to avoid making, or inviting, moral or policy judgments. Soviet 'muckrakers' expose 'shortcomings' or 'mistakes' but they do not spotlight outright failures. This has the effect of appeasing the masses by conveying the impression that problems are recognized on high, without ever letting on that some policy may be wrong, that different elements of society have conflicting interests, or that something is fundamentally amiss with Soviet life.

'It may sound strange to you,' one Soviet journalist commented to me privately, 'but the kind of criticism that we print in our press has the effect of increasing popular acceptance of the idea that the Soviet system is sound, and that it is only a few officials who are bad.' A persuasive observation, I found, one echoed by people I knew who had close contact with ordinary working people – Gennadi, the state farm accountant, and Yuri, the young metal worker. Soviets privately grouse about their living conditions, complain about corruption, mock the pretenses of their ideology, and privately joke about their leaders, but they accept the system as fundamentally sound, as paradoxical as that may seem. It never seems to strike more than a mere handful of dissidents and perhaps some hidden loyal oppositionists within the establishment that anything major is on the wrong track.

Moreover, contrary to what many people think in the West, the Soviet press does offer a safety valve for minor grass roots dissatisfaction – letters to the editors. I was surprised to discover that it is big business. *Pravda* gets close to 40,000 letters a month and has 45 people in its letters department. *Literary Gazette* gets 7,000 letters a month and one of the reform efforts in which its chief editor, Aleksandr Chakovsky, takes the greatest pride was prompted by reader letters several years ago. After so many readers had complained about bad mail service, *Literaturka* decided to experiment for itself. It sent out test batches of mail, found it took nearly five days for a letter to reach Leningrad (comparable in distance from New York to Chicago), six days to Tbilisi, and nearly eight to Novosibirsk. *Literaturka* ran several articles chastising the Communications Ministry and now claims credit for helping to establish the Soviet postal code to speed the sorting of mail (though more recent articles suggest that mail service is not much faster now.)

'We're not afraid of criticism,' Chakovsky rumbled at several American reporters one afternoon in his office. Chakovsky is a large, portly man with an ego to match his girth, a fondness for smoking cigars down to the nub and then spraying ash over the table as he lisps in quite competent but heavily accented English, affecting confidentiality about Soviet life with comments like, 'I'll tell you candidly,' or 'Let me give you a sophisticated answer.' As a ranking Party man, he invites ideological combat and kiddingly calls himself 'a shark of socialism' (for all its liberalism on some domestic issues, his paper has spear-headed vitriolic attacks

452

on Sakharov, Solzhenitsyn, emigrating Jews, and Western journalists).

'*The New York Times* thinks its task is over after a reader's letter is printed,' Chakovsky puffed at me. 'But we think the task begins with printing letters. After that, we expect an immediate reply from the responsible agency, and this reply is also printed in our newspaper. If the reply does not satisfy us or seems too formal, we write an editor's note that we consider the reply of this particular ministry or agency unsatisfactory and demand a more detailed and thorough answer.' Sometimes it does work out that way (if the Party wants) but Chakovsky made it sound considerably more fearless and independent-minded than his own staff later described it to me in private. They cited cases where reporting had been stopped or articles killed because they ran afoul of some Party official, even at a pretty low level. One writer recalled repeated efforts merely to expose a Party-backed scholar guilty of fraudulent work which had ended in the wastebasket. This was not to mention all the topics like frictions among Soviet nationalities or the privileges of the Soviet elite which editors and reporters know are taboo from the outset.

But the regime generally finds letters useful. They give ordinary Soviets a chance to vent their frustrations at the notoriously inefficient bureaucracy, to sound off about poor consumer goods, and to let off steam generally. In the process, they give the Party an excellent means for monitoring the behavior of officialdom as well as the morals and attitudes of the general citizenry. In effect, letters trigger the press in its watchdog role. And for editors, they sometimes provide some sauce to season the dry ideological noodles.

Nor is there any great risk taken. Most letters that get into print are fairly innocuous: the woman in Dnepropetrovsk who is angry because her apartment walls are like iron and she cannot drive in a nail or a hook to hang pictures and curtains; the Moscow teacher irked by the long hair and rumpled outfits of Soviet soccer players; the workers at Bratsk supposedly irate to discover that their factory is supporting a bunch of professional athletes who theoretically work at the factory but actually play soccer – and poorly; the mother in Odessa disturbed by her teenage daughter's acquisitive instincts; women complaining about drunken husbands.

Sometimes, as two writers for *Literary Gazette* told me, newspapers deliberately stir up readers with 'provocative articles' intended to generate letters. Then they manipulate the responses to keep debates sputtering on uselessly for years. One perennial topic is alcoholism; another is whether husbands should help working wives more with the housework and shopping. A third dead-ender, flogged during my three years by *Literary Gazette*, was whether more flunking grades should be given in Soviet schools. This is not to mention the inspired letters which staffers told me were actually written by the newspapers themselves or by Communist Party activists and then foisted on ordinary workers or big-name intellectuals to sign, in order to make it appear as though the Party line was riding a groundswell of popular support. 'We used to have lists of people to call – some of them very important writers – and we would simply tell them what the Party expected them to say,' said one former *Literary Gazette* staffer.

Suicidal as it sounds, people also send letters that oppose the Party line. 'I know for sure that during the campaign against Solzhenitsyn and Sakharov (1973), *Literaturka* got some letters supporting these two men and other letters saying that it was wrong for people to denounce them without even knowing what they have said or without printing what they have written,' one staff writer told me. 'But of course these letters are not printed. Once a month, a KGB official comes to our office and goes through our letters. Always he takes some away with him, usually the *anonymkas* [anonymous ones].' Other letter writers are sometimes publicly denounced for wayward views. *Leningradskaya Pravda* once scolded four readers by name for their letters – one for abusive language, a second for opposing the policy of détente with the United States, a third for declaring that it was 'our duty to help Israel in its defensive war against Arab extremists and nationalists', and a fourth for saying that Soviet society was divided into rich and poor classes.

Occasionally, editors themselves seem to veer mistakenly toward touchy topics and are steered back on course by some higher authority. The newspaper *Soviet Russia* once opened a new column on 'The Female Problem' with a letter from a distraught lady economist who complained bitterly about the double burden of women and proposed that women get more pay, shorter hours, and be given more time

454

to raise their children. The newspaper invited reader responses, but no follow-up column ever appeared. Obviously, the Party had no intention of reducing women's working hours because they are too essential to the economy to be let off with part-time jobs.

Some who have worked with readers' mail on the inside told me they regarded the show of debate on social issues a charade because it is so thoroughly manipulated behind the scenes. There are exceptions, one writer said, when some leadership faction wants to use reader complaints to advance a viewpoint or to put pressure on other officials for its own purposes. On rare occasions, other letters slip by censors and raise important issues. But the entire process is crippled by the dictum: 'Criticize but Don't Generalize' and it is here, perhaps, that Soviet censorship is playing its most vital function.

In the West, Soviet censorship has a reputation for suppressing bad news like airplane crashes or political purges, or for turning Trotsky, Khrushchev, and other foes of the regime into nonpersons. But what is more important is that on behalf of the Soviet elite, the system of censorship suppresses the facts of life in many areas that seem to have no obvious connection with national security or the political secrets of Soviet rulers – and this cripples independent public discussion of almost any serious issue.

I was once given five pages of typed notes summarizing the basic censor's list. It was a tiny fragment from the huge looseleaf notebooks used by *Glavlit*, the Soviet censorship organization left over, curiously enough, from czarist times. It contained the expected prohibitions against printing certain material about the military, the operations of the secret police, the system of correctional labor camps, about censorship itself, about foreign aid doled out by the Soviet Union and foreign credits received by it, or about putting out advance word on the movement and whereabouts of Soviet leaders.

But what intrigued me far more were the bans on more innocent sounding things: data on the amount of crime and numbers of arrests; the number of uncared-for children; the number of people engaged in vagrancy or begging; the number of drug addicts; about illness in the population from cholera, the plague and other diseases including chronic alcoholism; about industrial poisonings and vocational illness; about occupational injuries; about human victims of accidents, wrecks and fires; about the consequences of earthquakes, tidal waves, floods and other natural calamities; about the duration of training camps for athletes, 'their rates of pay, the money prizes paid to them for good performances', and the financing, upkeep and staff of sports teams.

Anyone who has followed the Soviet press for any length of time can expand that list from simple observation. The information gaps in the press are enormous – nationwide statistics on the number of people still living in communal apartments; on the amount of labor turnover; on how successful women really are in their careers; on who gets to go abroad; on the social breakdown of those who get into universities; on the real earning power of members of the Soviet elite (including pay, bonuses, prizes, and other perquisites); on the relative costs and standards of living in various parts of the country (which a Siberian journalist admitted to me were deliberately suppressed 'because it might bring pressure from people who feel at a disadvantage'); on the relative availability of social services in rural areas compared to cities; on just what percent of the applicants for hospital beds, rooms in sanatoria, subsidized vacations, or other welfare benefits, get satisfaction; on class attitudes of various strata of Soviet society or the attitudes of various minority nationalities toward Russians and each other.

What is striking about such a list is that the Soviet people are being denied an accurate general picture of their own life and their own society, let alone a chance to compare it with other societies. Censorship prevents that. Some articles, often based on localized sociological studies, do appear from time to time touching on some of the important social issues that I have mentioned. But by and large the Party's monopoly of the means of communication makes it not only exceedingly difficult for divergent viewpoints to find public expression but also for independent public opinion to form on any issue. In consequence, as the young Karl Marx observed, censorship breeds public hypocrisy, political skepticism and people 'become a crowd of individuals, each living only his own private existence.' I have heard that sad cry from Soviet intellectuals.

'We are an atomized society,' a bearded writer lamented to me from his daybed one afternoon. 'We do not know what is really happening in our own society and what other people really think. I know what my own small circle thinks, and a bit about other intellectuals in Moscow maybe. But I do not know what workers really think or much about their lives, or what collective farmers really think or much about their lives. We live in separate worlds and we have no common world except the one the Party gives us to read about. The only time I mix with people of other classes is when my old military unit holds its annual reunion and we all get drunk together remembering the war. Otherwise we are strangers to one another.'

PART THREE

Issues

XV

CULTURE
Cat and Mouse

In this country, all real poetry is outrageous.
Nadezhda Mandelshtam
Hope Against Hope

The scene outside the Moscow Writers' Club was a mad-house, like New York at the return of Bob Dylan or bobby-soxers mobbing Frank Sinatra in his heydey as a matinee idol. University coeds in slick imported raincoats ignored the spring drizzle and swarmed around late-comers, begging for a ticket. Celebrities were beginning to gather and the police, to keep order, called internal security troops as reinforcements. Squeezing through the crush, I lost Ann's grip, barely caught it again, and literally had to haul her through the human whirlpool to make it into the building.

Inside, the audience of several hundred was restlessly expectant. People were crowding the aisles or snatching each other's seats. We saw Maya Plisetskaya, the Bolshoi Ballet's prima ballerina, and her husband, Rodion Shchedrin, a few rows ahead. Near them was Arkady Raikin, the comedian, and Viktor Sukhodrev, Brezhnev's handsome, wavy-haired personal interpreter for summit meetings with Presidents and Prime Ministers. But mostly it was a young audience, gently mod or shaggy-haired, the sons and daughters of the cultural and political elite, drawn by one of those special rituals of Russian cultural life – a rare poetry reading by one of the leading liberal poets – Andrei Voznesensky.

The evening began, in a bow to convention, with Voznesensky's modern patriotic oratory to Russia performed by about eighty voices from the Soviet Radio and Television Chorus. It was well performed but the audience was only mildly appreciative. This was not what they had come for. Gingerly, a half dozen actors and actresses edged into singing and reading some of Voznesensky's whimsical and non-controversial verses, and the assembly was politely amused, growing more expectant. Then suddenly came an upward, daring vault toward the political high wire with a poem, read by one actor, about Vsevolod Meyerhold, the avant-garde theater director who perished in a Stalinist camp in 1940. Without mentioning Stalin or the purges directly, Voznesensky's verse evoked Meyerhold's desolate death somewhere in the Gulag Archipelago:

> Where is your grave —
> or maybe just a mound,
> Vsevolod Emilyevich Meyerhold?
> Where can we put a monument?
> There is no grave . . .
>
> You cannot be frozen into a statue,
> Like some docile teacher's pet.
> You blaze
> From the pedestals of the world stage,
> Vsevolod Emilyevich Meyerhold.

Just as in the wave of poetry readings that swept Moscow in the late Fifties and early Sixties, the sudden fusion of art and politics and the poet's resurrection of a forbidden topic brought the audience to life. This was what they had come to see — how far Voznesensky would test and challenge the taboos. For Meyerhold, one of the most gifted and radical innovators of the early Soviet theater world, is officially canonized. But his death and the fact that he was punished for the heresy of anti-ideological artistic formalism are buried in silence. At Voznesensky's allusion to Meyerhold's free spirit, the audience broke into rhythmic applause. Yuri Lyubimov, director of the Taganka Theater which reveres Meyerhold as the godfather of its own experimentalism, rushed to embrace Voznesensky warmly. More waves of applause.

Through the first half of the performance, the poet himself sat on stage but off to one side, his face – still boyish at 41 – showing pained embarrassment. But, dapper in a houndstooth sport jacket, blue velvet slacks and a foulard scarf, he emerged after intermission to hush a new flow of gate crashers. By then, the overflow crowd was standing in the aisle near center stage, rapt and enthusiastic.

Voznesensky's shyness melted. He answered their un-spoken expectations with his hip-lingo satire on the anti-humanism of the technological revolution, ending on a nicely turned poetic plea not to make artificial caviar out of oil but to make oil flow from natural caviar. He touched them deeply with his celebration in verse of the return to Russia of Marc Chagall, so long a Soviet pariah. And then from an early work, *Anti-Worlds*, Voznesensky invoked his perennial protest against censors who have choked the throats of poets from Cervantes to Pasternak:

> Amen.
> I have killed a poem. Killed it unborn.
> To hell with it.
> We bury,
> Bury poems. Come see.
> We bury.

The audience was completely his by now. He dallied with some whimsical ditties and then tickled them with a poem that made fun of the endless queuing up in Soviet life, the signing-up years in advance for *defitsitny* goods, and even inking numbers on your wrist to prove your place to the self-appointed busybodies who monitor Soviet lines:

> I am 41st for Plisetskaya,
> 33rd for the theatre at Taganka,
> 45th for the graveyard at Vagankovo.
> I am 14th for the eye specialist
> 21st for Glazunov, the artist,
> 45th for an abortion
> (When my turn comes, I'll be in shape),
> I am 103rd for auto parts
> (They signed me up when I was born),
> I am 10,007th for a new car
> (They signed me up before I was born).

What pleased them most, however, was the irreverence of his retort to cultural watchdogs and prudish Party hacks who had been chiding him for sexual imagery and pornographic language in some of his verses. Hoisting them on their own petard, Voznesensky denounced *Pornography of the Spirit:*

> A girl friend dances in public
> With a naked admirer.
> Hail, pornography of the flesh!
> But there is also a pornography of the spirit.
> Sometimes, during a lecture, a functionary
> Is as competent in his art as a cook,
> And reveals to his audience
> His pornography of the spirit.
> In a Picasso, to him
> Everything is unclear
> And Shostakovich has no ear.
> This kind of humbug would embarrass
> Even a Paris whore!

The crowd in the aisles surged forward, passing flowers of adulation up to Voznesensky, who was allowed to give only three such performances during our time in Moscow. He was besieged by autograph-hunters while rhythmic applause echoed in the hall.

The enthusiasm that night, it seemed to me, symbolized the craving of the Soviet intelligentsia for a few moments of mischievous disobedience and candor, little morsels of free expression liberated from the cheap cheerfulness and stifling dogmatism of orthodox writing. Beside the stark moral probing or lacerating social criticism of such Western writers as Beckett, Pinter, Albee, or Baldwin, Voznesensky and other Soviet establishment liberals often seem like boys sticking out saucy tongues at the authorities rather than delivering literary body blows to the moral *solar plexus* of their society. Yet there is so much in Soviet culture that is hackneyed, false, and crudely sloganistic that any quiet voice of honesty or fleeting independence from the dictates of politics catches the ear like a whisper in a library.

Nowhere else in the world is poetry accorded such religious reverence or the poet so celebrated as priest and oracle as

461

in Russia. If ordinary people escape into alcoholism, intellectuals flee into books, especially poetry, finding there the spiritual compensation for the ennui of ordinary life. 'We have no philosophers or political commentators in your sense, no folk singers with moral messages, and no religion for most people,' Voznesensky observed to Ann and me one evening as he sat drinking Georgian wine in his favorite costume, a leather jacket and jeans, lounging on a low couch in his untidy high-ceilinged apartment. 'So there is a vacuum. People need something for their spirit, and they turn to poets. Some come for entertainment and others for religion or politics or philosophy. They expect all this from the poet. That's why he is so important in Russia.' And he always has been, under czarism as well as Communism. For daring poetry – or daring art of any kind – teeters on the line of confrontation between tyranny and talent, where censorship and creativity inevitably collide. People come to a poetry reading to see how far the poet dares defy the political laws of gravity and whether he will keep his balance on the high wire or lose it and suffer the political consequences. This becomes a cat-and-mouse game between Authority and the intelligentsia, natural enemies throughout Russian history. For Russian audiences this game provides the main source of tension and flavor and amusement in the otherwise muted and muffled Soviet cultural scene.

It is, of course, an unequal game, just as it was in Pushkin's day or Dostoyevsky's, in which the state and its cultural watchdogs have the ultimate sanctions of approval or punishment and the intelligentsia can arm themselves only with wit, courage and imagination. It is a game of cunning played with ruses and subterfuge, allegories and Aesopian language, hidden meanings and significant inflections, with dramas performed one way to soothe the censors and another way to excite live audiences. Strangely, it is a game in which, writers told me, the rules in Moscow differ from those in the provinces because censors in some provincial cities are more lenient or more awed by big-name authors than are the hardnosed censors of Moscow. This sometimes makes certain issues of provincial magazines more interesting than the better-known journals of Moscow. In the same way, what often passes as underground, nonconformist art in the stricter ideological climate of Moscow has long been discreetly accepted in Estonia, Lithuania or Latvia where the arts had already absorbed modernist abstract trends before the Baltic states were joined during World War II to Stalin's Russia, which had been stolidly plodding along with Socialist Realism as its cultural banner. It is a game where the size of the audience is vitally important because the watchdogs can afford a margin of error at small theaters where the audience is reckoned in hundreds rather than millions. 'The larger the audience, the tighter the controls,' a movie script writer groaned to me. 'They worry a great deal about anything for a mass audience. That's why our television is so terribly dull and the movies are not much better.' The game is a constant struggle between liberals maneuvering for more elbow room and conservatives trying to hold the line, in which the outcome can depend on influence, personality and collusion among factions more than on actual content. Just as the economy muddles along aided by endemic corruption, so cultural life profits from illicit alliances between writers, editors or theater directors and their sympathizers and patrons among the politically powerful.

Sometimes sheer luck blesses a work of art so that to everyone's amazement it breaks through the labyrinth of controls – as with *The Red Snowball Tree*, one of the best recent Soviet movies, which created a cultural sensation in the spring of 1974. It was written, directed and starred in by Vasily Shukshin, a tall, lanky, diamond-in-the-rough writer-director with the squint-eyed toughness of a Jack Palance and a reputation for short stories that sympathetically portray rough country folk and even criminals. Its artistic excellence impressed many people I knew but beyond that, all were astonished at how many rules it broke. Not only did it put pimps, leggy hussies, and underworld thugs on the Soviet screen, but its hero was an exconvict who wavered between going straight and lapsing into habitual criminality before he was brutally bumped off by his old gang. Its country characters, from a drunken collective farm chairman to the hero's aging mother forced to live on a pitiful 20-ruble monthly pension, were richly authentic. In one scene Shukshin dared show the total boredom of people at a compulsory political lecture. In others, my friends were intrigued to see ikons in the corners of rural homes or the ruins of Russian churches, fleeting but unusual allusions to the persecution of religious faith as well as its hold among the peasantry.

463

As a rural romanticist, Shukshin had his hero kissing the Russian birches while the camera lovingly caressed the flowing rivers and rambling fields of the Russian countryside. A good-hearted country woman helped the excon try to go straight and toward the end he was getting a grip on a tractor. But the film's whole thrust – crime growing in the supposedly pure soil of Communist society, the hero's tragic ending, doubts about the perfectibility of man, and the clear implication that it was the depravity of modern city life which had made a good country boy go bad, all ran counter to the canons of Soviet Socialist Realism.

Word quickly spread among Moscow intellectuals that Shukshin had battled a couple of years to get the film cleared and that some of the best scenes had been cut by censors. In the public version that I saw, jumps and omissions were raggedly evident. Still, enough had survived to leave people asking how this film had managed to appear at all when so many others, reputedly less daring, had been blocked.

Some knowledgeable Muscovites I knew speculated that Shukshin had developed credit and good standing from earlier, more orthodox works and that the film industry desperately needed an unusual, top quality film to show at international competitions. Probably true, I thought, but not enough to explain the chorus of favorable reviews the film was getting in the Soviet press. Shukshin, who was lionized overnight, seemed to have someone smiling on him from on high and it was not clear why. Months later, I was told by an intellectual with good friends at the Party Central Committee that Shukshin's mystery fan was Brezhnev himself. My friend said that while censors were holding *The Red Snowball Tree* in limbo, Brezhnev had seen it at a private Kremlin showing and had been moved to tears by the authentic scenes of rural Russia, the well-told tragedy of the hero, and by the moving portrayal of simple people whose faith in Russia was unshaken by their hard lives. Brezhnev's tears, my friend said, 'guaranteed the film's success.' It was not the kind of explanation that could be positively confirmed but it was plausible and it illustrates the capriciousness with which the Soviet system sometimes operates. Sadly, Shukshin died within months of his great success.

I never met Shukshin but I did meet another author who

464

was helped to overcome the queasiness of censors by high-level patronage – Chingiz Aitmatov, an unusual Communist writer who is praised both by Brezhnev and some dissident intellectuals. With four other American journalists, I was traveling in Central Asia in spring 1974, and all of us wanted to meet Aitmatov because of his reputation as a liberal writer. When we tried to arrange an official interview with him during our visit to his hometown of Frunze, we were given the run-around. Luckily, we managed to contact him directly, and he took the risk of graciously inviting us to his out-of-town dacha, a large comfortable, well-furnished country home that would not have been out of place in bourgeois Scarsdale or Greenwich. He took us around his brickwalled garden where he had lovingly gathered several old primitive stone statues of women, which he said had been done by Turkic artisans in the sixth century and had legendary or religious meaning. Aitmatov, a husky, soft-spoken, middle-aged man of the hills whose dark eyebrows and oriental eyes immediately mark him as a Central Asian, is fascinated by the myths, legends and remote history of his own people. Over a lavish, heaping table of his wife's excellent Kirghiz cooking, he talked to us with feeling deep into the night about mankind's common problems of protecting nature, of industrialists both East and West who misuse it, and of betrayals of man by man from Richard III to the Soviet present. When someone observed that both he and Solzhenitsyn were concerned with themes of betrayal, he did not disagree but said, 'Each sees it in his own way, each depicts it in his own way.' Later, he criticized Solzhenitsyn – in keeping with the Party line and backed away from open discussion of the penalties imposed against iconoclastic writers.

To the Party leadership, Aitmatov is a convenient success story for the Soviet policy toward minority nationalities because, coming from Kirghizia and writing in Russian, he represents a minority writer who has hit the top. As such, he is a rarity celebrated by the Party in its struggling effort to weld minority groups more firmly to their union with Russia. His political credentials, moreover, are impeccable. His parents were high-level Kirghiz Communist Party activists and, joining the Party practically as a matter of inheritance, Aitmatov himself was rapidly advanced by the Party as one of its leading representatives among intellectuals. In early years his well-crafted but fairly conventional fiction set in the Kirghiz mountains won him state prizes and formal recognition. As a mature writer he had made his compromises – leaving certain things unsaid or going along with collective denunciation of a dissident like Andrei Sakharov. But in recent years, he has won a liberal following by using his protected position to write more unorthodox works on moral issues that lesser writers shy away from.

The liberal wing of the intelligentsia took it as their victory when in 1970 he published *The White Steamer*, a novel. It was a moving allegory of good and evil in which a seven-year-old boy commits suicide in protest over the rape of nature by modern man, symbolized by the killing of a prized mountain deer. Conservatives protested that the boy's mood and suicide was too pessimistic for Soviet literature. Aitmatov's next challenge to establishment conservatives came in 1973. He co-authored a play, *The Ascent of Fujiyama*, which raised for the first time in several years the moral guilt of people who had secretly betrayed others by informing on them in the Stalinist era. In keeping with the rules of the game, Aitmatov avoided explicit mention of Stalin or the purges. He chose for his setting the picnic reunion of four old wartime friends who spend their outing haunted by the lingering mystery: which of them had secretly denounced a missing colleague whose life was ruined as a consequence. 'Tell the truth, tell the truth,' Aitmatov's most attractive characters keep saying to each other and to the sympathetic audience. In an implied reproach of the establishment, his two most negative characters are rapaciously successful careerists, a world-traveling journalist and the director of a scientific institute. I found the play stronger in theme than in dramatic finesse, but the mere treatment of such issues as personal betrayal, dishonesty, and the allusions to Stalinist repressions were daring and unusual enough for the Soviet stage to keep the audience at the edge of its seats on the night I saw the play. Aitmatov's position is not so impregnable that he does not occasionally pay for his independence. I was told that he was officially reprimanded for having agreed to see our group without getting official permission and as a result was banned from traveling abroad for about a year. But later, when Washington's Arena Stage put on *Fujiyama* in translation, he was allowed to come to America; for purposes of détente the Party found in him a useful image.

On other occasions the balance in the game of cat-and-mouse is tipped in favor of the intelligentsia by the attention and pressures of the outside world. In 1970, for example, the Cannes Film Festival awarded a prize to *Andrei Rublev*, a mercilessly realistic film about the sufferings of medieval Russia seen through the life and art of Andrei Rublev, a legendary 15th-century monk and ikon painter. Filmed in the naturalistic style of Ingmar Bergman by Andrei Tarkovsky, Moscow's most talented film director, the movie was intended for release in 1967 as part of the 50th anniversary celebrations of the Bolshevik Revolution. But its vivid portrayal of the violent Mongol conquest, the internecine fighting among Russians, the mass nudity of a pagan midsummer night's festival, and its admiring representation of Rublev's religious art and his urge for creative freedom in a hostile environment of informers and authoritarian rule, all ran afoul of censors. For four years they held back the film, chopping away scenes while the movie was being marketed in the West earning hard currency and a reputation for Soviet culture. Eventually, the international recognition at Cannes evidently proved such an embarrassment that Soviet authorities felt they could no longer hold back the film from their own people. A cut version was released to a few theaters in Moscow and then given a modest run around the country.

An even more striking reversal, thanks to détente, was the change in official policy in the fall of 1974 when a group of unofficial artists – none of them members of the Artists' Union – tried to stage an outdoor art show in Moscow for their nonconformist and mildly abstract paintings. When they gathered in an open lot on September 15, they were brutally dispersed by plainclothes police dressed as workers and operating bulldozers and dump trucks to scatter the artists and several hundred friends, foreign diplomats and correspondents. My *Times* colleague, Chris Wren, was beaten up and had a tooth broken when police goons assaulted several newsmen. Other onlookers were arrested and interrogated. More than a dozen paintings were seized, torn and tossed into a dump truck with other debris. Some of my artist friends said they saw paintings burned as well. The artists were quick to exploit and publicize this overkill by the authorities. The resulting international outcry, recalling Nazi book-burning, caused the Kremlin to reverse the tactic of repression, while high-level journalists privately tried to blame the whole affair on Moscow Party officials rather than higher-ups – though my own hunch is that it was fairly high-level conservatives who had ordered the crack down. Ultimately, permission was given for an outdoor exhibition near Izmailovo Park a couple of weeks later, on September 29.

That was easily the most unusual cultural event during my years in Moscow. Russians themselves were amazed by it. More than 10,000 people gathered in a huge open field on a gorgeous sunny Sunday afternoon. The air was festive, the atmosphere astonishingly free in spite of KGB cameramen with fancy Japanese equipment photographing Russians who dared to mingle openly with Western correspondents. It was, as one French diplomat remarked, 'a Russian Woodstock,' a grand outdoor happening, more important because the authorities had felt compelled to let it take place or lose face internationally, than for the intrinsic merit of the art exhibited. Among the 200 canvases exhibited by 65 artists, I saw styles ranging from whimsical realism and religious symbolism to surrealism, pop art, coloristic abstractions or the acid art of the psychedelic era, along with more conventional painting. Few artists showed their most far-out works. They didn't want to spoil things by going too far. The crowds edged cheerfully across the field studying the canvases. People scrambled up and down ditches, held children aloft on their shoulders, applauded some artists, heckled others and argued into the evening, after the canvases were gone, whether a painting should be considered art if the common man could not understand it. The entire scene was very un-Soviet.

By world standards, the art was pretty tame. Several of the more prominent underground artists like Oskar Rabin, Vladimir Nemukhin and Lidiya Masterkova, had for years been discreetly allowed by authorities to show and sell paintings privately to foreign diplomats. The art which reached the West had caused only mild interest, and then chiefly because it emanated from the Soviet Union but violated the canons of Socialist Realism in either modernistic style or ironic content. It was certainly far less striking and daring than the work of the Russian avant-garde of the Twenties and generally less abstract or modernistic than graphic art long shown in the Soviet Baltics. 'The art is not what was most important,' an experienced Moscow literary critic remarked to me a few days later. 'I saw only one or two paintings that I thought were good. It was the atmosphere I liked, the sense of freedom. It made me proud to be a Russian for once, just to be there.'

The underground artists exploited the international attention they had won and pressed for other, smaller exhibits. At times, the authorities gave way and at other times played upon differences among the artists to contain them. A year after the first big show, the artists insisted on having another big exhibition, this time with close to 800 works; and when some conservative officials took down 41 of them, the artists created another furor by threatening to shut down the entire exhibit and informing the Western press. Again, fearing an international scandal, higher, more pragmatic officials gave way, allowing some paintings to be returned and barring only the ones with obvious political import. 'It was a good philistine reaction,' commented an American official. 'The Soviet authorities seem to think that if they leave it alone, the novelty of this stuff will wear off and it will go away. Probably they're right.' For though this group of painters had cleverly made the most of their opening, there was no evidence that the Party was relaxing controls on the mainstream of Soviet art.

Sometimes the watchdogs of culture are simply outplayed on their own territory because of competition among the more liberal magazine editors who are desperate for readable material to spice up the volumes of predictable propaganda they are obliged to run. The science fiction fantasies of the Strugatsky brothers, Boris and Arkady, for example, are widely read by the cogniscenti as critical allegories about Soviet Russia set on other planets or in the West. In *Predatory Things of the Epoch*, the Strugatskys projected a future society where material needs were met but people were overcome with boredom and a spiritual vacuum. In *It's Difficult to be God*, an earth expedition to another planet witnesses a religiously inspired coup d'etat and the setting up of a medieval, fascist society with features quite recognizable to Russian readers. Their fantasy, *The Snail on a Slope*, offered so telling a caricature of the useless paper-work, inefficiency and uncaring hypocrisy of Soviet bureau-crats represented by the fictional 'Office of Forest Affairs' that *Pravda* attacked the work as 'a libel and defamation of Soviet reality,' and the Strugatskys ran into serious problems getting published after that.

Soviet intellectuals take delight in spotting and sharing any such items that slip past the censors. One of the most stunning goofs occurred when Yevgeny Markin published a symbolic poem, 'Weightlessness', in *New World* magazine in late 1971 and used it as an allegory to repent for having joined the official campaign to expel Solzhenitsyn from the Russian Writers' Union. But when that interpretation of the poem became common gossip among Moscow intellectuals, the game was over and retribution was swift. I was told that the responsible censors and editors were reprimanded and Markin himself was thrown out of the Writers' Union for his poetic heresy and thereby denied a living as a writer.

The theater probably more than any other medium lends itself to the duel between artist and censor which is a prime reason why drama was the most lively and popular of the Soviet arts in the early Seventies. I knew Russians who would come home relishing the extra meanings they had read into nuances, inflections, and gestures. They would go to plays and wait for these few lines or that single soliloquy that titillated them, forgiving the rest of the performance for being pedestrian or orthodox. *Rock and Roll at Dawn*, for example, was an anti-American Soviet musical written by two *Pravda* editors who used a few recorded tunes from *Jesus Christ, Superstar* and an American ambience as a come-on. Its portrayal of the United States essentially fit the cliché Soviet view of American society as money-grubbing, immoral, bent on the arms race, intriguing with the Chinese and repressive toward its idealistic youth. But this gambit did manage to get *Superstar* officially accepted and toward the end, when a police detective protested to his chief about lying among officialdom, the director got off a commentary on Soviet life by having his actor face the Soviet audience and declare: 'We lie, level by level. I lie to you. You lie to your chief. And he lies to the very top. A pyramid of lies. What holds it up – I don't know. Perhaps it is built on the fear that someone will get out of the pyramid and it will collapse. But sometime all this must end. I personally am quitting the game.' At the premiere of the play, which I saw, that was an electric moment. The police detective was saying something intellectuals would only say in private, but not outside a trusted group. To have pulled it off in public was a real coup. Written about America, of course, it was innocent enough, but delivered fullface to the Russian audience, it was pregnant with meaning. The audience, savoring it fully, responded with strong applause.

So prone are Russians to read significance into every art form that they can find political overtones even in musical performances. In December 1972, Mstislav Rostropovich was under a ban against foreign travel and was severely restricted in his home concerts. The Kremlin, angered over his giving refuge in his home to Aleksandr Solzhenitsyn, nonetheless permitted him to appear several evenings during the Moscow Winter Festival of the Arts. One highlight was his performance of a new composition by Poland's leading composer, Witold Litoslawski, written especially for Rostropovich. By Moscow standards it was very modern, dissonant, unorthodox. Rostropovich took the precaution of rehearsing it discreetly with the orchestra only a few times before performing it at the Moscow Conservatory, a favorite haven of the liberal intelligentsia.

Russian friends of mine who saw the performance interpreted it as more than the bold airing of provocatively modern music. They saw it as a deliberate statement of the cellist's and the composer's philosophy. In several passages the lone lyrical voice of Rostropovich's cello struggled to be heard against a crashing and cacophonous orchestra. To Rostropovich's friends and enthusiasts, the message was that of a free and unbowed musical and intellectual spirit struggling to make himself heard against the din of cultural orthodoxy and in spite of official censure of his behaviour.

One favorite ploy of leading liberal theaters is to perform unchallengeable classics but give them a modern twist that makes them more politically potent than anything contemporary Soviet dramatists could get away with. Yuri Lyubimov, the talented and imaginative director of Moscow's Taganka Theater, is a past master of this technique. His version of *Hamlet*, with the players in modern slacks and turtleneck sweaters and the grave diggers unmistakably cast as Russian peasants, puts the atmosphere of medieval Danish intrigues and eavesdropping into a Soviet setting. To add to the Russianness, Lyubimov had one actor read, as a prologue, Boris Pasternak's poem about Hamlet from the still-banned novel *Doctor Zhivago*. His Hamlet, moreover, is no self-doubting prince but an enraged young man struggling against an evil ruler in an evil time (King Claudius as Stalin?).

This rendering was sufficiently touchy for Lyubimov to have had to fight hard for permission to stage it. I was fairly new to Moscow when I saw it and was uncertain how much to read into it. After the performance, I asked Lyubimov how deliberately he had pointed his *Hamlet* at the Soviet present. Still playing the game in order to protect himself, he answered me elliptically: 'The play is a classic because it is so eternal. If it ever stops sounding contemporary, if it does not stir a contemporary response, if it does not make people think about themselves, there is no point in playing it.' He paused to make sure I had gotten his meaning and then illustrated his point with the 'to be or not to be' speech. In his version, it is less a philosophical soliloquy than a moral sermon to the audience not to cooperate with evil, given twice over for emphasis. 'Hamlet is a very decent man, severe in criticizing himself for inaction,' Lyubimov said. 'He is afraid of death. We are all afraid of death, of losing careers, of the unknown. That is why we tolerate evil.'

The most cunning dramatic exercise in double-entendres that I saw in Moscow, however, was *Balalaikin and Company*, which many intellectuals I knew took as a deliciously apt and funny commentary on their lives – the timid silence of the intelligentsia, their fawning fear of the police and political authority, their turning to walks, to feasting and to drinking as a substitute for intellectual freedom and activity, their penchant for philosophizing during drunken bouts and their inaction afterward, their compulsion for hiding the flaws of Russian life from foreigners, the double-talk they use to appease the powers-that-be, their readiness to toady to Authority.

What especially piqued the fancy of Moscow intellectuals was that this provocative satire was written by Sergei Mikhalkov, the lumbering millionaire children's writer, known as a leader among the conservative watchdogs of the literary scene. The fact that Mikhalkov would author a play like *Balalaikin* is one of those Soviet paradoxes that made it difficult for me ever to be confident of characterizing someone as an unreconstructed hard-liner. It prompted endless gossip among other intellectuals. Some of my friends saw the play as proof of the supreme ideological cynicism of which they had long suspected Mikhalkov. Others said they had heard he had been pushed into doing the play because his liberal-minded sons had challenged him to produce something honest and daring. I often wondered whether one of his sons had actually written it and had gotten his father to front for him.

The cover for *Balalaikin* was that it was a dramatic adaptation of the novel, *A Modern Idyll*, by the great 19th-century Russian satirist Mikhail Saltykov-Shchedrin. As a precaution, the Sovremennik Theater which presented the play hoisted a huge banner over the stage which read: 'It is impossible to understand the history of Russia in the second half of the 19th century without the help of Shchedrin.' Stage and costuming were from the last century. But all that only made my Russian friends enjoy the entire spectacle even more as a spoof on their own lives. It opens with two liberal intellectuals who have just heard the warning, as if in a modern Soviet crackdown, to 'keep quiet and wait'. No reason is given but the two men retreat indoors, give up all liberal activities and contacts, and sit quietly in the drawing room, devoid of resistance. The contemporary audience is right at home with them. 'If you try to hide somewhere, *they* will find out,' cautions one of the men. '*They* will find you and ask what you are doing. Even innocent people will become guilty.' Like Russians today, the two men start whispering to each other for fear of being overheard, even though they are saying nothing of consequence. 'The main thing is to fight the wildness of the spirit,' affirms the first pompously. 'We will surprise the world with our lack of action and the purity of our sentiments,' echoes the second. Gradually their lives lose content and meaning. They drink, eat, sit in silence, stare at each other, talk nonsense, go for long walks and then, in the ritualistic phrase of so many Russians today, proudly proclaim to each other, 'We have everything.' When a police informer appears, they purposely lose to him at cards to ingratiate themselves. When the forbidding Chief of Police appears, they quake in terror, mask their opinions in double-talk, and begin echoing his comments. Quite willingly they make themselves his tools. Staged by Leningrad's masterful director, Georgi Tovstonogov, *Balalaikin* is beautifully played, richly appreciated by the intelligentsia for portraying their predicament, and privately mistrusted by Party conservatives.

A leading journalist told me that Mikhalkov's satire struck so close to home that in spite of the author's exalted position, he was called on the carpet by the Communist Party Central Committee to explain why he had produced a work with so many anti-Soviet innuendos. But Mikhalkov proved himself a masterful tactician. According to the journalist's account, he insisted that this was Shchedrin writing about czarist times and he was surprised that Party officials would read anti-Soviet sentiments into it. On this occasion, he was let go. But he was summoned again later. The journalist told me that this time Mikhalkov went armed with citations from czarist officials who had roundly denounced Shchedrin for the original work. So that when the Party officials censured Mikhalkov, he quoted the parallel comments of czarist officialdom. That, the journalist told me, proved to be an effective rebuttal, and *Balalaikin* survived.

The political and intellectual tension over *Balalaikin* and similar works of art, commented Galya, a middle-aged Moscow linguist and playwright, 'is what gives our cultural life pockets of vitality. In the West everything is possible and so almost nothing is desperately precious. In Russia, almost nothing of great merit is possible and so anything of value is immediately treasured. The choice of good books is so small that you appreciate every single one of them. I know a man who used to carry his favorite books around with him – Pasternak, Mandelshtam, Akhmatova. When he visited America he was overwhelmed to see stacks of Mandelshtam in book stores. At first he was impressed by how many copies were available and then he was depressed that no one was buying them. He told me, "I could not live in a country where Mandelshtam was not properly appreciated." '

Galya was right. Russian intellectuals do keenly prize artistic excellence, because they are so starved of it, and this unstinting appreciation is one of the most attractive features of Soviet cultural life. They are like the Soviet consumers who display newlywed excitement about some modest new purchase that would be taken for granted in the West. Russian intellectuals treasure any unusual poetry reading, concert or foreign film and talk about it for months afterward as a major event in their lives. I remember one morning in Tbilisi coming upon a line of people half-a-block long and learning from some of them that they were waiting for a bookstore to open because they had heard that a new volume of Dostoyevsky's writings was going on sale. Many were the evenings that Ann and I sat among enraptured audiences at the Moscow Conservatory where the music was superb and where, as one Moscow friend said, 'I can find refuge from our politicized life.' The intelligentsia would come unpretentiously in their plain sweaters and slacks and warmly cheer their local heroes – Shostakovich, Oistrakh, Rostropovich, Richter, Khachaturian. Modern atonal trends were all but forbidden but these Russians were thrilled to savor Tchaikowsky, Borodin, Rimsky-Korsakov and other classics. In spite of its limited repertoire and the constant foreign tours of its stars, the Bolshoi could sometimes be a place of excitement especially when some leading ballerina like Plisetskaya was dancing. Both inside the hall and outside the crowds were electrified. Whether Plisetskaya was a liquid graceful black swan or a wry, angular bullfighter's moll in *Carmen Suite*, the bouquets would shower down from the balconies. Nor were these mere cultural diversions in a flood of offerings, as they might be in New York, London or Paris. These were rare treats and Russians absorbed each one of them as an occasion to be remembered.

Nonetheless, many of the intellectuals I knew regarded high points like the underground art show, Voznesensky's rare poetry readings or *Balalaikin* as sporadic titillations, flowers in a cultural desert, piecemeal sops from the authorities. To them, the caricature of intellectual life in *Balalaikin*, though an exaggeration, was all too painfully appropriate for the early Soviet Seventies. The ferment and excitement of the Khrushchev thaw in the late Fifties and early Sixties had kindled hopes for real, long-term cultural relaxation and freedom, but in the retrenchment that followed the invasion of Czechoslovakia, Soviet intellectuals found their own cultural climate sterile.

Individual stories, plays, readings flashed momentarily from time to time because since Stalin's death, the Party felt the need to allow safety valves in order to enlist gifted writers and other intellectuals in its cause with the offer of some flexibility though it curbed their most rebellious pro-

475

clivities. My liberal intellectual friends admired not only Shukshin, Aitmatov, and Tarkovsky, among their contemporaries, but to name only a few of the others – Vasil Bykov with his unorthodox picture of the aimless brutality of World War II; Fazil Iskander with his sardonic short stories reminiscent of William Saroyan; and Yuri Trifonov with his trenchant tales of philistinism of the rising middle class, or Fyodor Abramov with his realistic portrayal of the hard life and the degenerating moral values of the Russian countryside. But the focus of each was limited and narrow, their treatment more subtle than daring.

For the first half of the Seventies lacked the thrust, direction and above all, the sense of community and hope of the Khrushchev era. 'There were ten years of my life, 1955–1965, when I thought that today is not so good but tomorrow will be better,' Galya, the playwright, told me. 'For others maybe this went on a bit longer, a bit later. But for me, these ten years had a very nice feeling. I felt it was possible to be published eventually. I wrote things that could not be published at the time but I thought this was temporary and they would be published later. But then the trial of Sinyavski and Daniel [in 1966] was like a crash. Others had their own crash later. The Six-Day War. Czechoslovakia. It got harder to publish. We lost hope.'

Under Khrushchev, what was known as the 'Tribune of Poets' – Yevtushenko, Voznesensky, Bella Akhmadulina, Robert Rozhdestvensky – fired the imagination of the young. New theaters like Taganka and Sovremennik burst into life. Periodically, Khrushchev would scold and rein in the liberals but his erratic lurches of policy and his de-Stalinization campaign provided flexibility that could be exploited more readily by the intelligentsia than the grayer, more controlled atmosphere of Brezhnev's Russia in the years after Czechoslovakia.

Probably the most painful setback to literary liberals was the forced removal in early 1970 of Aleksandr Tvardovsky as chief editor of *New World* magazine, long a liberal beacon. It was Tvardovsky, himself a successful and ironic poet, who had discovered Solzhenitsyn and most other unorthodox writers. '*New World* was finished as a magazine when Tvardovsky was removed,' a successful satirist lamented to me. 'If you had read it for ten years while he was editor, you could have learned much about Soviet life.

But after that, not much. He was a wonderful editor. He suffered greatly for that magazine and for his writers. He printed much that without him would never have seen the light of day.' This man told me that when he had tried to put together a book of collected articles recently, the censors blocked the most daring ones – although they had been published earlier by Tvardovsky.

This sense of retrenchment in the early Seventies was felt by many others with whom I talked. Writers like Lidiya Chukovskaya and Vladimir Voinovich were kicked out of the Writers' Union for supporting Solzhenitsyn or publishing works abroad that the authorities found offensive, like Voinovich's *Ivan Chonkin*, a satire of bumbling inefficiency in the Soviet bureaucracy and the Army which the author tried vainly to publish in Moscow for a decade. Other writers privately complained of what had been cut from works of theirs that did appear. 'Never judge what a Soviet writer thinks by what appears in his books,' a middle-aged dramatist bitterly warned me one evening. 'We have all learned to submit to censorship and, what is worse, to censor ourselves. You and your heroic *New York Times* wouldn't be so brave if you knew that the price of exposing Nixon or of editorials your government doesn't like was [exile to] Siberia or being blacklisted for life. When you see people here getting excited over Aitmatov or someone else, it is because he has found a way to eke out a bit more honesty than usual. But it is a matter of degree only. If someone manages to be 20 or 30 percent honest about our life, it is considered a sensation.'

From someone in a Moscow publishing house I heard of another writer who was ordered to cut offensive allusions from a science fiction story by the Strugatsky brothers to meet the objections of book censors. The man, who was a friend of the authors, hated the task but reasoned that he would probably be gentler and more sympathetic than someone who did not care. 'It was either cut or not be published and the Strugatskys needed the money,' the publishing official said. In 1971, when I first met Yuri Lyubimov, the Taganka Theater director, he enthusiastically ticked off three plays then in rehearsal: *Guard Your Faces*, a theatrical review by Voznesensky that had been shut down in 1970 by censors after two performances; an unorthodox play by Boris Mozhayev about an independent-minded farmer who wants to do the unthinkable – quit his collective farm; and a theatrical adaptation of Mikhail Bulgakov's satirical fantasy, *The Master and Margarita*. But none of these cleared the censors in the next three seasons. At Moscow Art Theater, I was told, objections of politically conservative Party members in the troupe blocked an interesting and unconventional drama about Pushkin and Czar Nicholas I. A movie scenarist told me that probably ten or a dozen movies were stopped each year after being filmed, not to mention numerous scripts rejected before filming on political grounds. Not only liberal writers like Fazil Iskander but established conservatives like Mikhail Sholokhov, I was told, had large chunks of works removed because of allusions the watchdogs disapproved of. The editors of the conservative youth monthly, *Young Guard*, I heard from one former editor, suppressed a whole flood of manuscripts dealing openly with sex, pacifist sentiments or cynicism among youth about military service.

Westerners often picture a single censor in a publishing house ferreting out the unacceptable works, but Russian writers described to me a much more complex process. Frequently, they fear censors less than their editors, who are anxious to protect themselves from political repercussions and thus inclined to do vigorous precensoring and cutting. One internationally known poet, angry about *The New York Times* characterization of one of his works as stridently anti-American, took me to lunch and explained for five hours the labyrinth of checks which had whittled away what he claimed was his most interesting material and left him with a naked propaganda piece. For 18 months, he bleated, he dragged himself to a Committee for the Russian Republic's Ministry of Culture, to the All-Union Ministry of Culture, to a district Communist Party Committee, to the ideological section of the Moscow Party Committee, and to the Culture Ministry's Administration of Theaters to get his script okayed – all before it even went to *Glavlit*, the official censorship agency. At just one of the preliminary stages, he groaned, 'They made 100 changes – I counted them myself, and they promised that was all they would do – but it wasn't. They did more later.'

More than one writer observed to me, however, that it was the attraction of big royalties, large editions and big audiences, or of country dachas, and the chance to travel abroad and other perquisites – as much as censorship – that has bought off many would-be 'liberals'. Ideological stalwarts who write patriotic themes are usually the most richly rewarded. Vadim Kozhevnikov, an author of many war novels and cold war spy thrillers – some picked up by movies and television, has reputedly piled up a million-ruble fortune. Other writers have bargained for much less but the materialist mood of the Seventies has affected many. 'Who's going to worry about daring poetry,' quipped one successful poet, 'when he's anxious to get in line for a new Zhiguli car?'.

By the early Seventies, all kinds of people were complaining privately that the liberal poets of the Sixties had lost their fire: Yevtushenko with his lean-limbed, self-serving charm had become a poetic huckster for the regime, chanting civic verses of Soviet loyalty, attacking the Chinese or the Chilean junta; Rozhdestvensky was writing pop tunes or rhapsodizing about space heroes and construction projects; Voznesensky had surrendered the clear ring of youth and retreated into more caution, complex, and stifled projects; Akmadulina had trouble getting into print at all. That difficulty plagued others – like the Strugatsky brothers with their politicized science fiction, or Vasily Aksyonov, a leader of the youth prose movement in the early Sixties. Worse, I kept hearing, the only interesting writing in the Seventies came from 'the Khruschchev generation' now in middle age, and the younger generation of the Seventies had not produced any striking new talent or writers with a dash of disobedience to replace the older ones. 'You have to be someone already to get away with saying anything at all,' shrewdly observed one literary critic in his twenties. 'Nowadays, daring young writers are crushed before they get started,' added an older man. Privately, Voznesensky acknowledged that he could never have gotten a liberal start and reputation in the conservative climate of the Seventies.

Moreover, Soviet cultural life was being drained of vitality and its characteristic talent. Not only was Solzhenitsyn forcibly ejected from the country but other important writers went into exile: Joseph Brodsky, perhaps the most talented living Russian poet; Viktor Nekrasov, celebrated author of *In the Trenches of Stalingrad*; Andrei Sinyavsky, a brilliant literary critic and dissident satirist; and Vladimir

Maximov, a strident dissident novelist, among others. A sense of cultural claustrophobia drove inventive, creative intellectuals in other fields to exile as well. Mstislav Rostropovich tired of the official 'quarantine' imposed on him for supporting Solzhenitsyn and went West with his wife, the operatic singer, Galina Vishnevskaya, in order to recapture his artistic career. Even such a nonpolitical figure as young Mikhail Baryshnikov, the leading dancer of Leningrad's Kirov Ballet and one of the most privileged of all artists in the Soviet Union, defected in Canada in 1974 and later let it be known that it was the deadening cultural conservatism that drove him out. He had wanted in Leningrad to dance Schoenberg and Webern but the ideological committee of the Ministry of Culture had ruled out such modern classics as 'not suitable for ballet.' Valery Panov, another Kirov star, mounted his campaign to emigrate for the same kind of reason.

These cases illustrate not only the stifling cultural controls but the stodginess of the entire cultural environment: in its public cultural life today, the Soviet Union, as a nation, has opted out on most of the cultural development of the 20th century – abstract art, modern dance, stream-of-consciousness prose. Dmitri Shostakovich stood until his recent death practically alone as an important composer in the medium of twelve-tone music, and this from a nation which overwhelmed the world with the richness of its musical as well as literary outpouring in the 19th and early 20th centuries. Today, the Bolshoi Ballet and the Soviet symphony orchestras for all their technical magnificence – and they are a treat to see and hear – are still performing essentially 19th-century repertoires.

In literature and drama as well, it is the 19th-century classics that set the standard. The common denominator of contemporary Soviet culture is still a banal, propagandistic factory drama like *Steelworkers* put on by the Moscow Art Theater, home of Chekhov and Stanislavsky. The plot of *Steelworkers* revolves around who will become the new leader of a work-brigade in a steel mill; its most dramatic moment occurs when the curtain parts to reveal four blast furnaces roaring realistically at the rear of the stage. As I was leaving Moscow, the most widely promoted movie was *The Hottest Month*, another steel plant saga where the drama focused on whether the Plan could be fulfilled. The biggest book editions go to stories of youth joyously marching off to the draft or to construction projects in Siberia, Communist patriots heroically fighting off the Whites during the Russian Civil War or heroically written war stories about the struggle against the fascists.

The brilliant stagecraft of such theater directors as Yuri Lyubimov at Taganka Theater, Anatoli Yefros at Malaya Bronnaya Theater, or Georgi Tovstonogov at Leningrad's Gorky Theater, and their new interpretations of the classics, diverts attention from the paucity of modern dramatic talent. In literature, people burrow into the 19th-century writers, one well-read engineer commented, 'because they are so much better, more honest, more revealing than anything that is being written today. All this Yevtushenko-Voznesensky-Shukshin doesn't interest me.' A university coed, an enthusiast of the classics, told me of the real panic in her Russian prose class at Moscow State University when the professor announced an upcoming test on literary style based on recognition of unidentified passages from contemporary writers supposedly read outside of class. 'I haven't read any modern Soviet authors in three years,' she moaned, 'and neither have my friends.' A slight exaggeration, perhaps, but her disinterest and that of other young people in contemporary Soviet writing was genuine. So tame and disappointing did some young people find the muffled art of Soviet establishment liberals in the early Seventies that they would hungrily ask for any Western writing, almost regardless of quality, because it was both exotic and unrestrained. I heard other intellectuals, more radical, complain that the liberals were doing a disservice because they were playing with half-truths and pulling their punches while pretending to speak out daringly. Ironically, it was Voznesensky who captured this turned-off mood of the young as well as expressing his own frustrations in some laconic ruminations which he published in 1972, called, *An Ironic Treatise on Boredom*:

> Boredom is a fast of the spirit,
> It is a solitary supper.
> The carousing of your enemies is boring,
> And your comrade is doubly boring.
> Art lies, thought is scant.
> Impudent rhymes are boring.

And your darling is as boring
As a whore who plays the nun.
A great fast of the spirit:
The applauding audiences are boring.

XVI

INTELLECTUAL LIFE
The Archipelago of Private Culture

Culture in Russia has been dispersed into tiny islets.
Lev Navrozov, 1972

The most vital and bracing cultural life in Russia is outlaw, and therefore private. It is the art least adulterated by official canons, the most original, the least compromised, and most threatening to the official cultural world. The State knows of its existence and fearing it has, in the words of the writer-in-exile Lev Navrozov, dispersed it into tiny islets.

These islets form a hidden archipelago whose life is far less well known than the life of the gulag archipelago so powerfully portrayed by Solzhenitsyn. Yet its existence is every bit as characteristic of Soviet society. In this private realm survives great art and literature – the richness of the pre-Revolutionary Silver Age of Russian culture, the brilliant abstract art of the early Soviet period, the incomparable writing of poets pilloried or persecuted to death in the Thirties. This art is not only purposefully excluded from official culture but is being intentionally forgotten. It survives because a few undaunted individuals have nominated themselves as keepers of culture otherwise lost to contemporary Soviet society.

Mostly, it is the elderly who preserve a human link with the past and nourish a younger generation curious to know their full cultural heritage. For in a nation where history is constantly written and rewritten to suit the present needs of rulers and where controversial cultural figures are frozen into vulgarized caricatures of themselves to fit the procrustean mold of State Culture, the tradition of oral history is not just a luxury to aid future scholars but a vital and trusted source of cultural continuity. The old Russian saying that the education of a child begins with his grandfather's education takes on special meaning when grandfathers preserve so much lore and knowledge that would be lost without their presence.

Widows and sons of great poets like Osip Mandelshtam and Boris Pasternak sustain the memory not only of those remarkable men but a tactile flesh-and-blood feel of the times in which they moved. Sometimes unexpected guardians of the past emerge. Naum Kleiman, a dedicated young admirer of the great Sergei Eisenstein, has not only single-handedly kept alive an apartment museum of that genius of cinema but has initiated such projects as the careful reconstruction of an Eisenstein movie from a few extant film clips. The original movie (*Bezhin Lug*) had so enraged Stalinist censors with its ideological heresies that they burned all the reels both times Eisenstein made the film. As Solzhenitsyn's writings have shown, self-appointed unofficial historians have preserved the personal documentation of the Stalinist repressions that the Party has tried assiduously to banish from public recollection, and underground balladiers now preserve the mood and memories of those years.

Russians are great people for remembering anniversaries and in the private archipelago of culture, important anniversaries are often occasions for the gathering of the modern equivalent of the 19th-century literary salons. I remember well one cool spring day, May 30, going to the writers' hideaway village of Peredelkino where scores of Muscovites, young and old, were making their annual pilgrimage to the grave of Boris Pasternak. One of the peculiar aspects of the Soviet system is that a man like Pasternak can be quoted, cited and honored as a poet because the regime finds it convenient to number such a famous lyrical writer within its official family. But the inconvenient half of Pasternak, the free spirit who wrote *Doctor Zhivago*, is simply denied any public existence. Tourists, when they ask about visiting his grave, are always given excuses about why that is impossible.

Yet so tranquil was the scene in Peredelkino that day that the ugly campaign against Pasternak, over *Zhivago* and the Nobel Prize that he was forced to decline, seemed only a distant memory. A cool breeze wafted through the three tall pines and the cove of birches that shelter his grave. Small boys were playing on piles of prefabricated slabs of concrete left out in the open and barefoot country women were quietly spading the rich chocolate earth near the graveyard. A huge black crow paused to peck in the freshly furrowed field.

On the white tombstone designed by Pasternak's friend, the sculptress Sara Lebedeva, people quietly laid their unpretentious bouquets – tulips, buttercups, hand-picked lilies of the valley, even dandelions. The tombstone, handsome in its stark simplicity, bore the clean, pure indented impression of the poet's craggy head and the simple legend, 'Boris Pasternak, 1890–1960.' The family had provided a miscellaneous assortment of water-filled jars for the overflow of flowers. 'There are not enough jars,' a family friend gently chided Alyonya Pasternak, the writer's daughter-in-law.

'Not to worry,' she replied, 'usually there are mountains of flowers on the grave.'

Those who came ranged from elderly women in baggy coats and the thick gray socks that Russian matrons prefer in the colder months, to modish young women in zipper-pocketed jeans or young men carrying attaché cases or wearing Western-cut raincoats. All had reached Peredelkino by the suburban *electrichka* train from Moscow and had walked nearly a mile to the grave. Pasternak's admirers began coming to the grave in midmorning and their gentle procession stretched into the evening. They would lay down their flowers and stand for a few moments in the rectangle of pilgrims around the grave until they saw that newcomers needed their places. At one point while we were there, a youth who wore a wreath of dandelions recited what was apparently his own poetry in praise of Pasternak and encouraged others to follow suit. Most preferred silence. A few hours later, another group, some of them professional writers, read Pasternak's poetry, including verses from *Doctor Zhivago.*

I wandered into the neighboring graveyard which had for decades been reserved for Old Bolsheviks – one reason why there had been controversy over Pasternak's being buried there. Each tombstone bore not only the normal dates of birth and death but the loyal record of when each person had joined the Communist Party. When I observed to one of Pasternak's relatives that Pasternak and the Old Bolsheviks made strange bedfellows, he smilingly commented, 'Pasternak was the Old Bolsheviks' link with the people.'

The writer's grave, and that of his wife nearby, look down a gentle slope across a broad meadow, already plowed and planted that Spring, to the rambling old wooden dacha where Pasternak lived out his final years. There his sons, Zhenya and Leonid, gathered with their friends in the evening while modern writers like Voznesensky, Yevtushenko, Aksyonov and many others came to pay their tribute and to read richly from the Pasternak that is still partly forbidden. In a society where the state ritually causes millions to mark so many anniversaries and holidays for its own political ends, this seemed all the more meaningful an occasion because it had been forgotten by the state and remembered by private individuals.

I recall another such gathering, at the home of the late Kornei Chukovsky, a brilliant and much-loved children's writer, where the level of the discourse, the spontaneous dramatic readings, the recited poetry and the ad-lib humor was refreshingly free of the cant and hypocrisy of the tortured mainstream of public culture and the rancid bitterness that is so often its private echo. There was nothing counter-revolutionary in what was said, but one sensed a pure and honest community, the Russian intelligentsia in its natural setting.

The company itself was interesting, perhaps because Chukovsky in his lifetime had ranged so broadly. Not only had he been the genial author of wonderful children's stories, as well known to Russians as Hans Christian Andersen to the rest of the world, but early in life he had been the charming, but sharp-witted *enfant terrible* among the literary critics during the luminous flowering of the Silver Age of Russian culture a few years before World War I. Tolstoy, Blok, Gorky, Bunin, Chaliapin, Mayakovsky had peopled his life and scribbled whimsy and irreverences in a marvelous album he kept through his life. The censors have not yet seen fit to permit the album to be published even posthumously. Late in life, in the Khrushchev-Brezhnev years, Chukovsky defended younger, liberal writers from Aksyonov and Aleksandr Galich to Solzhenitsyn, when they had come under fire from conservatives.

On that day his daughter, Lidiya Korneyevna, an important writer in her own right, had assembled an unusual company – Lev Kopelev, a scholar of Brecht and German culture who, as an Army officer, had objected to looting and raping by Soviet troops in Germany and for that had been sent to the camps for ten years where he met Solzhenitsyn and became a model for Rubin, one of the characters in *First Circle*; his wife, Raisa Orlova, a warm and talented literary critic and specialist in American literature; Venyamin Kaverin, a writer who had been a leader in the Serapion Brothers movement of the Twenties, attempting to free literature from all political and social commitment; Volodya Kornilov, a middle-aged poet and writer, husky and bearded as Hemingway; Natalya Ilyina, a prominent and very able satirical writer and journalist; Rina Zelenaya, a popular and delightfully amusing television actress; Klara Lozovsky, Chukovsky's devoted secretary who developed and maintained the museum which his house had become, despite the lack of customary assistance from the state; and two younger linguists and critics, Erik Khanpira and Vladimir Glotser. The three generations present were the physical embodiment of the transfer of culture from past to future.

It was a damp, cold day – October 28. The little hillside cemetery near the Peredelkino church, where Chukovsky was buried not far from Pasternak and the Old Bolsheviks, was a sea of coffee-colored mud and we slithered around the pathways, clinging to fenceposts to keep from sliding downhill. 'It was the kind of day on which he died,' someone whispered to me. But unbowed and straightbacked, Lidiya Chukovskaya stood by the grave, tall, white-haired and erect, like some New England Calvinist heroine. Of her, another writer remarked, 'When there is a flood in the countryside, there is usually a stick which stands upright in the stream and shows the level of the flood. Lidiya Korneyevna is like that. Always the same. Rigid. Uncompromising.' And for that unbending independence – her novels published in the West about the Stalinist period, her public defense of dissident physicist Andrei Sakharov when he was under severe attack in the fall of 1973 and her giving shelter to Solzhenitsyn in his final months in the Soviet Union – she was expelled from the Writers' Union in 1974.

After the penetrating dampness of the brief cemetery vigil, the warmth of Chukovsky's home museum was a welcome relief. A huge well-filled table had been set for twenty or more, and people plopped unceremoniously on an odd assortment of chairs, sofas padded with extra pillows, and stools. The Russians did not mind – it was company and conversation that mattered. Lidiya Chukovskaya, determined that the remembrance should be not only for the man but more significantly for a cultured spirit and an era of cultural elegance, had arranged for some readings. One was an amusing yet taut and telling essay by Chukovsky written in 1910 about several writers of the period. Another, done in 1911 by the writer Vasily Rozonov, graphically depicted Chukovsky's charm as a lecturer and then fiercely debated his highbrow contention that the mass media, especially the movies, were a corrupting influence that would cheapen Culture, with a capital C. Rozonov accused Chukovsky of being too far removed from the masses.

The two readings were a catalyst around the table for feverish discussion of well-remembered elements of Russian cultural life in the Silver Age. I could not follow it all, but clearly everyone had been stimulated by the richness of the essayists' linguistic styles and the openness of the debate six decades earlier. One by one, the writers around the table were coaxed into giving their own remarks, readings and performances for the others. Toasts were raised and the generous portions of food surrendered to the common appetite.

Rina Zelenaya, a little wag of a woman with a hoarse voice, rolling eyes and a plastic face that made her imitations of children on television a delight to all, gave a puckish parody of Soviet propaganda. She had come armed with a book of her own stories, including one satirizing the cult of 'hero workers' in the Soviet press.

Her story was about a small boy who had helped his grandmother wash the dishes once. When this became known at his Young Pioneers camp, he was promptly asked to give a speech to the camp, 'How I helped grandmother wash the dishes.' Soon, he was written up in the camp newspaper and then his school newspaper. His school was then deluged with letters from children in other cities asking him how dishes are washed and how one is most helpful to grandmother – all of which Rina Zelenaya read with a wonderful mixture of slurs, lisps, burps, mock seriousness, and the gawkish awkwardness of a nine-year-old, her eyes rolling and a hand on her hip, the elbow stuck jauntily outward. By that time the company had made a substantial dent in the vodka as well as the food, and people were laughing so hard at her performance that some found it hard to breathe.

But the little hero campaign rolled onward. The boy himself was asked to write testimonials about dishwashing for other schools to post on their bulletin boards and to print in their newspapers. His life became one great testimonial. Finally, one evening, the grandmother asked him to help her wash the dishes once more. But the young hero could not. He was so busy writing letters to others about how to wash dishes and how to help grandmother, that he had no time to do it any more himself.

Of all the self-appointed carriers of culture, Nadezhda Mandelshtam personifies most clearly the living conduit of knowledge that is officially dead. Her frail husband, Osip Mandelshtam, perhaps the greatest Russian poet of the century, paid with his life for a 14-line poem that mocked Stalin as 'the Kremlin mountaineer, the murderer' with a 'cockroach whiskers leer' and 'fingers fat as grubs'. Mandelshtam vanished in the Stalinist camps, died roughly in 1938 – no one has pinpointed the date. In 1973, delayed by censors for 13 years, a collection of some of his poetry was published and marketed almost entirely abroad, in callous disregard of the hunger for Mandelshtam's work among his own people. The volume was bereft, not surprisingly, of his most trenchant verses, those either too virile or too tragic for Soviet censors. Those poems have appeared only in the West, thanks to his widow's tenacious efforts to insure that the legacy did not perish. Like a hunted rabbit, as Joseph Brodsky put it, she dodged about the country for years after his death, avoiding arrest and preserving the treasure of Mandelshtam's poetry by scattering it among friends for safekeeping and memorizing practically every line, thus making herself a living archive.

'If you get me started,' she said to me once, 'I can recite for three hours without stopping.' It would have been impossible that afternoon, for Nadezhda Yakovlevna, as her Russian friends call her, was rasping and coughing from a variety of ailments aggravated, I am sure, by the pungent tobacco of the strong, foul-smelling Russian *papirosy*, the tube cigarettes to which she was addicted in spite of her ulcer and her 72 years. She would puff and cough, puff and cough, put out one vile tube and light another, twisting its hollow stem, Russian style, for a filter. But judging from her coughing, it did not filter much. Sometimes she looked as pale and ancient as death, but in fact she was unquenchable as life itself – short, sturdy, 'tough – as women have to be', she herself liked to boast.

Nadezhda Yakovlevna was also flattered by anything that allowed her to play the role of poet's widow and to recall her anguished but halcyon martyrdom with her beloved Osip. One evening, I remember how a pilgrimage to her apartment by Jan Meyer, a slavic specialist from the University of Utrecht, prompted her to rattle off from memory and later aided by dossiers secreted under her bed, ten variations of one of Mandelshtam's longer poems, while Meyer scribbled away furiously and I held her wobbly, porcelain-topped kitchen table steady for him to write upon.

Young Russian intellectuals hovered around her like acolytes, attending to her housekeeping, while she preached or lectured as long as energy held out. She would either lie on her side in bed when an ailing leg kept her from getting up or, wrapped in a faded green housecoat, would sit on the high-backed settee that occupied half of her tiny kitchen. Her one bedroom-living room was absolutely crammed with a disorderly clutter of books, ikons, records, paintings, furniture – more books than furniture – and dried flowers, brought to her long ago by admiring friends and evidently too precious a remembrance of them or of nature to be thrown away. It was impossible for more than three or four people to gather around her without someone knocking over a vase of dried flowers.

In such a setting, she would open up an entire universe to her listeners with her vivid recollections not only of Mandelshtam but of legendary Russian poets like Akhmatova, Tsvetayeva, Pasternak and Bely, or writers like Bulgakov, Zoshchenko, Platonov, or Pilnyak, an entire constellation of Russian culture for half a century, all of whom she had known personally. More than anything, she relished a chance to have others confirm her husband's preeminent place in the firmament, but not cheaply. One of her favorite intellectual sports was to challenge someone else to come up with a great intellectual figure or a writer from anywhere in the world, in order to undercut the candidate and reassure herself that no one was a match for Mandelshtam and to reaffirm her own judgment that not only Russian culture but world culture was irreversibly in decline.

Her own vinegary judgments of art and people were rendered as unsparingly as by the Old Testament Jehovah. In the incestuous world of the Moscow intelligentsia, where important writers not only know each other but are often related or married to each other's former wives or husbands, this trait turned many old friends away from her permanently when her naked verdicts appeared in her two remarkable books, *Hope Against Hope* and *Hope Abandoned*. Especially after the second book was published in the West, we knew several free-spirited intellectuals who so resented her having dismissed people as weak-willed toadies, informers, or the like, that they would no longer join her coterie or visit her apartment. Some were embittered that she had criticized others from the relative safety of her world prominence while other people, less well known and hence more vulnerable, could not afford to speak out candidly in reply without jeopardizing themselves or giving ammunition to the authorities against her, which they were loath to do.

Perhaps her tartness was a sign of age. Once, when I was talking with Nadezhda Yakovlevna about the problem of being Jewish in the Soviet Union, the discussion touched the late Ilya Ehrenburg whose famous novel *The Thaw* lent its name to the period of Khrushchevian cultural liberalism of the late Fifties and early Sixties. I recalled Ehrenburg's remark that, 'It is impossible not to feel Jewish when there is anti-Semitism in one's homeland.'

'That's the only good thing he said,' Nadezhda Yakovlevna declared. The acidity of her comment surprised me not only because Ehrenburg had been a lifelong friend of the Mandelshtams but also because he had presided in 1965 at a rare evening in Osip Mandelshtam's honor. I suggested that for foreigners, Ehrenburg was a more complex figure, but she came back quickly: 'His specialty was deceiving foreigners.' She meant, deceiving them into thinking that he was more liberal than in fact he was, which is still a much-practiced technique of writers, journalists, scientists and intellectuals interested in ingratiating themselves with Westerners. When I asked her by whom we were being deceived now, unhesitatingly she replied, 'You are now being deceived by Yevtushenko and Voznesensky.'

Equally harsh was she in her judgment of the Western world whose literature she knew fairly well for she had read widely in English, French and German and had talked with a number of Western scholars and writers who had visited the Soviet Union. In her estimation, T. S. Eliot was 'a great poet' and William Faulkner a 'great prose writer'. She admired them both for their Christian belief as well as their art, for Christianity was a vital matter to her. 'Tell me a great American writer since Faulkner,' she would demand. Saul Bellow she found tedious. Nabokov was only a craftsman. W. H. Auden and Robert Lowell were not on a par with the greats. Hemingway was shallow. F. Scott Fitzgerald she felt was better because he captured the spirit of an age and he loved America.

Although Nadezhda Yakovlevna had the tensile strength of steel and the authorities had not harassed her in recent years, treating her as a non-person, the fear that followed her for years after her husband's arrest in May 1943 still haunted her. One evening, when Ann and I were alone with her, she was constantly phoning friends, talking to each for only a couple of minutes, like a blind person reaching for the walls in a room, seeking the reassurance of contact with some known point on the compass. The apartment searches and the interrogations of other intellectuals, particularly pronounced in 1972 and 1973 during the secret police crackdown against the unofficial *Chronicle of Current Events*, worried her greatly. 'I'm always shivering in the evening but after half an hour I'll stop,' she said, rather clinically. I glanced at my watch. It was 8.30. 'After nine, *they* don't come,' she advised. '*They* are not allowed to come after that.' Why she thought that the secret police had a nine o'clock curfew, I don't know. But she was then as convinced of that as she had been earlier that they would get her before she could write Mandelshtam's story and get it out to the West to be published. 'I was greatly afraid when I was writing both my books but I kept going,' she said. 'I had to – there was nothing else to do. It was my duty to my husband.'

Americans, she protested, had no idea how others lived, especially Russians. She had heard from the poet Robert Lowell who had read *Hope Against Hope* and remarked, in response to her searing descriptions of the hell of informing, repressions, interrogations, suspicions, midnight arrests, and oppressive fear of the Stalinist era, that things were much the same everywhere, evidently in some effort to console her. 'You Americans are wonderful liars,' she growled with a knowing smile.

At the time when the exodus of Soviet Jewish intellectuals to Israel and the West was at its peak in 1972 and 1973, Nadezhda Yakovlevna liked to tease herself and others with the notion of going into exile. But she was far too deeply rooted in Russia, too deeply devoted to her task of passing on to the younger generation what she knew of the past, for anyone to take seriously her threatened departure. But her one wish for many years was to be sure that the complete collection of Mandelshtam's papers would finally find some safe repository, preferably abroad with some Western scholar whom she could trust. That accomplished, she told a friend, 'then I could die in peace.'

So it was arranged for a young American to help convey them out of the country. Nadezhda Yakovlevna had not dared keep them all in her own apartment because she feared a raid by the secret police. They were farmed out to the most trusted young scholars and students. So she had them assembled, perhaps 25 pounds of papers in all, and when they were all at her place, word was passed indirectly to the American to come take them. A day or two later, he arrived and Nadezhda Yakovlevna, who never had patience for trivia, went right to the business.

'You've come,' she said, lying in her bed. 'I had them all here, but I have sent them away.'

Her large brown eyes, searching for a reaction, the creases in her full, masculine head deeper than ever, her wispy hair neatened but not combed, showed how much she had been tested by the decision. To part with that lifeblood legacy was as anguishing for her as to part from Russia itself.

'Do you despise me for being so two-minded?' she asked the young man, in that characteristic, uncompromising Biblical way of hers. He shook his head.

'I couldn't do it,' she said, this living vessel of Russian culture. 'These young people love them. You see, there is always Russia . . . ' And, regardless of risk, that was where she felt they belonged.

It is hard to imagine two individuals more different than Nadezhda Mandelshtam and George Costakis, the Russian-born Greek who had assembled what must be the world's foremost collection of the brilliant painting of the first Russian avant-garde that was so firmly suppressed in the Twenties. Where she is bold and blasphemous, brazenly confronting power, Costakis has been cautious and calculating, defensive and diplomatic, courting power and seeking to beguile it. But like her, he is an important atoll in the uncharted archipelago of private culture for he has managed to accumulate an enormous lode of Russia's forgotten cultural wealth and to preserve it when the natural ravages of an antagonistic system would have destroyed it.

By all the logic of Soviet realism even today, George Costakis and his private art collection should not exist. It is a measure of the idiosyncrasies of the Soviet system, which permits in private what it censures in public, that one can step into the ample, well-appointed seven-room apartment of Costakis and be transported to a world utterly beyond the boundaries of the stodgy, placard world of official Soviet art.

Not once, but several times, Ann and I went there and on each occasion we were overwhelmed from the instant we entered by the fireworks of modern art – dazzling in a country which has so little aesthetic beauty and color in its public life. The apartment is literally ablaze with the colors of nearly 300 works of Kazimir Malevich, Vasily Kandinsky, Marc Chagall, Vladimir Tatlin, Lyubov Popova, Ivan Klyun, Kliment Ritko, Aleksandr Rodchenko and many others – in every room, on every wall, in almost every inch of space. Here, an entire wall of Chagall blue fantasies and fairytale country figures in lyrical woodcut style. There, nine Kandinskys, including the well-known psychedelic abstraction of Red Square. Opposite, a large and pivotal canvas by Malevich at the juncture when he was leaving cubism to create his new geometrical suprematism and to chart a new course for art.

Very few people, Russian or foreigners, are aware of the multimillion dollar collection of Russian suprematism, constructivism, cubism and abstract modernism that this 63-year-old Greek has assembled. But such art experts as Princeton's Frederick Starr compare its impact to that of the famous Armory Show in New York in 1913 which first opened American eyes to new trends in European art. 'What is interesting for foreigners when they see my collection,'

Costakis remarked, 'is that they find that in some paintings the Russians were 30, 40, 50 years in advance. Something that was done in Russia in 1917, 1918, 1919 was done in America in the Fifties and Sixties.'

Not only are foreigners amazed. So is Costakis. I remember one wintry afternoon as he was showing around a group of people from Western embassies, Costakis recalled his own joy of discovery at his first glimpse of a single-stripe white and green abstraction by Olga Rozonova done in 1917. 'My heart was beating wildly,' he said. 'It was like finding a rocket ship built in 1917 and stored in someone's shed. Impossible! Because they were just making such a rocket ship 10 or 15 years ago. But there are the markings. It was really done in 1917.'

The suprematist designs of Klyun, with circles superimposed on geometric shapes and layers of translucent color passing through each other foreshadowed, in Costakis' view, some experimentation by American artists 40 years later. Over a bed, he has hung a painting of drips and splashes by Rodchenko which he feels predated Jackson Pollock's first such ventures. 'Don't think I am putting Russian art way up here and American art way down there,' Costakis said, raising one sturdy hand over his head and pushing the other down to his knee, 'because today, the most important art – the most interesting things – are being done in America. But it happened, you see, that some things were done in Russia first.'

Physically, George Costakis seems an unlikely man to collect dazzling modern art. If one had a palette, the instinct would be to paint him in subdued browns and olives, catching the weight of his shoulders, his dark hair, his drooping eyes, his heavy hands. As a person, too, he is an unusual combination. Blended with his passion for bright, unconventional art, I sensed not only the natural instincts of a collector, wealth inherited from his father's prosperous tobacco business, a keen Greek mercantile eye for value, and the special status of a foreigner (who since 1943 has worked for the Canadian Embassy) enjoying protection that Russians do not have, but also the inbred conservative canniness of a ward politician who has studied the prevailing political winds and ferreted out allies within the Establishment to help him navigate the shoals.

Paradoxically, Costakis' passion for art was born about the

time that Kandinsky and Chagall fled West as the avant-garde was being snuffed out in the mid-Twenties. As a lad of 13, he became a choirboy at the Orthodox Church on Pushkin Square where the great Chaliapin occasionally sang. 'Sometimes, I would not have time to get home and I would sleep at the church on the robes of the priests,' he said. 'The robes, the ikons, and the paintings were very beautiful. These gave me a taste for art.'

His collector's instinct got its boost about the same time. His brother-in-law, a member of the aristocratic Greek Metaxas family, had a set of rare stamps which he left to his widow. No one appreciated their value and they were given to young George who raced off to sell them to get money toward a bicycle. He was astonished when a Japanese tourist outside the stamp store 'gave me all the money in his wallet – enough for six bicycles'. By the time he was 22, Costakis was seriously collecting antiques, old Russian silver and paintings by traditional French and Dutch masters. In the prewar period, as the families of the old czarist nobility, deprived of their fortunes, sold off their art works, Moscow was full of treasures at bargain prices.

The sea change in Costakis' life came after World War II when traditional art began to pall. 'Little by little, I got tired of all the grays and browns,' he explained one afternoon over very strong black coffee. 'I wanted some color around me. Bright modern art is like medicine for me. If I feel bad, I can come into the room, sit surrounded by it and it cures me. Also, I wanted to do something new. I knew that anyone could collect Dutch masters. I thought to myself, "The Louvre is full, and every city has four or five museums of classical art." I had always wanted to do something – write a book, invent a machine. Then accidentally, I came across two or three avant-garde paintings. To me, they were dynamic and colorful. I got them for nothing. I put them with my other paintings, and it was as if I had been living in a dark room and suddenly the sun came in.'

Not only was he unusual and daring, but lucky. That was the era when Stalin's henchman, Andrei Zhdanov, was vigorously stamping out formalism and liberalism in all the arts. 'Stupid Greek – collecting junk!' is what Costakis recalled other collectors saying about him then. Like a detective he began to track down the art of the avant-garde. Some paintings came from widows and families of artists.

Others, like his favorite of Olga Rozonova, were given to him by collectors who had no use for abstract art. Rodchenko had done six modernistic mobiles but, out of fear of discovery under Stalin, destroyed five. The sixth survived, collapsed and hidden on top of a wardrobe, and Costakis retrieved it. A Popova abstraction, painted on plywood, hung for years in a barn. Another painting was under oilcloth on someone's kitchen table, either hidden in ignorance or deliberately secreted.

When Costakis had to pay, he bought at tremendous bargains. A big Malevich cubist-suprematist work, now worth possibly $1.5 million, cost him roughly $400. He paid the same for a lovely Chagall still life 'Lilacs on a table' and half that much for a cubist work by Popova. Those were years, he explained, when names like Kandinsky and Chagall were known, but not fully appreciated, and when he himself was branching out from what he likes to call the marshals and generals of the Russian avant-garde to 'find the colonels, and captains and the privates'. In all, he estimated that about 300 painters took part in the avant-garde movement from 1910–1925 and about 40 are in his collection.

To Western eyes, there is nothing politically incendiary in this art, with one exception, though Soviet conservatives can find mutinous meaning in anything unorthodox. The exception, a striking one, is a prophetic Kafkaesque canvas called 'Uprising' done by Kliment Ritko at the time of Lenin's death in 1924. Chillingly, it conveys the Red terror and the regimentation of Stalinist totalitarianism to come and the civil war just past. Like a political ikon, it sets out the main figures of the Revolution – Lenin, Stalin, Trotsky, Bukharin and others, in a diamond pattern against a blood-red background. Around this centerpiece move somber funeral bands and truckloads of troops, shooting defenseless people in the streets. In the rest of the collection, however, the only visible political sentiment, if any, is the exuberant idealism of the artists of the revolutionary period. Still, the collection hangs in a peculiarly Soviet kind of limbo.

The art itself remains taboo. Yet discreetly and without official interference, Costakis has shown it to foreigners, from resident diplomats to art scholars and such distinguished visitors as Marc Chagall, Nina Kandinsky, David Rockefeller, Averell Harriman and former French premier Edgar Faure. More gingerly yet, he has opened this rich heritage to select groups of Russians. As many as 90 at a time have come from the Moscow Institute of Architecture, Pushkin Museum, Tretyakov Gallery or the Russian Museum in Leningrad. Costakis, who is careful not to mix foreigners and Russians in his private showings, thrives on giving guided tours, explaining the art or softly playing a melancholy guitar while his blonde wife, Zina, sings old Russian romances. In June 1972 he loaned 27 cubist and abstract paintings by Klyun and Popova to senior scientists at the Kurchatov Institute of Physics who were interested in modern art. On another occasion, he organized a similar closed exposition of work by Mikhail Larionov at the institute.

His patient goal has been to gain recognition for the avant-garde art, first abroad and then through Western influence, in Moscow. In 1959 he got his first break when sympathetic officials in the Ministry of Culture helped him send five paintings to a Chagall exhibition in West Germany. Since then, other small groups of his paintings have been loaned briefly to the Metropolitan Museum in New York, Tate Gallery in London, Los Angeles County Museum of Art, and galleries in Japan, Italy, Germany and elsewhere, but Soviet authorities have always rejected requests for a loan of the entire collection. Some Soviet officials, including the late Minister of Culture, Yekaterina Furtseva, his secret patron, have been flattered that his showings abroad and to limited circles in Moscow have helped publicize Russian artistic achievements in a way that has added to Soviet prestige in the West without challenging official canons of art at home. In return, Costakis has been allowed to sell off some lesser works of modern painters and possibly part of his magnificent and valuable collection of classic religious ikons.

As part of an obvious accommodation with some authorities, he has played the politics of art with careful conservatism in recent years. In the late Fifties and early Sixties, he used to collect the works of the contemporary unofficial artists like Oskar Rabin, Dmitri Plavinsky, and Vasily Sitnikov. Curious Westerners in that period often had Costakis as a guide leading them to the subterranean world of nonconformist artists. But as his semiofficial stature grew, Costakis broke with those artists and sold off many of their paintings. When in September 1974 they boldly attempted to hold their outdoor art exhibits, Costakis was privately alarmed by their tactics of confrontation, fearing that they would jeopardize his world. 'That is not the way to help art,' he complained. For a time, he stopped allowing Russians to see his own collection until 'the scandal' blew over.

He became defensive, too, about Western contentions that the Soviets killed the avant-garde movement with political suppression. 'That is not true,' he asserted to a group one afternoon, somewhat inconsistently with his own tales of the difficulties of finding the hidden art. 'The avant-garde sent paintings abroad. They exhibited here. They had freedom. But people did not understand their art. Nobody recognized them or appreciated them. Everywhere – in England, in America, in France – people lost interest in avant-garde art. Cubism was accepted. So was Fauvism. But not avant-garde. Only in the last ten or fifteen years has it come back.'

His ardent advocacy of Russian artistic achievement and his deliberate effort to avoid offending the authorities have helped him win some official favor. Mme Furtseva, when she was alive, led Costakis to believe that when the new Tretyakov Gallery opened in 1977, some of his works might be displayed there. Whether or not she could have won the necessary approval of the Party leadership, her death has raised new uncertainties. As a final hope, Costakis has talked of some arrangement permitting him to keep and sell off a small portion of his paintings as an inheritance for his family, if he were to bequeath the rest to Russia. 'I don't want this collection to be destroyed,' he said to me one afternoon with the earnest concern of a man growing old and caught in a delicate dilemma. 'When the Russians are ready to recognize this art, I will give it to the state.'

Although lowbrow in comparison with the Costakis collection, a medium with far wider impact in the private world of the intelligentsia is music – the music of the underground balladiers. Circulating unpublishable writing in Russia is as old as Pushkin who did it 150 years ago when the Czar and his censors blocked the publication of some of his poetry. The Russians call it *samizdat*, literally, self-publishing. The advent of the electronic age with its handy portable cassette recordings has revolutionized *samizdat*, and made the job of ideological watchdogs infinitely more complicated. A writer or humorist with a guitar can sing some amusing, politically off-color songs to friends at a small party and, if someone has brought along a tape or cassette recorder (which the Russians call a *magnitofon*), the process of uncensored reproduction begins at once and its outward ripples continue endlessly. Wryly, the Russians call this *magnitizdat*, magnetic self-publishing. Through that medium, the modern outlaw minstrels of Soviet society have developed an audience of millions, not only the young and disgruntled intelligentsia, but technocrats and even government and Party officials, all clandestine admirers.

Since about 1960, when *magnitizdat* got its start as Khrushchev was letting people out of the Stalinist camps, a couple of dozen balladiers have become known. Of these, by far the best-known figures of the underworld of music are Bulat Okudzhava, Vladimir Vysotsky and Aleksandr Galich.

Okudzhava is a well-established liberal poet and writer now in his early forties. His *Gulp of Freedom* is a funny, bawdy, and highly unconventional historical novel about the 19th-century Russian revolutionaries known as the Decembrists, presenting them not as a band of fearless heroes in the stereotype of Soviet propaganda, but as a confused and beaten lot, however admirable their democratic impulses. His underground songs have a similar, lyrical mood of melancholy alienation. As a war veteran who was wounded, Okudzhava has many songs about the cruel and aimless brutality of war decidedly at odds with official panegyrics. 'Don't believe in war, little boy,' goes one, 'it is sad, little boy, and as tight as boots. Your dashing steed can accomplish nothing, and you will wind up getting all the bullets.'* Several times, Okudzhava was called down by the ideologists for his 'uncivic' ballads, but he continued to compose them until, in June 1972, he was expelled from the Communist Party for 'anti-Party behavior and refusal to condemn the publication of some of his works abroad'. Since then, he has been less active.

The most popular of the balladiers by far is Vysotsky, a jaunty, sandy-haired, nationally famous movie star and actor

---

* Translation by Gene Sosin, 'Magnitizdat: Uncensored Songs of Dissident,' in Rudolf L. Tokes, ed., *Dissent in the U.S.S.R.* (Baltimore, 1975). In these excerpts from songs by Okudzhava and Galich, I have used Sosin's excellent translations.

500

at Moscow's liberal Taganka Theater where I saw him perform several times. Vysotsky, who is married to French film star Marina Vlady, has become something of an idol to all young people. In his own youth, he did a stretch in the penal camps, got out during the Khrushchev period, and made his peace with the regime by playing movie roles calculated to inspire idealistic Soviet youth – mountain climbers, geologists, or patriots headed off to conquer Siberia. On television or at the Taganka, Vysotsky, now in his early forties, has gained status playing Hamlet, the lead role in Brecht's *Galileo* and Pechorin in Lermontov's classic, *Hero of Our Time*.

Deftly Vysotsky has plied an ambivalent course. His five officially released records include wholesome Soviet tunes about alpinists, friendship, space heroes and the war dead. Even his unofficial repertoire is sprinkled with humorous tunes mocking Bobby Fischer, the rough play of Canadian hockey pros, or Chairman Mao, all themes with a healthy dollop of patriotism that he can use at concerts and an army of young Soviet guitarists can play safely on the streets. The more private his audience, especially if it is a group of actors drinking into the wee hours after a show, the more risks he takes. One writer raved to me about a Vysotsky routine aping the clumsy, ungrammatical talk of a factory director, an act with calculated appeal for the Moscow intelligentsia who look down their noses at 'our peasant bosses'. Rarely does he go that far in song, however. One Vysotsky tune, playing on the 'inequality of sounds' on the musical scale, pokes fun at the rank consciousness of Soviet officialdom. Another, 'The Ballad of the Currency Store', mocks the cultural elite trooping off to special stores to buy carpets, fur coats and caviar with special certificates which ordinary rubles cannot buy. Yet another, named for a mythical 'Seryozhka Fomin', lampoons officials who sat out World War II on the home front, awarding themselves the nation's highest decorations:

While I shed my blood for the country and for home,
Something always burned me up inside:
I was bleeding for Seryozhka Fomin,
While he sat back and did not risk his hide.
At last the war was over,
The heavy burden from our shoulders passed,

> I met Seryozhka Fomin. Lo – Hero of the Soviet
> Union – on his breast.*

Vysotsky has many tunes about the miseries of prison
camp life, the fate of penal battalions in the war and one
daring 'song of the madhouse', telling of the trauma of a
sane man put in a mental hospital where real lunatics menace
him – 'and if Gogol could be told about our life in grief,
even Gogol would gaze on it, in utter disbelief'. But Vysotsky,
a slick performer with a knock for suggestive innuendo,
leaves it unclear whether the prisoners have landed in the
penal camps or the mental hospital for political crimes or
something less subversive. And this takes the sting out of
many of his songs.

Like Okudzhava, he has been publicly chastized, bawled
out for 'profiteering' in 1973 by giving 16 concerts in four
days in the city of Novokuznetsk, when the legal limit is
one a day, and barred from traveling to France to see or
accompany his wife. But ever agile, he has always managed
to bounce back, protected in part by his mass following and
his loyal ballads. 'He is clever,' observed a woman journalist.
'Vysotsky makes it because he knows the limits. The KGB
themselves collect his songs. They know all those camp tunes
of his. They like the jargon of thieves that he uses – they
are thieves themselves. Vysotsky knows you can criticize different things here and there, but you can't criticize the
system, the Party, and you can never touch *them* (the
bosses) personally. His songs aren't political. That is what
finished Galich.'

Unlike Vysotsky, Aleksandr Galich, who is from an older
generation, did not spend time in the camps but for 30 years
was a successful writer, before disillusionment and a sense of
guilt moved him into the ranks of the underground balladiers. He is the only one I heard and came to know personally. And he is by far the most barbed in his satire, the most
desolate in his view of Soviet society, and the most daring in
theme. Born in 1918, he was trained as an actor in the
Stanislavsky school and later became a successful dramatist.
Ten of his plays and several screenplays, described by official
Soviet publications as dealing with 'the romance of the

* Vladimir Vysotsky, 'Seryozhka Fomin,' from 'Ballads from the
Underground,' in *Problems of Communism* (USIA, Washington, Vol. XIX,
No. 6, 1970, p. 28), selected and translated by Misha Allen.

struggle and creative labor of Soviet youth', were performed before he fell out of favor, though a handful of his best scripts did not make it past the censor. The sharp edge of moral dissent in his underground ballads later earned him the nickname as 'the Solzhenitsyn of Song'.

With a receding hairline and a prominent moustache, Galich looks like a stouter, taller, sadder Xavier Cugat. Hunched over his little guitar and singing in a light, un-musical bass, he can transform a smoke-filled apartment, jammed with sweating people, into a political cabaret. 'First I have a housekeeping matter,' he will begin. 'If anybody telephones me, please ask them to call back in an hour or hour and a half.' The obvious allusion to telling the KGB to wait while Galich sings his political songs gets a laugh. Then, deadpan and sardonic, he launches into 'The Ballad of the Clean Hands', mocking the political lot of the Soviet citizen as the obligation 'to chew, to moo and to listen'. While campfires burn in the Siberian labor camps and Soviet armored trains stand near Prague, Galich pictures Russians repeating their school grammar lesson: 'I wash my hands, you wash your hands, he washes his hands . . .'

So minimal is Galich's guitar playing that it often comes across as a musical prop for a raconteur whose tales turn on masterful parody of the bureaucratic language of public life, historical allusions, and the argot of the underworld. To drive home an image, Galich will come up with grotesque combinations like casting Stalin as Herod in the story of the Nativity or forcing Johann Sebastian Bach, as the symbol of the creative individual, to endure the daily grind of Soviet life. He has sung movingly about anti-Semitism in Warsaw and trains leaving for Auschwitz, or prisoners off in the Stalinist camps. But where Galich was most daring and most different from the others was in singing not only about the oppressed little people of Soviet society but their high and mighty oppressors – challenging the contemporary generation of leaders.

In several tunes he suggested that the Stalinist mood is not dead and that hangmen are nostalgic for the old days. One eerie vocal fantasy, *Night Patrol*, imagines a monument of Stalin and thousands of other statues coming back to life in the dark of night and stalking the sleeping city while drums roll. Another characteristic Galich lyric takes aim at successful careerists who made their way to the top by silently riding with the tide:

> Let others cry out from despair,
> From insult, from hunger and cold!
> In silence we know there's more profit,
> And the reason is – silence is gold.
> That's how you get to be wealthy,
> That's how you get to be first,
> That's how you get to be hangman!
> Just keep mum, keep mum, keep mum.

Galich has peopled his repertoire of more than 100 underground tunes with several stock Soviet characters. On the night that I heard him, people were calling for songs about Klem Petrovich Kolomytsev, 'workshop foreman, holder of many decorations, and deputy of the city Soviet'. In one ballad, Klem Petrovich goes to plead with higher officials for proper recognition of the outstanding performance of his factory in fulfilling all economic plans up to 1980, but they beg off saying it would be too embarrassing to make a public commendation – the West would raise a fuss because the plant produces barbed wire! Another Klem Petrovich escapade that delights Russians is a lovely lampoon on the canned propaganda lectures everyone is called upon to make at various meetings. In the Galich rendition, Klem Petrovich is handed a prepared text, mistakenly meant for a woman, but gamely delivers it unknowingly:

> The Israeli militarists, I say,
> Are well known to the whole world.
> As a mother, I say, and as a woman:
> I demand they be brought to answer.

Astonished, Klem Petrovich checks the audience and the Party officials as he rolls on verse after verse of this feminist appeal, but he finds everyone too numbed from so many lectures to notice the mistake. Afterwards, the Party Secretary praises him: 'You gave it to 'em good – like a worker.'

Surprisingly, given his daring, Galich had one mass public concert – only one – in early 1968 at the House of Scientists in Novosibirsk's Academic City, then a haven of liberalism, where 2,500 people heard him sing for three hours or more.

His songs in tribute to Pasternak, his political tunes about Stalinism and his adventures of Klem Petrovich were enthusiastically received, he told me. But later he said, he was summoned by the heads of the Writers' Union and forbidden to make more appearances. 'Well, no one forbade me,' he smiled. 'You know their hypocritical way: "We don't recommend it. You have a bad heart, dear boy. No need to strain yourself . . ." '

Galich's downfall came, however, in December 1971 at a private party where he was not even singing. According to Galich, Vysotsky was singing Galich's songs at the wedding party of a young actor, Ivan Dykhovichny, who had married Olga Polyansky, the blonde daughter of Dmitri Polyansky, a member of the Politburo. Polyansky, who has a very conservative reputation, was said to have chuckled at some of Vysotsky's own lighter tunes but to have been outraged at Galich's sharp satires. Surprisingly, Polyansky's son, a naval officer, tried to offer a defense by saying that these songs were not that unusual, that they were sung even by Navy officers. But that only enraged Polyansky more.

According to Galich, Polyansky telephoned that very night to Pyotr Demichev, the Party's chief watchdog over cultural affairs and within ten days, on December 29th, Galich was expelled from the Writers' Union on the pretext that he was propagating Zionism, encouraging people to emigrate to Israel, and refusing to renounce the publication of his songs in the West. He lost his rights as a filmwriter, too. Some of his films were withdrawn and his credits were removed from others. 'Not only am I untouchable but I am unmentionable,' Galich later protested. He was left without work to live on a 60-ruble-a-month state disability pension granted on the grounds of his several heart attacks. In early 1974, finding the black-listing unbearable, Galich applied for a visa to visit a cousin in New York City but the government rejected his application 'for ideological reasons'. In an open letter to the International Committee on Human Rights, he protested that he had been deprived of all rights except 'the right to resign myself to my complete lack of rights, to admit that at 54 my life is practically over, and to get my invalid's pension and shut up'. But as a result of an international campaign over his case he was allowed to emigrate in mid-1974.

XVII

RELIGION

Solzhenitsyn and the Russianness of Russia

Russia cannot be understood by wit alone.
Common measures cannot be applied to her.
She has a special character.
One must simply believe in Russia.

Fyodr Tyutchev
(19th-century Slavophile poet)

The West has fallen into belated disenchantment with Aleksandr Solzhenitsyn, a mark of its earlier misconception of the man and of the Russianness of Russia itself. Solzhenitsyn confounded Western expectations. People were disconcerted that the heroic dissident who had documented the terrors of a police state should also scorn democracy. It became a nuisance that he was such a moral absolutist, so obsessed with his holy mission to purge Mother Russia of Stalinism and Marxism that he would not stay the volcanic flow of his works when foreigners were sated. It was a shock that when his own manifesto appeared, it offered not a model of an open, urban, scientific society joining the modern world but a mystic vision of a future-past, a dream of Holy Russia resurrected by turning inward into itself and pulling away from the 20th century. Westerners, quick to focus on dissent from the left in their own image, too easily disposed to ignore the Russian right, found his prescription awkwardly archaic. Yet his strain of religious Russophilism articulates a whole syndrome of feelings and sentiments that have strong pull on large numbers of Russians.

Solzhenitsyn himself, I found on first encounter, never

fits preconceptions. Dissidents are not supposed to be dictatorial, yet the willful Russian autocrat in him manifested itself almost at once and produced the most baffling interview that I have ever had.

It took place in early 1972, when such undertakings were not without peril. For Solzhenitsyn then lived in the very jaws of the leviathan, a solitary, defiant soul with the audacity to assert his full freedom as a writer and to challenge the entire apparatus of the Soviet state by publishing works like *Cancer Ward* and *First Circle* abroad when Soviet authorities suppressed them. For ideological heresy he had been excommunicated from the Writers' Union. To contact him was to venture into a politically radioactive zone: the aftereffects were uncertain.

Our meeting was arranged with conspiratorial precautions to avoid tipping off the authorities. Secret negotiations were conducted through Zhores Medvedev, the dissident biologist. Never was the topic mentioned indoors for fear of bugs. Medvedev himself occasionally resorted to code language. Bob Kaiser of the *Washington Post,* my partner in the endeavor, once overheard Medvedev telling someone by phone that he had forgotten his briefcase. Noticing that Medvedev had the briefcase, Kaiser inquired, 'What was that all about?' and Medvedev said it was the signal to fix the meeting with Solzhenitsyn for Thursday, March 30th. On a night when Solzhenitsyn was out of Moscow, we were given a dry run past the old cream-colored apartment building where the interview would take place. To prepare questions in privacy, Kaiser and I went skating at a deserted outdoor rink near Lenin Stadium.

So blasé have Westerners become about Solzhenitsyn's exile in Zurich that they have forgotten the breathtaking vulnerability of his existence in those years – the constant fear that each new act of defiance would hurl him back to slow death in Siberia where he had languished for eight years and contracted cancer after his arrest for some critical remarks about Stalin in a wartime letter to a friend.

In those days, Solzhenitsyn was a totally secluded figure. Almost no one saw him, let alone for an interview. In magnificent silence, he had created a sensation by appearing bareheaded at the wintry funeral of Aleksandr Tvardovsky in December 1971. Tvardovsky, as the liberal editor of *New World* Magazine, was the man who had persuaded Khrushchev to permit publication of Solzhenitsyn's first searing novella of the Stalinist camps, *One Day in the Life of Ivan Denisovich*. Again, the excitement was electric when in mid-March, Solzhenitsyn went to the Moscow Conservatory for a concert by Mstislav Rostropovich, the cellist who had brooked the Kremlin's anger by giving shelter to Solzhenitsyn in his dacha. Controversy was building around *August, 1914*, just published in Russian. A new confrontation loomed because Solzhenitsyn was defiantly bent on having a private ceremony in Moscow to receive the Nobel Prize for literature which he had won in 1970. He had never dared leave the country to collect it for fear that Moscow would slam the door on his return.

By prearrangement, Kaiser and I met a few minutes before noon on March 20th at a food shop not far from apartment 169 at No 12 Gorky Street, curiously located not on Gorky Street but a block behind it. As we edged down the side street, our gaze fixed on a uniformed police officer at the entrance. We froze like a couple of bank robbers caught burgling a safe. A stake-out, we had expected, but not a sentry. For contact with lesser dissidents, other reporters had been interrogated by the KGB or thrown out of the country. We did not want to be nabbed even before seeing him.

'How could they have found out?' Kaiser whispered.

'Don't know,' I stalled. 'Maybe they just move with him and he's "brought" one in from Rostropovich's country house.'

We walked on a few paces, then decided to reverse course and go around the block on the odd chance that the policeman was there purely by coincidence. Luckily, when we came out of the alley, the policeman had moved down the block and only a *babushka* was hobbling past the door. We slipped into the entryway, flew up half a flight of stairs, rang the bell, and waited for an eternity.

Solzhenitsyn himself opened the door – but only a few inches. His eyes, dark and penetrating, peered out intently, searching, checking, questioning. I could see his full, rust-brown beard and beneath it a soft gray pullover. He looked like the few pictures I had seen, but bigger, taller. He kept the chain latched while we muttered uneasily about Medvedev sending us. Satisfied, he unlatched the door quickly to permit entry. Just as quickly, he shut and bolted it again.

508

That sense of conspiratorial wariness never lifted. When I saw him nearly three years later in Zurich, he was still on guard. Even among the Swiss, he had a special lock on his garden gate and he was mistrustful of the telephone.

Inside the apartment, his greeting was warm. He introduced us to Natalya Svetlova, a dark-haired woman with a round face, large, soft eyes, and about 20 years younger than he, as his wife. He was then 53, she was 32, and a mathematician. It was her family's high-ceilinged old apartment where we were meeting. Legally, she and Solzhenitsyn were not yet married because Soviet courts were engaged in highly irregular delaying tactics preventing his divorce from his first wife. Eventually it came through. But already, Solzhenitsyn and Natalya were extremely close. He openly depended on her for advice, research help, and moral support. Far better than he, she had a gentle capacity for reaching out to others, yet with this sympathetic side went an inner toughness and contempt for the Soviet system that matched his own. I would come to see it in the strenuous weeks after his enforced exile in 1974 when she was left behind to gather his archives and bring them and his three sons safely to him in Switzerland. Nightly, the family would gather in the kitchen, listening to Western radio broadcasts telling how he had gone to Norway, followed by reporters and they would ask me and other newsmen about the West. With the family's fate still uncertain, the strain on her was immense but she did not waver. Doggedly, she fought for every scrap of material of value to him and refused to leave Russia until all was ready.

Clearly, Natalya had created for Solzhenitsyn something for which he had ached throughout his life – a sense of family. His own father had died before he was born and he had no children by his first marriage. Now, he drew strength from biological procreation as well as from his literary work. When I happened to catch him by phone after his harrowing deportation just as he arrived at the home of Heinrich Böll in West Germany, Solzhenitsyn's first question to me was: 'Have you seen my family today? How many hours ago? How are they?' He made me promise to relay to them the news that he was well and unharmed and when I did, Natalya said that it was the first time she had believed since his arrest that he was still alive and had not been shot or carted off to Siberia again. In 1972, at our first meeting, they already had one son, Yermolai, a blond, 15-month-old toddler who played on the floor and babbled with his parents in some private family language. Solzhenitsyn was terribly proud of his son.

The easy informality of those first few minutes disarmed me for I had expected to be over-awed by this living classic of Russian literature. Solzhenitsyn was warm and engaging. He was also physically more dynamic than I had expected, bounding out of chairs, moving with athletic ease across the room. His enormous energy was palpable. For a man who had suffered so much, he looked well. But his face was etched beneath its surface ruddiness by the trauma of camp and cancer. It reminded me of a well-worn table, its scratches, nicks and scars visible through a veneer. Steel molars flashed when he smiled. A dark tobacco stain on his index finger marked him as a heavy smoker.

The spell of easy informality lingered as long as we dallied in the smalltalk of first acquaintance, sitting in the book-lined den, a Sony tape recorder and several stacks of papers on the writing table. But as soon as we turned to substance, we confronted his imperial will. (I can still hear his voice, taut and hard, in the tense days before his final arrest and enforced exile, summoning me on the phone: 'This is Solzhenitsyn. I have something I want to discuss with you.' The way he said it he might as well have been saying, 'This is the Czar. Come quickly to the palace.')

It was unfortunate, he told Kaiser and me that first day, that he had needed to advance the timing of our interview because that kept him from receiving our written questions as planned. He had gotten a gist of our interests from Medvedev, and so, to help things work smoothly, he had prepared some material. *A statement?* I thought incredulously. *All this trouble and we wind up with a prepared statement?*

But it was not a statement. He handed us each a fat copy of written material from the writing table, headed, 'Interview with *The New York Times* and the *Washington Post*.' And there it was, the whole thing, questions and answers – all prepared by Solzhenitsyn. I was stunned. What an irony, I thought. This is the way it is done at *Pravda* and here is Solzhenitsyn, whose entire being reverberates with his furious battle against censorship, a man who in the great tradition of Pushkin and Dostoyevsky had dared to assert the writer's independence, producing a prepackaged interview. How could he be so blind or so vain? I thought of walking out.

'This is outrageous,' I muttered to Kaiser. 'We can't do this.'

Kaiser was more practical. 'Let's read it first,' he suggested. That was what Solzhenitsyn was urging. So I read. It began like a patsy Soviet interview: 'Aleksandr Isayevich, what are you working on now?' Eventually, we would have gotten to that, but we wanted to open with broader themes about the general fate of writers in Russia from Pushkin to himself: Was censorship, exile and disgrace the inevitable condition of Russian writers regardless of regime? What had happened to the cultural vigor and ferment of the Khrushchev thaw period? What other Russian writers were now composing secretly, as he had once done, and would burst upon us in the years ahead? I handed him our questions and argued with him to go over them while we read his material. He withdrew leaving us alone with Natalya.

It was fortunate she stayed behind. Solzhenitsyn's prose is a dense, complex form of Russian, hard for the best translators to handle because he deliberately avoids the many words that have seeped into modern Russian from German, French or English. One element of his Russophilism is to employ the purest Russian. For both of us, in the country less than six months, it was a struggle to skim, let alone read, 25 pages of his heavy archaic prose. Natalya was an immense help, translating his Russian into more ordinary Russian we could understand. The process was tortuously slow. Periodically Solzhenitsyn would stick his head in the room, surprised at our plodding pace but humoring us. After an hour or so, when Natalya went off to get us a pitcher of berry juice and homemade fruitcake I protested to Kaiser again about the whole artificial procedure.

'But he doesn't understand that,' Bob observed. 'This is his first interview in years – nine years, he says himself. Maybe he doesn't understand.' The irony was cruel but it showed how much Solzhenitsyn had been conditioned by Soviet life. It was a reflection of the myopia of Soviet dissidents who were as ignorant of the ways of the West and as unprepared for the untidiness of democracy and the awkward probing questions of the Western press as Soviet authorities themselves. Here was Solzhenitsyn, an uncompromising foe of the Soviet system, using Soviet methods because they were only ones he knew.

The material, however, was anything but Soviet – a poignant story of his harassment as a writer, how he was barred from government archives, how elderly survivors of World War I 'shutup' out of fear of talking to him, how he was prevented from hiring research assistants and how he had to rely on haphazard voluntary help, how his mail was checked, his living quarters bugged, his friends shadowed 'like State criminals' and his wife Natalya illegally dismissed from work when an institute director found out her relation to Solzhenitsyn. 'They decided to suffocate me in 1965,' he wrote. 'You Westerners cannot imagine my situation. I live in my own country. I write a novel about Russia. But it is as hard for me to gather material as it would be if I were writing about Polynesia ... A kind of forbidden, contaminated zone has been created around my family ... The plan is either to drive me out of my life, or out of the country, to throw me into a ditch or to send me to Siberia, or to have me dissolve in an alien fog.' It was charged with the compelling detail about the demeaning harassments of Soviet life that made his novels world famous.

Then followed page after page of esoteric arguments about the social background of his grandparents and about his father's death – Solzhenitsyn's angry rebuttal to slurs against his family in the Soviet press suggesting that he came from wealthy forebears and that his father, a czarist army officer, had committed suicide. He had been especially stung that the West German weekly, *Stern*, had printed this material, too, and felt it was a KGB plant. He was expecting another broadside in the Soviet press within a week and was determined to strike before new slanders were launched.

Here we were face to face with Solzhenitsyn, the grand antagonist, condemned in the Soviet press because the West so often picked up his criticisms of Soviet society, taking it for granted that the Western press was his vehicle. If he had to be his own defense attorney, he assumed that the West would provide him partisan witnesses and a partisan jury. He was obsessed with the tactics of combat against those who were out to discredit and destroy him.

I was amazed: Not only did he want the 'interview' printed in full but immediately – several days before his planned Nobel Prize ceremony. This was certain to give Soviet authorities a pretext for not issuing a visa to the Swedish Academy representative who was to bring him the Nobel Award. Perhaps some martyr complex impelled him to risk something he so deeply cherished. Perhaps he reckoned the ceremony would be blocked in any case. Perhaps his combative temperament made him want to fling down a challenge for he said he intended to invite the Culture Minister and two Soviet journalists to his ceremony. Perhaps it was some deepseated arrogance that made him believe he could get away with releasing the interview and also holding the Nobel celebration for he gave us our invitation to the small private ceremony which was fated never to be held.

The crucible of the camps had given him not only immense moral courage and authority as a writer but had forged, diamond-hard, the single-mindedness of an autocrat. He was incredulous and unyielding when I said that *The New York Times* could use only about half of the 7,500-word text he had prepared and that we must put some of our own questions to him. 'We don't even guarantee the American President to print his every word,' I reminded him. Kaiser, too, was concerned by Solzhenitsyn's demands. 'He thinks the world is hanging on his every word,' Bob whispered to me. The *Post*, he said, could handle little over half. Both of us felt that Solzhenitsyn's arguments about his family were of only limited interest in America, but that was what Solzhenitsyn wanted to print most.

He left the room again and we tried to explain our problems and our way of journalism to Natalya. When Solzhenitsyn reappeared, he offered to let us take what we wanted so long as we pledged to have the rest printed in some other Western publications. We explained we had no power to promise that. He left again and reappeared with a compromise: Suppose, he said, that a Swedish correspondent had taken part and the Swede agreed to print the parts we omitted.

'But there is no Swedish correspondent,' Kaiser objected.

With that Solzhenitsyn disappeared again and returned with a slender, sandy-haired young man whom he introduced as Stig Frederikson, the Scandanavian News Agency man in Moscow. 'Now,' he declared, 'here is a Swedish correspondent and he promises to print the entire text, but he will do it a day after you release your stories.' Once again, I was stunned by Solzhenitsyn's highhandedness. We had not met Frederikson before. Nor had we seen him enter the apartment. But he was obviously the reason for Solzhenitsyn's shuttling in and out of the den. Clearly he had arrived without expecting an interview – possibly with news from Stockholm – for he quickly assented to Solzhenitsyn's conditions and was speedily ushered out of the room while we wrangled with Solzhenitsyn and his wife for another couple of hours.

We found a few places where his material meshed with our questions. Natalya seemed to glean how artificial his text sounded to Western ears and eventually he agreed to substitute our formulation of several questions. We argued long and hard about our broader queries which he found too sweeping, too political and evidently too precarious, for he was careful to control every word attributed to him to insure that it could not be used against him in unexpected ways. Finally, he relented and vaguely responded to four questions, recording his answers on his tape recorder. Reluctantly, I concluded we had made a passable compromise but later I learned how it had angered and frustrated Solzhenitsyn. For after the 'interview' appeared, he wrote me a personal letter complaining that I had indulged in unnecessary fictionalizing in my description of the setting and the way he had opened the door, and that I had destroyed the coherence of his material by placing our questions ahead of his 'interview' (which he later released in Russian since the Swede, too, was unable to publish it fully enough to satisfy him). But that day, Solzhenitsyn relaxed and let us photograph him with Natalya and Yermolai. When I shot pictures of him alone, he wore a solemn face and would not be coaxed into a smiling portrait. 'There is nothing to be happy about,' he insisted.

After more than four hours, Kaiser and I left exhausted. We made our way nervously to my car. On the way home, I missed a turn and when I stopped to make a legal U-turn, someone rammed me from behind. Immediately, both of us suspected an accident staged by the KGB to catch us with tapes, cameras, film and Russian texts. Kaiser scooped up all the material in an instant and fled in the confusion, while I occupied the police who were slow in materializing. To my relief and amusement, it turned out to be only a reckless cabbie who had plowed into my trunk and whose passengers, like Kaiser, had fled to avoid any entanglement with the authorities. The police were very polite and helpful, totally unaware of our contact with Solzhenitsyn. Our stories went out a couple of days later on schedule.

It was nearly two years before I had another private audience with Solzhenitsyn – on the eve of his arrest and deportation in February 1974. He called me to release ahead of time a section from *Gulag Archipelago* in which he acidly charged that retroactive decrees, fixed trials, and judges given secret instructions by political bosses made a sham of Soviet justice in political cases, not only under Stalin but today, too. That day, the air was heavy with omens of Solzhenitsyn's impending doom. More abuse had been heaped upon him as a traitor and renegade by the Soviet press than on anyone else since the purge trials. The streets near the Gorky Street apartment were thick with police agents loitering on the sidewalks or sitting in foursomes in their black Volga sedans. Walking among them was like swimming through jellyfish in late August. Brazenly, Solzhenitsyn had defied two warrants. He had taken the precaution to prepare a survival kit for the inevitable arrest, including the old sheepskin jacket he had worn in his first Siberian exile. Now, he was deliberately sounding the alarm to the West by firing off statements. His courage at the eye of the gathering storm was remarkable.

We talked for a while about the difficult prison jargon in the segment of *Gulag* that he gave me. 'No interviews,' he insisted, smilingly remembering our first encounter, and refusing the entreaties of Murray Seeger of the *Los Angeles Times* and Erik de Mauny of the BBC, who came with me. De Mauny did, however, get him to read aloud the segment of *Gulag* for a recording. With Natalya standing behind him, resting her hands on his shoulders, his own hair flying in his face, Solzhenitsyn sat at the writing table. His mood changed. His voice, often quick, high and taut, dropped to deep and moving resonance as if he imagined an audience before him. His reading rustled with the richness of the Russian language and bristled with his own sarcastic barbs. His implicit warning to the West was that it would not heed the lessons of the police state until Western liberals themselves had to jump to the bark of prison guards commanding, 'hands behind your back' – in Russian, *ruki nazad*. And he sharply rolled the 'r's' as if hearing an inextinguishable echo

515

of the years when he had bent to that command.

A day later he was gone. Carted off by seven agents, stripped down, interrogated, held incommunicado, accused of treason, threatened with death, and then forcibly exiled, like a character from one of his own novels. The entire drama seemed a re-enactment of the stage managed 'execution' of Dostoyevsky in the 19th century, who was spared by the Czar as the firing squad was about to take aim, and then banished to Siberia. Except that Solzhenitsyn was deported to the West, a fate he once described as 'spiritual castration'. By the time I next saw him in Zurich in December 1974, he had endured what he had described to friends as the first withering agonies of being uprooted from his beloved Russia and being separated from his family, uncertain whether he could go on writing, and fearful that he literally would perish without family and work. By then he had released his 'Letter to the Supreme Leaders', the personal manifesto that stunned the West.

Previously, only glimpses of Solzhenitsyn's Russophile philosophy had come through; now it was explicit. In the most stridently anti-Communist statement by a major Russian figure since the Revolutionary period, he turned his back on the 20th century. Like Count Leo Tolstoy, he spoke with the voice of a mystical apostle of Holy Russia, a religious fundamentalist, a back-to-the-unspoilt-village Russian patriot. His vision of the apocalypse was an unwinnable war with China brought on by foolish ideological rivalry, or the Russian people threatened with extinction because modern, urban technological society was devouring natural resources and defiling the precious Russian landscape.

He pictured the West as the source of evil importations – the false god of modern technology and 'the dark, un-Russian whirlwind' of Marxist ideology. America was 'democracy run riot', a culture in decline because it lacked moral underpinning. Russia – not the Soviet Union, but Russia proper – could find salvation by casting off Marxism, shedding its East European empire and the non-Russian republics of the Soviet Union, and turning inward away from Europe to develop the Russian interior in the Northeast. Let it remain authoritarian, he said, so long as Marxism were scrapped as the state creed and Orthodox Christianity became the moral foundation of a new order.

Solzhenitsyn invoked the soul-soothing silences, the

516

human scale, and the moral goodness of the Russian village. He urged the leaders to give up mass production and reduce the economy to small-scale and manual production, to abandon internal combustion engines in favor of electric cars and horses, to remember the glories of two-story homes ('the most pleasant height for human habitation'), and to stop destroying old Russian architecture. 'Build new towns of the old type,' he commanded. 'Make the Northeast the center of national activity and settlement, and a focus of aspiration of young people.' Recognize as Stalin had in World War II, he told the Kremlin, that the nation should be rallied around the banner of Russian patriotism – Russian, not Soviet – and around the Orthodox Church. And, he reminded them, when Stalin made those appeals in war against Hitler – 'we conquered'.

However far-fetched Solzhenitsyn's ideas sounded to Western ears, his was not as isolated a voice as many Westerners assumed. He had placed himself in the mainstream of classic Russian Slavophiles, that part of the Russian national mentality that has suspiciously rejected passive imitation and admiration of the West, that has proclaimed a sacred and unique mission for a Russia standing apart from Europe, and has vaunted Russia's spiritual superiority over other nations. The trinity of church, soil, and Mother Russia that Solzhenitsyn held aloft was earlier professed by Dostoyevsky. His rural populism echoed the 19th-century People's Will Movement, the *narodniki.* Even today, after half a century of Communist indoctrination, other Slavophile dissenters have put forward similar views. (Actually, Solzhenitsyn is more Russophile than Slavophile because Slavophilism embraces other Slavic peoples and projects an imperial role for Russia.) Perhaps more important, Solzhenitsyn articulated a broader undercurrent of nostalgia for the Russian past, a reviving interest in Orthodox religion, a rural romanticism, and resurgent Great Russian nationalism – companions of modern ideological apathy. His letter seemed almost intended to offer the rationale and patriotic ideology for a military takeover. He also seemed to imply the suspicion that even one member among the current leadership might sympathize.

Indeed, the 35-billion-ruble program for developing the

depressed North and Central Russian farmlands that Brezhnev announced in April 1974, had a ring similar to Solzhenitsyn's preaching and was supposedly pushed by a Russia-first faction within the leadership. When the Kremlin decided to postpone for several years an offer of large, long-term Siberian oil sales to Japan, I heard muted official expressions of economic nationalism like those Solzhenitsyn advanced. In spite of détente, the isolationist strain in Solzhenitsyn has great resonance among Russians in the hinterlands, a people more isolationist and more provincial than so-called Middle Americans.

Solzhenitsyn's romantic evocation of provincial Russia and its village life is echoed in a flow of officially published works idealizing the moral purity and the 'genuine Russia' to be found in the countryside. What Solzhenitsyn and dissident Slavophiles like Vladimir Osipov have stated explicitly, an establishment film director like Vasily Shukshin has conveyed implicitly in his film, *The Red Snowball Tree*; the Russian nation cannot be saved without the moral force of the peasantry to halt the cultural disintegration brought on by modern urban life. In a similar vein, an entire school of officially published village writers like Fyodor Abramov, Vasily Belov and Viktor Astafyev have written tales subtly decrying the crude collectivist transfiguration of rural Russia by the violent intrusion of the modern Soviet state. Yuri Lyubimov, the director of Moscow's avant-garde Taganka Theater, took two of Abramov's stories to stage *Wooden Horses*, a moving and effective representation of the moral goodness of the old peasantry, before collectivization and 'progress' transformed their lives. It had generated a strong following among urban intellectuals.

'We have a mixture of the psychology of Asia and the culture of Europe and we are now slowly returning to our Russian sources,' Vladimir Maximov, a Slavophile writer told me before hounding by the authorities forced him into exile in Paris. 'If it were not for the Chinese problem, we would do it more boldly. But the Chinese force our leaders to defend our ideology.'

Solzhenitsyn's instinctive urge to protect Mother Russia from the intrusion of alien influences from the West also has resonance in official Russian life. At the very time he was being deported, no less worldly a figure than Nikolai Fedorenko, the former Soviet representative to the United

Nations and editor of the magazine *Foreign Literature*, published an article lamenting the wholesale borrowing of foreign terms that were polluting the purity of the great Russian language. In an echo of the 19th-century Slavophiles, Fedorenko was distraught at the intrusion of such terms as nonconformism, or *nonkonformizm* as Russians render it – *populizm, akedemizm, detant, mass mediya, sekularizatsiya, isteblishment,* and *kheppening.* 'The word *eskalatsiya* entered usage with the light touch of Pentagon strategists who used it in connection with American aggression in Vietnam,' Fedorenko fumed. 'Then various combinations of words were used. From *eskalatsiya* of war and *eskalatsiya* of aggression, a transition was made to word-eskalatsiya, ideological eskalatsiya, intellectual eskalatsiya, emotional eskalatsiya and later de-eskalatsiya, and kontre-eskalatsiya.'

'Is the Russian language so poor, has it become so impoverished?' Fedorenko wailed. Though insisting he did not want to build a 'Chinese wall' around the Russian tongue, he called for an urgent campaign to promote pure Russian and to curb 'uncontrolled borrowing' from Western languages.

To many modern-minded Russians, this is a hopeless rearguard action because Russian is already saturated with words like *press relis, kredit, tranzistor, khokkei, krizis, dzhass,* and *dzhinsy* pants, not to mention entire vocabularies in the natural and social sciences and in literary criticism. Nor is the trend new. Peter the Great and Catherine the Great brought Dutch and German borrowings. In the 19th century, the influx of Gallicisms permeated art, literature, military life. It is purists like Solzhenitsyn and Fedorenko who want to turn back the clock to prevent what Fedorenko derisively termed 'weeds of barbarism' from sprouting in rich Russian soil.

They are not alone. Even such a prominent organ of Soviet ideology as *Komsomolskaya Pravda* was vexed enough to protest that Russian children did not know about *lapta* but were hearing about baseball 'which essentially is nothing but Americanized *lapta* brought to California in the old times by Russian settlers'. It advocated reviving old Russian national games just 'as we lovingly restore monuments of the past'.

*   *   *

The undertow of Russophilism today is palpable but difficult to gauge because it is more mood than movement, more hidden than open. Its milder forms are tolerated, even officially encouraged as Russia proper presses its cultural and political influence outward among other nationalities which have been absorbed into the Soviet Union and which now outnumber ethnic Russians – a demographic fact that worries ethnic Russians so much that some government officials and specialists advocate higher birth rates in Russia proper to stem the trend.

A subtle political manifestation of Russophilism is the special praise that Brezhnev, an ethnic Russian raised in the Ukraine, sometimes bestows on ethnic Russians as leaders in the formation and development of the Soviet state and the tribute he pays to the Russian Republic as 'first among equals'. (Technically, it is one of 15 union republics, but it carries preponderant weight – over half the population and three-fourths the land area of the country.) Similarly, President Podgorny, a Ukrainian, has asserted that the Russian language 'is a mighty instrument of unification and interconnection' among the diverse Soviet peoples. In many minority areas that we visited we found persistent official efforts to promote learning of Russian, as the modern, scientific language, 'the language of Lenin', and schools, organized so that in big cities more children were often being encouraged to take Russian as a compulsory course than their own native language. From 1959–1970, millions of ethnic Russians moved into the Baltic Republics, Central Asia, and the Ukraine (more than two million to the Ukraine alone).* The resettlement was concentrated in major cities so that in some republics, ethnic Russians outnumbered the main local nationality, causing serious underlying frictions against Russians. (I remember an Estonian poet, in despair, lamenting to me that 'we are like your Indians, a dying breed', over the slow persistent Russification in his area.)

Party leaders across the country are constantly on the attack against local nationalist sentiments in places like Lithuania, Georgia, Armenia, the Ukraine, Uzbekistan, be-

* In late 1973, Radio Liberty did a series of detailed studies, based on the 1959 and 1970 census figures, showing the marked rise in the ethnic Russian population in these areas, from which I have drawn these statistics.

cause such feelings have broad latent popular support and contain the most serious threat of decentralization and disloyalty faced by the Russian-dominated Soviet state. At times, too, Russian nationalists are officially rapped on the knuckles. But with all nine top Communist Party Secretaries being ethnic Russians and with Russians dominant in key administrative posts throughout Soviet society, it is more acceptable to promote Russian nationalism than the nationalism of any minority group.

Strictly speaking Russophilism goes against the grain of Marxist-Leninist ideology. The undertones of narrow Russian patriotism and religious feeling conflict with the proletarian internationalism, militant atheism and multinational unity of Soviet peoples preached by the Party. But the line of tolerance is often fuzzy because Soviet Communism, during and since the war, has contained a fair quotient of Russian super-nationalism sometimes veering off into a Russian equivalent of Ku Klux Klan chauvinism with reactionary, anti-Semitic and antiforeign prejudices. Jews I knew were especially sensitive to super-patriotic *Russity*, as they were called, publishing and promoting books like *Caution Zionism* by Yuri Ivanov.

Time and again, liberal Soviet intellectuals insisted privately to me that Russophiles could count among their hidden protectors important officials in the Communist Party, the secret police, Armed Forces, and Komsomol youth league, men who were ardent Russia-firsters, some of them neo-Stalinists and anti-Semites and others with vaguer right-wing Slavic mistrust of the West and détente, and a yen for glorifying the mystique of Russia. With this kind of official sympathy and protection, two conservative monthly magazines pitched toward youth, *Young Guard* and *Our Contemporary*, have become known as centers of right-wing Russianism, outlets for paeans to the Russian village, neo-Stalinist fiction, essays idealizing Russian conquests, or eulogies to 'the majesty and loftiness of the Russian soul'. One Soviet journalist confided that after Khrushchev's devastating exposé of Stalin, 'the Armed Forces desperately needed something for indoctrinating young soldiers and appeals to Russian patriotic pride offered a good alternative' to ideology, though only in the Russian Republic because elsewhere it would generate resentment among minorities. Under the former leadership of Sergei Pavlov, a staunch conservative, the Komsomol League organized *rodina* – Motherland – clubs in the mid-Sixties to study pre-Revolutionary Russia as an antidote to Western cultural influences among youth and to try to fill the ideological vacuum left by Khrushchev.

Not until I fell into conversation one day with a little old doorman at the 69th Parallel Hotel in Murmansk did I discern how the blood-and-soil patriotism of ordinary Russians differed from that of Americans or Britons. So flattered was he to find an American speaking Russian that he launched into a peroration about the beauty and richness of the Russian language and an explanation of how this richness of the tongue and the strength of the Russian nation came from the soil. With his age-softened hand holding mine and friendly eyes relishing my attention, he related a mystic story about an ancient sage who advised Russians to take the good Russian earth and put it in their mouths, to eat it and take in its nourishment directly because the very soil was the source of Russian character and culture. Later, reading Slavophile writings with similar passions, I thought of the little doorman.

A West German diplomatic friend told me, too, of an Easter evening Orthodox service to which he had been taken by a Communist Party member. They had not gone inside but stood among a crowd of onlookers at the church on Lenin Hills, watching the midnight procession of priests and believers. 'Look, at that!' the Russian said excitedly. 'I am a Communist, not a believer. But it is good to see these old Russian customs preserved and coming back.'

The most innocent manifestations of this traditionalist mood are the faddish hunger for collecting and hanging religious ikons or the craze for czarist antiques, hobbies that establishment figures from writers and generals to ministers indulge in. 'In the early Sixties, under Khrushchev, buying antiques was frowned upon,' a journalist's wife told me as she showed off a handsome Alexandrine chest of drawers and an armchair from another imperial period. 'We wouldn't have thought of buying these things then. But the situation has changed and all kinds of people are doing it.'

Paradoxically, it was Stalin, Georgian by birth but Great Russian in mentality, who made the reclamation of the Russian past respectable. After the suppression of Russian nationalist feelings in the first 15 years of Bolshevism, Stalin encouraged the revival of czarist heroes – movies glorifying Peter the Great, Ivan the Terrible, and Aleksandr Nevsky's heroic battles against the German knights – themes perpetuated today. He put epaulets back on military uniforms, reestablished ranks and czarist decorations, lavished special praise on the Great Russians for their leading role in the war against Hitler, and allocated postwar reconstruction funds for restoring the treasures of the Hermitage and the grandeur of czarist palaces.

Since Stalin, Soviet policy has ebbed and flowed, treating the Russian heritage ambivalently. The great music, literature, and ballet of the 19th century are revered. Monuments have been raised to such purely Russian triumphs as Marshal Kutuzov's victory over Napoleon. Some major cathedrals and churches have been restored as monuments but hundreds of other architectural treasures have been razed and history has still been written in Communist stereotypes.

When official policy flagged, the renascent Russianism among the intelligentsia sometimes stepped in. One celebrated case occurred in 1973. Word leaked that the Kremlin, decreeing that Moscow should be made 'a model Communist city', was about to approve a plan to rebuild its central district and rip down such architectual landmarks as the old czarist municipal hall and Museum of History next to Red Square, Stanislavsky's Moscow Art Theater and the 18th-century Maly Theater next to the Bolshoi. Some of the nation's most prestigious scientists, artists, musicians and other intellectuals banded together to protest and succeeded in blocking this plan. Earlier, in the mid-Sixties, students from Moscow State University's Archaeological Faculty rushed out to provincial towns in northern Russia and managed to save some old churches slated for destruction, by recategorizing them as top priority historical monuments.

In those years, musical groups like the Russian Republic Academic Choir under Aleksandr Yurlov or the madrigal group formed by composer Andrei Volkonsky resurrected church chants and canticles. Other composers drew on old religious motifs for modern works. I knew writers, artists and other intellectuals who roamed the Russian countryside visiting monasteries, church ruins and distant rural settlements, collecting artifacts of Old Russia from ikons and books written in church slavonic, to antique pots, wooden objects and farm implements. The ikon fad caused enormous inflation in that field. Black market prices also skyrocketed in the past decade for books by such early 20th-century Russian religious philosophers as Nikolai Berdyayev and Pavel Florinsky, who not only opposed Marxism but advocated a radical renovation of social life on the basis of Christian faith – themes that Solzhenitsyn has now sounded again.

Joseph Brodsky captured the mood of the nostalgic Russian revival in a lovely poem called, *A Halt in the Desert:*

> The dogs, moved by old memory, still lift
> their hind legs at a once-familiar spot.
> The church's walls have long since been torn down,
> but these dogs see the church walls in their dreams –
> dog-dreams have cancelled out reality...
> And if I were to speak in earnest of
> the 'relay race of human history',
> I'd swear by nothing but this relay race –
> this race of all the generations who
> have sniffed, and who will sniff, the ancient smells.*

No ancient smell is more vividly unforgettable than the exotic incense of an Orthodox mass and no institution more central to renascent Russianism than Orthodox Christianity. For centuries the Church has been a special guardian of Russian culture. To a foreigner accustomed to picturing the Soviet Union as a land of militant atheists, the magnetism of Orthodox services on such high feast days as Easter is hard to believe. It astonished me to see that it was primarily young people, in their late teens and twenties, who congregated outside the old cathedrals for a glimpse of the rich pageantry within. But anyone who knows Russia understands that churches are her artistic glory.

One Easter eve Ann and I were swept up among a crowd in Vladimir, once a medieval capital of Russia and now a provincial city. Thousands of people were swarming to the imposing 12th-century Cathedral of the Assumption, trimmed with stone carvings and serene beneath its decorative domes and the rhythmic repetition of its rounded arches.

Driving to Vladimir we had stopped at a farmhouse on the road cutting through the flat, barely budding farmlands

* Joseph Brodsky, *Selected Poems*, translated by George L. Kline (New York, Harper & Row, 1973), pp. 132–133.

that sweep eastward from Moscow, and watched a strong-armed farm woman kneading dough for the traditional *kulich* Easter cake. She had already made *paskha*, a rich and tasty mixture of sweetened cheese curds, butter and raisins, and had dyed her Easter eggs a soft russet color by boiling them with onion skins. Later, we had seen old women bring their holiday food to the Cathedral for blessing. In the flickering candlelight, they laid out bread and cakes on a long, low table, flowers adorning their dishes.

According to the Eastern Orthodox rites, Russians celebrate Easter with a Saturday midnight mass that lasts for several hours. In Vladimir, secular authorities had organized an outdoor dance in a park near the old stone cathedral, obviously to distract the young. But this expedient worked only temporarily. By 11.30, when the dance broke up, 3,000–4,000 young people had encircled the church and were pressing against lines of police and auxiliary police who held them back.

Inside, where we were, the ceremony of Christ's Resurrection had transformed the Cathedral into a place of mystical enchantment. It was ablaze with forests of candles that illuminated innumerable ikons, encased in gold or silver and lavished with the kisses of the faithful. Bearded priests in gilded robes were swinging censers or passing an ornamented Bible studded with pearls and precious stones. The repetitive litany and the melancholy, disembodied chants of the choir, somewhere up in the lofts, had a hypnotic effect. Churchgoers craned to see the choir and to glimpse the carved baroque ikonostasis or the world-famous frescos of Andrei Rublev.

It was a terribly Russian scene with its Eastern, Byzantine emphasis on the beauty and power of the ritual creating a pious state of mind rather than Western Protestant sermonizing to appeal to the individual conscience. There were no pews. The worshippers, hundreds strong, filled the cathedral, watching, waiting, listening patiently for two or three hours. As the climactic moment approached, the church was so jammed I found it impossible to move, even a few inches. Yet there was something soothing in the communal presence, in the mesmerizing hum of the priests' chants and the quiet crackling of waxed candles burning before the ikons. The candles reinforced the communal bond of the service. People bought them at the rear of the church and then passed them forward, shoulder to shoulder, hand to hand, and instructions were whispered, stranger to stranger so that each new candle would be lit before the chosen ikon of its distant, invisible owner.

When the priests emerged from the cathedral followed by the faithful in a candlelight procession to pass three times around the church, symbolizing the search for Christ's body in the sepulchre, this produced an irresistible surge among the throngs of young people outside. Just as the procession returned into the cathedral to celebrate the Resurrection, several hundred broke through the human wall of police.

Theoretically, the police lines were there to shield the believers from interference from young hooligans though just as surely their function was to screen off the young from the attraction of the forbidden ceremony. As the dam broke, I heard a couple of *babushkas* worrying that the young would break the ikons or laugh at worshipers. But from what I saw, those who made it inside were quiet, respectful and above all, curious. A few squirmed into the congregation for a look at the priests and ikonostasis, the five-tiered altar screen of ikons, or to hear the choir. One or two had tape recorders to record the ceremony, a far more colorful pageant than anything offered in Soviet secular life.

'Why did you want to go in?' I overheard one police officer later asking a slender blonde girl who had come outside carrying a lighted candle, glowing with excitement.

'I wanted to see it,' she replied firmly, uncowed. 'It was very interesting. Very beautiful.'

I saw that sort of scene several times and it left me feeling that, left to their own devices, the common folk would heed Solzhenitsyn's call to turn to the Church. Its grandeur, its ceremony, its communal feeling suit the Russian soul.

In Vladimir, as elsewhere, older women comprised the main body of regular worshipers (70–80 percent) though as one middle-aged man – a believer but not a churchgoer – smilingly remarked to me, 'When each generation of old women dies off, there always seems to be another generation to take their place.' At ordinary church services, I have seen a fair sprinkling of middle-aged men and women, an occasional military uniform, or a few young people carrying a prayer book, lighting a candle or crossing themselves, not to mention the intermittent stream of curious young onlookers. But the pressures and controls of the Soviet system still makes it risky for people from 20–50, especially those with career ambitions, to attend church. Old women go fairly freely because the system has given up on them.

Nonetheless, there is evidence of a modest religious revival in recent years among the middle and younger generations. No less authoritative source than *Pravda* complained in a long article in 1974 of a 'notable increase' of religious interest among young men and women coupled with widespread ideological apathy. Other Soviet publications like the magazine *Science and Religion* have let slip information that in recent years as many as half of the newlyweds in some areas, including Moscow, were having church weddings and more than half of the newborns were being baptized. Baptisms are a regular target for the Party press. To combat them, authorities began requiring that priests demand domestic passports from parents, as a form of intimidation. But people told me you could get around that by going out of town and renting the documents of other people.

One encounters manifestations of hidden interest in the Church or in religion in various little ways – an Intourist guide asking an American businessman for a Bible; a Russian priest confiding to a Western pastor that he has little time to counsel young people because he is so busy doing 1,000 baptisms a year; a young woman who carefully draws out a visiting Catholic priest to explain his faith and then expresses her admiration for it; a young engineer who keeps ikons in the corner, the traditional place of worship, and who knows verses from the scriptures. Periodically, Communist publications berate Party members or Komsomol members for participating in weddings, funerals and other religious ceremonies. In 1973, *Pravda Ukrainy* reported that while one Party official was lecturing on atheism, his children were being taken for baptism by his wife and mother-in-law. Some sensational incidents are hushed up. A writer told me that when Alla Tarasova, a leading actress of the Moscow Art Theater, a Party official there for 19 years and a deputy in the Supreme Soviet, died in 1972, she shocked Party officials by leaving a will requiring a religious burial and her husband, a secret police official, fulfilled her wish. The late Ivan Petrovsky, for 22 years rector of Moscow State University, was another secret believer for years, this same writer informed me.

Once, noticing that a highly educated woman, a computer expert in her mid-forties, was wearing a cross, I asked if she was a believer. She glanced down at the cross, smiled at me with embarrassment, and tried to sidestep the question. 'It's an Armenian cross – I don't go to church,' she said. 'I don't like a crowd of people.'

'I understand about your not going to church – it's a big risk,' I said. 'But what I meant is, are you a believer?'

We were in her Moscow apartment, alone among her family, but she was still hesitant. Finally, she acknowledged, 'Yes, in the sense of believing in Something [her eyes glanced upward] and not going to church, I am a believer, but I have no Bible. Some time ago, I got little books of four of the gospels.' She went and fetched four little books, not much larger than matchboxes, from behind an overstuffed chair. 'I read them quite a bit and I find they help me,' she said. 'Sometimes I read them to my children.'

'Are there many scientists your age and with your level of training who are also believers in your sense?' I asked.

'Many,' she nodded. 'Like me, they do not go to church, but they believe.'

'Why?' I asked.

'Most of all, out of frustration with the emptiness of life here, the emptiness in our contemporary life. Religion gives something to hold on to. That is how I feel it.'

Vladimir Osipov, a Slavophile dissident, has written that some middle-aged intellectuals turned to religion in recent years because of the shattering experience in the late Fifties and early Sixties of Khrushchev's de-Stalinization campaign. 'All of us future "heretics" were Stalinists in the prime of our youth,' he wrote. Without Stalin, he said, they felt lost. I found it impossible to judge how widely either Osipov's or the lady scientist's views were shared, but I am skeptical that there are very many religious converts, even loose ones, among scientists. Of those with whom I talked most were drawn toward the Orthodox Church as a vessel of Russian culture, a link with their suppressed heritage.

The relation of the Church and the Party is a curious one. As an institution vigorously repressed in the Twenties and

Thirties, allowed to revive by Stalin during World War II to rally Russian patriotism, and later roughly suppressed by Khrushchev, the Orthodox Church has accepted uneasy accommodation with the Brezhnev leadership. Throughout Russian history, the Orthodox establishment has reinforced secular power by preaching submission to the state among its faithful, and it does so now. Patriarch Pimen and other Orthodox prelates make obligatory speeches praising Soviet policy at home and abroad. The Church donates millions of rubles to the Soviet Peace Committee and other Communist causes. With such tactics, it has survived and claims 30 million churchgoers, twice the number of card-carrying Communists in the country – though the numbers have limited meaning since it is the Party that sets the terms under which the churches can exist, not vice versa. (Other smaller churches like the Roman Catholic Church in Lithuania and Baptists elsewhere have more vigorously asserted themselves and have been subject to more repressions.)

Tacitly, the Party has acknowledged Orthodoxy as an essential ingredient in the peculiar mixture of loyalties that holds the Soviet State together, a vital element of its Russianness. But it has hemmed in the Church with restrictions: priests can celebrate mass but not preach or proselytize; new cities are built without churches; and in some old regions, like the Western Ukraine, established churches are shut down. The more outspoken priests are defrocked or disciplined. There is a shortage of priests and though the rector of the Zagorsk Theological Seminary told a group of us foreign correspondents that they have four applicants annually for each seminary opening, the state does not permit the four Orthodox seminaries to expand beyond the 1,000 places they now have.

Dissidents like Solzhenitsyn chafe at this kind of accommodation by the Church and manipulation by the Party. In 1972, Solzhenitsyn sent a stinging letter to Patriarch Pimen charging that the Church had forsaken its flock, let houses of worship be razed or ruined by neglect, and had become a tool of the atheist state. Some defrocked priests, refusing to submit to the Party's dictates, have set up 'underground monasteries' for more radical believers, I was told by a Western churchman with considerable contacts among Russians. One, he said, was composed entirely of scientists. On rare occasions, an ordained churchman dares openly to pursue aggressive priesthood.

The most striking 'preaching priest' during my experience in Moscow was Father Dmitri Dudko, a short, balding cleric in his fifties who had spent eight years in the Stalinist camps after his arrest in 1948 for writing religious poetry. Later, he became Solzhenitsyn's priest. In early 1974, he created a sensation with a series of extremely candid question-and-answer sessions at the small old Church of St Nicholas in Moscow. On Sunday evenings, 500 or 600 people, many of them intellectuals and young people, packed the church. They were drawn by his sincere and untrammeled preaching, his moral questions about 'how to live' and his comments on the state of Christianity in the Soviet Union. Often, his daring remarks brought gasps.

I remember myself, barely squeezed inside the creaky door of the church, wondering if I were in Moscow when I heard his blunt attacks on atheism. Without the usual circumlocutions, he asserted that Russia had suffered moral and spiritual decline during the half century of Soviet rule. It was time, he said, to speak out for Christianity. He told simple tales of religious conversions, recalled the strength of believers in prison camps, and protested 'the interference by the godless in the internal affairs of the church'. Finally, one evening, he charged that the Church hierarchy was so penetrated and the Patriarch so surrounded by informers that 'he sighs and it is heard by all the organs' – a Russian euphemism for the KGB.

People went away asking how long this could last. After ten such sessions, the authorities intervened. Father Dmitri was silenced, made to apologize to the Patriarch, and shipped off to an out-of-the-way rural parish. The international notoriety that his case attracted may have protected him from much harsher punishment.

A number of religious Slavophile dissidents have met sterner destinies. Long before Solzhenitsyn's exile, the authorities cracked down on a group of right-wing, reactionary, militantly anti-Soviet Slavophiles calling themselves the All-Russian Social Christian Alliance of Liberation of the People. Their writings, circulating in Leningrad, Tomsk, Irkutsk and other cities in the late Sixties not only had Slavophile but anti-Semitic and neo-Fascist overtones. Russian friends told me that some of them had supposedly jotted down license plate numbers of Communist Party officials and talked of violence. In 1968, a score or more were tried secretly and given long sentences. In 1971, another group anonymously circulated an underground 'Manifesto of Russian Patriots' that rejected Marxism, favored a return to an Orthodox Christian State, preached a strong brand of Russian nationalism, and white supremacy – unlike Solzhenitsyn, but they shared his preference for authoritarian rule, a common feature of the Russian right. If they were caught and punished, it never came to light. But Vladimir Osipov, a square-jawed, broad-shouldered, pacifist Slavophile writer, who had edited a series of underground publications like *Veche* (the name of a medieval Russian assembly) and *Zemlya* (Earth), has faced persistent repression despite assertions that he does not oppose the established order. In 1961, he was sent off to Siberia for seven years and then, after a period of exile outside Moscow, was arrested again and sentenced in 1975 to eight more years in a strict labor camp for circulating his journals in the West.

In late 1974 several of Solzhenitsyn's followers collaborated with him in publishing a book in the West, entitled *From Under the Boulders*. It is a series of essays analyzing the moral decline in Soviet society from a religious viewpoint, rejecting Marxism and reviving the thought of Berdyayev and other early 20th-century Russian religious philosophers. One obvious objective was to provoke debate of Russophile views among Soviet intellectuals. Even before it appeared, two contributors, Vadim Borisov, a church historian, and Yevgeny Barabanov, an art historian, both in their early thirties, were fired from work and Borisov was also kept from defending his academic dissertation. Igor Shafarevich, another contributor, has evidently been protected by his eminence as a world-renowned mathematician in his early fifties and a corresponding member of the Soviet Acadamy of Sciences, though I was told of repeated efforts to dismiss him from the Mocow University faculty.

The dilemma of Soviet authorities so far has been not in dealing with blatantly dissident Russophiles but in managing the broader, more amorphous renascent Russianism and religious interest within the establishment. Cultural watchdogs periodically berate writers for dwelling too much on the past, book illustrators for idealizing peasant life under the czars, or musicians for reviving so much old church music. But the

Party itself seems to be split on how to strike a proper balance evidently because of the Russophile influence within its own ranks. In late 1972, for example, the head of the Central Committee's powerful Department of Agitation and Propaganda, Aleksandr Yakovlev, published a major commentary condemning various magazines and writers for romanticizing Russia's past, glorifying traditional village life, and showing excessive respect for old churches and historic monuments. His article seemed a signal that the Party wanted to curb Great Russian nationalism.

But a few months later, Yakovlev was quietly dismissed and demoted to a diplomatic post abroad. Russian intellectuals told me that a behind-the-scenes argument had taken place in high Party circles over whether his article should have been printed. The message to some of them was that 'someone up top' in the very inner circle disapproved of his approach and wanted to protect the renascent Russian nationalist mood.

XVIII

DISSENT
The Modern Technology of Repression

It is very important to silence the man who first
cries out, 'the king is naked', before others pick up
the cry.

> Valentin Moroz, Ukrainian dissident

Lost in the unfolding sensations of Aleksandr Solzhenitsyn's
sudden exile in early 1974 was the extraordinary fact that for
a brief moment in time, the Soviet Union's three leading
dissidents had begun to debate their nation's future. For a
country devoid of real political discourse for half a century,
it was a remarkable turn of events. It was widely overlooked
in the West because the West had long indiscriminately
lumped all dissidents together. Yet here were three men out
of a population of 250 million – Solzhenitsyn, the classic
Slavophile moralist, Andrei Sakharov, the 20th-century
scientific liberal, and Roy Medvedev, the reform-minded
Marxist historian – daring to infringe publicly on the Communist Party's declared monopoly of social thought to argue
about their own prescriptions for Russia in statements to
the Western press that were beamed back to their own people
through the instant replay of Western radio broadcasts.

It was a development unimaginable a decade earlier, made
possible by the protective umbrella of détente and their own
fame. Yet this debate of the super dissidents was misleading
in its way, too. It obscured the fact that dissent as a movement, probably never more than a thousand activists at
most, had waned. The technology of Soviet repression had
become more sophisticated and more effective as détente
proceeded. The unexpected irony was that détente, instead
of spawning more general ferment among the Soviet intelligentsia as the West had hoped and the Kremlin had feared,

became a reason for tighter controls and sometimes provided new techniques for quieting disaffected intellectuals. Only those of the stature of Solzhenitsyn, Sakharov and Medvedev could use its shield to deepen the substance of their dissent.

In those final months before Solzhenitsyn was forcibly ejected, Sakharov was often automatically paired with Solzhenitsyn – vilified in the Soviet press as a 'renegade and turncoat' who had slandered and betrayed with 'black ingratitude' the Motherland which had nurtured him; sanctified in the West as the champion of individual rights, a symbol for humanizing détente and opening up the Soviet Union to greater democratization. Solzhenitsyn had won the Nobel Prize for Literature in 1970, and Sakharov would win the Nobel Prize in 1975.

Yet I found Sakharov and Solzhenitsyn immensely different men. In person, Sakharov hardly seems the man to stir an international uproar. He does not have the imposing presence, the commanding personality or the combative temperament of Solzhenitsyn. Where Solzhenitsyn would thrust self-confidently to the center of the conversational stage, Sakharov would hover in the wings, a shy, almost homely, unpretentious man, content to listen and reflect, head rolled thoughtfully to one side, until he felt sufficiently at home with some newcomer to converse freely.

Their physical presence was entirely different. The Solzhenitsyn of barrel chest, lined and ruddy face, work-worn hands, mahogany beard and penetrating eyes is physically as well as mentally powerful. He fought for eminence late in life as he had earlier fought for life itself; and when it suited him, he relished prestige and the limelight. By contrast, Sakharov emanates vulnerability. He is a tall but slightly stooped figure, with high intellectual forehead, and two patches of thinning gray hair bordering his baldness, large hands unscarred by physical labor, and sad, compassionate eyes. He is an inward man, a Russian *intelligent*, an intellectual through and through.

In his reticence and his conversational lapses, one senses the solitary thinker. His own natural penchant for privacy was reinforced by two decades of enforced privacy in the Soviet nuclear research program where outside contacts were forbidden and a personal bodyguard moved with him everywhere, even when he went swimming. (Puckishly, he told me, he had once given the guard the slip to go off skiing in the woods.) His unprecedented Soviet awards and decorations won him no public fame, since they were bestowed in secrecy. His picture has not been printed in the press. My colleague Ted Shabad saw him walk into a grocery, unshaven and in a rumpled raincoat, looking for something to celebrate the birth of his first grandchild, and pass all but unnoticed and unrecognized.

A theoretical physicist of the stature of Oppenheimer and Teller, Sakharov gained eminence naturally, easily and early in life as one of the fathers of the Soviet hydrogen bomb. His meteoric scientific career (Doctor of Science at 26, full member of the Academy of Sciences at the unheard-of age of 32), earned him high position, an early fortune of nearly 140,000 rubles, and direct access to the pinnacle of the Soviet system. One of his first acts of dissent was a note scribbled to Khrushchev during a Kremlin meeting, in which he objected to a 100-megaton nuclear test as technically unnecessary, politically risky and biologically harmful because of radioactive fallout. For a decade he voiced such misgivings only within the rarefied atmosphere of the Soviet elite.

Abroad, Sakharov's name was unknown until 1968 when his memorandum, *Progress, Peaceful Coexistence and Intellectual Freedom*, advocating an end to the arms race, proposing détente, and urging convergence of the socialist and capitalist systems, leaked out to the West. Only thereafter did Sakharov begin to use his intellectual eminence in a public way, and then sparingly at first. Unlike Solzhenitsyn, his instinct is to avoid the limelight. For months, I tried – as did others – to persuade him to allow an interview or a journalistic portrait but he shied away from personal publicity. Only with reluctance, feeling cornered and falsely accused by a shrill propaganda campaign in the Soviet press, did he take his personal problems to the world press in the fall of 1973.

A kind of Grant Wood-American Gothic simplicity and modesty permeate Sakharov's life. He is modest in gesture, in manner, in dress, in surroundings. He gave away his accumulated fortune for cancer research, feeling that it was blood money earned from weapons of mass destruction. As plain as an off duty night-watchman, he would pad around his modest apartment in baggy pants strung from pencil-thin suspenders and in stockinged feet, not bothering to change when guests arrived. As a concession to social convention, he would don a charcoal gray suit with a nondescript, clip-on, four-in-hand tie over a white, or even a gray work shirt, to go to the theater.

His apartment was as unpretentious as Sakharov himself. He shared two rooms and a kitchen with his second wife Yelena, her mother and her son. For morning callers, bedclothes were tucked away to convert a modest main bedroom into an equally modest living room: a foam rubber, double bed-couch on a faded oriental rug; a typewriter and an old fashioned phonograph piled near a glass-front bookcase jammed with papers; a pan tied to a window radiator to catch drips. Because of the inevitable apartment space-squeeze, skis were stored next to the flush bowl in a tiny toilet. Ice skates dangled closely overhead.

The first time someone took me to his apartment, we arrived to find it in a total turmoil for repairs. With instinctive Russian hospitality and a brief apology for the mess, Sakharov led us directly to the kitchen where an enamel-topped table was littered with dishes, teacups and stray saucers. Andrei Dmitriyevich, as Russians call him, using his first name and patronymic, was drinking tea sweetened – or rather flavored – with chunks of little hard, green apples.

'It's my favorite way of drinking tea,' he remarked in answer to my curious glance.

'They used to say that the nobility had tea with lemon and the cooks had tea with apples,' volunteered his wife. 'So this is cook's tea.'

Gently, Sakharov urged me to try his cook's tea and I did. One cup was enough. I had the next cup with sugar. A carton of plain biscuits was produced and then a small box of assorted candies, a few odd chocolates mixed with other sweets. Everything was very plain. Seven people squeezed around a little table. In a thoroughly Russian way, visitors were absorbed into life as it was and made to feel at home. No one made any effort to dress things up. It was that way every time I went, for Sakharov is utterly devoid of pretension. Yet private, reticent, and soft-spoken as he is, Sakharov is direct in his emotions. When moved, he has a vibrant sense of outrage at injustice, a quick and deep compassion for the suffering of others, a naive directness of action and speech, heedless of the personal consequences

536

though threats and harassment against his family have pained him acutely.

Over the years, the authorities have played up his streak of naive idealism when trying to discredit his unorthodox views among other intellectuals. Party spokesmen in private lectures to scientists have ridiculed him as a naive eccentric, a well-meaning but hopelessly unrealistic, unworldly thinker. In September 1973, when the Soviet press flowed with daily denunciations against Sakharov signed by leading Soviet scholars and public figures, the propaganda crescendo stirred sentiments for putting him in a mental hospital, recalling the treatment of the dissident nineteenth-century biologist and philosopher, Pyotr Chaadayev, whom the czar had declared insane for his dissenting views.

I have heard Sakharov, who has a good enough sense of humor to smile at the tragic irony of being a prophet without honor in his own country, joke about being treated as a half-sainted, half-demented maverick. And he showed enough perspective about his own limited influence and that of the Human Rights Committee which he formed with two other physicists in 1970, to have kiddingly dismissed it as 'The Pickwick Committee', a jibe at its windy inefficacy.

Some Westerners who have met him have come away wondering why so powerful a state as the Soviet Union treats a man like Sakharov as a political threat. Others have asked aloud how so meek-mannered a soul brought down on his own head the orchestrated wrath of the Soviet establishment as he did in late 1973. The questions underestimate the force of Sakharov's heretical views and the jealousy with which the Communist Party guards its monopoly over social thought. To challenge this monopoly as Sakharov has done is to threaten the bedrock foundation of the system. For if in the modern age managers and engineers can run the economy, and administrators and bureaucrats can manage the government and diplomacy without ideological guidance, the Party is left without legitimacy and *raison d'être*. That is why the Party reacts so violently to Sakharov's ideological opposition.

His own radicalization over the years, reflecting his mounting despair over the possibilities for reform within the system, has sharpened the confrontation. He has been influenced, too, by his second wife, Yelena Georgevna Bonner, an Armenian-Jewish dissident activist whose mother spent 16 years in the camps. She and Sakharov married in 1971 and his dissent has since taken on some of her fire.

As a prestigious government scientist in 1968, Sakharov began his unofficial protests with a philosophical, carefully reasoned memorandum marshaling rational arguments for détente, and greater intellectual freedoms. It condemned the 'foulness of Stalinism' and the influence of neo-Stalinists, but it balanced criticism of Soviet repression with critiques of capitalism and American policy, and strongly affirmed Sakharov's 'profoundly socialist' viewpoint. For this 1968 memorandum, Sakharov was fired from the Soviet nuclear program. But his ideas circulated widely and his prestige soared among scientific liberals for whom he had emerged as a daring spokesman.

Within five years, however, he had become a pariah who was raising an anguished cry for persecuted dissenters in mental hospitals, for Armenians secretly tried and jailed for advocating national separatism, for Jews who wanted to emigrate, for nonconformist Baptists persecuted for giving their children religious training. He had been arrested for joining in the protest vigil at the Lebanese Embassy over the killing of Israeli athletes at the 1972 Munich Olympic games. And his censure of Soviet society had become harsh and sweeping.

'I am skeptical of socialism in general,' Sakharov declared in July 1973 to Olle Stenholm, a Swedish radio correspondent, in an interview that caused Stenholm's expulsion and led to the press campaign against Sakharov. 'I don't find that socialism has brought anything new in the theoretical plane, or a better social order . . . We have the same kinds of problems as the capitalist world: criminality and alienation. The difference is that our society is an extreme case, with maximum lack of freedom, maximum ideological rigidity, and – this is most typical – with maximum pretensions about being the best society, although it certainly is not that.'

Already, in a series of statements, Sakharov had advocated wide reforms – an electoral system with multiple candidates, establishment of newspapers and publishing houses free of Party and state domination, decentralization of economic controls, development of a private service industry, abolition of Party control of key appointments, and honest acknowledgment of negative aspects of Soviet life as a basis for reforms. He attacked the vaunted Soviet system of free education and medical care as an 'economic illusion' based on underpaid doctors and teachers and offering 'very low' quality of services; he condemned the 'pernicious' effects of the hierarchical class structure in which the Party-government-intellectual elite enjoys 'open and secret privileges' such as better schools, clinics, special stores and 'a system of supplemental salaries in special envelopes'; and he protested that 'militarization of the economy' posed a threat to peace because 'in no other country is the proportion of national income which goes to military expenditures as high as in the U.S.S.R. – over 40 per cent'.

Most controversially, he came to regard Western pressures as the main hope for liberalizing Soviet society. Privately, I heard him plead for Western liberals to protect harassed Soviet freethinkers with their public protests, and to keep their own countries strong and united as a counterweight to growing Soviet might. Publicly, he issued appeals for Congress to exact a price for trade concessions to Moscow (no equal tariff treatment or large long-term credits unless the Kremlin opened wide the doors to free emigration). He reasoned that if the Soviet leadership could buy high technology from the West without being forced by the West to liberalize internally, the Kremlin would lose all incentive to free its own scientists and intellectuals. On the fifth anniversary of the August 21, 1968 Soviet invasion of Czechoslovakia, he called foreign reporters to his apartment to read a chill warning about the dangers of a false détente:

Détente without democratization [in the Soviet Union], détente in which the West in effect accepts the Soviet rules of the game, would be dangerous, it would not really solve any of the world's problems and would simply mean capitulating in the face of real or exaggerated Soviet power. It would mean trading with the Soviet Union, buying its gas and oil, while ignoring other aspects. I think such a development would be dangerous because it would contaminate the whole world with the anti-democratic peculiarities of Soviet society, it would enable the Soviet Union to bypass problems it cannot resolve on its own and to concentrate on accumulating still further strength. As a result, the world would become helpless before this uncontrollable bureaucratic machine. I think that if détente were to proceed totally without qualifications, on Soviet terms it would pose a serious threat to the world as a whole. It would mean cultivating a closed country where anything that happens may be shielded from outside eyes, a country wearing a mask that hides its true face.

Yet when Solzhenitsyn issued his manifesto attacking the Soviet system, Sakharov was aghast. He did not rush to agree, for they were poles apart, like the Westernizers and Slavophiles of 19-century Russia.

I remember Sakharov, sitting in a faded bathrobe and slippers on his daybed one evening, distraught at the news from an academic friend that a group of his university students were enthralled by Solzhenitsyn's vision of a Holy Russian renaissance. What alarmed him was the powerful potential appeal of such a vision. He felt impelled to challenge Solzhenitsyn publicly, though theretofore they had been careful to stand together because of the relentless pressures both faced. In that very Russian way, Sakharov spoke of how he 'bowed deeply' before Solzhenitsyn's morally powerful exposés of Stalinism in *Gulag Archipelago* and other works. But he was appalled by Solzhenitsyn's 'religious patriarchal romanticism', as he put it, Solzhenitsyn's mystic mistrust of modern science, his Slavophile aspersions on the West, his isolationist retreat into Mother Russia away from world trade and from global cooperation on world problems of hunger, health, and the environment.

In his public rebuttal, Sakharov praised Solzhenitsyn, the novelist, as he had in private. He found common points in their rejection of Marxism as the official ideology, in their hope that Eastern Europe would be relinquished by the Kremlin, and their desire for intellectual and cultural freedoms, including freedom of religion. But he attacked Solzhenitsyn's authoritarian streak as anathema and charged that his Great Russian nationalism was a leaf 'entirely out of the arsenal of semiofficial propaganda'. He said it smacked of 'the notorious military-patriotic indoctrination' of the Soviet populace throughout the Cold War. He went so far as to suggest that the thrust of Solzhenitsyn's Slavophilism, though advanced with peaceful intent, bore echoes of Stalin's approach. 'During the war and up to his very death, Stalin

gave broad rein to "tamed" Orthodoxy,' Sakharov warned.
'These parallels with Solzhenitsyn's proposals are not only
striking, they should put us on guard.'

The breach between the right and the left wings of Soviet
dissent had been opened and was irreparable.

Roy Medvedev, the third corner in the triangular debate, is
the personification of the cool dissident. He is queasy at the
combative mentality of rebels like burly, bearded Pyotr
Yakir who had been schooled in the Stalinist camps. Quite
deliberately, he steers clear of the passionate moral indignation of either Solzhenitsyn or Sakharov. He has always
maintained the sober, dispassionate stance of the thoughtful, armchair reformer. With practical pragmatism, he has
issued statements both with an eye to their impact and to
timing them so that it would be awkward for the authorities
to strike back without embarrassing themselves in the West
or raising an undesirable scandal at home.

Long before meeting him, I sensed that Roy was a study
in carefully calibrated nonconformism. He did not seem to
say all that was on his mind. His protests were often couched
in the stilted rhetoric of Soviet Communism, framed to
appeal to hidden moderates within the Party *apparat*, protected by his declared devotion to reviving some true, purer
form of Marxism-Leninism purged of the sinful deviations
of Stalinism and neo-Stalinism. Privately, some other dissidents scoffed that he was merely an establishment liberal
seeking more flexibility to permit him and his ilk greater
access to information and publications from the West and
a less restricted life for themselves, without really trans-
forming Soviet society. More than once, I heard more
radical dissidents comment sarcastically that the Medvedev
brothers – Roy and Zhores – were 'the only true believers
left' because in their idealism they envisioned Soviet Communism with a human face.

But the implication that this somehow reduced their
dissent to nil was unfair. Roy Medvedev took the risk of
publishing in the West his book, *Let History Judge*, a fat,
thoroughly documented, scholarly indictment of the Stalinist
police state, two years before Solzhenitsyn's *Gulag Archipelago* appeared. His twin brother Zhores has written books
chronicling the suppression of Soviet genetics under the

scientific dictatorship and false biology of Trofim Lysenko; exposing Soviet controls hindering East-West scientific exchanges; and dissecting the unseen workings of Soviet mail censorship. Together they wrote *A Question of Madness*, a shocking yet antiseptically told account of how Zhores was lured into a mental hospital in 1970 to silence his dissent and how Roy raised an international scandal to get him out. During the final torrent of hostility against Solzhenitsyn over *Gulag Archipelago*, Roy dared circulate essays praising the book for its accuracy and condemning Solzhenitsyn's deportation as a 'moral defeat for those in power who were neither willing nor able to answer his accusations' about Stalinist terror.

Stalinism is the issue that drives Roy Medvedev's dissent. At 13, with Zhores, he saw his father, a former political commissar in the Red Army during the Russian Civil War and later a Party instructor at Tomachev Military-Political Academy, dragged away in the middle of the night by Stalin's secret police in 1938. Their last contact with him was a bristly, unshaven hug. They never saw him again.

Stalinism was the issue when I first met the Medvedevs, or rather met Zhores, because Roy preferred to stay in the background. Zhores was born 20 minutes earlier than Roy and for a long time it seemed to me that perhaps this narrow seniority made him the bolder and more daring of the two. Zhores was the first to get into scrapes with the authorities – publishing his dissident works abroad first, venturing far sooner to meet Westerners unofficially, acting as a go-between for Solzhenitsyn, trying to maneuver his way into an international gerontology conference in Kiev in July, 1972, only to be carted away by the KGB. Roy joined the Party in 1961 (Zhores never did) but was thrown out in 1969 for a statement that had warned against plans to rehabilitate Stalin. Yet it is Roy who has produced the more sustained political critique of Soviet society and offered proposals for reform, especially in a new book, *On Socialist Democracy*, much of which I had read in Russian while I was in Moscow.

In late 1971, when I met Zhores, he was trying to help Roy escape the secret police, an episode that had comic moments. Roy had suddenly quit his job at the Institute of Pedagogical Sciences where, as a former teacher and school principal, he had written tracts on education. His unauthorized book on Stalin was about to appear in the West and, with good reason, he feared reprisals. His theory was that if he waited for the axe to fall, he would be blacklisted for life and harshly punished. So he had decided to quit first, go into hiding and lay low until the controversy cooled. But before he could make a move the secret police had a stakeout on his apartment building.

Roy and Zhores are look-alike twins: trim, nearly six-feet tall, with handsome oval faces, and silvering hair yet far younger looking than most Soviet men at 50. So closely do they resemble each other that even good friends have mistaken one for the other. Reveling in the gamesmanship, Zhores explained how he had tried to outwit the stakeout by passing in and out of Roy's apartment building several times in hopes that the secret police would follow him off by mistake and let Roy escape. But the ploy had not worked. 'I guess they have assigned good men to the job,' he chortled. Nonetheless, Roy did manage to slip off, in a wig and disguised as a woman. He hid out for several months in the south. When he returned, he could not get back his job or any official work. He lived on Western royalties and his wife's salary. His immunity from harsher punishment left me wondering if he had sympathetic protectors in the governing *apparat*.

It was close to two years before I met Roy. By then, Zhores had gotten out to England to pursue his career as a biologist and to represent both brothers to Western publishers. Roy, working still as a freelance historian and essayist, was the most meticulous, most organized Russian I ever encountered. (Actually, his father was Russian and his mother was Jewish.) He followed a disciplined work routine and did not let his strictly limited social life interfere. He rarely went out, totally avoided movies and television, read voraciously, and kept voluminous files in extraordinarily good order. His habitat was an immaculate little study lined with books on three walls, where we used to talk, sitting only five or six feet apart with two shortwave radios playing different programs in the background to foil any 'room-bugs'.

Roy was as fastidious as an accountant, and terribly proud of it. Once when I remarked on how precise and organized he was, a smile curled the corners of his mouth. 'When I was a senior in high school, I had already figured out how I was

543

going to organize my files,' he explained. 'I have changed my system a number of times, but I have always known how to lay my hands on any piece of paper.'

Even the KGB had been impressed with his archives when they searched his apartment in 1972. 'They took only three hours,' Roy recalled with pride. 'They immediately understood that they had found a businesslike man and that the files contained what the labels said they contained. That is why they could get done so quickly.' By comparison, he said, a search at the home of another dissident whom I knew, a writer of enormous vitality and charm but deliciously disorganized, 'would have taken them four days.' Even more astonishing to me was the fact that Roy had not had to engage in an endless wrangle with the secret police to reclaim his files – a hopeless task in any case – because years before he had developed the practice of duplicating all his material and keeping a spare set in a safe place. So after the secret police had carted off his archives, he fished out the second set and was back in business.

This unruffled equanimity was Roy's trademark. It was of a piece with the careful calibration of his protest, his calculated tactic of refraining from extremes that would make the authorities feel compelled to garrot him. Unlike Sakharov and Solzhenitsyn, he pointed out to me, he had not been attacked in the Soviet press. Moreover, he said he had let officialdom know his basic lines of research. Indeed, the Stalin book was launched in 1962 during Khrushchev's de-Stalinization with the idea of having it officially published in Moscow. But by the time it was finished in 1968, the Party line had changed and Stalin's rehabilitation was under way. Still, the manuscript was shown to Party officials. In part, this explains why Roy took pains to make it palatable, treating Stalinism as 'pseudo-Communism', a perversion 'profoundly alien to Marxism-Leninism' rather than a fundamental flaw of the system, and why he so gingerly treated the 'little Stalins' of Soviet life, now high officials, who had fattened their own careers with the help of the Stalinist purges. Even when writing about contemporary Soviet life, Roy has avoided attacking the Party head-on but has criticized neo-Stalinist 'deformations' and conservative dogmatism.

In short, Roy Medvedev is an unusual phenomenon among dissidents. He constitutes the loyal opposition. Publicly he has chided other dissidents, including Sakharov and Solzhenitsyn, for 'provocative' behavior or 'extremist' views. Although his own dissent has deepened in recent years, he is above all a pragmatist, a gradualist who envisions reform evolving slowly in the Soviet system, essentially decreed from on high but in response to pressures from 'an alliance between the best of the intelligentsia and the most forward-looking individuals in the governing *apparat*' but not without periodic backtracking and retrenchment forced by neo-Stalinists. Again, his approach made me wonder, as others have, whether Roy speaks for a hidden liberal faction inside the Party. But Roy was careful with me to insist that he spoke only for himself, though he made no secret of long-time Party connections.

Modernization, he used to tell me, will impel the system toward greater democracy over the long run. Copying machines and eventually television broadcasts relayed from abroad by satellites, as well as foreign radio broadcasts, will make it impossible for authorities to keep the lid on the spread of information and ideas. The needs of the modern economy, he felt, would force decentralization of economic management and relaxation of what he regarded as the 'clumsy, cumbersome' overcentralized mechanism of state planning and control. Over two or three generations, he predicted, the Soviet Union will evolve toward a multiparty system.

Some of his criticisms of the Soviet system sound very much like those of Sakharov in earlier years. Indeed, in 1970, they joined in one important critique of the Soviet system along with Valentin Turchin, a Soviet physicist, mathematician and author of one of the few Soviet computer languages. Roy has directed his fire against the ruling bureaucratic oligarchy, against ideological controls that he feels have fossilized Communist ideology by suppressing genuine debate, against the system of privilege and administrative rigidity. He has called for reducing the size and power of the swollen Party apparatus, for experimenting with Yugoslav-style worker self-management in industry, and freedom for the non-Marxist opposition to come legally into the open rather than being forcibly repressed. He has urged far greater freedom of information in science and academic life, offering to a hidden audience of Party liberals the lure that greater flexibility and relaxed controls will put new life into Soviet Communism which he feels has lost popular appeal. 'A process of normal political debate will only promote the development of Marxist-Leninist ideology and the formation of a new, more capable generation of Communist leaders,' he contended in *On Socialist Democracy*, published in English in 1975.

At times, Medvedev has sounded as though he was preaching Dubcek communism (though he criticized the Czechoslovak reformers for pushing too hard, too fast). At one point, answering Solzhenitsyn in the spring of 1974, he called for 'absolute freedom of speech and convictions', freedom of organization and assembly, freedom to propagate religion, free elections open to candidates from a variety of political groups and parties, but always within the framework of a socialist system. But at other times, he has hedged. He has ridiculed Soviet censorship for being so rigid that even Marx and Engels could not pass the censors if they were writing today, but asserted that press freedoms must be limited to protect not only state secrets but Party secrets and professional secrets. And for all his talk of other parties, he leaves in doubt whether any but the Communist Party could actually wield power.

More important, the whole temper of his dissent differs from both Solzhenitsyn and Sakharov. Medvedev strikes a detached philosophical pose and an air of patience where they are trying to mobilize others to speak out and press for changes today. His differences of viewpoint with Solzhenitsyn are fundamental. He dismisses Solzhenitsyn's religious Russophilism as both unappealing and unrealistic. Religion, he reasons, cannot attract enough people in the modern age to serve as the underpinning for society, and if Solzhenitsyn's scheme were imposed, it would run the danger of degenerating into a repressive theocratic state, an echo of the Spanish Inquisition.

Roy Medvedev's disagreement with Sakharov has emerged more subtly. For several years, they stood together publicly, despite private differences, joining in appeals for liberalization and relaxation of controls in all walks of life. But when Sakharov urged the West to pressure Moscow into reforms, Roy's pragmatic, loyalist streak forced him to break with Sakharov. When Sakharov was warning the West against a false détente in which it risked being hoodwinked into helping the Soviet regime strengthen itself and narrow the technological gap, I heard Roy insisting privately that if the United States put preconditions on trade and credits, the insult of ultimatums would anger the Kremlin and backfire. Come December 1974 he held up Moscow's cancellation of the Soviet-American trade agreement as evidence.

Roy's position was that the West could influence Soviet handling of individual cases but that Sakharov and others were overestimating Western influence on the general situation inside the Soviet Union. In the long run, Roy reasoned, Western leaders would lose interest in Soviet internal reforms and problems. His hope was that over 10–15 years tendencies toward reform within the Soviet leadership would be fostered by increased contact with the West through détente. But he was an honest enough historian to acknowledge that during the first couple of years of détente, 'the pressures against dissent even increased' and repressive measures tightened.

Sakharov's own position is a case in point. He was vacationing on the Black Sea in August 1973, when the flood of officially inspired vilification against him broke loose. He and his wife were lying on a beach near Sochi, his wife told me, when they overheard transistors broadcasting a stream of vitriol against this 'renegade' scientist who had sold his soul to the West (no mention of his role in helping make the Soviet H-bomb). Around them, knots of vacationers fell into the mood, talking about Sakharov, cursing his disloyalty and his supposed opposition to détente, while he lay among them unrecognized. Sakharov's wife wanted to get away quickly but Sakharov lingered on. He approached one group and after listening to them scold him, inquired whether anyone actually knew Sakharov or had read what he had written. No one had. Yet for all the conventional skepticism about Soviet propaganda on other matters, these people had taken it at face value on Sakharov. Quietly, still anonymous, he suggested that it would be worth knowing what Sakharov had actually said because 'perhaps he is a man with good intentions after all.' Unable to bear it any longer, his wife hustled him off the beach out of fear that he might be hurt if people discovered his identity.

The propaganda onslaught against Sakharov ended abruptly on September 9 after protests from Willi Brandt,

Austrian Chancellor Bruno Kreisky, Swedish Foreign Minister Krister Wickman, and a warning telegrammed to the Soviet Academy of Sciences from Philip Handler, the head of the American Academy of Science. 'Harassment or detention of Sakharov,' Handler apprised sternly, 'will have severe effects upon relationships between the scientific communities of the U.S.A. and U.S.S.R. and could vitiate our recent efforts toward increasing interchange and cooperation.'

That touched a vital nerve. The Kremlin obviously felt that the price of carrying the campaign against Sakharov to its ultimate conclusion had become too high. Western intervention had thus proven a deterrent against the possible arrest of Sakharov (he had been questioned and warned by the Deputy Procurator General and the secret police) or detention in a mental hospital and expulsion from the Soviet Academy, which the Party *apparat* had desperately been trying to engineer behind the scenes.

It was a victory but a pyrrhic one, for the Kremlin had already succeeded in crippling Sakharov's influence among his natural constituency, the Soviet scientific world. He had become an isolated and demoralized man. Tens of thousands of scientists had read his first memorandum on peaceful coexistence in 1968, according to Moscow scientists whom I knew, and yet very few had seen any of his major subsequent declarations, which had been sharper. I heard this not only in Moscow but from a physicist in Novosibirsk in Western Siberia and a biologist in the Moldavian capital of Kishinev, among others. Both the public propaganda campaign accusing him of opposing détente and the private whisper campaign that he was a bit whacky took their toll.

'Respect for Sakharov has fallen over the past couple of years,' a medical scientist told me in late 1974. 'People consider him an eccentric, a bit feebleminded, strange, emotional, unpredictable.' When this man learned that I knew Sakharov personally, he questioned me closely about whether Sakharov seemed mentally normal and what he was like. He wanted to be sympathetic to Sakharov but he was wary. His attitude recalled that apt observation of Lidiya Chukovskaya, the writer, so little understood by outsiders and so revealing about the way Soviet life actually moves: 'That soundproof wall, built by the authorities methodically and with malice, between the creators of spiritual values and those for whom those values are created, has grown higher and stronger.'

Assiduously, intellectuals were driven into one of two camps by the authorities: either into open dissent, to be prosecuted or made social outcasts, or to become collaborators of repression. This, according to Valentin Turchin, the dissident scientist, was one of the main purposes of the regime in getting so many prominent scientists, writers, scholars and intellectuals to join in the collective vilification of Sakharov and Solzhenitsyn. His reasoning was that these people felt morally compromised by that act, so guilty that no matter what their private views, they would go on participating in denouncing all nonconformists.

Turchin, a slender, soft-spoken and self-effacing scientist, had felt the heat of this hounding personally. He paid dearly for his own loyalty to Sakharov. During the virulent outpouring of late 1973, he had been almost alone in defending Sakharov. Retribution was swift. A mass meeting was organized at his institute, the Institute for Computer Systems in the Construction Industry. It was one of those classic criticism-sessions where the Institute Director, the Party Secretary and other workers publicly chastised Turchin for siding with Sakharov. Some called for him to be fired, though he was temporarily spared when the campaign against Sakharov ended. But immediately he felt the chill of ostracism from colleagues who privately sympathized with him. And he fell to analyzing what he called the 'technology of repression' in the era of détente.

'There is an unbelievable cynicism among people,' he remarked one evening. 'The honest man makes the silent ones feel guilty for not having spoken out. They cannot understand how he had the courage to do what they could not bring themselves to do. So they feel impelled to speak out against him to protect their own consciences. In the second place, they feel that everyone everywhere is deceiving everyone else, based on their own experience. *Homo Sovieticus* is like the prostitute who believes that all women are whores because she is. Soviet man believes that the whole world is divided into parties and that every man is a member of one party or another, and there is no real honesty. No one stands for the truth. And if anyone says he is above Party and is trying to speak the truth alone, he is lying. This cynicism greatly helps the authorities keep the intelligentsia in line and exclude the "wild dissidents" from society. People can travel to the West and hear Western radio broadcasts and it makes no difference, so long as there is this persuasive cynicism that it is just the other side speaking. This cynicism provides the stability of the totalitarian state today in place of the fear of the Stalinist years.'

Sakharov himself told me that he had been effectively ostracized by all but a few friends like Turchin. Hardly any of the other top scientists who used regularly to frequent his dacha still paid him visits after the 1973 campaign. For establishment figures, private contact with him had become poisonous. His own friends and supporters suffered. Valery Chalidze and Andrei Tverdokhlebov, the two younger physicists who had joined him in forming the Human Rights Committee, were fired from their jobs. Tverdokhlebov was eventually arrested. Threats of Siberian exile became so intimidating to Chalidze that he accepted the 'out' of going to America. In the summer of 1974, Turchin was fired from his job for 'social reasons', as the euphemism went, and effective economic blacklisting forced at least four other institutes to reject him because he would not pledge to keep quiet. When I last heard from him in October 1975, he still had no work. The KGB had interrogated him several times, searched his apartment and seized his typewriter and many of his private papers. He was trying to come to America as a visiting scholar before being arrested and carted off to Siberia. But the path to emigration was being blocked, too.

Sakharov admitted privately to me that after the 1973 campaign against him, he had become so disheartened that he had applied for permission to go to Princeton's Institute of Advanced Studies and had tried to arrange for his stepson, stepdaughter and her husband to be admitted to M.I.T. for what would obviously be permanent exile. Theoretically, his own appointment would be for a year but he recognized he might never get back to Moscow if he ever got out. Mainly for that reason, he dropped the idea of going abroad himself after Solzhenitsyn had been forcibly deported. He felt morally obliged to remain rather than leave Soviet dissent without any commanding voice. But the tensions of anonymous death threats against his children and his grandson, the administrative harassments against his family, the refusal for many months to let his wife go to Italy for medical treatment to keep her from going blind, were wearing him down. Although the award of the Nobel Peace Prize in October 1975 undoubtedly gave him and his small band of friends a lift, his protests were increasingly those of a single voice rather than one joined by a chorus of supporters. In mid-1975 he cried out in pain against threats and 'thuggery' against his family who, he said, were being used as 'hostages' against him.

Nor was this merely Sakharov's personal plight. It reflected a more general retrenchment of Russian dissent. Various nationalist groups in Lithuania or Armenia, or religious groups like the nonofficial Baptists issued periodic collective appeals and protests, but dissent among the liberal Russian intelligentsia was disintegrating as the Seventies wore on. If the great debate of the super dissidents briefly displayed the substance and vitality of their ideas, it also demonstrated that such outspoken nonconformism had increasingly become a luxury of the world famous. What had rather pretentiously called itself the Democratic Movement, a loose coalition of a few hundred dissident intellectuals, had been dispersed, deported and demoralized by the mid-Seventies. Many people who had once shared Roy Medvedev's hope of liberalizing Soviet society from within were overcome by a sense of futility.

The contrast was striking with the early Sixties when crowds gathered in Pushkin Square for open poetry readings in defiance of authority, or the mid-Sixties when literally hundreds of establishment scientists, writers, scholars, and cultural notables took the risk of signing petitions protesting the trial against Andrei Sinyavsky and Yuli Daniel, who were charged with illegally publishing 'anti-Soviet' works abroad under pseudonyms. This triggered a wave of mass protests from 1965–1968. 'We all had hoped then that by openly opposing the system things would eventually get better,' an elderly Moscow writer told me. 'It was an uneven struggle and we knew it. We had hope. But it got us nowhere. Now, what's the use?'

I remember in the fall of 1972, in the first flush of détente after the Nixon-Brezhnev summit, talking with a successful Moscow mathematician who was explaining why he was so reluctant to sign a protest against a new round of political trials in Czechoslovakia. This was a change for him because formerly he had been active in circulating petitions. 'It's another "nothing" paper,' he said in despair. 'Your conscience tells you that you cannot be silent. But you know nothing will come of it. We tried it and it made no difference except that more people got hurt.' He was referring to the scores who were ousted from the Party and fired from jobs for signing the earlier protests.

The sense of futility and disenchantment affected even the most hard-core activists. When Sinyavsky and Daniel returned from long years in Siberia, they did not rejoin the ranks of active dissenters but kept quietly to themselves. Natalya Gorbanyevskaya, a young poet put in a mental hospital for her part in the brief Red Square demonstration against the Soviet invasion of Czechoslovakia, came out of the hospital and went back to poetry and raising her child rather than activism. Others too laid low, like Larissa Bogoraz, Anatoly Marchenko, and Aleksandr Ginzberg, all forbidden by the authorities to return to Moscow. Marchenko was eventually sent back to the forced labor camps in 1975 for coming back into Moscow, and Andrei Amalrik, another prominent dissident, was threatened with the same fate when in the fall of 1975 he tried to resume his activism after six years in Siberia.

To me, it would have seemed logical that the very dawning of détente would have encouraged Soviet intellectuals, especially scientists and scholars, to rally to the ideas of Sakharov and the Medvedevs for much freer and more direct exchanges of visits and information with the West. Yet the silence on such issues was deafening. What happened was that the authorities closely controlled all channels of travel and contact with the West and used the opportunities for East-West exchange as a new source of leverage for enforcing ideological conformity.

Often, I was told, stepping out of line, let alone open dissent, was an immediate pretext for dropping a scientist from a delegation going abroad or excluding a scholar from taking part in meetings with visiting Western groups. I knew personally of cases where those who fraternized too freely and were too talkative with Westerners were dropped on the next trip. People became anxious to keep their records clean and to demonstrate reliability.

'You Americans really don't understand how our system works,' a young biologist chided me. 'You assume that détente will automatically open up our system. For the reliable "Party" scientists, it is a "good thing". They get to travel again and again. The rest of us have to be on our best behavior if we want to stand any chance. So you see, détente gives the authorities a new way to reward and punish us.'

A middle-aged movie script writer who had traveled to Eastern Europe but never had been permitted to go to the West was acid in his comments. 'I know writers who will sign any statement, make any denunciations of Sakharov or whomever the authorities want, to get something published or to get a trip abroad,' he said angrily. 'I know a scientist who will stop at nothing for a trip to Japan. You should understand what an insidious thing this is. Ninety percent will do that. They would inform even on their own colleagues for a three-week trip to Japan.'

'The technology of repression has become more refined in recent years,' Roy Medvedev commented to me. 'Before, repression always went much further than necessary. Stalin killed millions of people when arresting 1,000 would have enabled him to control people. Our leaders have never known how to go just far enough and not too far. But they have found out eventually that you don't have to put people in prison or in a psychiatric hospital to silence them. There are other ways.'

The very emphasis of Solzhenitsyn and others on Stalin's mass terror has blinded outsiders to the more subtle yet powerfully coercive mechanisms of the Soviet Seventies. Modern Soviet authoritarianism is more efficient – though not as totally effective – as Stalin's brand, because the near-perfect conformism of public life is achieved with much less physical violence. People are already conditioned to conform.

The KGB remains a formidable apparatus – some 500,000 strong by knowledgeable Western estimates. Here and there, I became aware of it as I was tailed on the streets of Yerevan or Riga, entertained by police plants in Central Asia who muscled more normal citizens away from my dining tables, or had my tires punctured outside Sakharov's apartment under the watchful eye of a late night 'taxi'.

My strongest visual impression of the awesome human resources of Soviet security services came when President Nixon arrived in Moscow in late May, 1972. He landed at Vnukovo Airport, about 20 miles southwest of the heart of

Moscow. Thousands of gray-uniformed policemen lined the route out to the city limits. Behind them, you could see a second line of men in plain clothes whose ranks continued out past the militia, all the way to the airport. Mile after mile, these shadowy figures hovered amongst the trees every 20 yards or so. I couldn't help wondering what this enormous manpower pool did in normal times – tailing people, bugging telephones, compiling dossiers, interrogating, blackmailing, searching, arresting.

The Bolshoi Ballet gave a special gala performance of *Swan Lake* in Nixon's honor and the hall, I was told later by Russians, was packed with KGB officials and their families plus a sprinkling of other government and Party faithful. According to people in the Bolshoi company, some KGB contingents were bused in from provincial cities to insure an absolutely reliable audience. A musician in the Bolshoi orchestra complained later to friends that it was 'a dead hall' that night with no warmth. 'You could feel that these people had not come for the performance,' he said. 'They simply didn't respond.'

The archipelago of Soviet labor camps in the 1970s has a population of one to two million, depending on which Western estimates you believe (the Soviets never say), including 10,000 to 20,000 political prisoners – from Ukrainian, Lithuanian, Armenian and other nationalists, to religious believers who refuse to serve in the armed forces or insist on giving their children religious training, to the democratic dissidents known in the West. It is a sizable contingent but a far cry from the millions of political prisoners incarcerated by Stalin.

Not only are the numbers lower but the totally unpredictable and arbitrary terror of the Stalinist era has abated. Most ordinary people can keep clear of the KGB, though complete dossiers are kept on everyone by the personnel section, *pervy otdel*, 'The First Department,' in every Soviet factory, institute, agency, or collective farm. Even dissidents will admit that they know they are consciously taking the risk of arrest with their protests, whereas ordinary people who stick to the Party line and avoid political nonconformism are not normally harassed by political police.

For those who stray out of line politically, the most effective and widely used method of control is economic blacklisting. A technique used in the West during the witchhunts and Red Scares of the past but far more crippling in a centralized economy where the state is effectively the sole employer and where the individual has a workbook that carries his lifetime work history showing his status, political as well as professional, and where every institution has its *pervy otdel* checking on the political background of new employees.

Westerners may have largely forgotten the Soviet invasion of Czechoslovakia, but Soviet liberals are very conscious of that year as a time of repression – and especially economic reprisals and blacklisting – because the Kremlin feared that the infection of Czechoslovak liberalism was spreading among the Soviet intelligentsia. Brezhnev seems to have been particularly vexed by what he saw in Prague on a visit in late February 1968, for he came home to make a major speech warning that Soviet 'renegades cannot expect immunity'. Russians took it as an omen of an imminent crackdown. Indeed, Mikhail Agursky, the systems analyst, who had related some of the inner workings of Lenin Library, told me that he and other Jews suddenly found that jobs promised them were withdrawn that spring. For Jews had been prominent among the protest-signers and administrators were more wary of taking them on. Several mathematicians at Moscow University were reprimanded and some were eased out of their jobs that summer. The same with non-conformist scientists in institutes from Leningrad to Novosibirsk, in West Siberia. Waves of dismissals and demotions put a chill on intellectual life.

I have heard of too many such cases to enumerate, but a couple will convey the power of the state, as a monopoly employer, to bring non-conformists to heel. A friend told me about Leonid Petrovsky, a Communist Party member from a family of loyal Bolsheviks whose grandfather had been the first president in 1922 of what was to become the Supreme Soviet. Petrovsky himself had a good research post at the Institute of the Museum of Lenin in Moscow. As events were unfolding in Czechoslovakia and in Moscow, Petrovsky like others feared a new Stalinist wave. He spoke against neo-Stalinism in various closed meetings and privately circulated writings that warned of a trend toward rehabilitating Stalin. One of his articles was published abroad, in Sweden.

Instantly, Petrovsky was expelled from the Party and fired from work. Previously he had made money on the side by doing newspaper articles on Soviet history and ideology for central newspapers but now that avenue was blocked. For a while, he slipped a few articles into distant provincial newspapers where his blacklisting was not yet known. But soon that, too, dried up.

'His family had a hard life,' a mutual friend told me. 'His wife was an ordinary teacher. She made less than 100 rubles a month and they had two children. It is impossible for four people to live on so little in Moscow. Petrovsky could not get any work at all. They were desperate. Because of his family background, Petrovsky appealed to the Central Committee to give him a job somewhere. There was no answer. Many times he appealed. Still no answer. Finally, after a long while – at least a year, I know – they called him in and gave him work at the state archives. Now he is in no mood to make any protests. He is a good man, honest, but quiet. He is afraid.'

The permutations of this technique are infinite but the intent and effect are almost always the same. I met a sad-faced art historian, a large, lumbering man with melancholy eyes and a look of hurt innocence, who had been driven mercilessly from every job he had found in the course of seven years because he had signed one petition – only one – on behalf of Sinyavsky and Daniel. Illegally he had been fired in 1966 from the art publishing house where he had worked for many years. He went to court to contest the bureaucratic maneuver by which he was euchred out of his post. It was useless. He told me the judge privately admitted being ready to decide the case in his favor until secret instructions came from higher up to rule against him. Later, the man got occasional jobs – in a school, in an institute, as an archivist in a library, and eventually he was so desperate he even took a job carrying books in the stacks. But always the political police caught up with him and he was fired. When I met him, he was out of work, numbed by his hopeless position and dependent on his wife's modest salary as a university language teacher for support. He had a lifetime of unemployment ahead of him, for he was far less well connected than Petrovsky.

I knew writers blacklisted for nearly a decade who survived only because of working wives or because friends in the literary world smuggled them work to be published under pseudonyms. Other people, though not fired, had careers stunted merely for guilt by association. Take Anatoly, a talented, promising, and likable young physicist of 30 at an institute in Obninsk, about 80 miles from Moscow. In 1969, as a Party member, he wrote a letter to the provincial Party committee in Kaluga gently suggesting that they re-examine the cases of two scientific colleagues sternly reprimanded for minor political deviations. His was a private, confidential letter in conformity with the Party rules that members address higher-ups with problems. The politically savvy understand, of course, that this is a myth and they keep quiet. But Anatoly was conscience-driven to defend his friends.

The Scientific Council at his institute was convened. Its chairman instructed the other 32 council members that Anatoly's letter showed he was politically immature and recommended that he be demoted (for that, I was told, was what Party headquarters had ordered). Although the other council members liked Anatoly and knew his professional talents, only one man spoke on his behalf, asking why such a fuss was being made over a mild letter. Immediately, several others turned on this man, attacking him for going against the line laid down by the chairman. No one else dared defend Anatoly. A vote was taken, by secret ballot. All 33 members voted for demotion, even the man who had originally defended Anatoly. I heard several other stories of collective sanctions, where everyone did the Party's bidding even against his own conscience and despite the protection of secrecy. Some dissidents called that pliant uniformity 'our greatest shame'.

None of these three – Petrovsky, the art historian, or Anatoly – were hard-core dissidents. Like many others, they were passively disaffected except for an occasional overt act. Yet blacklisting, demotions and economic pressures were enough to bring them to heel and to intimidate an entire segment of Soviet society which would otherwise have provided a constituency for Sakharov and undoubtedly would have joined the trend of the late Sixties toward increasingly open debate and dissent. But over the past five years, the Brezhnev-led coalition effectively turned back the clock from the ferment of the early Sixties and the greater activism of the mid-Sixties, and reimposed effective controls on this amorphous but important element of the intelligentsia.

In its tactics toward hard-core dissidents, the regime was much harsher but less inclined to overkill than previously. Some dissidents attributed this greater sophistication to Yuri Andropov, who became head of the secret police in 1967, and who is widely regarded as the most intelligent member of the Politburo. Détente, too, imposed a need for greater circumspection. Crackdowns were avoided at sensitive moments, such as the impending visit of a major Western leader, a critical period in East-West negotiations, or before a trip by Brezhnev to the West. Out in the provinces where foreign diplomats and newsmen had no access, round-ups and trials could go ahead without hindrance. But in Moscow, the secret police timed their reprisals carefully and cannily distinguished between famous dissenters whose tribulations would arouse sympathy and protest in the West and the minor, obscure figures whose demise would pass unnoticed and without danger to the climate of détente.

Sakharov and Solzhenitsyn might be spared the harshest sentences, but their friends fared less well. I have already mentioned the harassment of Sakharov's colleagues. After Solzhenitsyn was exiled, one of his friends, a cyberneticist named Aleksandr Gorlov, who had accidentally come upon police agents ransacking Solzhenitsyn's summer cottage in 1971, was unceremoniously fired from his job and thus blacklisted for life for his one act of friendship. Far worse, a frail young archivist named Gabriel Superfin, who had worked part time as an amanuensis for Solzhenitsyn, was dragged off to the provincial city of Orel, held incommunicado for eight months, and then after emerging in court to repudiate a confession extracted during relentless interrogations, was sentenced to seven years in camp and Siberian exile – for doing far less than Solzhenitsyn himself.

Such cases are innumerable, for Soviet authorities with perverse consistency recognize rank and importance among dissidents just as among the hierarchy of officialdom itself. People of prestige simply get away with actions or statements that would send unknown dissidents to their doom. Lidiya Chukovskaya, the inconoclastic writer who was eventually expelled from the Writers' Union for sheltering Solzhenitsyn and supporting Sakharov, pointed out several times that 'little people' in outlying cities were being tried and convicted for merely possessing some of her anti-Stalinist writings and protests whereas she, partially protected by notoriety and family connections, was still free. This deliberate double standard not only isolates but torments the more famous dissidents who are haunted with the sense of guilt that others risk more for speaking their minds than they do.

Another demoralizing technique used by the KGB with enormous effectiveness has been to set various factions of dissidents against each other and to play upon the natural, self-protective wariness of dissidents who must always be on guard against informers. I remember the pained look of one writer as he described how the secret police had planted the cancerous slander that he was one of their agents, poisoning his relations with others. The Sakharov-Solzhenitsyn-Medvedev debate, though not of the KGB's making, had a tragic acrimonious personal side that set the shrinking band of dissidents at odds with each other. But the most celebrated and devastating case was that of Pyotr Yakir, whose father had been one of the top Soviet Army generals purged and executed by Stalin in 1937.

As a boy of 14, Yakir had been sent to the camps where he spent 16 of his 30 years. By the time I met him, he was nearly 50, a bold, shaggy-haired, friendly, hard-drinking, roguish dissident whose earthy outspoken anti-Stalinism and fearlessness made him a father figure to younger dissidents. For correspondents, he had become an important channel of information and for obtaining the bimonthly *Chronicle of Current Events*, the main dissident publication, a dispassionate record of their activities and repressions against them. Yakir's flamboyance and indiscretions worried more careful dissenters who feared his circle was penetrated by informers. Sadly, they turned out to be right.

In late 1971, the leadership decided to crush the *Chronicle* and its network of 'correspondents' and distributors. By mid-1972, they focused on Yakir and his friend, Viktor Krasin, another veteran of the camps. Both were arrested, held incommunicado for months, and eventually broken by interrogators to the point where they falsely confessed links with anti-Soviet emigré groups abroad and implicated many other people. Scores of intellectuals in several cities, perhaps as many as 200, were interrogated and some forced into soul-wrenching confrontations with Yakir and Krasin who urged them to admit activities, some real, some false, because the KGB 'already knows everything'. The impact on dissident morale was shattering. Too many had regarded Yakir as a rock of reliability and were unbearably disillusioned when he began to talk, disillusioned not only with him but with any hope for cooperative efforts to liberalize Soviet society.

'It is so painful – too painful to talk about,' a Leningrad dissident told me.

'No more for me,' said a gray-haired Moscow translator. 'It shows that organizations are dangerous politically and morally – politically because you can be arrested by the police and morally because any organization can be infiltrated and corrupted from inside.'

Paradoxically, détente provided a final windfall to the secret police for dealing with dissidents too well known to be easily suppressed without scandal and too strong-willed to be turned into informers. For them, the new technique was expulsion. Actually, it was not entirely new as a tactic: Lenin and the early Bolsheviks had gotten rid of important anti-Communist intellectuals the same way in the post-Revolutionary period. Stalin banished his rival Trotsky in 1929. In the Seventies, Solzhenitsyn was the prime target. In a swift maneuver, Soviet authorities deported him and rid themselves of their most prickly internal critic. However troubled the West might be, it was powerless to reverse his deportation and relieved that Solzhenitsyn had not ended up with a bullet in his brain or condemned to rot away his final years in Siberia. For Moscow, his deportation was an extremely successful move. Six months later, his books were still hot contraband among disaffected intellectuals, but he was a far less palpable force and influence.

Without many people in the West taking notice, an entire school of the more defiant or outspoken intellectuals was dealt with this way – pushed out to the West, like Solzhenitsyn, most of them lost in the flow of Jewish emigrants, though some were not Jewish: Mstislav Rostropovich, the cellist; Joseph Brodsky, the poet; writers like Viktor Nekrasov, Vladimir Maximov, and Anatoly Jacobson; Andrei Sinyavsky, the satirist and literary critic; Valery Chalidze, the physicist; Aleksandr Yanov, the publicist; Aleksandr Galich, dramatist and underground balladier; Yefim Etkind, noted philologist and friend of Solzhenitsyn, among others. Some people were bluntly warned by the KGB that they could either get out to the West or be shipped off to Siberia on an

560

endless cycle of trials and convictions.

Pavel Litvinov's case is a classic example of the new tactic. The grandson of Stalin's foreign minister, Maxim Litvinov, Pavel is a tall, husky, rather Irish-looking young man with a gregarious smile and unaffected directness of manner. He was exiled to a squalid, distant, and miserably cold village in Siberia near the Manchurian border as one of seven participants in the August 25, 1968 demonstration in Red Square against the Soviet invasion of Czechoslovakia. Although trained as a physicist and sent to an exile village which had no physics teacher in its local school, Pavel had to work as a manual laborer in a fluorspar mine. When he returned to Moscow in December 1972, he found it impossible to get regular work or to get re-registered for residence in Moscow with his wife and two small children. In the Yakir investigation, he was interrogated and blackmailed with offers of work and a residence permit if he would cooperate with the KGB. He refused. Somehow he managed to get private jobs tutoring high school students in physics and translating scientific works from English, and also to regain his Moscow registration. But he was drawn back into his human rights campaigning and had several run-ins with the secret police.

Events reached a climax on the evening of December 5, 1973, as Pavel headed for the brief, annual human rights vigil in Pushkin Square. Half a block from the square, he was surrounded by four men who said they were from the KGB. They ordered him to go with them. 'I refused,' Pavel later told me. 'I asked to see their identification. They refused to show me anything. The leader – a short, stocky man with wide shoulders and a boxer's face, an unpleasant face with his nose pushed in – told me, "if you do not come, there will be a fight and then you will get 15 days in jail for hooliganism." So I agreed to go.' They led him to a local police station where the leader took Pavel to a little room and talked to him for 20 minutes. Rather humorously, Pavel called the pug-nosed agent 'my sponsor' in the KGB for 'he knew everything about my case, my life history, my private life, my family. He was probably in charge of me.'

'Oh, Litvinov,' the KGB man said, 'you are really going back to your old business again. Of course, you must understand that we will not tolerate this. We will not stand for such things. It is better for you to stop this business or you will be in much worse conditions than last time – and for many years.' Pavel took this as a clear warning of a long term in the labor camps. But then came the alternative. 'I know you have an invitation from the West and from Israel,' the KGB man said. 'If you apply for an exit visa, it will be the best solution for all. Otherwise, you will go East.'

The alternatives were clear. 'He didn't promise me, but there was mutual understanding of course,' Pavel said. 'They must have known how I was feeling because I had made no secret of how discouraged I was about my future prospects. I had even talked with friends about going abroad. Of course, the KGB prefer for people who are well known in the West to go abroad rather than to send them to Siberia because there is less of a scandal.'

Within a month, Pavel had applied to emigrate and two months later he was in America. It was a pattern repeated in a number of important cases with the same choice – go West into oblivion or see yourself slowly destroyed here. A fair number, like Litvinov, chose the West and the dissident movement lost them for good.

'We are so alone,' lamented one woman who stayed behind. 'First, Solzhenitsyn; then, Nekrasov, Galich, Litvinov, and all these others. Living in Moscow now is like living on the moon.'

XIX

THE OUTSIDE WORLD
Province of the Privileged
and the Pariahs

> Soviet society is divided into two groups – those
> who are allowed to go abroad and those who are
> not.
>
> Russian scientist, 1973

The *Litva* is one of a small but exclusive class of Soviet cruise
vessels that ply the warm Mediterranean in summer and
cater mostly to foreign tourists to earn hard currency. But in
the summer of 1974, the *Litva* set sail from Odessa on a 15-
day sortie to Istanbul, Naples, Athens, Marseille, and other
ports with a special manifest of select Communist Party
officials and their families from Moscow, Kiev, and other
big cities – the key *apparatchiki* of the big city Party
machines. Nigel Broomfield, a British diplomatic friend, was
booked by chance on that voyage and returned educated in
the folkways of Soviet foreign travel and amused by the
brazenly bourgeois tastes and life-styles of these Party men
who at home so vociferously run down the decadent world
of capitalism.

'Not a single person – man, woman, or child – was dressed
in Soviet clothes and they were all Party bigshots,' Broomfield said to me in amazement. 'They were all in Western
outfits from tip to toe. The family who sat near us for meals
were from Kiev. The father was some big Party man there.
The children were fitted out in Western slacks and shirts
and the wife was just groaning because she had been
squeezed into trim Western clothing that was not meant for
her ample Ukrainian figure.'

At each port of call, Broomfield related, these captains of

Communism were like coiled springs, leaping at the department store cornucopias of the West. 'When we landed at Naples, the few Western tourists on the ship would all troop off to Pompeii to see the sights, but the Russians would go off in the opposite direction,' he said. 'They weren't interested in touring. They would produce great bundles of American money – ten dollar bills, twenty dollar bills, 100 dollar bills. Lots of money. Obviously the kind of money that only special people get. And they would head for the cambio, exchange the dollars for lira and head off in a great horde on a shopping spree. When the Westerners got back to the ship, some might have bought a few cameos or knick-knacks, but the Russians came back incredibly laden with new dresses, slacks, shoes, shirts, radios, the whole kit. It was that way all through the trip. The Westerners would tour and the Russians would shop.'

In short, travel to the forbidden West has become an exotic privilege for an entire slice of Soviet society – the power elite and that veneer of officials, propagandists, technocrats, athletes, writers, ballerinas, and violinists who constitute the face the Soviet system shows the world. Travel abroad – especially to the West – has become the status symbol *par excellence* of the Soviet privileged class, the surest mark of political reliability. And for those who are permitted to indulge in this addictive habit regularly, it has become a pretty lucrative business.

The Moscow black market feeds on the Western transistors, rock records, fine foreign fabrics, stereo sets, platform shoes, and other fashions brought home by the corps de ballet of the Bolshoi, the Soviet national basketball team, or a delegation of paunchy foreign trade officials. Private commerce is well established as one of the perquisites of official travel abroad.

A short story writer told me of a colleague who had approached the administrator of the Exit Commission of the Writers' Union (every organization of note has its Exit Commission to filter out those acceptable and those unacceptable for foreign travel) to plead for a trip to the West. The writer told the Party man that he needed to keep up his contacts and to get fresh material for his writing. The Party official was cool to this approach, but he happened to glance at the writer's suit and remarked, 'What's the matter, Vanya, are your clothes wearing out?'

'Yes, yes,' the writer responded, instantly getting the pitch and playing to that theme. 'I'm in bad shape and my wife is after me for some new things, too.'

At that, the Party man sympathetically helped arrange the trip.

Those who are trusted and fortunate enough to go abroad regularly begin to count on steady income from the goods they buy on foreign jaunts. A friend of mine knew a senior editor of *New Times*, the Party's leading foreign language weekly on international affairs, who had a very solid salary of 300 rubles ($390) a month. This editor told him that he nearly doubled his annual income from the proceeds of two trips to the West each year. A leading ballet dancer explained to me that with any business acumen at all, he could parlay savings from his modest hard currency *per diem* from a two-month tour in the West into about 6,000 rubles ($8,000) profit just from items carried back in his suitcases. 'A little $100 tape recorder, duty free, in some Western airport brings 800–1,000 rubles in Russia,' he said. Nor was this just casual trade. He lined up customers in advance and knew the right selection of goods. In addition to electronics, Western fabrics for women's dresses and men's suits were hot items. With the kind of profit you could make, he said, 'people would kill their own mother to go abroad.'

The greatest privilege of all, of course, is to get an assignment abroad. The Soviet government pays special salaries to its foreign employees but holds back 40 percent to be paid out at the end of the foreign tour in 'certificate rubles' spendable in Moscow's own hard currency stores where the buying power of the certificates is four to eight times the normal ruble. This procedure is a great incentive for people to return home at the end of the assignment. I was told of one Novosti Press Agency man in Tokyo (possibly an intelligence cover) who was getting $1,400 a month over and above expenses and living allowances, almost all banked in certificate rubles. 'At that rate, he's earning a car a month!' said my Russian informant.

Even with that 40 percent withheld, some official Russians manage to return home from years overseas loaded with Western goods. A graying Moscow writer told me that a former Soviet official at the United Nations lived in his building and had an apartment full of American appliances down to a flush toilet, which was his proudest item. A journalist, also formerly posted in New York, showed off his complete Maytag built-in kitchen, his Lord & Taylor living room, and the lollipop curtains in his child's room to some diplomatic friends of mine.

The key, of course, is being a trusted official or a member of the official delegations which are waved through Soviet customs without a glance. Otherwise, Western goods may be confiscated. I have had my luggage well searched at times (for black market rubles or foreign literature) and have watched Soviet customs agents, especially the women, go through the luggage of others like peasant women doing a vigorous wash, kneading every item. I saw an elderly, sun-burnt worker from Bulgaria stripped of ten pathetic two-ounce balls of mohair wool (worth 15 rubles apiece on the black market). Customs officials are not above seizing desirable, resalable items like that wool or *Playboy* magazines for their own profiteering. Once, a friend of mine noticed two customs men glancing at a forbidden Western skin magazine carried by a tourist and debating what to do. 'Do we have that one?' one official asked the other, who shrugged uncertainly. So they took it. But official delegations usually skim by without a worry. A journalist for the government newspaper *Izvestia* told me of returning once from the West with suitcases loaded with contraband literature – Solz-henitsyn, Pasternak, *Playboy*, and lots of others. A young customs man asked him and the other newsmen in his delegation whether they had any literature.

'No,' the *Izvestia* man said with authority. 'No literature.' The others made similar denials.

'Really?' the customs man asked with a knowing smile. 'You are journalists and journalists don't need literature?'

'We are journalists,' the *Izvestia* man told him, 'so we know what is permitted and what is forbidden.'

The customs man let them go without opening a bag.

The West has long held the fascination of the unattainable for educated Russians. The declaration of détente has merely quickened their appetite to see it for themselves. Westerners have been so acutely conscious lately of their economic world falling to pieces that they have been unaware of how greedily Russians scrounge and scheme to arrange a visit to the crumbling citadels of capitalism. Permission to go abroad – anywhere – is enough to transport a Soviet citizen into giddy excitement. It is a giddiness far more exhilarating to a Soviet than the pleasure Westerners feel at signing up for a package tour to Athens and the Greek Isles, for implicit in the permission to travel abroad is the immediate status of knowing you can do something that very few other Russians can. 'At the Writers' Union, the moment you are told that you can go to *Argentina*, things change,' one writer told me. 'People start saying, "Oh, so you are going to Argentina. Very good." And everyone talks about it enviously. It is a big thing. Even before you go, you are already up in the air.' And she sat there, beaming, as if riding a magic carpet to Argentina.

Among those who stay behind, I found an insatiable hunger to hear about the West from Westerners themselves. Russian interest in America, for example, far exceeds the interest of Americans in Russia. And Russian attitudes are a schizophrenic mixture of love and hate. America is both rival and model, the one country against which Russians feel compelled to measure themselves, the one worthy standard in the world. They may run it down as a harsh, money-grubbing country of crass materialism devoid of moral values or civic responsibility, but many – especially the urban intellectuals – speak admiringly of American technology, efficiency, creature comforts – of America's unassailable modernism.

I have often had the experience of Russians flashing from hot to cold about America in conversation. I spent an evening in Bratsk with Yevgeny Vereshchagin, a tense, spare, combative Komsomol official, who told me about his visit to America in 1961. He had been impressed by the highways, material wealth, and warm friendliness of most people. But he alternated between memories of heartwarming reunions with American pilots whom he had known during the war and denunciations of capitalism, the cynicism of American businessmen who built obsolescence into their products and the stupidity of American workers who thought of themselves as middle class instead of the proletariat. He would raise a toast to the hope that Russia and America would never fight a war and that our children would never fight. Then, in the next breath, he would bait me by telling me that my children would live under Communism.

Vereshchagin was unusual because he had seen the West

567

with his own eyes. The ignorance of most other Russians about real conditions in the West had bred either excessive admiration of Western life (generally among intellectuals) or a baffling, parochial sense of Soviet superiority (among more ordinary folk). Russian intellectuals have long been sensitive to the provincialism of their own people and are prone to joke about it. From several I heard the old anecdote about the Jew in the Ukrainian town of Zhmerinka who came across a friend wearing a nicely tailored suit. He inquired where it had come from and was told Paris. 'How far is Paris from Zhmerinka?' the Jew asked. About 1,500 miles, he was told. 'Imagine Paris being that far from Zhmerinka,' he said, 'and their knowing how to make such nice suits.'

I ran into many a modern version of that old joke. Once in the Central Asian city of Bukhara, an ancient center of Moslem culture, I wandered into a small metal-working shop and two workmen, spotting me as a foreigner, began pumping me about America – typical questions about wages, prices, cars, and so on. Pretty soon, one of them cut off the conversation with the defensive rejoinder that America had unemployment and lacked free public education. Besides, he said with a final thrust, 'the ruble is worth more than the dollar.'

The questions of ordinary Soviets often provided the most revealing insight into what they knew or thought. In Frunze, another Central Asian city, several American correspondents were surrounded in a park one evening by young people who showered us with questions. Does J. P. Morgan have 92-billion dollars? Did Rockefeller build a special car for his daughter? Is it true that President Kennedy's father made his money by selling pornographic movies? Why did Edward Kennedy refuse to run for the Presidency? Can you kill your President and still not be arrested? What does the foreign affairs committee of Congress do? Is it better to send a man to the moon or just a mechanical moon-rover? What 'nationality' are you? Why aren't more American books and magazines sold here? Is it safe in America with all the shootings and the fires in skyscrapers?

Among some people I found astonishing pockets of knowledge about Western life. Deep in Siberia, a musician asked me whether American accordions had four or five rows of buttons, for he knew practically everything else about the makes and varieties of Western instruments. Almost anywhere I went I ran into Soviet young people who knew far more than I about the social and professional lives of The Beatles, Mick Jagger, and other Western rock stars. They were anxious for the latest gossip and disappointed when I could not oblige them. In Moscow, Americans whom I knew were surprised to find Russians at the Union of Architects who were thoroughly familiar with the most modern Western trends publicized in a very mod magazine, *Architecture-Plus*, and who asked knowledgeable questions about Moshe Safdie's construction at Montreal Expo. In general, I found Soviet intellectuals more *au courant* about elements of contemporary American and Western life than Westerners are about Soviet life and culture.

What is missing, however, is a sense of the fabric of Western life. From the Soviet press people knew about unemployment, high medical costs, or poverty statistics, but they had never heard about unemployment insurance, medicare, or what constitutes the poverty-level in America (a figure well above the average Soviet wage). Those who had never been abroad tended to project their own system onto the outside world and were often skeptical of things that did not match this picture.

A young linguist, very attentive to things Western but oblivious of the Watergate scandal and the Pentagon Papers, asked another American correspondent which censorship was stricter – Soviet or American. A customs inspector after leafing through an American magazine on hotrod cars, handed it back to an American friend of ours with the comment, 'Of course, they don't really have all those cars. It's just pictures made up for children.' A scholar who knows several foreign languages and has followed Western academic affairs for years was nonetheless startled to find on his first visit to the West – to Rome – that newsstands not only sold the Italian Communist newspaper *Unita* but also *Pravda*. A young Ukrainian woman told another American friend that she found it hard to believe that people in other countries were learning English rather than Russian as a foreign language and that young people in the West regarded the Soviet Union as a conservative power rather than the pillar of world progressivism. An American exchange student told me of her surprise at discovering that fairly sophisticated students at Leningrad and Moscow universities took at face value

Soviet television newscasts that workers all over the West were striking and demonstrating in support of Communist causes. 'One student at the Institute of International Relations simply couldn't believe me when I said that workers in America are generally conservative and the students are the radicals,' this girl said. 'He asked me, "Who reads *The Daily Worker* and other Communist papers?" and I said, "Practically no one." He said, "You mean, no one besides the workers," and I said, "No, not the workers – the workers wouldn't touch it." He couldn't believe me.'

Those who travel to the West on delegations are officially supposed to help maintain *Pravda*'s picture of the West when they return. They often have to give obligatory lectures on life in the West which, I was told, differ dramatically from their frank reactions to friends in private. So prevalent is this practice that Russians have a joke about it, told to me with great amusement by a bureaucrat. It concerns a Russian official returning from the West and telling his fellow employees about the decadence, corruption, and decline of capitalism. 'It simply rots before your eyes – you can smell it rotting,' the official asserted. Then a blissful expression passed over his face and he sighed, 'But, oh, what a smell!'

The temptation is strong in this era of détente to believe that the Cold War vigilance has relaxed and borders are opening up between East and West. But in my experience, there is still a very palpable line at Soviet frontiers that marks Russia off as a world apart. One little sign is the unconscious habit of veteran travelers not to speak of going 'to' and 'from' Russia but of going 'in' and 'out'. Like many other foreign residents, I felt a palpable sense of apprehension as I returned to Moscow because of the pressures of the police state. At airports, Soviet document checks seem to take much longer than elsewhere and the guard always makes sure to examine your face and carefully to compare it with your passport. Buses from the terminal to the aircraft pull close to the foot of the ramp, as if fearing someone would make a break for it. A soldier stands beneath the tail and another by the ramp – not on the lookout for terrorists, as in the West, but for stowaways.

My most tangible sense of this wary vigilance at the border came on a train trip from Helsinki to Moscow. When we passed the Finnish frontier, a lone Finnish guard, in gray, watched without interest as the train moved through stands of dark green pine and yellowing birches into the Soviet Union. Almost immediately beyond, we saw a maze of barbed wire. Then, a sudden open slash cut through the woods, stretching off in both directions as if nature had been shaved to mark the frontier. From over the next hill peeped the top of a watchtower on stilts. A few hundred yards further the train halted in the trackless woods. Ten Russian border guards materialized in their sea-green uniforms and high boots, some armed with hip pistols and others with submachine guns. They looked like teenage lads but they went about their business in all seriousness. Two marched down each side of the train inspecting the undercarriages. Two others took up posts, one by the engine and the other by the rear car. Overhead we could hear the footsteps of another heavy-booted pair. Passengers popped their heads out of opened windows to watch the proceedings and were quickly advised to get back in their compartments. Before we knew it, other soldiers came through the train in pairs – tall, nice-looking blonds. One politely gathered up passports. The other checked in our washroom, climbed up on one bunk to peer in the large overhead luggage rack, and finally, asking us to stand, lifted our bunks to examine the storage space beneath them. It was a very thorough search.

The border also has its paper barrier for those Russians who are permitted to go abroad legally. The procedures for obtaining a passport for foreign travel are intricate beyond belief, more probing than to get a top secret security clearance in the West. A Ukrainian construction worker, a Party member who had been sent to Egypt to work on the Aswan Dam, told me that he and his comrades had gone through intensive KGB investigations to get those jobs. 'They check everything back to your grandfather and your great-grandfather,' he said, 'and if there is any dirt, they will find out about it – you can be sure of that.' From others I heard of cases where respected scientists or seemingly trustworthy scholars had simply fallen by the wayside during the screening process and others in their group had made no whimper of protest for fear of jeopardizing their own chances. Western academicians who have regular contacts with Russians become accustomed to delegations arriving minus a couple of people, supposedly taken sick or kept by other pressing business, though everyone knows nothing would actually divert a Russian from a foreign trip if he could help it.

Moreover, before each trip abroad, several people told me, Soviet citizens have to go through special political indoctrination and sign a little booklet saying they have been informed of the government's recommendations and rules of conduct for Soviet citizens abroad. A writer described to me the process even for going to a fellow Communist country like Czechoslovakia. A party lecturer, she said, tells the group: 'Now, you are Soviet citizens leaving your Motherland. You must understand what a heavy responsibility rests on you. You should know that there are many provocative people who ask provocative questions. You must know how to answer them.' Those going to non-Communist countries, she said, are sternly warned to stay away from Russian emigrés and to keep together in a group. If they take a stroll, they are advised to go in twos and threes. Galina Ragozina, the Kirvo ballet dancer who later emigrated with her husband, Valery Panov, told me that the Kirov troupe was given special political topics to study and little quizzes before each trip to make sure they knew how to answer awkward questions according to the Party line. It was like cramming for an examination, she said. A scientist who had been through a similar routine told me: 'You are supposed to know what to say if a foreigner asks you what you think about Israel or how you relate to American society. You are supposed to say that you approve of such and such a [dissident] trial because the convicted person was truly an enemy of the people, but that the gravest injustice is done to Luis Corvalan, [the Communist leader in Chile] because he is unjustly held by the fascists in Chile. There are a whole list of standard phrases you must simply memorize.'

I have heard some Russians assert that because of such procedures and because of the KGB men and the informers who travel among all groups (from cross country skiers to cosmonauts), they do not want to go abroad. But these are rare individuals indeed. The yen to travel, especially to the West, is almost irresistible to the urban intelligentsia. Being denied a chance to travel is the frustration that chafes them most today. One Party propagandist, a man who had traveled abroad in the past but was having trouble now, bitched at having to wait six or eight months for permission, though he was among the more fortunate in counting on going at all. 'Our life is getting better,' he whined. 'Why do we have to wait? What are they worried about?'

Soviet officials like to talk about the increase in travel since the Sixties but it has been very modest indeed. In 1974, Soviet citizens made 2.2 million trips to all countries, less than half as many as from little Czechoslovakia and under one tenth the number of trips abroad by Americans. The great bulk of Soviet trips were to Eastern Europe. Almost all trips are official – not only for government officials and diplomats, but ballet troupes, sports teams, scientific delegations – mostly the same people year in and year out. There are selected worker and student groups that visit Eastern Europe, but individual tourism is practically unheard of. 'It is only the *mayaki* [the beacons] of Communism who get to go,' a disappointed writer remarked bitterly. A computer specialist, turned down for a trip to take his family to see friends in East Germany, angrily denounced the travel controls as '20th-century slavery'. Actually, it is an old tradition of Russian rulers to dole out the right of traveling abroad to privileged servants of the state. In her charter of 1785, Catherine the Great institutionalized the right to travel abroad as a privilege of the nobility and gentry.

Now, the KGB and Party capitalize on the urge of the intelligentsia to travel abroad as one of the main controls for keeping liberal intellectuals in line at home. I have heard personally of several occasions when poets or playwrights had their foreign trips canceled because authorities took offense at some misstep of theirs. But sometimes travel permission is refused without explanation, like a Kafka story, and people suffer terrible fears.

'The worst thing is that when they turn you down for something, they never give you a reason,' said a well-placed scientist who had made previous trips and was shattered by an unexpected rejection for an official visit to Poland. 'If they say anything, it has nothing to do with the actual problem. You cannot get the real reason. It is a terrible feeling – to know you are not trusted and yet not to know why and not to be able to find out.'

Strange as it may sound to Westerners who quite properly agonized over the ordeals of many emigrating Soviet Jews, the Jews must paradoxically be counted among the privileged – for even as pariahs they have succeeded as no other Soviet ethnic group in opening up an opportunity for reaching the forbidden territories beyond the Soviet frontiers.

Jews themselves took ironic satisfaction in the envy of other ethnic groups and the alacrity with which Russian, Latvians, Ukrainians, Georgians, and others latched onto Jews through marriage as a means of geting abroad themselves. Amused by the twist of fate that had put them in an advantageous position for change, Jewish activists loved to tell the joke about Abramovich being called to OVIR for questioning. It is OVIR, the Office of Visas and Registration, which decides on applications for exit visas.

'Abramovich,' says the OVIR colonel, 'you have a good position as a professor. Why do you want to go to Israel?'

'It's not me who wants to go,' Abramovich says defensively, 'it's the wife and children.'

'But Abramovich,' insists the colonel, 'you have a nice apartment and a dacha. Why should you want to leave your socialist motherland?'

'It's not me who wants to go,' Abramovich shrugs, 'it's the mother-in-law.'

'Tell me, Abramovich, what is it?' the colonel implores. 'You have even bought yourself a car. Why should you want to give up this good life?'

'I told you,' Abramovich insists, 'it's not me who wants to go. It's the aunt and the cousins.'

'Well, if you don't want to go, why did you apply?' asks the colonel.

'Don't you see?' Abramovich replies. 'I'm the only Jew in the family.'

The exodus of the Jews – Abramovich, relatives and hangers-on – was easily the most implausible phenomenon of my time in Moscow. So much have people now come to take the emigration movement for granted that they have forgotten how incredible the entire course of events has been – seen from the perspective, say, of 1968. Not only was the departure of 100,000 Jews from 1971–1974 unforeseeable but the protests that accompanied it were wholly unprecedented for Soviet life – the startling spectacle of young Jews staging sit-ins at the Central Post and Telegraph Office or wearing yellow Stars of David and carrying placards (*Let My People Go*) in demonstrations at the reception room of the Supreme Soviet or outside the gray headquarters of the Communist Party Central Committee.

With a brazenness that startled the Kremlin, the emigration movement created the illusion that the Party and the KGB were not omnipotent after all. Of course, this depended not only on the determined opposition of Jews with the clear-cut objective of emigration and with powerful, organized support abroad, but it also depended on the Brezhnev leadership's refusal to resort to the stark terror of Stalinism that would have finished the emigration movement in a trice. The Kremlin was caught in a dilemma because it did not want too nakedly to appear the strong-arm police state while it pursued détente. Its tactics were rough, but they did know limits.

There is no need here to rehearse the vacillations of Kremlin policy from the get-tough periods of trying Jewish hijackers and other would-be emigrants or imposing astronomical emigration taxes on educated Jews to periods of moderation when the outflow of Jews rose to sweeten the climate before Nixon came to Moscow, Brezhnev went to America, or Congress was about to take up trade legislation. What struck me as the most out-of-character moment was the time when the Kremlin was tempted to strike a deal with Senator Henry Jackson of Washington who was seeking firm guarantees for free emigration in return for credits and lower tariffs for Soviet goods. Although the Kremlin had lots of administrative loopholes for getting around the provisions, such a deal was still a great concession. In retrospect, it is not so surprising that Brezhnev drew back, feeling that the American credits were too miserly and the unwanted disclosure of the private-deal-made-public, too humiliating.

Only reluctantly and by costly trial and error did the Soviet leadership arrive at what it felt was a livable combination of selective intimidation and limited emigration. This seemed to suit its complex and conflicting objectives – to appease the West, to prevent a serious scientific and technical brain-drain, to put a damper on the whole trend toward emigration yet discreetly rid itself of disaffected Jewish intellectuals and dissidents, and to let other ethnic groups know through subtler, more remote crackdowns in the Ukraine, Lithuania, Armenia, and elsewhere that Jews were a special case not to be emulated.

Willy-nilly, too, the Soviet leaders came to realize that the

West would take pride in the departure of 100,000 Jews and exult in the ultimate liberation of celebrated figures like dancer Valery Panov, but not understand that other ballet dancers would remember Panov, as I do, pacing his tiny Leningrad apartment like a caged panther for two years in utter despair. Yevgeny Levich, the handsome dark-haired young astro-physicist, could be hailed in Israel but the Kremlin knew that Soviet scientists were aware that his eminent father, Ben Levich, the highest ranking Soviet scientist to apply for emigration, was still captive in Moscow months later, and they remembered that Yevgeny himself was sent to Tiksi on the Arctic Coast of Siberia to clean latrines in an Army outpost while he prayed for a visa. The majority of visa applicants were processed at reasonable speed – no more slowly, at least, than normal Soviet citizens trying to make a trip abroad. But there was always a deterrent to the talented. There were always a few tormented people whose ordeals made applying to emigrate like playing Russian roulette. Westerners, as one intellectual observed to me, are impressed with overall statistics but for Soviet citizens, 'the language of events', as he so nicely phrased it, often speaks most powerfully through individual examples.

The number of departing Jews has now sloped off dramatically since the peak of 35,000 departures in 1973. It could rise again if a new Soviet-American trade deal were struck. But one of the imponderable mysteries of Soviet life is how many Soviet Jews want to go to Israel. For wanting or not wanting to go always depends, as Jewish friends reminded me, on how easy it is to go at the moment and what kind of life exists for the Jews who stay behind. It also depends on the mood and character of Soviet Jewry, and they are more complex than I had imagined and less easily definable than the emigration movement suggests.

A million or more, perhaps many more, have already opted for assimilation in Soviet life and have left themselves no way out. The 1970 Soviet census recorded 2,151,000 Jews but this does not count hidden Jews who have been passing for years as Russians or members of some other ethnic group. Roy Medvedev, the dissident historian whose father was Russian and mother was Jewish, guessed their number at anywhere from one to ten million. The drop in the 1970 census figure for Jews from 1959 (down 117,000) when activists were predicting it would rise along with other ethnic groups, was evidence that even in the Sixties many young Jews took advantage of mixed parentage to claim some other ethnic affiliation and bury their Jewishness. It is an old game in Russia. In the years after the Revolution, the practice of outright name-changing was easy and fairly common. Medvedev told me that Jewish Party members would pay the police ten rubles and choose any name and ethnic group that suited them, usually Russian, to be entered on their documents. Panov confessed to me that when he reached 16, the age of decision, he picked Byelorussian since he was born in Byelorussia and his mother wanted him to escape the stigma of being Jewish. Other prominent people like Maya Plisetskaya the prima ballerina of the Bolshoi Ballet, Georgi Arbatov the head of the Institute of the U.S.A. and Canada, or Valentin Zorin the Moscow television commentator, keep as discreet a silence as possible about one or the other of their parents being Jewish.

I was told by an American doctor at Mount Sinai Hospital in New York, a world-famous Jewish hospital, that Russian officials at the United Nations come there sometimes to have babies delivered by an old emigré doctor. Even though they have clearly Russian names, some quietly ask him, 'Would you mind circumcising my baby?' After he agrees there follows the pregnant question, 'Would you mind, by chance, arranging to do the circumcision on the eighth day?' Since this is so obviously in keeping with Jewish practice, the American doctor takes such requests as tacit acknowledgment that in some cases these are hidden Jews who have been passing for years as Russians and only that way had they risen to positions of trust in the Soviet foreign service or the KGB.

The mood and character of Soviet Jewry remain elusive, too, because even the mood and character of the emigration movement itself have evolved as it passed through several 'generations' of departing Jews. There was an early wave of strongly Zionist and rather religious Jews who spearheaded the movement as it took form in 1968–1970. But they had left the country or had been jailed by the time I arrived in Moscow in August 1971. And though large numbers of religious Jews continued to flow out of Soviet Georgia, a region with special traditions of religious tolerance, Jews of another character had taken the lead in Moscow. For me, it was strange to learn how secular these activist leaders were, how little religious pull they felt. I might find the younger ones gathered outside the pillared Moscow synagogue on Saturdays swapping the latest gossip about the emigration movement or on holidays like Simchas Torah, celebrating into the night with dances or songs of the Jewish diaspora like *Hava Nagila*. But very few if any of them had had bar mitzvahs or were at ease in yarmulkes or prayer shawls. Almost none understood Yiddish or Hebrew. For them, Jewishness was a genetic fact of life, a matter of inheritance reinforced by negative forces of Russian life, rather than a function of religious attraction or identity.

Roman Rutman, a short, quiet, well composed middle-aged mathematician, told me not long before his departure for Israel in 1973 that he had been brought up in a Communist Party family and had learned about Judaism backwards – piecing it together by reading between the lines of atheistic attacks on religion. As a boy, he had never been to synagogue or church. 'It was almost impossible for someone to have a Bible then [the Stalin years],' he said. 'When I was about 20, I felt some moral vacuum. I wouldn't call it a religious longing, just a sense of something missing from life. I would read antireligious literature to find out about the Bible. I would read, for example – and this is very rough – about the Flood in one place and about Noah in another place, and I would put them together.' By the time I knew him, Rutman went fairly regularly to the synagogue but that was to maintain contacts with other Jewish activists, not to attend services. Not until almost the eve of his departure, Rutman confided, did a rabbi persuade him to don a prayer shawl. 'I found the Bible beautiful,' he said. 'It's really poetry. Quite lovely.' He began to study Judaism and to teach it to his son.

Rutman was unusual in having moved that close to religion. But in another way he was typical of many whom I met in the emigration movement – Volodya Slepak, Mikhail Agursky, Leonid Tsipin, Volodya Kozlovsky, Alex Goldfarb, and others whom I prefer not to name to spare their relatives repercussions. They were children of successful Soviet establishment families. Like Rutman, many were the sons of staunch Party members, brought up in the traditions of the atheistic state. Their turn to Jewish activism was often a personal act of rebellion against the system or their own parents as sharp and dramatic as the revolt of young American anti-Vietnam protesters who spurned the upper middle-class affluence of their successful American parents.

Yet I found it hard sometimes to get at what drove these people to leave for Israel while others, very much like them, stayed behind. Sometimes, it was difficult to discern what tipped the balance. In 1972 and 1973, emigration was in the air. The trend was snowballing. Some people were leaving because suddenly it had become possible to leave. A few people I met were genuine Zionists, saying they wanted to go live with their own people in their true homeland. Many more, however, seemed no more fundamentally attracted to Israel or alienated from Soviet society than people of other ethnic groups who also were privately fed up with police controls, censorship, and the tribulations of Soviet consumer life. A minority thought they saw some soaring personal future in the outside world and for many of these, I heard afterwards, the tough competitive life in the West provided a cruel and disillusioning experience.

It was puzzling to me that so few activists told anti-Semitic horror stories as justification for their decisions to emigrate. It was not, of course, that anti-Semitism was not a palpable part of the climate in Russia or had not touched them, for each could recall personal slurs or derogatory remarks about Jews in general. As Yevgeny Yevtushenko intimated in his celebrated poem about Babi Yar, Russians imbibe anti-Semitism from their mother's milk.

'Look at the press,' said a Jewish linguist. 'If a Russian steals, he is a thief. But if a Jew steals, he is a Jew.' Nina Voronel, a writer born in Kharkov in the Ukraine, remembered with horror the moment in childhood when another girl came home from school and discovered her nationality. 'Ohhhh,' groaned the other girl, pointing at Nina, 'you are a Jew.' The way she said that word, Nina recalled, 'made me feel that if there were a hole, I would just die and fall into it. The next day, this girl told everyone in school. All my life, I was ashamed that my parents had such names as Avraam and Izrailevna.'

The public incident in recent years that Moscow Jews seemed to recall most vividly was the occasion when someone in the audience shouted *zhid* – kike – at Arkady Raikin, the Soviet Union's most famous and popular comedian, during a performance in the Ukraine. Raikin interrupted his skit and demanded, 'Who said that?' Dead silence. 'Whoever said that put up your hand,' Raikin insisted. No one confessed. Raikin walked off the stage, canceling the performance.

Ukrainians, especially in the provincial villages, have a reputation for the most outspoken anti-Semitic feelings of any group, but I have on occasions heard entirely unprompted slurs against Jews from Russians. An artist's wife once told me she liked a place in the countryside because of the real raw milk, the homemade bread, and because it was 'unspoilt by the Jews'. The most unattractive outburst that I heard came from a Bolshoi Opera bass, a hulking great giant bursting from the turtleneck sweater that he wore under his suit. He had been a railroad worker during the war until someone discovered his powerful voice and sent him to voice school. We met on a train and fell to talking about foreign policy. Suddenly, after lacerating the Chinese, this Russian patriot lit into the Jews without any pretext.

'They are the most dangerous people in the world, more dangerous than the Chinese,' he warned me. 'You Americans think they have problems here but they are really privileged people. Everywhere you look, you see the Jews. Eighty-four percent of the Bolshoi Company is Jews. Who do you think plays the violins in the orchestra? The poor peasants take their children and teach them how to work in the fields or sit them behind the wheel and they become collective farmers or tractor drivers. They don't earn much. And what do the Jews do? They teach their children to play the violin and they end up in the Bolshoi Theater making 400 rubles a month. And they are dissatisfied. They are rabble, the Jews.'

Not only did he grossly exaggerate the pay scale of violinists, many of whom earn less than tractor drivers, but also I have heard Jews ruefully describe discrimination they have faced in education and at work. A Jewish graduate student once protested to a senior scientist whom I knew that he had been ordered by a Russian professor to give flunking grades to several Jewish applicants for Moscow State University despite their excellent examination results. A man who was formerly senior editor at a publishing house said that when the annual list of books for the coming year was sent to the Communist Party Central Committee for approval, it would invariably be returned with several titles by Jewish authors crossed off. No explanation was needed;

a Jewish 'quota' had been imposed. The head of a laboratory, a Russian, told me that his superiors explicitly rejected some highly qualified Jewish scientists whom he had proposed hiring on grounds that 'we already have enough Jews.'

Jews point out that with a few notable exceptions, widely trumpeted by the Soviet regime, they are effectively disqualified from such careers as diplomacy, political journalism, the armed forces, the Communist Party apparatus, and high-ranking Party jobs. Yet it is also true that through their abilities Jews have succeeded in Soviet life far out of proportion to their numbers. In 1970, official figures showed that 134 Jews per 1,000 had received higher education, far ahead of ethnic Russians with 22 per 1,000. Despite discrimination, Jews have fared extremely well in such creative fields as art, literature, music, drama, and the cinema, and in the high prestige area of science. In the economy, having a Jewish deputy is a tradition with many Soviet administrators, just as Party functionaries in key positions often use Jewish scholars as their ghost writers. Since job status in Soviet life determines life-style, Jews by and large have done pretty well by Soviet standards.

What is more, as some Jewish activists acknowledged to me, anti-Semitism in Soviet life today is far milder than under Stalin and not as bad as it was under the czars. It provides some motivation for emigration but it is not decisive, for the provincial towns and villages where anti-Semitism supposedly is most oppressive have generally produced only a trickle of emigrants, whereas a region like Georgia, with a reputation for tolerance towards Jews, has produced a large proportion of those who have left. Although I knew quite a number of Jews, I heard very few cases where some ugly, unconcealed manifestation of anti-Semitism was the catalyst for an individual to emigrate.

The most powerful motive, I found, was a newly vibrant sense of Jewish nationalism. But it was a nationalism different from the militant Zionism that I had expected. It seemed less a zealous devotion to Israel than a drive for self-affirmation in Soviet life after decades of self-denial. For if Soviet Jews had accommodated to anti-Semitic slurs and job discrimination, the most glaring grievance to the activists of the Sixties and Seventies was that they were being denied positive outlets for their own ethnic identity. 'I am a man without a nationality in a very nationalistic country,' declared Alex Goldfarb, a biologist who later left for Israel. In the Soviet system, being a Jew – and asserting Jewishness – implicitly conflicts with being a loyal Soviet citizen. It is here that Jews feel at a disadvantage compared to other ethnic groups.

Foreigners, especially Americans, often miss the critical importance of ethnic identity among Soviet people. If they happen to ask a Soviet his ethnic background and he replies Russian, Armenian, Uzbek, Latvian, Ukrainian or Jew, Americans often mistake this as something equivalent to their own habit of announcing their home states to a new acquaintance. Britons with centuries of thinking of themselves as Scottish, Welsh, Irish, or English understand that this is something that goes much deeper. It is a fundamental form of identity. It communicates language, tradition, culture, values, heritage.

At heart, it is the denial of this cultural, ethnic outlet that Jewish activists have been protesting with their emigration movement. Historically, Jews had great hopes after the Bolshevik Revolution in which they played a considerable role. In the early years of the Soviet state, Yiddish language enjoyed a renaissance. By the Thirties more than 1,200 Yiddish schools and university departments of Jewish studies had been set up. There were Yiddish newspapers and theaters. Some Jews like Leon Trotsky held important political and governmental positions – more than today's tokenism.

It was Stalin's purges and his wartime thrust toward ardent Russian nationalism that halted this upward trend. With the establishment of the state of Israel in 1948, he launched his final paranoiac campaign against 'rootless cosmopolitans' – the Jews. Writers were murdered, doctors persecuted, and all traces of Yiddish culture erased. That is roughly where the Jews stand today. Other ethnic groups complain privately that creeping Russification is depriving them of their cultural identity and heritage, but they have their geographic regions, their 'governments', schools, ethnic theaters, and literary and cultural traditions. Jews have almost none of this. There is one Yiddish-language publication – a monthly government-controlled mouthpiece called *Sovetish Heimland* (Soviet Homeland) and one tiny, barely active Yiddish theater group. The officially designated Jewish Autonomous Republic of Birobidzhan in East Siberia is only 18 percent Jewish by population and is regarded by most Jews as an irrelevant farce. It was Jewish frustration over this ethnic-cultural vacuum that was ignited by the Israeli victory in the Six Day War of 1967. That war, I was told over and over again, 'made us proud to be Jews'. Because many Jewish intellectuals were prominent in liberal cultural and scientific circles and in the dissident movement, they felt particularly crushed and suffocated after the Soviet invasion of Czechoslovakia in 1968. This quick succession of new hope and sharp despair fired their push to get out.

What about those who stayed?

In my private contacts, I found successful, assimilated Jews who shared those feelings of resurgent Jewish pride and cultural frustration, yet kept their feelings to themselves or shared them only with trusted friends. What was it that held them back?

Through some departing Jews, we met one couple who teetered for months on the brink of deciding to leave Russia. Tanya, the wife, was a petite character actress, dark and attractive, and her husband, Mark, a slender, sour playwright of 50 whose eyes wore a quizzical frown when he took off his glasses. By Soviet standards they were well off but both were unsparingly critical of Soviet society. They were proud of the Israelis and mocked Soviet aid to the Arabs. They asserted their Jewishness with us but, I suspect, soft-pedaled it in the company of Russians. Mark's writing gave little hint of his private feelings. When I asked about it, he was greatly embarrassed and rather awkwardly refused to lend me anything he had written. 'You can't tell what a Soviet writer really thinks by what gets published,' he said. I gathered he was not one who often fought the censors head-on. Mostly his anguish came during the self-censorship that made his writing officially palatable, though I heard him complain a few times about the butchering he had suffered. 'I am ready to give up everything,' he said disconsolately. 'The permanent quibbling and fighting over any little phrase. That feeling of never "belonging" here. This idiotic secrecy in our lives. It is terrible.'

Mark had lost his father in the Stalinist purges and was haunted by the thought that another dark period of reaction might be coming. He would ask me my views and then pour out his worst fears. Tanya fluctuated between bitter comments about the incompetents and cynics in the theater and a defensive love and pride in Russian culture. Mark intimated that he wanted to leave and Tanya thought it would be best for the children – one university-age son, a talented linguist, and a much younger daughter, who was interested in theater. They questioned us intensively about life in the West, in very personal terms.

Always, there was a hesitancy to let go. 'Life in Israel is no rose garden,' Mark would say, and then, drawing on my critical comments about Western life, turn the bitterness he normally vented on his own country against Israel and the West. He was well enough read to know the problems anywhere. Other Jews would discover, he predicted, that adjustment in Israel would be impossible. As a few letters trickled back with disillusioned comments from some new settlers in Jerusalem, he felt vindicated. But still, it seemed to torment him. Indirectly, he would hint at what was really affecting his decision. Although he knew German and English, he was unsure at his age whether he could make a new start in life. He was afraid that if he applied for an exit visa, the authorities would let him dangle, uncertain and unemployed, for a couple of years before letting him go. 'I feel terribly tired,' he told me one night. 'That is why I have decided to stay.' That was his way, I think, of saying that the fear of the unknown was too great, and so was his attachment to the pretty comfortable niche in Soviet society that he had made for himself.

I encountered other 'tame Jews', as the more ardent activists called them, who were resentful or openly hostile toward the emigration movement. Those whom I met officially, like Aleksandr Chakovsky the Jewish editor of *Literary Gazette* and a high-ranking candidate member of the Party Central Committee, were vitriolic in their condemnation of departing Jews and vehement in their insistence that Jews had full opportunity, free of discrimination in the Soviet Union. Some of this was undoubtedly propaganda. But it struck me, too, as the self-defensive reflex of people who had achieved success by downplaying their Jewishness. Any movement that called upon them, in effect, to assert themselves as Jews was a threat to their whole pattern of life. 'They [the activists] are troublemakers,' a cinema translator told me caustically one day. 'They have made it harder for the rest of us.'

584

There was considerable merit to her claim that the emigration movement had caused anti-Semitism and discrimination to rise. I heard from scientists that as the exodus proceeded, it became harder for Jews to get good positions and promotions in the better scientific institutes. Administrators were wary of them. 'If a Jew applies for a job, he is asked first, "Are you planning to leave?" ' a computer specialist said. A medical scientist told me this increased suspicion toward Jews had finally prompted him to apply for an exit visa. He had been denied a promotion that he felt he had earned and a superior, a good friend and an ethnic Russian, had intimated promotion was impossible because of fears that he might later emigrate. A successful science writer, who had published several books under a Russian pseudonym, related a similar sequence. In early 1974 an editor with whom he had worked closely suggested a book idea to him and got preliminary approval from the firm's director. But when the contract was submitted, including both the writer's Russian pseudonym and his real Jewish name, the publisher refused to sign and told the editor that the author did not have 'the right kind of name'. Hearing this and fearing matters would get steadily worse, the writer decided to emigrate.

The most striking evidence that official discrimination has risen since the inception of the Jewish movement in 1968 is the annual statistics on enrollment in higher education. In the peak year of 1968, there were 111,900 Jews, a figure that followed steady rises in previous years. Since 1968, the number of Jews has persistently declined to 88,500 in 1972. When the 1973 statistical yearbook came out, it was missing that table, a possible sign that a more dramatic drop took place that year. Even on the street, some Jews told me, they sensed Russians speaking with more open hostility than in the past. One middle-aged woman with a Jewish profile said that when she got impatient with a store clerk one afternoon, the clerk turned on her and snapped, 'If you don't like it here, why don't you go to your Israel.'

Families who stayed behind have often paid a price for the activism of those who left. Several young Jews reported that their fathers had been demoted or transferred from key administrative jobs, told as writers they would no longer get such choice assignments, or informed that they could not travel abroad any more because of relatives emigrating to

Israel. One woman had a brother in the KGB who was demoted because of her. I heard that when Viktor Yakhot, a nervously handsome young physicist, decided to leave, immense pressure was put on his father, a long-time Party member with a high-level job as full professor in the Moscow Institute of Finance, to block him. Like Mark, the playwright, the father felt too old to start a new life in Israel and decided against going, but he was understanding of his son's feelings and simply let him get away. The director of the institute was furious. The elder Yakhot was read out of the Communist Party, demoted step by step, his academic degrees stripped from him one by one as lifelong colleagues and subordinates denounced him. So humiliated was he after this hurricane had crashed through his life that he, too, reluctantly decided he had no choice but to emigrate. Other Jews have found that lifelong friends turned against them overnight, evidently in self-protection. I knew a ballerina whose career was strangled by officials merely because she made the mistake of publicly befriending a man who had applied to emigrate when the Party demanded he be completely shunned.

Once I witnessed the quixotic emotions of an assimilated Jew. At the airport in Samarkand, I met a Jewish tailor who said he had relatives who had gone to Israel and now talked of coming back. So assimilated was this Jew that he called himself a 'nonparty Communist' and had named his son Vladimir Ilyich (for Lenin). Still, when he began talking about his relatives, he was rather apologetic and understanding of them. His explanation was that other Jews had talked them into going. He wondered if I wrote a story about them whether that might help them get back. But when my Soviet escort moved nearby and overheard our conversation, this man began smearing his relatives and disavowing them. 'They put us in a difficult position,' he said. 'They spit in the mug they had drunk from. They betrayed the Motherland.'

No one, however, was more tragically trapped by strife within the family than Volodya Slepak who, throughout my time in Moscow, was the patient elder, the Gibraltar, the most renowned and unsuccessful visa applicant in the entire emigration movement.

Slepak's story reads like a capsule history of the movement. His activism began in 1969 and since filing his application for an exit visa in 1970, he has been fired from several jobs, harassed, tailed, searched, had his front door bashed in, been held or interrogated on at least twenty occasions, and put in preventive detention both times President Nixon went to Moscow, though when he protested the second time to the Moscow prosecutor that he had been illegally imprisoned, he was officially informed that his imprisonment had never taken place. For all that, it seemed to me that Slepak bore his troubles with remarkably little open rancor and took great satisfaction in helping others. The last time I saw him, sitting in a heavy, overstuffed chair in his communal apartment, he was raising toasts to my future in scotch, which we drank neat from shot glasses since there was no vodka to celebrate my departure. But his wife Mariya, a large, patient woman with a beatific face, admitted ever so quietly that waiting was getting hard after nearly five years.

Slepak was hesitant to voice his worst fears – that his father was preventing him from leaving. But as he talked, the story unfolded like a Greek tragedy. His father, born Solomon Izrailevich Slepak, had lived the history of the Russian Revolution. Jailed under the czars as a radical, he went like Ho Chi Minh and other Communists of the early 20th century to the West where he worked as a stevedore in New York. Come the Revolution, he rushed home and by 1920 he was a top Party leader in Sakhalin after leading a partisan brigade against the Japanese. In the early Twenties, he became the first Soviet representative to Japan, as a journalist. At the suggestion of Soviet Foreign Minister Maxim Litvinov, he changed his name to one less obviously Jewish – Semyon Ignatyevich Slepak. Eventually, he was named to the Presidium of the Comintern, the association of world communist parties founded by Lenin. He had the proud biography of a true Old Bolshevik and the unshaken convictions to match.

As Volodya recalled, his first sharp break with his father came in the early Fifties when Stalin was on his anticosmopolitan campaign. Mariya, his wife, who was working in a hospital, was very upset by the charges of the Doctors' Plot and the innocent victims of Stalin's paranoia. Volodya began arguing with his father about it.

'If you chop wood, the sparrows fly,' the old man replied with a proverb, dismissing Mariya's worries. 'So let there be

587

innocent victims. Just be sure to destroy the one real enemy.'

'Father, you're dead!' Volodya bellowed at him. 'I'll never join your Party.'

The old man was stunned. 'For you and the little grandchildren, I was in hard-labor prison,' he recalled. 'I fought for Soviet power and helped build it, and you use such words.' After the mutiny of his son, he had a heart attack. 'He had to take those drops all the time,' Volodya remembered.

In those years, the family all lived together. Later they separated and the wounds healed after Stalin died. But in 1968, after the Six Day War and the Soviet invasion of Czechoslovakia, Volodya told his father he was thinking of going to Israel. The father refused to listen. In early 1969, Volodya quit his job at the Scientific Institute of Television Research where he had headed a laboratory, hoping that this step would make his departure easier since he had had access to some secret materials. He informed his father just before he actually applied to emigrate. 'The argument was terrible,' Mariya Slepak told me. 'It was civil war in the family.'

Volodya Slepak is a big, powerfully built man in his late forties. He has the large hands of a workman, the build of a prize fighter, the heavy beard of a prophet, and an inner calm behind his sad brown eyes. I have never met his father but from the description of Volodya and his wife, he, too, is solid as a rock. They are both headstrong. I can imagine the rage that greeted Volodya's decision to go to Israel.

'It's not right – it's treason,' the old man yelled at Volodya. 'You were born here. You can't go.'

'We have thought it over,' Volodya insisted. 'We won't change our minds.'

'Then we are on different sides of the trenches,' the father declared. Coldly he announced that he never wanted to see Volodya and his family again. 'Don't you or your children call on me,' he said. 'Stay away so they can forget me and I can forget them and forget you.'

Mariya's mother, who has since emigrated to Israel, tried to intervene. She reminded the old man that he had carried the two boys, then entering their teens, from the hospital in his own arms when they were babes. She told him that he could not cut himself off in one blow from his blood relatives.

'No,' said the elder Slepak, adamant as stone. 'I will cut it off now. If you cut, you have to cut all at once.'

This harsh verdict was precisely what the Soviet system prescribes – immediate and total severance with the spiritual traitors who want to emigrate. Old man Slepak was not unique, but he was unusually severe in his verdict and in sticking to it.

In close to six years since the cataclysmic family confrontation, Volodya Slepak and his boys have seen the old man, now in his eighties, only three times – whenever he has been taken seriously ill, twice with heart failure. One or all of them have journeyed by subway and bus to Hospital No. 60, colloquially known as the Hospital of the Old Bolsheviks, fittingly located on the Boulevard of Enthusiasts. Each time the old man was glad to see his son and grandsons and to exchange pleasantries with them. But each time, he would turn to the inevitable question, 'Have you changed your mind?'

'No,' Volodya would reply.

'Then go away and don't come back,' the old man would command.

Other relatives told Volodya that his father had been to KGB headquarters at Lubyanka Prison several times to protest against letting Volodya and his family go to Israel. 'He's been there,' Volodya sadly acknowledged to me, 'but it's only someone's guess what he told them. I asked him about it once but he refused to talk about that subject at all. He just told me, "Go away and don't come back until you change your mind." '

Both Slepaks, father and son, are far more single-minded than the majority of Jews I met. Most had ambivalent feelings like Mark, the playwright, and his wife, Tanya. Among the departing Jews, even among activists, I found a fair number who had ambivalent feelings about Russia when the final moment approached. Suddenly, they were seized with the impulse to linger and look backward, a reluctance to tear themselves away, a sense of sadness mixed with the elation of having finally achieved what they had struggled for so long.

'I'm not ready to go yet – there's not enough time,' was a phrase that I heard again and again when final approval came. In a sense, it was literally true that they were not ready because the authorities usually allotted them only a week, sometimes only four or five miserably short days, to accomplish a mountain of bureaucratic clearances – 'returning' their apartment to the state, obtaining innumerable documents approved, stamped, and signed, getting approval from local police, paying final utility bills, having their belongings inspected and checked, paying 900 rubles for their exit visas. But it was also true that they were not ready emotionally to cut themselves off totally from their former lives. They might have rejected Soviet life and felt rejected by it themselves, but they were unprepared to let go totally.

Nina Voronel, a middle-aged writer and linguist whose girlish face and large curious eyes give no clue that she writes one-act plays with the brutal despair of Beckett, confided that she had been secretly relieved the first time her family's visa applications were rejected. It was hard for me to believe at first. For I knew how terrified Nina had been when her husband, Aleksandr Voronel, a lean, crewcut, articulate nuclear physicist and leader among dissident Jewish scientists, had been repeatedly interrogated and threatened by the KGB. She had been deathly afraid when he had gone into hiding once and she was constantly tailed by the secret police. Yet, she said, 'I wasn't ready to go. I had all my friends. It was my world. I didn't want to leave it. I would stroll along the streets near Pushkin Square thinking "I will never see these places again." Especially in autumn when the leaves were falling, I used to go to special places in the forest that I loved and think how I would miss these places.' For Nina and for other writers, the wrench was perhaps more painful than for others because as writers denied a Jewish culture of their own, they had immersed themselves in Russian culture, its traditions, its language, its richness. I knew some people who literally broke down under the final strain when, with guillotine suddenness, the realization came that they had to part with a lifetime. Roman Rutman told me: 'It is like a rehearsal for death.'

Some, having survived that experience, rose like the phoenix and adjusted well, but others found the outside world a more treacherously complicated place than it had been in their imaginings.

'You've already achieved communism here,' Aleksandr Yanov, the publicist, told me two days after landing in New

York, still in culture shock from the incredible material abundance of the West. I remember that same feeling myself in coming out of Moscow for the last time in December 1974 and landing in Zurich. I walked around the streets like Scrooge awakened by the ghost of Marlowe, literally chuckling at the fabulous bunches of bananas in wintertime, huge salamis displayed like spokes of a wheel, electric lamps, furniture, cars, antiques, clothes, all in so many varieties and bright colors that it seemed impossible to make a choice. I encountered Jews who in their first days in Vienna had gone on touch-and-feel binges, trying on pants, dresses, sweaters, shoes, popping toasters, testing appliances, sitting in cars and smelling the fresh upholstery, indulging the pent-up frustrations of a lifetime.

But several months later, I learned that Yanov, like many others, was overcome by the conundrum of furnishing an apartment and had discovered the agonies of finding a steady job in America. There was no government to provide work automatically for the qualified specialist and no network of old friends to help out, Russian style. The ways of America were strange. One woman I knew had trouble really understanding why a typist's job was so hard to obtain in New York after she had completed a typist's course. In Moscow a graduation certificate was a guarantee of some job. People talked with nostalgia about Moscow. If they had been overwhelmed at first by the unbelievable armies of private cars, they were let down later by the inadequacies and high cost of public transportation. From Israel, too, came letters of former Moscow friends laboring with the problems of and appalled or impatient with the disorderly processes and endless public debates of a democracy. One friend quoted the incredible sounding prescription of another Soviet Jew: 'They have a rotten government [in Israel]. They need a Stalin.'

Wonder of wonders to me, I began to hear Jews calling themselves Russians. In the Soviet Union I had not heard that. Officially, the Soviet system distinguishes between Russians and Jews, as it does among other nationalities, making a point of having people identified by nationality in their domestic passports. Jews are derisively called *pyaty punkty*, 'fifth pointers', because it is point No. 5 in the passport where nationality is listed. Especially with the activism of recent years, the Soviet Jews whom I knew would not think of calling themselves Russians in Moscow or Lenin-grad. But in New York, and in Israel, too, many Jews feel their Russianness. Even without leaving Russia and suffering that homesick nostalgia, Larisa Bogoraz, one of the best-known dissidents of the Sixties, a full-blooded Jew, wrote, 'I am accustomed to the color, smell, rustle of the Russian landscape, as I am to the Russian language, the rhythm of Russian poetry. I react to everything else as alien.'

It is a jolt for many Soviet Jews, coming to Israel or the West, to discover this about themselves. It is a jolt for many Westerners – accustomed to thinking of Soviet Jews in stereotypes of fervent Zionists or practicing religious Jews – to make this discovery, too. But it tells much about the mood and character of the Jews who stayed as well as the Jews who have left. The mark of Russia is powerful even on those who reject her. Nina Voronel cited Andrei Sinyavsky, the brilliant Russian satirical writer who settled in Paris after coming out of the Soviet labor camps where he had been sentenced for publishing works abroad. Someone had asked Sinyavsky, a man who had become the symbol of dissidence, which he found harder – his first six months in the camps or his first six months in Paris.

'The first six months in Paris,' Sinyavsky replied. 'When I was in the camps, I was still in Russia.'

To which a Jewish intellectual who had also just emigrated to New York appended the shrewd observation that 'people like Sinyavsky, and there are many of us, left Russia not really looking for Israel or the West, but for Russia without a police state.'

XX

CONVERGENCE
Are They Becoming More Like Us?

> I believe we can have her [Russia] by trade. Commerce has a sobering influence. . . . Trade, in my opinion, will bring an end to the ferocity, the rapine, and the crudity of Bolshevism surer than any other method.
>
> British Prime Minister Lloyd George
> February 10, 1922

Like a snowfall that commences with a few uncertain flakes, thickens gradually into flurries, and then becomes a blizzard, the word that the Soviet Government had stopped unacknowledged jamming of the broadcasts of the Voice of America, the BBC, and the West German radio spread to the Russian people.

It was mid-September 1973. A few days later we visited the apartment of some Russian friends, people who had long since evolved the intricate arrangements for obtaining jeans and French perfumes from abroad, for putting Western paperbacks on their bookshelves, and getting a Beatles poster for their kitchen wall. Their ten-year-old son Vasya drifted into the sitting room with a transistor pressed to his ear, his brown eyes aglow and a satisfied grin on his face. 'He's been like that for the last few days, going around everywhere with his transistor listening to the Voice of America,' his mother explained. 'We all have.'

Another friend, a computer specialist, told me that in his research institute some of the staff were assembled for a political lecture about Andrei Sakharov by a Communist Party propagandist. After his opening talk, someone asked

38

the Party official to tell precisely what Sakharov had said since none of his works or statements had been published in the Soviet press. Without hesitation, the lecturer replied, 'Maybe someone has been listening to the foreign radio broadcasts and can tell us what they say about Sakharov.' No one took up his offer, but it was a striking example of the overnight change that had taken place.

Not that some people had not been listening furtively to Western radio stations all along. Within weeks of my arrival in the Soviet Union, I had been ushered into a cramped, walkdown apartment in Kishinev, the capital of Soviet Moldavia, and behind drawn shades, I had watched a couple work the dials of a bulky, old-fashioned, short-wave cabinet radio on spindly legs. In the Siberian city of Bratsk I had been taken to see the amazing library of Western rock recordings compiled from Voice of America transmissions by a young pop group. They could not really understand English but they mimicked the mellow-toned disc jockey's 'This is Willis Conover bringing you Music U.S.A.,' and broke into laughter. Walking or picnicking in the woods around Moscow, staying in their country cottages, or living in the smaller cities and towns from the Carpathian Mountains in Byelorussia to the Pacific Far East, Soviet people had been discreetly tuning in to foreign stations for years. But in big cities jamming had made it not only difficult but risky.

Now suddenly, with the jamming halted, people could not only listen but also admit to each other that they had done so. The young could quite brashly make cassette recordings from the foreign pop music shows and then swap or sell them. At work, their parents could only share the latest reports on the Arab-Israeli fighting in the Yom Kippur War of 1973. For the first time, the middle-aged computer specialist said to me, he felt personally affected by détente. Of course, he had been relieved by the improvement in Soviet-American relations 'because everyone wants peace', he said. But until the jamming ended, he had felt that détente had been 'for the big bosses and not for us'.

It was vignettes like those, reported in the Western press and brought home by Western tourists or visiting business delegations, that reawakened the two perennial and irresistible questions: Are they becoming more like us? Has life inside Russia changed – is it being liberalized?

These are natural enough assumptions. I had leaned

toward them myself when I left for Moscow. With the instant radio communications of the 20th century, constant world travel, broadening trade and the declaration of East-West détente, we tend to assume that the world is becoming more homogeneous, a global village. It seems almost axiomatic that if leaders East and West get along better and ordinary people fly similar jets, land at similar airports, ride cars, wear suits and ties (or platform shoes and jeans), launch their astronauts into space, build atomic power plants, turn over their problems to computers and find their young people keeping time to a common rock beat, that the ways of life under capitalism and communism are growing similar. Scholars have even coined a name for it: *convergence*, the comforting and tempting thesis that the mass production, vast scale, complex organization, and modern technology of today's economies will impel them along similar paths. Economic and political systems, so the theory goes, converge because they must cope with the same kind of problems and naturally tend to evolve similar techniques and institutions.

At almost every turn of Soviet history since the death of Stalin, we in the West – and many in Russia itself – have sought confirmation for the hope that the harsh totalitarianism built by Stalin was eroding. Khrushchev's stark condemnations of Stalinist terror in 1956 and 1961 seemed at the time to have demolished the myth of the Communist Party's infallibility. Russians thought, some in hope (and others in panic), that its unchallenged supremacy over Soviet life would never again be the same. The cultural ferment of the Khrushchev thaw – the first flowering of Yevtushenko, Voznesensky, Solzhenitsyn, and others – appeared to put liberalization of Soviet cultural and intellectual life on a new, promising, and seemingly irreversible course. In the Fifties, the West encouraged this trend by developing cultural exchanges with Moscow. We were astonished and sanguine when Pasternak's *Doctor Zhivago* was published abroad. True, he was vilified, forced to renounce the Nobel Prize, and left to die in solitude. But he had not been liquidated as he surely would have been under Stalin. The liberalization seemed to strengthen in the mid-Sixties when hundreds of scientists and other liberal intellectuals – some of them Communist Party members – risked putting their names to written protests against the trial of writers like

595

Andrei Sinyavsky and Yuli Daniel who had smuggled out their writings to the West, and were being punished by Khrushchev's successors. When that phase of letter protests faded and retrenchment followed, more sober heads reasoned that the education of a generation of engineers, technocrats, and computer specialists was bound to dilute the influence of ideology and bring economic and political reforms. Finally there was détente, the formal acknowledgment of strategic stalemate accompanied by Moscow's decision to seek trade with the capitalists it had so long maligned. Once again, it seemed that the Soviet system was undergoing fundamental change.

So many are the hidden undercurrents of Soviet life, and so frequently flowing in opposite directions, that no outsider can be confident of knowing whither goes Soviet Russia. But some forces of change are visible and some changes have clearly taken place. Most dramatically, of course, Stalin's arbitrary, lunatic mass terror that irrationally decimated the top ranks of the Communist Party and the military high command as well as eliminating millions of ordinary citizens has been halted. Khrushchev did that. And though the memory of Stalinist terror and its legacy remain, for most Russians today the sense of liberation from the unrelieved uncertainty of the Stalinist purges is a vital fact of life. Once, as I was coming out of our foreigners' apartment ghetto with two young couples who had been courageous enough to enter past the secret police guards at the gate, one young man heaved a sigh of relief and confessed, 'If it had been under Stalin, I would never have dared try that. We would have been finished.' Whether they entirely escaped without retribution in Brezhnev's Russia I'll never know because I was unable to make contact with them again. But I am confident that even if discovered, they were not as harshly punished as they would have been under Stalin.

Almost equally important, it seemed to some Russians I knew, has been the radical improvement in Soviet living standards since the death of Stalin. Under the dictator, they had literally been bled white and denied decent food, housing and clothing. They had been squeezed to the utmost as a corvée work-force for national construction. Now, in the Seventies, they are enjoying what is materially the best decade of Soviet history. They are still poorly off by the standards of the industrialized West and they have to endure a shopping gauntlet that would wither the will of a weaker race. But their only real standard of comparison is the past and, as many Russians said to me, they are grateful 'for how much better off we are than our parents'.

What is more, among the upper middle class of intellectuals, administrators, engineers, writers, ballerinas, the officially sanctioned consumerism has let loose acquisitive bourgeois instincts that Russians had been suppressing for decades. In the private car, the privately owned apartment, the private country dacha (no matter if it is no bigger than a toolshed), they have found a niche of life independent from all-embracing collectivism. The very fact of ownership has generated an appetite for more and has sharpened dissatisfaction with the poor quality of Soviet consumer goods and services. It has also given new impetus to the black market, the entire counter-economy that has become a fixture of the Soviet system.

The new materialism, just as older, more orthodox Communists feared, has contributed to the erosion of the Communist ideology. Everyone pays lip-service to the Party slogans, yet I do not recall in three years of living in Moscow hearing anyone convincingly echo the sentiments of Yevgeniya Ginzburg, an idealistic Bolshevik revolutionary jailed by Stalin, who remembered her youth thus: 'I don't want to sound pretentious but, quite honestly, had I been ordered to die for the Party, not once but three times . . . I would have obeyed without a moment's hesitation.'* That was four decades ago. Today, such zeal is not to be found. Nor is it essential. What matters is the façade of political conformity. For the Party, alert to the ebbing of ideological conviction, insists nonetheless on a show of faith and young ambitious careerists comply, whatever their private thoughts, because they have learned that Party membership is a ticket to a good job, a comfortable life, and maybe a chance to travel abroad.

Probably the greatest as yet unrealized force for change within the Soviet system is the impulse for major economic reform. Quite apart from the few outspoken dissenters who

* Yevgeniya Ginzburg, *Journey Into the Whirlwind*. Translated by Paul Stevenson and Max Hayward (New York: Harcourt Brace Jovanovich), 1967.

advocate an open, multiparty, democratic political system, there exists a sizable latent loyal opposition within the economic establishment, a strata of managers and technocrats worried about what they deplore as 'the stagnation' of the Soviet economy. These are people content to keep the political structure but who want to modernize the economy, make it operate more rationally, and with less interference from the Party high command and the central planners. One group of modern-minded mathematical economists has challenged the highly centralized planning inherited from Stalin, with its rigid production targets to be implemented at all costs, and has pushed for a more flexible approach. In the mid-Sixties, Prime Minister Kosygin promoted some economic decentralization and experimented with using profits and sales, rather than sheer volume of output as a gauge of economic success. Other more limited experiments in economic pragmatism were tried in agriculture and construction to try to increase productivity.

A parallel drive to turn away from ideology and toward greater realism that has intrigued Western scholars has been the development of Soviet sociology since the late Fifties, a trend that saw several Soviet sociologists chip away at Marxist shibboleths. Brezhnev, for example, might boast that with each victorious year, Soviet society was becoming more classless and distinctions between white- and blue-collar labor were disappearing, but sociological studies began showing the opposite.

Actually, sociology had some tender beginnings in the Soviet Twenties until Stalin proscribed it officially as anti-Marxist. Until 1958, it remained almost nonexistent, at best a very weak stepchild of economics and philosophy. It was not taught as a separate discipline because its empirical methods were an implicit challenge to Marxist-Leninist ideology and the Party's monopoly on social information. Sociology got its real start in the late Fifties as part of the general intellectual ferment of the Khrushchev era. Even some moderate Communist Party figures saw it as a modern tool for managing society and encouraged it. By the mid-Sixties, some sociologists were optimistically toying with the idea of venturing into political science as an empirical academic discipline apart from established, heavily ideological courses in Marxism-Leninism. By 1968, the Institute for Applied Social Research had been set up in Moscow and was said to be doing some secret research for the Party and the military.

But long before then – and more striking actually – was the appearance of field studies that had begun to show that Soviet society was becoming more stratified (not more classless as Brezhnev claimed), that it was getting harder for blue-collar working-class children to move up the social ladder, that in spite of all the propaganda about the land of the victorious proletariat and the high esteem for physical labor, young people from all social classes looked down on blue-collar jobs and aspired to be physicists, engineers, medical scientists, mathematicians, chemists, or radio specialists. One study revealed that the offspring of the intelligentsia had at least eight times as good a chance of getting into university as farm children, and Western scholars extrapolating from that data reckoned the odds as possibly 24 to 1.

Some sociologists began to report that blue-collar workers were alienated from their factory jobs (theoretically impossible according to Soviet dogma since alienation was supposed to be the result of the capitalist system of ownership). Other scholars began studying the sociology of religious beliefs and practices. Still others showed that young people were interested in material well-being, satisfying careers, or foreign travel and were turned off by political indoctrination. These were all limited studies, done in one small region or another, because Soviet sociologists had – and still have – no known capability for national opinion polling. Often the findings were printed in limited circulation academic journals and obscured in charts. But the implications were there to be seen. Moreover, theorists began to formulate concepts for Soviet sociology that were closely related to Western theories. The whole phenomenon was followed with hopeful approval by a knowledgable segment of the liberal intelligentsia, who regarded the development of sociology – and the empirical facts it was turning up about Soviet life – as a touchstone for liberalization and an important avenue toward eventual reforms.

But in 1971, the clock was turned back and empirical sociology was put on the defensive. Like other areas of Soviet intellectual life, it was hit by the backlash over Czechoslovak liberalism, by the conservative Soviet reflex against 'revisionist' thinking and liberalization at home, and the general crackdown against intellectuals – especially Jews – who had been signing protest petitions in the earlier ferment of the mid- and late Sixties.

'There were too many inquisitive minds at work – and *they* [the authorities] decided *they* had to muzzle them,' I was told by Sasha, a dark-haired young Soviet sociologist. We met in an ill-lit room of a communal apartment in downtown Moscow. Sasha was nervous about meeting an American correspondent but anxious to tell the story of the purge at the Institute of Applied Social Research in Moscow, by far the most important such center in the country. Investigating commissions set up by the Party in late 1971 and 1972 questioned staff members and announced their intention to 'weed out the bad apples', he said. The director was forced into retirement and, by Sasha's count, about one-third of the 300 professional sociologists were purged, including the most daring and dynamic researchers, who fled to institutes of other disciplines. Conservatives then put on pressure to expunge Western concepts and terminology. The new institute director, M. N. Rutkevich, sounded a stern note by reasserting the primacy of Marxist-Leninist ideology and Party control. 'Sociology is a Party science,' Rutkevich declared in *Pravda* in September 1973. 'The Marxist sociologist, be he scientist, Party official, or economic official, cannot pose as an "impartial researcher".'

The purge at the Moscow Institute was a major setback for sociology nationally because that Institute had collected many of the best researchers and had played a central role in the field. Publication of new work dropped off. Sociologists were split up and felt they had to lay low. I tried to meet with several of them but all except Sasha were too scared to take the risk. 'It's a bad situation for the development of sociology,' Sasha said. 'People feel isolated.'

Still, to regain some international standing, Soviet sociology was allowed to recover organizationally. In the fall of 1974, a regular sociological journal appeared for the first time and the Moscow Institute was renamed the Institute for Sociological Research, a step forward. A new batch of research studies appeared, but Western sociologists were unimpressed with them. Though sometimes more carefully done than the work in the Sixties, the new work seemed more limited in scope, more cautious and generally less revealing. Word passed that the best research was being kept secret, unpublished, while publicly Soviet sociology became more ideologically conservative. It faced an uncertain future. Other Soviet intellectuals were disheartened. 'It's a shame,' said a physicist, disconsolately. 'They are doing narrower studies now. It's too bad not only for them but also for the rest of us.'

The fate of Soviet sociology tells a lot about the political temper of Brezhnev's Russia: first, the pattern of early experimentation and later retrenchment; and second, the watershed for Soviet internal life that was the result of the Kremlin's decision to invade Czechoslovakia in August 1968 to crush the liberal reforms there. The liberal Russians I knew regarded the Soviet Seventies under Brezhnev as a period of gray, stand-pat conservatism at home – a less venturesome, stimulating, promising time than the reign of Khrushchev. The Brezhnev era has brought the partial rehabilitation of Stalin and the suppression of Khrushchev's criticism of Stalinist terror – a shift of great symbolic importance to all Russians. For Westerners to comprehend what this means, they would have to imagine that in America, for example, it became impossible to write or talk openly about the Vietnam War, the Watergate scandal, the whole controversy over the domestic political activities of the C.I.A. and F.B.I. As Russians remarked to me, when the dark side of history is shut off, it darkens the present as well.

Not only was the past placed beyond criticism, but a campaign of repression was directed against intellectual dissidents to curtail the ferment that Khrushchev's thaw had released. In the late Sixties the drive seemed to focus against the scientists and other scholars who had participated in the letter protests. Enough of them were expelled from the Party, pressured or fired from jobs and permanently blacklisted to force establishment liberals to retreat from direct, open criticism. In the early Seventies, despite détente, there was a sharper crackdown against active dissidents – the deportation of Solzhenitsyn, the effective isolation of Sakharov, a campaign to suppress underground publications and to jail nationalists in the Ukraine, Lithuania, Armenia, and elsewhere, and continuing trials and exile to Siberia or abroad of less well-known dissenters.

601

In the wider cultural world as well there was a reflexive tightening that squeezed off the hopes spawned under Khrushchev for steady cultural liberalization and freer expression. By 1970–1971, its effects were fairly clear. After that, several published writers complained to me, works that had gotten into print in the Khrushchev era and the early Brezhnev years were no longer printable. 'Under Khrushchev, our literature was better,' one novelist advised me. 'It was easier to breathe then. In *New World* [magazine] you could read real literature – Solzhenitsyn, Dudintsev, others. Now, Solzhenitsyn is gone and you can't read Dudintsev.' Others thought, however, that the theater had become more active and interesting. But even they acknowledged that while individual films, plays, or books might stir temporary interest, the Brezhnev period had choked off the sense of ferment, direction, and hope of the Khrushchev thaw. The real measure of the cultural claustrophobia was that in a country that has historically issued forth a volcanic flow of creative talent, no writer of real stature has emerged publicly since Solzhenitsyn and Pasternak.

Conservatives obstructed change in other fields as well. The economic reforms intended by Kosygin in the mid-Sixties to give industrial managers more incentives and more flexibility were gutted and smothered by the powerful Party and government bureaucracies in Moscow. Central planners fought off proposals of mathematical economists for more flexible planning. In agriculture, the experiment with the farming-link groups was sidetracked and effectively abandoned.

In short, despite the fascinating eccentricities of Russian life beneath the surface, most of the basic economic and political structure inherited from Stalin remains intact today. In spite of the political earth tremors caused by Khrushchev, the dominance and infallibility of the Communist Party are still the pillars of the Soviet edifice. 'Any small organization, even a club of dog lovers or cactus-growers is supervised by some appropriate body of the Party,' groused Roy Medvedev, the dissident historian. Within the Party, there has been precious little new blood at or near the top. Khrushchev's plan for enforced rotation of choice Party jobs has been scrapped. The leadership has become conservative with age (the average age of the Politburo in 1975 was 66), and so have the echelons of bureaucrats beneath it.

The bloody purges have ended but not the system of coercion with its Siberian camps and secret police. Occasionally criticized in Khrushchev's time, the secret police have been restored to respectability and are now even lauded by the press as 'our brave *Chekists*' (Lenin's name for them). Yuri Andropov, the head of the KGB, was elevated into the Politburo in April 1973, the first such appointment since Lavrenti Beria, Stalin's secret police chief, enjoyed such rank. And while it is a vital fact of Soviet life that Stalin's control by mass terror has been abandoned, it is also true that more subtle techniques of repression seem quite adequate – Stalin's overkill has been streamlined. As one dissident observed, the regime has found that several thousand selected arrests and blacklisting have a chilling effect and that mass terror is not necessary. 'People are cautious, not so much from fear of being thrown in prison,' a movie script writer confessed, 'but because of more subtle pressures – jobs, travel, little privileges, and opportunities. The system works – quietly, quietly.'

Nor has there been any automatic cause-and-effect, as many in the West presumed, between economic improvements and the development of political democracy and liberalization in Soviet life. In time, the rising expectations of Soviet consumers and the emergence of a selfconscious middle class may affect the Soviet system, but so far the burgeoning of bourgeois tastes has not forced any realignment of national priorities or shifts of power. Publicly, the Brezhnev coalition has made a great show of attentiveness to consumers, and Soviet consumers are unquestionably better off. After the meat riots by Polish dockworkers in the Baltic seaports in December 1970, the Kremlin was sufficiently shaken to promise the Soviet people the first Five-Year-Plan in their history (1971–75) that would strive for more growth in the consumer sector than in heavy industry. But by 1972 the priorities had been quietly reversed and by 1974 the Soviet leadership was openly admitting that top priority was again going to heavy industry.

In other countries such a shift might have been risky. But one distinguishing feature of Russian life is the leadership's ability to hold consumer expectations in check. Paul Hollander, an American sociologist, made the shrewd observation that 'the Soviet people have been told of approaching utopia for over 50 years and yet there has been no appreciable growth of a utopian mentality among them'.* The regime has failed to make good on all kinds of promises, yet Russian consumers are appeased if there is a steady supply of bread, cabbage, potatoes, and vodka, an occasional shipment of oranges, and a chance once in a while to go to a Western movie. They will settle for less than consumers in any other industrialized nation – and that is an important element of the regime's stability.

What is more, the very mood of consumer materialism among Soviet intellectuals seems to have sapped their energy for reform and diverted their urge for a freer cultural and political climate. The earlier idealism of the Khrushchev period has given way to a cynical mood. 'Cynicism,' observed a disillusioned mathematician, 'is the ultimate method of control.' People are on the make for themselves and care little about broader social issues, echoed a highly-placed Party journalist. The *nachalstvo*, the class of bosses, and the cultural and scientific elite enjoy their covert creature comforts and those just beneath them lust after the same privileges. A surprising number of intellectuals are corrosively disaffected, judging by their private remarks to me, but feel impotent and prefer escape into their private lives to jousting with the system. Not long before I left Moscow, Yevgeny Yevtushenko caught the mood in a little poem that mocked the way that liberal writers (himself included, I presume) were being tamed by the trappings of affluence into toning down their works. That internal villain of self-censorship, Kompromis Kompromisovich, he said:

> Whispers from within:
> 'Well, don't you be too choosey.
> Alter a line a bit.'
> Calculating everything with an abacus,
> This recruiter of compromises
> Buys us off with things,
> Like big children –
> He buys us off with flats,
> Furniture, showy fashions,
> And we're no longer belligerent.
> We raise a noise – only when we're drinking.

* Paul Hollander, *American and Soviet Society* (Oxford, New York, 1973), pp. 388–389.

'You have to understand that we are years behind you in the West,' a magazine editor mused. 'Right now, I suppose we are about where you Americans were after the war, when you were gorging yourselves on the material things that you had been denied during the war – cars, houses, clothes. There was no radical political movement in America then, no hint of what was to come 20 years later though the intellectual dropouts from your society now owe something to those people and that time. So right now there is a rush in our society to get dachas, cars, and I don't know what. People are talking about these things, not caring about anything else. But maybe after a while people will have enough of these material things and they will start thinking more about the quality of life – maybe, in a generation or two.'

That was a phrase I heard rather frequently – 'maybe, in a generation or two'. The Russian sense of time is so different from that in the West, so much more patient. And Russians, unlike Americans and other Westerners, do not assume that progress toward a more liberal, open society is inevitable.

Even so, détente has had an impact on the Soviet scene. Without détente, for example, it would have been impossible for an American President to address the Soviet public twice on nationwide television and difficult to imagine Senator Edward Kennedy being sped by a Soviet secret police escort to a midnight rendezvous in Moscow with leaders of the Jewish emigration movement. As the vignettes about radio listening suggest, détente gained millions of new listeners for Western radio broadcasts and gave them some glimmering of the outside world. Soviet agreements on scientific, technical, and cultural exchanges with the West have markedly expanded the numbers of contacts between Soviet and Western specialists in recent years. The Soviet desire to maintain these contacts has also made the Kremlin sensitive to the outcry in the West against its campaign of vilification against dissident physicist Andrei Sakharov in the fall of 1973 and the crude, police-state bulldozing of the mildly iconoclastic art exhibit a year later. To appease the West, the Kremlin called off the anti-Sakharov drive and permitted a substitute art show to be held. Later as a humanitarian gesture it allowed chess grandmaster Boris Spassky to marry a Frenchwoman, a cosmetic concession that had little effect on less celebrated individuals.

Occasionally, détente has caused the Soviet leaders to lift some shrouds of secrecy. In their campaign to woo France into greater independence from the Western alliance, they honored President de Gaulle in 1966 as the first Westerner permitted to visit the secret Soviet space-launching site at Baikonur in Kazakhstan. And nine years later, it was the momentum of the Apollo-Soyuz mission with the Americans plus the firm insistence of the American Apollo commander, Brig. Gen. Thomas Stafford, that forced the Soviets to open Baikonur to a few Americans and even to let American officials and newsmen visit mission control outside Moscow as well. (I remember on our visit to the cosmonauts' 'Star City' thinking how much it reminded me of the old Kremlin of Pskov with walls not only surrounding the whole space complex but walls within walls, shutting off still more secret areas that we could not enter.) To compete with the openness of the American space program, the Russians had to let their own people for the first time see a live space launch and follow the progress of the Apollo-Soyuz mission as it proceeded. Again, after great delay, some American technical specialists were allowed to visit Siberian natural gas fields that Moscow wanted to develop with American credits. And, after Washington was three times caught ill-prepared for the effects of sizable Soviet grain purchases, Moscow was willing in 1975 to negotiate some long-term arrangements to cushion the shock of more big grain-buying.

But by far the most dramatic example of the human impact of détente was the willingness of the Kremlin under strong pressure from the American Congress to permit about 100,000 Soviet Jews to emigrate to Israel and the West in the first half of this decade. (Under similar though less publicized and controversial pressures from West Germany, several thousand ethnic Germans were also allowed to leave the country.) Given the Kremlin's acute sensitivity to the proud image of the Soviet Union abroad as the promised land of socialism, permitting such an exodus was an unprecedented concession – a measure both of the severe disaffection among Soviet Jewry and of the intense desire of Leonid Brezhnev and his supporters within the leadership to secure the benefits of trade with the United States.

'You have no idea how important it is to have this "third alternative",' said a Jewish science writer who eventually emigrated. 'Ten years ago, if you could not stomach living under the Soviet system, you could – ' and he drew a finger across his throat. 'Now, thanks to the American policy of détente and the Soviet need for these little kernels of grain, there are three choices. Either as before [the finger at the throat], or you can struggle for some little bit of freedom because you know there exists a third alternative – to leave the country.'

It is important, however, to recognize where Moscow drew the limits. As this science writer pointed out, Soviet Jews were being allowed to emigrate 'as an exception' to the normal Soviet restrictions on travel and migration. Jews and ethnic Germans were being allowed to go, he said, but that did not mean this right was being granted permanently to them or that the other hundred-odd Soviet nationals shared this privilege. 'The Jews are an exception,' he emphasized. 'That is what you have to remember. Whenever our authorities have a difficult problem to deal with and they must make concessions, they make exceptions. But they do not like to change the rules themselves.'

It was an important point, it seemed to me, in assessing the impact of other Soviet concessions to détente as well. Western outrage could spare Andrei Sakharov from jail or expulsion from the Academy of Sciences, but it had not protected many less well-known dissidents. Nor had it won intellectual freedom for other Soviet scientists. Trials of anonymous dissenters continued steadily through détente. The Western outcry over the crude bulldozing of the modern art exhibit could shame Soviet authorities into allowing another special exhibit or two to take place but it did not alter the fundamental controls on Soviet art. 'A bit of steam has to be let off,' a gaunt young writer commented to me after the art show, 'but in ways that cause the least trouble – a bit of long hair, jazz, Western-style clothes for young people, a small art exhibition. But make no mistake: they are not about to sanction abstract art. No great change in cultural life is coming.'

The Jewish emigration has not changed the fact that well over 90 percent or more of the 250 million Soviet citizens have never spent a day of their lives outside their country and probably never will. The opening of the Baikonur cosmodome to American astronauts did not signal a shift to an open policy for the Soviet space program in general.

Even the end of radio jamming was merely a return to the situation under Khrushchev who had ended jamming in 1963 under a previous flowering of Soviet-American détente. Brezhnev had reimposed the jamming after the Soviet invasion of Czechoslovakia in 1968, and even after it was partially lifted in 1973, it still remained in force against Radio Liberty, the Western station most devoted to Soviet news. As détente wore on, moreover, some of my Soviet friends contended that Voice of America had toned down its political content to avoid ruffling the Kremlin's feathers. Others merely got bored with the preoccupation of Western stations with the West's own economic plight. 'We can read about that in our own press,' a teacher commented drily. 'We want the other news, the news we can't read in our own newspapers.'

Nor were the increased contacts with the West being allowed to get out of hand. Every outgoing scientific or cultural delegation was carefully screened and so were Soviet participants for joint sessions in the Soviet Union. 'Getting into a meeting with the Americans is practically like getting access to a closed [defense] institute,' one natural scientist complained. Not surprisingly, those outside the privileged circle feel more isolated than ever. 'Hurry up and invite all our bosses to America,' one Soviet scientist told an American who was arranging scientific exchanges. 'Only after they have been there will there be space on our delegations for real practicing scientists.' All these group contacts are monitored by informers, often just scientists who want to earn the privilege of still more trips to the West.

In other words, the Brezhnev leadership was making certain not to repeat what it obviously regarded as the mistake made by Khrushchev – allowing some relaxation at home to accompany the easing of tensions abroad. Despite détente, vigilance against foreign ideological subversion remained a paramount concern in the Soviet press. At closed lectures or even in little outdoor movies in public parks, Russians were told or shown how foreign tourists, scholars, or businessmen were trying to bring religious or political literature or other 'contraband' into the Soviet Union to subvert the Russian people. Although the July 1975 Conference on European Security and Cooperation did agree on exchanging observers to monitor large-scale military maneuvers in Europe, Moscow still resisted the principle of on-site inspection in arms agreements. It gained formal recognition of the *de facto* boundaries of Eastern Europe, just as it had previously used the more relaxed atmosphere of détente to promote acceptance of East Germany, Cuba and North Vietnam into the family of nations. The Russians accepted the conference proclamations about reunification of families and freer travel East and West but Brezhnev openly warned the West that 'no one should try to dictate to other people, on the basis of foreign policy considerations of one kind or another, the manner in which they ought to manage their internal affairs'. Politburo members like Yuri Andropov and Mikhail Suslov underscored the message that Moscow was not changing internally to accommodate the West by contending that Western concern about human rights was no more than a cover for 'ideological sabotage'. Georgi Arbatov, a leading spokesman on Soviet-American relations contended that the Russians had 'far surpassed the West, and particularly the United States' in honoring humanitarian provisions of the Security Conference proclamation. In other words, the Kremlin was eager to push détente abroad to take advantage of what Soviet Marxists are fond of calling 'the changing correlation of forces', but it sought to contain the impact of détente at home. Brezhnev was reaching out to the world abroad, but trying to hold it at bay at home. Thus far, he has been very successful.

The notion persists in the West nonetheless, that trade leaps ideological barriers and will become the catalyst for the convergence of the two systems. In America, particularly, there is the feeling that in the long run the nexus of commerce will soften the Soviet police state and sow the seeds of eventual liberalization. The concept is not new. Back in 1922, British Prime Minister Lloyd George told Parliament that the 'sobering influence' of trade would 'bring an end to the ferocity, the rapine, and the crudity of Bolshevism surer than any other method'. (As a matter of fact, Britain, Germany, and the United States all traded quite heavily with Stalin's Russia in the Twenties and Thirties.) The modern variant is that as the Soviet Union does more and more business with the capitalist West, some of capitalism's ways will rub off and the Kremlin will have to loosen up and move toward some kind of market socialism. As Soviet industrial managers are exposed to Western technology and the Russian public is exposed to Western life-styles, they will see the strength of the Western system, so the theory goes, and this will feed the appetite for greater freedom and kindle grass-roots pressures for fundamental changes in the Soviet Union.

When I arrived in Moscow in 1971, I was intrigued by this possibility myself but after three years of living there, I came home much more skeptical. In the first place, the Brezhnev coalition only turned to the West for new technology as an alternative to having to liberalize its own economy. When the domestic economic reforms of 1965 failed, Brezhnev and Kosygin decided that the short cut to modernizing the Soviet system was to buy computers, petrochemical plants, and other high technology from the West and to plug these facilities, ready-made into the Soviet system, rather than granting the necessary freedom to Soviet managers, scientists, and engineers to develop such technology themselves. One of my Russian friends commented sarcastically that the Western technology would modernize the Soviet system so that 'we can have Stalinism with computers' – a still centralized, controlled economy rather than a more flexible one.

Over a long period of time, of course, this could change. But the Soviet rulers themselves do not seem uneasy at the prospect of exposure to Western businessmen. Any number of times I was told rather pointedly by Soviet officials or Party journalists that they welcomed Western businessmen more than Western politicians, journalists, or writers because, as one official said, 'they accept our system as it is' without ideological objections. In other words, the Kremlin found that the profit motive could be trusted because Western businessmen were too busy doing business to be passing on the infectious virus of democracy. Nor did the Russians themselves have any ideological qualms about whom they dealt with. Among Americans, some of their favorite partners in trade were the biggest American defense contractors. But where East European countries have been willing to experiment with new forms of cooperative enterprises and various lease-back arrangements, the Russians have been quite firm about not altering the fundamental machinery of the Soviet economy.

The basic objection, I believe, is less one of ideology than the refusal to permit the dispersal of power. When all is said and done the Kremlin falls back on the tradition of holding all real power of decision at the center. For the Western notion that trade will somehow arouse irresistible grass-roots pressure for greater freedoms in Soviet life rather naively ignores Soviet – and Russian – history. It is Western concept based on Western experience. In the past, the major changes in the Soviet system have not come about because of pressures from the Soviet public but through decisions from on high. It was Stalin who initiated the industrial five-year-plans in 1928 and ordered collectivization of agriculture; Khrushchev in 1956 who unmasked Stalin, later shook up the Party structure and imposed regional economic management on the country; and the Brezhnev-Kosygin leadership which promulgated the half-hearted and ill-fated economic reforms of 1965.

Détente itself was a policy launched by the leadership for its own purposes and it has been carefully controlled by the leadership ever since. What little change it has brought has been kept in check within parameters that precluded fundamental reforms. What has been at work is a process of grafting on, of adapting techniques from the West, or making exceptions and piecemeal adjustments but not of radical transformation. Western technicians may now be allowed to look at some gas and oil fields in Siberia to encourage Western investment, but they are kept away from scores of other industrial sites to which their business would logically take them. I.B.M. may be asked to install computerized type-setting for *Pravda* and *Izvestia* and computerized control systems for the Kama River Truck Plant, but it is required to house most of its specialists in Western Europe and fly them periodically into the Soviet Union to do their jobs because Moscow will not grant visas for more than two I.B.M. men to live in the country at one time. Security and control of contacts take precedence over convenience or efficiency. The result is that so far, one cannot see any germ which has been taken in – either through nuclear standoff, cultural exchange, or broadened trade, all loosely lumped together as détente – that has flowed on its own and is visibly beginning to transform the Soviet system. For the Kremlin has proven itself remarkably adept at insulating its population from the contagion of free ideas from the West.

*   *   *

Far more is at work, however, than the Soviet system of controls. For détente confronts the accumulated weight of Russian history, the built-in inertia and attitudes of centuries. Those in the West captivated by the notion of convergence often lose sight of the essential Russianness of Russia today. We are aware that Russia is a very old nation but nonetheless we are quick to forget its past when we think about its present and its future. It would be foolish, of course, to maintain that nothing was changed by the Bolshevik Revolution which was one of the cataclysmic events of this century. Royalty and the old aristocracy were swept away and later, under Stalin, an entire continental economy was transformed. The rhetoric of public life today is unambiguously Communist. Yet the longer I stayed in Moscow, the less impressed I was by how Communist the country was and the more I thought how Russian it was. Rather than alter the centralized authoritarian system of rule inherited from the czars, the Communists have strengthened it, made it more pervasive and efficient. Their dramatic, built-from-scratch construction projects were not entirely new departures but modern variations of Peter the Great's brutal construction of St Petersburg. The violent social upheavals of the first two decades of Soviet rule wrought great changes but now a new ruling class has emerged, as jealous of its power and privilege as the czarist nobility. Paradoxically perhaps Russia has seemed gradually to be returning to many of its old ways.

The Cold War legacy, as well as Moscow's economic isolationism during the postwar period, has mistakenly led many Americans to assume, for example, that trade with the West is a new game for the Russians. But it is actually striking how Leonid Brezhnev is pursuing a path and a policy used by his czarist predecessors and how little authoritarian rule in Russia through the centuries has been affected by its episodic contacts with the West. For buying high technology from the West in exchange for Russian raw materials is a pattern of Russian commerce that predates the discovery of America.

Five hundred years ago, Ivan the Great, the Grand Prince of Muscovy, hired Italian architects and engineers to build two of the great Kremlin cathedrals, a palace, and the Kremlin walls and towers, much as today's Kremlin rulers are hiring Western firms to construct truck and car factories, metal foundries, and petrochemical plants. Other Italians ran the imperial mint and managed the casting of cannons for the Grand Prince, while Greek masters were imported to teach art. The next Czar, Ivan the Terrible, persuaded some Englishmen to set up the first Russian printing press, used German military engineers to help him mount the siege of Kazan against the Tatars in 1552, and had the Dutch set up an ironworks to support the armaments industry. Yet he was one of the bloodiest despots in all Russian history. At the turn of the 18th century, Peter the Great conducted a Western technology hunt on an even grander scale (today, some Russians jokingly call Brezhnev a modern Peter), bringing to Russia thousands of foreign craftsmen in all fields and recruiting hundreds of Swedes and Germans to work in his civil service because he admired their efficiency, self-discipline, and honesty. He, too, ruled with an iron hand.

Some of the very practices that Westerners attribute today to the obsessive secrecy and xenophobia of the Communist police state developed under the czars. In those days, too, the Russians imposed ideological controls on trade and segregated foreign merchants from the local population. Like the Communist Party today, the Russian Orthodox Church in the 15th century was on guard against alien heresies. Books brought along by Western traders were confiscated by the customs agent of the Grand Prince, stirred to action by a vigilant and defensive church, just as Soviet customs agents today take away political literature, skin-magazines, or certain rock records from indiscreet Western travelers. Then, as now, resident foreigners were shunted off into isolated ghettos apart from the mass of Russians with whom they had little contact. The most important of these enclaves, called *Kitaigorod*, was located outside the Kremlin walls where now stands the Rossiya Hotel, one of the lodgings most frequented by foreign businessmen and Western delegations today. Russian history even contains a precedent for Leonid Brezhnev's efforts to sweeten the climate for trade with America by letting larger numbers of Soviet Jews emigrate. Around 1600, Czar Boris Godunov released a number of German merchants captured during the battle of Novgorod in a deliberate ploy to cajole the German princedoms into commerce.

Not only in its patterns of trade but also in its political system, the Soviet state owes a debt to the traditions of czarist Russia, traditions that today constitute a powerful impediment to change. The great celebrations of Communist holidays when the leadership assembles on the Lenin Mausoleum and throngs of people march through Red Square in a ritual declaration of fealty evoke Tolstoy's rich descriptions of the religious processions through Red Square by the masses humbly parading their homage before the czar. Under Communism, the masses carry aloft the portraits of the Party Politburo members; under the czars, they carried huge religious ikons. The censorship of poets like Pushkin, the Siberian exile of Dostoyevsky, the illegal publication in the West of later works by Tolstoy all foreshadowed Soviet repression of free-thinking writers today. In much the same way that Khrushchev and Brezhnev snuffed out incipient revolts in Hungary and Czechoslovakia, the czars crushed rebellions in Hungary and Poland in the 19th century. Then, as now, the rulers were supported by a service class of nobility who were rewarded for service to the state with grants of land and other privileges, translated today into the system of special stores, hospitals, rest homes, dacha communities for the Soviet elite. Then, as now, the state supported the Imperial Ballet to project the image of cultured elegance at home and abroad.

Perhaps more fundamental than these abiding arrangements and rituals of public life is the deep-seated influence of history on Russian character and institutions – the centralized concentration of power, the fetish of rank, the xenophobia of simple people, the futile carping of alienated intelligentsia, the passionate attachment of the Russians to Mother Russia, the habitual submission of the masses to the Supreme Leader and their unquestioned acceptance of the yawning gulf between the Ruler and the Ruled. The longer I lived in Soviet Russia, the more Russian it seemed to me and hence the less likely to undergo fundamental change. Whenever I would see signs of change, Russian intellectuals would disabuse me. Gradually, it came through to me that Russians – unlike Westerners – do not take it for granted that Russian dictatorship must inevitably evolve into democracy for they know its power and its permanence; they recognize its ability to adapt without surrendering its essence; they find comfort in the stability and order that it provides. Fearing what seems to them the chaotic turbulence of Western liberal democracies, most of them do not want democracy for Russia. Even those intellectuals who long for it will say their society is not ready for the give-and-take, the political tolerance and compromise, the self-restraint that democracy requires. Even they draw back from it or say that it must take generations to evolve.

Perhaps one reason that Westerners do not grasp such feelings and so readily assume that Russians are 'like us' is that Russian life offers no obvious tourist exotica – women in saris or kimonos, figures of Buddha in temples, camels on the desert – to remind the outsider that here is an alien culture, one which did not pass through the Renaissance, Reformation, and the era of constitutional liberalism which shaped the West. But here is a culture that absorbed Eastern Orthodox Christianity from Byzantium, endured Mongol conquest and rule, and then developed through centuries of czarist absolutism with intermittent periods of opening toward the West followed by withdrawal into continental isolation. That pattern was repeated again and again. The forays into the West brought some changes but did not fundamentally dilute the strong authoritarian strain in the Russian body politic in any lasting way. If anything, Western innovations were simply used to reinforce Russian methods. Peter the Great could win the reputation as Russia's greatest Westernizer and yet he also laid the foundations of the modern police state and was ruthless in his intolerance of dissent and his bloody punishment of wayward nobility. Catherine the Great could begin her détente with the West in fascination with Voltaire and the French Encyclopedists and end it by imposing controls to stamp out the infection of liberal French ideas in her court. In short, there often have been unsettling influences from the West but Russia's rulers have coped with them over time. Brezhnev's tactics today may differ slightly, but his strategy is the same as that of the czars: to extract the best technology from the West without having to absorb the critical cast of mind or the way of life that produced it. As did the czars before him, Brezhnev takes a risk. But so far there is no visible reason to expect that the ancient patterns of Russian life will be fundamentally altered.

Often the powerful sense of continuity with the Russian past comes through in funny little ways. Right after Nixon's first visit to Moscow in 1972, Ann and I took a car trip to Yaroslavl to see the Russian countryside in summertime.

About halfway, we stopped at a Soviet service station for gasoline – the first time I had ever gassed up in a Soviet car on the highway and I was intrigued by the routine. First I had to pick my pump, guess how many liters of gas I needed, and inform a chubby girl in the office. Then I paid her in advance with special coupons and she dialed me the desired number of liters on a console in the office. Finally I went back to pump my own gas. It was strictly do-it-yourself.

To me, it was a mildly comic scene to see everyone pumping his own gas – the bread man, two motorcyclists, truck drivers servicing massive vehicles, and a few people bent over Soviet compacts like the Moskvich or the Zaporozhets. That station was a scene of great disorder. People wheeled up to a pump or backed into a pump from any possible direction and parked at any angle that suited them. It was a minor mayhem getting in and out, and it struck me as a great scene for pictures. I had only shot about four or five when I was confronted by a bull-necked Russian in shirtsleeves and a hat who was waving his arms in front of my camera and angrily bellowing at me.

'Show me your documents,' he demanded. With his fleshy face, ample stomach, and baggy pants, he looked the epitome of the Russian worker, one step off the collective farm.

Since I knew of nothing in the Soviet regulations that forbade photographing a gasoline station and since he appeared to be no more than an over-zealous Soviet citizen (of whom there are many), I tried to ignore him. 'It's all right,' I said soothingly, 'excuse me.' I side-stepped him so that I could shoot pictures in another direction.

Again, he loomed in front of me and demanded my documents – a standard Soviet method of intimidation.

'Who are you?' I asked.

'Show me your documents,' he repeated. By now he was fairly exercised, evidently because I had not immediately succumbed. We argued back and forth. I half expected a crowd to reinforce him, but the other motorists went on gassing up. They stared but did not take part. It turned out that my burly friend was the manager of the service station. I explained to him that I was an American correspondent – which he undoubtedly knew already from the special coded license plates on our car – and that I had just finished writing stories about the meetings between Nixon and Brezhnev and was taking my wife on a trip.

'Which way are you going?' he demanded suspiciously. 'I am going to call the police.'

I said we were driving toward Yaroslavl and, trying to humor him, I asked whether he had seen Nixon and Brezhnev on television. Yes, he had seen it all. Was he happy about détente? I asked. Yes, of course. He wanted peace between our peoples – but it was forbidden to take photographs. Then I said that since he was interested in peace, he must have read the arms agreements. Yes, of course, he had. And I asked whether he had noticed that each side had agreed to let the other side fly sputniks over its territory to take pictures of its missiles so that there would be no danger of surprise attack. He looked puzzled. But after a couple of minutes, he seemed to absorb the idea that Russian sputniks were taking pictures of American rockets and American sputniks were taking pictures of Soviet rockets from the sky.

'Well,' I said finally, 'if our leaders can be so friendly and agree on those sputniks taking pictures of missiles, there can't be anything wrong with taking pictures of a gas station, can there?'

He frowned with peasant wariness. 'It's forbidden,' he fumed, his former indignation returning. He wagged an angry finger at my camera. 'It's forbidden. I am going to call the police to come after you.' And he stormed off to telephone them. I took a couple of last snapshots, and drove off. The police never troubled us, but I still muttered at what I took to be the exaggerated Communist vigilance of this gas station manager keeping watch against a wandering imperialist.

Ann, who was then reading Henri Troyat's biography of Tolstoy, recalled the episode after his death when Tolstoy's body was lying in a provincial railroad station. Some Russian photographers wanted to take pictures of the great man's body, but the stationmaster would not permit any photography on his premises. He was suspicious of photography and vaguely aware of rules against it. Without special permission from St Petersburg, he was adamantly opposed to any photography in his station.

'So you see,' said Ann, 'it's nothing new. It was the same under the czars. They're the same people.'

Index

Chou En-lai, 244

Chronicle of Current Events, 211, 492, 559

Chukovskaya, Lidiya Korneyevna, 477, 486-7, 488, 548, 558-9

Chukovsky, Kornei, 57, 486-9

Cinema *see* Motion pictures

Circuses, 148, 194

Cliburn, Van, 145

Clinical Medicine, 316

Clothing, 76, 81, 89, 117-22, 429; price-scalping, 118; privileged class, 42, 54; shortages, 83-5; Siberia, 401, 415; speculators, 117-21; underground industry, 125, 128; youth, 223-4, 235-6

Club of Young Technicians, 197

Cold War, 37, 202, 411, 427, 570, 612

Collective (*kollektiv*), 375-6

Collective farms, 124, 190, 191, 249, 251-2, 254, 255, 260-1, 262

Collectivisation, 204, 249, 611

Communist of the Armed Forces (*Kommunist Vooruzhennykh Sil*), 293

Communist Party, 21, 22, 35, 195, 276-7, 304, 334-68; Central Committee of, 43, 46, 47, 50-1, 60, 170, 294, 295, 341, 357, 358, 431, 580; Communism as a secular religion, 337-41; convergence and, 595, 596, 597; corruption in, 114, 129-31, 358-9, 363-4, 367; cult of Lenin, 301, 317, 337-41, 343-6, 352; dissidents and, 341-2, 537, 538-9, 541-7, 550, 555-8; elections, 319, 350-2; ideological indifference, 341-68; intelligentsia and, 343-4, 351-4, 533, 537, 541-7, 550, 555-8; Jews and, 573-7, 580-1, 584, 586, 587-9; jokes about, 345-6, 348, 354, 363-4, 367; Komsomol, 203, 204, 205, 213, 216, 220, 226, 233-6, 241; Lenin on, 334; loyalty to, 358-9; Medvedev and, 541-7; meetings of, 352-4, 435; membership statistics, 356n; number of members, 355; parades, 328, 348-9, 614; patriotism, 371, 375-6; power of, 46-7, 355-7, 359; as

privileged class, 41-3, 45-9, 50-1, 54-7, 64-5, 68, 70, 71; propaganda of, 347-8, 349, 356, 357, 372, 376, 434-5; reasons for joining, 342, 355-8, 363-4; rites and rituals, 349-50; Russian Orthodox Church and, 341, 348, 371, 528-32; Russophilism and, 521; Sakharov and, 341, 538-9, 593-4; slogans, 202, 347-8, 354, 446; sociology and, 598-600; split in Central Committee structure, 358; sports and, 372; travel and, 343, 346, 563-4; *Upravleniye Delami*, 48; women and, 166, 169-70; work passes, 321

Computers, 291, 353, 610, 611; Conference on European Security and Cooperation, 608, 609

Conference on European Security and Cooperation, 608, 609

Construction, 270-3, 283-4; counter-economy, 110, 124, 130; dams, 405, 406, 412, 413-15

Consumers, 74-107, 597; airlines, 39, 63, 117, 126; alcoholic beverages, 81, 95; appliances, 75, 79, 82, 83-4, 88-9, 174-5; automobiles, 75, 77-9, 95-6, 120-1; clothing and shoes, 76, 82, 83, 84, 86, 89, 93, 95, 96, 118-22, 125, 128; deferred expectations, 106-7, 603-5; Five-Year Plans and, 603; food, 76, 80, 83, 89-90, 94, 95, 96; household furnishings, 139; housing, 74-5, 81, 93, 94, 100-7; imports, 86-7, 93, 96; inflation, 93, 94, 95-6; information, 428-33, 434-40; job security, 93-4; kitchenware, 82; medical services, 93, 96-100; quality of goods, 83; railroads, 53-4, 63; retirement, 94, 169; savings deposits, 79-80; services, 91-2, 122-4, 131; shopping, 81-93, 95-6, 106; cash carrying, 85; daily ordeal, 81-2, 84-93; queueing, 87-91, 106; shopping pools, 85-6; shortages (*defitsitny tovary*), 82-3, 84, 117-18; standard of living, 76, 79-81, 93-4, 105-7, 597; television, 79; theater

621

627

Medical services, 93, 96–100, 539; black market, 113; bureaucracy at Jaunkemeri Sanatorium, 329–30; dentists, 113, 123; doctors, 96–8, 182; foreign comparisons, 93, 96–7; Kremlin Clinic, 51–2, 53, 98; life expectancy, 96; for privileged class, 51–3, 60; women and, 166, 170–1, 181–3

Medicines, 52–3, 97, 99–100

Medvedev, Roy, 70, 72, 129, 155, 441, 533, 541–7, 553, 559, 576, 577, 602; Stalin and, 541–3, 544

Medvedev, Zhores, 437, 440–1, 507, 508, 510, 541–3

The Medvedev Papers (Medvedev), 437

Mein Kampf (Hitler), 436

Mental hospitals, dissidents sent to, 308, 537, 538, 542, 552

Meyer, Jan, 490

Meyerhold, Vsevolod, 459

Mikhalkov, Sergei Vladimirovich, 21, 57, 62, 472–4

Mikoyan, General Aleksei, 50

Mikoyan, Anastas, 50, 55, 60, 62

The Military, 44, 67, 68, 289–93; détente and, 608–9; indoctrination of youth, 390; invasion of Czechoslovakia and, 382–3; patriotism and, 390–3; science and, 442, 443; special production for, 289–93; themes in literature, movies and television, 386–8; Voluntary Committee for Assistance to the Armed Forces (D.O.S.A.A.F.), 391–2; Voyentorg (Army-Navy store), 44; war game (*zarnitsa:* lightning), 391; World War II themes in propaganda, 386–8

Miller, Wright, 136

Millionaires, 21, 127–9, 472–3

Minorities, 36, 520–1; *see also* Jews

Mirkhalov, Sultan, 196

A Modern Idyll (Saltykov-Shchedrin), 473

Modern Industrial State (Galbraith), 436

Moiseyev Dance Troupe, 65, 388

Molotov, Vyacheslav, 59, 62, 244

Money, 71, 85, 94–5; attitudes toward, 22, 168–9, 274; millionaires, 21, 127–9, 472–3

Montesquieu, Baron de La Brède et de, 308

Monuments, 138

Moroz, Valentin, 533

Morozov, Pavel, 204

Morton, Henry, 100n, 101n, 105n

Moscow Art Theater, 136–7, 181, 225, 478, 480, 523, 527

Moscow Conservatory, 471, 475, 508

Moscow Film Studios, 65

Moscow Institute of Architecture, 498

Moscow Institute of International Relations (MIMO), 68–9

Moscow Jazz School, 216

Moscow Physical-Engineering Institute, 216

Moscow State University (MGU), 68, 198, 237, 239–40, 241, 393, 523, 528

Moscow Winter Festival of the Arts, 471

Moscow Writers' Club, 458–61

Moskva Department Store, 88

Moskvich automobile, 120–1

Motherland Clubs (*rodina*), 522

Motion pictures, 413, 480, 484; censorship, 463–4, 467, 478, 505; for children, 194; privileged class and, 65–6; on Russian heritage, 518; Western, 65, 134; on World War II, 386–7

Mozhaisky, Aleksandr, 381

Mozhayev, Boris, 251, 260, 477

Mushroom-picking, 149–50

Music, 320, 475, 480, 523; agitprop songs, 219; electronic, 25, 499; jazz, 25, 135, 216–17; politics and, 343–4, 471; pop, 215–23; religious, 523, 531; rock, 25, 215–23, 243, 413; self-publishing, 499–505

My Country and the World (Sakharov), 443

Mzhavanadze, Vasily, 127, 128

Na Levo ('under the table'), 108, 114, 123, 131

Nabokov, Vladimir, 492

Napoleon I, 135, 308, 523

Napravleniye see Job assignment

631

636

All Sphere Books are available at your bookshop or newsagent, or can be ordered from the following address: Sphere Books, Cash Sales Department, P.O. Box 11, Falmouth, Cornwall.

Please send cheque or postal order (no currency), and allow 19p for postage and packing for the first book plus 9p per copy for each additional book ordered up to a maximum charge of 73p in U.K.

Customers in Eire and B.F.P.O. please allow 19p for postage and packing for the first book plus 9p per copy for the next 6 books, thereafter 3p per book.

Overseas customers please allow 20p for postage and packing for the first book and 10p per copy for each additional book.